PEARSON

FOUNDATIONS SERIES

AMERICAN
GOVERNMENT

PEARSON

Boston, Massachusetts   Chandler, Arizona   Glenview, Illinois   Upper Saddle River, New Jersey

Acknowledgments appear on pages 741–743, which constitute an extension of this copyright page.

PEARSON

ISBN 13: 978-0-78-546852-3
ISBN 10:   0-78-546852-8
Student Edition with Online Student Center 6-year access   ISBN: 0-78-546856-0
1 2 3 4 5 6 7 8 9 10   13 12 11 10 09

Authors

Jane Wilcox Smith received her master of arts in teaching as a reading specialist from Emory University in Atlanta, Georgia. She taught basic reading skills at the Schenck School in Atlanta, Georgia, and remedial English and reading skills at Forsyth Central High School in Cumming, Georgia. She serves on Emory University's Woodruff Library's Special Collection Board.

Carol Sullivan received her bachelor of science degree from Jersey State College of New Jersey. She taught at Forsyth Central High School in Cumming, Georgia, in the content areas of English, social studies, vocational skills, and science. She also taught special education at Sandburg Middle School in Elmhurst, Illinois.

Program Consultant

Grant Wiggins is the President of Authentic Education in Hopewell, New Jersey. He earned his Ed.D. from Harvard University and his B.A. from St. John's College in Annapolis. Grant consults with schools, districts, and state education departments on a variety of reform matters; organizes conferences and workshops; and develops print materials and Web resources on curricular change. He is the coauthor, with Jay McTighe, of *Understanding by Design* and *The Understanding by Design Handbook,* the award-winning and highly successful materials on curriculum published by ASCD. His work has been supported by the Pew Charitable Trusts, the Geraldine R. Dodge Foundation, and the National Science Foundation.

Over the past 20 years, Wiggins has worked on some of the most influential reform initiatives in the country, including Vermont's portfolio system and Ted Sizer's Coalition of Essential Schools. He has established statewide Consortia devoted to assessment reform for the states of North Carolina and New Jersey. Grant is the author of *Educative Assessment* and *Assessing Student Performance,* both published by Jossey-Bass. His many articles have appeared in such journals as Educational Leadership and Phi Delta Kappan.

iv

Unit 1

Foundations of American Government

1

Essential Question What should be the goals of government?

Go online with Unit 1
Find these interactive resources at PearsonSuccessNet.com

⟩ **GOVERNMENT** ONLINE
How Government Works

- Checks and Balances
- Amending the Constitution

⟩ **GOVERNMENT** ONLINE
Government on the Go

- Political Dictionary
- Audio Review
- Downloadable Interactives

⟩ **GOVERNMENT** ONLINE
WebQuest

- Explore Essential Questions online

⟩ **GOVERNMENT** ONLINE
Government Online

- Interactives
- In the News
- Citizenship Activity Pack
- Online Self-Test
- Audio Tours
- Updates
- Documents

Unit 2

Political Behavior: Government By the People

99

Essential Question In what ways should people participate in public affairs?

Go online with Unit 2
Find these interactive resources at
PearsonSuccessNet.com

GOVERNMENT ONLINE
How Government Works

- Minor Parties in History
- Five Methods of Nomination
- What Happens to a Ballot
- Grass-roots Organizing

GOVERNMENT ONLINE
Government on the Go

- Political Dictionary
- Audio Review
- Downloadable Interactives

GOVERNMENT ONLINE
WebQuest

- Explore Essential Questions online

GOVERNMENT ONLINE
Government Online

- Interactives
- In the News
- Citizenship Activity Pack
- Online Self-Test
- Audio Tours
- Updates
- Documents

Unit 3

The Legislative Branch

229

Essential Question What makes a successful Congress?

Go online with Unit 3
Find these interactive resources at PearsonSuccessNet.com

⑦ GOVERNMENT ONLINE
How Government Works

- **Choosing Their Voters**
- **The Impeachment Process**
- **Congressional Checks on the Presidential Treaty-Making Power**
- **How a Bill Becomes a Law**

⑦ GOVERNMENT ONLINE
Government on the Go

- **Political Dictionary**
- **Audio Review**
- **Downloadable Interactives**

⑦ GOVERNMENT ONLINE
WebQuest

- **Explore Essential Questions online**

⑦ GOVERNMENT ONLINE
Government Online

- **Interactives**
- **In the News**
- **Citizenship Activity Pack**
- **Online Self-Test**
- **Audio Tours**
- **Updates**
- **Documents**

Unit 4

The Executive Branch

311

Essential Question What makes a good President?

Go online with Unit 4
Find these interactive resources at PearsonSuccessNet.com

⑦ GOVERNMENT ONLINE
How Government Works

- Who Is Next in Line?
- The Race to the Presidency
- The Executive Branch
- The Executive Departments
- Regulatory Commissions
- The State Department
- Civilian Control of the Military
- Department of Homeland Security

⑦ GOVERNMENT ONLINE
Government on the Go

- Political Dictionary
- Audio Review
- Downloadable Interactives

⑦ GOVERNMENT ONLINE
WebQuest

- Explore Essential Questions online

⑦ GOVERNMENT ONLINE
Government Online

- Interactives
- In the News
- Citizenship Activity Pack
- Online Self-Test
- Audio Tours
- Updates
- Documents

Unit 5

The Judicial Branch — 441

Essential Question What should be the role of the judicial branch?

Go online with Unit 5
Find these interactive resources at PearsonSuccessNet.com

GOVERNMENT ONLINE
How Government Works

- The Appellate Path in the Federal Courts
- How a Case Reaches the Supreme Court
- The *Lemon* Test
- Freedoms of Speech and Press

GOVERNMENT ONLINE
Government on the Go

- Political Dictionary
- Audio Review
- Downloadable Interactives

GOVERNMENT ONLINE
WebQuest

- Explore Essential Questions online

GOVERNMENT ONLINE
Government Online

- Interactives
- In the News
- Citizenship Activity Pack
- Online Self-Test
- Audio Tours
- Updates
- Documents

Unit 6

Political and Economic Systems 549

Essential Question How should a government meet the needs of its people?

Go online with Unit 6
Find these interactive resources at
PearsonSuccessNet.com

⭐ **GOVERNMENT** ONLINE
How Government Works

- The Federal Reserve System

⭐ **GOVERNMENT** ONLINE
Government on the Go

- Political Dictionary
- Audio Review
- Downloadable Interactives

⭐ **GOVERNMENT** ONLINE
WebQuest

- Explore Essential Questions online

⭐ **GOVERNMENT** ONLINE
Government Online

- Interactives
- In the News
- Citizenship Activity Pack
- Online Self-Test
- Audio Tours
- Updates
- Documents

Unit 7

Participating in State and Local Government 601

Essential Question What is the right balance of local, sOtate, and federal government?

Go online with Unit 7
Find these interactive resources at PearsonSuccessNet.com

GOVERNMENT ONLINE
How Government Works

- Amending State Constitutions
- Initiative and Referendum
- Choosing Executive Officers
- Criminal and Civil Law
- Municipalities and Townships
- Alternate Forms of City Government
- State and Local Spending
- State and Local Revenues

GOVERNMENT ONLINE
Government on the Go

- Political Dictionary
- Audio Review
- Downloadable Interactives

GOVERNMENT ONLINE
WebQuest

- Explore Essential Questions online

GOVERNMENT ONLINE
Government Online

- Interactives
- In the News
- Citizenship Activity Pack
- Online Self-Test
- Audio Tours
- Updates
- Documents

Learning With Essential Questions

Foundations of American Government is organized around Essential Questions. An essential question is a launching pad for exploring ideas. It doesn't have just one right answer. The answer to an essential question changes as you learn more or as circumstances change.

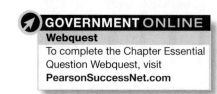

GOVERNMENT ONLINE
Webquest
To complete the Chapter Essential Question Webquest, visit
PearsonSuccessNet.com

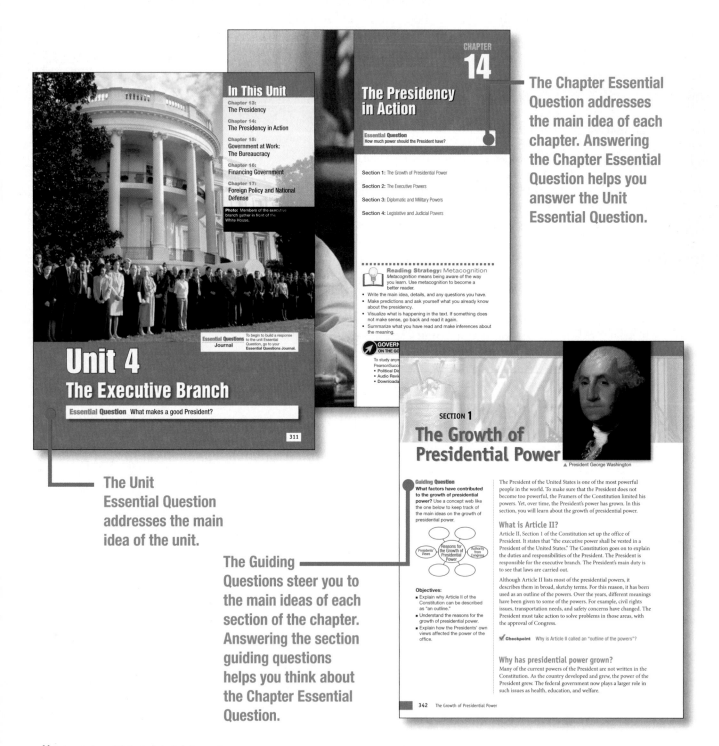

In This Unit

Chapter 13:
The Presidency

Chapter 14:
The Presidency in Action

Chapter 15:
Government at Work: The Bureaucracy

Chapter 16:
Financing Government

Chapter 17:
Foreign Policy and National Defense

Photo: Members of the executive branch gather in front of the White House.

Essential Questions Journal To begin to build a response to the unit Essential Question, go to your *Essential Questions Journal.*

Unit 4
The Executive Branch

Essential Question What makes a good President?

311

CHAPTER 14

The Presidency in Action

Essential Question
How much power should the President have?

Section 1: The Growth of Presidential Power

Section 2: The Executive Powers

Section 3: Diplomatic and Military Powers

Section 4: Legislative and Judicial Powers

Reading Strategy: Metacognition
Metacognition means being aware of the way you learn. Use metacognition to become a better reader.
- Write the main idea, details, and any questions you have.
- Make predictions and ask yourself what you already know about the presidency.
- Visualize what is happening in the text. If something does not make sense, go back and read it again.
- Summarize what you have read and make inferences about the meaning.

GOVERNMENT ON THE GO
To study anyw... PearsonSucc...
- Political Dic...
- Audio Revie...
- Downloada...

SECTION 1

The Growth of Presidential Power

▲ President George Washington

Guiding Question
What factors have contributed to the growth of presidential power? Use a concept web like the one below to keep track of the main ideas on the growth of presidential power.

Presidents' Views — Reasons for the Growth of Presidential Power — Authority from Congress

Objectives:
- Explain why Article II of the Constitution can be described as "an outline."
- Understand the reasons for the growth of presidential power.
- Explain how the Presidents' own views affected the power of the office.

The President of the United States is one of the most powerful people in the world. To make sure that the President does not become too powerful, the Framers of the Constitution limited his powers. Yet, over time, the President's power has grown. In this section, you will learn about the growth of presidential power.

What is Article II?
Article II, Section 1 of the Constitution set up the office of President. It states that "the executive power shall be vested in a President of the United States." The Constitution goes on to explain the duties and responsibilities of the President. The President is responsible for the executive branch. The President's main duty is to see that laws are carried out.

Although Article II lists most of the presidential powers, it describes them in broad, sketchy terms. For this reason, it has been used as an outline of the powers. Over the years, different meanings have been given to some of the powers. For example, civil rights issues, transportation needs, and safety concerns have changed. The President must take action to solve problems in those areas, with the approval of Congress.

✓ **Checkpoint** Why is Article II called an "outline of the powers"?

Why has presidential power grown?
Many of the current powers of the President are not written in the Constitution. As the country developed and grew, the power of the President grew. The federal government now plays a larger role in such issues as health, education, and welfare.

342   The Growth of Presidential Power

The Chapter Essential Question addresses the main idea of each chapter. Answering the Chapter Essential Question helps you answer the Unit Essential Question.

The Unit Essential Question addresses the main idea of the unit.

The Guiding Questions steer you to the main ideas of each section of the chapter. Answering the section guiding questions helps you think about the Chapter Essential Question.

"Once you have learned to question and to persist in your questioning, nothing can stop you. That's why a curriculum framed around Essential Questions is so important."

—Grant Wiggins, coauthor of *Understanding by Design*

▲ Grant Wiggins talks with high school students.

Essential Questions Journal

Use your Essential Questions Journal to build answers to Essential Questions.

Also available online at PearsonSuccessNet.com

Learning Online

▶ Online Student Center

It all starts with the Online Student Center! There you can access a wide array of 21st century learning tools to help personalize learning.

Access *Foundations of American Government* online

Go to the Online Student Center at PearsonSuccessNet.com to find your textbook.

Connect with content using Government ▶ on the Go Audio and Video

Study anywhere, anytime, with downloadable audio and video files.

- Political Dictionary Audio in English
- Political Dictionary Audio in Spanish
- Audio Review in English
- Audio Review in Spanish
- Audio Tour Animations

GOVERNMENT ONLINE
Interactive
For an interactive version of actu confirmation hearings, visit
PearsonSuccessNet.com

Fig. 14.2 **How Government Works**

Who Gets the Job?

Some high-level positions, such as Supreme Court justice, require Senate approval. The multistep process can be long and drawn out. *Why is this multistep process necessary?*

The President Nominates a Candidate

- The White House staff conducts a search for the candidate.
- Experts provide the White House with information.

◀ **Interact with online activities**

Online features such as "How Government Works" help you visualize key concepts and information.

Research online with Webquests

Research current and relevant information using a wide range of preselected, reliable Web sites.

Monitor progress with online assessment

Online self-tests help you monitor your learning.

Study Skills

▶ Prepare to Read

Get more from your reading by answering the guiding questions and completing note-taking graphic organizers that appear at the beginning of each section.

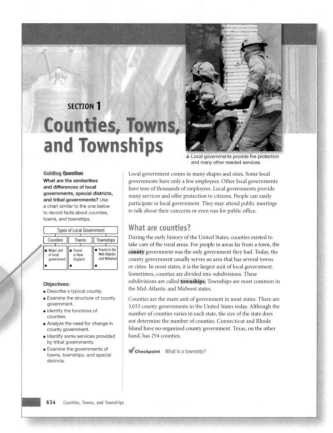

Graphic organizers help you answer the guiding question at the beginning of each section.

▶ Quick Study Guide

Prepare for tests with charts that organize unit and chapter Essential Questions.

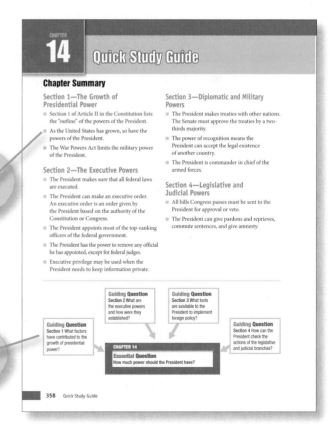

Bulleted section summaries provide key information.

A graphic organizer helps you see how the guiding questions for each chapter help you answer the chapter's Essential Question.

Special Features

▶ Issues of Our Time

**Confront key issues from new perspectives.
Learn the facts behind today's debates.**

GOVERNMENT ONLINE
with Online Enhancement

Many charts, graphs, diagrams, and illustrations are expanded online with interactivities, audio tours, and updates. To view these enhanced graphics, go to **PearsonSuccessNet.com** The ⟶ on these pages indicates an online enhancement.

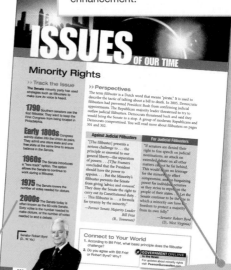

A timeline shows the connection between today's debate and past events.

Consider the viewpoints of prominent Americans on the issues that impact our lives.

▶ Citizenship 101

Practice your citizenship skills with online activities.

Learn to to be an active citizen.

Focus on the Supreme Court

▶ Landmark Decisions of the Supreme Court

Learn the complete story behind groundbreaking decisions of the U.S. Supreme Court.

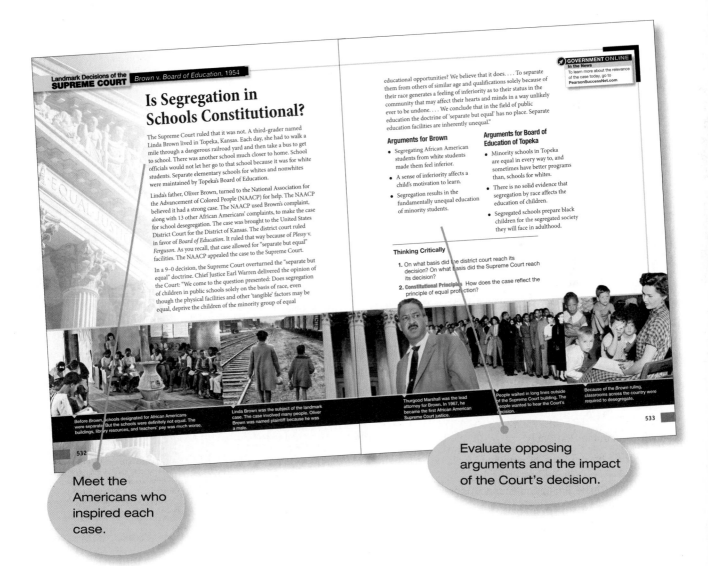

Landmark Decisions of the SUPREME COURT — *Brown v. Board of Education, 1954*

Is Segregation in Schools Constitutional?

The Supreme Court ruled that it was not. A third-grader named Linda Brown lived in Topeka, Kansas. Each day, she had to walk a mile through a dangerous railroad yard and then take a bus to get to school. There was another school much closer to home. School officials would not let her go to that school because it was for white students. Separate elementary schools for whites and nonwhites were maintained by Topeka's Board of Education.

Linda's father, Oliver Brown, turned to the National Association for the Advancement of Colored People (NAACP) for help. The NAACP believed it had a strong case. The NAACP used Brown's complaint, along with 13 other African Americans' complaints, to make the case for school desegregation. The case was brought to the United States District Court for the District of Kansas. The district court ruled in favor of *Board of Education*. It ruled that way because of *Plessy* v. *Ferguson*. As you recall, that case allowed for "separate but equal" facilities. The NAACP appealed the case to the Supreme Court.

In a 9–0 decision, the Supreme Court overturned the "separate but equal" doctrine. Chief Justice Earl Warren delivered the opinion of the Court: "We come to the question presented: Does segregation of children in public schools solely on the basis of race, even though the physical facilities and other 'tangible' factors may be equal, deprive the children of the minority group of equal

educational opportunities? We believe that it does. . . . To separate them from others of similar age and qualifications solely because of their race generates a feeling of inferiority as to their status in the community that may affect their hearts and minds in a way unlikely ever to be undone. . . . We conclude that in the field of public education the doctrine of 'separate but equal' has no place. Separate education facilities are inherently unequal."

GOVERNMENT ONLINE
In the News
To learn more about the relevance of the case today, go to PearsonSuccessNet.com

Arguments for Brown

- Segregating African American students from white students made them feel inferior.
- A sense of inferiority affects a child's motivation to learn.
- Segregation results in the fundamentally unequal education of minority students.

Arguments for Board of Education of Topeka

- Minority schools in Topeka are equal in every way to, and sometimes have better programs than, schools for whites.
- There is no solid evidence that segregation by race affects the education of children.
- Segregated schools prepare black children for the segregated society they will face in adulthood.

Thinking Critically

1. On what basis did the district court reach its decision? On what basis did the Supreme Court reach its decision?
2. **Constitutional Principles** How does the case reflect the principle of equal protection?

Before *Brown*, schools designated for African Americans were separate. But the schools were definitely not equal. The buildings, library resources, and teachers' pay was much worse.

Linda Brown was the subject of the landmark case. The case involved many people. Oliver Brown was named plaintiff because he was a male.

Thurgood Marshall was the lead attorney for Brown. In 1967, he became the first African American Supreme Court justice.

People waited in long lines outside of the Supreme Court building. The people wanted to hear the Court's decision.

Because of the *Brown* ruling, classrooms across the country were required to desegregate.

532

533

Meet the Americans who inspired each case.

Evaluate opposing arguments and the impact of the Court's decision.

See the Supreme Court Glossary, p. 685, for summaries of key cases.

▶ Government in Your Life

Understand the way government relates to the world around you.

Government in Your Life

Do Young People Vote?

In 1971, the voting age was lowered from 21 to 18. That year, many young people were fighting in Vietnam or involved in the civil rights movement but could not vote. Those young people successfully lobbied for the passage of the 26th Amendment, which changed the voting age. In the 1972 presidential election, 48 percent of young people under the age of 30 voted. From 1972 until 2006, the number of younger voters dropped. In the 2008 presidential election, approximately 52 percent of voters under the age of 30 went to the polls.

However, there are more than 30 million Americans between the ages of 18 and 24. Many young people report they do not vote. They claim political leaders do not meet their needs. Others say they are too busy or know little about the candidates. Some young people say they do not know how to register or where to vote. Some of these problems may easily be solved by looking up the candidates online, or by using mail-in or absentee ballots to vote. For young people unhappy with politics, voting is the easiest way to make a difference.

▶ Biography

Meet people who have made contributions to American government.

Biography

Two Famous Children of Immigrants

Cesar Chavez was born in 1927 in Arizona. His parents were born in Mexico and had come to the United States. When Cesar was a boy, he and his family became migrant farm workers in California. Migrant farm workers pick crops and move from place to place as crops need picking.

Chavez later dedicated his life to helping underpaid farm workers. Using peaceful means, he helped them get better pay and better working conditions. Chavez led the United Farm Workers. Under Chavez's leadership, grape pickers refused to work for almost five years. Finally the farm owners agreed to give the workers higher pay. After Chavez died in 1993, President Clinton awarded him the Presidential Medal of Freedom in 1994. His family and others carry on the work he did for migrant farm workers.

Colin Powell was born in 1937 in the Harlem area of New York City. His parents were immigrants from Jamaica and had little education. Powell attended the City College of New York. He enrolled in the Reserve Officers Training Corps (ROTC). When he graduated, he was the top student in his ROTC class. After many years in the army, Powell became a four-star general. He worked hard to settle problems in peaceful ways. Powell was chairman of the Joint Chiefs of Staff during Operation Desert Storm in 1992. During this time, the American people came to know and admire Powell. In 1996, many people encouraged Powell to run for President. Colin Powell served as Secretary of State beginning in 2001.

▶ How Government Works

Find out about the processes by which our government functions, through detailed diagrams and infographics.

Complex content is displayed visually to explain how our government works.

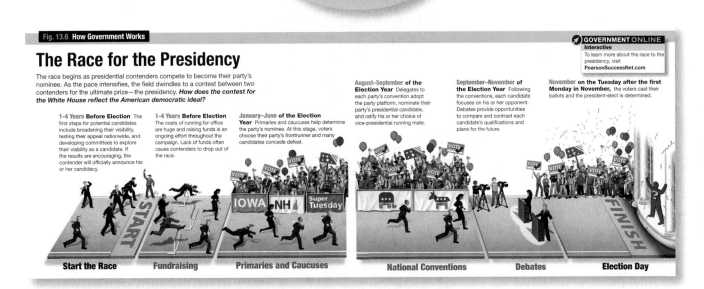

Fig. 13.6 **How Government Works**

The Race for the Presidency

⊘ **GOVERNMENT** ONLINE
Interactive
To learn more about the race to the presidency, visit
PearsonSuccessNet.com

The race begins as presidential contenders compete to become their party's nominee. As the pace intensifies, the field dwindles to a contest between two contenders for the ultimate prize—the presidency. *How does the contest for the White House reflect the American democratic ideal?*

1-4 Years Before Election The first steps for potential candidates include broadening their visibility, testing their appeal nationwide, and developing committees to explore their viability as a candidate. If the results are encouraging, the contender will officially announce his or her candidacy.

1-4 Years Before Election The costs of running for office are huge and raising funds is an ongoing effort throughout the campaign. Lack of funds often causes contenders to drop out of the race.

January–June of the Election Year Primaries and caucuses help determine the party's nominee. At this stage, voters choose their party's frontrunner and many candidates concede defeat.

August–September of the Election Year Delegates to each party's convention adopt the party platform, nominate their party's presidential candidate, and ratify his or her choice of vice-presidential running mate.

September–November of the Election Year Following the conventions, each candidate focuses on his or her opponent. Debates provide opportunities to compare and contrast each candidate's qualifications and plans for the future.

November on the Tuesday after the first Monday in November, the voters cast their ballots and the president-elect is determined.

Start the Race | **Fundraising** | **Primaries and Caucuses** | **National Conventions** | **Debates** | **Election Day**

▶ Infographics, Charts, Graphs, and Tables

Visualize key government concepts and interpret relevant data through infographics, charts, graphs, and tables.

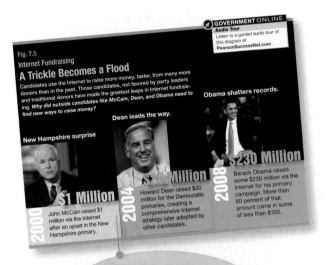

Charts, graphs, and diagrams help deepen your understanding of important concepts.

The rights established in these landmark documents were revolutionary in their day. They did not, however, extend to all people when first granted. Over the years, these rights have influenced systems of government in many countries. **How might the right to petition stop the abuse of power by a monarch?**

The English Bill of Rights is presented to William and Mary.

	1215 Magna Carta	1689 English Bill of Rights	1776 Virginia Bill of Rights	1791 U.S. Bill of Rights
Trial by jury				
Due process				
Private property				
No cruel punishment				
No excessive bail or fines				
Right to bear arms				
Right to petition				
No unreasonable searches or seizures				
Freedom of speech				
Freedom of the press				
Freedom of religion				

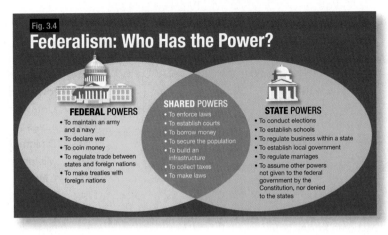

Fig. 3.4
Federalism: Who Has the Power?

FEDERAL POWERS
- To maintain an army and a navy
- To declare war
- To coin money
- To regulate trade between states and foreign nations
- To make treaties with foreign nations

SHARED POWERS
- To enforce laws
- To establish courts
- To borrow money
- To secure the population
- To build an infrastructure
- To collect taxes
- To make laws

STATE POWERS
- To conduct elections
- To establish schools
- To regulate business within a state
- To establish local government
- To regulate marriages
- To assume other powers not given to the federal government by the Constitution, nor denied to the states

▶ Political Cartoons

Examine historical and modern political cartoons for insights into American government.

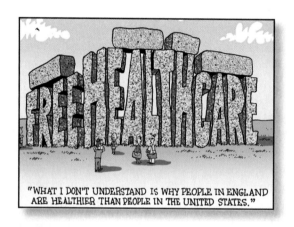

▶ Document-Based Assessment

Analyze enduring issues and prepare for high-stakes tests by examining important historical documents.

▶ Maps

Explore the intersection of government and geography.

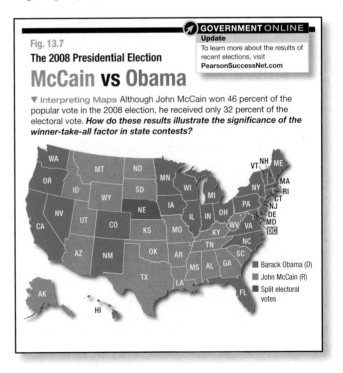

GOVERNMENT ONLINE
Update
To learn more about the results of recent elections, visit PearsonSuccessNet.com

Fig. 13.7
The 2008 Presidential Election

McCain vs Obama

▼ **Interpreting Maps** Although John McCain won 46 percent of the popular vote in the 2008 election, he received only 32 percent of the electoral vote. *How do these results illustrate the significance of the winner-take-all factor in state contests?*

- Barack Obama (D)
- John McCain (R)
- Split electoral votes

Constitution Quick Study Guide

UNITED STATES CONSTITUTION: Constitution Quick Study Guide

The Preamble The Preamble describes the purpose of the government as set up by the Constitution. Americans expect their government to defend justice and liberty and provide peace and safety from foreign enemies.

Section 1 The Constitution gives Congress the power to make laws. Congress is divided into the Senate and the House of Representatives.

Clause 1 <u>Electors</u> refers to voters. Members of the House of Representatives are elected every two years. Any citizen allowed to vote for members of the larger house of the state legislature can also vote for members of the House.

Clause 3 The number of representatives each state elects is based on its population. An <u>enumeration</u>, or census, must be taken every ten years to determine population. Today, the number of representatives in the House is fixed at 435. Clause 3 contains the Three-Fifths Compromise worked out at the Constitutional Convention. <u>Persons bound to service</u> meant indentured servants. <u>All other persons meant slaves</u>. All free people in a state were counted. However, only three fifths of the slaves were included in the population count. This three-fifths clause became meaningless when slaves were freed by the Thirteenth Amendment.

Clause 4 <u>Executive authority</u> means the governor of a state. If a member of the House leaves office before his or her term ends, the governor must call a special election to fill the seat.

Note: The black lines indicate portions of the Constitution altered by later amendments or that no longer apply.

The United States Constitution

PREAMBLE

We the People of the United States, in Order to form a more perfect Union, establish Justice, insure domestic Tranquility, provide for the common defence, promote the general Welfare, and secure the Blessings of Liberty to ourselves and our Posterity, do ordain and establish this Constitution for the United States of America.

Article I ★ Legislative Department

Section 1. Legislative Power, the Congress

All legislative Powers herein granted shall be vested in a Congress of the United States, which shall consist of a Senate and House of Representatives.

Section 2. House of Representatives

1. **Election of Members** The House of Representatives shall be composed of Members chosen every second Year by the People of the several States, and the Electors in each State shall have the Qualifications requisite for Electors of the most numerous Branch of the State Legislature.

2. **Qualifications** No Person shall be a Representative who shall not have attained to the age of twenty-five Years, and been seven Years a Citizen of the United States, and who shall not, when elected, be an Inhabitant of that State in which he shall be chosen.

3. **Apportionment** Representatives ~~and direct Taxes*~~ shall be apportioned among the several States which may be included within this Union, according to their respective Numbers, ~~which shall be determined by adding to the whole Number of free Persons, including those bound to Service for a Term of Years and excluding Indians not taxed, three fifths of all other Persons.~~ The actual Enumeration shall be made within three Years after the first Meeting of the Congress of the United States, and within every subsequent term of ten Years, in such Manner as they shall by Law direct. The Number of Representatives shall not exceed one for every thirty Thousand, but each State shall have at Least one Representative; and, until such enumeration shall be made, the State of New Hampshire shall be entitled to choose three, Massachusetts eight, Rhode Island and Providence Plantations one, Connecticut five, New York six, New Jersey four, Pennsylvania eight, Delaware one, Maryland six, Virginia ten, North Carolina five, South Carolina five, and Georgia three.

4. **Filling Vacancies** When vacancies happen in the Representation from any State, the Executive Authority thereof shall issue Writs of Election to fill such Vacancies.

5. Officers; Impeachment The House of Representatives shall choose their Speaker and other Officers; and shall have the sole Power of Impeachment.

Section 3. Senate

1. Composition; Term The Senate of the United States shall be composed of two Senators from each State ~~chosen by the Legislature thereof~~ for six Years; and each Senator shall have one Vote.

2. Classification; Filling Vacancies Immediately after they shall be assembled in Consequences of the first Election, they shall be divided, as equally as may be, into three Classes. The Seats of the Senators of the first Class shall be vacated at the Expiration of the second Year; of the second Class, at the Expiration of the fourth Year; and of the third Class, at the Expiration of the sixth Year; so that one-third may be chosen every second Year; ~~and if Vacancies happen by Resignation, or otherwise, during the Recess of the Legislature of any State, the Executive thereof may make temporary Appointments until the next Meeting of the Legislature, which shall then fill such Vacancies.~~

3. Qualifications No Person shall be a Senator who shall not have attained to the Age of thirty Years, and been nine Years a Citizen of the United States, and who shall not, when elected, be an Inhabitant of that State for which he shall be chosen.

4. President of the Senate The Vice President of the United States shall be President of the Senate but shall have no Vote, unless they be equally divided.

5. Other Officers The Senate shall choose their other Officers, and also a President pro tempore, in the Absence of the Vice President, or when he shall exercise the Office of President of the United States.

6. Impeachment Trails The Senate shall have the sole Power to try all Impeachments. When sitting for that Purpose, they shall be on Oath or Affirmation. When the President of the United States is tried, the Chief Justice shall preside: And no Person shall be convicted without the Concurrence of two thirds of the Members present.

7. Penalty on Conviction Judgment in Cases of Impeachment shall not extend further than to removal from Office, and disqualification to hold and enjoy any Office of honor, Trust, or Profit under the United States: but the Party convicted shall nevertheless be liable and subject to Indictment, Trial, Judgment and Punishment, according to Law.

Clause 5 The House elects a Speaker. Only the House has the power to <u>impeach</u>, or accuse, a federal official of wrongdoing.

Clause 2 Every two years, one third of the senators run for reelection. The Seventeenth Amendment changed the way of filling <u>vacancies</u>, or empty seats. Today, the governor of a state must choose a senator to fill a vacancy that occurs between elections.

Clause 5 *Pro tempore* means temporary. The Senate chooses one of its members to serve as president <u>pro tempore</u> when the Vice President is absent.

Clause 6 The Senate acts as a jury if the House impeaches a federal official. The Chief Justice of the Supreme Court presides if the President is on trial. Two thirds of all senators present must vote for conviction, or finding the accused guilty. No President has ever been convicted. The House impeached President Andrew Johnson in 1868, but the Senate acquitted him of the charges. In 1998–1999, President Bill Clinton became the second President to be impeached and acquitted.

Clause 1 Each state legislature can decide when and how congressional elections take place, but Congress can overrule these decisions. In 1842, Congress required each state to set up congressional districts with one representative elected from each district. In 1872, Congress decided that congressional elections must be held in every state on the same date in even-numbered years.

Clause 1 Each house decides whether a member has the qualifications for office set by the Constitution. A <u>quorum</u> is the smallest number of members who must be present for business to be conducted. Each house can set its own rules about absent members.

Clause 4 Neither house can <u>adjourn</u>, or stop meeting, for more than three days unless the other house approves. Both houses must meet in the same city.

Section 4. Elections and Meetings

1. **Election of Congress** The Times, Places and Manner of holding Elections for Senators and Representatives, shall be prescribed in each State by the Legislature thereof; but the Congress may at any time by law make or alter such Regulations, except as to the Places of choosing Senators.

2. **Sessions** The Congress shall assemble at least once in every Year, ~~and such Meeting shall be on the first Monday in December, unless they shall by Law appoint a different Day.~~

Section 5. Legislative Proceedings

1. **Organization** Each House shall be the Judge of the Elections, Returns and Qualifications of its own Members, and a Majority of each shall constitute a Quorum to do Business; but a smaller Number may adjourn from day to day, and may be authorized to compel the Attendance of absent Members, in such Manner, and under such Penalties, as each House may provide.

2. **Rules** Each House may determine the Rules of its Proceedings, punish its Members for disorderly Behavior, and, with the Concurrence of two thirds, expel a Member.

3. **Record** Each House shall keep a Journal of its Proceedings, and from time to time publish the same, excepting such Parts as may in their Judgment require Secrecy; and the Yeas and Nays of the Members of either House on any question shall, at the Desire of one fifth of those Present, be entered on the Journal.

4. **Adjournment** Neither House, during the Session of Congress, shall, without the Consent of the other, adjourn for more than three days, nor to any other Place than that in which the two Houses shall be sitting.

Note: The black lines indicate portions of the Constitution altered by later amendments or that no longer apply.

Section 6. Compensation, Immunities, and Disabilities of Members

1. Salaries; Immunities The Senators and Representatives shall receive a Compensation for their Services, to be ascertained by Law, and paid out of the Treasury of the United States. They shall in all Cases, except Treason, Felony, and Breach of the Peace, be privileged from Arrest during their Attendance at the Session of their respective Houses, and in going to and returning from the same; and for any Speech or Debate in either House, they shall not be questioned in any other Place.

2. Restrictions on Other Employment No Senator or Representative shall, during the Time for which he was elected, be appointed to any civil Office under the Authority of the United States, which shall have been created, or the Emoluments whereof shall have been increased during such time; and no Person holding any Office under the United States, shall be a Member of either House during his Continuance in Office.

Section 7. Law-Making Process

1. Revenue Bills All Bills for raising Revenue shall originate in the House of Representatives; but the Senate may propose or concur with amendments as on other Bills.

2. How a Bill Becomes Law; the Veto Every Bill which shall have passed the House of Representatives and the Senate, shall, before it become a law, be presented to the President of the United States: If he approve, he shall sign it, but if not he shall return it, with his Objections to that House in which it shall have originated, who shall enter the Objections at large on their Journal, and proceed to reconsider it. If after such Reconsideration two thirds of the House shall agree to pass the Bill, it shall be sent, together with the Objections, to the other House, by which it shall likewise be reconsidered, and if approved by two thirds of that House, it shall become a Law. But in all such Cases the Votes of both Houses shall be determined by Yeas and Nays, and the Names of the Persons voting for and against the Bill shall be entered on the Journal of each House respectively. If any Bill shall not be returned by the President within ten Days (Sunday excepted) after it shall have been presented to him, the Same shall be a law, in like Manner as if he had signed it, unless the Congress by their Adjournment, prevent its Return, in which Case it shall not be a Law.

3. Resolutions Passed by Congress Every Order, Resolution, or Vote to which the Concurrence of the Senate and House of Representatives may be necessary (except on a question of adjournment) shall be presented

Clause 1 Congress decides the salary for its members. While Congress is in session, a member is free from arrest in civil cases and cannot be sued for anything he or she says on the floor of Congress. This allows for freedom of debate. However, a member can be arrested for a criminal offense.

Clause 2 Emolument means salary. A member of Congress cannot hold another federal office during his or her term. A former member of Congress cannot hold an office created while he or she was in Congress. An official in another branch of government cannot serve at the same time in Congress.

Clause 1 Revenue is money raised by the government through taxes. Tax bills must be introduced in the House. The Senate, however, can make changes in tax bills.

Clause 2 A bill, or proposed law, that is passed by a majority of the House and Senate is sent to the President. If the President signs the bill, it becomes law.

A bill can also become law without the President's signature. The President can refuse to act on a bill. If Congress is in session at the time, the bill becomes law ten days after the President receives it.

The President can veto, or reject, a bill by sending it back to the house where it was introduced. If the President refuses to act on a bill and Congress adjourns within ten days, then the bill dies. This way of killing a bill without taking action is called the pocket veto.

Congress can override the President's veto if each house of Congress passes the bill again by a two-thirds vote.

Congress's power is expressed directly in the Constitution. Numbered from 1 to 18, these powers are also known as enumerated powers.

Clause 1 Duties are tariffs. Imposts are taxes in general. Excises are taxes on the production or sale of certain goods.

Clause 3 Only Congress has the power to regulate foreign and interstate commerce. This allows a "common market" with a unified set of laws governing trade. This clause has also been interpreted as giving the federal government authority over Native American nations.

Clause 4 Naturalization is the process whereby a foreigner becomes a citizen. Bankruptcy is the condition in which a person or business cannot pay its debts.

Clause 6 Counterfeiting is the making of imitation money. Securities are bonds. Congress can make laws to punish counterfeiters.

Clause 11 Only Congress can declare war. Declarations of war are granted at the request of the President. Letters of marque and reprisal were documents issued by a government allowing merchant ships to arm themselves and attack ships of an enemy nation. They are no longer issued.

Clauses 15, 16 The militia is a body of citizen soldiers. Each state has its own militia, today called the National Guard. Normally, the militia is under the command of a state's governor. However, it can be placed under the command of the President.

Note: The black lines indicate portions of the Constitution altered by later amendments or that no longer apply.

to the President of the United States; and before the Same shall take Effect, shall be approved by him, or, being disapproved by him, shall be repassed by two thirds of the Senate and House of Representatives, according to the Rules and Limitations prescribed in the Case of a Bill.

Section 8. Powers of Congress
The Congress shall have Power

1. To lay and collect Taxes, Duties, Imposts and Excises to pay the Debts and provide for the common Defence and general Welfare of the United States; but all Duties, Imposts and Excises, shall be uniform throughout the United States;

2. To borrow Money on the credit of the United States;

3. To regulate Commerce with foreign Nations, and among the several States, and with the Indian Tribes;

4. To establish an uniform Rule of Naturalization, and uniform Laws on the subject of Bankruptcies throughout the United States;

5. To coin Money, regulate the Value thereof, and of foreign Coin, and fix the Standard of Weights and Measures;

6. To provide for the Punishment of counterfeiting the Securities and current Coin of the United States;

7. To establish Post Offices and post Roads;

8. To promote the Progress of Science and useful Arts, by securing, for limited Times to Authors and Inventors the exclusive Right to their respective Writings and Discoveries;

9. To constitute Tribunals inferior to the supreme Court;

10. To define and punish Piracies and Felonies committed on the high Seas, and Offences against the Law of nations;

11. To declare War, grant Letters of Marque and Reprisal, and make Rules concerning Captures on Land and Water;

12. To raise and support Armies; but no Appropriation of Money to that Use shall be for a longer Term than two Years;

13. To provide and maintain a Navy;

14. To make Rules for the Government and Regulation of the land and naval Forces;

15. To provide for calling forth the Militia to execute the Laws of the Union, suppress Insurrections and repel Invasions;

16. To provide for organizing, arming, and disciplining the Militia, and for governing such Part of them as may be employed in the Service of the United States, reserving to the States respectively the Appointment of the Officers, and the Authority of training the Militia according to the discipline prescribed by Congress;

17. To exercise exclusive Legislation in all Cases whatsoever, over such District (not exceeding ten Miles square) as may, by Cession of Particular States, and the Acceptance of Congress, become the Seat of the Government of the United States, and to exercise like Authority over all Places purchased by the Consent of the Legislature of the State in which the Same shall be, for the Erection of Forts, Magazines, Arsenals, Dockyards and other needful Buildings;—And

18. To make all Laws which shall be necessary and proper for carrying into Execution the foregoing Powers and all other Powers vested by this Constitution in the Government of the United States, or in any Department or Officer thereof.

Clause 18 Congress has the power to make laws as needed to carry out the first 17 clauses. It is sometimes called the elastic clause because it lets Congress stretch the meaning of its power.

Section 9.   Powers Denied to Congress

1. **The Slave Trade** ~~The Migration or Importation of such Persons as any of the States now existing shall think proper to admit, shall not be prohibited by the Congress prior to the Year one thousand eight hundred and eight, but a Tax or duty may be imposed on such Importation, not exceeding ten dollars for each Person.~~

2. **Writ of Habeas Corpus** The Privilege of the Writ of Habeas Corpus shall not be suspended, unless when in Cases of Rebellion or Invasion the public safety may require it.

3. **Bills of Attainder; Ex Post Facto Laws** No Bill of Attainder or ex post facto Law shall be passed.

4. **Apportionment of Direct Taxes** No Capitation, or other direct, Tax shall be laid, unless in Proportion to the Census of Enumeration hereinbefore directed to be taken.

5. **Taxes on Exports** No Tax or Duty shall be laid on Articles exported from any State.

6. **Special Preference for Trade** No Preference shall be given by any Regulation of Commerce or Revenue to the Ports of one State over those of another: nor shall Vessels bound to, or from, one State, be obliged to enter, clear or pay Duties in another.

Clause 1 Such persons means slaves. In 1808, as soon as Congress was permitted to abolish the slave trade, it did so.

Clause 2 A writ of habeas corpus is a court order requiring government officials to bring a prisoner to court and explain why he or she is being held. A writ of habeas corpus protects people from unlawful imprisonment. The government cannot suspend this right except in times of rebellion or invasion.

Clause 3 A bill of attainder is a law declaring that a person is guilty of a particular crime. An ex post facto law punishes an act that was not illegal when it was committed. Congress cannot pass a bill of attainder or ex post facto law.

Clause 7 The federal government cannot spend money unless Congress appropriates it, or passes a law allowing it. The government must publish a statement showing how it spends public funds.

Clause 1 The writers of the Constitution did not want the states to act like separate nations, so they prohibited states from making treaties or coining money. Some powers denied to the federal government are also denied to the states.

Clauses 2, 3 Powers listed here are forbidden to the states, but Congress can pass laws that give these powers to the states.
Clause 2 States are forbidden from taxing imports and exports without the consent of Congress. States may charge inspection fees on goods entering the states. Any profits go to the United States Treasury.

Clause 3 States are forbidden from keeping an army or navy without the consent of Congress. States cannot make treaties or declare war unless an enemy invades or is about to invade.

Clauses 2, 3 Some writers of the Constitution were afraid to allow the people to elect the President directly. Therefore, the Constitutional Convention set up the electoral college. Clause 2 directs each state to choose electors, or delegates to the electoral college, to vote for President. A state's electoral vote is equal to the combined number of senators and representatives. Each state may decide how to choose its electors. Members of Congress and federal officeholders may not serve as electors. This much of the original electoral college system is still in effect.

Note: The black lines indicate portions of the Constitution altered by later amendments or that no longer apply.

7. **Spending** No Money shall be drawn from the Treasury, but in Consequence of Appropriations made by Law; and a regular Statement and Account of the Receipts and Expenditures of all public Money shall be published from time to time.

8. **Titles of Nobility** No Title of Nobility shall be granted by the United States: And no Person holding any Office of Profit or Trust under them, shall, without the Consent of the Congress, accept of any present, Emolument, Office, or Title, of any kind whatever, from any King, Prince, or foreign State.

Section 10. Powers Denied to the States

1. **Unconditional Prohibitions** No State shall enter into any Treaty, Alliance, or Confederation; grant Letters of Marque and Reprisal; coin Money; emit Bills of Credit; make any Thing but gold and silver Coin a Tender in Payment of Debts; pass any Bill of Attainder, ex post facto Law, or Law impairing the Obligation of Contracts, or grant any Title of Nobility.

2. **Powers Conditionally Denied** No State shall, without the Consent of the Congress, lay any Imposts or Duties on Imports or Exports, except what may be absolutely necessary for executing its inspection Laws; and the net Produce of all Duties and Imposts, laid by any State on Imports or Exports, shall be for the Use of the Treasury of the United States; and all such Laws shall be subject to the Revision and Control of the Congress.

3. **Other Denied Powers** No State shall, without the Consent of Congress, lay any Duty of Tonnage, keep Troops, or Ships of War in time of Peace, enter into any Agreement or Compact with another State, or with a foreign Power, or engage in War, unless actually invaded, or in such imminent Danger as will not admit of delay.

Article II ★ Executive Branch

Section 1. Executive Power: The President; Term; Election; Qualificatiions; Compensation; Oath of Office

1. **Chief Executive; Term** The executive Power shall be vested in a President of the United States of America. He shall hold his Office during the Term of four Years, and, together with the Vice President, chosen for the same Term, be elected as follows:

2. **Electoral College** Each State shall appoint, in such Manner as the Legislature thereof may direct, a Number of Electors, equal to the whole Number of Senators and Representatives to which the State may be entitled in the Congress: but no Senator or Representative, or Person holding an Office of Trust or Profit, under the United States, shall be appointed an Elector.

3. **Former Electoral Method** ~~The Electors shall meet in their respective States, and vote by Ballot for two Persons, of whom one at least shall not be an Inhabitant of the same State with themselves. And they shall make a List of all the Persons voted for, and of the Number of Votes for each; which List they shall sign and certify, and transmit sealed to the Seat of the Government of the United States, directed to the President of the Senate. The President of the Senate shall, in the Presence of the Senate and House of Representatives, open all the Certificates, and the Votes shall then be counted. The Person having the greatest Number of Votes shall be the President, if such Number be a majority of the whole Number of Electors appointed; and if there be more than one who have such Majority, and have an equal Number of Votes, then, the House of Representatives shall immediately choose by Ballot one of them for President; and if no Person have a Majority, then from the five highest on the List the said House shall in like Manner choose the President. But in choosing the President, the Votes shall be taken by States, the Representatives from each State having one Vote; a quorum for this Purpose shall consist of a Member or Members from two thirds of the States, and a Majority of all the States shall be necessary to a Choice. In every Case, after the Choice of the President, the Person having the greatest Number of Votes of the Electors shall be the Vice President. But if there should remain two or more who have equal Votes, the Senate shall choose from them by Ballot the Vice President.~~

4. **Time of Elections** The Congress may determine the Time of choosing the Electors, and the Day on which they shall give their Votes; which Day shall be the same throughout the United States.

5. **Qualifications for President** No Person except a natural born Citizen, or a Citizen of the United States, at the

Clause 3 Each elector is called upon to vote for two candidates. The candidate who received a majority of the electoral votes would become President. The runner-up would become Vice President. If no candidate won a majority, the House would choose the President. The Senate would choose the Vice President. The election of 1800 showed a problem with the original electoral college system. Thomas Jefferson was the Democratic-Republican candidate for President, and Aaron Burr was the Democratic-Republican candidate for Vice President. In the electoral college, the vote ended in a tie. The election was finally decided in the House, where Jefferson was chosen President. The Twelfth Amendment changed the electoral college system so that this could not happen again.

National convention to nominate candidates for President and Vice President

> **Clause 6** The powers of the President pass to the Vice President if the President leaves office or cannot discharge his or her duties. The Twenty-Fifth Amendment replaced this clause.

> **Clause 7** The President is paid a salary. It cannot be raised or lowered during his or her term of office. The President is not allowed to hold any other federal or state position while in office.

> **Clause 1** The President is the head of the armed forces and the state militias when they are called into national service. So the military is under <u>civilian</u>, or nonmilitary, control. The President can get advice from the heads of executive departments. In most cases, the President has the power to grant reprieves and pardons. A reprieve suspends punishment ordered by law. A <u>pardon</u> prevents prosecution for a crime or overrides the judgment of a court.

time of the Adoption of this Constitution, shall be eligible to the Office of President; neither shall any person be eligible to that Office who shall not have attained to the Age of thirty-five Years, and been fourteen Years a Resident within the United States.

6. **Presidential Succession** ~~In Case of the Removal of the President from Office, or of his Death, Resignation, or Inability to discharge the Powers and Duties of the said Office, the Same shall devolve on the Vice President,~~ and the Congress may by Law provide for the Case of Removal, Death, Resignation or Inability, both of the President and Vice President, declaring what Officer shall then act as President, and such Officer shall act accordingly, until the Disability be removed, or a President shall be elected.

7. **Salary** The President shall, at stated Times, receive for his Services, a Compensation, which shall neither be increased nor diminished during the Period for which he shall have been elected, and he shall not receive within that Period any other Emolument from the United States, or any of them.

8. **Oath of Office** Before he enter on the Execution of his Office, he shall take the following Oath or Affirmation: "I do solemnly swear (or affirm) that I will faithfully execute the Office of President of the United States, and will to the best of my Ability, preserve, protect and defend the Constitution of the United States."

Section 2. President's Powers

1. **Military Powers** The President shall be Commander in Chief of the Army and Navy of the United States, and of the Militia of the several States, when called into the actual Service of the United States; he may require the Opinion, in writing, of the principal Officer in each of the executive Departments, upon any Subject relating to the Duties of their respective Offices, and he shall have Power to Grant Reprieves and Pardons for Offences against the United States, except in Cases of Impeachment.

Ronald Reagan takes the oath of office to become President.

2. **Treaties; Appointments** He shall have Power, by and with the Advice and Consent of the Senate, to make Treaties, provided two thirds of the Senators present concur; and he shall nominate, and by and with the Advice and Consent of the Senate, shall appoint Ambassadors, other public Ministers and Consuls, Judges of the supreme Court, and all other Officers of the United States, whose Appointments are not herein otherwise provided for, and which shall be established by Law: but the Congress may by Law vest the Appointment of such inferior Officers, as they think proper, in the President alone, in the Courts of Law, or in the Heads of Departments.

3. **Temporary Appointments** The President shall have Power to fill up all Vacancies that may happen during the Recess of the Senate, by granting Commissions which shall expire at the End of their next Session.

Section 3. President's Duties

He shall from time to time give to the Congress Information of the State of the Union, and recommend to their Consideration such Measures as he shall judge necessary and expedient; he may, on extraordinary Occasions, convene both Houses, or either of them, and in Case of Disagreement between them, with Respect to the Time of Adjournment, he may adjourn them to such Time as he shall think proper; he shall receive Ambassadors and other public Ministers; he shall take Care that the Laws be faithfully executed, and shall Commission all the Officers of the United States.

Section 4. Impeachment

The President, Vice President and all Civil Officers of the United States, shall be removed from Office on Impeachment for and Conviction of, Treason, Bribery, or other high Crimes and Misdemeanors.

Article III ★ Judicial Department

Section 1. Judicial Power; Courts; Terms of office

The judicial Power of the United States, shall be vested in one supreme Court, and in such inferior Courts as the Congress may from time to time ordain and establish. The Judges, both of the supreme and inferior Courts, shall hold their Offices during good Behavior, and shall, at stated Times, receive for their Services, a Compensation, which shall not be diminished during their Continuance in Office.

Section 2. Jurisdiction

1. **Scope of Judicial Power** The judicial Power shall extend to all Cases, in Law and Equity, arising under this Constitution, the Laws of the United States, and

Clause 2 The President has the power to make treaties with other nations. Under the system of checks and balances, all treaties must be approved by two thirds of the Senate.

The President has the power to appoint ambassadors to foreign countries and to appoint other high officials. The Senate must confirm, or approve, these appointments.

Section 4 Civil officers include federal judges and members of the Cabinet. High crimes are major crimes.

Misdemeanors are lesser crimes. The President, Vice President, and others can be forced out of office if impeached and found guilty of certain crimes.

Clause 1 Jurisdiction refers to the right of a court to hear a case. Federal courts have jurisdiction over cases that involve the Constitution, federal laws, treaties, foreign ambassadors and diplomats, naval and maritime laws, disagreements between states or between citizens from different states, and disputes between a state or citizen and a foreign state or citizen.

Note: The black lines indicate portions of the Constitution altered by later amendments or that no longer apply.

Treaties made, or which shall be made, under their Authority;— to all Cases affecting Ambassadors, other public ministers, and Consuls;— to all Cases of Admiralty and maritime Jurisdiction;— to Controversies to which the United States shall be a Party;— to Controversies between two or more States;— between a State and Citizens of another State;— between Citizens of different States;— between Citizens of the same State claiming Lands under Grants of different States, and between a State, or the Citizens thereof, and foreign States, Citizens, or Subjects.

> **Clause 2** Original jurisdiction means the power of a court to hear a case where it first arises. The Supreme Court has original jurisdiction over only a few cases, such as those involving foreign diplomats. More often, the Supreme Court acts as an appellate court. An appellate court does not decide guilt. It decides whether the lower court trial was properly conducted and reviews the lower court's decision.

2. **Supreme Court** In all Cases affecting Ambassadors, other public Ministers and Consuls, and those in which a State shall be a Party, the supreme Court shall have original Jurisdiction. In all the other Cases before mentioned, the supreme Court shall have appellate Jurisdiction, both as to Law and Fact, with such Exceptions, and under such Regulations as the Congress shall make.

3. **Trial by Jury** The trial of all Crimes, except in Cases of Impeachment, shall be by Jury; and such Trial shall be held in the State where the said Crimes shall have been committed; but when not committed within any State, the Trial shall be at such Place or Places as the Congress may by Law have directed.

Section 3. Treason

> **Clause 1** Treason is clearly defined. An overt act is an action that has been seen by other people.

1. **Definition** Treason against the United States shall consist only in levying War against them, or in adhering to their Enemies, giving them Aid and Comfort. No Person shall be convicted of Treason unless on the Testimony of two Witnesses to the same overt Act, or on Confession in open Court.

> **Clause 2** Congress has the power to set the punishment for traitors. Congress may not punish the children of convicted traitors by taking away their civil rights or property.

2. **Punishment** The Congress shall have Power to declare the Punishment of Treason, but no Attainder of Treason shall work Corruption of Blood, or Forfeiture except during the Life of the Person attainted.

Article IV ★ Relations Among the States

Section 1. Full Faith and Credit

Full Faith and Credit shall be given in each State to the public Acts, Records, and judicial Proceedings of every other State. And the Congress may by general Laws prescribe the Manner in which such Acts, Records and Proceedings shall be proved, and the Effect thereof.

Section 2. Privileges and Immunities of Citizens

> **Section 1** Each state must recognize the official acts and records of any other state. For example, each state must recognize marriage certificates issued by another state. Congress can pass laws to explain how to do this.

1. **Privileges** The Citizens of each State shall be entitled to all Privileges and Immunities of Citizens in the several States.
2. **Extradition** A Person charged in any State with Treason, Felony, or other Crime, who shall flee from justice, and be found in another State, shall on Demand of the executive Authority of the State from which he fled, be delivered up, to be removed to the State having Jurisdiction of the Crime.
3. **Fugitive Slaves** ~~No Person held to Service or Labor in one State, under the Laws thereof, escaping into another, shall, in Consequence of any Law or Regulation therein, be discharged from Service or Labor, but shall be delivered up on Claim of the Party to whom such Service or Labor may be due.~~

Section 3. New States and Territories

1. **New States** New States may be admitted by the Congress into this Union; but no new State shall be formed or erected within the Jurisdiction of any other State; nor any State be formed by the Junction of two or more States, or Parts of States, without the Consent of the Legislatures of the States concerned as well as of the Congress.
2. **Federal Lands** The Congress shall have Power to dispose of and make all needful Rules and Regulations respecting the Territory or other Property belonging to the United States; and nothing in this Constitution shall be so construed as to Prejudice any Claims of the United States, or of any particular State.

Section 4. Protection Afforded to States by the Nation

The United States shall guarantee to every State in this Union a Republican Form of Government, and shall protect each of them against Invasion; and on Application of the Legislature, or of the Executive (when the Legislature cannot be convened) against domestic Violence.

Article V ★ Provisions for Amendment

The Congress, whenever two thirds of both Houses shall deem it necessary, shall propose Amendments to this Constitution, or, on the Application of the Legislatures of two thirds of the several States, shall call a Convention for proposing Amendments, which, in either Case, shall be valid to all Intents and Purposes, as Part of this Constitution, when ratified by the Legislatures of three fourths of the several States, or by Conventions in three fourths thereof, as the one or the other Mode of Ratification may be proposed by the Congress; Provided ~~that no Amendment which may be made prior to the Year One thousand eight hundred and eight shall in any Manner~~

Clause 2 <u>Extradition</u> means the act of returning a suspected criminal or escaped prisoner to a state where he or she is wanted. State governors must return a suspect to another state. However, the Supreme Court has ruled that a governor cannot be forced to do so if he or she feels that justice will not be done.

Clause 3 <u>Persons held to service or labor</u> refers to slaves or indentured servants. This clause required states to return runaway slaves to their owners. The Thirteenth Amendment replaces this clause.

Clause 1 Congress has the power to admit new states to the Union. Existing states cannot be split up or joined together to form new states unless both Congress and the state legislatures approve.

Section 4 In a <u>republic</u>, voters choose representatives to govern them. The federal government must protect the states from foreign invasion and from domestic, or internal, disorder if asked to do so by a state.

Article V The Constitution can be <u>amended</u>, or changed, if necessary. An amendment can be proposed by (1) a two-thirds vote of both houses of Congress or (2) a national convention called by Congress at the request of two thirds of the state legislatures. (This second method has never been used.) An amendment must be <u>ratified</u>, or approved, by (1) three fourths of the state legislatures or (2) special conventions in three fourths of the states. Congress decides which method will be used.

Congress has proposed each of the 27 amendments to the Constitution by a vote of two thirds in both houses. The only amendment ratified by constitutional conventions of the states was the Twenty-First Amendment. State legislatures have ratified all other amendments.

~~affect the first and fourth Clauses in the Ninth section of~~ ~~the first Article; and~~ that no State, without its Consent, shall be deprived of its equal Suffrage in the Senate.

Article VI ★ Public Debts; Supremacy of National Law; Oath

Section 1. Validity of Debts

All Debts contracted and Engagements entered into, before the Adoption of this Constitution, shall be as valid against the United States under this Constitution, as under the Confederation.

Section 2. Supremacy of National Law

This Constitution, and the Laws of the United States which shall be made in Pursuance thereof; and all Treaties made, or which shall be made, under the Authority of the United States, shall be the supreme Law of the Land; and the Judges in every State shall be bound thereby, anything in the constitution or Laws of any State to the Contrary notwithstanding.

Section 3. Oaths of Office

The Senators and Representatives before mentioned, and the Members of the several State legislatures, and all executive and judicial Officers, both of the United States and of the several States, shall be bound by Oath or Affirmation, to support this Constitution; but no religious Test shall ever be required as a Qualification to any Office or public Trust under the United States.

Article VII ★ Ratification of Constitution

The ratification of the Conventions of nine States, shall be sufficient for the Establishment of this Constitution between the States so ratifying the same.

Done in Convention by the Unanimous Consent of the States present the Seventeenth Day of September in the Year of our Lord one thousand seven hundred and Eighty-seven and of the Independence of the United States of America the twelfth. In witness whereof We have hereunto subscribed our Names.

Section 2 The Supremacy Clause in this section establishes the Constitution, federal laws, and treaties that the Senate has ratified as the <u>supreme</u>, or highest, law of the land. Thus, they outweigh state laws. A state judge must overturn a state law that conflicts with the Constitution or with a federal law.

Article VII During 1787 and 1788, states held special conventions. By October 1788, the required nine states had ratified the United States Constitution.

Nine states had to approve the Constitution before it became law.

Note: The black lines indicate portions of the Constitution altered by later amendments or that no longer apply.

Attest:

William Jackson, *Secretary*

George Washington, *President and Deputy from Virginia*

New Hampshire

John Langdon

Nicholas Gilman

Massachusetts

Nathaniel Gorham

Rufus King

Connecticut

William Samuel
  Johnson

Roger Sherman

New York

Alexander Hamilton

New Jersey

William Livingston

David Brearley

William Paterson

Jonathan Dayton

Pennsylvania

Benjamin Franklin

Thomas Mifflin

Robert Morris

George Clymer

Thomas Fitzsimons

Jared Ingersoll

James Wilson

Gouverneur Morris

Delaware

George Read

Gunning Bedford, Jr.

John Dickinson

Richard Bassett

Jacob Broom

Maryland

James McHenry

Daniel of St. Thomas
  Jenifer

Daniel Carroll

Virginia

John Blair

James Madison, Jr.

North Carolina

William Blount

Richard Dobbs Spaight

Hugh Williamson

South Carolina

John Rutledge

Charles Cotesworth
  Pinckney

Charles Pinckney

Pierce Butler

Georgia

William Few

Abraham Baldwin

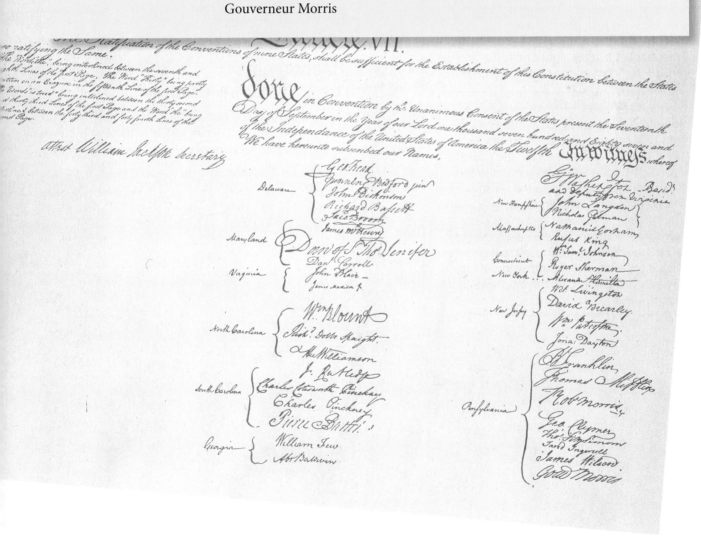

The Amendments Amendments are changes. The Constitution has been amended 27 times since it was ratified in 1788. The first 10 amendments are referred to as the Bill of Rights. These amendments give rights to the people and states, thus putting limits on the power of government.

First Amendment The First Amendment protects five basic rights: freedom of religion, speech, press, assembly, and petition. Congress cannot set up an established, or official, church or religion for the nation. It cannot forbid the practice of religion, nor can it force the practice of religion.

Congress may not abridge, or limit, the freedom to speak and write freely. The government may not censor, or review, books and newspapers before they are printed. This amendment also protects the right to assemble, or hold public meetings. Petition means to ask. Redress means to correct. Grievances are wrongs. The people have the right to ask the government for wrongs to be corrected.

Second Amendment Each state has the right to maintain a militia, an armed force for its own protection—today, the National Guard. The national government and the states can and do regulate the private possession and use of firearms.

Third Amendment In colonial times, the British could quarter, or house, soldiers in private homes without permission of the owners. The Third Amendment prevents such abuses.

The United States Constitution

Amendments

1st Amendment
(1791) Freedom of Religion, Speech, Press, Assembly, and Petition

Congress shall make no law respecting an establishment of religion, or prohibiting the free exercise thereof, or abridging the freedom of speech, or of the press; or the right of the people peaceably to assemble, and to petition the Government for a redress of grievances.

2nd Amendment
(1791) Right to Keep, Bear Arms

A well-regulated Militia being necessary to the security of a free State, the right of the people to keep and bear Arms, shall not be infringed.

3rd Amendment
(1791) Lodging Troops in Private Homes

No Soldier shall, in time of peace be quartered in any house, without the consent of the Owner, nor, in time of war, but in a manner to be prescribed by law.

4th Amendment

(1791) Search, Seizures, Proper Warrants

The right of the people to be secure in their persons, houses, papers, and effects, against unreasonable searches and seizures, shall not be violated, and no Warrants shall issue, but upon probable cause, supported by Oath or affirmation, and particularly describing the place to be searched, and the persons or things to be seized.

5th Amendment

(1791) Criminal Proceedings; Due Process; Eminent Domain

No person shall be held to answer for a capital, or otherwise infamous crime, unless on a presentment or indictment of a Grand Jury, except in cases arising in the land or naval forces, or in the Militia, when in actual service in time of War, or public danger; nor shall any person be subject for the same offence to be twice put in jeopardy of life or limb; nor shall be compelled in any criminal case to be a witness against himself, nor be deprived of life, liberty, or property, without due process of law; nor shall private property be taken for public use, without just compensation.

6th Amendment

(1791) Criminal Proceedings

In all criminal prosecutions, the accused shall enjoy the right to a speedy and public trial, by an impartial jury of the State and district wherein the crime shall have been committed, which district shall have been previously ascertained by law, and to be informed of the nature and cause of the accusation; to be confronted with the witnesses against him; to have compulsory process for obtaining witnesses in his favor, and to have the Assistance of Counsel for his defence.

7th Amendment

(1791) Jury Trials in Civil Cases

In Suits at common law, where the value in controversy shall exceed twenty dollars, the right of trial by jury shall be preserved, and no fact tried by a jury, shall be otherwise re-examined in any Court of the United States, than according to the rules of the common law.

Fourth Amendment This amendment protects Americans from unreasonable searches and seizures. Search and seizure are permitted only if a judge has issued a warrant, or written court order. A warrant is issued only if there is probable cause. This means an officer must show that it is probable, or likely, that the search will produce evidence of a crime.

Fifth Amendment This amendment protects the rights of the accused. Capital crimes are those that can be punished with death. Infamous crimes are those that can be punished with prison or loss of rights. The federal government must obtain an indictment, or formal accusation, from a grand jury to prosecute anyone for such crimes. A grand jury is a panel of between 12 and 23 citizens who decide if the government has enough evidence to justify a trial.

Double jeopardy is forbidden by this amendment. This means that a person cannot be tried twice for the same crime. However, if a court sets aside a conviction because of a legal error, the accused can be tried again. A person on trial cannot be forced to testify, or give evidence, against himself or herself. A person accused of a crime is entitled to due process of law, or a fair hearing or trial. Finally, the government cannot seize private property for public use without paying the owner a fair price for it.

Sixth Amendment In criminal cases, the jury must be impartial, or not favor either side. The accused is guaranteed the right to a trial by jury. The trial must be speedy. If the government purposely postpones the trial so that it becomes hard for the person to get a fair hearing, the charge may be dismissed. The accused must be told the charges and be allowed to question all witnesses. Witnesses who can help the accused can be ordered to appear in court. The accused must be allowed a lawyer.

Seventh Amendment Common law refers to rules of law established by judges in past cases. This amendment guarantees the right to a jury trial in lawsuits where the sum of money at stake is more than $20. An appeals court can set aside a verdict only if legal errors made the trial unfair.

Eighth Amendment <u>Bail</u> is money that the accused leaves with the court as a pledge to appear for trial. If the accused does not appear, the court keeps the money. This amendment prevents the court from imposing bail or fines that are <u>excessive</u>, or too high. The amendment also forbids cruel and unusual punishments, such as physical torture.

Ninth Amendment The rights of the people are not limited to those listed in the Bill of Rights. In the Ninth Amendment, the government is prevented from claiming these are the only rights people have.

Tenth Amendment Powers not given to the federal government belong to the states. Powers reserved to the states are not listed in the Constitution.

Eleventh Amendment A private citizen from one state cannot sue the government of another state in federal court. However, a citizen can sue a state government in a state court.

Twelfth Amendment This amendment changed the way the electoral college voted as outlined in Article II, Clause 3. This amendment provides that each elector choose one candidate for President and one candidate for Vice President. If no candidate for President receives a majority of electoral votes, the House of Representatives chooses the President. If no candidate for Vice President receives a majority, the Senate elects the Vice President. The Vice President must be a person who is eligible to be President.

This system is still in use today. However, it is possible for a candidate to win the popular vote and lose in the electoral college. This happened in 1888 and in 2000.

Note: The black lines indicate portions of the Constitution altered by later amendments or that no longer apply.

8th Amendment
(1791)Bail; Cruel, Unusual Punishment

Excessive bail shall not be required, nor excessive fines imposed, nor cruel and unusual punishment inflicted.

9th Amendment
(1791) Unenumerated Rights

The enumeration in the Constitution, of certain rights, shall not be construed to deny or disparage others retained by the people.

10th Amendment
(1791) Powers Reserved to the States

The powers not delegated to the United States by the Constitution, nor prohibited by it to the States, are reserved to the States respectively, or to the people.

11th Amendment
(1795) Suits Against the States

The Judicial power of the United States shall not be construed to extend to any suit in law or equity, commenced or prosecuted against one of the United States by Citizens of another State, or by Citizens or Subjects of any Foreign State.

12th Amendment
(1804) Election of President and Vice President

The Electors shall meet in their respective States and vote by ballot for President and Vice President, one of whom, at least, shall not be an inhabitant of the same State with themselves; they shall name in their ballots the person voted for as President, and in distinct ballots the person voted for as Vice President, and they shall make distinct lists of all persons voted for as President, and of all persons voted for as Vice President, and of the number of votes for each, which lists they shall sign and certify, and transmit sealed to the seat of the government of the United States, directed to the President of the Senate;— The President of the Senate shall, in the presence of the Senate and the House of Representatives, open all the certificates and the votes shall then be counted;— the person having the greatest Number of votes for President shall be the President, if such number be a majority of the whole number of Electors appointed; and if no person have such a majority, then, from the persons having the highest numbers not exceeding three on the list of those voted for as President, the House of Representatives shall choose immediately, by ballot, the President. But in choosing the President, the votes shall be taken by States, the representation from each State having one vote; a quorum for this purpose shall consist of a member or members from two thirds of the States, and a majority of all the States shall be necessary to a choice. ~~And if the House of Representatives shall not choose a President whenever the right of choice shall devolve upon them, before the fourth day of March next following, then the Vice President shall act as President, as in case of death or other constitutional disability of the President.~~ The person having the greatest number of votes as Vice President, shall be the Vice President, if such number be a majority of the whole number of Electors appointed, and if no person have a majority, then from the two highest numbers on the list, the Senate shall choose the Vice President; a quorum for the purpose shall consist of two thirds of the whole number of Senators, a majority of the whole number shall be necessary to a choice. But no person constitutionally ineligible to the office of President shall be eligible to that of Vice-President of the United States.

13th Amendment

(1865) Slavery and Involuntary Servitude

Section 1. Slavery and Involuntary Servitude Neither slavery nor involuntary servitude, except as a punishment for crime whereof the party shall have been duly convicted, shall exist within the United States, or any place subject to their jurisdiction.

Section 2. Power of Congress Congress shall have power to enforce this article by appropriate legislation.

14th Amendment

(1868) Rights of Citizens

Section 1. Citizenship All persons born or naturalized in the United States and subject to the jurisdiction thereof, are citizens of the United States and of the State wherein they reside. No State shall make or enforce any law which shall abridge the privileges or immunities of citizens of the United States; nor shall any State deprive any person of life, liberty, or property, without due process of law; nor deny to any person within its jurisdiction the equal protection of the laws.

Section 2. Apportionment of Representatives Representatives shall be apportioned among the several States according to their respective numbers, counting the whole number of persons in each State, excluding Indians not taxed. But when the right to vote at any election for the choice of electors for President and Vice President of the United States, Representatives in Congress, the Executive and Judicial officers of a State, or the members of the Legislature thereof, is denied to any of the male inhabitants of such State, being twenty-one years of age and citizens of the United States, or in any way abridged, except for participation in rebellion,

Thirteenth Amendment The Emancipation Proclamation (1863) freed slaves only in areas controlled by the Confederacy. This amendment freed all slaves. It also forbids <u>involuntary servitude</u>, or labor done against one's will. However, it does not prevent prison wardens from making prisoners work. Congress can pass laws to carry out this amendment.

Fourteenth Amendment, Section 1 This amendment defines citizenship for the first time in the Constitution. It was intended to protect the rights of the freed slaves by guaranteeing all citizens "equal protection under the law."

Fourteenth Amendment, Section 2 This section replaced the three-fifths clause. It provides that representation in the House of Representatives is decided on the basis of the number of people in the state. It also provides that states that deny the vote to male citizens over age 21 will be punished by losing part of their representation in the House. This provision has never been enforced.

or other crime, the basis of representation therein shall be reduced in the proportion which the number of such male citizens shall bear to the whole number of male citizens twenty-one years of age in such State.

Section 3. Disqualification of Officers No person shall be a Senator or Representative in Congress, or elector of President and Vice President, or hold any office, civil or military, under the United States, or under any State, who, having previously taken an oath, as a member of Congress, or as an officer of the United States, or as a member of any State legislature, or as an executive or judicial officer of any State, to support the Constitution of the United States, shall have engaged in insurrection or rebellion against the same, or given aid or comfort to the enemies thereof. But Congress may, by a vote of two thirds of each House, remove such disability.

Section 4. Public Debt The validity of the public debt of the United States, authorized by law, including debts incurred for payment of pensions and bounties for services in suppressing insurrection or rebellion, shall not be questioned. But neither the United States nor any State shall assume or pay any debt or obligation incurred in aid of insurrection or rebellion against the United States, or any claim for the loss or emancipation of any slave; but all such debts, obligations and claims shall be held illegal and void.

Section 5. Power of Congress The Congress shall have power to enforce, by appropriate legislation, the provisions of this article.

15th Amendment
(1870) Right to Vote—Race, Color, Servitude

Section 1. Suffrage Not to be Abridged The right of citizens of the United States to vote shall not be denied or abridged by the United States or by any State on account of race, color, or previous condition of servitude.

Section 2. Power of Congress The Congress shall have power to enforce this article by appropriate legislation.

16th Amendment
(1913) Income Tax

The Congress shall have power to lay and collect taxes on incomes, from whatever source derived, without apportionment among the several States, and without regard to any census or enumeration.

Fifteenth Amendment, Section 1
Previous condition of servitude refers to slavery. This amendment gave African Americans, both those who were former slaves and those who were free, the right to vote. In the late 1800s, southern states used grandfather clauses, literacy tests, and poll taxes to keep African Americans from voting.

Fifteenth Amendment, Section 2 Congress can pass laws to carry out this amendment. The Twenty-Fourth Amendment barred the use of poll taxes in national elections. The Voting Rights Act of 1965 gave federal officials the power to register voters where there was voting discrimination.

Sixteenth Amendment Congress has the power to collect taxes on people's income. An income tax can be collected without regard to a state's population. This amendment changed Article 1, Section 9, Clause 4.

Note: The black lines indicate portions of the Constitution altered by later amendments or that no longer apply.

17th Amendment
(1913) Popular Election of Senators

Section 1. Popular Election of Senators The Senate of the United States shall be composed of two Senators from each State, elected by the people thereof, for six years; and each Senator shall have one vote. The electors in each State shall have the qualifications requisite for electors of the most numerous branch of the State legislatures.

Section 2. Senate Vacancies When vacancies happen in the representation of any State in the Senate, the executive authority of such State shall issue writs of election to fill such vacancies: Provided, That the legislature of any State may empower the executive thereof to make temporary appointments until the people fill the vacancies by election as the legislature may direct.

Section 3. Inapplicable to Senators Previously Chosen ~~This amendment shall not be so construed as to affect the election or term of any Senator chosen before it becomes valid as part of the Constitution~~

18th Amendment
(1919) Prohibition of Intoxicating Beverages

Section 1. Ban on Alcohol ~~After one year from the ratification of this article the manufacture, sale, or transportation of intoxicating liquors within, the importation thereof into, or the exportation thereof from the United States and all territory subject to the jurisdiction thereof for beverage purposes is hereby prohibited.~~

Section 2. Concurrent Power to Enforce ~~The Congress and the several States shall have concurrent power to enforce this article by appropriate legislation.~~

Section 3. The Limit on Ratification ~~This article shall be inoperative unless it shall have been ratified as an amendment to the Constitution by the legislatures of the several States, as provided in the Constitution, within seven years of the date of the submission hereof to the States by Congress.~~

19th Amendment
(1920) Equal Suffrage—Sex

Section 1. Suffrage Not to be Abridged The right of citizens of the United States to vote shall not be denied or abridged by the United States or by any State on account of sex.

Section 2. Power of Congress Congress shall have power to enforce this article by appropriate legislation.

Seventeenth Amendment, Section 1 This amendment replaced Article 1, Section 2, Clause 1. Before it was adopted, state legislatures chose senators. This amendment provides that senators are directly elected by the people of each state.

Eighteenth Amendment This amendment, known as Prohibition, banned the making, selling, or transporting of alcoholic beverages in the United States. Later, the Twenty-First Amendment <u>repealed</u>, or canceled, this amendment.

Nineteenth Amendment Neither the federal government nor state governments can deny the right to vote on account of sex. Thus, women won <u>suffrage</u>, or the right to vote. Before 1920, some states had allowed women to vote in state elections.

Twentieth Amendment, Section 1. The date for the inauguration of the President was changed to January 20, and the date for Congress to begin its term changed to January 3. Prior to this amendment, the beginning of term date was set in March. The outgoing officials with little or no influence on matters were not effective in office during the time after the election. Being so inactive, they were called "lame ducks."

Twentieth Amendment, Section 3. If the President–elect dies before taking office, the Vice President–elect becomes President. If no President has been chosen by January 20 or if the elected candidate fails to qualify for office, the Vice President–elect acts as President, but only until a qualified President is chosen.

Finally, Congress has the power to choose a person to act as President if neither the President-elect nor the Vice President–elect is qualified to take office.

Twenty-First Amendment, Section 1
The Eighteenth Amendment is repealed, making it legal to make and sell alcoholic beverages. Prohibition ended on December 5, 1933.

Note: The black lines indicate portions of the Constitution altered by later amendments or that no longer apply.

20th Amendment
(1933) Commencement of Terms; Sessions of Congress; Death or Disqualification of President-Elect

Section 1. Beginning of terms The terms of the President and Vice President shall end at noon on the 20th day of January, and the terms of Senators and Representatives at noon on the 3d day of January, of the years in which such terms would have ended if this article had not been ratified; and the terms of their successors shall then begin.

Section 2. Sessions of Congress The Congress shall assemble at least once in every year, and such meeting shall begin at noon on the 3d day of January, unless they shall by law appoint a different day.

Section 3. Death or Disqualification of President-Elect If, at the time fixed for the beginning of the term of the President, the President elect shall have died, the Vice President elect shall become President. If a President shall not have been chosen before the time fixed for the beginning of his term, or if the President-elect shall have failed to qualify, then the Vice President elect shall act as President until a President shall have qualified; and the Congress may by law provide for the case wherein neither a President elect nor a Vice President elect shall have qualified, declaring who shall then act as President, or the manner in which one who is to act shall be selected, and such person shall act accordingly until a President or Vice President shall have qualified.

Section 4. Congress to Provide for Certain Successors The Congress may by law provide for the case of the death of any of the persons from whom the House of Representatives may choose a President whenever the right of choice shall have devolved upon them, and for the case of the death of any of the persons from whom the Senate may choose a Vice President whenever the right of choice shall have devolved upon them.

Section 5. Effective Date ~~Sections 1 and 2 shall take effect on the 15th day of October following the ratification of this article.~~

Section 6. Time Limit on Ratification This article shall be inoperative unless it shall have been ratified as an amendment to the Constitution by the legislatures of three fourths of the several States within seven years from the date of its submission.

21st Amendment
(1933) Repeal of Prohibition

Section 1. Repeal The eighteenth article of amendment to the Constitution of the United States is hereby repealed.

Section 2. Transportation/Importation of Intoxicating Liquors The transportation or importation into any State, Territory, or possession of the United States for delivery or use therein of intoxicating liquors, in violation of the laws thereof, is hereby prohibited.

Section 3. Time Limit on Ratification This article shall be inoperative unless it shall have been ratified as an amendment to the Constitution by conventions in the several States, as provided in the Constitution, within seven years from the date of the submission hereof to the States by the Congress.

22nd Amendment
(1951) Presidential Tenure

Section 1. Presidential Elections for District No person shall be elected to the office of the President more than twice, and no person who has held the office of President, or acted as President, for more than two years of a term to which some other person was elected President shall be elected to the office of the President more than once. But this Article shall not apply to any person holding the office of President, when this Article was proposed by the Congress, and shall not prevent any person who may be holding the office of President, or acting as President, during the term within which this Article becomes operative from holding the office of President or acting as President during the remainder of such term.

Section 2. Power of Congress This article shall be inoperative unless it shall have been ratified as an amendment to the Constitution by the legislatures of three fourths of the several states within seven years from the date of its submission to the States by the Congress.

23rd Amendment
(1961) Presidential Electors for Inclusion of District of Columbia in Presidential Election Systems

Section 1. Determining the Number of Electors The District constituting the seat of Government of the United States shall appoint in such manner as the Congress may direct:

A number of electors of President and Vice President equal to the whole number of Senators and Representatives in Congress to which the District would be entitled if it were a State, but in no event more than the least populous State; they shall be in addition to those appointed by the States, they shall be considered, for the purposes of the election of President and Vice President, to be electors appointed by a State; and they shall meet in the District and perform such duties as provided by the twelfth article of amendment.

Section 2. Power of Congress The Congress shall have power to enforce this article by appropriate legislation.

Twenty-Second Amendment, Section 1
This amendment provides that no President may serve more than two terms. A President who has already served more than half of someone else's term can serve only one more full term. Before Franklin Roosevelt became President, no President had served more than two terms in office. Roosevelt broke with this custom and was elected to four terms. The amendment, however, did not apply to Harry Truman, who became President after Franklin Roosevelt's death in 1945.

Twenty-Third Amendment, Section 1
This amendment gives the residents of Washington, D.C., the right to vote in presidential elections. Until this amendment was adopted, people living in Washington, D.C., could not vote for President because the Constitution had made no provision for choosing electors from the nation's capital. Washington, D.C., now has three electoral votes.

Twenty-Fourth Amendment, Section 1
A poll tax is a tax on voters. This amendment bans poll taxes in national elections. Some states used poll taxes to keep African Americans from voting. In 1966, the Supreme Court struck down poll taxes in state elections.

Twenty-Fifth Amendment, Section 1 If the President dies or resigns, the Vice President becomes President. This section clarifies Article 2, Section 1, Clause 6.

Twenty-Fifth Amendment, Section 3 If the President declares in writing that he or she is unable to perform the duties of office, the Vice President serves as acting President until the President recovers.

Twenty-fifth Amendment, Section 4
Two Presidents, Woodrow Wilson and Dwight Eisenhower, fell gravely ill while in office. The Constitution contained no provision for this kind of emergency. Section 3 provided that the President can inform Congress he or she is too sick to perform the duties of office. However, if the President is unconscious or refuses to admit to a disabling illness, Section 4 provides that the Vice President and Cabinet may declare the President disabled. The Vice President becomes the acting President until the President can return to the duties of office. In case of a disagreement between the President and the Vice President and Cabinet over the President's ability to perform the duties of office, Congress must decide the issue. A two-thirds vote of both houses is needed to find that the President is disabled or unable to fulfill the duties of office.

Note: The black lines indicate portions of the Constitution altered by later amendments or that no longer apply.

24th Amendment

(1964) Right to Vote in Federal Elections—Tax Payments

Section 1. Suffrage Not to Be Abridged The right of citizens of the United States to vote in any primary or other election for President or Vice President, for electors for President or Vice President, or for Senator or Representative in Congress, shall not be denied or abridged by the United States or any State by reason of failure to pay any poll tax or other tax.

Section 2. Power of Congress The Congress shall have power to enforce this article by appropriate legislation.

25th Amendment

(1967) Presidential Succession, Vice Presidential Vacancy, Presidential Inability

Section 1. Presidential Succession In case of the removal of the President from office or of his death or resignation, the Vice President shall become President.

Section 2. Vice Presidential Vacancy Whenever there is a vacancy in the office of the Vice President, the President shall nominate a Vice President who shall take office upon confirmation by a majority vote of both Houses of Congress.

Section 3. Presidential Inability Whenever the President transmits to the President pro tempore of the Senate and the Speaker of the House of Representatives his written declaration that he is unable to discharge the powers and duties of his office, and until he transmits to them a written declaration to the contrary, such powers and duties shall be discharged by the Vice President as Acting President.

Section 4. Vice President as Acting President Whenever the Vice President and a majority of either the principal officers of the executive departments or of such other body as Congress may by law provide, transmit to the President pro tempore of the Senate and the Speaker of the House of Representatives their written declaration that the President is unable to discharge the powers and duties of his office, the Vice President shall immediately assume the powers and duties of the office as Acting President.

Thereafter, when the President transmits to the President pro tempore of the Senate and the Speaker of the House of Representatives his written declaration that no inability exists, he shall resume the powers and duties of his office unless the Vice President and a majority of either the principal officers of the executive department or of such other body as Congress may by law provide, transmit within four days to the President pro tempore of the Senate and the Speaker of the House of Representatives their written declaration that the President is unable to discharge the powers and duties of his office. Thereupon Congress shall decide the issue, assembling within forty-eight hours for that purpose if not in session. If the Congress, within twenty-one days after receipt of the latter written declaration, or, if Congress is not in session, within twenty-one days after Congress is required to assemble, determines by two-thirds vote of both Houses that the President is unable to discharge the powers and duties of his office, the Vice President shall continue to discharge the same as Acting President; otherwise, the President shall resume the powers and duties of his office.

26th Amendment

(1971) Right to Vote—Age

Section 1. Suffrage Not to Be Abridged The right of citizens of the United States, who are eighteen years of age or older, to vote shall not be denied or abridged by the United States or by any State on account of age.

Section 2. Power of Congress The Congress shall have the power to enforce this article by appropriate legislation.

27th Amendment

(1992) Congressional Pay

No law varying the compensation for the services of the Senators and Representatives, shall take effect, until an election of Representatives shall have intervened.

Twenty-Sixth Amendment, Section 1 In 1970, Congress passed a law allowing 18-year-olds to vote. However, the Supreme Court decided that Congress could not set a minimum age for state elections.

Twenty-Seventh Amendment If members of Congress vote themselves a pay increase, it cannot go into effect until after the next congressional election. This amendment was proposed in 1789. In 1992, Michigan became the thirty-eighth state to ratify it.

21st Century Skills

Skills Handbook

The following pages provide you with the skills you need to learn about and demonstrate your knowledge of American government.

Writing

Writing is one of the most powerful communication tools you will use for the rest of your life. The written word inspires, informs, and entertains. Research shows that writing about what you read helps you learn new information and form new ideas. A systematic approach to writing—including prewriting, drafting, revising, and proofreading—can help you write better.

Narrative Essay

Narrative writing tells a story, often about a personal experience. In a government or civics course, this story might be a narrative essay that recounts, for example, how participation in a campaign affected you.

① Prewriting

Choose a topic. The focus of your essay should be an important experience to you. Use these suggestions as a guide.
- Look at photos that show you with friends or family. Perhaps you attended a political rally or worked on a community event for a cause you cared about.
- Scan the news in print or through electronic media. Consider how current events, court decisions, or election results have affected you or people you know. Brainstorm with family or friends. How did you react or respond to these events? Write down ideas like the ones below.

Consider audience and purpose. As you write, think about who your reader will be.
- Think about what your audience already knows about the topic. Make sure you provide any necessary background information.
- Think about the purpose of the essay. Is your goal to entertain or inform? If your goal is to inform, you might share your thoughts, describe what you learned, or tell how the experience changed you.

Connections to Government and Politics This Year
- participated in a mock legislative assembly
- watched debates between candidates on television
- attended a climate change rally and started a petition for stricter controls on greenhouse emissions

Gather details. Collect the facts and details you need to tell your story.
- Conduct research. Include any background information about the experience that readers might need to understand how it affected you.
- List details about your own thoughts and feelings about the experience.

② Drafting

Organize information. Narratives are usually told in chronological order. Identify the climax, or high point, in your story. Then logically organize your work into a beginning, middle, and end.

Write an opening sentence. Begin with an engaging sentence that will catch your reader's attention.

Use sensory details. Use sights, sounds, or smells to make the story come alive for readers. Describe people's actions and body language. Tell about the setting.

Write a conclusion. Sum up the importance of the experience.

A strong opening engages the reader. → Practicing my speech in front of my bedroom mirror wasn't so bad. Now, however, I was saying these same words out loud in a crowded high school auditorium. It was filled with seniors who would rather be somewhere else.

Sensory details make the moment come alive. → My heart pounded wildly. My first thought was "What am I doing here?" As I began to talk, some of those bored expressions began to change. Other people, however, whispered to their neighbors or stared off into space. Couldn't they see that climate change might someday have a dramatic effect on their lives?

Your thoughts tell the reader what this event means to you. → I learned that day that knowing how you feel about an issue is easy. Convincing others to take that issue seriously is much tougher. My political education was just beginning.

③ Revising

Add dialogue or description. Dialogue (a person's thoughts or feelings in his or her own words) can make a narrative more convincing. Look for places in the story where the emotions are especially intense. In the model, this might be when the speaker first faces the bored audience.

First Draft	Revision
Despite the many times I had practiced my speech in front of a mirror, I was still nervous. My heart was beating fast as I looked out at the auditorium.	Practicing my speech in front of my bedroom mirror wasn't so bad. Now, however, I was saying these same words in a crowded high school auditorium. It was filled with seniors who would rather be somewhere else. My heart pounded wildly.

Revise word choice. Replace general words with more specific, colorful ones. Choose vivid action verbs and specific adjectives and nouns to convey your meaning. In the example above, notice how much more effective the revised version is at telling the experience.

Read your draft aloud. Listen for grammatical errors and for statements that are unclear. Revise your sentences as necessary.

④ Publishing and Presenting

Highlight text you want to emphasize. Then read your essay aloud to the class. Invite questions and then respond to them.

Expository Writing

Expository writing explains ideas or information in detail. The strategies on these pages examine different types of expository writing.

① Prewriting

Choose a topic. In a government course, the focus of your writing might be to explain the process of a bill becoming law. It might be to examine the causes and effects of policy changes. The following suggestions are a guide.

- For writing about a process, consider the question *how*. For example, you might ask, "How does a bill become a law?" Then you would identify the steps or procedures involved to answer the question.

> **Question:** How does a bill become a law?
>
> **Answer:** A proposed law is introduced in the House or Senate. It is then sent to the appropriate committee to be studied. If the committee votes to pass the bill, it is debated by the full House or Senate. After debate, members vote on the bill. If passed, it is sent to the other house and goes through the same process. If it passes that house, it is sent to the President for his approval or veto.

- With a partner, visit the Web sites of two candidates for office. Choose three issues that both candidates address. Note each candidate's viewpoint on the issues you've chosen.

- With a small group, write problems related to each of these challenges on slips of paper: global warming, universal healthcare, and energy alternatives. Have each person take a slip of paper and brainstorm possible solutions to each problem with the group.

- Write down questions to ask a school board member about changes they are considering. Ask why these changes are being considered. Understanding *why* is the basis of a cause-and-effect essay.

Consider audience and purpose. Consider how much your readers know about the topic you will address. Adjust your writing to your audience's knowledge or provide explanations of unfamiliar ideas.

Research the topic. Use library and Internet resources and interviews with local officials or experts if possible. Also consider your personal experience. You might know about a local community problem from first-hand experience.

Candidate A
- Favors expanding free trade agreements
- Wants government subsidies for private insurance companies
- Supports oil drilling on public lands to increase energy independence

Shared by Both Candidates
- Favors expanding healthcare benefits
- Supports increased energy independence

Candidate B
- Opposes international trade agreements
- Favors government-run healthcare programs
- Wants government to fund alternative energy programs to increase energy independence

Create a graphic organizer. For cause-and-effect or problem-solution essays, use a two-column chart. When writing about a process, make a bulleted list of the steps. A Venn diagram, like the one above, can help you compare and contrast.

Fine-tune your ideas. For a problem-solution essay, choose a solution that it is achievable in cost, effort, and time. If your solution has been tried by others, describe successes or failures and how your approach will differ. Keep in mind that problem-solution and process writing often involve cause-and-effect relationships. Look for causes and effects as you organize your material.

② Drafting

Match structure to purpose. Typically, problem-solution essays benefit from block organization. This structure presents the entire problem and then proposes a solution. Put process and cause-and-effect essays in sequential order. Organize compare-contrast essays by subject or by point.

By subject: Discuss the issues and viewpoints of Candidate A, and then compare and contrast them with those of Candidate B.

By point: Introduce each issue, such as healthcare or trade agreements. Give the views of both candidates on the issue, comparing or contrasting them in your discussion. Then move on to the next issue.

Give background. Provide the reader with context. Ensure that readers know why a law was passed or what the court case was about. Choose the important facts, but don't overwhelm the reader with too many details.

Elaborate for interest and emphasis. Give details about each point in your essay. To show a cause-and-effect relationship, explain the link between the reason for a decision or action and its consequences. In a problem-solution essay, readers are more likely to support proposed solutions if you show how the solutions will solve the problem. Sum up in a brief conclusion.

One of the most serious problems Americans face today is the rising cost of healthcare. For several decades, the cost of healthcare has risen much faster than personal wages. At the same time, the number of Americans without health insurance continues to rise. In 2006, 14.8 percent of Americans were uninsured. To further complicate the problem, the baby boom generation is just starting to retire. Experts predict that in the decade ahead these changes will greatly increase the demand for healthcare.

Healthcare policy analysts offer several strategies for reducing costs. First, allow the government to negotiate with drug companies for lower prescription prices. Also, allow cheaper drugs to be brought in from other countries. Second, pay doctors and other providers lower fees similar to those in other industrialized nations. Finally, make consumers pay more of their own healthcare costs so that they will consider the necessity of treatments. A careful plan to put these ideas into action will give more Americans access to quality healthcare.

Identify the topic for readers.

Point out causes of the problem.

List possible solutions.

Conclude by summarizing the goal of the solution.

③ Revising

Remember purpose. Your essay should answer the question or thesis with which you began. In a problem-solution essay, your purpose is to convince readers to support your solution. Think about the opposing arguments and respond to them.

Review organization. Number your main points. Reorganize these points so that they flow in a logical order.

Add transition words. Make cause-and-effect relationships clear with such words as *because* and *so*. To compare and contrast, use linking words, such as *similarly* or *in contrast*. Use words such as *first* and *next* to show steps in a process.

First Draft	Revision
The Federal Drug Administration monitors small clinical trials. These trials show the drug to be safe, and FDA officials conduct larger trials.	First, the Federal Drug Administration monitors small clinical trials. Next, if the results of these trials show the drug to be safe and effective enough for further study, FDA officials conduct larger trials.

Add details. For a process essay, be sure to include all steps. Don't assume readers will make connections. When writing about cause and effect, stress the way one event leads to the next. Add more background if necessary for clarity.

Revise. Vary sentence length. Scan for vague words, such as *good*, and replace them with specific words. Do not overuse technical terms, and be sure to define them.

Peer review. Ask a classmate to review your draft. Revise areas of confusion.

④ Publishing and Presenting

Create a government manual. Contribute your explanation of a government process to a class manual of Government How-Tos.

Skills Handbook **S5**

Research Writing

A research paper gives information about a topic from several different sources. The writer must then tie this information together and present it to the reader.

① Prewriting

Choose a topic. Often, a teacher will assign your research topic. If not, you may be allowed to choose your focus. The following suggestions are a guide.

- Using an online or electronic library catalog, search for topics that interest you. When a title looks promising, find the book on the shelves. Because libraries group research materials by subject, you should find other books on similar subjects.

- Review your class notes. Jot down topics that you found interesting. For example, you might find a starting point for research into students' legal rights in schools from a Supreme Court case that you studied in class.

- Brainstorm topics with a group. List interesting current events issues such as the economy, healthcare, the environment, and privacy. Within each category, take turns adding subtopics. The chart below looks at different topics related to the Internet, politics, and government.

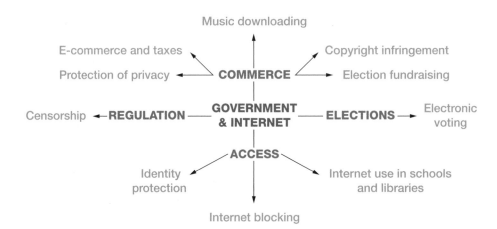

Music downloading

E-commerce and taxes

Copyright infringement

Protection of privacy ← **COMMERCE** → Election fundraising

Censorship ← **REGULATION** — **GOVERNMENT & INTERNET** — **ELECTIONS** → Electronic voting

ACCESS

Identity protection

Internet use in schools and libraries

Internet blocking

Analyze the audience. Your research and your paper should be strongly influenced by the audience. How much will readers already know about this topic and how much will you have to teach them?

Gather details. Collect the facts and details you need to write your paper. Use a variety of resources. Search the Internet for reliable information and opinions on your topic. Start with online encyclopedias and news organizations. Look for interviews with experts on your topic.

Organize evidence and ideas. Create notecards or a computer file on your topic. They will help you to record information and organize your thoughts. Start by writing down a possible thesis statement. Then begin reading and taking notes. Write a heading at the top of each notecard and add subtopics below. List your information sources on a separate card, giving each a number. Use that number to identify the source for each subtopic on your cards. In the examples below, the number 3 is used to identify the information source. Use the same number for additional topic cards from the same source.

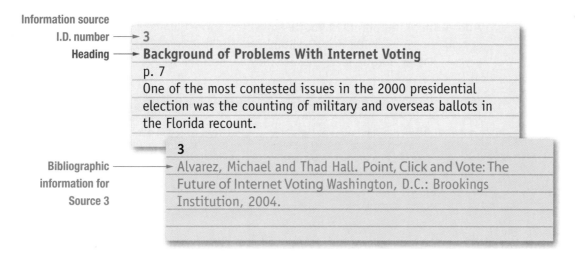

Information source
I.D. number → **3**
Heading → **Background of Problems With Internet Voting**
p. 7
One of the most contested issues in the 2000 presidential election was the counting of military and overseas ballots in the Florida recount.

3
Bibliographic information for Source 3 → Alvarez, Michael and Thad Hall. Point, Click and Vote: The Future of Internet Voting Washington, D.C.: Brookings Institution, 2004.

❷ Drafting

Fine-tune your thesis. Review your notes to find relationships between ideas. Shape a thesis that is supported by the majority of your information. Then check that the thesis statement is specific enough to address thoroughly. You can fine-tune your thesis further as you draft or even when you revise.

Organize the information to fit your purpose. Consider your reason for exploring this topic. Then identify the structure that will best help you reach this goal. For example, do you want to compare and contrast aspects of a topic? Do you want to persuade readers to support your position on an issue or policy? Or do you want to argue for a particular solution to a problem? Then organize appropriately. For example, if your goal is to persuade readers that electronic voting should be allowed in national elections, begin by stating arguments in favor of your position. Present opposing views and give your counterarguments to those points.

Make an outline. Create an outline in which you identify each topic and subtopic in a single phrase. Turn these phrases into sentences. Then organize them into the topic sentences and supporting sentences of your draft paragraphs. Write an introduction, at least three body paragraphs, and a conclusion. Support all of your statements with the facts and details you gathered.

An outline helps you organize your information.

Each paragraph in the body examines a part of the main topic.

Internet Voting
Outline
I. Introduction
II. What are the benefits of Internet voting?
A. Appeal to young voters and increased voter turnout
B. Ease and convenience of voting
III. What are the risks of Internet voting?
A. Inequality of access (Counterargument: Computers in schools and libraries provide access.)
B. Potential for voter fraud and tampering (Counterargument: Technological improvements make Internet voting more secure.)
IV. Conclusion: Benefits outweigh risks.

❸ Revising

Add detail. Find points in your essay where more details would strengthen your statements. In the following example, notice the added details in the revised version. When adding facts, be sure they are accurate.

First Draft	Revision
Internet voting can increase voter participation by making it easier to cast a ballot. Even people who don't own computers can vote in schools and libraries.	Internet voting can increase voter participation by making the process more convenient, especially for citizens with disabilities and Americans living abroad. Critics argue that online voting unfairly favors wealthier Americans who are more likely to own computers. In many places, however, voters who do not own computers will be able to cast their ballots on computers in public schools and libraries.

Make the connection for readers. Help readers find their way through your ideas. First, check that your paragraphs flow in a logical sequence. If they do not, revise to correct this. Then add transition words to link ideas and paragraphs.

Give credit. Check that you have used your own words or given proper credit to other sources. For quoted text, add parenthetical notes that include the author's last name and the page number from the source. For example, you could cite the notecard on page 57 as "(Alvarez and Hall, p. 7)." The surest way to avoid plagiarism is to take notes in your own words and then write from your notes. Avoid writing from the original source.

❹ Publishing and Presenting

Share your research. Gather a group of classmates and present your research projects. If time allows, create visual materials for your presentations. After you share your papers, hold a question-and-answer session.

Persuasive Essay

Persuasive writing is meant to convince readers to support your opinions. Persuasive essays in government often argue for or against government policies, candidates, or political issues.

① Prewriting

Choose a topic. Choose a topic that sparks discussion and has at least two sides. Use these suggestions as a guide.

- Talk with classmates about issues you have studied recently. Outline pro and con positions on these issues.
- Scan the table of contents or flip through the pages of your textbook. Focus on issues that interest you.
- Look at blogs, editorials, or Op-Ed pieces online or in current newspapers. Develop a position on an issue of importance today.

Narrow your topic. Choose a subsection of the topic to focus on if the subject is broad. Write for five minutes on the general topic. Circle the most important idea. Then write for five minutes on that idea. Continue looping until the topic is manageable.

Consider your audience. Choose arguments that will appeal to your audience and that are likely to persuade readers to agree with your views.

Gather evidence. Collect evidence that will help you support your position convincingly.

Identify pros and cons. Use a graphic organizer like the one below to list points on both sides of the issue.

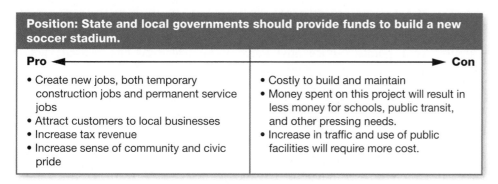

Position: State and local governments should provide funds to build a new soccer stadium.	
Pro ←	**→ Con**
• Create new jobs, both temporary construction jobs and permanent service jobs • Attract customers to local businesses • Increase tax revenue • Increase sense of community and civic pride	• Costly to build and maintain • Money spent on this project will result in less money for schools, public transit, and other pressing needs. • Increase in traffic and use of public facilities will require more cost.

② Drafting

State your thesis. Clearly state your position, as in this example:

> Local and state government officials should provide funding for the construction of a new soccer stadium because of the economic and social benefits it will bring to the city and the region.

Write your introduction Use your introduction to provide context. Tell your readers when and why the issue arose, and identify the key decision makers involved.

Acknowledge the opposition. State opposing arguments. Then refute them.

Use facts and details. Include quotations, statistics, or comparisons to build your case. Include personal experiences or reactions to the topic, such as the opinions of officials who were interviewed.

Write a conclusion. Return to your thesis and close with a strong, compelling argument or a brief summary of the three strongest arguments.

Background orients readers.	A plan to build a world-class soccer stadium has been proposed at both the state and local levels. Is this a good idea for our city? I believe that
Thesis identifies your main argument.	it is. Local and state government officials should provide funding for construction of a new soccer stadium because of the economic and social benefits it will bring to the city and the region. Those who oppose the
Acknowledging opposing argument and then refuting it solidifies your position.	stadium project focus mainly on its costs to the public. The new stadium will bring many benefits that don't show up on a balance sheet— entertainment, excitement, and, most importantly, a sense of community pride. Studies show that cities with professional sports teams attract
Supporting argument clarifies your thesis and sums up your position.	more tourists. Equally important, residents get a positive message about their community every time they turn on their TVs and see the local team on the new playing field.

③ Revising

Add information. Extra details can generate interest in your topic. For example, add a quotation from a news article supporting your argument.

Review arguments. Make sure your arguments are logical and clear. Avoid arguing a point by merely restating it differently. Evidence is the best way to support your points. Notice how much more effectively the revised version supports the argument in the following example.

First Draft	Revision
Building a new stadium will bring money to the city, which will help residents.	A 2008 study commissioned by the city manager estimated that stadium construction would create 1,700 construction jobs and provide $2 million in tax revenues. The study also concluded that spending at local hotels, restaurants, and shops by visiting soccer teams and fans would bring in an additional $1.1 million per year.

Use transition words to guide readers. To show contrast, use *although* or *despite*. To point out a reason, use *because* or *if*. To signal a conclusion, use *so* or *then*.

④ Publishing and Presenting

Persuasive speech. Many persuasive essays are delivered orally. Prepare your essay as a speech. Highlight words that you will emphasize.

Writing for Assessment

Assessment writing allows fewer choices than other writing. It usually imposes a time limit as well. In government and political science courses, you will be required to write both short-answer and extended responses.

1 Prewriting

Choose a topic. Short-answer questions seldom offer a choice of topics. For extended response, however, you may have a choice of more than one question.

- Analyze what each question is asking. Identify key words such as those listed below.

Key Words	What You Need in an Answer
• Explain	• Give a clear, complete account.
• Compare/Contrast	• Show how two or more things are alike and different.
• Define	• Give examples to explain meaning.
• Argue, Convince, Support, Persuade	• Take a position on an issue and present strong reasons to support your opinion.
• Summarize	• Provide the most important elements.
• Evaluate/Judge	• Assign a value or explain an opinion.

- Notice that the key words are underlined below.

> **Short-Answer Question:** Explain why the ability to communicate is an important aspect of presidential leadership.
>
> **Extended-Response Question:** What leadership qualities have the nation's most outstanding Presidents displayed? Give examples to support your choices.

- After choosing a question, try to answer it quickly in your mind. If you cannot do so easily, choose another question.

Measure your time. Divide your time: one quarter on prewriting, half on drafting, one quarter on revising. For short-answer questions, decide how much of the overall test time you can spend on each question.

Organize your response. For extended-response questions, divide your topic into subtopics that fit the type of question. Jot down facts and details for each. For a question on presidential leadership, consider the following.

Leadership Qualities of Outstanding Presidents
1. ability to communicate and build consensus on major policies
2. ability to gain the trust and respect of the American public
3. vision or clear idea of where to lead the nation
4. openness to new ideas; flexibility in changing conditions

Example of President Exhibiting Specific Leadership Qualities
• Franklin Roosevelt: ability to communicate, gain trust, try new ideas (New Deal)

② Drafting

Choose an appropriate organization. For short-answer responses, write one to three complete sentences. Extended responses require a more elaborate structure. For an extended response on presidential leadership, describe the leadership qualities of each President, and give examples. For problem-solution questions, describe the problem, and propose a solution. For compare-contrast questions, present similarities first, then differences.

Open and close strongly. Start by using the words in the question to state your position. This helps you focus and shows that you understand the question. Conclude by restating your position. For short answers, include language from the question in your response.

Support your ideas. Each paragraph should support your main idea.

> The opening restates the question and presents the main idea.
> The writer uses information from the graphic organizer to build an argument.
> The writer supports the second subtopic.
> The conclusion recaps the main idea and uses the question's language.

By itself, no single quality makes an exceptional leader. In the careers of the nation's most outstanding Presidents, many of their qualities built upon and complemented one another. Franklin Roosevelt was a highly effective communicator and flexible leader. (1) Despite his privileged upbringing, his skills as a communicator enabled him to convey his compassion for the poor and earned him the trust and respect of the American people. He used his communication skills to convince the people in his administration to work together. Roosevelt showed flexibility in responding to the difficult economic and social challenges of the Depression (2) by his advocacy of the many experimental programs and policies of his New Deal initiative. President Roosevelt provides an excellent example of several key qualities of an exceptional leader.

③ Revising

Examine word choice. Replace general words with specific words. Add transitions where they improve clarity. Read the following examples. The revised version shows the relative importance of the writer's supporting evidence.

First Draft	Revision
No single quality makes a good leader. Qualities build upon and complement one another. Franklin Delano Roosevelt was a highly effective communicator because he won the trust and support of the American people. He convinced people to work together.	By itself no single quality makes an exceptional leader. In the careers of the nation's most outstanding Presidents, many qualities built upon and complemented one another. For example, Franklin Delano Roosevelt was a highly effective communicator who won the trust and support of the American people; in addition, the President convinced the people in his administration to work together.

Check organization. Make sure your introduction includes a main idea and briefly defines each subtopic. Review each paragraph for a single main idea. Check that your conclusion summarizes the information you have presented.

④ Publishing and Presenting

Edit and proofread. Check spelling, grammar, and mechanics. Make sure that tenses match, subjects agree with verbs, and all sentences include a subject and verb. Confirm that you have responded to all the questions you were asked.

Writing Rubric

Use this chart, or rubric, to evaluate your writing.

Criteria	Exceeds standard	Meets standard	Approaches standard	Does not meet standard
Thesis	Sharp, well-developed thesis with clear connection to topic	Sharp and mostly developed thesis with clear connection to topic	Somewhat clear thesis with limited connection to topic	No thesis, or unclear thesis, with little connection to topic
Introduction	Clear, direct focus; highly interesting and engaging; provides excellent context for discussing topic	Focused and interesting, provides context for discussing topic	Somewhat focused and interesting, provides some limited context for discussing topic	Too broad, provides little context for discussing topic; uses throwaway phrases like "throughout history"
Organization	Recognizable beginning, middle, and ending; logically organized with a variety of transitions	Clear beginning, middle, and ending; generally logical organization with some transition words used	Beginning, middle, and ending unclear; connections between ideas weak and few transition words used	No beginning, middle, or ending; no connections between ideas and no transition words used
Supporting evidence and facts	Substantial facts and evidence	Sufficient facts and evidence	Uneven use of facts and evidence	Insufficient facts and evidence
Analysis	Effective, logical, sophisticated analysis supported by facts and evidence; demonstrates keen insight into and understanding of topic	Effective, logical analysis supported by facts and evidence; demonstrates clear understanding of topic	General and/or somewhat illogical or inconsistent analysis; facts and evidence somewhat enhance analysis; demonstrates basic understanding of topic	Limited and/or illogical analysis; uses descriptive and storytelling format rather than analysis; demonstrates limited understanding of topic
Conclusion	Ties together main ideas to arrive at a logical and insightful conclusion that shows deep understanding of the topic	Ties together main ideas to arrive at a logical and insightful conclusion	Demonstrates some understanding of the topic and/or relies heavily on summary	Demonstrates general and shallow understanding of the topic or is summary only
Mechanics	Extremely few or no grammatical, spelling, punctuation, or other mechanical errors	A few grammatical and spelling errors, which do not distract from the overall quality of the paper	Some errors in spelling, grammar, punctuation, word choice, and capitalization; includes repetition, fragments, conversational prose	Many grammatical, spelling, punctuation, and other errors, which detract from the quality of the paper

Critical Thinking

Analyze Sources

A primary source is a firsthand account of an event. Examples include letters and photographs. A secondary source is an account based on primary sources. Follow these steps to analyze primary and secondary sources.

1 Identify the document. Determine when, where, and why it was written. Is the document a primary or secondary source?

2 Find the main idea. After identifying the main idea, identify details or sections of text that support the main idea.

3 Evaluate the source for point of view and bias. Primary sources often have a strong point of view or bias. It is important to analyze primary sources critically.

> For three weeks in September 1957, . . . Little Rock became the focus of a showdown over integration as Gov. Orval Faubus blocked nine black students from enrolling at all-white Central. Although the U.S. Supreme Court had declared segregated classrooms unconstitutional in 1954 . . . Faubus said he feared violence if the races mixed in a public school. The showdown soon became a test for President Dwight D. Eisenhower, who has been derided by some historians as being silent on civil rights. . . .
>   David A. Nichols, author of *A Matter of Justice: Eisenhower and the Beginning of the Civil Rights Revolution*, argues that the showdown . . . showed the 34th president's true feelings about desegregation. "I think the intervention in Little Rock revealed who Eisenhower really was on this issue," . . .
>
> —*USA Today*, September 22, 2007

> Newport, Rhode Island,
> September 27, 1957
>
> The Honorable Richard B. Russell [Georgia]
> United States Senate
> Washington, D.C.
>
> Few times in my life have I felt as saddened as when the obligations of my office required me to order the use of force [federal troops] within a state to carry out the decisions of a Federal Court. . . . [H]ad the police powers of the State of Arkansas been utilized not to frustrate the orders of the Court but to support them, the ensuing violence and open disrespect for the law would never have occurred. . . . When a State, . . . refuses to utilize its police powers to protect against mobs persons who are peaceably exercising their right under the Constitution . . . the oath of office of the President requires that he take action. . . . "
>
> —President Dwight D. Eisenhower

Practice and Apply the Skill

Use the sources above to answer the following questions.

1. What makes the letter a primary source and the article a secondary source?

2. Based on the letter, what are Eisenhower's reasons for sending federal troops?

3. What point does the article make about Eisenhower's role in the Little Rock crisis? How is this point supported by the letter?

Compare Viewpoints

Many factors shape a person's viewpoint. These factors include values, age, prejudices, gender, and past experiences. Comparing viewpoints will help you understand issues and form your own opinions. Use the following steps to learn about comparing viewpoints. Then analyze the speeches below and answer the questions.

1 Identify the authors. Determine when and where each person was speaking. Identify the intended audience for each speech and the speech's purpose.

2 Determine the author's frame of reference. Consider how each speaker's values; social, economic, or political concerns and affiliations; and past experiences might affect his or her viewpoint.

3 Determine the author's bias. Bias may be revealed through emotionally charged words, faulty logic, or exaggerated claims. In written or spoken materials, be sure to identify which statements are facts and which are opinions.

4 Compare and contrast. Determine how the viewpoints are similar and different. Consider factors that might have contributed to differing positions.

Passage A

It is time to check and reverse the growth of government which shows signs of having grown beyond the consent of the governed. It is my intention to curb the size and influence of the Federal establishment . . . . Now . . . it is not my intention to do away with government. It is, rather, to make it . . . . stand by our side, not ride on our back. . . . It is no coincidence that our present troubles . . . are proportionate to the intervention and intrusion into our lives that result from unnecessary and excessive growth of government.

—Ronald Reagan, First Inaugural Address, January 20, 1981

Passage B

My view is to . . . recognize that [the federal government] has a role in our lives and a partnership role to play. We have made the Government smaller. . . . We have . . . been working . . . to reduce the burden of unnecessary regulation. But we believe Government has important work to do, to expand opportunity, to give people the tools they need to make the most of their own lives, to enhance our security. That's why we support adding 100,000 police . . . more affordable college loans . . . the minimum wage legislation now before Congress. . . .

—Bill Clinton, Press Conference, March 4, 1995

Practice and Apply the Skill

Use the passages above to answer the following questions.

1. Who are the speakers, where did they speak, and who was the intended audience?

2. What issue are both Presidents addressing? How do their viewpoints differ?

3. How do you think each President's political background influenced his viewpoint?

4. How does Reagan's statement that government should "not ride on our back" reflect a bias, if any, on this issue?

Analyze Cause and Effect

Recognizing a cause-effect relationship means examining how one event or action brings about others. Government decision makers face choices and often need to understand relationships among events to set or improve policy. Use the following steps to learn how to understand the relationships between causes and effects. Then read the passage below and answer the questions.

1 Identify the central event. Determine what event is the most important and decide if it is a cause or an effect.

2 Look for signal words and phrases. Words and phrases such as *because, due to,* and *on account of* signal causes. Words and phrases such as *so, thus, therefore,* and *as a result* signal effects.

3 Decide if an event has more than one cause or effect. Most events have multiple causes and many have more than one effect.

4 Identify events that are both causes and effects. Events can form a chain of causes and effects. For example, a decrease in taxes might result in a decrease in state funding for new highway construction. The decreased funding might cause increased traffic delays.

Fewer Youths Jump Behind the Wheel at 16
by Mary Chapman and Micheline Maynard, *The New York Times*, February 25, 2008

For generations, driver's licenses have been tickets to freedom for America's 16-year-olds, prompting many to line up at motor vehicle offices the day they were eligible to apply.

No longer. In the last decade, the proportion of 16-year-olds nationwide who hold driver's licenses has dropped from nearly half to less than one-third, according to . . . the Federal Highway Administration.

Reasons vary, including tighter state laws governing when teenagers can drive, higher insurance costs and a shift . . . to expensive private driving academies. . . .

[E]xperts also add parents . . . willing to chauffeur their children to activities, and pastimes like surfing the Web that keep them indoors. . . .

The way students learn has undergone a major change, too. Twenty-five years ago most teenagers took driver's education in their local schools. But the number of school systems offering the program has plummeted to about 20 percent today, from 90 percent in the 1980s, said Allen Robinson, of American Driver and Traffic Safety Education Association. . . .

"High schools are out of the business because of the cost," said Henning Mortensen, owner of Bond Driving School in Sacramento. Commercial driving academies have stepped in to fill the gap. . . .

Driving schools charge higher rates. . . .

Graduated driver-licensing laws, which delay awarding a full license until a teenager spends time . . . driving under certain conditions, are also keeping down the number of 16-year-olds on the road, said Frederik R. Mottola . . . of the National Institute for Driver Behavior. . . .

Practice and Apply the Skill

Use the article above to answer the following questions.
1. What is the issue discussed in this article?
2. What two causes are cited in paragraph four?
3. Why have many high schools stopped offering driver's education?

Problem Solving

Every year elected officials at all levels of government face problems. The ability to solve problems is a valuable skill. Use the following steps to learn more about problem solving. Then read the passage below and answer the questions.

① Identify the problem. Begin by clearly identifying the problem. Write a statement or question that summarizes the problem you are trying to solve.

② Gather information and identify options. Collect information and data, considering both the causes of the problem and strategies for addressing it. Most problems have multiple solutions. Identify as many options as possible.

③ Consider advantages and disadvantages of each option. Analyze each option by predicting benefits, drawbacks, and possible outcomes.

④ Choose, implement, and evaluate a solution. Pick the option with the most benefits and fewest drawbacks. Once the chosen option has been implemented, evaluate the outcome to decide if the strategy worked.

> Like most large cities in America today, Minneapolis continues to face violent crime . . .
>
> We have met the challenge of crime with a multi-faceted plan of attack . . . The most . . . powerful tool in our crime fighting strategy has been increasing the visibility and presence of police officers on the street. We are growing our police force by over 100 officers . . .
>
> To a larger more diverse, more visible police force, we added groundbreaking public safety technology . . . The addition of dozens of safety cameras and dramatically increased police patrol has made our downtown one of the safest in America. The safety cameras . . . have helped provide essential evidence to arrest and successfully charge criminals. . . .
>
> The technology we are implementing increases prosecutions by providing needed court evidence, but we also invested in better prosecution with more funding for community prosecutors. . . . The number of our most chronic criminals . . . who were convicted has increased from 81 convictions in 2005 to 129 convictions in 2006—a 60% increase in one year. . . .
>
> Working . . . with our juvenile crime unit, we are identifying young offenders early and getting them into programs that offer a productive alternative to gangs. . . .
>
> We have also focused . . . efforts to get illegal guns off the street. . . . The results . . . are beginning to be seen. After a surge of crime during the summer of 2005 and first half of 2006, violent crime began trending down in the later months of 2006. As we end the first quarter of 2007, for the first time in years, violent crime is falling, down 22 percent city-wide. . . .
>
> —Minneapolis mayor R.T. Rybak,
> State of the City Address,
> March 19, 2007

Practice and Apply the Skill

Use the passage above to answer the following questions.

1. What problem is the mayor concerned about, and what is his problem-solving goal?

2. What options does the mayor identify for solving this problem?

3. What are the advantages and drawbacks of the safety camera option?

4. How did the mayor assess the effectiveness of efforts to prosecute criminals?

5. What kinds of information can the mayor use to evaluate his solutions?

Decision Making

Decision making plays a key role in the political process in every branch of government. Although the types of decisions Presidents, cabinet heads, governors, and city councilors make differ, they all involve the steps below.

1 Identify the problem and gather information. Define and clarify what needs to be decided. Consider the goal or the intended outcome. Decide what information is needed to make an informed decision. Apply existing knowledge and research about the subject. Consider strategies others have used to address the issue.

2 List and review possible options. A decision requires choosing among two or more alternatives. List all possible options.

3 Identify possible consequences and make a decision. Consider the possible outcomes and predict the consequences of each option. Then review all options. Choose those with the fewest drawbacks and greatest number of benefits. Read about one school's tardiness problem and its possible solutions.

The Problem
Many students have been tardy [late] more than usual this semester.
- The city has canceled bus service to the school due to budget cuts. The school is located on a low-use bus route, and student discount passes did not generate enough revenue to keep the bus route going.
- Since many parents now drive their children to school, traffic has increased. The traffic causes school buses and parents to be late.
- Many students are unable to walk because they live too far away from the school.
- Students are missing the first 5 to 20 minutes of their first-period class, when attendance is taken.
- Students are either marked as tardy or absent if they come in very late.

Potential Solutions
- Require all students to take school buses.
- Circulate a petition that demands the city continue its bus service.
- Work with city councilors to establish a reasonable fare.
- Create a carpooling program for students who live close to one another.
- Establish first period as a study hall, and take attendance at the end of the period in order to allow students time to arrive at school.

Practice and Apply the Skill

Use the list above to answer the following questions.

1. What is the major concern for the school?

2. What is the advantage of requiring all students to take the bus to school?

3. What are the disadvantages of turning first period into a study hall?

4. What do you think is the best solution to the problem? Why?

Draw Inferences and Conclusions

Drawing inferences means forming conclusions based on information that is not stated directly but only suggested. Use the following steps to learn how to draw inferences and arrive at conclusions. Then read the passage below and answer the questions.

1 Summarize information. Identify the main idea. To find information that is suggested but unstated in a passage, you have to understand the stated content of the passage.

2 Study the facts. Determine what facts and information have been given.

3 Apply other facts or prior knowledge. Consider what you know about the topic. Use this prior knowledge to evaluate the information. A combination of what you already know and what you learn from reading the passage can help you draw inferences.

4 Summarize the information to form a conclusion. Combine the inferences you made to form a conclusion about the topic.

A New GI Bill for a New Generation of Veterans
Editorial, *The Sacramento Bee*, 2008

. . . [W]e must accept our duty to care for those who have borne the battle. . . .

That's why the GI Bill of Rights, which President Franklin D. Roosevelt signed in June 1944, was so important. That law gave returning soldiers benefits to compensate for opportunities they lost while they served in the military. It eased their transition to civilian life.

Before World War II, less than 10 percent of Americans went to college and home ownership was unreachable for most. The GI Bill spurred [brought about] a college education and home ownership boom. It has been rightly called the "Magic Carpet to the Middle Class."

The nation should have a similar package ready when those who have served tours in Afghanistan and Iraq move . . . to civilian life. . . .

To that end, Sen. Jim Webb, D-Va., introduced a 21st century GI Bill of Rights (S. 22). Most soldiers in the current war enlisted right after high school, so 90 percent do not have a college degree. As Webb notes, current law is designed only for peacetime service. (It requires a $1,200 fee to enroll, provides no money for books and housing and covers only half the cost of the average public college education). . . .

The cost [of the new bill]: $2 billion a year. That's less than one week of the Iraq war. . . .

Many veterans say they're frustrated . . . a new GI Bill still hasn't [passed]. They should be. The two houses of Congress need to get their act together and get this done, . . .

Practice and Apply the Skill

Use the editorial above to answer the following questions.

1. What is the main idea in this editorial?

2. Why was Roosevelt's GI Bill called the "Magic Carpet to the Middle Class"?

3. What does the author of this editorial suggest when he says that the new GI bill will cost less than one week of the Iraq war?

4. What conclusion can you draw about the benefits of a new GI bill?

Note Taking and Active Listening

Note taking and active listening are two skills that can increase your ability to remember and understand a speech or lecture. Use the following steps to learn more about note taking and active listening. Then read the excerpted speech below and answer the questions.

1 Identify the topic and main ideas. The title of the text often gives clues to its content. Once you identify the topic, it is easier to identify main ideas. Many speakers start their speeches by listing the key points they will develop. At the conclusion of the talk, they often restate their main ideas and then summarize their conclusions.

2 Take notes selectively. Do not write down every word you hear. Instead, jot down important terms and summarize key points and details that support these points.

3 Practice active listening. Like all communication, active listening requires engaged participation. Look at and listen to the speaker. Think about what you hear and see.

4 Listen for transitions, repetition, and emphasis. Listen for words or phrases that indicate key points. Be alert for repetition. Statements that are repeated or said with emphasis are important points. Pay attention for phrases, gestures, or expressions that suggest strong opinions.

Speech on Stewardship of the Earth by James E. Hansen, NASA chief climate scientist, 2007

. . . Global warming differs from previous pollution problems in two fundamental ways. With water pollution or common air pollution, smog, the problems occur immediately. . . . If we . . . stop emitting them, the problem goes away. However, global warming is caused by greenhouse gases that have a lifetime of hundreds of years. . . .

The second major difference . . . is that the climate system responds slowly to the gases that we add to the air. . . .The Earth has warmed one and one-half degrees Fahrenheit so far. . . . Moreover, there are surely more gases in the pipeline, because of power plants . . . and vehicles. . . . One and one-half degrees! Who cares about that? . . . Well, we had better all care about it, because we have already brought the planet close to some tipping points. . . .

Let me mention three major consequences of global warming, if we go down the business-as-usual path. . . . First, there is the extermination of species. . . . [A] given mean temperature line is moving poleward, . . . about 35 miles per decade. That rate will accelerate under business-as-usual. Many species cannot migrate that fast. Besides, there is no place colder for polar species to go. . . . Second, there is potential instability of the ice sheets. If additional global warming exceeds two degrees Fahrenheit, the West Antarctic ice sheet and part of Greenland surely will become unstable, causing eventual sea level rise of several meters. . . . Third, there will be a noticeable increase in climate extremes. . . . Heavy rains and floods will increase, but so will . . . droughts and forest fires. . . .

Practice and Apply the Skill

Use the excerpt above to answer the following questions.

1. What is the topic of this speech?
2. What three main points would you list as consequences of global warming?
3. What statements in this speech suggest greater emphasis or strong emotion?

Give a Multimedia Presentation

Government officials are often asked to make presentations. You too will be asked to give presentations in school and at work. One key to an effective presentation is to combine text, video, audio, and graphics. Use these steps for an effective presentation.

❶ Define your topic. When choosing a topic, consider the time given for the presentation and the complexity of the subject. Multimedia presentations lend themselves to topics that have several subtopics. However, a topic that is too broad is hard to cover adequately in a limited amount of time. Consider how to narrow the topic.

❷ Determine what types of media are available for the presentation. Do you have a computer and the software to create a podcast, PowerPoint presentation, or slide show? Do you have access to video, film, or audio clips of speeches or historic events?

❸ Make a storyboard. Brainstorm ideas for covering your topic in various media. Then make a detailed outline of the information you will present. Identify the medium that will work best for each part of the presentation.

❹ Practice your presentation. A trial run gives presenters a chance to time each segment, identify technical problems, and make sure all participants know their roles.

Below is a storyboard for a presentation on reducing traffic congestion.

1 (2 mins)

Gridlock: Traffic cam of city at rush hour

Introduce issue by explaining how traffic congestion affects everyone in the audience.
- Wastes time
- Wastes gas
- Increases energy dependence

2 (3 mins)

Graphs
- Rise in peak period travel times
- Costs of congestion
- Smog and poor air quality

1996 2000 2004 2008

3 (4 mins)

Video clip of transportation expert or newscaster talking about possible solutions to traffic problems

4 (4 mins)

Solutions
- More emphasis on public transportation: buses, light rail, metro
- Contruction of Park and Ride lots
- Incentives by local businesses to encourage employees to carpool
- Fast passes

5 (4 mins)

Solutions
- Toll roads
- HOV lanes
- Better signal control
- Businesses encourage employees to commute at different times through flextime

6 (5 mins)

Summarize possible solutions in sections 4 and 5

What we recommend

Practice and Apply the Skill

Use the storyboards above to answer the following questions.

1. What media will be used in the presentation?

2. How did the presenters narrow or focus the presentation of their topic?

3. How did the storyboard help the presenters stay within the time limit of the presentation?

Analyze Political Cartoons

Political cartoons express the cartoonist's opinion on a recent issue or current event. Often the cartoon's purpose is to influence public opinion about political leaders and issues. To achieve this goal, cartoonists use humor and exaggeration. When analyzing a political cartoon, be sure to examine all words, images, and labels to help you fully understand the cartoon's intent. Use the following steps to analyze a political cartoon.

1 Identify the symbols in the cartoon. Analyze the cartoon to determine what each image or symbol represents. Read the title and any labels or captions.

2 Analyze the meaning of the cartoon. Consider how the cartoonist uses the images and symbols in the cartoon to express his or her opinion.

3 Draw conclusions about the cartoon's intent. Determine the main idea, message, or point of view expressed in the cartoon.

Medicare Cuts

Practice and Apply the Skill

Use the cartoon above to answer the following questions.

1. Who does the figure in the bed represent?
2. What symbol represents cuts to the senior insurance program, Medicare?
3. According to the cartoon, what will be the result of Medicare cuts?
4. What is the main idea of this cartoon?

Innovate and Think Creatively

An innovation is a new idea that improves on an existing product or process. Use the steps below to learn how to think innovatively and creatively. Then read the passage below and answer the questions.

1 Identify what it is that needs improving. Describe a specific problem to be solved. Are there faster, better, or more efficient ways of getting a job or task done? Consider the intended outcome.

2 Brainstorm solutions. Generate as many ideas as possible. Be open to all ideas. If you are working in a group, don't criticize the ideas of others. Also, don't hesitate to suggest ideas that might seem strange or impractical. Innovation often results from a chain of related ideas leading to an unexpected insight.

3 Understand how to achieve the innovation. Think about the skills, tools, or methods needed to reach the goal. Identify such factors as ease of use, resources, costs, and time. Get input from likely users. Involve people who are knowledgeable about the process, and work to build their support. Establish benchmarks for success and compare the results of the innovation with the original process.

Homeless Project's Army of Citizens Calls Year Success
by Kevin Fagan, *San Francisco Chronicle*, 10/19/05

Barry Cowart stood in front of the Bill Graham Civic Auditorium, staring at the 200 homeless people in a line. . . .

"Last April, that was me in that line," he said. "I'd been sleeping in the Greyhound bus station for months, and then I came here to this *thing* they do every month. That day, they got me into a residential hotel room. . . .

The "thing" he referred to is Project Homeless Connect, San Francisco Mayor Gavin Newsom's monthly gathering of volunteers to help his city's street people. . . .

On Oct. 13, 2004, the mayor kicked off his concept . . . with a handful of participants and street counselors . . . . By the end of the day, they had placed 24 into shelter and housing . . .

Since that first foray, Project Homeless Connect became a veritable citizen army that assembles between 1,000 and 2,000 community and government volunteers from all over the nation at the auditorium every other month to help more than 1,000 homeless people get into shelter, permanent housing, counseling and health care. While the homeless are being hooked up to those services, they get . . . food, clothing, blankets, and even kibble for their dogs or cats. . . .

. . . [R]epresentatives of cities from New York and Chicago to Los Angeles . . . have come to check out the past few gatherings. . . .

"It's daunting . . . to even consider doing something this big," said Kathleen Gardipee, a representative of Portland, Ore., who came to help prepare her city for its own Connect. . . . "But this is amazing. . . ."

Over the past year . . . the Connect efforts have helped 6,822 homeless people, putting 646 into shelter or housing, 1,583 into medical or mental health care, and the rest into legal counseling, food programs or other services. A total 11,382 individual volunteers pitched in.

Practice and Apply the Skill

Use the newspaper article to answer the following questions.

1. What problem did Mayor Newsom want to solve through the creation of PHC?

2. What was innovative about the mayor's solution?

3. Why do you think many cities are interested in San Francisco's innovation?

4. How did the mayor's office measure the effectiveness of this program?

Digital Age Literacy

The Internet is a valuable research tool. It provides links to millions of sources of information created by government agencies, schools, businesses, and people all over the world. E-mail, wikis, and blogs all provide ways for Internet users to share information and express opinions. Follow the steps below to learn how you can use e-mail, wikis, and blogs effectively.

Writing an E-mail

1 Identify the purpose of the e-mail. Clearly indicate the topic in the subject line. A busy recipient is more likely to open the e-mail promptly if the subject is stated.

2 Focus on why you are writing. Include the subject of your e-mail in the first sentence. State why you are writing and what you expect to receive in terms of information or action from the recipient. Try to limit messages to three or four key points and keep paragraphs short.

3 Respect your reader. If you are responding to or following up on an e-mail query or request that is more than a few days old, remind the recipient of why you are writing. It is often helpful to leave the original e-mail in your response for reference. Identify yourself clearly if the recipient is someone you don't know. If you are uncertain about whether your language and tone should be formal or informal, examine the e-mail received and take your cues from it.

4 Proofread e-mails before sending. Once you have composed your e-mail, use a spell checker or other tool to check grammar, punctuation, and spelling. Remember that e-mail is not private. Think carefully about sending messages that you would not want shared with others. Below is an example of an e-mail sent from one student to another.

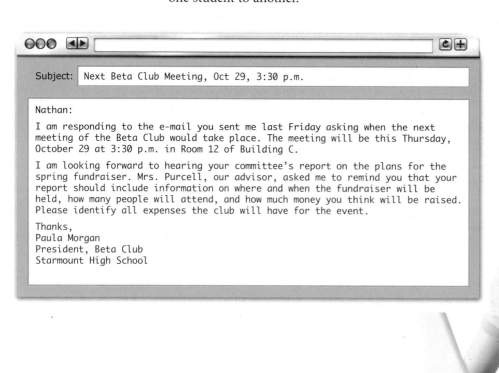

Subject: Next Beta Club Meeting, Oct 29, 3:30 p.m.

Nathan:

I am responding to the e-mail you sent me last Friday asking when the next meeting of the Beta Club would take place. The meeting will be this Thursday, October 29 at 3:30 p.m. in Room 12 of Building C.

I am looking forward to hearing your committee's report on the plans for the spring fundraiser. Mrs. Purcell, our advisor, asked me to remind you that your report should include information on where and when the fundraiser will be held, how many people will attend, and how much money you think will be raised. Please identify all expenses the club will have for the event.

Thanks,
Paula Morgan
President, Beta Club
Starmount High School

Understanding and Evaluating Wikis

A wiki is a Web site that allows users to make, edit, and link Web pages to create an online document. As shared Web sites, many wikis are used for collaborative writing and research activities. Each entry includes a list of changes made by all the writers or editors. While many Internet users are enthusiastic about wikis, critics question their reliability. Critics also fear that users will accept information without verifying its accuracy.

Follow the steps below to learn about evaluating wikis.

① Identify the sources of the information on the Web site. Scan the entry to find out who provided the information. Consider whether the writer has expertise on or special knowledge of this topic.

② Determine when the article was written. Look for a date indicating when the article was written or last updated. Does the entry reflect changing events or provide current information on this topic?

③ Verify information by looking at other sources. Compare the information on the wiki with information from official sources. Do further research if your sources disagree.

Reading and Assessing Blogs

Blogs are online journals. The word *blog* is short for *weblog*. Most blogs are short posts expressing an author's opinions. Blog writers, or bloggers, typically focus on a particular subject. Blogs can be found on every topic from politics to fashion. Blogs usually include the writer's previous posts as well as links to posts on other blogs, Web sites, and news articles. Some also include photos and video or audio files. Most blogs are interactive, providing a space for readers to comment.

① Identify the writer. Look for the author's name, biographical information, and his or her professional affiliation, if any.

② Assess sources. Evaluate the credibility and accuracy of recommended sources.

③ Identify the writer's bias. Consider the arguments and evidence the writer presents. Are positions stated in rational language and presented in a balanced way? Do the posts contain frequent misspellings and grammatical errors? Scan reader comments to determine whether the blog allows opposing points of view.

Practice and Apply the Skill

Use the information above to answer these questions.

1. How might the language in a business e-mail differ from the language in an e-mail sent to friends?

2. How are wikis useful for projects with multiple participants?

3. How does a blog differ from an editorial in a newspaper?

Analyze Graphic Data

A graph is a useful way to visually present large amounts of data. Every day, people use different kinds of graphs to present and summarize data. Line graphs describe changes over time. Bar graphs show the relationships between two or more sets of data, and suggest trends. Circle graphs show how individual parts relate to a whole. Use the steps below to analyze graphic data.

1 Identify the type of information presented. Before you can interpret the information in a graph, you must identify what is being shown. Note the title, all labels, and the key, if there is one. On a bar or line graph, use the graph title, the axis labels, and the key to interpret the data. On a circle graph, examine labels of all segments of the graphs. Identify the source of the data for the graph.

2 Read the data. Look at specific elements on the graph. On line graphs and bar graphs, determine what the numbers on the x-axis (horizontal) and the y-axis (vertical) represent. Then determine the relationship between the numbers.

3 Interpret the graph and draw conclusions. Study the data in the graph to draw conclusions. Look for patterns or trends, such as changes over time or comparisons of different groups.

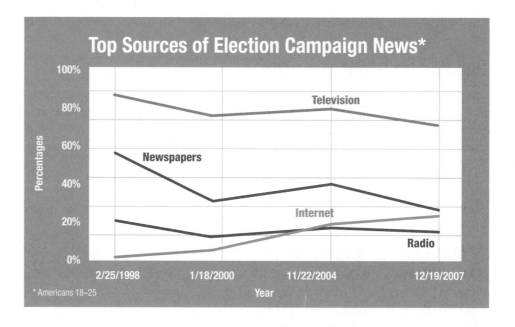

Practice and Apply the Skill

Use the graph above to answer the questions below.

1. (a) What is the subject of the graph? (b) What is the time frame? (c) What do the numbers on the x-axis and y-axis represent?

2. What could the relationship be between Internet use and newspaper readership among 18- to 25-year-olds?

3. Based on the graph, what prediction can you make about the use of Internet and television as sources in the future?

Analyze Maps

Maps bring information to life in a way that words alone cannot. Election maps, for example, can be valuable tools for identifying and understanding voting patterns. Political analysts often study voting patterns from previous elections to make predictions about winners and losers on election night. Use the steps below to analyze an election map.

2006 Missouri Senate Race Election Results by County

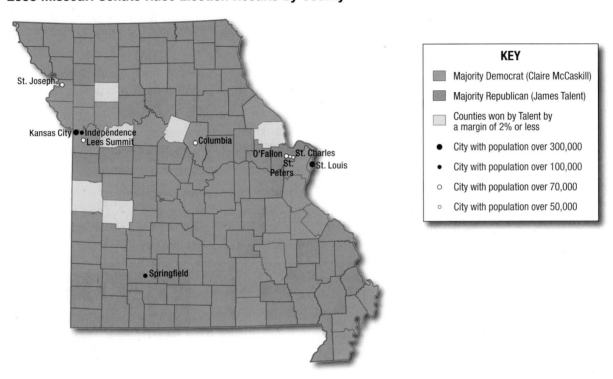

KEY

■ Majority Democrat (Claire McCaskill)
■ Majority Republican (James Talent)
□ Counties won by Talent by a margin of 2% or less
● City with population over 300,000
● City with population over 100,000
○ City with population over 70,000
○ City with population over 50,000

① **Identify the purpose of the map.** Study the title to identify the purpose of the map and to make sure that you understand what information is shown.

② **Determine the scope of the analysis.** For a national election map, analysis might focus on voting by state or region. Analysis of a map of a state's election data might focus on voter turnout by county or by precinct. Here, it is by county.

③ **Use the key.** Analyze and apply the information in the map key to determine what data is shown. In an election map, you might look for color patterns. These might include areas of the state where voter turnout was strong for one political party or the other.

Practice and Apply the Skill

Use the Missouri county election map above to answer the following questions.
1. What does the map's title tell you?
2. What does each color on the map represent?
3. What voting pattern can you find in the counties with the state's largest cities?
4. How was McCaskill able to win the election when she only won the city of St. Louis and 25 of Missouri's 114 counties?

Analyze Images

During elections, images of candidates and the issues they support fill television screens, newspapers, and Web sites. They seek to inform, persuade, and influence the viewer's opinion. It is important to be able to analyze an image in advertising for bias, emotional appeals, or inaccurate statements. Use the steps below to practice analyzing images.

1 Identify the content. When viewing an advertisement, look closely at the images and text. Determine which information is most important. Identify themes or issues that the advertisement highlights. Notice how the images reinforce the overall message.

2 Note emotions. In analyzing the images of people, study facial expressions and body positions. Consider the emotions these expressions or positions suggest.

3 Consider context. Determine the context in which the image was created. Evaluate the accuracy of any information and supporting facts presented. Read all captions and credits. When possible, gather information about who produced or paid for the image or advertisement.

4 Identify the purpose. Determine whether the advertisement provides mostly factual information or opinions about a candidate or an issue. Does it emphasize a candidate's positive features or present an issue in a positive or balanced way? Or is it intended to show an opponent or decision in a negative light?

Image A
This advertisement was paid for by a national organization that represents large private nursing home chains. It refers to a congressperson who voted in favor of a bill that might have reduced Medicare funding.

Image B
This poster is from Ronald Reagan's 1980 presidential campaign.

Practice and Apply the Skill

Use the political ads above to answer the following questions.

1. (a) What issue does Image A focus on? (b) What is the purpose of Image A?
2. Why do you think the producers of Image A chose this image?
3. In what ways could Image A be considered a negative, or attack, ad?
4. (a) Does Image B make the candidate seem presidential? How? (b) What is the impact of the phrase at the bottom of the poster?
5. How does the purpose of Image B differ from the purpose of Image A?

Analyze Timelines

A timeline allows readers to analyze a sequence of historical events. Use the steps below to analyze a timeline.

1 Identify the topic and time period. Read the timeline's title. Then determine the span of time represented by the entire timeline.

2 Determine how the timeline is divided. Most timelines are divided into equal segments, or increments, of time—years, decades, or centuries.

3 Read each entry. Read each caption carefully. Where possible, connect each one to the events before and after it. Be sure to note the date when each event occurred.

4 Look for relationships. Decide if any of the events fall into a common category. Identify any recurring events. Look for events that might be causes and/or effects of other events.

Voting Rights in the United States, 1964–2008

1964 Civil Rights Act abolishes poll tax for federal elections and bans discrimination in voter registration.

1965 The first Voting Rights Act outlaws literacy tests and other practices that discriminate against voters.

1971 26th Amendment lowers voting age from 21 to 18.

1975 Voting Rights Act is amended to include language assistance to voters who are limited English speakers.

1982 Congress reauthorizes Voting Rights Act.

1990 Americans with Disabilities Act requires access to polls for people with disabilities.

1993 Motor Voter law allows citizens to register to vote while getting driver's licenses.

2001 National Commission on Election Reform recommends adoption of more reliable and accurate electronic voting machines.

2006 The Voting Rights Act is extended for 25 more years.

2008 Supreme Court considers legality of Indiana's Voter Identification Law requiring voters to present a government-issued photo ID in order to vote.

Practice and Apply the Skill

Use the timeline above to answer the following questions.

1. What span of time does the timeline cover?

2. How many years is each segment of the timeline?

3. What was the impact of the Americans with Disabilities Act on voting rights?

4. What event is repeated on the timeline?

5. How many years passed between the two renewals of the Voting Rights Act?

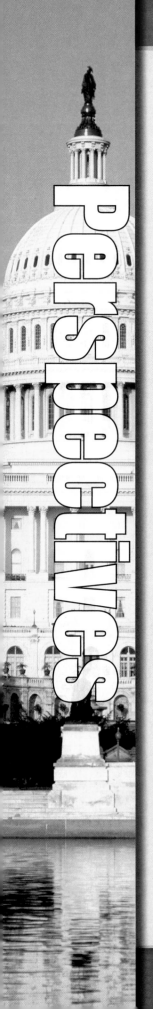

PREFACE

You may wonder why it is necessary to learn about national, state, and local government. The answer is that the government touches your life every day. You can attend public school because your local or country government has raised money to run the school. If you have a driver's license, you earned it according to the laws of your state. If you have a job, you pay part of your earnings to the government in taxes.

And consider this: Suppose you have written a book or posted a song you wrote on the Internet. If you want to make a profit from your work, you need a copyright. This would establish you as the owner of your work. The Constitution protects your rights by providing a copyright office where you can register your creative work.

Being an American offers both rights and responsibilities. For example, you have the right to speak your mind publicly. Freedom of speech is protected by the United States Constitution. But you have obligations, as well. For instance, you must obey the law and pay your taxes.

You also have an obligation to become educated about the government and about current events. When it comes time to vote, you have a responsibility to understand the issues and to think critically about the statements of candidates. This way, you make an informed choice when you vote. Then, you must continue to stay informed and become involved, whether you support a certain cause or you oppose a proposed law. In the end, you must do your part to keep our nation working as a healthy democracy. As Thomas Jefferson said over 200 years ago, "If a nation expects to be ignorant and free, … it expects what never was and never will be."

Photo: U.S. Capitol dome

Essential Questions Journal
To begin to build a response to the unit Essential Question, go to your **Essential Questions Journal.**

Unit 1 Foundations of American Government

Essential Question   What should be the goals of government?

▲ The Statue of Liberty is a symbol of democracy in the United States.

Principles of Government

Essential Question
Is government necessary?

Section 1: Government and the State

Section 2: Forms of Government

Section 3: Basic Concepts of Democracy

Reading Strategy: Summarizing
When readers summarize, they restate what they read in their own words. As you read this chapter, ask yourself the following questions:
- Who or what is this about?
- What is the main point being made about this topic?
- What details are important to the understanding of this chapter?

When you can answer these questions, begin to write your summary.

To study anywhere, anytime, download these online resources at PearsonSuccessNet.com
- Political Dictionary
- Audio Review
- Downloadable Interactivities

Government and the State

▲ Flags representing several countries fly outside of the European Parliament in Strasbourg, France.

Guiding Question

What is government, and what is its purpose? Use an outline like the one below to take notes on the definition and purposes of government.

> A. Definition of Government
>   a. Laws and policies
>   b. _____
> B. Characteristics of a State
>   a. _____
>   b. _____
> C. Purposes of Government
>   a. _____
>   b. _____

Objectives:

- Define government and the basic powers every government holds.
- Describe the four characteristics of the state.
- Identify four different ideas that attempt to explain the origin of the state.
- Understand the purpose of government in the United States and other countries.

All people share a common need for rules and laws to lead peaceful and safe lives. Families have rules for their children. Schools have rules for their students. Governments have rules for their citizens. These rules protect citizens and provide for their needs.

What is government?

Government is the group of people and agencies entrusted with making and carrying out laws and policies agreed upon by the larger population. Early groups of people lived simply. They shared food, punished people who did wrong, and joined together for protection. As these groups grew into larger communities, life became more difficult. Governments grew in size and power in order to meet the needs of the new communities. As land and property became more important to people, rules were needed to protect people's possessions.

Every government has three kinds of power. **Legislative power** is the power to make laws. **Executive power** is the power to carry out laws. **Judicial power** is the power to settle arguments and decide on the meaning of laws. See Figure 1.1 on the next page.

Many countries outline these powers in a **constitution.** If the responsibility to carry out governmental power is in the hands of one person or a small group of people, the country is a **dictatorship.** In a **democracy,** the people hold the power. The process by which a society decides how government is run and how the leaders are chosen is called politics. Politics is the way that a society decides who will benefit from, and who will pay for, its **public policies.**

✓**Checkpoint** What is the difference between a dictatorship and a democracy?

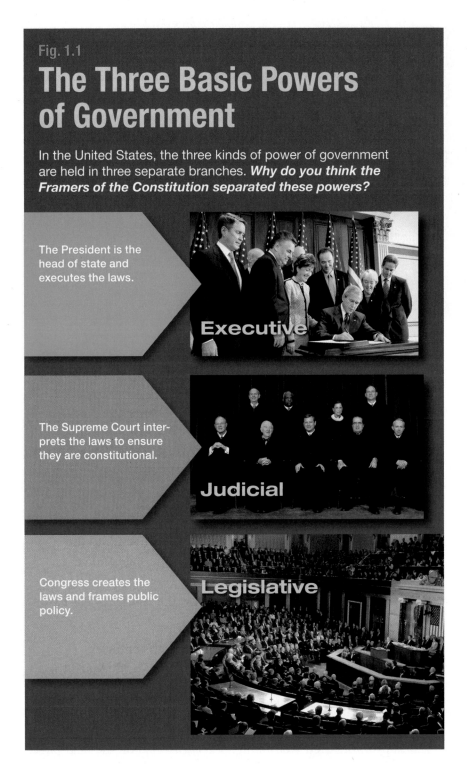

Fig. 1.1
The Three Basic Powers of Government

In the United States, the three kinds of power of government are held in three separate branches. *Why do you think the Framers of the Constitution separated these powers?*

The President is the head of state and executes the laws.

Executive

The Supreme Court interprets the laws to ensure they are constitutional.

Judicial

Congress creates the laws and frames public policy.

Legislative

Government
The group of people and agencies entrusted with making and carrying out laws and policies agreed upon by the larger population

Legislative power
The power to make laws

Executive power
The power to carry out laws

Judicial power
The power to settle arguments and decide the meaning of laws

Constitution
A plan for government

Dictatorship
A person or a small group of people ruling a country with total control

Democracy
A form of government in which people hold the power

Public policy
The laws and goals that government follows or pursues

State
A group of people, living in a defined territory, having a government with absolute power within its territory to decide its own policies

What is a state?

Throughout history, the **state** has emerged as the main political unit in the world. A state has four basic characteristics. First, a state is made up of a population, or the people who live there. Second, this group of people lives in a territory with clear borders. Next, a state has sovereignty, or absolute power within its territory. Finally, the government has the power to make and enforce laws. See Figure 1.2 on page 6 for summaries of the characteristics of a state.

Fig. 1.2
Four Characteristics of a State

What do you need to make a state?

GOVERNMENT ONLINE
Audio Tour
Listen to a guided audio tour of these characteristics at **PearsonSuccessNet.com**

Every state in the world has the following four characteristics. Each characteristic may vary widely from state to state. *Which of these characteristics is represented by the map in the background?*

Population

Large or small, every state must be inhabited—that is, have a population.

Territory

Every state must have land, with known and recognized borders.

Sovereignty

The state has absolute power within its territory. It can decide its own foreign and domestic policies.

Government

Government is the mechanism through which a state makes and enforces its policies.

Reading Strategy
Summarizing
Why do you think the divine right theory was popular among rulers for centuries?

What theories have tried to explain the origin of the state?

There are several ideas on how the state may have started. Some think the state began when a small group took over an area and forced others to follow their rules. This theory is called the force theory. Others think the state began as a family, with related families soon joining and cooperating to form a state. This idea is called the evolutionary theory.

The divine right theory was popular from the fifteenth to the eighteenth century. It held that God created the state and gave those of royal birth a "divine right" to rule. People were obligated to follow the ruler. If people did not follow the ruler, it was treason and a sin.

Philosophers in the seventeenth and eighteenth centuries developed the social contract theory. This theory influenced the American political system. It held that people came together with a common need for security and agreed to form the state. The people gave power to the government of the state so it could keep people safe and promote their well-being. See Figure 1.3 on the next page.

✔**Checkpoint**   When was the social contract theory developed?

What is the purpose of government?

What does government do? You can find an answer to this question in the Constitution of the United States.

The Preamble of the Constitution promised that government would serve many purposes:

" . . . form a more perfect Union . . . "
By joining together, the individual states hoped to protect the independence they had gained from Great Britain.

" . . . establish Justice . . . "
It was the government's role to create laws that were reasonable, fair, and impartial.

" . . . insure domestic Tranquility . . . "
Government's role was to provide peace and order for its people.

" . . . provide for the common defence . . . "
The government must protect the nation with a strong army.

" . . . promote the general Welfare . . . "
The government should provide for the things people need, such as schools, roads, and other services.

" . . . secure the Blessings of Liberty . . . "
The government should offer freedom to all.

Reading Strategy
Summarizing
What promises are made by the Preamble of the Constitution?

Fig. 1.3
Origins of the State

There are four theories for how the state came to be. Each theory brings together the four characteristics of the state in different ways. *Which of the theories best describes the origin of the United States? Why?*

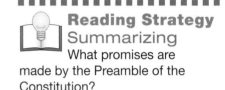

GOVERNMENT ONLINE
Audio Tour
To listen to a guided audio tour of theories about how the state formed, visit
PearsonSuccessNet.com

Force
Theory
An individual or group claimed control over a **territory** and forced the **population** to submit. In this way, the state became **sovereign,** and those in control formed a **government.**

Divine Right
Theory
God created the state, making it **sovereign.** The **government** is made up of those chosen by God to rule a certain **territory.** The people **(population)** must obey their ruler as they would God.

Evolutionary
Theory
A **population** formed out of primitive families. The heads of these families became the **government.** When these families settled in one **territory** and claimed it as their own, they became a **sovereign** state.

Social Contract
Theory
A **population** in a given place **(territory)** gave up as much power to a **government** as needed to promote the well-being of all. In doing so, they created a **sovereign** state.

Fig. 1.4

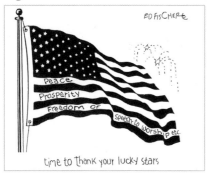

ED FISCHERE

Peace
Prosperity
Freedom of
speech to worship etc.

time to thank your lucky stars

▲ **Analyzing Political Cartoons** In this cartoon, some of the liberties secured by the Constitution are written on the flag. *What is the phrase "thank your lucky stars" referring to?*

Government in Your Life

Public Education in the United States

In 1647, the colony of Massachusetts passed a public school law. Under this law, towns of 50 or more families were required to set up schools and hire teachers. The money for the schools came from taxes. This law was an important step toward free public education. By the early 1800s, a system of free public education was common. Today, education is the responsibility of state and local governments. By law, every state requires young people to attend school until a certain age. In most states this age is 16.

Essential Questions Journal Go to your **Essential Questions Journal** to work on this chapter's Essential Question.

SECTION 1 ASSESSMENT

Word Bank

executive

government

legislative

state

Quick Write

Brainstorm a list of all of the different services that you can think of that government provides. While brainstorming, think about some of things you do each day. For instance, the roads you drive on to school are maintained by the government. Once you are done, share your list with the class.

1. **Guiding Question** Use your completed outline to answer this question: What is government, and what is its purpose?

Key Terms and Comprehension

On a sheet of paper, use the words from the Word Bank to complete each sentence correctly.

2. A(n) _____ is a group of people and agencies entrusted with making and carrying out laws and policies.

3. A group of people living in a territory with recognized borders, a government, and sovereignty is a(n) _____.

4. _____ power is the right to make laws.

5. _____ power is the right to carry out laws.

Critical Thinking

6. **Analyze Information** Why are rules and laws needed to protect people's possessions?

7. **Summarize** What are the four theories of the origin of the state?

Forms of Government

▲ Members of the House of Lords in the British Parliament wear traditional robes and wigs.

Guiding Question

What are some forms of government in the world today? Use a table like the one below to take notes on the different kinds of government in the world today.

Forms of Government	
Unitary	Parliamentary
■ Single, central group	■ Prime minister and cabinet
■	■
■	■
■	■

Objectives:

- Understand three different ways governments are classified.
- Define systems of government based on who can participate.
- Identify different ways that power can be distributed geographically within a state.
- Describe a government by the distribution of power between the executive branch and the legislative branch.

There are many forms of government. These forms of government are classified according to their basic features, which you will read about in this section.

How are governments classified?

There are three ways governments are classified: (1) by the number of people who are allowed to take part in the running of the government, (2) by the way the state divides government power geographically, and (3) by the relationship between the lawmakers and those who carry out the laws.

Who can participate?

The first classification of government is based on the number of people who are allowed to participate. Basically, a government is either a democracy or a dictatorship. The most important feature in a democracy is that the people have all the power. Government is conducted only by and with the consent of the people. The most familiar form of democracy is representative democracy. In this type, a small group of people is chosen by election to represent a larger group. This is also known as government by popular consent or indirect democracy.

Another form of democracy is direct democracy. See Figure 1.5 on page 10. In a direct democracy, the people themselves create laws and other policies. No national government in the world today uses direct democracy. A good example of local direct democracy can be found in New England. The citizens of towns meet regularly to take care of their town business.

Fig. 1.5

Direct and Indirect Democracy: Who Governs?

A democratic government gets its power from the people. The picture below shows citizens in a small town voting. To the right, a representative casts her vote. The board behind her records the votes of all the representatives. *Why might a direct democracy be better for a smaller community? Why might an indirect democracy be better for a larger community?*

Direct Democracy

- Also called pure democracy
- Occurs when the will of the people translates directly into public policy
- Works only on a local level in small communities

Image: Town meeting

Indirect Democracy

- Also called representative democracy
- A group of persons chosen by the people express the will of the people.
- Widely used on a national, state, and local level

Image: A legislator votes.

Autocracy
A government in which one person holds unlimited political power

Oligarchy
A government in which a small group of people hold unlimited political power

Unitary government
A system of government that gives all key powers to the national or central government

Federal government
A form of government in which powers are divided between a central government and several local governments

Confederate government
A form of government in which several states join together for a common purpose

Reading Strategy
Summarizing
What is the difference between an autocracy and an oligarchy?

A dictatorship is a form of government in which those who rule have complete authority over the people. Dictators are powerful and rule as they please. There is no limit to the length of time they rule. A dictatorship can be an autocracy or an oligarchy. In an **autocracy,** a single person holds the power. An **oligarchy** is government in which a small group of people holds the power. This small group may be self-appointed or chosen by the dictator. In many dictatorships today, the army, religious leaders, or others compete for power.

What is the geographic distribution of power?

In every system of government, the power to govern is located in one or more places geographically. There are three basic forms of government that exist as defined by geographic location: federal, confederate, and unitary. See Figure 1.6 on the next page.

In a **federal government,** as in the United States, there is a division of powers between a central government and several local governments. This means that the national government has certain powers and the 50 states have other powers. In a **confederate government,** several individual states join to form a group. This confederation helps the states with certain matters, such as foreign policy or trade. The confederation cannot make laws; only the individual states can. In a **unitary government,** a single, central group holds limited power. Areas of local government also exist, but only to help reduce the duties of the central government.

What is the relationship between the legislative and executive branches?

In terms of the relationship between the legislative and executive branches, there are two basic forms of government: presidential and parliamentary.

The United States has a presidential government. In a **presidential government,** the executive and legislative branches are separate and equal. The President is the elected leader of the executive branch, which makes sure the laws are carried out. The legislative branch makes the laws. Both branches have powers that can block the actions of the other branch. This system is called checks and balances. For example, the President can reject a law proposed by the legislative branch. This rejection can prevent it from becoming a law.

Great Britain and many other democratic nations have a parliamentary form of government. In a **parliamentary government,** the executive branch is made up of a prime minister and his or her cabinet. They are chosen by the parliament, which is the lawmaking branch. The prime minister and cabinet are themselves members of the parliament. There are fewer conflicts between the executive and legislative branches in a parliamentary government. However, only the presidential form of government has checks and balances.

✔ **Checkpoint** What is a presidential government?

Presidential government
A form of government in which the executive and legislative branches are separate but equal

Parliamentary government
A form of government in which the executive branch is made up of a prime minister and his or her cabinet and is part of the legislature

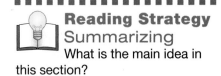
Reading Strategy
Summarizing
What is the main idea in this section?

Fig. 1.6

Distribution of Power

Power can be distributed between central (national) and local governments in three different ways. *Which diagram best describes the distribution of power in the United States?*

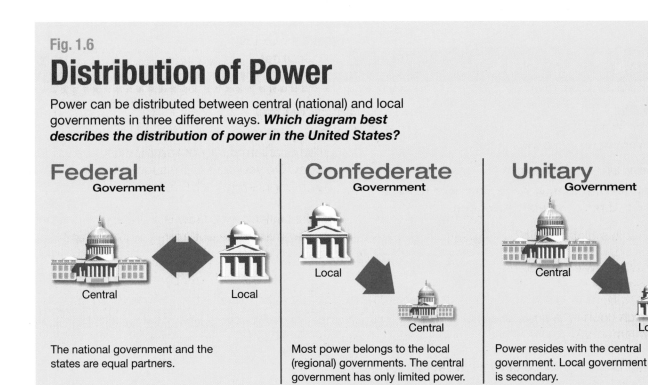

Federal Government

Central ⟷ Local

The national government and the states are equal partners.

Confederate Government

Local

Central

Most power belongs to the local (regional) governments. The central government has only limited power.

Unitary Government

Central

Local

Power resides with the central government. Local government is secondary.

Biography

Benjamin Franklin (1706–1790)

Benjamin Franklin was the son of a soap and candle maker. When Franklin was ten years old, his formal schooling ended. However, he continued to study throughout his life. Franklin became a printer and published his own newspaper. He was a witty and energetic man.

As the colonies grew, Franklin saw a need for a plan of government. As a delegate to the Second Continental Congress, he was part of the committee named to create the Declaration of Independence. Many of his ideas are in this important document.

The Revolutionary War ended and Great Britain formally recognized American independence when Franklin and others signed the Treaty of Paris in 1783. Later, Franklin became the first American ambassador to France. When Franklin returned to the United States, he served as a delegate to the Constitutional Convention. He was one of the signers of the Constitution in 1787. Throughout his life, he made many scientific discoveries in electricity, sailing, farming, and other fields.

SECTION 2 ASSESSMENT

Essential Questions Journal — Go to your **Essential Questions Journal** to work on this chapter's Essential Question.

1. **Guiding Question** Use your completed table to answer this question: What are some forms of government in the world today?

Key Terms and Comprehension

On a sheet of paper, write the answer to each question. Use complete sentences.

2. What is a dictatorship?

3. How is power distributed in a federal government?

4. Which country is an example of a parliamentary government?

5. What is the difference between an autocracy and an oligarchy?

Critical Thinking

6. **Recognize Forms of Government** There are many parliamentary governments in the world today. Do you agree or disagree with this form of government? Explain.

7. **Make Comparisons** How is a unitary government different from a dictatorship?

Volunteering

During his presidency, George W. Bush asked people to volunteer. He also announced the creation of the USA Freedom Corps. This organization links Americans to thousands of volunteer opportunities. USA Freedom Corps has helped many volunteer organizations gain support for their causes.

Many students volunteer their time and skills each year. According to the Department of Labor, about one in five citizens between the ages of 16 and 24 has volunteered in recent years.

Volunteering is not required. But it is an important responsibility that many students fulfill in their spare time. Most recently, people between the ages of 16 and 24 have been volunteering less. Many programs suffer when people stop giving their time and money.

All citizens of the United States benefit from services provided by the government.

People can go to public schools, receive mail, and enjoy national parks. However, sometimes the government lacks funding or people to provide these services. Volunteers provide the services that government does not have the time or money to provide. For instance, a volunteer group might maintain hiking trails in a national park.

In addition, volunteers provide services that the government is not required to provide. These include visiting the elderly, or starting a community theater. Volunteers are very necessary during times of war. The United Service Organizations (USO) support troops overseas. The USO provides entertainment, packages from home, and phone cards to call people back in the United States.

1. Make a List To volunteer, make a list of activities that you like and talents that you have. Many people find it fun to share their talents and interests with others. For example, if you like to play soccer, you might be able to coach a youth soccer team.

2. Seek Out Opportunities Look for volunteer opportunities that are connected to your strengths and interests. Ask your teacher or use the Internet to find an organization that interests you.

3. Make Contact E-mail or call the contact person for your chosen organization. Some organizations require a list of past experiences. They might also want a list of references. Make sure you have these with you when you contact the organization.

▶▶ What do you think?

1. How does volunteering benefit all citizens?
2. Why do you think there has been a drop in the number of volunteers in recent years?
3. What might be a way to get people more interested in volunteering? Why?

GOVERNMENT ONLINE
Citizenship Activity Pack
For an activity to help you explore volunteering, go to **PearsonSuccessNet.com**

Basic Concepts of Democracy

▲ Children gather to celebrate Flag Day in New York City.

Guiding Question

What are the basic concepts of democracy? Use a concept web like the one below to take notes on the basic concepts of democracy.

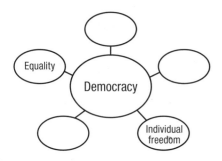

Objectives:

■ Understand the foundations of democracy.
■ Analyze the connections between democracy and the free enterprise system.

The word *democracy* means "rule by the people." Early American leaders formed a democratic government based on ideas learned from older governments. They believed democracy was the best form of government. A democratic government strives to treat citizens equally and offers them protection. In return, citizens must act with responsibility.

What are the foundations of democracy?

Most Americans believe in the basic ideas of democracy. Democracy will exist only as long as the people continue to believe in those ideas, which are listed below.

1. Every person has worth and dignity. Sometimes society demands a person to do certain things for the common good, however. Following laws and paying taxes are examples.

2. Every person is equal. All people must be treated the same under the law. Each person should have the same chance to be educated or to hold a job.

3. We believe in the **majority rule.** Democracy holds that the majority will usually be just. At the same time, we must insist on minority rights.

4. **Compromise** is the best way to settle differences. Compromise is a process in which opposing sides come to an agreement on an issue.

5. Every person must have freedom, but must not take away the freedom of others. The actions of one person should not cause harm to another. Democracy works to keep a balance between freedom and law.

What are the responsibilities and duties of citizenship?

A **citizen** is one who holds certain rights, duties, and responsibilities within a state. Duties include paying taxes, going to school, and obeying laws. These duties benefit all citizens. Citizenship also comes with responsibilities. Responsibilities are different than duties. Duties are required of all citizens. Responsibilities are only strongly encouraged. Responsibilities of citizens may include voting at election time and helping in the community.

✓**Checkpoint**   What is one duty of citizenship? What is one responsibility?

What is the free enterprise system?

The economy of the United States is a **free enterprise system.** Free enterprise in the United States is also called capitalism. In this system, goods and services are bought and sold. Competition in the market is the driving force of the free enterprise system. Laborers and workers compete for jobs. Businesses compete to produce goods and services that can be sold for a profit. Consumers benefit by being able to buy goods and services at the lowest possible prices. People, not the government, make most of the economic decisions in the free enterprise system of the United States. However, the government has always played a role in the system by passing laws and regulations.

Majority rule
A belief that a majority will be just more often than it will be unjust

Compromise
A settlement of differences in which each side gives up some of its demands

Citizen
One who holds certain rights, duties, and responsibilities within a state

Free enterprise system
System in which businesses are privately owned and operated with little government involvement

Reading Strategy
Summarizing
Why is a free enterprise system good for consumers?

Essential Questions Journal   Go to your **Essential Questions Journal** to work on this chapter's Essential Question.

SECTION 3 ASSESSMENT

1. **Guiding Question** Use your completed concept web to answer this question: What are the basic concepts of democracy?

Key Terms and Comprehension

On a sheet of paper, write the answer to each question. Use complete sentences.

2. What do most Americans think is the best system of government?

3. What is the role of government in the free enterprise system?

4. What is the free enterprise system?

5. What is competition and why is it important?

Critical Thinking

6. **Make Comparisons** What is the difference between a duty and a responsibility? Why is each important in a democracy?

7. **Make Connections** Why do you think a free enterprise system goes well with democracy?

Chapter Summary

Section 1—Government and the State

- Government has three basic kinds of power: legislative, executive, and judicial.

- The state is a group of people living in a territory. The state is sovereign and is controlled by the government.

- The purpose of government in America is described in the Preamble of the Constitution.

Section 2—Forms of Government

- Governments may be classified in three ways: by the number of people who are allowed to take part; by the way power is divided geographically, and by the relationship between the lawmakers and those who carry out the law.

- A democratic government receives its power from the people. In an indirect democracy, a small group of people is elected to represent a larger group.

- In a dictatorship, one person or a small group of people runs the government. There is no limit to the length of the dictator or group's rule.

- In a federal form of government, powers are divided between a central government and several local governments.

- In a confederate form of government, several individual states join together. The confederation cannot make laws but may help the states with foreign policy or trade.

- In a unitary form of government, power is held by a central organization, such as a parliament.

- In a presidential form of government, the power is divided between a legislative and an executive branch. The United States has a presidential form of government.

- In a parliamentary form of government, the leader and his cabinet are part of the legislative branch, which is called the parliament. Great Britain has a parliamentary form of government.

Section 3—Basic Concepts of Democracy

- There are five basic ideas of democracy: Every person has worth and dignity; every person is equal; majority rules; compromise is the best way to settle differences; every person must have freedom but must not take freedom away from others.

- The United States has a free enterprise system. The government has always played a role in this free enterprise system but does not control it.

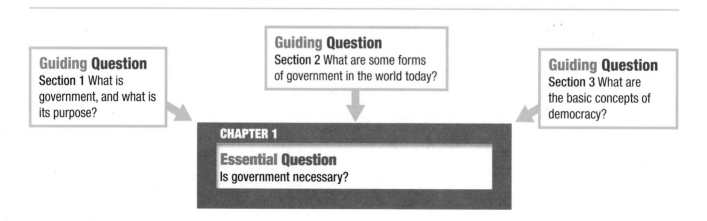

Guiding Question
Section 1 What is government, and what is its purpose?

Guiding Question
Section 2 What are some forms of government in the world today?

Guiding Question
Section 3 What are the basic concepts of democracy?

CHAPTER 1

Essential Question
Is government necessary?

Document-Based Assessment

The Political Ideas of John Locke

John Locke was an important English philosopher who lived from 1632 until 1704. He studied medicine and philosophy at Oxford University. He worked as a doctor and for the government.

In his time, kings and queens ruled many countries. In 1690, Locke wrote a book called Two Treatises of Government. *His book supported democracy as a form of government. These passages are from a section of his book.*

Document at a Glance

- Philosopher John Locke
- Supported democracy
- Against monarchs

Men being . . . by nature all free, equal, and independent, no one can be put out of this estate and subjected to the political power of another without his own consent. The only way whereby any one divests [take away from] himself of his natural liberty . . . is by agreeing with other men to join and unite into a community for their comfortable, safe, and peaceable living . . .

Locke wrote that there was a type of government that men, not monarchs, could form to protect the natural rights of people. The passage below is also from his book.

The liberty of man in society is to be under no other legislative [lawmaking] power but that established by consent in the commonwealth [a community]; nor under the dominion of any will or restraint of any law, but what that legislative shall enact according to the trust put in it . . .

Freedom of men under government is to have a standing rule to live by, common to every one of that society, and made by the legislative power erected [built] in it . . .

The majority [more than half of a total] having . . . the whole power of the community naturally in them, may employ all that power in making laws for the community . . . and then the form of the government is a perfect democracy . . .

Document-Based Questions

1. Locke did not believe in a monarchy. Why?

2. What does the author say is the natural state of man?

3. According to the author, what gives governments their power?

4. How does Locke think that rules for society should be made?

5. **Summarize** What was Locke's feeling about democracy?

SOURCE: *Two Treatises of Government* by John Locke, 1690

Chapter Assessment

Directions: Choose the letter of the best answer or write the answer using complete sentences.

Section 1—Government and the State

1. What is the term for the laws and goals of a country?
   - **A.** constitution
   - **B.** democracy
   - **C.** public policy
   - **D.** state

2. What are the three basic powers of government?
   - **A.** judicial, state judicial, state executive
   - **B.** democracy, public policy, legislative
   - **C.** legislative, democracy, executive
   - **D.** legislative, executive, judicial

3. What is legislative power?

4. What is the social contract theory?

5. Where in the U.S. Constitution can you find the purpose of government?

6. **Critical Thinking** Government is a mixture of laws and policies. What do you think life would be like without government?

Section 2—Forms of Government

7. In what kind of government is limited power held by a single, central group?
   - **A.** unitary
   - **B.** autocracy
   - **C.** confederation
   - **D.** representative

8. What kind of government receives its power from the people?
   - **A.** dictatorship
   - **B.** unitary
   - **C.** democracy
   - **D.** confederate

9. Who is the power divided between in a presidential form of government?

10. What are the three basic forms of government that exist when defining government by the geographic division of power?

11. **Critical Thinking** Why do you think most national governments do not use direct democracy?

Section 3—Basic Concepts of Democracy

12. The government has always played a role in the free enterprise system by doing what?

13. Who makes most of the decisions in a free enterprise system?

14. What is the difference between a duty and a responsibility?

15. What is the majority rule?

16. Why did early American leaders form a democratic government?

17. **Critical Thinking** What do you think is the most important basic idea of democracy? Why do you think so?

Apply What You've Learned

Exploring the Essential Question

You have been chosen to run a new country. The country is very large and has many people. Think about how you want your new country to run. Work with a partner if you need help.

18. Will your country run using the free enterprise system? Why?

19. What major functions will you want the government to perform? List at least two.

Essential Questions Project

20. Write a plan for your country by answering the above questions. Present the plan to the class. Allow time for questions that your classmates might have at the end of your presentation. After all of the presentations have been completed, work with the class to answer the Essential Question: **Is government necessary?**

Essential Questions Journal

Go to your **Essential Questions Journal** to work on this chapter's Essential Question.

Test-Taking Tip

Pace yourself. If you are unsure about a question, put a check next to it and move on. If you have time left, go back and try to answer the checked questions.

▲ The colonists meet the British army at Lexington, Massachusetts.

Origins of American Government

Essential Question
How does the Constitution reflect the times in which it was written?

■ ■

Reading Strategy: Questioning
Asking questions as you read will help you find answers and remember more of the information. Questioning the text will also help you to be a more active reader. Ask yourself,

- What will I learn about the origins of American government?
- What decisions can I make about the facts and details?
- How does information about the origins of American government connect to my life?

ON THE GO

To study anywhere, anytime, download these online resources at PearsonSuccessNet.com
- **Political Dictionary**
- **Audio Review**
- **Downloadable Interactivities**

Our Political Beginnings

▲ King John signs the Magna Carta, limiting his own power to rule.

Guiding Question

What ideas and traditions influenced government in the English colonies? Use a concept web to take notes on the ideas that shaped American colonists' concepts of government.

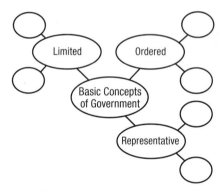

Objectives:

- Identify the three basic concepts that influenced the English colonies.
- Explain the following English documents: the Magna Carta, the Petition of Right, and the English Bill of Rights.
- Describe the three types of colonies that the English established in America.

The early settlers, or **colonists,** in America wanted to make rules and laws that were fair. The rights of people were considered and written into the law. All **political,** or governmental, ideas used by the settlers had their roots in older forms of government. **Ancient** civilizations such as those in Greece and Rome had an influence. European political thinkers who wrote about government did as well. The greatest influence, however, came from the governments in England at that time.

What are the basic concepts of government?

The English colonists used an **ordered government** based on what they knew. They created offices to serve their needs at the time. Some of these offices, such as sheriff and justice of the peace, are still used today. Our modern government also has a grand jury, counties, and townships as the colonists did.

The colonists did not want government to take away basic individual rights such as freedom of speech and the right to worship. The idea of a **limited government** was important to the colonists.

England had had a **representative government** for centuries, which the settlers also wanted. They believed people should have a say in government decisions. The colonists, under English rule, were not allowed to make decisions for themselves. Eventually, the idea of government "for and by the people" became a reality in America. The colonists worked very hard to have a representative form of government.

What were the landmark English documents?

In early times, only the English king and his lords could make laws. In the 1200s, King John was the ruler of England. He was a cruel and unfair king. He imposed heavy taxes on the people.

The nobles, or rich people in the country, decided something had to be done. A group of determined barons forced King John to sign a document called the **Magna Carta.** *Magna Carta* means "great charter." A **charter** is a written agreement.

The Magna Carta gave certain rights to the English people and limited the king's power. It stated the following:

- The king must ask the advice of the nobles in important matters.
- No special taxes could be raised unless the nobles agreed.
- No free man could be put in prison without first being judged by his peers (equals).
- Judges and other officials were to be appointed to serve the kingdom.
- The common people were allowed to elect people to represent them in government. This type of lawmaking body in England was called Parliament.

By the mid-1300s, Parliament had two parts. The House of Lords included nobles and church leaders. The House of Commons included knights and common people.

Parliament was used by some rulers and ignored by others. Finally Parliament was allowed to make laws on its own. The system that Parliament used to make laws worked very well. The colonists followed the same system. Today the United States Congress and state legislatures are based on this system.

By 1628, the members of Parliament felt that the power of the king had become too strong. In the **Petition of Right** they listed the actions that a king could not take. The Petition said that a king could not force rich people to loan him money. It also stated that people could not be put in prison without a jury trial.

In 1689, during the rule of William and Mary, Parliament passed the **English Bill of Rights.** This bill stated the powers of a king or queen. Under this bill of rights, Parliament had to approve all taxes. The king was not allowed to suspend, or stop, the work of Parliament. The people could ask the king for help. A person accused of a crime had the right to a jury trial.

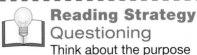

Reading Strategy
Questioning
Think about the purpose of this text. Ask yourself, "Am I finding out the information I expected to when I began reading?"

Colonist
Person who lives in a new land that keeps ties with the home country

Political
Having to do with government or the actions of the government

Ancient
Many years ago; belonging to early history

Ordered government
A regulated government that consists of specific offices and units

Limited government
A government that has certain restrictions and gives certain rights to individuals

Representative government
A government in which the people have a say

Magna Carta
Great Charter; a document that grants rights

Charter
A written agreement

Petition of Right
A written document asking for a limit to the king's power

English Bill of Rights
Document written by Parliament to prevent abuse of power by English rulers

The settlers who came to America knew about the rights in the English Bill of Rights. When the settlers wrote a plan for their own government, they added a Bill of Rights. The Bill of Rights was similar to the English Bill of Rights and the earlier Petition of Right. See Figure 2.1. You will learn more about the United States Bill of Rights in Chapter 3.

✔ **Checkpoint** What were two rights that the Magna Carta gave to the English people?

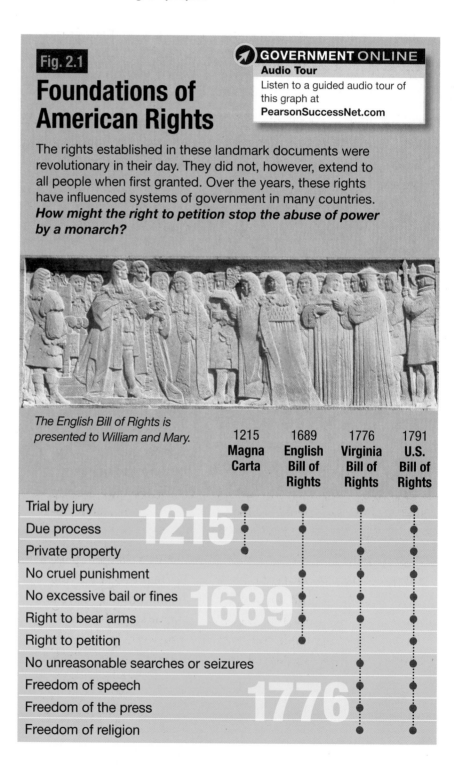

Fig. 2.1

Foundations of American Rights

GOVERNMENT ONLINE
Audio Tour
Listen to a guided audio tour of this graph at
PearsonSuccessNet.com

The rights established in these landmark documents were revolutionary in their day. They did not, however, extend to all people when first granted. Over the years, these rights have influenced systems of government in many countries. *How might the right to petition stop the abuse of power by a monarch?*

The English Bill of Rights is presented to William and Mary.

	1215 Magna Carta	1689 English Bill of Rights	1776 Virginia Bill of Rights	1791 U.S. Bill of Rights
Trial by jury	●	●	●	●
Due process	●	●	●	●
Private property	●	●	●	●
No cruel punishment		●	●	●
No excessive bail or fines		●	●	●
Right to bear arms		●	●	●
Right to petition	●	●	●	●
No unreasonable searches or seizures			●	●
Freedom of speech		●	●	●
Freedom of the press		●	●	●
Freedom of religion			●	●

What were the thirteen colonies?

There were 13 colonies that rebelled in the American Revolution. (Great Britain had other colonies—notably Quebec, Barbados, and Jamaica.) In 1775, eight were royal colonies, three were proprietary colonies, and two were charter colonies. See Figure 2.2.

The king named a governor for each royal colony. The king also named a council and a lower house. Royal governors were strict and made the people angry. This anger was one of the causes of the revolution.

The **proprietary** colonies were Maryland, Pennsylvania, and Delaware. A proprietor, who was given land by the king, ran the colony. He also appointed the governor.

■ ■ ■ ■ ■ ■ ■ ■ ■ ■ ■ ■ ■ ■ ■
Proprietary
Organized by a person who was given land by the king

Fig. 2.2 The Thirteen Colonies, 1775

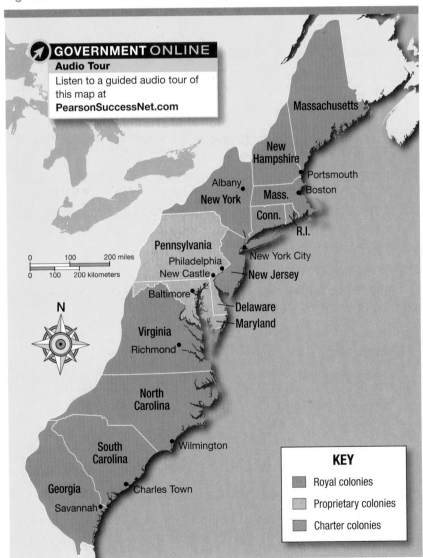

▲ Analyzing Maps Despite the differing government systems within the colonies, they were all influenced by their English roots. *How was a royal colony different from a proprietary colony?*

The charter colonies were Connecticut and Rhode Island. They were successful, self-governing colonies with a governor elected by the property owners. These colonies had fair laws and judges. The charter colonies had more freedom and self-government than the other colonies.

The Connecticut and Rhode Island charters were so liberal for their time that, after independence, they were kept with only minor changes as state constitutions for many years. Many historians say that if Britain had allowed the other colonies the same freedoms and self-government found in these charter colonies, the Revolution might never have occurred.

✔ **Checkpoint** What were the three types of colonies that were created?

Essential Questions Journal Go to your **Essential Questions Journal** to work on this chapter's Essential Question.

SECTION 1 ASSESSMENT

Word Bank

limited government

Magna Carta

ordered government

representative government

1. Guiding Question Use your completed flowchart to answer this question: What ideas and traditions influenced government in the English colonies?

Key Terms and Comprehension

On a sheet of paper, use the words from the Word Bank to complete each sentence correctly.

2. The _____ gave certain rights to the English people and limited the King's power.

3. The idea of _____ was important because colonists wanted basic individual rights.

4. A(n) _____ is a type of government "for and by the people."

5. Creating offices, such as sheriff, is an example of a(n) _____.

Critical Thinking

6. **Make Comparisons** What do the Magna Carta, the Petition of Right, and the English Bill of Rights have in common?

7. **Draw Conclusions** What part of English government do you think had the most influence on American government? Explain.

ISSUES OF OUR TIME

Does a country need a constitution?

▶▶ Track the Issue

The need for a constitution has been debated by many nations. Some nations have chosen to use a constitution, while others have not.

1788 The U.S. Constitution is approved after much debate.

1861 After breaking away from the Union, the Confederate States of America approved a constitution that was like the federal constitution.

1949 Germany makes a constitution based on the U.S. Constitution and the British government.

2005 The constitution of the European Union is defeated after France and the Netherlands reject it.

October 2005 The Iraqi people vote to approve their constitution.

The Iraqi Governing Council held their signing on March 8, 2004.

▶▶ Perspectives

On July 13, 2003, twenty-five people in Iraq came together to write a constitution. This group was called the Iraqi Governing Council. This group's task was to create a constitution that would serve the needs of the country's diverse population. After more than two years of debate, the constitution was written and approved. There were many arguments about it. For example, the Sunni Arab community in Kirkuk did not like the plan. They feared that the constitution would divide the nation instead of making it stronger.

An Incomplete Constitution	Dividing the Country
"The constitution will not be complete or legitimate unless those who did not participate in the previous elections or those who are not represented in the National Assembly are involved in it. Among these are the Sunni Arabs. If they do not take part in writing the constitution, the constitution will not be at all legitimate. It will be a lame constitution which will be met with objection and rejection by a large sector of the Iraqi society." *—National Dialogue Council Head Shaykh Khalaf Salih al-Ulayyan, "The Iraqi Scene," broadcast by Al-Jezeera, reproduced by the BBC, July 29, 2005*	"Kirkuk's Arabs refuse any constitution that would divide the country by different names, which is at odds with Islam and with the Arabic nation of Iraq." *— Sheik Abdul Rahman Mished, leader of Kirkuk's Arab Assembly from "Sunni Arabs Rally to Protest Iraqi Constitution," by Robert F. Worth, The New York Times, August 27, 2005*

Connect to Your World

1. Why does Sheik Abdul Rahman not like the idea of a constitution?
2. Why would the constitution not be complete if the Sunni Arabs refused to take part in writing it?

GOVERNMENT ONLINE
In the News
To find out more about the Iraqi constitution, visit
PearsonSuccessNet.com

SECTION 2

The Coming of Independence

▲ Benjamin Franklin was a leading member of the Second Continental Congress.

Guiding Question

What events and ideas led to American independence?

Use a flowchart to record major events that led to American independence.

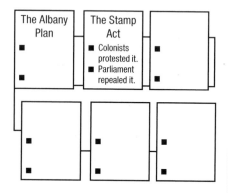

The Albany Plan	The Stamp Act
■	■ Colonists protested it.
■	■ Parliament repealed it.

Objectives:

- Describe how Britain's policies led to the growth of self-government in the colonies.
- Identify some of the steps that led to colonies uniting.
- Understand the First and Second Continental Congresses.
- Describe the ideas in the Declaration of Independence.
- Summarize the first state constitutions and how they were alike.

England became Great Britain in 1707. The 13 American colonies belonged to Britain and were ruled by British law. Many things happened under these laws that upset the colonists. The colonists did not like the way they were treated by Britain. They felt they were taxed unfairly and were not represented in Britain. Soon the colonists decided to form their own government. They broke away from Britain. In this section, you will learn how the United States gained independence.

What were Britain's colonial policies?

Britain did not interfere with the government in the colonies for nearly a century. Then Britain needed money to pay its debts and tried to raise money from the colonies. By the middle 1700s, the colonists felt that Britain was trying to gain control. The colonists did not like the high taxes collected on certain goods. Gradually feelings against British rule increased. In order to control the royal governors, the colonists would not vote to approve the money for their salaries. Soon the colonists began working together to gain control of their land.

How did the colonies unite?

Early attempts had been made in the colonies to come together. The New England Confederation was formed to help coordinate the efforts of the colonies to defend against the Native Americans. The danger soon passed and the confederation ended. The northern colonies then formed the **Albany Plan of Union.** They wanted to solve the problem of trade and were concerned about attacks by the French.

Benjamin Franklin suggested a congress be formed with representatives from all the colonies. It would have the power to make war, gather troops, and regulate trade. It was turned down by the colonies. Many of Franklin's ideas were used later when the colonists created the new government.

Britain continued its severe tax policies. The Stamp Act of 1765 required the colonists to pay for stamps to use on official documents. The colonists thought of this as "taxation without representation." The Stamp Act Congress was held in New York, and a protest was sent to the king. (See Figure 2.3.) Parliament repealed the Stamp Act, but more laws were soon passed. The colonists protested these laws by no longer using British goods. Then, in Boston, British troops fired on a mob that was taunting them. Five colonists were killed. This event became known as the Boston Massacre. More protests occurred, such as the Boston Tea Party. Colonists in disguise boarded British tea ships and threw the cargo into Boston Harbor to protest the Tea Act.

What was the First Continental Congress?

In 1774, a large meeting called the First Continental Congress was held in Philadelphia. At this meeting the colonists decided to take action against the king. Britain had passed a new set of laws known as the **Intolerable Acts.** The colonists sent the king a list of the rights they demanded. They also said that they would refuse to buy all British goods, including tea.

The Continental Congress met for two months and sent a Declaration of Rights to King George. They did not like Britain's colonial policies. The delegates suggested all trade with England be stopped. This action of the First Continental Congress made no difference in the way Britain treated the colonists. Trouble continued between the colonists and Britain. The final result was the Revolutionary War.

The Revolutionary War between the colonists and Britain started on April 19, 1775. The first battle of the war took place in Massachusetts. It started at Lexington when British soldiers ordered the colonists to lay down their guns. When they would not, the battle began. The armed colonists were called **minutemen** because they had promised to be ready to fight at a minute's notice. Eight minutemen were killed. The British then marched to Concord. They burned buildings until the minutemen forced them to retreat. Many more battles were fought that spring.

✔ **Checkpoint**   What caused the start of the Revolutionary War?

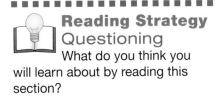

Reading Strategy
Questioning
What do you think you will learn about by reading this section?

Albany Plan of Union
Plan made by Benjamin Franklin that would unite colonies for trade and war decisions

Intolerable Acts
New laws passed by British Parliament to punish the colonists

Minutemen
A group of armed men who fought in the Revolutionary War

Fig. 2.3

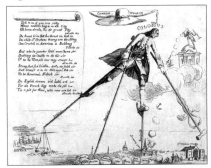

▲ Analyzing Political Cartoons
A colonial cartoonist mocks a British lord on stilts fishing for popularity after the Stamp Act disaster. *Why were the British losing popularity in the colonies?*

What was the Second Continental Congress?

The Second Continental Congress ran the government of the colonies and supported the colonists during the war. The Congress met in May, 1775. They organized an army to be led by George Washington. Not all Americans supported the war. It was difficult to get soldiers to join the army. Other countries such as Spain and France helped the Americans.

The Continental Congress wanted to end British rule and to have a government run by the people. They asked Thomas Jefferson to write their ideas to send to the king. The document Jefferson wrote was called the Declaration of Independence. It was the greatest contribution of the colonial period to the future form of democratic government in America. (See Figure 2.4.) With the adoption of the Declaration of Independence, the United States was born. The 13 colonies became free and independent states.

At the Second Continental Congress, a committee wrote a plan to join the states together. This plan was called the Articles of Confederation. It was popular with the states because it did not make the national, or central, government too strong. However, it took several years for the Articles to be approved by all the states. It went into effect in 1781.

Fig. 2.4 The Road to Independence

The New World	The Colonies Unite	War Begins	Independence
1607 Jamestown, Virginia, the first successful English settlement, is founded.	**1754** The Albany Congress proposes that the colonies unite.	**1775** The battles of Lexington and Concord sparks the American Revolution.	**1776** The Declaration of Independence is signed.
1620 The Pilgrims sign the Mayflower Compact.	**1765** The Stamp Act is passed.		
1669 John Locke writes the constitution for the Carolina colony.	**1770** Five colonists are killed by the British at the Boston Massacre.		
	1773 The Tea Act is passed. Colonists respond with the Boston Tea Party.		

▲ Interpreting Timelines *How did early events contribute to the colonists' fight for independence?*

What is the Declaration of Independence?

The first part of the Declaration of Independence says all people have certain rights. These rights include "life, liberty, and the pursuit of happiness." It also says that if a government denies these rights to the people, then its rule must end.

The middle section of the Declaration lists all the **grievances** (complaints) the colonists had against King George III. See the Declaration of Independence in the appendix of this book.

The last paragraph says that the colonists were free from the rule of England.

" . . . these United Colonies are, and of Right ought to be, Free and independent States; that they are absolved from all Allegiance to the British Crown, and that all political Connection between them and the State of Great Britain, is and ought to be totally dissolved."

On July 4, 1776, Congress approved the Declaration of Independence. In October 1781, the British surrendered at the Battle of Yorktown. This battle marked a turning point in the war. By 1783, the war was over. Many lives had been lost on both sides.

✔**Checkpoint** What does the first part of the Declaration of Independence guarantee?

How were the first state constitutions written?

In the 1600s, the Jamestown, Virginia, colony was the first to have an assembly of representatives. This assembly, called the House of Burgesses, made decisions for the people. The people elected the representatives. The plan for the assembly did not come from the settlers. The plan was set up by England.

The idea of voting and electing representatives was later used as the states wrote their constitutions. New Hampshire was the first state to write a constitution; South Carolina was the second. By 1777, most states had adopted written constitutions. **Conventions** were called to write and then adopt these constitutions.

✔**Checkpoint** How did the English government influence the government in Jamestown?

Grievance
A complaint

Convention
A formal meeting called for a special purpose

What are the common features of constitutions?

Most states created constitutions shortly after the Declaration of Independence had been written. The new documents were brief. The terms of elected officials were kept short. Most power was given to the legislatures. These state constitutions had an influence on the Constitution of the United States (Figure 2.5).

Fig. 2.5

The state constitutions shared many features.	
Popular Sovereignty	Government can only exist with the consent of the people. The people hold the power.
Limited Government	The power of government has many restrictions.
Civil Rights and Liberties	People have certain rights that the government must respect.
Separation of Powers Checks and Balances	Power of government is divided among three branches. Each branch has a way to control the power of the others.

Essential Questions Journal Go to your **Essential Questions Journal** to work on this chapter's Essential Question.

SECTION 2 ASSESSMENT

Word Bank

convention

Declaration of Independence

New England Confederation

representation

1. **Guiding Question** Use your completed flowchart to answer this question: What events and ideas led to American independence?

Key Terms and Comprehension

On a sheet of paper, use the words from the Word Bank to complete each sentence correctly.

2. The _____ was formed to defend against Native Americans.

3. Colonists felt that the Stamp Act was taxation without _____.

4. A formal meeting called for a special purpose is a _____.

5. On July 4, 1776, the _____ was adopted. A new nation was formed.

Critical Thinking

6. **Summarize** What events led to the First Continental Congress?

7. **Make Comparisons** What were the goals of the First and Second Continental Congresses?

▲ Daniel Shays' rebellion made the need for a stronger government clear.

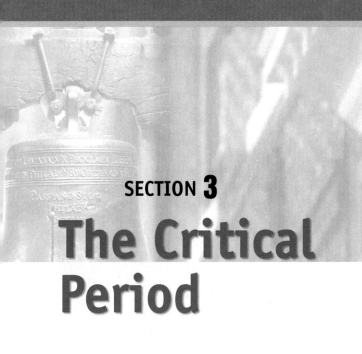

SECTION 3

The Critical Period

Guiding Question

What weaknesses in the Articles of Confederation made a lasting government impossible? Use an outline to take notes on the reasons why the Articles of Confederation failed.

I. The Articles of Confederation
   A. Weaknesses
      1. Congress had no power to tax.
      2. _____
   B. Effects of the Weaknesses
      1. _____
      2. _____

Objectives:

- Describe how government was set up under the Articles of Confederation.
- Explain why the Articles of Confederation were too weak.
- Understand that a need for a stronger national government led to the Constitutional Convention.

The ties between the colonies and Britain were broken after the Revolutionary War. A new nation formed, but it was a nation of separate and individual colonies. The colonies needed a government to join them together as a country.

What were the Articles of Confederation?

The Articles of Confederation set up a national Congress made up of **delegates** from the 13 states. A delegate is a person chosen to speak or act for others. This Congress could make war. It could also agree to **treaties** with other countries, borrow money, and set up a money system. Each state sent delegates to the Congress. The Articles did not provide for a president as a national leader or for a system of **justice.** The Articles also did not allow Congress to raise money.

At first most people were satisfied with the Articles of Confederation. The Articles allowed the states to control most of their own affairs. The Articles limited Congress's power over the states. However, over time, issues arose that indicated the Articles were too weak. See Figure 2.6 on page 34.

What was the critical period?

The war with Britain cost a great deal of money. Congress had no money of its own. It had no way of raising money. Most of the money should have come from the states. Many states refused to pay. Congress had no system of law to force the states to pay.

Fig. 2.6
Weaknesses of the Articles of Confederation

- Congress did not have the power to tax.

- Each state had only one vote, regardless of size.

- Congress could not regulate trade.

- Congress had no executive power to enforce its acts.

- There was no national court system.

- Amendments required the approval of states.

▲ The Articles were too weak to hold the states together. *What was one result of the weaknesses listed above?*

Delegate
A person chosen to speak or act for another person or group

Treaty
An agreement between two or more countries or states about trade, peace, or other matters

Justice
Fair and equal treatment under the law; the use of authority to uphold what is right and lawful

Besides the war debt, the nation was faced with many financial problems. Businesses and farmers were out of money. Congress had no funds to pay an army or navy to defend the nation. Soldiers who had fought in the Revolutionary War had not been paid. Individual states were printing their own money. Some states even asked for foreign aid. States fought over trade. There were protests and rebellions over taxes and debts. One such uprising was Shays' Rebellion in Massachusetts. Daniel Shays was a Revolutionary War officer who led a violent attack on a federal arsenal. As a result of this, Massachusetts passed some laws to help those with no money to pay their debts. Shays left the state but was later forgiven for his rebellion.

✔ **Checkpoint**   What was Shays' Rebellion?

Why was there a need for a stronger government?

Many plans were proposed to strengthen the new nation's government. Maryland and Virginia had a meeting at Mt. Vernon to work out their differences. This meeting proved to be successful. The Virginia General Assembly then suggested a joint meeting of all states. This meeting was held in Annapolis, Maryland, in September 1786. It was not well attended. However, this convention called for another meeting of the states. Congress then called upon the states to send delegates to a meeting in Philadelphia. The purpose of this meeting was to revise the Articles of Confederation. It became known as the Constitutional Convention.

▲ Independence Hall in Philadelphia, Pennsylvania, served as the meeting place for both the Second Continental Congress and the Constitutional Convention. *What importance might this building have had for the Constitutional Convention?*

Reading Strategy
Questioning
What details are important to understand what this section is about?

SECTION 3 ASSESSMENT

Essential Questions Journal Go to your **Essential Questions Journal** to work on this chapter's Essential Question.

1. **Guiding Question** Use your completed outline to answer this question: What weaknesses in the Articles of Confederation made a lasting government impossible?

Key Terms and Comprehension

On a sheet of paper, write the letter of the answer that correctly completes each sentence.

2. What was the goal of the Articles of the Confederation?

3. What was the result of Shays' Rebellion?

4. What were some of the reasons for the financial problems after the war?

5. What was the purpose of the Constitutional Convention?

Critical Thinking

6. **Predict Consequences** What problems could arise with each state printing its own money?

7. **Identify Alternatives** How do you think the Articles of Confederation could have been made stronger?

▲ General George Washington served as president of the Constitutional Convention.

Creating the Constitution

Guiding Question

What compromises enabled the Framers to create the Constitution? Use a flowchart to record details about the Framers' compromises.

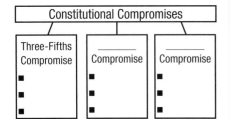

Objectives:

- Identify the Framers of the Constitution and discuss how they organized the Philadelphia Convention.
- Understand the Virginia Plan and the New Jersey Plan.
- Summarize the major compromises that the delegates agreed to make and their effects.
- Describe the delegates' reactions to the Constitution.

When the Constitutional Convention was held, the doors to Philadelphia's state house were guarded. Only the official delegates to the Convention were allowed inside.

Each delegate had agreed ahead of time not to discuss Convention business with outsiders. They knew they had difficult decisions to make. The delegates wanted to meet in private to settle their differences. They wanted to form their ideas for the new government. They did not want the public to be allowed to judge their ideas until they were finished.

Who were the Framers?

The 55 delegates who attended the convention in Philadelphia, Pennsylvania, in 1787 were well-educated men. George Washington was the leader at the convention. Like Washington, the other delegates were important people in their own states. The delegates came from different sections of the country. Even so, they shared many of the same ideas about government.

These delegates were known as the Framers of the Constitution. Most had a record of public service and many had fought in the Revolutionary War. Many had also been members of other conventions. Eight had signed the Declaration of Independence. Most of the delegates were a new generation of young men. See Figure 2.7 on the next page. Missing from the convention were Thomas Jefferson and John Adams. They were serving as ministers to Europe. Jefferson was in France and Adams in Britain.

The delegates worked in secret in the same room where the Declaration of Independence was signed. William Jackson kept a journal, but it was not complete. Most of what we know today comes from James Madison's record of the events. He became a leader at the convention and contributed more to the Constitution than any other delegate. He is known as the "Father of the Constitution."

What plans of government were considered?

The delegates considered two plans of government—the Virginia Plan and the New Jersey Plan.

The Virginia Plan called for a strong central government with three branches: legislative, executive, and judicial. The legislature (Congress) would be **bicameral,** meaning it would have two parts. The House of Representatives would have members elected from each state. The Senate would have members chosen by the House. Also, under this proposed plan, Congress would choose a "National Executive" and a "National Judiciary." Other conditions of the Virginia Plan were that states were required to take an oath to support the Union. States also would have representative governments and Congress would admit new states to the Union.

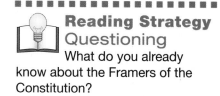

Reading Strategy
Questioning
What do you already know about the Framers of the Constitution?

Bicameral
A legislative body made up of two parts, or chambers

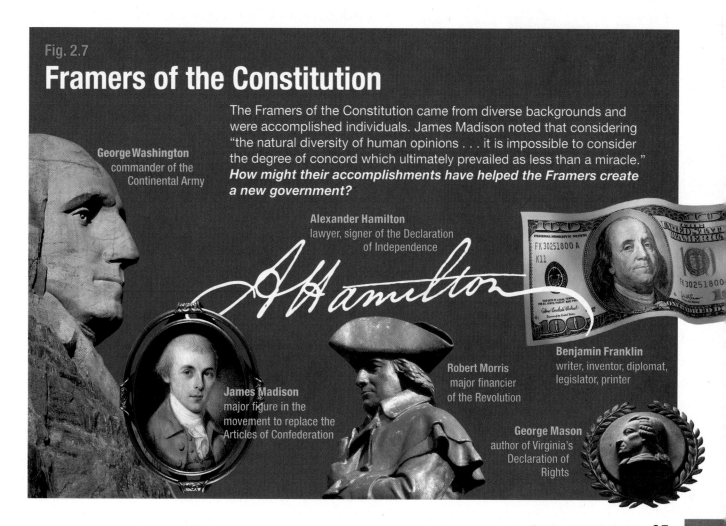

Fig. 2.7

Framers of the Constitution

The Framers of the Constitution came from diverse backgrounds and were accomplished individuals. James Madison noted that considering "the natural diversity of human opinions . . . it is impossible to consider the degree of concord which ultimately prevailed as less than a miracle." *How might their accomplishments have helped the Framers create a new government?*

George Washington
commander of the Continental Army

Alexander Hamilton
lawyer, signer of the Declaration of Independence

James Madison
major figure in the movement to replace the Articles of Confederation

Robert Morris
major financier of the Revolution

Benjamin Franklin
writer, inventor, diplomat, legislator, printer

George Mason
author of Virginia's Declaration of Rights

■ ■ ■ ■ ■ ■ ■ ■ ■ ■ ■ ■ ■ ■ ■ ■

Compromise
A settlement of differences in which each side gives up some of its demands

The New Jersey Plan was suggested by the smaller states. It called for one Congress with the states represented equally. Congress could impose taxes and regulate trade. The New Jersey Plan also called for a "federal executive" of more than one person.

The two plans did not agree about how the states should be represented in Congress. The delegates had to decide if representation would be by population, by financial contributions, or by state equality. After a lot of debate, the delegates made **compromises** to solve their problems. A compromise is when each side gives up some of its demands to reach an agreement.

What compromises were made at the Convention?

At the Constitutional Convention, each side had to compromise some of its plan to reach an agreement. Four major compromises were made.

How would the states be represented?

The most important compromise was about how to create a legislature (lawmaking body) for the new government. A group of delegates from Connecticut suggested a two-part legislature. The delegates said it should be a two-part legislature to please both the larger and smaller states. The members of one part of the legislature would be chosen according to population. The other part would have two representatives from each state, no matter how large or small the state was. This idea became known as the Connecticut Compromise or the Great Compromise.

How would slaves be counted?

The second compromise settled a problem about slaves. The problem was whether the slaves should be counted for tax collection and population purposes. The compromise said that every five slaves would count the same as three free men. This was called the Three-Fifths Compromise. This formula was used in fixing the amount of money raised in each state by any tax levied by Congress. In short, the Southerners could count their slaves, but they would have to pay for them. See Figure 2.8.

Fig. 2.8 **Slavery in the United States, 1790**

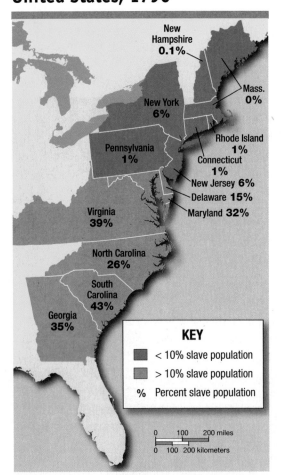

New Hampshire 0.1%
Mass. 0%
New York 6%
Rhode Island 1%
Pennsylvania 1%
Connecticut 1%
New Jersey 6%
Delaware 15%
Maryland 32%
Virginia 39%
North Carolina 26%
South Carolina 43%
Georgia 35%

KEY
■ < 10% slave population
■ > 10% slave population
% Percent slave population

0   100   200 miles
0   100   200 kilometers

▲ Analyzing Maps The southern states had a larger slave population than the northern states at the time of the Constitutional Convention. *How might this have influenced their opinion on the Three-Fifths Compromise?*

Who would control trade between states?

The third compromise had to do with **interstate** trade, or trade between states. The delegates debated how much power Congress should have over trade. They decided Congress would control trade between states. The states were given control of trade within their own territories.

Who would control trade between countries?

The northern and southern states did not agree on the issue of foreign trade, or trade with other countries. The northern states wanted Congress to control all foreign trade. The southern states sold large amounts of rice and tobacco to foreign countries. They were afraid they would lose this trade if Congress taxed these goods. The northern and southern states also disagreed about slaves. The Southerners worried that Congress would stop the slave trade.

The two sides compromised. The delegates gave Congress the power to control foreign trade. Congress could tax **imports** (goods brought in) but not **exports** (goods shipped out). The delegates also said that Congress could not end the slave trade for 20 years.

✔ **Checkpoint** What were the four major compromises made at the Constitutional Convention?

Interstate
Between or connecting two or more states

Imports
Goods bought from foreign countries

Exports
Goods sold and shipped to foreign countries

Biography

James Madison: 1751–1836

Born in Virginia, James Madison attended Princeton University and studied history and government. He was also well-read in the law and was an excellent farmer. Madison was a member of the Continental Congress and the Virginia Assembly, where he helped form the Constitution of Virginia in 1776.

Madison was a delegate to the Constitutional Convention in Philadelphia. He argued to scrap the Articles of Confederation. Instead, he wanted a national government that served individual citizens rather than the states.

Madison took a leading role in shaping the Constitution and was the author of the basic plan of government adopted by the delegates.

After ratification, Madison became known as the "Father of the Constitution." As a congressman from Virginia, Madison helped create the Bill of Rights. In 1808, James Madison was elected the fourth President of the United States.

How did the Framers complete their work?

The Framers all agreed the country needed a new national government. They wanted government's power given to it by the people. They also agreed that government should be limited. They wanted separation of powers to allow checks and balances among the branches of government. It was the smaller issues that caused the disagreements among the delegates. The method of choosing a President, the structure of Congress, and the way trade should be handled were all argued.

After compromises were made, the Constitutional Convention was finally over. On September 17, 1787, thirty-nine delegates signed the Constitution and created a new plan of government. Because not all of the delegates were willing to sign the Constitution, the final paragraph was worded carefully. It was written to give the impression of unanimity. "Done in Convention by the Unanimous Consent of the States present . . ."

✔ **Checkpoint** What were three issues of government on which the Framers agreed?

SECTION 4 ASSESSMENT

Essential Questions Journal Go to your **Essential Questions Journal** to work on this chapter's Essential Question.

1. **Guiding Question** Use your completed flowchart to answer this question: What compromises enabled the Framers to create the Constitution?

Key Terms and Comprehension
On a sheet of paper, write the answer to each question. Use complete sentences.

2. Why did the Framers want to keep their discussions at the Constitutional Convention secret?

3. Who is the "Father of the Constitution"?

4. What is the Three-Fifths Compromise?

5. What event happened on September 17, 1787?

Critical Thinking

6. **Analyze Information** What do you think was the most important compromise? Explain your answer.

7. **Identify Central Issues** Explain the Virginia Plan and the New Jersey Plan. How were the plans different?

Ratifying the Constitution

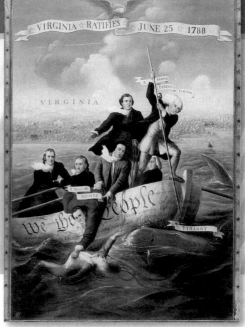

▲ This poster celebrates the 200th anniversary of Virginia's ratification of the Constitution.

Guiding Question

What issues aroused vigorous debate over the ratification of the Constitution? Use an outline to keep track of the issues debated during ratification.

I. Ratification of the Constitution
  A. Federalist Arguments
    1. Favored the Constitution
    2. _____
  B. Anti-Federalist Arguments
    1. _____
    2. _____

Objectives:

- Identify the arguments for and against the Constitution.
- Describe the start of the new government in the United States.

Once the Constitution was completed, the states had to approve it. Most delegates at the Constitutional Convention had signed the Constitution. These delegates now worked hard to persuade the states to **ratify,** or approve, it.

What was the fight for ratification?

Some people, called **Federalists,** favored the Constitution because it provided for a strong national government. The Federalists believed a strong central **authority** was necessary to defend the nation and keep it united.

Alexander Hamilton, James Madison, and John Jay were three well-known Federalists. They sent their messages to the people of New York by writing 85 **essays** in the New York newspapers. The authors all used the same name, Publius. These essays became known as the *Federalist Papers.* The three writers explained how the new government would work under the new Constitution and why this type of government was the best choice for the country. For example, *The Federalist* No. 51 told readers about the principle of checks and balances. *The Federalist* No. 78 explained the importance of an independent judicial branch.

The *Federalist Papers* told readers about the **rule of law.** Under the rule of law, government leaders must act according to the law. The *Federalist Papers* explained that the military would be under **civilian** control. This meant that the chief civilian, the President, would be in charge of the military. The *Federalist Papers* also told readers about the **enumerated powers,** or the 18 powers of Congress written into the Constitution.

■ ■ ■ ■ ■ ■ ■ ■ ■ ■ ■ ■ ■ ■ ■ ■ ■ ■ ■ ■

Ratify
To approve

Federalist
A person who favored the Constitution

Authority
The power or right to command or make final decisions

Essay
A short writing on a subject

Rule of law
Government leaders must act according to the law

Civilian
A person not on active duty in a military, police, or firefighting force

Enumerated powers
The 18 powers of Congress numbered from 1 to 18 in the Constitution

Anti-Federalist
A person who favored state and individual rights

Guarantee
An agreement to protect a possession or right

Another group, known as the **Anti-Federalists,** favored stronger state governments than the Constitution permitted. Anti-Federalists opposed the Constitution because they thought it would take away many state and individual rights. Patrick Henry, a famous Anti-Federalist, thought the Constitution would create a national government that was too powerful.

The Federalists agreed to add amendments to the Constitution to protect people's basic rights. Many Anti-Federalists then favored it. These amendments were added two years later. This addition is known as the Bill of Rights. It **guarantees** such rights as freedom of speech, freedom of religion, and freedom of the press.

Discussions continued throughout the winter at the state conventions. Nine states were needed to ratify the Constitution. Delaware was the first state to ratify. When New Hampshire ratified six months later, the number was brought to nine.

The new government still needed the support of Virginia and New York. Those two states had both ratified the Constitution by the end of July 1788. There was a long struggle in Virginia. Ratification was only by a small margin, 89 to 79. George Washington's strong support, along with the support of Madison, finally convinced Virginia to ratify. By 1790, all 13 states had ratified the Constitution. See Figure 2.9 on the next page.

✔**Checkpoint**   How did the positions of the Federalists and the Anti-Federalists differ on the role of government?

■ ■ ■ ■ ■ ■ ■ ■ ■ ■ ■ ■ ■ ■ ■ ■ ■ ■ ■ ■

Reading Strategy
Questioning
Why do you think it took six months for the states to ratify the Constitution?

Government in Your Life

Free Press in the United States

In 1733, the royal governor of New York suspended a judge who ruled against him. The judge and others started a newspaper that spoke out against the governor and the replacement judge. The editor of this paper, *The Journal,* was Peter Zenger. He accused the governor of breaking the law. Peter Zenger was arrested and sent to trial for libel, or a false use of the printed word. The jury found Zenger not guilty because he had printed the truth. The case was important to the freedom of the press that we now have in America.

What was the new government like in the United States?

Congress began putting the Constitution into use as soon as it was ratified. The first action Congress took was to name New York City the temporary national capital. Later the capital was moved to Philadelphia. In 1800, the capital was moved to Washington, D.C.

Congress gathered for the first time on March 4, 1789. They met in Federal Hall on Wall Street in New York City. At that time, the states elected 26 senators and 65 representatives to serve in the new Congress. Because it lacked a quorum (majority), it could not count the votes for President until April 6. On that day, George Washington was the unanimous choice for President. John Adams was elected Vice President. Then, on April 30, 1789, Washington traveled from his home in Mount Vernon, Virginia, to the capital in New York. He took the oath of office as the first President of the United States.

Fig. 2.9

Ratification of the Constitution

State	Date	Vote
Delaware	Dec. 7, 1787	30–0
Pennsylvania	Dec. 12, 1787	46–23
New Jersey	Dec. 18, 1787	38–0
Georgia	Jan. 2, 1788	26–0
Connecticut	Jan. 8, 1788	128–40
Massachusetts	Feb. 6, 1788	187–168
Maryland	April 28, 1788	63–11
South Carolina	May 23, 1788	149–73
New Hampshire	June 21, 1788	57–46
Virginia	June 25, 1788	89–79
New York	July 26, 1788	30–27
North Carolina*	Nov. 21, 1789	195–77
Rhode Island	May 29, 1790	34–32

* Second vote; ratification was originally defeated on August 4, 1788, by a vote of 184–84.

▲ Interpreting Tables Virginia's ratification came only after a long struggle. *In which states was ratification won by a narrow margin?*

Essential Questions Journal — Go to your **Essential Questions Journal** to work on this chapter's Essential Question.

SECTION 5 ASSESSMENT

Quick Write

Choose one of the 13 original colonies. Using the library or a trusted Web site, research the colony. Find information about the founding of the colony, its original government, and how it changed over time. When you have completed your research, write a short essay describing your colony.

1. **Guiding Question** Use your completed outline to answer this question: What issues aroused vigorous debate over the ratification of the Constitution?

Key Terms and Comprehension

On a sheet of paper, write the answer to each question. Use complete sentences.

2. What is the rule of law?

3. What were the 85 essays written by the Federalists called?

4. What freedoms does the Bill of Rights protect?

5. What did Patrick Henry believe about the Constitution?

Critical Thinking

6. **Draw Conclusions** What do you think people were afraid might happen if the Bill of Rights was not added to the Constitution?

7. **Recognize Cause and Effect** How do you think a written constitution protects individual rights?

Quick Study Guide

Chapter Summary

Section 1—Our Political Beginnings

- The American colonists broke away from England. They formed a government using the basic concepts of ordered government, limited government, and representative government.

- English government influenced the formation of American government. Ideas were used from the Magna Carta, the Petition of Right, and the English Bill of Rights.

- There were royal, proprietary, and charter colonies in America.

Section 2—The Coming of Independence

- When England tried to increase control of the colonists, they came together in protest. The First and Second Continental Congresses helped unify the colonists' cause.

- The Declaration of Independence declared the colonists free from English rule.

- The states wrote constitutions using the principles of popular sovereignty, limited government, and separation of powers.

Section 3—The Critical Period

- The Articles of Confederation was the first plan of government. Written at the Second Continental Congress, it proved to be too weak.

Section 4—Creating the Constitution

- The Constitutional Convention met to revise the Articles of Confederation in 1787. Instead, a new constitution was written.

- The larger states favored the Virginia Plan, while the smaller states wanted the New Jersey Plan. The delegates made compromises to reach an agreement.

Section 5—Ratifying the Constitution

- Before the Constitution could take effect, states had to ratify it.

- The Federalists favored the Constitution. The Anti-Federalists opposed the Constitution.

- After the Federalists agreed to add amendments to protect people's rights, the Constitution was ratified.

Guiding Question
Section 2 What events and ideas led to American independence?

Guiding Question
Section 3 What weaknesses in the Articles of Confederation made a lasting government impossible?

Guiding Question
Section 4 What compromises enabled the Framers to create the Constitution?

Guiding Question
Section 1 What ideas and traditions influenced government in the English colonies?

Guiding Question
Section 5 What issues aroused vigorous debate over the ratification of the Constitution?

CHAPTER 2

Essential Question
How does the Constitution reflect the times in which it was written?

Document-Based Assessment

The Federalist No. 51

The Federalist Papers *was a series of 85 essays written under the pen name of* Publius. *James Madison, Alexander Hamilton, and John Jay actually wrote the essays.*

The three men were well-respected leaders. Madison would later go on to become President of the United States. Hamilton would become a major force in setting economic policy for the United States. Jay would become the first Chief Justice of the United States Supreme Court.

Some states such as New York and Virginia were deeply split over ratifying the Constitution. Madison, Hamilton, and Jay wrote the Federalist Papers *to gain popular support for the proposed Constitution. This passage is from* The Federalist *No. 51, written by James Madison in 1788.*

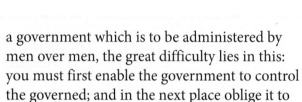

Document at a Glance
- One of the *Federalist Papers*
- Written by James Madison
- Supports the Constitution

To what expedient, then, shall we finally resort, for maintaining in practice the necessary partition [division] of power among the several departments, as laid down in the Constitution? . . . I will hazard [make] a few general observations . . .

It may be a reflection on human nature, that such devices should be necessary to control the abuses of government. But what is government itself, but the greatest of all reflections on human nature? If men were angels, no government would be necessary. If angels were to govern men, neither external [outside] nor internal [inside] controls on government would be necessary. In framing a government which is to be administered by men over men, the great difficulty lies in this: you must first enable the government to control the governed; and in the next place oblige it to control itself.

A dependence on the people is, no doubt, the primary control on the government; but experience has taught mankind the necessity of auxiliary [helpful] precautions . . . the constant aim is to divide and arrange the several offices in such a manner as that each may be a check on the other . . .

Document-Based Questions

1. According to the author, how might human nature abuse a weak government?

2. How does the author think that government reflects human nature?

3. What did the author mean by "a government which is to be administered by men over men"?

4. In your own words, write what this statement means: "If men were angels, no government would be necessary."

5. **Question** Why do you think Madison thought it was important that the government be forced to control itself?

Source: *The Federalist* No. 51, James Madison, 1788

Chapter Assessment

Directions: Choose the letter of the best answer or write the answer using complete sentences.

Section 1—Our Political Beginnings

1. How many colonies were there in 1775?

A. 8   **B.** 3   **C.** 5   **D.** 13

2. The greatest governmental influences on the colonists were Europe and _____.

A. Greece   **C.** England

B. Rome   **D.** Mexico

3. Why was the English Bill of Rights written?

4. Critical Thinking Why do you think the royal governors in the royal colonies made the people angry?

Section 2—The Coming of Independence

5. The first state to write a constitution was _____.

A. Connecticut   **C.** Delaware

B. Massachusetts   **D.** Maine

6. Why was the Albany Plan of Union formed?

7. Critical Thinking Why do you think the Stamp Act was viewed as "taxation without representation"?

Section 3—The Critical Period

8. The Articles of Confederation set up a Congress made up of _____.

A. delegates   **C.** judges

B. treaties   **D.** conventions

9. What were two of the weaknesses of the Articles of Confederation?

10. Critical Thinking How did Shay's Rebellion highlight the weaknesses of the federal government?

Section 4—Creating the Constitution

11. The _____ Plan called for a strong central government with three branches.

    A. Virginia   **C.** Connecticut

    B. New Jersey   **D.** Massachusetts

12. What is interstate trade?

13. What compromises were made concerning foreign trade?

14. Critical Thinking Why were southerners worried that Congress would stop the slave trade?

Section 5—Ratifying the Constitution

15. Why was there a struggle in Virginia over ratifying the Constitution?

16. Who were the writers of the *Federalist Papers*?

17. Critical Thinking Why do you think a bill of rights was not included in the original Constitution?

Apply What You've Learned

Exploring the Essential Question

18. Why was the first national government formed?

19. Why did the Framers replace the Articles of Confederation?

Essential Question Project

20. Use the content of this chapter to answer the Essential Question: **How does the Constitution reflect the times in which it was written?** Write a paragraph and share it with a classmate.

Essential Questions
Journal

Go to your **Essential Questions Journal** to work on this chapter's Essential Question.

Test-Taking Tip

When a teacher announces a test, listen carefully. Write down the lessons that will be included. Write down any specific topics the teacher says to review. Remember to write down the date the test will be given.

▲ Sculptures of the Framers at the National Constitution Center in Philadelphia

The Constitution

Essential Question
How has the Constitution lasted through changing times?

Reading Strategy: Predicting
Predicting helps readers think about what they already know about a subject. It also prepares them to look for new information. It helps readers think about what will come next. In other words, it gives them a purpose for reading. Keep this in mind as you begin this chapter.

- Look at the chapter words and images for clues about what you will read.
- As you read, make your best guess about what will come next. Decide why you think so.

To study anywhere, anytime, download these online resources at PearsonSuccessNet.com
- Political Dictionary
- Audio Review
- Downloadable Interactivities

SECTION 1

Basic Principles

▲ Voters express their will to the government. This concept is called popular sovereignty.

Guiding Question

What are the main principles on which the Constitution is based? Use a concept web like the one below to take notes on the six basic principles of the Constitution.

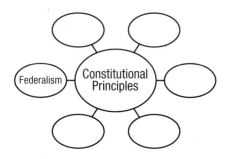

Objectives:

- Outline the important elements of the Constitution.
- List the six basic principles of the Constitution.

Written in Independence Hall in Philadelphia, Pennsylvania, the Constitution became the new plan of government for the United States. The Constitution was written in 1787 and took effect in 1789. It explained how the new government should be set up and run. The Constitution has been in use for over 200 years. It has continued to work even though the country has grown and changed.

What is the outline of the Constitution?

The Constitution of the United States outlines the basic **principles** of government. It explains the organization of the federal government. It tells how the leaders are chosen. The government also must follow certain rules. The Framers wrote these rules and the limits of the government into the Constitution. Knowing about the Constitution will help Americans better understand government and become responsible citizens.

The Constitution is a short document. Ten amendments were added soon after the Constitution became effective. Seventeen more have been added since then. The Constitution contains about 7,000 words. You can find the text of the Constitution at the back of this textbook. The basic principles of this brief document have guided our country successfully for over 200 years.

The Constitution begins with a Preamble, or introduction. The rest of the document is divided into seven sections called **articles.** (See **Figure 3.1** on the next page.) The first three articles outline the three branches of the federal government—executive, legislative, and judicial. Article IV outlines the relationship between the national government and the states. It also outlines the states' relationships to each other. Article V explains how amendments are added to the Constitution. Article VI says that the Constitution is the law of the land above any other law. Article VII explains ratification of the Constitution by the states. The last part of the Constitution contains the 27 amendments, in the order in which they were adopted. You will learn more about amendments in Section 2.

The writers of the Constitution built the new plan on certain principles they felt were necessary for a democratic government. These six principles are popular sovereignty, limited government, separation of powers, checks and balances, judicial review, and federalism. Figure 3.2 on pages 52–53 outlines these six basic principles of the Constitution.

What is popular sovereignty?

In the United States, the people hold all political power. This is called **popular sovereignty.** It means the people choose the leaders who will represent them and who do what the people want. The Preamble clearly states that it is the people who "ordain and establish" the Constitution. The Constitution was written and ratified to express the will of the people. Therefore, the federal government gets its power from the people. The same is true of state governments. The state leaders are also elected to represent and act according to the people's wishes.

Principle
A basic truth, law, or ideal of behavior

Article
A numbered section of a document such as the Constitution

Popular sovereignty
A basic principle of American government in which the people hold all of the political power

Fig. 3.1

The Seven Articles

The body of the Constitution is made up of seven articles. These articles lay the foundation for American government. *What is the purpose of the first three articles?*

Articles of the Constitution

Section	Subject
Preamble	States the purpose of the Constitution
Article I	Creates the Legislative branch
Article II	Creates the Executive branch
Article III	Creates the Judicial branch
Article IV	Relations among the States
Article V	Amending the Constitution
Article VI	National debts, supremacy of national law, and oaths of office
Article VII	Ratifying the Constitution

Fig. 3.2

Basic Principles of the Constitution

Throughout this section you will learn about the scope of the six basic principles of the Constitution. *According to these cartoons, what is the role of the judicial branch?*

Popular Sovereignty	Limited Government	Separation of Powers

Reading Strategy
Predicting
Predict the main idea of this section. Ask yourself if you are learning what you expected to when you began reading.

Limited government
The principle that government has only those powers given to it by the people

Rule of law
The principle that government must obey the law

Separation of powers
The division of government into three branches—the legislative, executive, and judicial branches

What is limited government?

Government must obey the law and conduct business according to the principles of the Constitution. The government and its officers are never above the law. The government is not all-powerful. The people have the power to give authority to the government. The government must follow the principles which have been authorized by the people. This idea of **limited government** is described as the **rule of law.**

What is separation of powers?

The Constitution divides the power of government into three different branches. This division is called the **separation of powers.** The Congress is the legislative, or lawmaking, branch. The executive branch (the President) carries out the laws. The judicial branch (the courts) applies the laws made by Congress.

Only Congress can make laws. It cannot give anyone else the power to do so. It also must approve appointments the President makes. The President and the executive branch see that the laws are carried out. The President can veto bills and appoint officials, including ambassadors and judges.

Checks and Balances

Judicial Review

Federalism

The court system is made up of the United States Supreme Court and the lower courts. The courts can settle disagreements or disputes brought to them by the government or by any person. The judicial branch tells what the laws mean. The courts also decide whether a law agrees with the Constitution.

✓ **Checkpoint** How does the separation of powers keep the government from becoming too powerful?

What are checks and balances?

The three branches of government have separate duties, but they must all work together. They are connected by a system of **checks and balances.** Figure 3.3 on page 54 shows the system of checks and balances. Limits are placed on each branch to prevent one branch from becoming too powerful. Each branch has power to check the actions of the other two branches.

Here are a few examples of how the system of checks and balances works. The President cannot make laws but must approve the laws Congress passes. The President can also **veto** a law passed by Congress. This means the law is rejected. Congress can override a President's veto by a two-thirds majority. Congress must approve all money the country spends.

Checks and balances
A system in which each branch of government checks the others to prevent one branch from becoming too powerful

Veto
To reject a proposed law

Fig. 3.3 **How Government Works**

Checks and Balances

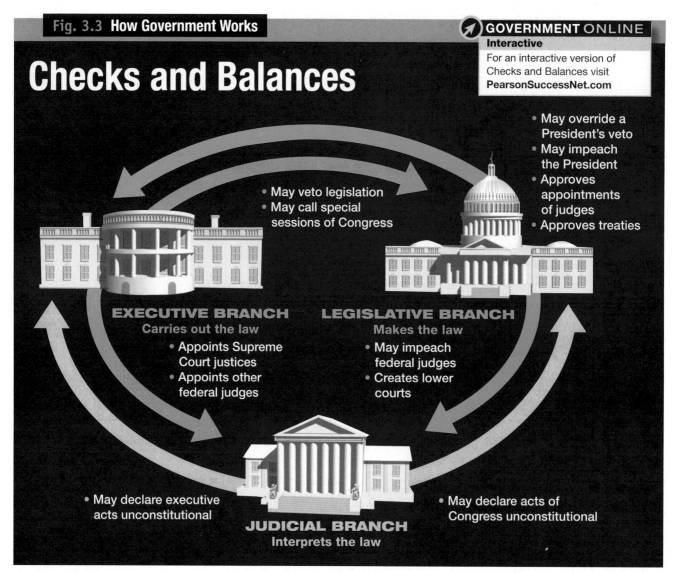

May veto legislation
- May call special sessions of Congress

- May override a President's veto
- May impeach the President
- Approves appointments of judges
- Approves treaties

EXECUTIVE BRANCH
Carries out the law
- Appoints Supreme Court justices
- Appoints other federal judges

LEGISLATIVE BRANCH
Makes the law
- May impeach federal judges
- Creates lower courts

- May declare executive acts unconstitutional

- May declare acts of Congress unconstitutional

JUDICIAL BRANCH
Interprets the law

▲ **Interpreting Diagrams** Under the system of checks and balances, each branch of government can check the actions of the others. *In what ways can the power of the executive branch be checked by the other two branches?*

Unconstitutional
Against the Constitution

Judicial review
The power of the courts to decide whether or not a government action is constitutional

The President has power to name federal judges, but the Senate must approve each appointment. The Senate must also approve the President's appointments of other important government jobs. The Supreme Court cannot make laws, but it can decide if a law is **unconstitutional.** If it does, Congress then has to change the law or write a new law.

The checks-and-balances system means that the three branches of government must compromise if they want to get anything done. This is what the Framers intended. For example, when appointing people to government jobs, the President usually picks someone he knows Congress will approve. In a similar way, when Congress passes a law, its members try to make sure the law is constitutional. These compromises keep government operating smoothly most of the time.

Note, however, that the working relationship between the President and Congress runs more smoothly when they are of the same political party. Throughout most of our history, this has been the case. For the past 50 years, however, the American people have become familiar with divided government. But most recently, the Democrats won control of both branches of government. In 2008, Barack Obama recaptured the White House for the Democrats, and the Democratic party strengthened their slim majorities in Congress.

What is judicial review?

The courts have the power to decide whether or not an action of the government is constitutional. This principle is called **judicial review.** The federal courts, as well as most state courts, have this power. Judicial review is not identified as such in the Constitution. However, it seems clear that the Framers intended for the courts to have this power.

An 1803 landmark case, *Marbury* v. *Madison,* firmly established the power of judicial review. Since the *Marbury* case, the Supreme Court and other federal courts have used this power of judicial review in thousands of cases. The Supreme Court has found part or all of an act of Congress unconstitutional in about 150 cases. The Court has also struck down several actions of Presidents and hundreds of state and local laws. You will read more about *Marbury* v. *Madison* in the Landmark Decisions of the Supreme Court feature on pages 58–59.

✔**Checkpoint**   Which case established the power of judicial review?

Government in Your Life

Gun Control

The Second Amendment says: "A well-regulated militia, being necessary to the security of a free state, the right of people to keep and bear arms shall not be infringed."

Some Americans use guns for hunting and other recreational purposes. Because many people are hurt and killed by guns each year, however, other Americans favor gun control laws. Gun control laws have been proposed to ban the sale and use of handguns or to make the rules more difficult to buy them.

In 1994, the Brady Handgun Violence Prevention Act went into effect. This national law requires a five-day waiting period to buy a handgun. It also requires local law-enforcement agencies to check the backgrounds of people who want to buy handguns. Convicted criminals, minors, drug abusers, and illegal immigrants cannot buy handguns.

The "Brady Law" is named for Jim Brady, President Ronald Reagan's press secretary. Brady was shot when someone tried to kill President Reagan in 1981. Brady and his wife, Sarah, campaigned very hard for Congress to pass this law.

Federalism
A government system in which power is divided between the federal government and the state governments

Reading Strategy
Predicting
Based on what you just read, what do you think the rest of the chapter will be about?

What is federalism?

Federalism is a government system in which power is divided between the federal government and the state government. When the Constitution was written, the Framers felt it would be difficult to have an effective national government and still preserve the rights of the states to govern independently. The colonists had fought to win independence from the British. They did not want to set up another government that would take away their rights. Federalism was their solution. It was a compromise between independent states with little connecting them and a central government that was too powerful. Both levels of government would have their own agencies and officials. Both levels would pass laws that directly affected citizens. Figure 3.4 below shows the shared powers as well as the individual federal and state powers. Federalism was another way in which the Framers limited the power of the federal government. See Figure 3.5 on the next page.

✔**Checkpoint** What are two powers given to the state governments that the federal government does not have?

Fig. 3.4
Federalism: Who Has the Power?

FEDERAL POWERS
- To maintain an army and a navy
- To declare war
- To coin money
- To regulate trade between states and foreign nations
- To make treaties with foreign nations

SHARED POWERS
- To enforce laws
- To establish courts
- To borrow money
- To secure the population
- To build an infrastructure
- To collect taxes
- To make laws

STATE POWERS
- To conduct elections
- To establish schools
- To regulate business within a state
- To establish local government
- To regulate marriages
- To assume other powers not given to the federal government by the Constitution, nor denied to the states

▲ Interpreting Diagrams The Constitution divides power between the state and the federal government. *Why might the Constitution give the federal government the power to regulate trade among the states?*

Fig. 3.5

The Six Basic Principles

Popular Sovereignty	The people give the government its power.
Limited Government	Government has only those powers that the people give it.
Separation of Powers	The powers of government are split among the judicial, legislative, and executive branches.
Checks and Balances	Each branch has the power to check the other two branches.
Judicial Review	The Court has the power to determine if government actions violate the Constitution.
Federalism	The powers of government are divided between the federal government and the states.

SECTION 1 ASSESSMENT

Essential Questions Journal Go to your **Essential Questions Journal** to work on this chapter's Essential Question.

Word Bank

federalism

popular sovereignty

rule of law

separation of power

Quick Write

Imagine you are one of the Framers of the Constitution. Write a short essay explaining why you created the Constitution as a brief outline so open to interpretation.

1. **Guiding Question** Use your completed concept web to answer this question: What are the main principles on which the Constitution is based?

Key Terms and Comprehension

On a sheet of paper, use the words from the Word Bank to complete each sentence correctly.

2. _____ gives certain duties to the executive, legislative, and judicial branches of government.

3. The _____ says that the government and its actions must follow the law.

4. The principle of _____ says that all political power belongs to the people.

5. The principle of _____ gives power to both the national and the state governments.

Critical Thinking

6. **Summarize** How was the idea of judicial review officially established?

7. **Express Problems Clearly** What problems might occur if the legislative and executive branches are split between the two political parties?

What is judicial review?

Since 1803, the Supreme Court has exercised the power of judicial review. It does this by declaring acts of Congress or the President constitutional or unconstitutional. The Court assumed this power when it decided the case of *Marbury* v. *Madison*. What began as a dispute over a small piece of federal law became, arguably, the most important decision in the history of the Supreme Court.

"It is emphatically the province and duty of the Judicial Department to say what the law is. . . .

If, then, the Courts are to regard the Constitution, and the Constitution is superior to any ordinary act of the Legislature, the Constitution, and not such ordinary act, must govern the case to which they both apply."

—Chief Justice John Marshall, *Marbury* v. *Madison*

In the 1800 presidential election, Thomas Jefferson defeated John Adams, the sitting President. Shortly before he left office, Adams signed the Judiciary Act of 1801. This act created several new federal judgeships. Adams then filled these positions. He also appointed John Marshall, his former secretary of state, to be chief justice of the Supreme Court.

While he was still secretary of state, Marshall's duty was to make sure that all appointments were delivered to the appropriate persons. Unfortunately, a few appointments were never delivered in the last days of the Adams administration.

Secretary of State James Madison refused to issue Marbury's appointment.

William Marbury requested a writ of mandamus from the Supreme Court.

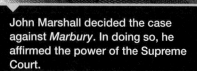

John Marshall decided the case against *Marbury*. In doing so, he affirmed the power of the Supreme Court.

One of those appointments was intended for William Marbury. Marbury was to be a justice of the peace in Washington, D.C. When the appointment did not arrive, Marbury requested it from the new secretary of state, James Madison. He was refused. President Jefferson had ordered Madison not to issue the lost appointments made by President Adams.

Marbury brought his case before the Supreme Court. He demanded a writ of mandamus. (This is an order from a higher court to a lower court or department of government to carry out a duty.) Chief Justice Marshall wanted to avoid a direct conflict with the executive branch. He also knew that he could not directly order the President to do anything. If he did and Jefferson ignored him, the case would destroy the power of the judicial branch.

Instead, Marshall criticized Madison and Jefferson for not following through on an appointment. He declared that Marbury's rights had been violated. Marshall went on to write that it was not the duty of the Supreme Court to issue a writ of mandamus. Marbury had asked for such a writ under the Judiciary Act of 1789. The act gave the Supreme Court the power to issue writs of mandamus without the request first moving through the lower courts.

However, the Constitution does not allow such cases to come directly to the Supreme Court. Under the Constitution, most cases brought to the Supreme Court must come through the lower courts first. Therefore, Marshall found the Judiciary Act of 1789 unconstitutional. The Court could not rule in favor of Marbury.

With this ruling, the Supreme Court had applied the Constitution to an existing law. It had also declared the Constitution the supreme law. The Supreme Court had practiced judicial review.

Although Jefferson was opposed to judicial review, there was not much he could do to restrict it. He and Madison had, in effect, won their case. Marbury never got his appointment. However, the Supreme Court gained a power that they have used in every case that has come before them for more than 200 years.

Thinking Critically

1. Did the Supreme Court overstep its boundaries when it interpreted the Constitution in *Marbury* v. *Madison?* Why or why not?

2. This case fully established the principle of judicial review. How does judicial review fit into the checks and balances system?

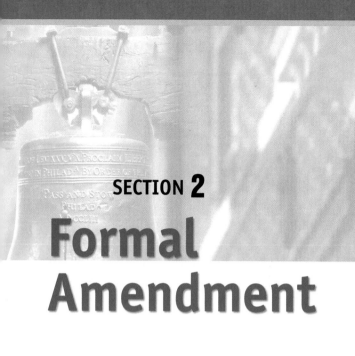

SECTION 2

Formal Amendment

▲ Inez Milholland fought to amend the Constitution to allow women to vote.

Guiding Question

How has the Constitution been amended through the formal amendment process? Use an outline like the one below to take notes on how the Constitution can be amended.

I. Formal Amendment Process
   A. First Method
      1. A proposed amendment must be approved by two thirds of Congress.
      2. _____
   B. Second Method
      1. _____
      2. _____

Objectives:

- Identify the four ways the Constitution may be formally changed.
- Explain the formal amendment process and how it reflects the principles of federalism and popular sovereignty.
- Outline the 27 amendments to the Constitution.

The Constitution of the United States has been in use for over 200 years. As the needs of the country have changed, the Constitution has also changed. Many words are the same, as is much of their meaning. However, some words have been added. Others have been removed. This has been done by formal **amendment** and by informal means. In this section, you will learn about formal amendments and how they are added to the Constitution.

What is the formal amendment process?

Any change to the Constitution is called an amendment. The writers of the Constitution knew that changes might have to be made over time. However, changes to the Constitution are not made easily.

Article V outlines how changes can be made to the Constitution. It gives two methods to propose amendments and two ways to **ratify** each proposal. When Congress proposes an amendment, it also chooses how the amendment will be ratified. **Figure 3.6** shows the four ways for amending and ratifying the Constitution.

In the first method, Congress proposes an amendment. The amendment must be proposed by a two-thirds vote in both the Senate and the House of Representatives. Then the amendment is sent to all the states. At least three-fourths of the state legislatures must ratify the amendment for it to become part of the Constitution. So, 38 of the 52 states must ratify. Of the Constitution's 27 amendments, 26 were adopted in this manner.

In the second way, the amendment is also proposed by Congress. But, rather than being sent to the state legislatures it is sent to state conventions, called together to consider the amendment. If it is ratified by three-fourths of those conventions, it becomes a part of the Constitution. The 21st Amendment is the only amendment that was ratified by state conventions. This amendment which repealed the 18th Amendment banned the manufacture, use, and transportation of alcoholic beverages.

The second method for proposing an amendment is done by a national convention. Congress calls this type of convention at the request of two-thirds of state legislatures. The proposed amendment must then be ratified by three-fourths of the state legislatures. So far, Congress has not called such a convention.

The other way to ratify this type of amendment proposal is for it to be proposed at a national convention and then ratified by conventions in three-fourths of the states. The Constitution itself was adopted in a very similar way.

Amendment
A change in, or addition to, a constitution

Ratify
To give approval of an amendment

Reading Strategy
Predicting
Think about the purpose of this section. What do you think you will learn by reading it?

✔ **Checkpoint**　How was the 21st Amendment ratified?

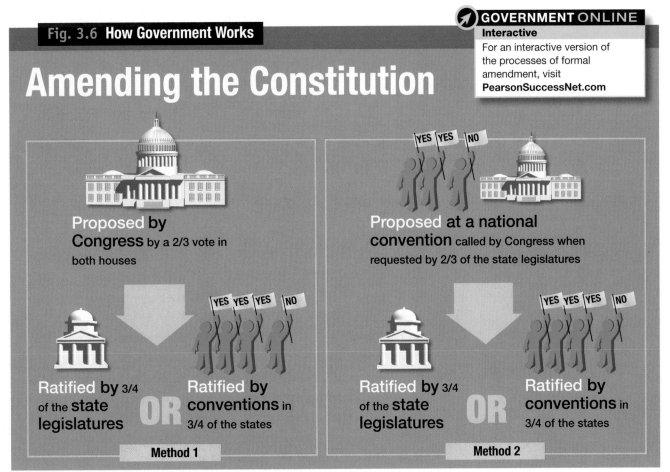

Fig. 3.6 How Government Works

GOVERNMENT ONLINE
Interactive
For an interactive version of the processes of formal amendment, visit **PearsonSuccessNet.com**

Amending the Constitution

Proposed by Congress by a 2/3 vote in both houses

Ratified by 3/4 of the **state legislatures**　OR　**Ratified by conventions** in 3/4 of the states

Method 1

Proposed at a national convention called by Congress when requested by 2/3 of the state legislatures

Ratified by 3/4 of the **state legislatures**　OR　**Ratified by conventions** in 3/4 of the states

Method 2

▲ **Analyzing Charts** There are two ways to propose an amendment. Each way has two means of ratification. **Which method has been used to ratify most amendments?**

■■■■■■■■■■■■■■■■■■
Reading Strategy
Predicting
What rights do you think
are given to Americans by the Bill
of Rights?

Fig. 3.7

The Bill of Rights

Amendment 1	• Freedom of religion, speech, and the press • Freedom to peaceably assemble and to petition the government
Amendment 2	• The right to maintain a militia • The right to bear arms
Amendment 3	• Protection from having to quarter (house) soldiers in time of peace without the consent of the owner, nor in time of war except as provided by law
Amendment 4	• Protection against arbitrary (unreasonable) searches and seizures without probable cause
Amendment 5	• Protection from prosecution without an indictment (accusation) • Protection from being tried for the same crime twice • Protection from having to testify against oneself • Protection from the loss of life, liberty, or property without due process of law • Protection from loss of property without just compensation
Amendment 6	• The right to a speedy trial by an impartial (fair) jury • The right to be informed of the charges, to cross-examine witnesses, and to present favorable witnesses • The right to an attorney
Amendment 7	• The right to a trial by jury in any civil case where the amount of money involved is $20 or more
Amendment 8	• Protection from excessive bail or fines • Protection from cruel and unusual punishment
Amendment 9	• The fact that the Constitution spells out a number of civil rights does not mean that there are not other, unwritten rights held by the people.
Amendment 10	• The powers not delegated to the federal government may be exercised by the states, as long as they are not prohibited by the Constitution.

▲ The Bill of Rights was added to the Constitution. It guarantees the protection of a person's basic rights. ***Why is it important to spell out these rights?***

How do federalism and popular sovereignty relate to amendments?

The formal amendment process reflects the federal character of our government. The national government proposes an amendment, and the state governments ratify it. When state legislatures or ratifying conventions vote, the principle of popular sovereignty is used. The people make the final decision. Some people believe only ratifying conventions, and not state legislatures, should ratify amendments. They say that because convention delegates are usually chosen based on their stand on the amendment, whereas members of the state legislatures are elected for many reasons.

The Supreme Court has held that a state cannot require an amendment proposed by Congress to be approved by the people before it can be ratified by the state legislature. However, a state legislature can ask for the people to advise the legislature before it decides on a constitutional amendment.

How are amendments proposed?

When Congress proposes an amendment, it does not send the amendment to the President. This is because amendments are not laws. The states must ratify an amendment. If a state rejects a proposed amendment, the state may later reverse its decision and ratify the amendment. If a state approves an amendment, however, that decision cannot be changed.

Congress has proposed more than 15,000 resolutions calling for amendments since 1789. Only 33 of them have been sent to the states, and only 27 have become amendments. One unratified amendment dealt with the distribution of seats in the House of Representatives. Another said that no amendments could be passed about slavery. A third amendment that failed was the Equal Rights for women (ERA) amendment of 1972. It almost passed but fell short by three states.

Congress can set a time limit on the ratification period for amendments. For example, the ERA proposal expired in 1982. There was a seven-year deadline set on the 18th Amendment. Since then, Congress has set a similar time limit on all amendments, except the 19th Amendment.

✔ **Checkpoint** Why doesn't Congress send proposed amendments to the President?

What are the 27 amendments to the Constitution?

The Bill of Rights

Some people did not like the new Constitution because it did not guarantee individual rights. These people, including Thomas Jefferson, agreed to support the Constitution only if a listing of basic rights was added immediately. These amendments were ratified in 1791, less than three years after the Constitution was adopted.

The first ten amendments are known as the Bill of Rights. See Figure 3.7 on page 62. These amendments guarantee basic freedoms to the people. These include freedom of religion, freedom of speech, freedom of the press, and the right to trial by jury. The Bill of Rights also limits the powers of the federal and state governments. Figure 3.8 is a cartoon about a 4th Amendment right. The 4th Amendment protects citizens from having their personal property searched illegally.

Fig. 3.8

▲ Analyzing Political Cartoons **What is this cartoon saying about the 4th Amendment?**

Fig. 3.9

The 27 Amendments

Since the Constitution was ratified, 27 amendments have been added to it. *How do the amendments keep the Constitution relevant to the times?* ▼

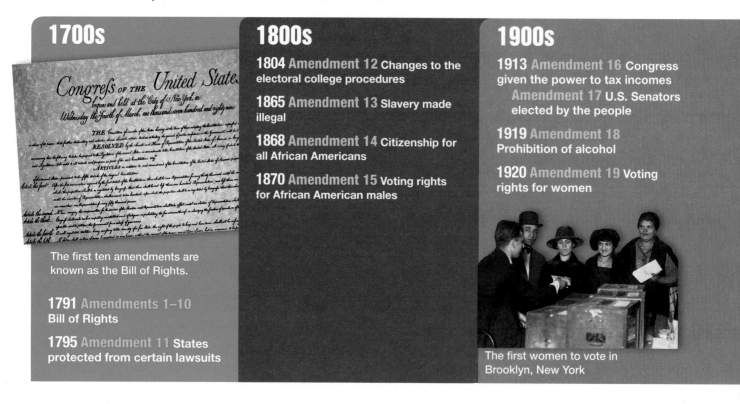

1700s

The first ten amendments are known as the Bill of Rights.

1791 Amendments 1–10 Bill of Rights

1795 Amendment 11 States protected from certain lawsuits

1800s

1804 Amendment 12 Changes to the electoral college procedures

1865 Amendment 13 Slavery made illegal

1868 Amendment 14 Citizenship for all African Americans

1870 Amendment 15 Voting rights for African American males

1900s

1913 Amendment 16 Congress given the power to tax incomes
Amendment 17 U.S. Senators elected by the people

1919 Amendment 18 Prohibition of alcohol

1920 Amendment 19 Voting rights for women

The first women to vote in Brooklyn, New York

The Later Amendments

Each of the remaining 17 amendments have been added to the Constitution as the result of interesting circumstances. The 11th Amendment, for example, says that states cannot be sued by citizens of other states. This amendment was proposed in 1794 and ratified in 1795. The matter came up when a man from South Carolina sued the state of Georgia. In 1804, the 12th Amendment changed the system for electing the President and Vice President. The 13th Amendment, added in 1865, outlawed slavery in the United States. This amendment was a direct result of the Civil War. The 14th Amendment (1868) defined citizenship, and the 15th Amendment (1870) gave African American men the right to vote. Both of these amendments also resulted from the Civil War.

After the 15th Amendment, 43 years passed before more changes were made to the Constitution. Then twelve amendments were added from 1913 to 1992. Since 1971, several amendments have been proposed, but most have failed to pass. All 27 amendments are highlighted in Figure 3.9.

64   Formal Amendment

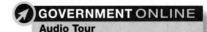
1933 Amendment 20 Change of dates for presidential and congressional terms

Amendment 21 Ends Prohibition (Amendment 18)

1951 Amendment 22 Limits a President to two terms

1961 Amendment 23 Allows citizens of Washington, D.C., to vote in presidential elections

1964 Amendment 24 Ends poll taxes in federal elections

1967 Amendment 25 Identifies who becomes President if the office becomes vacant

1971 Amendment 26 Voting age changes to 18

1992 Amendment 27 Congressional pay raises not effective until the next congressional election

Below: A young woman rallies for the ratification of the 26th amendment.

The 18th Amendment was ratified in 1919. This amendment banned the making, use, and transportation of alcohol. What came to be known as "the noble experiment" lasted fewer than 14 years. The 18th Amendment was **repealed** by the 21st Amendment in 1933.

The 22nd Amendment (1951) limited the number of terms a President may serve to two. It was proposed in 1947 after Franklin D. Roosevelt had served four terms as President. The 26th Amendment was added in 1971. It lowered the voting age to 18 in all elections in the United States. Its ratification was brought on by the war in Vietnam.

The most recent amendment, the 27th, was written by James Madison. It was among the first to be offered by Congress in 1789. This amendment forbids members of Congress from raising their own pay during the same term. It finally became a part of the Constitution in 1992, when the 38th state, Michigan, ratified it.

Repeal
To recall or take back

✔**Checkpoint** Which amendments were adopted because of the Civil War?

Biography

Two People and the ERA

Patricia Schroeder and Phyllis Schlafly greatly influenced the course of the Equal Rights Amendment, also called the ERA.

Patricia Schroeder supported the ERA. After graduating from the University of Minnesota, she received her law degree from Harvard University. Schroeder was elected as Colorado's first woman in Congress in 1972. She served for 24 years. She thought the Constitution should guarantee certain rights for women such as equal pay, family leave, and adequate healthcare. She believed women should have the same rights as men in the military and in the workforce.

Phyllis Schlafly opposed the ERA. Schlafly received a master's degree in political science from Harvard and a law degree from Washington University in 1978. A political activist, Schlafly thought the ERA would take away certain rights of women. She said women should not serve in the military or work in certain jobs. To defeat the ERA, Schlafly organized the conservative Stop ERA and Eagle Forum groups during the 1970s and 1980s.

SECTION 2 ASSESSMENT

Essential Questions Journal Go to your **Essential Questions Journal** to work on this chapter's Essential Question.

1. **Guiding Question** Use your completed outline to answer this question: How has the Constitution been amended through the formal amendment process?

Key Terms and Comprehension

On a sheet of paper, write the answer to each question. Use complete sentences.

2. Which method of formal amendment has been used only once?

3. How is the formal amendment process an example of federalism?

4. How is the ratification process an example of popular sovereignty?

5. Why was the Bill of Rights added to the Constitution?

Critical Thinking

6. **Predict Consequences** How might news reports be different if freedom of speech and freedom of the press were never added to the Constitution?

7. **Identify Central Issues** For what reason has the amendment ratification process been criticized?

Political Roots and Attitudes

What is your position on the following questions?
- **Should all Americans have the right to free healthcare?**
- **Should the government do more to save the environment?**
- **Is outsourcing jobs to other countries good for America?**

Your position on these issues probably reflects a number of factors, especially your background and personal experiences. Family, friends, and teachers, as well as their party affiliations, may also be influences. The part of the country where you live may affect your political attitudes, too.

Political attitudes come from many sources. People settle in different parts of the country. They belong to different ethnic and cultural groups. Career paths and education are also major influences.

1. Choose a Question Look at the questions above. Do you have opinions about these issues? Where do you think

your opinions came from? Did you read articles about these issues? Did you hear others talking about them?

2. Choose One Question Choose one of these questions. Then look at opinion polls from various sources to see how people across the country feel about the issue. Can you notice trends? For example, how do people in the city feel about the environment? How do people in rural areas feel about it? What are the opinions of each of the political parties?

3. Create Polling Questions Now, create your own polling questions on the issue.

4. Ask Questions Ask fellow students their opinion on the subject. Ask them how

much they have read or heard about the subject. Also, ask how they think of themselves politically. Are they conservative? Liberal? With which party do they most identify?

Collect your information to present to the class. Review all that you have learned through this process. Where do your political roots fall? Has your opinion on this issue changed? Understanding your own political roots and attitudes can help you judge where you stand on an issue. It can also help you make the best choice when voting.

▶▶ What do you think?

1. What experiences and individuals have influenced your political attitudes?
2. What has had the greatest effect on your political attitudes: where you live, your family's party views, or your religious background? Explain your answer.

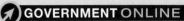
GOVERNMENT ONLINE
Citizenship Activity Pack
For an activity to help you explore your political roots and attitudes, go to **PearsonSuccessNet.com**

▲ Delegates play an important role in shaping the U.S. government.

SECTION 3
Change by Other Means

Guiding Question

How have the day-to-day workings of government affected how we interpret the Constitution? Use a cause-and-effect chart like the one below to take notes on how the workings of government affect how we interpret the Constitution.

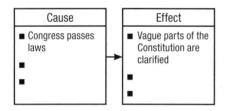

Cause		Effect
■ Congress passes laws	→	■ Vague parts of the Constitution are clarified
■		■
■		■

Objectives:

- Identify how basic legislation has helped to clarify the Constitution over time.
- Describe how the Constitution has been interpreted by executive and judicial actions.
- Analyze how political parties and customs have affected the meaning of the Constitution.

As you learned in Section 2, only 17 amendments have been added to the Constitution since the Bill of Rights. However, formal amendments are only one way the Constitution has changed. The meaning of the Constitution can also be affected through the daily operations of the government. This can happen through five different ways: (1) basic legislation; (2) executive action; (3) Court decisions; (4) party practices; and (5) custom and usage.

How does basic legislation affect the Constitution?

Congress has the power to pass laws. Some of these laws have helped explain the meaning of parts of the Constitution. Take the federal court system as an example. The Constitution sets up the Supreme Court, but leaves the creation of all other federal courts to Congress. In 1789, Congress passed the Judiciary Act. Since then, all the federal courts, except the Supreme Court, have been created by acts of Congress. The Constitution creates the presidency and the vice presidency. Beyond that, it was Congress that set up the agencies, departments, and offices that make up the executive department.

Congress has also added to the Constitution by the way in which it has used many of its powers. For example, the Constitution gives Congress the power to regulate commerce. What exactly does this mean? Congress has answered that question by passing thousands of laws. In doing so, it has expanded the meaning of the Constitution.

✓ Checkpoint What are two ways that legislation has expanded the meaning of the Constitution?

Fig. 3.10
The State of the Union Address

"The President shall from time to time give to Congress information of the State of the Union and recommend to their Consideration such measures as he shall judge necessary and expedient.

—Article II, Sec. 3

FROM THE CONSTITUTION

The State of the Union Address The President is required by the Constitution to address Congress. The method of address is left to each President. George Washington spoke to Congress in person, while Thomas Jefferson wrote his address down. After this, a written address became common practice for 112 years. Woodrow Wilson brought back the speech in 1913. Calvin Coolidge delivered his address on the radio in 1923. Harry Truman's State of the Union was on television in 1947. Today, the State of the Union is televised annually. *How does the State of the Union address reflect the checks and balances between Congress and the President?*

▲ President Harry Truman delivers the first televised State of the Union.

How does executive action affect the meaning of the Constitution?

The basic outline of executive powers in the Constitution has been expanded by many of our Presidents. In 1803, Thomas Jefferson did so when he authorized the Louisiana Purchase, which doubled the size of the country.

Another example of expanded power concerns **executive agreements.** These agreements between the President and the leader of a foreign country do not have to be approved by Congress. Only treaties must be approved by Congress, according to the Constitution. Recent Presidents have used executive agreements rather than the treaty-making process outlined in the Constitution.

Finally, the Constitution says that only Congress can declare war. However, the Constitution has also made the President **commander in chief** of the armed forces. Many times in our history, troops have been sent into combat on the President's orders alone.

Executive agreement
A pact between the President and the leader of a foreign country

Commander in chief
The top person in charge of a nation's armed forces

▲ President George W. Bush sits with his Cabinet members Gail Norton (far left), Colin Powell (left), and Donald Rumsfeld. The Cabinet advises the President.

■ ■ ■ ■ ■ ■ ■ ■ ■ ■ ■ ■ ■ ■ ■ ■ ■

Reading Strategy
Predicting
Based on the red headings, what do you think the rest of the section will be about?

■ ■ ■ ■ ■ ■ ■ ■ ■ ■ ■ ■ ■ ■ ■ ■ ■

Electoral college
A group of people chosen from each state to formally select the President and Vice President

How do court decisions affect the Constitution?

The nation's courts interpret and apply the Constitution in many of the cases they hear. You have already read some examples of how the courts interpret the Constitution. Recall that the Court established the power of judicial review even though it is not specifically mentioned in the Constitution. You will find many more examples of court decisions throughout the pages of this book. President Woodrow Wilson once said the Supreme Court is "a constitutional convention in continuous session."

How do political parties interpret the Constitution?

The Constitution makes no mention of political parties. They developed as the country expanded. George Washington and many Framers feared that political parties would divide the country. Still, political parties have helped shape the country and the Constitution.

The Constitution does not say how candidates for President should be nominated. Political parties have taken this matter into their own hands. Political parties have also changed the **electoral college.** At first this group elected the President. Because of the influence of political parties, however, the electoral college today simply reflects each state's popular vote. Congress is organized and conducts business on the basis of party. The President, too, considers political parties when making appointments.

✓ **Checkpoint** What is the main job of the electoral college?

How have custom and usage changed the Constitution?

Unwritten customs are as important to our government as law. For example, the heads of the 15 executive departments make up the **Cabinet,** a group of advisors to the President. This is not part of the Constitution, but has developed by custom. Also, each time a President has died in office, the Vice President has taken over. This has happened eight times in history. However, the custom was not written in the Constitution until the adoption of the 25th Amendment in 1967. Until then, the Constitution stated that the powers and duties of the presidency—not the office itself—should be given to the Vice President.

Another custom that was closely followed but not written into the Constitution was the "no-third-term tradition." It began with George Washington, who refused a third term as President. All Presidents after President Washington followed the custom until Franklin D. Roosevelt. President Roosevelt was elected for a third and then a fourth term. As a result, the 22nd Amendment was added to the Constitution in 1951. It states that a President can be elected for only two terms.

✔ Checkpoint Which President established the "no-third-term tradition"?

Cabinet
A group of advisors to the President made up of heads of the executive departments

---

SECTION 3 ASSESSMENT

Essential Questions Journal Go to your **Essential Questions Journal** to work on this chapter's Essential Question.

1. **Guiding Question** Use your completed cause-and-effect chart to answer this question: How have the day-to-day workings of government affected how we interpret the Constitution?

Key Terms and Comprehension
On a sheet of paper, write the answer to each question. Use complete sentences.

2. How has Congress helped to expand the meaning of the Constitution?

3. How have Supreme Court decisions changed the Constitution?

4. How might our history be different if political parties had not changed the electoral college?

5. What two customs were added to the Constitution with the 22nd and 25th amendments?

Critical Thinking

6. **Predict Consequences** Presidents have sent troops to other countries without a declaration of war. How do you think this might upset the system of checks and balances?

7. **Draw Conclusions** Why do you think customs are often as important to the government as amendments and laws?

Chapter Summary

Section 1—Basic Principles

- The Constitution is built on six basic principles—popular sovereignty, limited government, separation of powers, checks and balances, judicial review, and federalism.

- The people hold the power through popular sovereignty. The government is limited by the principles of the Constitution.

- The Constitution separates power into three branches—legislative, executive, and judicial.

- Each branch of the government has power to place limits on the other two branches. This is called the system of checks and balances.

- The Constitution is based on federalism. Power is divided between federal and state governments.

Section 2—Formal Amendment

- Congress proposes amendments to the Constitution. States must ratify the amendments in order for them to take effect. Since 1787, there have been 27 amendments added to the Constitution.

- There are four possible ways in formal amendment process—two for proposing an amendment and each has two ways for ratification.

- The formal amendment process is based on federalism and popular sovereignty.

- The first ten amendments to the Constitution are known as the Bill of Rights. These guarantee basic freedoms to Americans.

Section 3—Change by Other Means

- Laws passed by Congress and decisions of the Supreme Court can both affect the meaning of the Constitution.

- Political party actions, presidential decisions, and customs have had an impact on the Constitution.

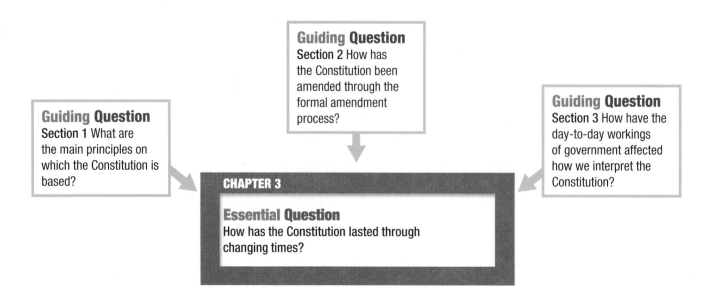

Guiding Question
Section 2 How has the Constitution been amended through the formal amendment process?

Guiding Question
Section 1 What are the main principles on which the Constitution is based?

Guiding Question
Section 3 How have the day-to-day workings of government affected how we interpret the Constitution?

CHAPTER 3

Essential Question
How has the Constitution lasted through changing times?

Document-Based Assessment

The 23rd Amendment

The District of Columbia has been the seat of government in the United States since the location was chosen in 1790. The new capital was to be called Washington, D.C. As a federal district, not a state, it had no votes in Congress. However, residents were required to pay taxes and serve in the military.

The population of Washington, D.C., grew to 760,000 by 1960. Some states had smaller populations than Washington, D.C., yet more voting rights. The 23rd Amendment was proposed in 1960 to give the district a voice in government. The district has members in the electoral college, but it does not provide for representatives in Congress. The 23rd Amendment was ratified in 1961.

Document at a Glance

- 23rd Amendment gave Washington, D.C. electoral votes.
- Proposed in 1960
- Ratified in 1961

Section 1. The District constituting the seat of Government of the United States shall appoint in such manner as the Congress may direct:

A number of electors of President and Vice President equal to the whole number of Senators and Representatives in Congress to which the District would be entitled if it were a state, but in no event more than the least populous state; they shall be in addition to those appointed by the states, but they shall be considered, for the purposes of the election of President and Vice President, to be electors appointed by a state; and they shall meet in the District and perform such duties as provided by the twelfth article of amendment.

Section 2. The Congress shall have the power to enforce this article by appropriate legislation.

Document-Based Questions

1. Which part of the United States does this amendment concern?

2. What were the electors expected to do?

3. What was the purpose of the 23rd Amendment?

4. What must the number of electors be equal to but not larger than?

5. **Draw Conclusions** Why do you think it took until 1960 for this issue to be addressed?

SOURCE: *The United States Constitution*

Chapter Assessment

Directions: On a sheet of paper, write the answer to each question. Use complete sentences.

Section 1—Basic Principles

1. Why did the Framers limit the powers of the federal government when they wrote the Constitution?

2. What are the six basic principles on which the federal government is built?

3. How is the rule of law related to the principle of limited government?

4. How does the system of checks and balances work?

5. What is the main duty of the Supreme Court?

6. **Critical Thinking** Which of the six principles do you think is the most important? Explain.

Section 2—Formal Amendment

7. Of the four processes for formal amendment, which has been used most often to change the Constitution?

8. What two basic principles are reflected in the formal amendment process? Explain.

9. How does the formal amendment process illustrate the goals of the Framers?

10. How might life today be different if the Bill of Rights had not been added to the Constitution?

11. What issue did the 22nd Amendment address?

12. **Critical Thinking** Why do you think only 27 amendments have been added to the Constitution since its ratification, even though thousands have been proposed?

Section 3—Change by Other Means

13. What are two ways in which laws have affected the meaning of the Constitution?

14. What two types of executive actions have impacted the Constitution?

15. How have political parties changed the way we interpret the Constitution?

16. How is the President's Cabinet an example of the ways that custom has influenced the meaning of the Constitution?

17. Critical Thinking What do you think President Wilson meant when he said the Supreme Court is "a constitutional convention in continuous session"?

Apply What You've Learned

Exploring the Essential Question

18. Should Congress and the states be allowed to change the Constitution by amendment or other means? Why or why not?

19. Does one branch of government have too much or too little power to change the Constitution? Explain.

Essential Question Project

20. Propose your own amendment to the Constitution. Research and choose a government issue that you feel should be made part of the Constitution. Write a list of arguments for and against the amendment. Then create a plan for how you would propose and ratify the amendment. Finally, present your amendment to your class and explain why it should be passed.

Essential Questions
Journal

Go to your **Essential Questions Journal** to work on this chapter's Essential Question.

Test-Taking Tip

Schedule short study periods that are easy to manage. Take breaks between study periods.

▲ President Obama talks about the economy with Virginia Governor Tim Kaine at John Tyler Community College.

Federalism

Essential Question
Is the federal system the best way to govern the United States?

Section 1: Federalism: Powers Divided

Section 2: The National Government and the 50 States

Section 3: Interstate Relations

Reading Strategy: Text Structure

Understanding how text is organized helps readers decide which information is most important.

Look at the title, headings, boldfaced words, and photographs. Also, consider the following:

- Description: Identify words that appeal to the five senses.
- Problem and Solution: Pay attention to problems and how they are solved.
- Compare and Contrast: Notice what is alike and what is different.

GOVERNMENT ONLINE
ON THE GO

To study anywhere, anytime, download these online resources at PearsonSuccessNet.com
- Political Dictionary
- Audio Review
- Downloadable Interactivities

▲ Members of the New York National Guard

SECTION **1**

Federalism: Powers Divided

Guiding Question

How is power divided between the federal government and the states? Use a Venn diagram like the one below to take notes on the powers of the federal and state governments.

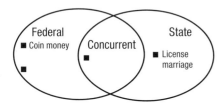

Objectives:

- Define federalism and explain why the Framers chose this system of government.
- Identify powers delegated to and denied to the national government, and powers reserved for and denied to the states.
- Explain the differences between exclusive and concurrent powers.
- Examine how the Constitution functions as "the supreme Law of the Land."

Federal laws, along with state laws, make the rules for most Americans. Federal laws apply to everyone in the country. For example, according to federal law, no person can be denied a job on the basis of his or her race or ethnicity. State laws regulate matters such as the age to obtain a driver's license. In this section you will read about the important arrangement between the national government and the 50 states.

Why did the Framers choose federalism?

The Constitution was created based on the idea of federalism. Under this system of government, power is divided between the national government and the states. Both levels have their own agencies and officials. Both levels pass laws that directly affect citizens. Most of the Framers of the Constitution did not favor the British model of government. The Revolutionary War was fought to free the colonies from strong British rule. The Framers believed that a government with divided powers would prevent the abuse of power.

What is federalism?

Federalism is a system of government with a **division of power** between a central government and several smaller governments, such as those of the states. The Constitution provides for this division. Each level of government has its own powers, ruling bodies, officials, and laws.

Each level has power to do things the other level cannot. For example, the federal government takes care of foreign policy. The state legislatures can decide on punishment for certain crimes and set some voting requirements.

The strength of federalism is that it allows local action in local matters and national action in matters of wider concern. It also allows the states to experiment with policies that are often later adopted by the nation as a whole. While federalism gives states the freedom to handle local matters, it also benefits them by belonging to a strong central union.

What are the powers of the federal government?

The national government has **delegated powers.** These powers are created by the Constitution. The three types of delegated powers are expressed, implied, and inherent.

The **expressed powers** are those described plainly in the Constitution. Most of them are written in Article I, Section 8. This article gives 27 powers to Congress. For example, Congress may collect taxes, declare war, and coin money. Other expressed powers are in Article II. These powers relate to the President. They include the power to make treaties, appoint federal officials, and do other things. Article III gives powers to the Supreme Court and other federal courts. A few expressed powers are found in the amendments.

Federalism
A government system in which power is divided geographically between the central government and several regional governments

Division of power
The constitutional provisions by which government powers are divided between the national government and the states

Delegated powers
Those powers—expressed, implied, or inherent—granted to the national government by the Constitution

Expressed powers
The delegated powers of the national government that are written plainly in the Constitution

Fig. 4.1

Expressed Powers

Implied Powers

▲ The federal government has the expressed power to print money. It has built many hydroelectric dams in the exercise of its many implied powers. *What is another implied power of the federal government?*

Reading Strategy
Text Structure
Compare and Contrast:
Notice what is alike and what is
different between expressed and
implied powers.

Implied powers
Powers the national government
is presumed to have because it
is the government of a sovereign
state in the world community

Inherent powers
Powers the Constitution is
presumed to have delegated to
the national government because
it is a government of a sovereign
state within the world community

Implied powers are not directly stated in the Constitution. Rather, they are suggested—or implied—by the expressed powers. (See Figure 4.1 on page 79.) The basis for the implied powers is found in Article I, Section 8, Clause 18—the Necessary and Proper Clause. This clause is sometimes called the "Elastic Clause" because its meaning has been stretched many times. This has been done to meet the needs of the country as it grew. The clause begins by saying Congress has the power "to make all laws which shall be necessary and proper . . ." Take, for example, the expressed power of Congress to regulate interstate commerce. Interstate commerce is business between states. Under this power, Congress has exercised many implied powers. It has made federal crimes of such acts as moving stolen goods and kidnapped persons across state lines. It has prohibited racial discrimination by granting all people access to public places. Congress has also provided for the building of the 42,000-mile interstate highway under its commerce power.

Inherent powers exist because the United States is a sovereign state. The Constitution does not put them in words, but these powers exist by tradition. For example, the government can regulate immigration, acquire territory, and protect citizens against rebellion and terrorism. (See Figure 4.2.)

✔ **Checkpoint**   What are the three types of delegated powers of the national government?

Fig. 4.2

Inherent Powers

▲ President George W. Bush meets with Chancellor Angela Merkel of Germany at the 2007 G8 Summit as part of his diplomatic role.

What powers are denied to the federal government?

The Constitution denies the federal government certain powers. It does this to preserve federalism. Most of these powers are listed in Article I, Section 9 and in the 1st through the 8th amendments. Among the powers denied to the federal government are the power to charge taxes on exports, or to prohibit freedom of religion, speech, press, and assembly. There are other powers denied to the federal government. For example, the federal government cannot deny a speedy and public trial to a person accused of a crime.

Many other powers are not given to the federal government because the Constitution does not list these powers. The federal government does not have the power to set up a public school system or to set up units of local government. Also, the federal government may not tax any state or its local units of government. This power is denied to prevent the government from bankrupting one or all of the states.

✔ **Checkpoint** What are two powers that are denied to the federal government?

■ ■ ■ ■ ■ ■ ■ ■ ■ ■ ■ ■ ■ ■ ■ ■ ■ ■

Reserved powers
The powers that the Constitution does not grant to the national government and does not deny to the states

What is the role of the states in a federal system?

The 50 states play an important role in the government of the United States. The individual state governments balance the power of the federal government. The states are governments of **reserved powers.** These are powers that the Constitution does not grant to the national government and does not deny to the states. For example, any state can require doctors, lawyers, or plumbers to be licensed. States can establish public schools and regulate public utilities, such as electric and gas.

The area of reserved powers is huge and also includes the important police power. This is the power of states to protect public health, safety, and welfare.

The Constitution does deny some powers to the states. Some are denied expressly. For example, no state can enter into a treaty with a foreign country. No state can print money or deny a person due process of law. Other powers are denied inherently. Because there is a federal system, for example, no state can tax the national government.

✔ **Checkpoint** What are reserved powers?

Exclusive powers
Powers that are only given to the
federal government

Concurrent powers
Powers that the national
government and the states share

Reading Strategy
Text Structure
Identify words in this
paragraph that tell the meaning of
concurrent powers.

What are exclusive and concurrent powers?

The national government has many **exclusive powers.** These are powers given only to the federal government. The states may not use these powers. Examples of exclusive powers are making treaties with other countries and collecting taxes on imports. The federal government always controls interstate commerce. This power is expressly denied to the states.

Concurrent powers are powers that the state and federal governments share (Figure 4.3). For example, both the federal government and state governments collect taxes. Both governments also set punishments for crimes. Figure 4.4 on the next page shows the division of powers between the federal government and the 50 state governments.

We often think of the United States as having three levels of government: national, state, and local. However, there are really only two levels of government in a federal system: the national government and the state government. The 87,000 local units of government have only the powers granted to them by their states. Because of this, each state is said to have a unitary form of government.

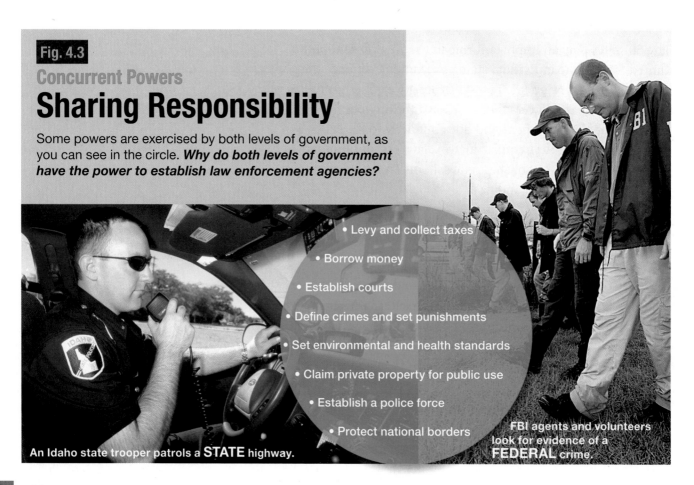

Fig. 4.3
Concurrent Powers
Sharing Responsibility

Some powers are exercised by both levels of government, as you can see in the circle. *Why do both levels of government have the power to establish law enforcement agencies?*

- Levy and collect taxes
- Borrow money
- Establish courts
- Define crimes and set punishments
- Set environmental and health standards
- Claim private property for public use
- Establish a police force
- Protect national borders

An Idaho state trooper patrols a **STATE** highway.

FBI agents and volunteers look for evidence of a **FEDERAL** crime.

Fig. 4.4
Division of Power

Federal Powers	Concurrent Powers	State Powers
Coin money	Levy and collect taxes	License marriage
Control commerce with foreign nations	Borrow money	License professionals
Determine standards of weight and measure	Establish courts	Establish public schools
Declare war	Define crimes and set punishments	License drivers
Make laws that are "necessary and proper"	Claim private property for public use	Regulate elections
Regulate interstate commerce	Set environmental and health standards	Oversee intrastate commerce
Control immigration		Set speed limits
Acquire territory		Exercise those powers not given to the federal government and not restricted by the Constitution
Conduct diplomatic relations with other countries		

Supremacy Clause
A clause in the Constitution that states that the Constitution is above all other laws

What is the supreme law of the land?

Conflicts between the federal government and the state governments do arise from time to time. The Framers knew this would happen and wrote the **Supremacy Clause** into the Constitution. It states in part, "This Constitution, and the Laws of the United States . . . and all Treaties . . . shall be the supreme Law of the Land; and the Judges in every State shall be bound thereby." This clause states that the Constitution stands above all other laws. Acts of Congress and treaties fall immediately below the Constitution. (See Figure 4.5 on page 84.)

In 1819, the Supreme Court first settled a dispute between a national and state law. The State of Maryland had placed a tax on the Baltimore branch of the Second Bank of the United States. Congress had created the bank and many people opposed it. The Maryland legislature hoped to destroy the bank. When a bank cashier refused to pay the tax, the Maryland courts convicted him. The Supreme Court cleared the cashier of all charges. The Court said the State of Maryland had no right to tax the federal bank, and it based its decision on the Supremacy Clause. Over the years, the Supreme Court has found thousands of state and local laws to be unconstitutional. It has also ruled that thousands of others were constitutional.

✔ **Checkpoint** What is the Supremacy Clause?

Fig.4.5

THIS LITTLE BOY WOULD PERSIST IN HANDLING BOOKS ABOVE HIS CAPACITY.

AND THIS WAS THE DISASTROUS RESULT.

▲ **Analyzing Cartoons** This cartoon ran in the magazine *Harper's Weekly* when Congress attempted to remove President Andrew Johnson from office. ***How does the "disastrous result" illustrate the Supremacy Clause?***

SECTION 1 ASSESSMENT

Essential Questions Journal Go to your **Essential Questions Journal** to work on this chapter's Essential Question.

Word Bank

concurrent powers

exclusive powers

expressed powers

implied powers

Quick Write

Compare and contrast state powers with the powers of the federal government. Research and take notes on the various powers held by the states and the federal government. Write about any powers that might have surprised you.

1. **Guiding Question** Use your completed Venn diagram to answer this question: How is power divided between the federal government and the states?

Key Terms and Comprehension

On a sheet of paper, write the words from the Word Bank to complete each sentence correctly.

2. _____ are powers only given to the federal government.

3. _____ allow state and federal governments to share the same power.

4. _____ are powers that are suggested by the expressed powers in the Constitution.

5. _____ are powers directly stated in the Constitution.

Critical Thinking

6. **Make Inferences** Why did the Framers want to reserve some specific powers to the states?

7. **Draw Conclusions** How does the Supremacy Clause support the system of federalism?

▲ Residents of Hawaii celebrate their newly acquired statehood in 1959.

The National Government and the 50 States

Guiding Question

According to the Constitution, what must the federal government guarantee to each state? Use a chart like the one below to take notes on the federal government's responsibilities.

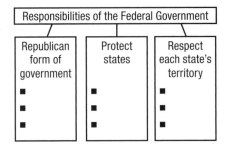

Responsibilities of the Federal Government

Republican form of government	Protect states	Respect each state's territory
■	■	■
■	■	■
■	■	■

Objectives:

- Summarize the responsibilities that the Constitution places on the national government for the benefit of the states.
- Explain the process for admitting new states to the Union.
- Examine the many and growing areas of cooperative federalism.

Have you ever focused on the words "United States"? What do they really mean? The Framers of the Constitution created a union of states and wanted to keep those states united. In order to do so, the Constitution requires the national government to guarantee certain things to the states. The Constitution also allows the national government to do certain things for the states.

What are the nation's obligations to the states?

The Constitution places several obligations on the national government to benefit the states. Most of these obligations are found in Article IV. This article states that the federal government guarantees each state a republican form of government. Although the Constitution does not explain what a republican form of government is, it is understood to mean a "representative government." Just as in the federal government, the leaders of the state are elected by the people and speak for the people of that state.

Article IV also promises that the federal government will protect each state from invasion and internal violence. Today, invasion is understood to mean an attack on the United States itself. However in the late 1780s, it was not certain if the original 13 states would join together if one state were attacked. So, before the states agreed to give up their war-making powers, they wanted to be guaranteed that an attack on one state would be considered an attack on all of the states.

✔ **Checkpoint** What is a republican form of government?

Enabling act
A congressional act directing the people of a territory to write a state constitution as a step toward admission to the Union

Act of admission
A congressional act admitting a new state to the Union

The federal system assumes that each state will keep peace within its borders. Therefore, the primary responsibility for preventing and stopping internal disorder rests within each state. In some situations, however, a state may need help. The Constitution guarantees protection against internal disorder, which it calls "domestic violence." The use of federal force to restore order in a state has been rare. It did happen in 1967 when racial unrest caused rioting in Detroit. President Johnson sent units of the United States Army to help state police. Chicago and Baltimore also needed help to control riots after the assassination of Martin Luther King, Jr. The federal government has also helped states during hurricanes, floods, and other natural disasters.

Finally, the national government is required to protect each state's legal existence and recognize each state's physical boundaries. In Article I, Sections 2 and 3, the Constitution declares that Congress must include members chosen from each of the states. Article V of the Constitution declares that no state can be denied equal representation in the United States Senate without its own consent.

How are states admitted to the Union?

The leaders of the new nation knew that more states would soon join the Union. To help that happen, they passed the Northwest Ordinance of 1787. The law focused on the Northwest Territory. This was the land north of the Ohio River and west of New York, Pennsylvania, and Virginia. The ordinance said that any area that had a population of 60,000 could become a state. Provisions were made for local government and for education.

When writing the Constitution, the Framers gave Congress the power to admit new states. Over the years, Congress has acted 37 times to admit new states to the country. In some cases, old states were divided to create new ones. Texas and Vermont were independent republics before they joined the country. Other states were formed from territories the United States acquired by wars and treaties. In fact, most states began as territories (Figure 4.6). To become a state, a territory applies to Congress for admission to the United States. If Congress agrees that a territory is ready to become a state, it passes an **enabling act.** This act directs the people of the territory to write a state constitution. The territory and Congress must approve the constitution. If the constitution is approved, Congress passes an **act of admission** to create a new state. If the President signs the act, the state is admitted to the United States.

What are the conditions for admission?

Congress has often set conditions a state must follow before being admitted to the Union. Alaska was admitted as a state with a condition concerning Native Americans. Alaska was not allowed to claim any lands held by any Native American. Congress cannot, however, set conditions of a political nature. When Oklahoma became a state in 1907, for example, Congress said the capital could not be moved from Guthrie until 1913. A few years later, however, the capital was moved to Oklahoma City. The move was challenged in the Supreme Court. The Court ruled in favor of the state of Oklahoma, saying that Congress must not interfere with a state's ability to manage its own affairs.

Fig. 4.6

Territorial Expansion of the U.S.

GOVERNMENT ONLINE
Interactive
To learn more about territorial expansion of the United States, visit **PearsonSuccessNet.com**

Analyzing Maps Until the early 20th century, the federal government steadily acquired land and admitted new states (indicated by years). *From which 19th-century acquisition were the most states created?* ▼

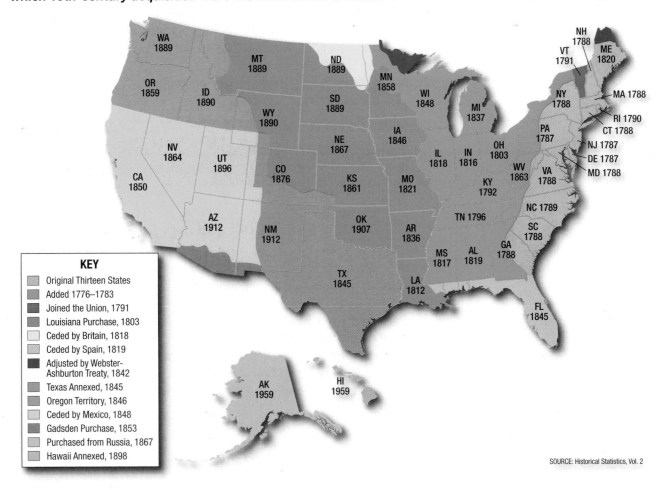

KEY
- Original Thirteen States
- Added 1776–1783
- Joined the Union, 1791
- Louisiana Purchase, 1803
- Ceded by Britain, 1818
- Ceded by Spain, 1819
- Adjusted by Webster-Ashburton Treaty, 1842
- Texas Annexed, 1845
- Oregon Territory, 1846
- Ceded by Mexico, 1848
- Gadsden Purchase, 1853
- Purchased from Russia, 1867
- Hawaii Annexed, 1898

SOURCE: Historical Statistics, Vol. 2

Grants-in-aid program
Grants of federal money or other resources to states, cities, counties, and other local units

Reading Strategy
Text Structure
As you read, look for descriptive words that help answer the question: what is cooperative federalism?

What is cooperative federalism?

The federal system is based on two levels of government (federal and state) working at the same time. This system means that power is often shared as the two levels of government cooperate. Federal **grants-in-aid programs** are a good example of this cooperation. Through these programs, money or other resources, such as land, is given to the states. These programs began with the Northwest Ordinance of 1787. Congress provided for the government of all territory beyond the Ohio River to set aside land for the support for public education there.

Federal lands were granted to the states throughout the nineteenth century. The land was used for schools and universities, roads, and other purposes. In 1808, Congress started to provide grants of federal money. Some of this money was used by the states to support the militia. The militia later became the National Guard, which is still in operation today. In the Depression years of the 1930s, Congress provided cash grants to states to help with the economic crisis. Since that time, Congress has set up hundreds of grants-in-aid programs. These programs help states in the areas of education, mass transit, highway construction, healthcare, and others. They account for about 25 percent of all state and local spending each year.

Some people do not like grants-in-aid programs. They say the programs cause interference in state affairs by the federal government.

✓ **Checkpoint**   What are grant-in-aid programs?

Government in Your Life

Safe Routes to School (SRTS)

The SRTS is a federally funded organization that provides money to state Departments of Transportation through grants. The grant money is used for improving the school environment. The focus is on schools that serve kindergarten through the 8th grade. The goal of this organization is to encourage children to walk or bike to school. In order for children to do this, the routes they use must be safe. Often the routes need to be improved or built, especially if there are no bike paths. The school routes also need to be maintained.

Funds are available for construction, planning, and maintenance of school routes through SRTS. The states must apply to the federal government for the grant money.

What are some types of federal grants?

Most grants are **categorical grants** and are made for special reasons, such as building roads or paying for school lunches. These grants usually require the states to contribute money as well and set up rules the states must follow. **Block grants** are made for broad areas, such as healthcare, social services, and welfare. The states have some freedom in using the money. **Project grants** are often made to support specific projects, like medical research. The Department of Health and Human Services makes many of the project grants. State and local governments may ask for these grants to pay for job training and other employment programs. The federal government helps the states in other ways as well. For example, the FBI helps state police, and states rely heavily on Census Bureau data.

✔**Checkpoint** What is a block grant?

Categorical grants
Grants made by the federal government for a specific purpose

Block grants
Grants made by the federal government for some particular but broadly defined area of public policy

Project grants
Grants made by the federal government for specific projects to states, localities, and private agencies that apply for them

How do states help the national government?

State governments help the national government in several ways. National elections are run by the states and funded with local money. States also take care of the naturalization process. Aliens who wish to become citizens must go through the naturalization procedures. These procedures take place most often in state courts. The federal government helps the states in other ways as well. For example, the FBI helps state police, and states rely heavily on Census Bureau data.

Essential Questions Journal Go to your **Essential Questions Journal** to work on this chapter's Essential Question.

SECTION 2 ASSESSMENT

1. **Guiding Question** Use your completed chart to answer this question: According to the Constitution, what must the national government guarantee to each state?

Key Terms and Comprehension
On a sheet of paper, write the answers to the following questions. Use complete sentences.

2. What is the purpose of an enabling act?

3. Why does the federal government make grants-in-aid to the states?

4. What are the three main types of federal grants?

5. What is the Northwest Ordinance?

Critical Thinking

6. **Draw Conclusions** Why might the Framers have included standards in the Constitution that each territory must meet before it can become a state?

7. **Summarize** What is cooperative federalism?

ISSUES OF OUR TIME

The Environment and States' Rights

▶▶ Track the Issue

Over time, the federal government has taken steps to protect the environment. Many of these steps have been controversial.

1872 Congress sets aside land in three states for Yellowstone National Park. Yellowstone was the country's first national park.

1907 President Theodore Roosevelt sets aside 16 million acres of new forest preserves.

1948 The Clean Water Act is passed by Congress. It is amended in 1972 and 1977.

1963 The Clean Air Act is passed by Congress. It is amended in 1990.

2004 The Supreme Court rules that the EPA can override states on issues of the environment.

EPA Administrator Stephen L. Johnson

▶▶ Perspectives

In 2008, California sued the Environmental Protection Agency (EPA) over the state's rights to restrict air pollutants. The state wanted stricter rules than the federal government had for air pollutants. The EPA, which controlled such restrictions, denied California's waiver. The case focused on this question: Should the federal government regulate environmental issues, or should the states make their own rules? California's governor, Arnold Schwarzenegger, and EPA Administrator, Stephen L. Johnson, disagree on the issue. Below are both arguments.

For State Control	For Federal Control
"The authority of states to address greenhouse gas emissions from motor vehicles has been clearly and unequivocally [unmistakenly] supported—by the Supreme Court, a federal court decision in Vermont, and in December by a federal court here in California. On this issue, the U.S. EPA has failed to lead, it has failed to follow the states' lead and we are prepared to force it out of the way in order to protect the environment." —*Governor Arnold Schwarzenegger, April 2, 2008*	"I believe that Congress by passing a unified federal standard of 35 mpg [miles per gallon] delivers significant reductions that are more effective than a state-by-state approach. This applies to all 50 states, not 1 state, not 12 states, not 15 states. It applies to all 50 states, and that's great for the economy, for national security and for the environment." —*EPA Administrator Stephen L. Johnson*

Connect to Your World

1. Why does Governor Schwarzenegger believe that states should control this issue? Why does Stephen L. Johnson believe that the federal government should control the issue?

2. Who do you agree with? Explain your answer.

GOVERNMENT ONLINE
In the News
For updates on environmental cases, visit
PearsonSuccessNet.com

ENERGY STAR

▲ A person stands where the borders of Utah, Colorado, Arizona, and New Mexico meet to create the "Four Corners."

SECTION 3

Interstate Relations

Guiding Question

How do the states work together to preserve the Union?
Use an outline like the one below to take notes on how the states cooperate.

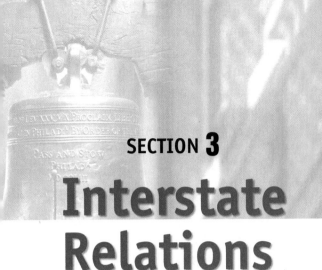

I. All States Work Together
   A. Interstate relations
      1. _____
      2. _____
   B. Full Faith and Credit
      1. _____
      2. _____
   C. Extradition
   D. Privileges and Immunities

Objectives:

■ Explain why states make interstate compacts.

■ Understand the purpose of the Full Faith and Credit Clause.

■ Define extradition and explain its purpose.

■ Discuss the purpose of the Privileges and Immunities Clause.

The states must interact with one another on many issues. Often this interaction causes conflicts. The Constitution contains provisions that help the states avoid and solve those conflicts. In this section you will read about those provisions and interstate compacts.

What are interstate compacts?

Interstate compacts are agreements the states make with one another and with foreign states. This provision is found in Article I, Section 10 of the Constitution. Congress usually must consent to all interstate compacts. By 1920, the states had made only 36 compacts. Since then, the number of interstate compacts has been growing. This began in 1921, when New York and New Jersey created the Port Authority of New York and New Jersey. The harbor serving both states is managed by both states.

Some interstate contracts involve several states. For example, the Compact on Juveniles allows all 50 states to share law enforcement data. Other compacts control tax collections, use of public universities, and conservation of wildlife.

What is the Full Faith and Credit Clause?

The Constitution declares that the laws, records, and results of court cases of one state are valid in all other states. This is the **Full Faith and Credit Clause.** If a person is sued in a state, he or she cannot flee the state to avoid paying damages. All states in our country recognize and obey the results of lawsuits in other states. Also, all documents issued by a state are recognized by all other states. These documents include birth certificates, marriage licenses, and titles to property.

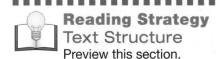
Interstate compact
Agreement made between two or
more states

Full Faith and Credit Clause
Constitution's requirement that
each state accept the public acts,
records, and judicial proceedings
of every other state

Extradition
The legal process by which a
fugitive from justice in one state is
returned to that state

**Privileges and Immunities
Clause**
Constitution's stipulation that all
citizens are entitled to certain
"privileges and immunities"
regardless of their state of
residence

There are exceptions to the Full Faith and Credit Clause. The first is that the clause applies only to civil matters. One state cannot enforce the criminal law of another state. The second exception relates to divorces. Certain divorces cannot receive full faith and credit in other states. Same-sex marriages are only recognized in some states. This causes problems when same-sex couples move to another state. Often the other state does not recognize the marriage. The Defense of Marriage Act, passed in 1996, declares no state can be made to recognize a same-sex marriage performed in another state.

What is extradition?

Article IV, Section 2, Clause 2 refers to **extradition.** It is the legal process by which a person fleeing justice in one state is returned to that state. Extradition prevents a person from fleeing a state to avoid being charged with a crime. A governor usually returns a fugitive without delay. Some requests are challenged, however. This often happens in cases concerning race, politics, or disputes over child custody. Before 1987, the Supreme Court had held that the government could not make a governor return a fugitive. Then, in 1987, the Court reversed its ruling.

What are privileges and immunities?

Citizens are protected by the **Privileges and Immunities Clause.** The clause forbids any state to discriminate unreasonably against people from other states. This means that any American may travel or live in any state. It also guarantees that any citizen, no matter where he or she lives, may use the courts in any state. The citizen may buy, own, rent, and sell property. Employers cannot be required by a state to hire only residents of that state. The Supreme Court has upheld this clause many times.

In some matters, such as voting, holding public office, or obtaining a license, a state can make rules based on a person's residence. For example, people must be residents for a specified length of time before running for public office. In most states, nonresidents have to pay higher fees for fishing and hunting licenses. This is because state residents pay taxes to maintain these natural resources. Also, out-of-state students usually pay higher tuition to attend state colleges or universities.

✔**Checkpoint**   In which matters can states discriminate between its
residents and those from other states?

Biography

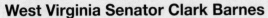

Clark Barnes (1950–)

West Virginia Senator Clark Barnes
is the minority whip in the West Virginia state
Senate. He is a Republican representing Randolph County.
He serves on the Natural Resources, Education, Transportation
and Infrastructure, Labor, and Judiciary committees. He is a
member of the NRA, the West Virginia Education Association,
and the United States Chamber of Commerce. He received his
degree from West Virginia University.

Barnes introduced a bill in the West Virginia Senate in January
2008 intended to block the federal Real ID Act. The act set up
new national standards for drivers' licenses (see page 95). He
had 15 cosponsors. Barnes is quoted as saying, "The Real ID
gives the [federal] government access in one fell swoop to a lot
of our information. . . the government hasn't told us exactly
what they want to do with all the information." Barnes says that
privacy rights are a constitutional guarantee. They are viewed
by West Virginians as "sacred."

Barnes lives in Elkin, West Virginia, with his wife, Deborah.
They are the parents of four children.

Essential Questions Journal   Go to your **Essential Questions Journal** to work on this chapter's Essential Question.

SECTION 3 ASSESSMENT

1. **Guiding Question** Use your completed outline
   to answer this question: How do the states
   work together to preserve the Union?

Key Terms and Comprehension

**On a sheet of paper, write the answers to the
following questions. Use complete sentences.**

2. What is an interstate compact?

3. What is an exception to the Full Faith and
   Credit Clause?

4. What is extradition?

5. Can an interstate compact be made between
   more than two states? Explain your answer.

Critical Thinking

6. **Synthesize Information** If a person commits
   a felony in one state and flees to another
   state, why might that person face extradition?
   Why wouldn't this person just be tried in the
   second state for the crime?

7. **Summarize** How are citizens protected by the
   Privileges and Immunities Clause? Give two
   examples.

Quick Study Guide

Chapter Summary

Section 1—Federalism: Powers Divided

- The United States has a federal system of government that divides power between a national government and state governments.

- The national government has three types of power: expressed, implied, and inherent.

- The state governments balance the power of the federal government. The states are governments of reserved powers.

- The federal government has many exclusive powers that may never be used by the states.

- Concurrent powers are those shared by the national government and the state governments.

- The Supremacy Clause declares that the Constitution and treaties are above all other laws.

Section 2—The National Government and the 50 States

- Article IV of the Constitution guarantees the states a republican form of government and protection by the national government.

- Congress admits a state to the union after approving a constitution written by the state.

- Under cooperative federalism, the federal government cooperates with state governments through grants-in-aid programs.

- The states aid the national government by carrying out certain duties. For example, states run national elections for the federal government.

Section 3—Interstate Relations

- Interstate compacts are made between states. These compacts are made to take care of matters shared by some states.

- The Full Faith and Credit Clause in the Constitution declares that each state must recognize the laws, records, and rulings of other states.

- Extradition is the legal process by which a fugitive from justice is returned to his or her home state. The extradition clause is part of Article IV in the Constitution.

- The Privileges and Immunities Clause allows Americans to travel, live, and do business in any state. A state cannot unreasonably favor its own residents over residents of other states.

Guiding Question
Section 1 How is power divided between the federal government and the states?

Guiding Question
Section 2 According to the Constitution, what must the federal government guarantee to each state?

Guiding Question
Section 3 How do the states work together to preserve the Union?

CHAPTER 4

Essential Question
Is the federal system the best way to govern the United States?

Document-Based Assessment

The REAL ID Act of 2005

The REAL ID Act of 2005 is a United States federal law. The Act established new national standards for driver's licenses and identification cards. The Act states that these standards must be met for people to use these cards to board commercial airlines. In 2008, Michael Chertoff, the former United States Secretary of Homeland Security, made remarks about the ID Act and what it means for the United States.

Document at a Glance
- Speech by Michael Chertoff
- REAL ID Act of 2005
- Obligation to Set National Standards

One of the biggest concerns we've had for the last several years . . . at the Department of Homeland Security is how we promote a secure form of identification across America . . . Congress has spoken to this by passing the REAL ID Act several years ago which provides that we have the obligation to set uniform security standards for . . . state driver's licenses . . . That is why the 9/11 Commission recommended that we enhance [improve] the security of our driver's licenses as a counterterrorism measure . . . First . . . secure identification is an essential way of ensuring that people are who they say they are . . . Second, secure identification [can] prevent illegal immigrants from pretending to be American citizens . . . Third . . . [it] protects us all from the . . . plague of identify theft.

. . . under the rule, people seeking driver's licenses must provide their state Department of Motor Vehicles documents that prove who they are and . . . that they are in this country legally. [The DMV] offices must verify that the documents . . . are legitimate . . . States have to work together to assure that individuals are not able to obtain driver's licenses from multiple states in an improper manner.

What is the cost going to be? . . . we estimate that the average cost for . . . a Real ID license will be about $8 per license . . . [A] a four-year license [will cost about] $2 a year.

Document-Based Questions

1. What are two of the reasons the 9/11 Commission recommended the higher standard for driver's licenses?

2. What does Chertoff say the cost will be per year for each person getting a four-year license?

3. What is the goal of the REAL ID Act?

4. What must those seeking licenses provide for the states' Department of Motor Vehicles?

5. **Text Structure** Does this document compare and contrast or present problems and solutions? Explain your reasoning.

SOURCE: http://www.studentnewsdaily.com/daily-news-article/real_id_implementation_delayed

Chapter Assessment

GOVERNMENT ONLINE
Self-Test
To test your understanding of
key terms and main ideas, visit
PearsonSuccessNet.com

Directions: On a sheet of paper, write the answers to the
following questions. Use complete sentences.

Section 1—Federalism: Powers Divided

1. What is federalism?

2. What are the three types of powers of the federal
government?

3. What is an example of an exclusive power of the federal
government?

4. What are concurrent powers?

5. What is the Supremacy Clause?

6. **Critical Thinking** Why do you think certain powers are given
to the states instead of the federal government? Explain your
answer.

Section 2—The National Government and the 50 States

7. What is an act of admission?

8. What are two examples of categorical grants?

9. What is the difference between a block grant and a
project grant?

10. What must a territory do before Congress will make it a state?

11. What are three ways states help the federal government?

12. **Critical Thinking** How might federal aid be used to heighten
the federal government's influence on state matters?

Section 3—Interstate Relations

13. What is one example of interstate compact?

14. What is the Full Faith and Credit Clause?

15. Is a governor required by law to return a fugitive in the extradition process? Why or why not?

16. What is the Privileges and Immunities Clause?

17. Critical Thinking What type of interstate compact might be made between two states? What type of interstate compact might be made between all the states? Give an example for each.

Apply What You've Learned

Exploring the Essential Question

Create a federal grant proposal.

18. As a class, brainstorm some local activities (education, law enforcement, traffic control, etc.) that could be supported by a federal grant.

19. As a small group, create a grant proposal for an activity. Write how much money you will need for your program. Also write what you will do with that money. Share it with the class.

Essential Questions Project

20. In groups or as a class, apply what you've learned about the grants and the grant process to talk about the Essential Question: **Is the federal system the best way to govern the United States?** Make sure to back up your opinions with facts from the textbook and from your research.

Essential Questions Journal

Go to your **Essential Questions Journal** to work on this chapter's Essential Question.

Test-Taking Tip

Organize a study group to study a subject. Each person can share his or her notes on a different part of the subject.

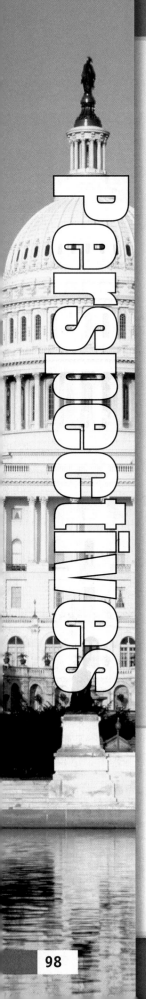

Perspectives

Essential Question
What should be the goals of government?

For every government, there exists a set of goals unique to the country's needs and history. For the United States government, those goals have been discussed and debated for the more than 200 years of the nation's existence.

ON THE GOALS OF GOVERNMENT:

A wise and frugal [thrifty] government . . . shall restrain men from injuring one another, shall leave them otherwise free to regulate their own pursuits of industry and improvement, and shall not take from the mouth of labor the bread it has earned. This is the sum of good government.

—Thomas Jefferson, First Inaugural Address, March 4, 1801

ON WHERE GOVERNMENT DERIVES ITS POWER:

Here, sir, the people govern; here they act by their immediate representatives.

—Alexander Hamilton, on ratifying the Constitution, June 27, 1788

ON WHAT MAKES A GOOD GOVERNMENT:

Good government is a trust, and the officers of the government are trustees; and both the trust and the trustees are created for the benefit of the people.

—Sen. Henry Clay,
  Speech at Ashland, Kentucky, 1829

Essential Question Warmup

Throughout this unit, you studied the origins and elements of various governments, including those of the United States. Use what you have learned and the quotations above to answer the following questions. Then, go to your **Essential Questions Journal.**

1. How might a government's goals be affected by that government's form?

2. What are some other factors that might determine a government's goals?

3. What are the goals of the U.S. government?

4. How did the Framers develop these goals?

Essential Questions Journal
To continue to build a response to the unit Essential Question, go to your **Essential Questions Journal.**

Photo: President Obama greets supporters.

| **Essential Questions** **Journal** | To begin to build a response to the unit Essential Question, go to your **Essential Questions Journal.** |

Unit 2 Political Behavior: Government By the People

Essential Question In what ways should people participate in public affairs?

▲ Republican convention delegates cheer their party's 2008 presidential and vice presidential nominees, Sen. John McCain (R., Arizona) and Gov. Sarah Palin (R., Alaska).

Political Parties

Section 1: Parties and What They Do

Section 2: Two-Party System in American History

Section 3: The Minor Parties

Section 4: Party Organization

Reading Strategy: Visualizing
Visualizing is like creating a movie in your mind. Use the following ways to visualize this chapter.

- Look at the photographs, illustrations, and descriptive words. Think about what these do and do not tell you.
- Think about experiences in your own life that may help you understand the images.
- Notice the order in which things are happening. Describe what you think might happen next.

GOVERNMENT ONLINE
ON THE GO

To study anywhere, anytime, download these online resources at PearsonSuccessNet.com.
- Political Dictionary
- Audio Review
- Downloadable Interactivities

SECTION 1

Parties and What They Do

▲ National party conventions are opportunities for party members to show their support.

Guiding Question

What are political parties, and how do they function in our two-party system? Use an outline to organize the main features of political parties, their roles, and the party systems.

I. What Parties Do
   A. Definition
   B. Functions
II. Types of Party Systems
   A. Two Party
   B. Multiparty
   C. _____

Objectives:

- Define a political party.
- Describe the functions of political parties.
- Identify why the United States has a two-party system.
- Understand different party systems and how they affect the government.

Political parties are an important feature of the American government system. Members of political parties work hard to get their **candidates** elected and their issues discussed in Congress. Voters can show support for a political party by displaying posters, wearing buttons, and attending political events.

What is a party?

A political party is a group of people that tries to control government by getting its candidates elected. Political parties are made up of groups of citizens who share common ideas about government. These groups try to get their candidates elected so they can develop the group's ideas on issues. Political parties also believe in certain principles. They try to present candidates who will support their beliefs. Individual citizens may also become involved in **campaigns** during elections. A campaign is all the activities connected to getting a person elected to public office.

The two **major parties** in American politics are the Republicans and the Democrats. Republicans are usually politically **conservative.** Conservatives believe in less governmental control and more individual responsibility. Democrats are usually more **liberal.** Liberals tend to be less concerned about the amount of governmental control and more open to change. Both parties have many of the same goals. They often have different ideas about reaching them.

Each party is an organization made up of three separate groups.

1. *The party organization.* These are the people who run the party at the national and state levels. These leaders, active members, and volunteers offer their time, skills, and money in support of the party.

2. *The party in government.* These are the people who serve in office at the national, state, and local levels of government for their party.

3. *The party in the electorate.* These are people who call themselves Republican or Democrat. They are loyal members of that party. They always vote in line with the party.

✔ **Checkpoint** What is the main goal of a political party?

What do parties do?

Political parties perform several functions that are necessary to our government. The main function of a political party is to choose candidates. Every four years, party members come together for a national convention. The convention takes place in the summer before a presidential election. At this meeting, the party **nominates,** or selects, candidates for President and Vice President. Each party agrees on a set of statements about what the candidates will do if elected. These statements of policy and promises are known as a **platform.** A platform committee is made up of delegates from each state and territory of the country. They listen to suggestions and ideas before the convention begins. They put these ideas together. During the convention, they present the platform. Sometimes it is accepted as presented. Sometimes parts of it are discussed and changed before the convention accepts it.

Political parties have a number of other duties. They educate the public about their candidate in hopes of convincing voters to choose that candidate on election day. Newspapers, television ads, the Internet, and rallies are some ways parties promote their candidates. (See **Figure 5.1** on the next page.)

The political party also acts as a "bonding agent." This means the party makes sure that candidates are well qualified and of good character. The party also encourages its officeholders to perform well. If elected officials do not succeed in office, the party may lose in the next election. Between elections, political parties work to see that **incumbents** will be reelected. An incumbent is a person who holds an office. Parties may send newsletters to voters to explain how the officeholder is working to help them.

Political party
A group of people that tries to control the government by getting its candidates elected

Candidate
A person who hopes to be elected to a public office

Campaign
The activities connected to trying to get a person elected to a political office

Major party
In American politics, the Republican and Democratic parties

Conservative
A person who believes in less governmental control and more individual responsibility

Liberal
A person who is less concerned about the amount of governmental control and more open to change

Electorate
All of the people allowed to vote in an election

Nominate
To select a candidate to run for a political office

Platform
A political party's statements of ideas, policies, and beliefs

Incumbent
A person who holds an office

Fig. 5.1 **How Government Works**

How Parties Communicate

For the better part of two centuries, political parties have used a variety of strategies to reach voters. Two ways candidates have tried to gain voter support are through personal Web sites and popular food products. *How do the pictures shown here reflect attempts to reach voters?*

▲ At recent national conventions, both parties gave these boxes of macaroni and cheese to the press and delegates.

▲ Candidates have created their own Web sites to connect with and inform voters.

Partisanship
Strong support of a political party

Members of Congress, state legislators, and other elected officials are members of political parties. They make decisions on the basis of **partisanship.** This means their policies or programs have the full support of their party. Appointments at all levels of government are often made on the basis of party connections.

The party not in power also has a function between elections. It acts as a watchdog over the party in power. It may criticize the other party's policies and candidates. The party not in power tries to convince the voters that its candidates can do a better job.

✔**Checkpoint** What is the purpose of a national convention?

Why is there a two-party system?

One reason the United States has a two-party system is because the nation began that way. This is true even though the Constitution did not set up parties, and the Framers did not want them. It was the struggle to ratify the Constitution that led to the formation of two parties. These two parties were called the Federalists and the Anti-Federalists. Since that time, America has been a two-party country.

Certain features of the American electoral system have encouraged only two parties. One such feature is single-member districts. In most elections, only one candidate is elected to each office on the **ballot.** Since only one candidate has a chance of winning, this discourages **minor parties** from placing a candidate on the ballot. A minor party is a political party that is not supported by a large number of people.

In order to discourage minor parties, the two major parties act in a **bipartisan** way. They find common ideas and work together so that minor party candidates have a harder time winning. A minor party candidate has been on all of the state ballots in only seven presidential elections.

Americans, for the most part, have always shared the same ideals and beliefs. Because of this, the two political parties are very much alike. Both are moderate and believe in a government as written in the Constitution of the United States. Even so, the two parties also have some major differences. For example, the Democrats tend to favor social welfare programs and more governmental control, especially in business practices. The Republicans support less governmental control in the economy and fewer social programs. See **Figure 5.2.**

Ballot
The tool voters use to select a candidate in an election

Minor party
A political party that is not supported by a large number of people

Bipartisan
Supported by two parties

Reading Strategy
Visualizing
Look at the political spectrum image on this page. Where do you think the political beliefs of many U.S. voters likely fall on this line?

GOVERNMENT ONLINE
Interactive
Check out a poll you can take at
PearsonSuccessNet.com

Fig. 5.2
Political Spectrum

Where Do the Parties Stand?

LEFT ⬅ CENTER ➡ RIGHT

Radical	**Liberal**	**Moderate**	**Conservative**	**Reactionary**
Favors great change to create an altered or new social system.	Believes that government must take action to change unfair policies.	Holds beliefs that fall between liberal and conservative views, including some of both.	Seeks to keep the economic, political, and social structures of society in place.	Favors great change to return society to an earlier, more conservative form.

Democratic Platform 2004

Healthcare

"We will provide tax credits to Americans who are approaching retirement age. . . .We will expand coverage for low income adults through existing federal-state health care programs. And we will provide all Americans with access to the same coverage that members of Congress give themselves."

Republican Platform 2004

Healthcare

"Shifting the cost-burden [of healthcare] onto the federal or state governments—costs that will ultimately be borne by the taxpayers—is not an effective solution to the problem. . .it is also important that we reaffirm our Party's firm rejection of any measure aimed at making health care a government-run enterprise."

▲ Critical Thinking Each party's platform reflects the political spectrum. *How are the party platforms different on the issues of healthcare? How are they similar?*

Multiparty system
A system in which several major and minor parties compete for and win public offices

Coalition
A temporary coming together of several groups to form a majority in order to control a government

One-party system
A political system in which only one party exists

What are multiparty and one-party systems?

Some Americans are in favor of a **multiparty system** to give voters a wide choice of candidates and ideas. In a multiparty system, many major and minor parties exist. Each has a special interest. Some of these interests are religion, economic class, or a political belief.

A multiparty system has several problems. One party may not be able to gain the support of a majority of the voters. Then the power must be shared in order to create a majority and control the government. This is known as a **coalition** and can weaken a party. Coalitions tend to dissolve quickly as new coalitions are formed.

Many European democracies have a multiparty system. Most Americans have not supported this type of system for the United States. American voters will usually only support a candidate from one of the two major parties, the Democrats or the Republicans. **Figure 5.4** on page 107 shows the differences between the multiparty and two-party systems.

One-party systems are usually dictatorships where only the ruling party is allowed to exist (**Figure 5.3**). In the United States, about one fourth of the states have a different type of one-party system. In these states, either the Republicans or Democrats have held power of most offices for a long time. For example, in the South from the 1860s to the 1960s, the Democratic Party was very powerful.

 Checkpoint   How is a two-party system different from a multiparty system?

Fig. 5.3

"My goodness, if I'd known how badly you wanted democracy I'd have given it to you ages ago."

Analyzing Political Cartoons ▶
What is the tone of this cartoon?

Fig. 5.4

Multiparty Versus Two-Party Systems

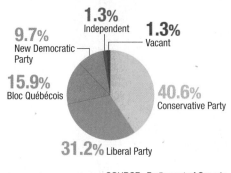

Canadian Parliament Today

9.7% New Democratic Party
1.3% Independent
1.3% Vacant
15.9% Bloc Québécois
40.6% Conservative Party
31.2% Liberal Party

SOURCE: Parliament of Canada

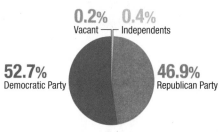

110th Congress

0.2% Vacant
0.4% Independents
52.7% Democratic Party
46.9% Republican Party

SOURCE: Clerk of the U.S. House of Representatives, U.S. Senate, House Press Gallery, 2007

▲ Canada is an example of government with a multiparty system. As you can see, power is shared among five different parties. *How is this system different from the American system?*

Essential Questions Journal Go to your **Essential Questions Journal** to work on this chapter's Essential Question.

SECTION 1 ASSESSMENT

Word Bank

candidates

convention

major

multiparty

1. **Guiding Question** Use your completed outline to answer this question: What are political parties, and how do they function in our two-party system?

Key Terms and Comprehension

On a sheet of paper, use the words from the Word Bank to complete each sentence correctly.

2. Political parties try to get their _____ elected to government offices.

3. One of the main duties of a political party is to prepare for the national _____.

4. In the United States, a _____ party is either the Republicans or the Democrats.

5. In a _____ system, many major and minor parties elect candidates to office.

Critical Thinking

6. **Draw Inferences** Why do you think there is often so much discussion and change before a party's platform is accepted?

7. **Compare Points of View** Explain why someone might vote for a minor party candidate even if that candidate will not win.

▲ James Madison (left) and Alexander Hamilton were members of the nation's earliest political parties.

SECTION 2

Two-Party System in American History

Guiding Question

How has the two-party system affected the history of American government? Use the table to record details of the history of the two-party system in American history.

Two-Party System in American History

Early Parties	Federalists, Anti-Federalists
1800–1860	
1860–1932	
1932–1968	Democrats
1968–Present	

Objectives:

- Understand the beginning of political parties in the United States.
- Identify the three major periods of single-party control, and describe the current divided government.

Political parties are not mentioned in the Constitution. They developed as the country grew. These groups formed because people had different ideas about how the government should work. The two political parties in the United States began in the late 1700s. For a summary of the major parties, see Figure 5.5 on the next page.

What were the nation's first parties?

Early forms of political parties began in the United States during colonial times. One group, the Whigs, was opposed to the English king and Parliament. The other group, the Tories, was loyal to the government of England.

During the ratification of the Constitution, two groups with differing political and economic beliefs formed. One group, the Federalist Party, supported a powerful central government and more liberal view of the Constitution. Alexander Hamilton led the Federalists. The other group, the Anti-Federalist Party, wanted a less powerful central government with strong, independent states. Thomas Jefferson led the Anti-Federalists.

The Federalists supported George Washington and John Adams, the first two Presidents of the United States. The Federalists worked hard to create a strong national government. This party was made up of businessmen and wealthy people. In 1800, the Federalists lost power when Thomas Jefferson defeated Adams. Jefferson and James Madison worked tirelessly to build the Democratic-Republican Party. Jefferson won the next few elections. His party favored a limited national government. It also favored more power for the average man.

As the country grew and changed, so did political parties. The Federalist Party lost most of its members and disappeared by 1816. The Democratic-Republican Party was also changing, and it split into different parts. Andrew Jackson led one part.

✓**Checkpoint**   Who started the nation's first political parties?

How did the Democratic Party begin?

In 1827, Andrew Jackson left the Democratic-Republican Party. Jackson felt the party was being used to help rich people. Jackson wanted the common people to be more active in making government decisions. His ideas started the Democratic Party. In 1828, Jackson was elected President. In 1860, the Democratic Party was challenged by another party—the Republican Party.

When did the Republican Party begin?

The Republican Party is the other powerful party in the United States. It began in 1854 when several groups combined. These people did not have the same beliefs as the Democratic Party. The Republican Party opposed slavery. In 1860, Abraham Lincoln won as the Republican candidate for President.

■■■■■■■■■■■■■■■
Reading Strategy
Visualizing
Think about what you already know about the Constitution. How does that information and what you are reading help you to make sense of the text?

Fig. 5.5

Major Parties

- Historically, one of two parties with a realistic chance to win elections

- Since 1800s, known as the Democratic Party and the Republican Party

- One party may dominate national elections at times.

- Both parties agree on many basic beliefs while disagreeing on some issues.

Government in Your Life

Political Party Symbols

The donkey and the elephant have long been the symbols of the two major political parties in the United States. The donkey, the symbol of the Democrats, began when Andrew Jackson was President. Cartoonist Thomas Nast, however, is the person given credit for making the donkey the Democratic Party's symbol. He first used the donkey in an 1870 *Harper's Weekly* cartoon. Nast is also given credit for the elephant, the symbol of the Republican Party. He used the elephant in an 1874 *Harper's Weekly* cartoon, and the symbol stuck. Since then, the Republicans have adopted the elephant as their mascot and use the symbol in many ways. The Democrats have never officially adopted the donkey, but they still think of it as the symbol of the party.

What are the four major eras of the American party system?

1800–1860

There have been four major eras in American party history (Figure 5.6). The Democrats controlled the era from 1800 to 1860. Andrew Jackson's administration brought changes such as voting rights for all white males. It also brought the spread of the **spoils system.** The spoils systems gave government jobs to those who supported the winning party. By the 1850s, the issue of slavery split the parties. The Whigs challenged the Democrats but fell apart after their leaders died. Within a short time, the Republican Party arose. Abraham Lincoln became the first Republican President in 1861.

1860–1932

The second era of the American party system lasted from 1860 to 1932. The Republicans were in power for much of this time. Farmers, laborers, businessmen, and newly freed African Americans supported the Republican Party. The Republicans lost the elections of 1884 and 1892. They took back power with the 1896 election. This election marked the movement of American politics back toward national, rather than regional, interests.

⊘ GOVERNMENT ONLINE
Interactive Timeline
For an interactive timeline of the parties in history, visit
PearsonSuccessNet.com

Fig. 5.6 Political Parties From 1800 Through Today

1800–1860	1860–1932	1932–1968	1968–Present
Era of Democrats	**Era of Republicans**	**Era of Democrats**	**Era of Divided Government**

1800 Thomas Jefferson is elected President.

1854 The Republican Party is formed. Many Whigs and antislavery Democrats are drawn to this new party.

1860 Abraham Lincoln is the first Republican to be elected President. The Civil War is the beginning of 75 years of Republican Party control.

1932 The Great Depression causes the role of government to shift. Democrat Franklin D. Roosevelt is elected President. The Democrats control most of this time period.

1968 Richard Nixon, a Republican, is elected President. Since 1968, however, neither the Republicans nor the Democrats have controlled the government for long periods of time.

▲ Analyzing Timelines This timeline shows which parties held the presidency since 1800. **Which two issues impacted elections from 1854 to 1932?**

The Republicans lost power again in 1912 and 1916 when the Democrats elected Woodrow Wilson. This happened because Republican support was divided between William H. Taft and the Progressive Party candidate, Theodore Roosevelt. Once again, the Republicans won power with victories in the 1920, 1924, and 1928 elections.

1932–1968

The third era of the American party system began in 1932 with the election of Franklin Roosevelt. The Democrats held power most of this time, which lasted until 1968. The Great Depression that began in 1929 affected all Americans and brought changes to American politics. When Franklin Roosevelt and the Democrats took power, they began a series of economic and social welfare programs. These New Deal programs helped the Democrats gain the support of African Americans and other minorities and changed the way people viewed government. Roosevelt was elected four times but died in office. Harry Truman, Roosevelt's Vice President, took over. Truman was elected to another term in 1948. The Republican and World War II hero, Dwight Eisenhower, won the 1952 and 1956 elections. The Democrats regained power in 1960 when John F. Kennedy was elected. After Kennedy was killed, the Vice President, Lyndon Johnson, became President until 1969.

1968–Present

The fourth era of the American party system began in 1968. This period continues today and is marked by divided government. Since Lyndon Johnson's presidency, neither of the two major parties has managed to hold both the presidency and a majority seat in Congress for very long. In 1968, Richard Nixon, a Republican, won the election by a small margin. He beat George Wallace, a minor-party candidate, and Hubert Humphrey, a Democrat. Nixon was reelected in 1972. Nixon was forced to **resign,** or leave office, in 1974 because of the Watergate scandal. Vice President Gerald Ford finished the term but lost the 1976 election to Democrat Jimmy Carter. In 1980, Republicans once again gained the White House by electing Ronald Reagan. The Republicans stayed in power by electing Reagan again in 1984. They elected George H. W. Bush in 1988. Then in 1992, Democrat Bill Clinton won the election and served two terms as President.

In 2000 and 2004, Republican George W. Bush was elected President. The 2000 election was very close. Bush lost the popular vote, but he won the electoral vote and therefore the election. The Democratic candidate, Vice President Al Gore, became the first candidate since 1888 to win the popular vote but lose the election. In 2004, President Bush defeated John Kerry.

Resign
To give up an office or position

Fig. 5.7

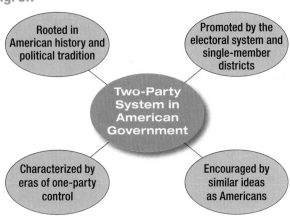

Rooted in American history and political tradition

Promoted by the electoral system and single-member districts

Two-Party System in American Government

Characterized by eras of one-party control

Encouraged by similar ideas as Americans

The Republican Party suffered big losses in Congress in 2006 because of unhappiness with President Bush's administration. Democrats won the Senate and the House of Representatives for the first time since 1992.

Democratic control of the federal government strengthened even more in 2008. A majority of voters turned to the Democrats, hoping that a change in party would help the country solve its economic problems. Democrats captured more seats in Congress, expanding their narrow majorities. Democrat Barack Obama defeated Republican John McCain for the presidency.

For over 200 years, the two-party system has been used in American government. Figure 5.7 shows a summary of this system.

Essential Questions Journal Go to your **Essential Questions Journal** to work on this chapter's Essential Question.

SECTION 2 ASSESSMENT

1. **Guiding Question** Use your completed table to answer this question: How has the two-party system affected the history of American government?

Key Terms and Comprehension

On a sheet of paper, write the answers to the following questions. Use complete sentences.

2. What were the first two political parties in the United States?

3. Why did Andrew Jackson start the Democratic Party?

4. In 1860, who was the first Republican to be elected President?

5. What event helped the Democrats win back power in 1932?

Critical Thinking

6. **Synthesize Information** How do you think political or economic crises help or harm candidates in getting elected?

7. **Draw Conclusions** What do you think the Framers would say about the recent history of divided government? Explain your answer.

▲ American Independent Party presidential candidate George C. Wallace campaigns in Culver City, California, in 1968.

SECTION 3
The Minor Parties

Guiding Question

What role have minor parties played in American politics? Use a flowchart to take notes on the role of minor parties in American politics.

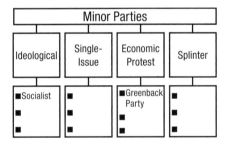

Objectives:

- Identify minor parties that have made a difference in American politics.
- Understand why minor parties are important.

You may have heard the names H. Ross Perot or Ralph Nader during recent elections. Political parties called Libertarian, Reform, Prohibition, American Independent, Green, and Constitution may be other names that you recognize. These are some of the candidates and minor parties that have appeared on recent election ballots. A minor party has never won a presidential election, but minor parties do play an important role in American politics.

What are the types of minor parties in the United States?

Minor parties in the United States are called third parties and the members of each share the same beliefs. These beliefs are often different from the beliefs of the two major political parties—the Democrats and the Republicans. Minor parties do not have the power of the major parties. Minor parties usually do not have enough money or support to get their candidates elected. The most they can do is take votes away from major party candidates. This has happened in several elections in our country's history. Although minor party candidates often have little chance of winning, they are still important.

There are four types of minor parties:

Ideological Parties: An ideological party is based on a certain set of beliefs. Some have been around a long time and are based on social, political, or economic issues. Three examples are the Socialist, Socialist Labor, and Communist parties. Others, such as the Libertarian Party, want more individual rights and less government control.

Reading Strategy
Visualizing
Read the descriptions of the four types of minor parties. With a partner, discuss which group you think might have the best chance of winning the next election in your community.

■ ■ ■ ■ ■ ■ ■ ■ ■ ■ ■ ■ ■ ■ ■ ■ ■

Ideological party
A political party based on a certain set of beliefs, such as political or economic issues

Single-issue party
A political party that focuses on one main concern

Economic protest party
A political party that forms during difficult economic times; often upset with current problems and demand reforms

Splinter party
A political party that has broken away from one of the major parties

Single-Issue Parties: These parties focus on only one main concern and usually do not last. One example is the Free Soil Party. It wanted to stop the spread of slavery in the mid-1800s. Today's Right to Life Party is another example. It opposes abortion.

Economic Protest Parties: These parties have appeared during periods of economic struggle. They have voiced their unhappiness with the major parties. They have focused on issues such as foreign imports or banking. An example was the Greenback Party of 1876–1884. This party wanted an income tax, labor laws, and regulation of the railroads. Economic protest parties usually fade after an economic crisis is over.

Splinter Parties: Splinter parties are parties that have broken away from a major party. Most of the more important minor parties have been splinter parties. Three examples are the Progressive Party (1912 and 1924), the States' Rights (Dixiecrat) Party (1948), and the American Independent Party (1968).

The Green Party led by Ralph Nader does not fit into the types of minor parties described above. The Green Party began with a single issue but has grown since 2000. The Green Party has taken on a number of issues including environmental concerns, healthcare, campaign finance reform, and opposition to free trade.

The Green Party refused to nominate Ralph Nader in 2004 and 2008. In 2004, they chose attorney and political activist David Cobb. In 2008, the Green Party nominated Cynthia McKinney, a former Congresswoman from Georgia. McKinney supported universal healthcare, an end to the war in Iraq, and repeal of the Patriot Act.

✔**Checkpoint**   What are the four different types of minor parties?

Why are minor parties important?

Although many Americans do not support them, minor parties play an important role in American politics. Minor parties can influence the outcome of elections. Their candidate may be popular and may take votes away from the major candidates. This has happened several times in history. For example, Ralph Nader and the Green Party took votes away from Al Gore, the Democratic candidate, in 2000. This can happen in state and local elections also. See Figure 5.8 to examine just how important minor parties can be in an election.

Fig. 5.8 **How Government Works**

Minor Parties in History

Minor parties have been important throughout the history of our country. They have given voters options other than the major party candidates. They have also caused the major parties to take another look at their own platforms. At certain times in history, minor parties have played an important role in presidential elections. *Have minor-party candidates had an impact on presidential elections in recent years?*

Significant Minor Party Efforts, 1848 to Today*

Year	Party	% Popular Vote	Electoral Votes
1848	Free Soil	10.13	---
1856	American	21.55	8
1860	Constitutional Union	12.64	39
1880	Greenback	3.36	---
1888	Prohibition	2.19	---
1892	Populist	8.54	22
	Prohibition	2.19	---
1904	Socialist	2.98	---
1908	Socialist	2.82	---
1912	Progressive (Bull Moose)	27.39	88
	Socialist	5.99	---
1916	Socialist	3.17	---
1920	Socialist	3.45	---
1924	Progressive	16.16	13
1932	Socialist	2.22	---
1948	States' Rights (Dixiecrat)	2.41	39
1968	American Independent	13.53	46
1996	Reform	8.40	---
2000	Green	2.74	---
2004	Libertarian	2.89	---

*Includes all minor parties that polled at least 2% of the popular vote
SOURCE: Historical Statistics of the United States, Colonial Times to 1970; U.S. Census Bureau

Minor parties often present issues that may appeal to a major party. The major party may then support those ideas. Usually this happens when many citizens see the need for change and support the minority ideas. Some issues that were originally brought to attention by a minor party were the income tax and voting rights for women. It was a minor party—the Anti-Masons—that first used a national convention to nominate a candidate. The Whigs and Democrats soon followed. Now both major parties use conventions to nominate candidates.

Despite their importance, minor parties have many problems to overcome. They usually do not have the money needed to promote their candidates and programs. Newspapers, television, and radio usually do not give minor party candidates much attention.

For a summary on minor parties, see Figure 5.9 on the next page.

✔ **Checkpoint** How can minor parties affect the outcome of an election?

Fig. 5.9

Minor Parties
• Have difficulty winning elections in the American party system
• May form based on an ideology or single issue, as a result of bad economic times, or from part of an existing party
• Though rarely successful, often influence elections and the major parties

Biography

Ralph Nader 1934–

Ralph Nader was born in Connecticut in 1934. After graduating from Princeton University and Harvard Law School, he worked as a lawyer. In 1965, Nader wrote a book on the American auto industry. His book prompted Congress to pass safety laws. Since that time, Nader has continued to push for laws that protect consumers, workers, taxpayers, and the environment. Nader has criticized the major parties for relying so much on wealthy supporters to fund their campaigns. Nader has run for President several times as a minor party candidate. In 1996 and 2000, he ran as the Green Party candidate. In 2004, he ran as the Reform Party candidate and collected over 400,000 votes.

Essential Questions Journal Go to your **Essential Questions Journal** to work on this chapter's Essential Question.

SECTION 3 ASSESSMENT

1. **Guiding Question** Use your completed flowchart to answer this question: What role have minor parties played in American politics?

Key Terms and Comprehension

On a sheet of paper, write the letter that correctly answers each question.

2. Which type of party focuses on one main concern?

   A. ideological　　**C.** single-issue
   B. major　　　　 **D.** coalition

3. Which type of party is one that often forms during difficult times?

   A. economic protest　**C.** splinter
   B. ideological　　　　**D.** partisanship

4. When members of a major party break away, what is it called?

   A. single-issue　　**C.** coalition
   B. splinter　　　　 **D.** leading

5. Which type of party focuses on social or economic beliefs?

   A. economic protest　**C.** platform
   B. single-issue　　　 **D.** ideological

Critical Thinking

6. **Draw Inferences** Why do you think there are so many types of minor parties? Explain your answer.

7. **Identify Central Issues** How do you think a minor party might gain support and become more successful in an election?

Working on a Political Campaign

Campaigning in Full Swing

"In the final days of the campaign, both camps worked for success on election day. Phone banks made thousands of calls trying to convince the few undecided voters. Supporters held campaign signs at almost every intersection. The candidates rushed from appearance to appearance, all in an exhausting sprint to the finish in this hotly contested election."

An election is a great celebration of our democratic system. Even if you cannot vote, you can still play a part in deciding who our leaders will be. While many political campaigns have paid staff, it is volunteers who perform much of the actual work. Indeed, a strong volunteer group can spell the difference between victory and defeat. Here's how to do it:

1. Get to Know the Candidate One excellent way to learn about the candidates is to visit their Web sites. Candidates might have a short biography, videos, press releases, and blogs posted. Typically they also provide a chance to ask questions and receive an e-mail response. If a candidate does not have a Web site, his or her campaign office can provide similar information. Another good option might be to see the candidate in person.

2. Choose a Candidate Once you are more familiar with a candidate and his or her positions, decide if that candidate's beliefs reflect your own. It is important to volunteer your time for a person you believe in. Be prepared to talk about his or her views.

3. Find Out About Volunteer Opportunities Political campaigns offer a wide range of volunteer opportunities. A candidate may be looking for people to go door-to-door to seek support. The campaign may need people to host or attend events. Most campaigns need people to make phone calls or send out mailings. Campaigns also appreciate financial contributions.

4. Choose a Task Before you choose a task, be sure you are able to fulfill it. For example, if you do not have access to a car or a ride, avoid a task that would need transportation. If your studies are demanding, do not commit to making phone calls every night. Though you may not be able to do every job, you will be able to find some way to get involved. Hopefully you will find it a rewarding experience.

▶▶ What do you think?

1. Whom should you contact to find out which candidates are running for office in your town or state?
2. How might volunteering for a campaign help you become a more informed voter?

GOVERNMENT ONLINE
Citizenship Activity Pack
For an activity about working on a political campaign, go to
PearsonSuccessNet.com

SECTION 4

Party Organization

▲ Howard Dean served as the Democratic Party's national chairperson in the 2008 election.

Guiding Question

How are political parties organized on the national, state, and local levels? Use a chart to take notes on how political parties are organized.

Party Organization		
National	State	Local
■ National Convention	■ Central Committee	■
■	■	■
■	■	

Objectives:

■ Understand why the major parties do not have a central structure.

■ Describe national parties and how parties are organized at the state and local levels.

You may have noticed television commercials for political candidates. Your family may have received mail that describes a certain candidate's view on important issues. Political parties may also have made telephone calls to your home asking for support in an upcoming election. These are just a few ways the party committees at the national, state, and local levels work to educate voters about their candidates.

Why do major parties not have a central structure?

Although it may seem hard to believe, the two major political parties are not well organized. Neither party has a chain of command from the national to the state to the local level. Each state and local unit of a political party also works independently. The groups usually cooperate more during election time.

The members of the President's party often work more closely together than the other party. The party not in power may have several strong, well-known political figures who act as leaders. These party members may be in competition with one another. This adds to the lack of organization. See Figure 5.10 on the next page.

Another reason the parties do not have a strong central structure is federalism. The United States has more than a half million elected offices. In our federal system, these offices and departments are located in all parts of the country. They are found at the national, state, and local levels. Each political party has members serving in these offices and departments nationwide.

The nomination process is another cause for a lack of central structure. The selection of party candidates often involves a struggle within the party. The process causes members of the same party to oppose one another. This can create divisions in the party.

✔ Checkpoint What are two reasons that political parties do not have a strong central structure?

How are the major parties organized at the national level?

Both parties are organized the same way at the national level. They focus on the national convention, the national committee, the national chairperson, and the congressional campaign committees. The national convention meets in the summer of presidential election years. At the convention, the candidates for President and Vice President are named. The delegates to the convention also write the party's platform and the party's rules.

Between the conventions, a national committee and a national chairperson run the party business. Both national party committees have grown over the years.

Fig. 5.10

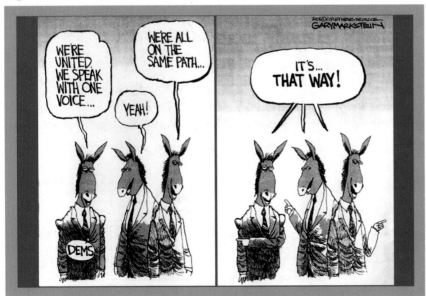

▲ Analyzing Political Cartoons *How does this cartoon show the decentralized nature of political parties?*

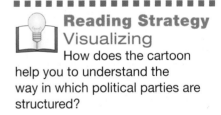

Reading Strategy
Visualizing
How does the cartoon help you to understand the way in which political parties are structured?

■ ■ ■ ■ ■ ■ ■ ■ ■ ■ ■ ■ ■ ■ ■

Reading Strategy
Visualizing
How could this text be written differently to help you better visualize the political party organization at the national level?

■ ■ ■ ■ ■ ■ ■ ■ ■ ■ ■ ■ ■ ■ ■

Primary election
An election to choose candidates or select delegates to a party convention

Caucus
A group of like-minded people who meet to select candidates they will support in an upcoming election

In each party, the national chairperson leads the national committee. This person serves for a four-year term. He or she works in Washington, D.C. The national chairperson runs the campaign and convention during elections. Between elections, the chairperson and the committee work to increase the power of the party. Other duties include raising money, getting new voters, and preparing for the next election.

Each party also has a campaign committee in each house of Congress. Members of these committees help with political campaigns in the Senate and House. They also try to win back seats from the opposing party when possible. Committee members are chosen by other members of their house of Congress. The committee members serve for a two-year term.

✓ **Checkpoint**   What is the role of the national party chairperson?

How are major parties organized at the state level?

State law sets up the structure of political parties at the state level. Like the national political parties, the state parties have a central committee. The state central committee is led by a state chairperson.

The members of the state central committee usually come from the counties located within the state. They are chosen by **primary elections,** local **caucuses,** or at state conventions. A primary election is an election to choose candidates or select delegates to a party convention. A caucus is a group of like-minded people who meet to select candidates they will support in an upcoming election.

The chairperson of the committee is often a well-known political figure. The chairperson and committee work to keep the party together. They also find candidates and bring in money for the election campaign. The committee's job is difficult. This is because members are often competing for power.

✓ **Checkpoint**   How are members of the state committee chosen?

▲ State delegates attending national conventions represent the population of a particular state.

How are major parties organized at the local level?

At the local level, the organization of the party follows the electoral map of the state. There is a party unit for congressional districts, counties, cities, towns, **wards,** and **precincts.** A ward is a unit into which cities are divided for the election of city council members. A precinct is a very small unit within which all voters report to one polling place.

In large cities, the local units may be divided into smaller areas such as blocks or large apartment buildings. In some places, local party organizations are active year-round. Most often they are busiest during the time before an election.

✔ **Checkpoint** What is a precinct?

Ward
A unit into which cities are divided for the election of city council members

Precinct
A very small unit where all voters report to one place

SECTION 4 ASSESSMENT

Essential Questions Journal Go to your **Essential Questions Journal** to work on this chapter's Essential Question.

Word Bank

caucus

chairperson

federalism

local

1. **Guiding Question** Use your completed chart to answer this question: How are political parties organized on the national, state, and local levels?

Key Terms and Comprehension

On a sheet of paper, use the words from the Word Bank to complete each sentence correctly.

2. _____ is one reason the parties do not have a strong central structure. Government offices and departments are located throughout the country.

3. The national committee and national _____ run each party's business between conventions.

4. Members of a state committee may be chosen by a primary election or a _____.

5. The _____ organization of a party follows the state's electoral map.

Critical Thinking

6. **Recognize Cause and Effect** Why do you think members of the party not in power have a more difficult time working together?

7. **Draw Inferences** Why do you think the Republican National Committee and the Democratic National Committee are such large organizations?

Chapter Summary

Section 1—Parties and What They Do

- Political parties are groups of people who share many of the same beliefs about government.

- Political parties have nominating, educating, bonding agent, governing, and watchdog functions.

- The United States has a two-party political system.

- Many European countries have a multiparty system. In a one-party system, only the ruling party is allowed.

Section 2—Two-Party System in American History

- Andrew Jackson formed the Democratic Party. He wanted common people to have more say in government. The Republican Party began in 1854. Members of the party opposed slavery.

- From 1800 to 1860, the Democrats won most presidential elections. From 1860 to 1932, the Republicans were in power most often. In 1932, the Democrats took back power, and this lasted largely until 1968. Since 1968, the government has been divided, with neither party controlling both the presidency and Congress for long periods of time.

Section 3—The Minor Parties

- There are four main types of minor parties. Ideological parties are often based on social or economic issues. Single-issue parties focus on one main concern. Economic protest parties appear during difficult times and demand change. A splinter party is a minor party that has broken apart from a major party.

Section 4—Party Organization

- At the national level, political parties focus on the national convention, the national committee, the national chairperson, and the congressional campaign committees.

- The State committee works to bring the party together, to find candidates, and to raise money for campaigns.

- Local committees are organized by the state's electoral map.

Guiding Question
Section 1 What are political parties, and how do they function in our two-party system?

Guiding Question
Section 2 How has the two-party system affected the history of American government?

Guiding Question
Section 3 What role have minor parties played in American politics?

Guiding Question
Section 4 How are political parties organized on the federal, state, and local levels?

CHAPTER 5

Essential Question
Does the two-party system help or harm democracy?

Document-Based Assessment

Theodore Roosevelt and the Progressive Party

In 1912, Theodore Roosevelt formed the Progressive Party, nicknamed the "Bull Moose" Party, and ran as its candidate. (Roosevelt had previously been elected President on the Republican ticket in 1900 and 1904.) He received so many votes that William H. Taft, the incumbent candidate, lost the election to Woodrow Wilson, the Democrat. Taft received only 8 electoral votes to Roosevelt's 88 votes.

The campaign speech that follows is one Roosevelt gave in Milwaukee, Wisconsin. Roosevelt had been shot in the chest just before entering the hall, but decided to go on with the speech. Although the bullet was lodged in his chest, it had hit his eyeglass case and his folded speech, thus saving his life.

Document at a Glance

■ Theodore Roosevelt's speech

■ Progressive Movement

■ Asked citizens for their votes

"Friends, I shall ask you to be as quiet as possible. I don't know whether you fully understand that I have just been shot; but it takes more than that to kill a Bull Moose. . . .

The bullet is in me now, so I cannot make a long speech, but I will try my best. . . .

I believe that the Progressive movement is making life a little easier for all our people; a movement to try to take the burdens off the men and especially the women and children of this country. I am absorbed in the success of that movement. . . . Now, friends, what we Progressives are trying to do is to enroll rich or poor, whatever their social or industrial position, to stand together for the . . . rights of good citizenship. . . ." I ask you to . . . read our platform about social and industrial injustice and then, friends, vote for the Progressive ticket . . . for only by voting for that platform you can be true to the cause of progress throughout this Union."

Document-Based Questions

1. Which party did Roosevelt belong to before he formed the Progressive Party?

2. How did Roosevelt prevent Taft from becoming President?

3. What did Roosevelt say the Progressive movement was doing?

4. At the end of his speech, what did Roosevelt ask people to do?

5. **Visualize** Based on Roosevelt's words, how do you picture people reacting to the speech?

SOURCE: *www.theodoreroosevelt.org/research/speech%20kill%20moose.htm*

Chapter Assessment

Directions: Choose the letter of the best answer or write the answer using complete sentences.

Section 1—Parties and What They Do

1. What type of party are the Republicans and Democrats?

A. major   **B.** minor   **C.** first   **D.** third

2. Which people at national conventions listen to the party's ideas and write the party's platform?

A. candidates   **C.** partisans

B. delegates   **D.** liberals

3. What is the main goal of a political party?

4. How do the two major parties use bipartisanship?

5. **Critical Thinking** Explain the differences among a two-party system, a multiparty system, and a one-party system.

Section 2—Two-Party System in American History

6. Which party supported a strong central government?

A. Whigs   **C.** Federalists

B. Tories   **D.** Anti-Federalists

7. Who was the Democratic candidate in 1828 that was elected President?

A. Jackson   **B.** Washington   **C.** Lincoln   **D.** Jefferson

8. What was the main issue of the Republican Party in 1854?

9. **Critical Thinking** How have the Republicans and Democrats controlled the government from 1800 to today? Explain.

Section 3—The Minor Parties

10. What is another name for a minor party?

A. third   **B.** major   **C.** recent   **D.** democracy

11. Who did Ralph Nader take votes away from in the 2000 election?

A. Bush   **B.** Perot   **C.** Clinton   **D.** Gore

12. What is the difference between an ideological party and an economic protest party?

13. **Critical Thinking** How can a minor party affect a major party's platform?

Section 4—Party Organization

14. Which process is one reason for a lack of national party structure because it pits members against one another?

    A. federalism

    B. delegate

    C. nomination

    D. campaign

15. What are the RNC and the DNC for each political party?

    A. members

    B. leaders

    C. candidates

    D. committees

16. What is the job of the political party national chairperson?

17. **Critical Thinking** Why do you think state and local political parties are important during a campaign and an election?

Apply What You've Learned

Exploring the Essential Question

18. Discuss how the two-party political system has changed over time. Create a graphic organizer to show how the two-party system began and what it looks like today.

19. If the United States moved from a two-party system to a multiparty system, do you think the federal government would change? Explain your answer.

Essential Question Activity

20. Based on your research, work with a partner to write an opinion paper that answers the Essential Question: Does the two-party system help or harm democracy?

Essential Questions
Journal

Go to your **Essential Questions Journal** to work on this chapter's Essential Question.

Test-Taking Tip

Study test material with a partner. Take turns quizzing each other on the material.

A college student casts her first-ever ballot in a presidential election in Springfield, Missouri.

Voters and Voter Behavior

Essential Question
Why do voters act as they do?

Section 1: The Right to Vote

Section 2: Voter Qualifications

Section 3: Suffrage and Civil Rights

Section 4: Voter Behavior

Reading Strategy: Inferencing
Sometimes the meaning of a text is not directly stated. You have to "read between the lines" to figure out what the text means. Use what you already know and what you just read to put the meaning together.

What I Know + What I Read = Inference

GOVERNMENT ONLINE
ON THE GO

To study anywhere, anytime, download these online resources at PearsonSuccessNet.com
• **Political Dictionary**
• **Audio Review**
• **Downloadable Interactivities**

▲ A volunteer helps a voter with instructions to vote.

SECTION 1

The Right to Vote

How have voting rights changed over the course of U.S. history?
Use a graphic organizer to take notes on the history of voting rights.

History of Voting Rights	
Early 1800s	
1870	
1920	Women have the right to vote.
1960s	
1970s	

Objectives:

- Summarize the history of voting rights in the United States.
- Understand constitutional restrictions on the states' power to set voting qualifications.

The right to vote is protected by the Constitution. United States citizens have the freedom to choose our country's leaders.

Although the United States is a government of, for, and by the people, the number of people who vote in elections is low. Most other democratic countries have higher voter turnouts than the United States. In a nonpresidential election, less than 40 percent of the eligible voters go to the polls. In local elections, sometimes only 10 percent of the people vote.

Many citizens choose not to use their right to vote. They have no interest in voting. They may feel that their vote would not make any difference. They may not know how to register to vote. Some people may feel that the government is running well and no change is needed.

What is the history of voting rights?

Voting rights were set in the Constitution in 1789. The states were given the power to set **suffrage** qualifications, or decide who would have the right to vote. Another word for suffrage is **franchise.**

In 1789, only white, male property owners were allowed to vote. Over the years, new laws were passed in some states that gave more people the right to vote. These laws said citizens could vote even if they did not own property or pay taxes. Later, new laws said citizens could no longer be kept from voting because of their race, gender, or religion. The federal government gradually took control over the right to vote during this time. Today in America, the **electorate** (people who may vote) includes nearly all citizens who are at least 18 years of age.

As shown in Figure 6.1 and in Figure 6.3 on page 131, changes in voting requirements occurred over the course of five eras:

1. During the 1800s, religious, property ownership, and tax payment requirements for voting were ended in most states.

2. After the Civil War, the 15th Amendment allowed all male citizens of legal age to vote. However, African Americans were still kept from voting in many states. After 1920, they were the largest group of **disenfranchised** citizens, which means citizens prevented from voting.

3. In 1920, the 19th Amendment allowed women to vote. Before that, women could vote in some states (Figure 6.2 on the next page). The territory of Wyoming had given women the right to vote in 1869.

4. In the 1960s, civil rights acts were passed, guaranteeing the right to vote. The Voting Rights Act of 1965 was the most important of these acts. Also during the 1960s, the 23rd Amendment added the voters of the District of Columbia to the electorate. In 1964, the 24th Amendment banned the **poll tax,** a special tax that people had to pay in order to vote.

5. In 1971, the 26th Amendment was passed. It set the minimum voting age at 18.

Suffrage
The right to vote

Franchise
A synonym for suffrage; the right to vote

Electorate
All the people that may vote

Disenfranchised
Not allowed to vote

Poll tax
A tax paid to vote

Fig. 6.1
The Five Stages of Expanding Suffrage

Suffrage was gradually expanded over a period of nearly 200 years.
As more and more Americans gained the right to vote, how have election results been affected?

Early 1800s	1870	1920	1965	1971
Religious, property, and tax qualifications begin to disappear in every state.	15th Amendment prohibits voting restrictions based on race or color.	19th Amendment removes voting restrictions based on sex.	The Voting Rights Act of 1965 enforces racial equality at polling places.	26th Amendment sets the minimum voting age at 18.

Fig. 6.2

Women's Suffrage in 1919

GOVERNMENT ONLINE

Audio Tour
To learn more about women's suffrage, visit
PearsonSuccessNet.com

▼ **Interpreting Maps** Before the 19th Amendment, several states and territories had given women suffrage in different forms. This map shows the type of suffrage granted in each state. *What can you tell about women's suffrage in the different regions of the United States?*

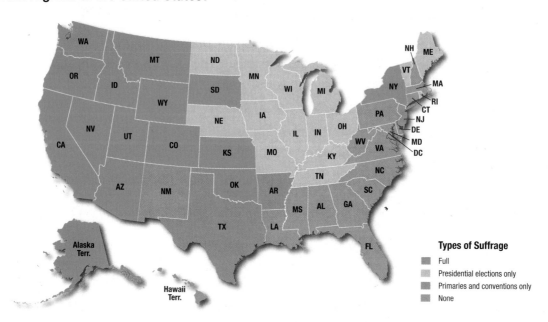

Types of Suffrage
- Full
- Presidential elections only
- Primaries and conventions only
- None

**Reading Strategy
Inferencing**
What do you already know about this topic?

Who has the power to set voter qualifications?

The Constitution does not allow the federal government to set voter qualifications. The Constitution does, however, place five restrictions on the states. These five restrictions are the following:

1. Voters of each state who vote for the "most numerous branch" can then vote for representatives and senators in Congress. This restriction has no meaning today. Voters, with a few exceptions, are allowed to vote in all elections in a state.

2. No state can deprive a person of the right to vote because of race or color (15th Amendment).

3. No state can deprive a person of the right to vote because of sex (19th Amendment).

4. No state can require payment of tax as a condition to vote for any federal officer: President, Vice President, or member of Congress (24th Amendment).

5. No state can deny a person who is at least 18 years old the right to vote (26th Amendment).

✔ **Checkpoint** What requirement did the 24th Amendment end?

Fig. 6.3

Expansion of Voting Rights in the U.S.

Original Electorate
Voting generally limited to white male property owners.

▼

Expansion Era #1
Religious qualifications and property-ownership requirements eliminated; by the mid-1800s, most white males could vote.

▼

Expansion Era #2
After the Civil War, the 15th Amendment was intended to protect any male citizen from being denied the vote because of race or color.

▼

Expansion Era #3
The 19th Amendment, ratified in 1920, gave women the right to vote in every state.

▼

Expansion Era #4
Court decisions and federal legislation, especially the Voting Rights Act of 1965 and its later extensions, finally made the 15th Amendment truly effective.

▼

Expansion Era #5
In 1971, the 26th Amendment lowered the voting age to 18.

Reading Strategy
Inferencing
After reading this section, what inference can you make about the right to vote? What words helped you make this inference?

Essential Questions Journal Go to your **Essential Questions Journal** to work on this chapter's Essential Question.

SECTION 1 ASSESSMENT

Word Bank

poll tax

suffrage

19th Amendment

26th Amendment

Quick Write
On a sheet of paper, describe why you think the right to vote is important. Use complete sentences. Before you begin your paragraph, brainstorm a list of reasons why voting is an important right in the United States. Share your paragraph with the class.

1. **Guiding Question** Use your completed graphic organizer to answer this question: How have voting rights changed over the course of U.S. history?

Key Terms and Comprehension
On a sheet of paper, use the words from the Word Bank to complete each sentence correctly.

2. The right to vote is called _____.

3. When people had to pay money to vote, it was called a _____.

4. The _____ gave women in every state the right to vote.

5. The _____ set the voting age in the United States at 18.

Critical Thinking

6. **Analyze Information** Why do you think only white male landowners were allowed to vote in 1789?

7. **Summarize** What five restrictions does the Constitution put on the states for voter qualifications?

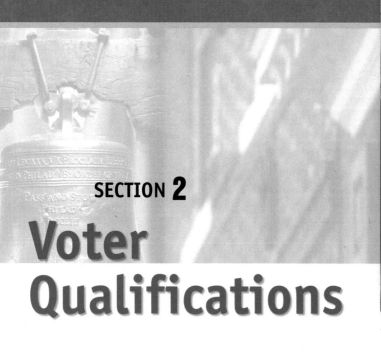

SECTION 2

Voter Qualifications

▲ Members of the armed forces stationed outside the United States vote by absentee ballot.

Guiding Question

What are the requirements for voting, and how have they changed over time? Use the flowchart to record information about voter qualifications in the United States.

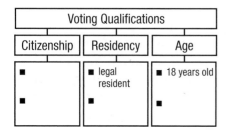

Voting Qualifications		
Citizenship	Residency	Age
■ ■	■ legal resident	■ 18 years old ■

Objectives:

- Identify the requirements for voting in the United States.
- Explain the other requirements that states have used or still use as voting qualifications.

In order to vote, a person must meet certain requirements or qualifications. All states have similar qualifications of citizenship, residency, and age. Most people can easily qualify to vote.

Citizens have a responsibility to take part in government. Voting is one of the easiest and most effective ways to become a good citizen. In this section, you will learn the qualifications for voting, now and in the past.

What are the universal requirements for voting?

In most states, a voter must register to vote in his or her own county. United States citizens have the right to vote if they are at least 18 years old. They also must have lived in a state for a period of time, usually 30 days. No person may be denied the right to vote because of race, color, sex, or religion. The right to vote is a civil right.

Each state requires a person to be a legal resident of that state in order to vote (Figure 6.4). States made this requirement to prevent voters from being brought in at election time, which had been done in the past. States also allow new residents time to learn about the issues and the candidates. For this reason, some states have a short waiting period for new residents, usually no longer than 30 days. The Voting Rights Act of 1970 and various Supreme Court decisions set 30 days as a reasonable waiting period. **Transients,** people living in a state for a short time, are usually not allowed to vote. In some states, college students may vote if they name their college as their residence.

The citizenship requirement for voting denies **aliens** the right to vote. Aliens are residents of the United States who were born in a foreign country. They have not yet become citizens. Only two states, Minnesota and Pennsylvania, have requirements for how long a new citizen must wait before voting. Minnesota requires three months. Pennsylvania requires only one month.

The 26th Amendment says that a citizen who is 18 years of age or older shall not be denied the right to vote. Every state must follow this amendment. Before this amendment was passed, the accepted age to vote in most states was 21.

During World War II, there was a movement to lower the voting age. Then, during the Vietnam War, the 26th Amendment was finally passed. Many people believed that if a person was old enough to fight in a war, the person was old enough to vote. The response to the 26th Amendment has not been great among 18- to 21-year-olds. In election after election, young voters are less likely to vote than any other age group.

✔ **Checkpoint**   What waiting period for voting did the Voting Rights Act decide on?

Transient
Person living in a state for only a short time, without legal residence

Alien
Foreign-born resident

Fig. 6.4
Residency Requirements

Where You Live Determines Where You Vote

In order to vote in elections today, voters must be citizens. They must have an established residence in their voting location. *Why do you think some states have different residency requirements?*

Large ceremonies (at right) are often held when people are sworn in as citizens. ▷

▸ States require voters to be residents.

▸ A person can have only one residence.

▸ Some states have provided registration qualifications that require people to have lived in a place for a certain amount of time.

▸ Naturalized citizens can vote once they become citizens.

■ ■ ■ ■ ■ ■ ■ ■ ■ ■ ■ ■ ■ ■ ■ ■
Reading Strategy
Inferencing
What do you already
know about voter registration?

What is registration?

Qualified persons must register to vote in the voting district where they live (**Figure 6.5**). A person may register at the courthouse of the voting district. Sometimes other places of **registration** will be set up. The names of persons who register are recorded on the district's list of qualified voters. This list is meant to prevent people from voting more than once.

Any citizen who votes regularly is considered an active voter. Citizens who no longer live in a district are removed from the voter list. This process, known as **purging,** is usually done every two or four years. A person who has been purged must register again in order to vote. When purging is not done, the **poll books** become clogged with people who are no longer eligible to vote. Poll books are the official lists of qualified voters in each precinct.

There have been controversies over the registration process. Those who oppose voter registration requirements think that voter turnout declined when most states adopted the registration process. European democracies have high voter turnout, but in those countries laws require voter registration. In the United States, each person may decide whether or not to register to vote.

Some feel that voter registration is necessary to avoid fraud. However, many want to make registration easier. In 1993, Congress passed a law that required every state (except North Dakota) to do so. That law, known as the "Motor Voter Law," became effective in 1995. It directs every state to (1) allow all eligible citizens to register to vote when they apply for or renew a driver's license, (2) provide for voter registration by mail, and (3) make registration forms available at state employment offices and social service agencies. The Federal Election Commission reported that by the year 2000, about eight million people had registered to vote as a direct result of the Motor Voter Law.

Fig. 6.5 How Government Works

Registering to Vote

Location, Location, Location

Registering to vote has become much easier in recent years. Mail-in forms are available in most schools, in public libraries, and on Web sites. Forms can even be found at public events, such as concerts. *Why do you think registration has been made easier in recent years?*

Getting a **LICENSE**

Since 1995, the Motor Voter Act has allowed people to register when applying for or renewing driver's licenses.

At **EVENTS**

Voter registration also occurs at concerts, rallies, fairs, or shopping centers, and on high school and college campuses.

LOCALLY

Most voters register locally, at the county clerk's office or with an officer usually called the registrar of elections.

The law also requires every state to mail a questionnaire to each of its registered voters every two to four years. This way, the poll books can be purged of names of people who have died or moved out of the state. It also forbids the states to purge for any other reason, including failure to vote.

There is usually controversy between Democrats and Republicans over the registration process. Many Republicans believe that firm rules on registration and voting are necessary to avoid illegal voting. A large number of Democrats say strict requirements often unfairly discourage elderly, disabled, poor, and minority groups from voting.

✔ **Checkpoint** What is one positive result of the Motor Voter Law?

What was the qualification of literacy?

Literacy means the ability to read or write. In the past, literacy was a requirement for voting in some states. Many African Americans, Native Americans, and Latinos were kept from voting using the literacy requirement. This requirement was different in each state. In some states, voters had to prove they could read and write. In other states, voters had to understand very difficult paragraphs and explain them.

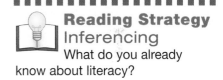

Registration
Procedure of voter identification intended to stop election fraud

Purge
The process of reviewing lists of registered voters and removing the names of those no longer eligible to vote

Poll book
A list of all registered voters in a precinct

Literacy
The ability to read or write

Reading Strategy
Inferencing
What do you already know about literacy?

Government in Your Life

Do Young People Vote?

In 1971, the voting age was lowered from 21 to 18. That year, many young people were fighting in Vietnam or involved in the civil rights movement but could not vote. Those young people successfully lobbied for the passage of the 26th Amendment, which changed the voting age. In the 1972 presidential election, 48 percent of young people under the age of 30 voted. From 1972 until 2006, the number of younger voters dropped. In the 2008 presidential election, approximately 52 percent of voters under the age of 30 went to the polls.

However, there are more than 30 million Americans between the ages of 18 and 24. Many young people report they do not vote. They claim political leaders do not meet their needs. Others say they are too busy or know little about the candidates. Some young people say they do not know how to register or where to vote. Some of these problems may easily be solved by looking up the candidates online, or by using mail-in or absentee ballots to vote. For young people unhappy with politics, voting is the easiest way to make a difference.

In 1855, Connecticut became the first state to have literacy requirements, followed by Massachusetts in 1857. The tests were intended to keep Irish Catholic immigrants from voting. By 1890, most southern states also had literacy requirements. These literacy requirements were intended to disenfranchise African Americans (Figure 6.6). White males who could not pass the literacy requirement were also kept from voting. Many states then decided to add a "grandfather clause" to their constitutions. The clause stated that any man, or his male descendants, that had voted before the 15th Amendment (1870) could become a legal voter. He did not have to meet the literacy requirement.

Several other states, beginning with Wyoming in 1889, also added the literacy requirement. Alaska was the last to adopt the requirement, in 1949. Finally, Congress banned the use of literacy tests as a requirement for voting. This was done with the Voting Rights Act of 1970. At this time, 18 states were using literacy as a requirement for voting.

✔ **Checkpoint**   Why were literacy requirements first used in Connecticut and Massachusetts?

Fig. 6.6
Registration Requirements

Literacy tests were used in many states. They were used to deny African Americans the right to vote. The questions below are from a literacy test that was used during that time. The tests were also changed many times. Changing the tests made it impossible to study for them. *How might these questions discourage eligible citizens from registering to vote?*

A voter fills out a registration form. ▷

Can you answer these?

1. If you have been employed by another employer during the last five years, state the nature of your employment and the name or names of such employer or employers and his or their adresses.

2. Give the names of the places, respectively, where you have lived during the last five years; and the name or names by which you have been known during the last five years.

3. Are you now or have you ever been affiliated with any group or organization which advocates the overthrow of the United States government or the government of any state of the United States by unlawful means?

4. Name some of the duties and obligations of citizenship. Do you regard those duties and obligations as having priority over the duties and obligations you owe to any other secular organization when they are in conflict?

Source: The Honorable Rufus A. Lewis Collection at Trenholm State Technical College Archives

How have taxes been used as a voting requirement?

For many years, some states used the payment of property taxes as a requirement for voting. A special tax, called the poll tax, was also used in the southern states. The poll tax was used in order to keep African Americans from voting. The poll tax was not very effective. By 1966 only four states still had a poll tax. In 1964, the 24th Amendment was passed. All taxes were banned as requirements for voting in a federal election. In *Harper* v. *Virginia Board of Elections* (1966), the Court declared the poll tax went against the 14th Amendment's Equal Protection Clause. The poll tax and all other taxes could no longer be used as requirements for voting.

■■■■■■■■■■■■■■■■■■■■
Reading Strategy
Inferencing
Read the paragraph. Why might the poll tax not have been effective?

✔**Checkpoint**   Which amendment outlawed the poll tax?

Are some people denied the right to vote?

Every state does deny the right to vote to certain people. People in mental institutions or those legally declared mentally unfit are usually not allowed to vote. Convicted criminals are temporarily denied the right to vote. Recently, some states have allowed most convicted criminals to get back their voting rights. A few states deny the right to vote to people who were dishonorably discharged from the military.

| **Essential Questions** **Journal** | Go to your **Essential Questions Journal** to work on this chapter's Essential Question. |

SECTION **2** ASSESSMENT

■■

1. **Guiding Question** Use your completed flowchart to answer this question: What are the requirements for voting, and how have they changed over time?

Key Terms and Comprehension
On a sheet of paper, write the answer to each question. Use complete sentences.

2. What is literacy?

3. What must a person who has been purged do in order to vote?

4. What is a poll book?

5. Which people can legally be denied the right to vote?

Critical Thinking

6. **Express Problems Clearly** What are the pros and cons of voter registration?

7. **Draw Inferences** Why do you think "grandfather clauses" were added to literacy requirements for voter registration?

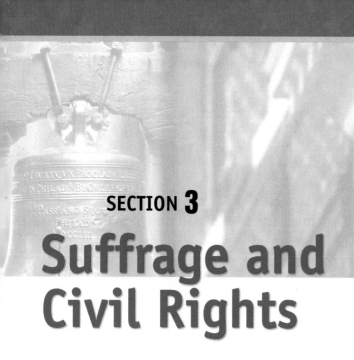

SECTION 3

Suffrage and Civil Rights

Dr. Martin Luther King, Jr., casts his ballot in Atlanta, Georgia, on November 3, 1964.

Guiding Question

How did the United States fulfill the promise of the 15th Amendment? Use the chart to record details of the history of voting rights for African Americans.

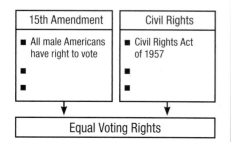

15th Amendment	Civil Rights
■ All male Americans have right to vote	■ Civil Rights Act of 1957
■	■
■	■

Equal Voting Rights

Objectives:

- Describe the passage of the 15th Amendment and the tactics used in an effort to keep African Americans from voting.
- Explain the importance of the civil rights legislation passed in 1957, 1960, and 1964.
- Analyze the Voting Rights Act of 1965.

Voting is very important in a democracy. In the past, not all Americans were granted suffrage. After a long, hard struggle, African Americans and other minority groups gained their civil rights.

What is the 15th Amendment?

The 15th Amendment was the last of the three amendments passed soon after the Civil War ended. It said that no one could be prevented from voting based on their race, color, or because they had been enslaved. The amendment was meant to ensure that all African American men of legal age could vote. The northern states approved the amendment right away. However, the southern states, except for Tennessee, would not implement the amendment. Congress, using military force, made the southern states hold constitutional conventions. The southern states had to rewrite their state constitutions so that African American men were guaranteed the right to vote.

Although the 15th Amendment was the law in the United States, most African Americans were unfairly kept from voting, especially in the South. This prevention often was done through threat of job loss or violence. Other methods used were literacy tests, poll taxes, and registration laws. Sometimes **gerrymandering** was used. Gerrymandering is the unfair drawing of district lines. These districts were formed to weaken the votes of African Americans. "White primaries" were another method used by political parties to exclude African American voters. Some political parties were called "private associations." Only party members could vote in the primaries to choose the candidates. The party could keep out anyone it wanted. Usually, the people kept out were African Americans.

What were the court rulings on the terms of the 15th Amendment?

The Supreme Court outlawed many of these unfair voting practices. In *Smith* v. *Allright* (1944), the Court ruled that primary elections are a part of the voting process. Therefore, primaries must follow the 15th Amendment rules and not exclude people due to race.

In *Gomillion* v. *Lightfoot* (1960), the Court struck down racial gerrymandering. In this case, a voting district had been drawn in Tuskegee, Alabama, to exclude African Americans. The Court ruled that this was done to deprive African Americans of the right to vote, therefore violating the 15th Amendment.

These two Court decisions concerning unfair voting practices led to many others. The lower federal courts struck down many of the practices designed to disenfranchise African Americans. Still, the courts could act only when those who claimed to be victims of discrimination sued. That case-by-case method was, at best, agonizingly slow.

✔ **Checkpoint** What unfair practice was struck down in *Gomillion* v. *Lightfoot?*

What was some of the early civil rights legislation?

Although the 15th Amendment was passed in the 1800s, it took the civil rights movement to finally make the amendment an effective part of the Constitution. (See **Figure 6.7** on page 140.) Dr. Martin Luther King, Jr., began working toward improving civil rights for African Americans. Congress acted by passing important civil rights legislation in the late 1950s. The first important legislation it passed was the Civil Rights Act of 1957. The act set up the United States Commission on Civil Rights. This group investigated all claims of voter discrimination. The Civil Rights Act of 1960 followed. This act allowed federal referees to be sent anywhere a federal court found voting discrimination. These federal officers also helped voters register to vote.

The Civil Rights Act of 1964 outlawed discrimination in voting practices and in the workplace. The act also outlawed unfair voter registration methods and literacy requirements. Federal court orders, called **injunctions,** were used to stop these practices.

Reading Strategy
Inferencing
Before reading this section, what do you already know about the 15th Amendment?

Gerrymandering
Unfair drawing of district lines

Injunction
A court order that forces or limits the performance of some act by a private individual or a public official

Fig. 6.7
African Americans and the Vote

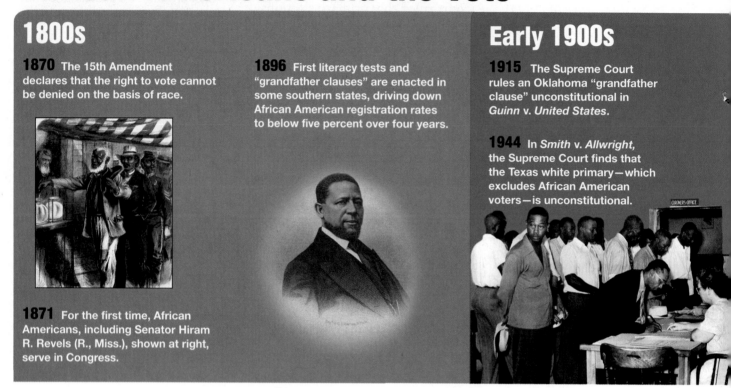

1800s

1870 The 15th Amendment declares that the right to vote cannot be denied on the basis of race.

1871 For the first time, African Americans, including Senator Hiram R. Revels (R., Miss.), shown at right, serve in Congress.

1896 First literacy tests and "grandfather clauses" are enacted in some southern states, driving down African American registration rates to below five percent over four years.

Early 1900s

1915 The Supreme Court rules an Oklahoma "grandfather clause" unconstitutional in *Guinn* v. *United States*.

1944 In *Smith* v. *Allwright*, the Supreme Court finds that the Texas white primary—which excludes African American voters—is unconstitutional.

In Selma, Alabama, in 1965, Dr. King began a movement to register African Americans to vote. Citizens, local police, and state troopers responded to his efforts with violence against his supporters. This violence was covered on national television when Dr. King's supporters tried to march to the state capitol. Two civil rights workers were murdered and many were beaten. The nation saw much of the drama on television and was shocked. President Lyndon Johnson was angry. He urged Congress to respond with new civil rights legislation. Congress quickly passed the Voting Rights Act of 1965.

✓ **Checkpoint** What did the Civil Rights Act of 1964 outlaw?

What is the Voting Rights Act of 1965?

The Voting Rights Act of 1965 made the 15th Amendment, at long last, a truly effective part of the Constitution. Unlike other laws before it, this act applied to all elections held anywhere in the United States. Originally, the act was to be in effect for a period of five years. Congress extended the act four times: in 1970, 1975, 1982, and 2006. The act is now extended until 2031.

GOVERNMENT ONLINE
Audio Tour
To learn more about African American voting rights over time, visit **PearsonSuccessNet.com**

Today

1965 The Voting Rights Act protects African Americans against various tactics intended to prevent them from voting.

1966 Edward W. Brooke III (R., Mass.) becomes the first African American elected to the Senate since the 1870s.

2008 Sen. Barack Obama (D., Ill.) is the first African American to be elected President of the United States.

Left: Civil rights marchers approach Alabama's state capitol during a voter registration protest march in 1965.
Right: Voter registration in New York City

The 1965 law directed the attorney general to challenge the remaining state poll tax laws in the federal courts. That provision led directly to *Harper* v. *Virginia Board of Elections,* in 1966, a case you may recall from Section 2. The Voting Rights Act ended literacy tests anyplace where less than half of the electorate had been registered in 1964. Federal officers were appointed to help register voters and watch over election procedures in those places.

The Voting Rights Act of 1965 added further restrictions for some states. States where a majority had not voted in 1964 could not change election laws without **preclearance.** This meant the election laws were reviewed and cleared by the Department of Justice before taking effect. Also, some states could be removed from the Voting Rights Act's coverage by a "bailout" process. This meant the state would not have federal officers overseeing its elections. This removal is allowed when a state can show that it has not used procedures that discriminate for at least 10 years. For example, some of the changes made in election procedures included adding new voting districts or changing location of polls.

Now several states and some counties have been removed from the law's coverage. Eight states are still covered.

■ ■ ■ ■ ■ ■ ■ ■ ■ ■ ■ ■ ■ ■ ■
Reading Strategy
Inferencing
Use what you know about the Voting Rights Act of 1965 to better understand the three paragraphs to the left.

■ ■ ■ ■ ■ ■ ■ ■ ■ ■ ■ ■ ■ ■ ■
Preclearance
Prior approval by the Justice Department of changes to or new election laws in certain states

Amendments to the Voting Rights Act of 1965 were added in 1970. These amendments provided that no state could use literacy as a requirement for five years. In 1975, the five-year ban on literacy became permanent.

The voter-examiner preclearance rules were also extended. Areas with more than five percent of the population belonging to "language minorities" were added. Ballots in these places must be printed in both English and the minority language. In 1992, the law was changed again. Now the provisions applied to any place where 10,000 or more citizens speak a minority language. At this time, eight states are subject to the Voting Rights Act of 1965. They are Alabama, Alaska, Arizona, Georgia, Louisiana, Mississippi, South Carolina, and Texas. Some counties in six other states are also covered by the statue. These states are California, Florida, New York, North Carolina, South Dakota, and Virginia. In addition, two townships in Michigan and ten towns in New Hampshire are subject to the statute.

✔ **Checkpoint**   When were literacy tests as voting requirements permanently banned?

Essential Questions Journal Go to your **Essential Questions Journal** to work on this chapter's Essential Question.

SECTION **3** ASSESSMENT

1. **Guiding Question** Use your completed chart to answer this question: How did the United States fulfill the promise of the 15th Amendment?

Key Terms and Comprehension

On a sheet of paper, write the answer to each question. Use complete sentences.

2. What is an injunction?

3. What right did the 15th Amendment provide?

4. What rights do non-English speaking citizens have when voting?

5. What tests ended when the Voting Rights Act of 1965 passed?

Critical Thinking

6. **Synthesize Information** What strategies were used in the South to keep African Americans from voting? Why was this done?

7. **Summarize** How has the Voting Rights Act changed since it was approved in 1965?

Casting Your Vote

Voting is one of the greatest rights a citizen enjoys. It means that you have a role in deciding who the elected officials will be. Yet voting is a big responsibility. It takes some planning to make sure you are eligible to vote. You also have to be an informed voter, and then cast your vote.

Casting your vote requires two different kinds of preparation. First, you must be aware of the rules and procedures for registering your vote and submitting your ballot. After that, you must consider all the issues and candidates involved in the election. This will help you make an informed decision.

1. Understand Eligibility Rules
In order to vote, you must be a United States citizen. You must be 18, although some states allow people to vote at a younger age. Be sure to find out what the rules are where you live. Also find out about residency requirements.

You must be a resident of the place you plan to vote. How you go about proving residence varies from state to state.

2. Register to Vote
You can register to vote by visiting the city or town election offices. You can also register to vote when you renew your driver's license. In some cases, you can even register to vote by mail or online. Find out how to register. Also find out how soon before an election you need to register. Pay close attention to whether or not you need to declare a political party when registering.

3. Educate Yourself
Research the candidates and issues that will appear on the ballot. Read newspapers and online news coverage. Watch televised debates. Review candidates' Web sites to learn about their views. Doing this preparation will help you be an informed voter.

4. Vote
To vote, you need to go to the polling place on election day to cast your ballot. Find out when the polls will be open. Make plans to take the time necessary to vote. If you think you will not be able to vote on election day, find out about absentee voting. If absentee voting is allowed where you live, make sure to understand the rules and procedures.

▶▶ What do you think?

1. Which step do you think is the most important in casting a vote? Why?
2. Why is it important to be an informed voter?

⊘ GOVERNMENT ONLINE
Citizenship Activity Pack
For an activity to help you learn more about voting, go to **PearsonSuccessNet.com**

▲ Reviewing a ballot on election day

SECTION 4

Voter Behavior

Guiding Question

What factors influence voter behavior? Use the outline to record details about voter behavior.

Factors That Influence Voters
A. Sociological
   1. Income
   2. _____
   3. _____
B. Psychological

Objectives:

- Examine why people do not vote in this country.
- Identify the groups of people who typically do not vote.
- Examine the behavior of those who vote and those who do not.
- Understand the sociological and psychological factors that affect voter behavior.

"Your vote is your voice. Use it." These words are the advice of Rock the Vote. This organization encourages voters between 18 and 25 to participate in the election process. After all, an important right in the United States essential to our democratic government is the right to choose or elect our leaders. Yet, the number of people who actually take part in elections is relatively low. In this section, you will look at voter behavior in the United States to discover why some people vote and others do not.

What is low voter turnout?

Millions of Americans do not vote or only vote for some offices. Most do not have a reason for not voting. In 2008, only 61 percent of the 227.8 million eligible people in the United States voted in the presidential election. Presidential elections do get the highest turnout of voters. Far fewer people vote during **off-year elections.** Off-year elections are congressional elections held in even-numbered years, between presidential elections.

During presidential voting years, some people who vote for the President fail to vote for the congressional candidates. This is known as **ballot fatigue.** Ballot fatigue also happens in state and local elections. Candidates at the end of the ballot get fewer votes. In an election for governor, the candidates for state offices at the end of the ballot get even fewer votes. Small elections, such as those for sheriff or district attorney, get the lowest percentage of voters.

✔ **Checkpoint** Which elections get the highest turnout of voters?

Why do people not vote?

Some people cannot vote. About 10 million people are resident aliens, 6 million are ill, 3 million reported they were traveling, 500,000 are in mental health facilities, and 2 million are in prison. There are about 100,000 who claim religious reasons for not voting.

It usually does not take much time to vote. Still, many people do not vote (Figure 6.8). Approximately 80 million eligible people did not vote for president in 2008. These people could vote but did not. Some of them believe their votes will not make a difference. Others think everything will be fine no matter who is elected. Many do not trust politicians or the government. Another group of people believe they do not have **political efficacy.** They believe their votes will have no impact at all in an election.

Sometimes complicated election methods turn people away. Long lines, complicated ballots, or even bad weather affect voter turnout. In the western states, the polls close later, and some voters believe the election is already decided before their votes could be counted. Lack of interest in politics is an important reason, too. It may be the real reason many Americans do not vote.

On average, voters and nonvoters have many differences. People who vote usually have a higher income, a better education, and a better job. They are involved in their communities and belong to a political party. Women tend to vote in larger numbers than men. Nonvoters are likely to be unmarried, young, and unskilled. People who live in the South and in rural areas are less likely to vote.

✓**Checkpoint** What are four reasons people do not vote?

■ ■ ■ ■ ■ ■ ■ ■ ■ ■ ■ ■ ■ ■ ■ ■ ■ ■

Reading Strategy
Inferencing
What do you already know about people who do not vote?

■ ■ ■ ■ ■ ■ ■ ■ ■ ■ ■ ■ ■ ■ ■ ■ ■ ■

Off-year election
Congressional election that occurs between presidential election years

Ballot fatigue
A general rule that the farther down the ballot an office is, the fewer the number of votes that will be cast for it

Political efficacy
One's ability to make a political difference

Fig. 6.8

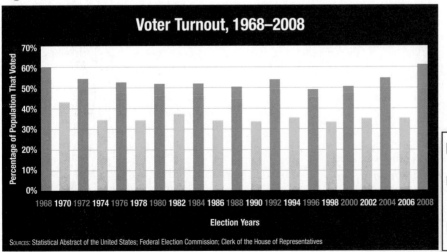

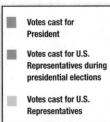

▲ **Analyzing Graphs** Voter turnout varies from election to election. Presidential elections always draw more voters than off-year elections. ***What factor does the blue at the top of each bar represent? What is this factor called?***

What is the behavior of voters?

Voting has been studied very closely in the United States. Areas where there are large ethnic or religious populations are studied the most. The Gallup Corporation does polling or surveys in certain areas. Other studies look at **political socialization.** Political socialization is the way people get their political attitudes and opinions. All the experiences in a person's entire life influence his or her political behavior.

✔**Checkpoint**   What is political socialization?

Fig. 6.9

Voting by Groups in Presidential Elections

GOVERNMENT ONLINE
Update
Check out recent voter data at
PearsonSuccessNet.com

Analyzing Charts This chart reports the voting behavior of several major segments of the American electorate in the 2008 presidential election. As you analyze this data, remember that every voter belongs to not just one but all of these groups. *How might a 45-year-old, college-educated, Hispanic woman who makes $60,000 per year vote? Explain your reasoning.* ▼

GROUPS (percentage of total)	REPUBLICAN	DEMOCRATIC
All voters (100%)	45%	53%
GENDER — Women vote Democratic more often than men.		
Men (46%)	48%	49%
Women (54%)	43%	56%
RACE — African Americans vote heavily Democratic.		
White (74%)	55%	43%
African American (13%)	4%	95%
Latino/a (9%)	31%	67%
Asian (2%)	35%	62%
AGE — Older people vote more heavily Republican.		
18–29 years (18%)	32%	66%
30–44 years (29%)	46%	52%
45–64 years (37%)	49%	50%
65 years (16%)	53%	45%
INCOME — People with higher incomes tend to vote Republican.		
Less than $50,000/year (38%)	38%	60%
$50,000 or more/year (62%)	49%	49%
EDUCATION — Republican voting increases with education, up to a point.		
No high school (4%)	35%	63%
High school graduate (20%)	46%	52%
Some college (31%)	47%	51%
College graduate (28%)	48%	50%
Postgraduate study (17%)	40%	58%
PARTY IDENTIFICATION — Most significant predictor of how one will vote.		
Democratic (39%)	10%	89%
Republican (32%)	90%	9%
Independent (29%)	44%	52%

Source: CNN exit poll

*Exit poll results may not match vote totals.

What are the sociological factors for voters?

Sociology is the study of groups of people and how these groups act. Sociological studies have shown many facts about voters in the United States. Voters in lower income groups are usually Democrats. Voters with higher incomes are usually Republicans. College graduates vote Republican more than high school graduates. Women tend to favor Democrats. Men seem to prefer Republicans. The differences between women and men is known as the **gender gap.** Young voters are more likely to be Democrats, and older voters often tend to be Republicans.

Religious views, race, and location also seem to play a part in political socialization. Protestants have most often favored Republicans. Catholics and Jews most often vote for Democrats. African Americans are usually Democrats, as are Latinos. Democrats are found in great numbers in northern states. Suburban areas, smaller cities, and rural areas have high Republican numbers. Family members tend to vote for the same political party. Figure 6.9 on page 146 shows how groups in different categories have voted in the 2008 presidential election. Gender, race, age, income, education, and party identification are all examined. Party identification as well as other psychological factors are discussed on the next page.

Figure 6.10 shows the different factors—both sociological and psychological—that go into voting decisions. In the end, no matter whom voters choose as their elected leaders, they are taking part in the political process and making their voices heard (Figure 6.11).

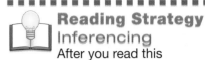

Gender gap
The difference between how men and women vote for candidates

Reading Strategy
Inferencing
After you read this section, make an inference about how different people might vote.

Fig. 6.10

Influences on Voter Behavior

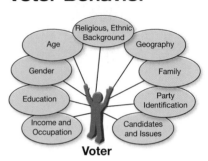

Fig. 6.11

▲ **Analyzing Political Cartoons** *Do you agree that only people who vote have a right to complain? Why or why not?*

■ ■

Party identification
Loyalty of people to a political party

Straight-ticket voting
Voting for candidates of only one party in an election

Split-ticket voting
Voting for candidates of different parties in an election

Independent
Person who does not belong to a political party

What are the psychological factors for voters?

Psychological factors that influence voters include a person's ideas about politics along with his or her opinions about candidates. Many people join a political party and never change their party affiliation. This loyalty is called **party identification.** These people usually vote for all of their party's candidates in every election. This practice is called **straight-ticket voting.** This trend has decreased in recent years.

Some people now vote for candidates from more than one party in elections. This practice is called **split-ticket voting.** Another recent trend is the increase in people who call themselves **independents.** These independents do not belong to any party. It is difficult to count the number of independents. It is guessed that about one third of all voters are independents. Independents are often well-informed, educated, and younger than the average voter.

Candidates and political events in America may influence voters who always vote within their parties. In the past 40 years, voters have become more aware of candidates and issues. The civil rights movement, the Vietnam War, and political scandals caused voters to be concerned. More recently, economic problems and the ongoing wars in Iraq and Afghanistan are most likely the reasons for voters' heightened concern. Issues like these may lead people to vote for a person outside of their political party.

▲ Family can influence party identification.

Biography

Carrie Chapman Catt (1859–1947)

Carrie Chapman Catt spent most of her life working for the rights of women. She began her work for women's voting rights in Iowa in 1887. She often traveled to organize women to campaign for a constitutional amendment allowing women to vote. Catt took over for Susan B. Anthony as the leader of the National American Women's Suffrage Association (NAWSA). In 1919, Catt established the League of Women Voters as a successor to NAWSA. This organization's purpose is to educate women to become informed voters. In 1920, the 19th Amendment giving women the right to vote was ratified and became part of the Constitution.

Carrie Chapman Catt was born in Ripon, Wisconsin, on January 9, 1859. Her family moved to Iowa when she was a child. She attended a one-room schoolhouse. Later, she taught school to earn money for college. She graduated from Iowa State Agricultural College with a class of 18 students. The other 17 were men. She spent a number of years in education before dedicating herself to the suffrage movement.

Essential Questions Journal Go to your **Essential Questions Journal** to work on this chapter's Essential Question.

SECTION 4 ASSESSMENT

1. **Guiding Question** Use your completed outline to answer this question: What factors influence voter behavior?

Key Terms and Comprehension
Choose the letter that best answers each question.

2. What are people called that usually vote for all of one party's candidates in an election?
   - **A.** straight-ticket voters
   - **B.** independents
   - **C.** split-ticket voters
   - **D.** presidential voters

3. Men favoring Republicans more than women do is an example of what?
   - **A.** split-ticket politics
   - **B.** socialization
   - **C.** the gender gap
   - **D.** party identification

4. During off-year elections, what happens to voter turnout?
   - **A.** Voter turnout goes up a large amount.
   - **B.** Voter turnout stays the same.
   - **C.** Voter turnout goes up a small amount.
   - **D.** Voter turnout goes down.

5. What is an example of a sociological factor of voters?
   - **A.** age
   - **B.** income
   - **C.** gender
   - **D.** all of the above

Critical Thinking

6. **Predict consequences** In some countries, voting is required of all eligible citizens. Do you think mandatory voting would work in the United States? Why or why not?

7. **Draw inferences** Why do you think factors like income and level of education affect voter participation?

Quick Study Guide

Chapter Summary

Section 1—The Right to Vote

- The electorate in America has expanded over the years. Citizens over the age of 18 cannot be kept from voting because of race, gender, or religion.

- Amendments to the Constitution and laws passed by Congress have ended most voting restrictions.

- The states set qualifications for voters. These qualifications must not violate the Constitution.

Section 2—Voter Qualifications

- All states require voters to be U.S. citizens and legal residents of the state.

- All states, except North Dakota, require voters to register.

- Literacy and the payment of a poll tax are no longer requirements for voting.

Section 3—Suffrage and Civil Rights

- The 15th Amendment gave all male Americans the right to vote. African Americans were still kept from voting in some southern states through unfair restrictions, such as literacy tests and gerrymandering.

- The Civil Rights Acts of 1957, 1960, and 1964 were passed by Congress to ensure that African Americans received their voting rights.

- The Voting Rights Act of 1965 made further changes to ensure that all eligible people had the right to vote.

Section 4—Voter Behavior

- Voter turnout in America is low for presidential elections. Voter turnout is even lower for other elections.

- Some people, such as aliens and people in mental health facilities, are not allowed to vote.

- Voter behavior is studied closely in the United States. This behavior often depends on the way people get their political opinions.

- Sociological and psychological factors affect political opinions and voting. For example, sociological factors may include gender, occupation, and ethnic background. Psychological factors may include party membership and interest in the issues.

Guiding Question
Section 2 What are the requirements for voting, and how have they changed over time?

Guiding Question
Section 3 How did the United States fulfill the promise of the 15th Amendment?

Guiding Question
Section 1 How have voting rights changed over the course of U.S. history?

Guiding Question
Section 4 What factors influence voter behavior?

CHAPTER 6

Essential Question
Why do voters act as they do?

Document-Based Assessment

The Voting Rights Act of 1965

The Voting Rights Act of 1965 was signed into law by President Lyndon Johnson in 1965. It said any voting practices used to discourage voting by citizens because of race or color were illegal. Certain states with large minority populations used reading tests, poll taxes, and redistricting to keep many people from voting. This act gave the federal government the right to act where these illegal practices were used.

Below are parts of the law.

Document at a Glance

- Made practices to discourage voters illegal
- Federal government had the right to act on unfair practices
- Gave Washington, D.C., voting rights

. . . Sec 2. No voting qualification or prerequisite to voting, or standard, practice, or procedure shall be imposed or applied by any State or political subdivision to deny or abridge the right of any citizen of the United States to vote on account of race or color.

. . . Sec 3. [the act] shall suspend the use of tests and devices in such State or political subdivisions as the court shall determine is appropriate and for such period as it deems necessary . . .

The act also states that certain areas of the country must get preapproval from the U.S. District Court

for the District of Columbia or U.S. Attorney General for any voting practice changes.

Sec. 5 . . . [any state or subdivision voting procedure] different from that in force or effect on November 1, 1964, . . . may institute an action in the United States District Court for the District of Columbia for a declaratory judgment that such qualification, prerequisite, standard, practice, or procedure does not have the purpose and will not have the effect of denying or abridging the right to vote on account of race or color . . .

Document-Based Questions

1. In this act, what are two of the restrictions that should not be imposed on a voter?

2. For what reason might these restrictions be illegally imposed?

3. Where is a request for a voting change to be made?

4. Who hears the request for action?

5. Inferencing From your reading of Chapter 6, what have you learned about the Voting Rights Act of 1965?

SOURCE: Voting Rights Act of 1965

Chapter Assessment

Directions: On a sheet of paper, write the answer to each
question. Use complete sentences.

Section 1—The Right to Vote

1. What is suffrage?

2. What is the electorate?

3. Why has the government slowly taken on a larger role in voting rights?

4. What are two restrictions that kept people from voting in the past?

5. **Critical Thinking** States, and not the federal government, set voter qualifications. Why do you think that is?

Section 2—Voter Qualifications

6. What is literacy?

7. What is a poll book?

8. What was the biggest reason people felt that 18 was the right age to be able to vote when the 26th Amendment was passed?

9. **Critical Thinking** What might be a reason that a person can now register to vote at a concert or other public event?

Section 3—Suffrage and Civil Rights

10. Which amendment gave all male citizens the right to vote?

11. Why was the amendment not very effective for nearly 100 years?

12. What were some of the ways used to keep African Americans from voting?

13. **Critical Thinking** Do you think there should be literacy requirements to vote? Why or why not?

Section 4—Voter Behavior

14. What is the gender gap?

15. What is ballot fatigue?

16. What are some of the sociological factors that make someone likely to vote?

17. Critical Thinking Do you think voters should consider candidates' personal qualities as well as their political views? Why or why not?

Apply What You've Learned

Exploring the Essential Question

18. What are the steps you have to take to vote?

19. Do you think it's hard or easy to register to vote? Why do you think so?

Essential Questions Project

20. Someone has just moved next to you in your community. Write a brochure that will help that person vote. Explain the registration process in your brochure. You should also include facts about why people do and do not vote. Those facts can be found in this chapter. You can include both sociological and psychological factors. Your brochure should help you answer the Essential Question: **Why do voters act as they do?**

Essential Questions
Journal

Go to your **Essential Questions Journal** to work on this chapter's Essential Question.

Test-Taking Tip

Pace yourself. If you are unsure about a question, put a check next to it and move on. If you have time left, go back and try to answer the checked questions.

▲ Governor Christine Gregoire (D., Washington) greets schoolchildren.

7

The Electoral Process

Essential Question
How fair and effective is the electoral process?

Section 1: The Nominating Process

Section 2: Elections

Section 3: Money and Elections

Reading Strategy: Metacognition

Metacognition means being aware of how you think and learn. Metacognition helps you figure out which strategy to use to better understand a text.

- Before you read, preview the chapter. Ask questions to identify your purpose for reading. Make predictions.
- As you read, identify the main idea. Visualize what is happening. Connect the text to your life. Ask questions about what you do not understand.
- After you read, summarize what you have read. Ask yourself what you learned and what you still want to know.

GOVERNMENT ONLINE
ON THE GO

To study anywhere, anytime, download these online resources at PearsonSuccessNet.com.
- Political Dictionary
- Audio Review
- Downloadable Interactivities

The Nominating Process

▲ Minnesota's Democratic-Farmer-Labor Party nominates a candidate for governor at a state convention.

Guiding Question

What methods are used to choose candidates for public office? Use the diagram to list the methods of nominating candidates for office.

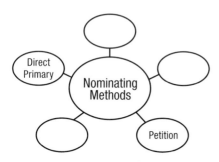

Direct Primary

Nominating Methods

Petition

Objectives:

- Explain why the nominating process is a critical first step in the election process.
- Describe the different nominating methods.
- Discuss the direct primary as the main nominating method used in the United States today.
- Understand why some candidates use the petition as a nominating tool.

If a teacher said to her class, "Here is a $1,000 bill. Who wants it?", most likely everyone in the class would say, "Me!" The teacher may then say, "We will hold an election, and the person who gets the most votes gets the money." Everyone in the class would probably vote for themselves. The election would probably end in a tie. But what if the teacher said, "We will have the election tomorrow"? Then what do you think might happen? As you think about the answer, you begin to see the importance of the nominating process.

What is the first step?

The election process begins with an important first step. It is the **nomination** of candidates. Nomination is the naming of those who will run for a public office. It is a major function of political parties. Nominating candidates is done at all levels of government.

In the United States, voters usually choose between two candidates, one from the Republican Party and one from the Democratic Party. This is because we have a two-party system in America. Those who make nominations place limits on the choices that voters have on election day.

In areas where one party is the dominant party, the **general election** is just a formality. In other words, the nominating process has already selected the winner. In these areas, the first step is the only one that really matters.

✔ **Checkpoint** What is a nomination?

Nominations are made in five ways in the United States. Candidates get their names on the ballot by self-announcement, caucus, convention, direct primary, and petition.

✔ **Checkpoint** What are the five ways in which nominations are made?

What is self-announcement?

Self-announcement is an old and simple method. A person simply declares that they are running for office. This is done frequently in small towns or rural areas. Self-announcement is also used by those who tried and failed to get their party's nomination or those who are unhappy with the candidate the party chose. Whenever an election includes a write-in candidate, the self-announcement method has been used. The most recent presidential candidate who used the self-announcement method was Ross Perot in 1992 (Figure 7.1).

What is a caucus?

A **caucus** is a group of people with similar views who meet to select a candidate. Originally, the caucus was a private meeting. It was closed to all but a few important people in a community. Political parties soon opened membership to more people. By 1800, the caucus was being used to nominate candidates for both state and national offices.

Criticism of the caucus arose because the meetings still represented the views of very few people. When Andrew Jackson ran for President in 1824, he and his supporters refused to use the caucus. This boycott reflected the views of many. As a result, the use of the caucus at the national level came to an end. Soon after, most caucuses at the state and local levels also ended. Today, a caucus is used to make local nominations in some places, such as New England. However, today's caucus is open to all members of the party.

✔ **Checkpoint** What is a caucus?

■ ■ ■ ■ ■ ■ ■ ■ ■ ■ ■ ■ ■ ■ ■
💡 **Reading Strategy**
Metacognition
Notice the structure of this chapter. Look at the titles, headings, and boldfaced words.

■ ■ ■ ■ ■ ■ ■ ■ ■ ■ ■ ■ ■ ■ ■
Nomination
The process of candidate selection in an electoral system

General election
The regularly scheduled election at which voters make a final selection of officeholders

Self-announcement
Nominating method in which a person announces an intention to run for public office

Caucus
A group of people who think alike and meet to select the candidates they will support in an upcoming election

Fig. 7.1

▲ **Analyzing Cartoons** Ross Perot, who ran for President in 1992, launched his campaign by using the self-announcement method. *Why might self-announcement attract candidates with enough personal wealth to finance their own campaigns?*

What is a convention?

As the caucus method died, the convention system took its place. In 1831, the Anti-Masons, a minor party, held the first national convention to nominate a presidential candidate. That same year, the National Republican (soon to become Whig) Party also held a convention. The Democrats followed the practice in 1832. Since that time, all national major party presidential nominations have been made at conventions.

The convention process begins at the local level where delegates are chosen to go to the county convention. At the county convention, delegates are chosen to go to the state convention. At the state convention, nominees for governor and other state offices are chosen, and delegates are then sent to the national convention. Presidential and vice-presidential candidates are chosen at this level. The convention seemed simple at first, but soon party bosses found ways to influence the delegates unfairly. The use of conventions declined as a result. By the 1910s, the direct primary replaced the convention in most states. Some states do continue to use the convention process. At the national level, both the Democratic and Republican parties continue to hold large conventions to nominate their presidential candidates every four years.

✔ **Checkpoint**   How does the convention process begin?

What is a direct primary?

The **direct primary** is an election within a political party to choose the party's candidates for the next election. It is one of the five methods of nomination. (See Figure 7.2 on page 160.) Every state now uses a primary election for at least some of its offices. In most states, the law requires that a primary be used to select candidates for the Senate and House of Representatives. Primaries are also used to select candidates for governor. In a few states, a mix of the convention and the primary is used to select candidates for some offices.

There are two basic forms of the direct primary: the closed primary and the open primary. The **closed primary** is a party's nominating election in which only party members can vote. The primary is closed to everyone else. In most states with closed primaries, voters must be registered with the party holding the election. When voters arrive at the polling place, their names are checked against the poll books. They are given the primary ballot for the party with which they are registered. The voter may mark only that party's ballot.

The **open primary** is a party's nominating election in which any qualified voter can vote. This method is now used in only 26 states. In some open primary states, voters are given two ballots, one from each party. Then in a private voting booth they make their choice of party by marking the ballot for that party. In other states, the voters must ask for the ballot of the party they want. This is done at the open check-in table before entering the voting booth.

A **blanket primary,** sometimes called a "wide-open primary," was used in three states: Washington, Alaska, and California. In this type of primary, every voter received the same ballot that listed every candidate. Voters could switch back and forth between parties to select candidates. They could also vote for just one party. The blanket primary is no longer used. The Supreme Court ruled that it was unconstitutional in 2000. The Court said this process violated the right of association because it forced a party to associate with members of other parties on the ballot. Alaska and California complied by changing to a regular open primary, but Washington did not.

Washington now provides for a top-two form of open primary. In this method, the names of all who seek nomination are listed on a single ballot. Then the top two winners, regardless of party, face one another in the general election.

In Louisiana, a similar form of the primary is used. All candidates are listed on a single ballot. As in Washington, the top two vote getters, regardless of party, run against each other in the general election. If any candidate gets a majority in the primary, however, that person is declared the winner. There is no general election in that case.

What is the debate between closed and open primaries?

Closed and open primaries both have strong supporters. Those who support closed primaries claim they are more fair, they make candidates more responsive to voters, and they require voters to give more thought to their choices. On the other hand, critics of the closed primary claim it violates a voter's privacy because voters must make their party preference known in order to vote. Independent voters are also excluded from this process. Those who support open primaries claim that they protect privacy because voters do not have to declare their party preference choice in public. Independent voters are included in open primaries and are part of the nomination process.

Direct primary
An election held within a party to pick that party's candidates for the general election

Closed primary
A party's nominating election in which only declared party members can vote

Open primary
A party's nominating election in which any qualified voter can vote

Blanket primary
An election in which voters receive a long ballot containing the names of all contenders, regardless of party, and can vote however they choose

Reading Strategy
Metacognition
Ask yourself if you understood what you just read about direct primaries. If not, go back and read the text again.

Fig. 7.2 How Government Works

Five Methods of Nomination

Candidates for federal, state, and local office have five ways to place their names on the ballot for the general election. *Which method of nomination is the most democratic?*

PRIMARY

>> Qualified voters cast ballots in private for their preferred candidate.

CAUCUS

>> Party members and supporters vote to select a nominee.

CONVENTION

>> Local communities select delegates to represent them at a higher-level meeting where the nominee is chosen.

SELF-ANNOUNCEMENT

>> The candidate announces his or her intention to run for office.

PETITION

>> Candidates collect signatures from voters to qualify for the general election.

GOVERNMENT ONLINE
Audio Tour
Listen to a guided audio tour of this table at **PearsonSuccessNet.com**

What is a runoff primary?

Runoff primaries are used in 8 states. In these states, candidates must win not just the most votes (a plurality), but an absolute majority (more than half) of the votes to win the primary. If a candidate does not receive a majority, then a **runoff primary** is held. In this type of primary, the two top vote getters run against each other. The winner becomes the party's nominee for that office.

✓**Checkpoint** When is a runoff primary held?

What are the nonpartisan and the presidential primaries?

The **nonpartisan election** is used in most states for electing school and city officers. About half of all state judges are also chosen this way. Candidates in these primaries are not identified by party. In any nonpartisan contest, a person who receives a clear majority runs unopposed in the general election. In some states, the candidate who wins a majority does not have to run again in the general election. They are simply declared the winner. When there is no majority winner, the top two candidates run in the general election.

The presidential primary is different from the other types of primaries. It is an election that is part of the process for choosing presidential candidates. It can be the way that a party selects its delegates to the national convention. It can also be an election in which voters choose their party's presidential nominee.

✔**Checkpoint** What is a nonpartisan election?

What are voters' views on the primary?

The direct primary came to the American political system after the convention system ended. Under the convention system, party bosses had been in control of the nominating process. The direct primary was meant to put party members in charge of nominating candidates.

Most people do not understand the facts about primaries. As a result, they dislike having to declare party preference in order to vote in a primary. They also disagree with excluding independent voters in closed primaries. Many voters object to not being able to support candidates in more than one party. These complaints, along with the idea that the primary is unimportant, have led to low voter turnout.

The high cost of primary campaigns, fights among party members, and uninformed voters are more problems with the primary. However, the primary does give party members a voice in selecting candidates.

What is a petition?

Nomination by petition is often used at the local level in American politics. In this method, candidates are nominated by gathering signatures from a certain number of qualified voters in their district. Nomination by petition is often used for school and city offices. It is also used for judges and minor party and independent candidates. The petition process is different from state to state. Usually, the higher the office or larger the area, the more signatures needed.

Runoff primary
A primary in which the top two vote getters in the first primary face one another

Nonpartisan election
Elections in which candidates are not identified by party labels

Biography

The Honorable Ron Paul (1935–)

Ron Paul was born in Pittsburgh, Pennsylvania. He graduated from Gettysburg College and Duke University Medical School. He served as a flight surgeon in the air force in the 1960s. He and his wife, Carol, live in Surfside, Texas.

Dr. Paul was first elected to Congress in 1976. There he became known for his beliefs about low taxes, free markets, and constitutional government. He has also supported limiting the terms of members of Congress. To show his belief in this idea, Dr. Paul gave up his seat in the House in 1984. In 1988, the Libertarian Party nominated Dr. Paul for President. In 1996, he was reelected to Congress. He was a candidate for the Republican presidential nomination in 2008.

SECTION 1 ASSESSMENT

Essential Questions Journal Go to your **Essential Questions Journal** to work on this chapter's Essential Question.

Quick Write
Using the Internet, find an example of a recent national, state, or local election. Write a brief summary of the election. Include names of the candidates and when the election took place.

1. **Guiding Question** Use your completed diagram to answer this question: What methods are used to choose candidates for public office?

Key Terms and Comprehension

On a sheet of paper, write the answer to each question. Use complete sentences.

2. What is a nomination?

3. What is the difference between a closed primary and an open primary?

4. What are two problems with primary elections?

5. What is a runoff primary?

Critical Thinking

6. **Draw Inferences** Why do you think voter turnout for primary elections is so low in some states?

7. **Draw Conclusions** Do you think each state should have the same type of primary election? Why or why not?

▲ Volunteers wave signs outside a polling place.

Elections

Guiding Question

How are elections conducted in the United States? Use the chart below to record information about how elections are administered and conducted.

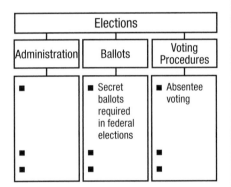

Elections		
Administration	Ballots	Voting Procedures
■	■ Secret ballots required in federal elections	■ Absentee voting
■	■	■
■	■	■

Objectives:

- Analyze how the administration of elections helps make democracy work.
- Define the roll of precincts and polling places in the election process.
- Describe the many ways voters can cast their votes.
- Outline the role that voting devices play in the election process.

Americans vote more often than most people realize. On almost every day of the year (except for Sundays and holidays), an election is being held somewhere in the United States. More than 500,000 officeholders are elected in this country at all levels of government. The United States has more elected officials than any other country in the world.

How are elections administered?

The government of the United States has passed very detailed and lengthy election laws. These laws were enacted to protect the honesty and quality of elections.

There are more than 89,000 units of government at the state and local levels. Because of this, it is the states, not the federal government, that make most election laws.

Still, there are some federal election laws in the Constitution. Congress has the power to fix the "Times, Places, and Manner of holding Elections" of members of Congress. Congress also sets the time for choosing presidential electors and the date for casting the electoral votes. Congress also regulates other parts of the presidential election process.

Congress has set the date for congressional elections as the first Tuesday following the first Monday in November of every even-numbered year. It has set the same date every fourth year for the presidential election.

✔ **Checkpoint** Why are election laws important?

Congress has required the use of secret ballots (Figure 7.3) and allowed the use of voting machines in federal elections. A ballot is the way a voter registers a choice in an election. Congress has also acted to protect the right to vote and regulates the financing of campaigns for federal office. Congress passed the Help America Vote Act in 2002. It was passed after the many problems that arose during the presidential election of 2000. The major provisions of the law direct the states to do the following:

- replace all lever-operated and punch-card voting devices;

- improve the training of local election officials and election day workers;

- centralize and computerize voter registration systems; and

- provide for provisional voting, so a person whose eligibility to vote is questioned can still vote. If it is found later that the person is qualified to vote, then the vote will be counted.

When is election day?

Most states hold elections for state offices on the same day Congress has set for national elections. Some states have chosen odd-numbered years for some elections. City, county, and other election dates vary from state to state. If elections are not held in November, they are usually held in the spring.

GOVERNMENT ONLINE
Audio Tour
Listen to a guided audio tour of this diagram at
PearsonSuccessNet.com

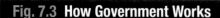

Fig. 7.3 How Government Works

What Happens to a Ballot?

The states offer voters different ways to cast their votes, both in paper formats and electronically, and on election day or earlier. *Why is it important for local officials to guard and track ballots after they are cast?*

Counting Facility
Ballots are usually counted in a central location and stored in case a recount is required.

Paper Ballot
Usually collected at polling place, taken to counting facility

Absentee Ballot
Mailed to the counting facility
OR
Brought to the polling place and combined with other ballots

Electronic Ballot
Data transported manually on discs or drives
OR
Votes transmitted electronically to counting facility

What is early voting?

Millions of Americans vote before election day. Many do so by **absentee voting,** the process by which people can vote without going to polling places on election day. Congress first allowed absentee voting during the Civil War. In the elections of 1864, federal troops were allowed to cast absentee ballots. Today, voters almost everywhere can apply for an absentee ballot weeks before an election. These ballots are then mailed back to the local election office before election day.

At first, these absentee ballots were meant for the ill, disabled, or those away from home on election day. Now almost anyone can apply if they want to vote that way.

Two thirds of the states now have regular, formal early voting as well. These states allow voters to cast regular ballots over a period of several days before election day. In many places, election day has become the last day you can vote.

✔ **Checkpoint** What is absentee voting?

What is the coattail effect?

The **coattail effect** happens when a popular candidate is at the top of a party's ballot. Voters who choose this candidate often will vote for other candidates from the same party. Even though these other candidates are less well-known, they get elected by "riding the coattails" of the popular candidate. The coattail effect is most often seen in presidential elections.

The reverse coattail effect can also happen. If a candidate is not popular, then other people from the party will not be elected. Because of the coattail effect, some people think state and local elections should not be held at the same time as federal elections. They claim people would pay more attention to state and local candidates and issues if they had a separate election day.

What are precincts and polling places?

A **precinct** is a voting district. This is the smallest area where elections are held. Usually it serves no more than 1,000 people. A **polling place** is where the voters who live in the precinct come to cast their votes. A county clerk or county board of elections sets the boundaries of the precincts and names the polling places. The board also selects precinct election boards that supervise the entire election process.

■ ■ ■ ■ ■ ■ ■ ■ ■ ■ ■ ■ ■ ■ ■ ■

Absentee voting
The process by which people can vote without going to polling places on election day

Coattail effect
The effect of a strong candidate running for an office at the top of a ballot helping to attract voters to other candidates on the party's ticket

Precinct
A voting district

Polling place
The place where the voters who live in a precinct go to vote

■ ■ ■ ■ ■ ■ ■ ■ ■ ■ ■ ■ ■ ■ ■ ■

Reading Strategy
Metacognition
Before you read this section, think about what strategies you can use to better understand the text.

■ ■ ■ ■ ■ ■ ■ ■ ■ ■ ■ ■ ■ ■ ■ ■ ■ ■

Reading Strategy
Metacognition
Ask yourself, What did
I learn by reading this section?
What do I still want to know about
this topic?

The precinct board opens and closes the polls according to state law. The board checks the ballot boxes or voting machines. It makes sure all voters are qualified. The election board often counts the votes and sends the results to the proper place. One poll watcher from each party is also allowed at the polling place.

✓ **Checkpoint** Who counts the votes and sends them to the proper place?

How do people cast their votes?

Today, all states require that ballots be cast in secret. In colonial times, voting was usually done by voice. Voters stated their choices aloud to an election board. As laws were changed to allow more and more people to vote, this method gave way to paper ballots in the mid-1800s. The voters themselves made those early ballots. Later, candidates and parties made ballots and gave them to the voters. Corruption crept into the process, however, and voters were sometimes bribed or threatened to make them vote a certain way. Today, votes are cast in secret. A ballot is provided at public expense only at the polls. This kind of ballot is called the Australian ballot, because it was first used in that country.

Today's ballot is often cast on some type of voting machine. For almost a hundred years, voting machines were lever operated. Voters had to pull levers to open the machine, cast their votes, and then close the machine. Although these machines did speed up voting and reduce fraud, they were costly. They were also difficult to store and move.

Electronic data processing (EDP) methods were first used in the 1960s. For years, the most common method was punch cards. These were sometimes hard to read. In the disputed presidential election of 2000, improper marking of punch cards caused problems when the ballots were read. This led to the passage of the Help America Vote Act, which required states to stop using punch card ballots.

Most states now use two other EDP-based systems. One involves optical-scanning technology. The other uses direct response electronic voting machines (DREs). They are much like cash machines. Voters use touch screens or buttons to make their choices.

Some states allow people to vote by mail. Critics fear this process may invite fraud. Others say it has proven to be safe and increases voter participation while cutting costs.

Online voting has attracted some support in recent years. It has been used in a limited way in some presidential primaries and caucuses. Supporters of online voting say it will increase voter turnout and reduce costs. Critics are fearful of such problems as digital disasters, jammed phone lines, and violations of voter security. All these voting methods, as well the nomination methods covered in Section 1, are listed in **Figure 7.4.**

Fig. 7.4

Path to Elected Office

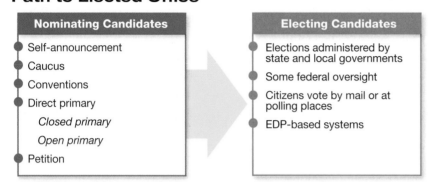

Nominating Candidates
- Self-announcement
- Caucus
- Conventions
- Direct primary
  - *Closed primary*
  - *Open primary*
- Petition

Electing Candidates
- Elections administered by state and local governments
- Some federal oversight
- Citizens vote by mail or at polling places
- EDP-based systems

Essential Questions Journal Go to your **Essential Questions Journal** to work on this chapter's Essential Question.

SECTION 2 ASSESSMENT

1. **Guiding Question** Use your completed chart to answer the question: How are elections conducted in the United States?

Key Terms and Comprehension

On a sheet of paper, write the answer to each question. Use complete sentences.

2. What is a precinct?

3. What does Congress do in the administration of elections?

4. How have absentee ballots changed over time?

5. What is the coattail effect?

Critical Thinking

6. **Predict Consequences** What might happen if people lost confidence that their ballots were being counted and recorded properly?

7. **Draw Conclusions** Do you think online voting will be a good way to vote in future elections? Why or why not?

ISSUES OF OUR TIME

Campaign Finance

>> **Track the Issue**

When regulating campaign finance, the federal government has tried to balance free speech rights against the potential for corruption.

1828 After winning a costly presidential race, Andrew Jackson replaces many government officials with his own campaign supporters.

1907 Congress bans corporate contributions to federal candidates.

1947 The Taft-Hartley Act blocks labor unions from donating to candidates. In response, unions donate through political action committees (PACs).

1974 Congress creates the Federal Election Commission to enforce strict new laws on campaign fundraising.

2002 The Bipartisan Campaign Reform Act becomes law. It places strict limits on the use of soft money.

Sen. John McCain
(R., Arizona)

>> **Perspectives**

Campaigns must raise money to organize and get their message out to voters. The boom in "soft money" in the 1990s made it easy for individuals to give campaigns unlimited donations. Soft money is money given to state and local party organizations for voting-related activities, but not limited to a particular candidate. Some believed that this soft money was out of control. Efforts to limit soft money were led by Senator John McCain. McCain's work sparked debate over government's proper role in regulating political activity.

For Campaign Finance Reform	Against Campaign Finance Reform
"This system of unregulated soft money . . . bred public cynicism [distrust] about the workings of our . . . government. At a minimum, the actions of Congress and the executive branch were severely tainted [damaged] by the specter [frightening vision] of six-figure soft-money donations by special interests with a stake in legislation and policies pending before the federal government." —Senator John McCain (R., Arizona)	"I think the practical effect of [limits on soft money] would dramatically push Americans out of the political process, putting restrictions on Political Action Committees means that Americans can't band together, pool their resources, and support the candidates of their choice. . . . [Under] the 1st Amendment of the Constitution, people are free to express themselves and the Supreme Court has said that campaign spending is speech. . . ." —Senator Mitch McConnell (R., Kentucky)

Connect to Your World

1. What argument does Senator McCain make? What argument does Senator McConnell make?

2. **Draw Conclusions** Who do you agree with on campaign finance reform? Explain your answer.

GOVERNMENT ONLINE
In the News
For updates about campaign finance, visit
PearsonSuccessNet.com

▲ Senator Russ Feingold (D., Wisconsin) has led efforts to regulate campaign contributions.

SECTION 3

Money and Elections

Guiding Question

What role does money play in electoral politics? Use a flow chart to record information about the role of money in electoral politics and the efforts of government to regulate it.

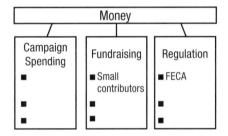

```
              Money
   ┌────────────┼────────────┐
Campaign    Fundraising   Regulation
Spending
   ■         ■ Small       ■ FECA
                contributors
   ■         ■             ■
   ■         ■             ■
```

Objectives:

- Explain the issues raised by campaign spending.
- Describe the various sources of funding for campaign spending.
- Examine the federal laws that regulate campaign finance.
- Outline the role of the Federal Election Commission in enforcing campaign finance laws.
- Describe the difference between hard money and soft money.

Running for public office costs a lot of money. This fact creates many problems. Candidates may try to buy their way into office. Some interest groups may try to buy favors from candidates. The getting and spending of campaign funds can corrupt the whole election process.

How much is spent on campaigns?

The money spent on campaigns in the United States totals billions of dollars. The presidential election costs the most money, including the primaries, conventions, campaigns, and more.

Congressional campaigns also spend huge amounts. A typical race for a seat in the House costs $1 million. A Senate campaign can cost up to $20 million.

Campaign funds are spent on many items. These include radio and television time, newspaper ads, buttons and posters, mass mailings, Web sites, and travel. The candidates also have managers and consultants who must be paid. The amount spent depends on several factors: the level of the office, whether the candidate is new or running again for the office (the incumbent), and how much money can be raised.

✔ **Checkpoint**   Which elections cost the most money?

What are the sources of campaign money?

Candidates and their parties get their money from private sources and from the public treasury. Private sources have always been the main source of campaign funds. They include the following:

- Small contributors who give $5 or $10. About 10 percent of people who vote give money to candidates or their party.

- Wealthy people and families who make large donations.

- Candidates themselves and their families. The candidate may be trying to get reelected or is a new candidate.

- The political part of special interest groups. These groups are called **political action committees** (PACs)

- Temporary organizations formed during a campaign. Their main purpose is fundraising.

Political parties and their candidates often hold fundraising events. These include luncheons, dinners, picnics, and similar events. People pay a certain amount of money to attend the event.

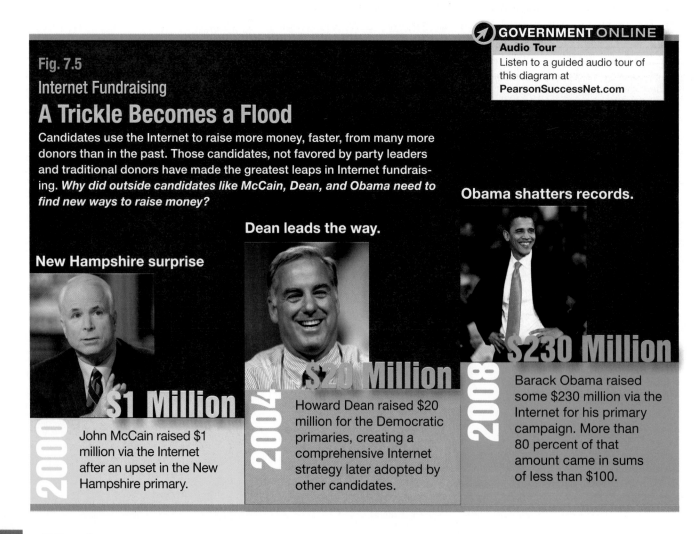

GOVERNMENT ONLINE
Audio Tour
Listen to a guided audio tour of this diagram at
PearsonSuccessNet.com

Fig. 7.5

Internet Fundraising

A Trickle Becomes a Flood

Candidates use the Internet to raise more money, faster, from many more donors than in the past. Those candidates, not favored by party leaders and traditional donors have made the greatest leaps in Internet fundraising. *Why did outside candidates like McCain, Dean, and Obama need to find new ways to raise money?*

Obama shatters records.

Dean leads the way.

New Hampshire surprise

$1 Million
2000
John McCain raised $1 million via the Internet after an upset in the New Hampshire primary.

$20 Million
2004
Howard Dean raised $20 million for the Democratic primaries, creating a comprehensive Internet strategy later adopted by other candidates.

$230 Million
2008
Barack Obama raised some $230 million via the Internet for his primary campaign. More than 80 percent of that amount came in sums of less than $100.

Funds are also raised through direct mail, telephone calls, or the Internet. The Internet has become by far the most successful way for candidates to raise money. (See Figure 7.5 on page 170.)

In addition to having private fundraising sources, campaigns now receive money from the public treasury in the form of subsidies. A **subsidy** is a grant of money usually given by the government. Subsidies are most important at the presidential level. Whatever the source, candidates welcome every contribution because the rising costs of campaigning demand more and more money. (See Figure 7.6.)

✔ **Checkpoint** What are two private sources of campaign funds?

Why do people give money to campaigns?
People give money to campaigns as a way to participate in government. They may believe in a party or a candidate. Others who give want something in return—perhaps a job in government. Some people donate to both parties to be sure to get what they want.

People who make large donations may be seeking appointments to public office. Labor, business, and professional organizations may want new laws passed. They may also seek changes in old laws or simply want some laws repealed.

How is campaign finance regulated?
In 1907, Congress began to regulate (control) the use of money in federal elections. That year it became unlawful for a corporation or a national bank to make "a money contribution in any election" to candidates for federal office. Today, there are many more regulations for presidential and congressional campaigns. A law passed in 1971 (the Federal Election Campaign Act) replaced many earlier laws. This law was amended in 1974 and 1976 in response to the Watergate scandal and a Supreme Court decision. Congress does not have the power to regulate money in state and local elections. The states do regulate campaign financing to some extent, however.

What is the role of the FEC?
The Federal Election Commission (FEC) is an independent agency that is part of the executive branch. Congress set up the FEC in 1974 to administer all federal law concerning campaign finance. These laws are detailed but not well enforced because the FEC does not have a large enough staff or enough funding.

■■■■■■■■■■■■■■■■■■■
Subsidy
A grant of money

■■■■■■■■■■■■■■■■■■
Reading Strategy
Metacognition
Note the main idea and important details of this paragraph. Summarize what you have read to make sure you understand it.

Fig. 7.6

Rising Campaign Costs

Candidates are raising and spending more money than ever, and no office demands more money than the presidential contest. John McCain and Barack Obama set new spending records in 2008, as data averages from both campaigns for just one month indicate. *How does campaign spending reflect the importance of television?*

GOVERNMENT ONLINE
Interactive
For an interactive view of campaign spending, visit **PearsonSuccessNet.com**

> TRAVEL $4,100,000   > TELEVISION AND RADIO ADVERTISING TIME $25,200,000   SOURCE: Federal Election Commission, September 2008
> CAMPAIGN WORKER SALARIES $2,000,000   > POLLING $800,000

The laws that the FEC is supposed to enforce cover four areas:

1. **Disclosure of campaign finance information.** This requirement is meant to spotlight the role of money in campaigns. Cash gifts of more than $100 are not allowed. Contributions must be made through a single campaign committee. This committee is in charge of spending. Contributions of more than $5,000 must be reported to the FEC.

2. **Limits on campaign contributions.** No person can give more than $2,300 to any federal candidate in a primary election. No person can give more than $2,300 to any federal candidate's election campaign. No person can give more than $5,000 to a political action committee, or $28,500 to a national party committee. The total of any person's contributions to federal candidates and committees must be no more than $108,200 in an election cycle. These numbers are adjusted every two years.

Some PACs are branches of business associations, labor unions, or professional organizations. These groups can only raise money from their members. There are a few hundred other PACs that are unconnected. They can raise money from anyone. PACs bundle the money they collect into a single large fund and give it to candidates. They may not give more than $5,000 to any one federal candidate in an election. They can give this amount to as many candidates as they choose. They may also contribute up to $15,000 a year to a political party.

PACs give hundreds of millions to presidential and congressional campaigns.

3. **Limits on federal campaign spending.** Most limits apply to presidential, not congressional, elections. This is due to the Supreme Court decision in *Buckley* v. *Valeo,* 1976. There, the Court struck down all but one spending limit. It said the other restrictions limited the right of free expression. In politics, the Court said, "money is speech." The one limit the Court upheld is a cap (limit) on spending if a candidate takes money from the FEC. A candidate can either take or reject that money.

4. **Public funds for presidential campaigns.** Congress provides for public funding of presidential campaigns. This practice began in 1971 with the Revenue Act, which created the Presidential Election Campaign Fund. Every person who files a federal income tax return can contribute to this fund. They simply check a box to give three dollars (six for a joint return) of their taxes to the fund. The money is used to pay for preconvention campaigns, national conventions, and presidential election campaigns.

Preconvention campaigns include all the campaigning done for primaries and caucuses. Preconvention campaigns are mostly paid for with private contributions. A candidate can also apply for public money from the FEC if he or she raises at least $100,000 from individuals. That $100,000 must be collected in $5,000 lots in at least 20 states. Individual donations can be no more than $250. This complicated method is meant to discourage candidates who are not serious.

The FEC matches part of the funds, and the candidate could receive about $21 million. In 2008, John McCain spent $100 million to win the Republican nomination and $7 million of that was from the FEC. Barack Obama refused the public money, but he raised $230 million on his own.

National conventions are also paid with public funds. If a major party applies for this money, it receives a grant to help pay for the national convention.

✔️ **Checkpoint** What are the four laws that the FEC is supposed to enforce?

Fig. 7.7

Total Campaign Spending, 1964–2008

Year	Estimated spending	Voter turnout*	Spending per voter
1964	$200 million	70.6 million	$2.83
1968	$300 million	73.2 million	$4.10
1972	$425 million	77.7 million	$5.47
1976	$540 million	81.6 million	$6.62
1980	$1.2 billion	86.6 million	$13.87
1984	$1.8 billion	92.7 million	$19.42
1988	$2.7 billion	91.6 million	$29.48
1992	$3.2 billion	104.4 million	$30.65
1996	$4.0 billion	96.5 million	$41.45
2000	$5.1 billion	105.4 million	$48.39
2004	$6.0 billion	120.2 million	$49.92
2008	$7.0 billion	131.2 million	$53.60

*Presidential elections
SOURCES: Federal Election Commission; Herbert E. Alexander, *Financing Politics*

▲ **Analyzing Charts** Total campaign spending has risen dramatically in recent elections. What factors account for this rise?

Hard money
Campaign money given directly to candidates and subject to FEC regulations

Soft money
Money given to parties or other political organizations in unlimited amounts

How are presidential elections funded?

Presidential election campaigns are, in part, paid with public funds. Each party nominee gets a public subsidy to pay for the general election campaign. In 2008, the subsidy was $84.1 million. If a candidate refuses the money, he or she can raise as much money as he or she can from private sources. John McCain took the FEC money in 2008. He was also backed by private organizations, such as the Republican National Committee. These groups contributed about $210 million to his campaign. Barack Obama did not take the FEC money, but he was able to raise $500 million for his post-convention campaign.

Some people think federal funding may soon end for several reasons: 1) so many candidates rejected the money for their preconvention campaigns, 2) taxpayers are not willing to finance the campaigns, and 3) the cost of campaign spending is rising.

✔**Checkpoint**   What are three reasons federal funding may end?

Fig. 7.7

Hard Money and Soft Money

Historically, hard money (right) was tightly regulated and more difficult to raise, while soft money (left) could be gotten easily from fewer people in larger sums. *How has regulation of hard and soft money changed since the 1990s?*

What is hard money? What is soft money?

Hard money is contributions that are given directly to candidates for their campaigns. This money is limited and must be reported to the FEC.

Soft money refers to funds given to parties or other political organizations, not limited to specific candidates, in unlimited amounts. This money is to be used for "party building." Party building includes voter registration or get-out-the-vote drives and campaigns for or against policies. As shown in Figure 7.7, soft money is much easier to come by than hard money.

In the 1980s, both major parties began to raise soft money. Millions of dollars came from wealthy people, labor unions, corporations, and other interest groups. These funds were supposed to be used for party-building. Instead, much of the money went into political campaigns.

Congress finally enacted legislation to reform the country's campaign finance laws in 2002. The Bipartisan Campaign Reform Act (BCRA) was passed after years of debate. The law is also known as the McCain-Feingold Law. It addresses the soft money problem by banning soft money contributions to political parties. The BCRA does not say that other groups cannot raise money, however. Soon, a number of independent groups, not connected to a political party, began to raise money. They raised hundreds of millions of dollars.

Figure 7.8 summarizes three important sources of campaign contributions: individual donors, political action committees, and public financing.

Fig. 7.8

Campaign Contributions
- Individual donors
- Political action committees (PACs)
- Public financing by government

SECTION 3 ASSESSMENT

Essential Questions Journal — Go to your **Essential Questions Journal** to work on this chapter's Essential Question.

1. **Guiding Question** Use your completed chart to answer the question: What role does money play in electoral politics?

Key Terms and Comprehension

On a sheet of paper, write the answer to each question. Use complete sentences.

2. Why do people contribute to political campaigns?

3. What is a political action committee?

4. What are two ways in which the FEC attempts to regulate campaign financing?

5. What is the difference between hard money and soft money?

Critical Thinking

6. **Summarize** Why does the huge amount of money needed for political campaigns concern many people?

7. **Identify Point of View** If you contributed a large amount of money to a candidate, would you want something (like a job or a new law passed) in return? Explain your answer.

Quick Study Guide

Chapter Summary

Section 1—The Nominating Process

- The nominating process is the important first step in an election.

- There are five ways nominations are made: self-announcement, caucus, convention, direct primary, and petition.

- The direct primary is an election within the political party to pick candidates for the general election.

- The two basic forms of the direct primary are closed primaries and open primaries.

- A petition must be signed by a certain number of qualified voters to place a candidate's name on the ballot.

Section 2—Elections

- Election laws protect the honesty and quality of the electoral process.

- States make most of the election laws. But Congress does regulate some aspects of elections.

- A precinct is a voting district. A polling place is where the voters of the precinct come to cast their votes.

- Voters may cast their ballots several ways: early voting, electronic data processing methods, direct response electronic voting (DRE), paper ballots, or voting by mail.

Section 3—Money and Elections

- Campaign spending in the United States costs billions of dollars.

- Candidates and their parties receive their money from private and public sources.

- People give money to candidates for many reasons. They may believe in the candidate, seek recognition, or want something in return.

- The Federal Election Commission (FEC) is an independent agency that administers all federal laws concerning campaign finance.

- Hard money is limited by law.

- The Bipartisan Campaign Reform Act, passed in 2002, bans soft money contributions to political parties.

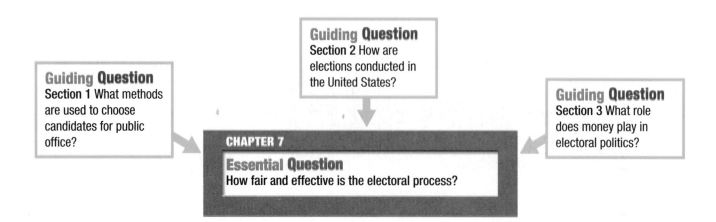

Guiding Question
Section 1 What methods are used to choose candidates for public office?

Guiding Question
Section 2 How are elections conducted in the United States?

Guiding Question
Section 3 What role does money play in electoral politics?

CHAPTER 7

Essential Question
How fair and effective is the electoral process?

Document-Based Assessment

Hillary Rodham Clinton's Presidential Candidacy Announcement

On January 20, 2007, Senator Hillary Rodham Clinton made a live announcement on her Web site to announce her candidacy for President of the United States. Here are excerpts from the announcement:

Document at a Glance

- Clinton's candidacy announcement for President
- Used Internet to announce candidacy
- Calls for supporters to get to work for America

I'm in. And I'm in to win . . . The stakes will be high when America chooses a new President in 2008. . . . Only a new President can renew the promise of America—the idea that if you work hard you can count on the healthcare and retirement security that you need to raise your family. . . .

This is a big election with some very big questions. How do we bring the war in Iraq to an end? . . . How will we ensure our children inherit a clean environment and energy independence? How can we reduce the deficits that threaten Social Security and Medicare?

No matter where you live, no matter what your political views, I want you to be a part of this important conversation right from the start . . . I'm going to spend the next several days answering your questions in a series of live video discussions . . . I'll sit down to answer your questions about how we can work together for a better future. And you can participate live at my Web site. . . .

This campaign is our moment, our chance to stand up for the principles and values that we cherish; to bring new ideas, energy, and leadership to a . . . challenging time. It's our chance to say "we can" and "we will." Let's go to work. America is calling us.

Document-Based Questions

1. What method did Hillary Clinton use to make her presidential candidacy announcement?

2. What did she say only a new President could do?

3. What did she say our children should inherit?

4. How did she say she was going to spend the next several days?

5. **Use Metacognition** What other questions do you have about this speech? Brainstorm ideas with the class.

SOURCE: *http://www.4president.org/speeches/2008/hillaryclinton2008announcement.htm*

Chapter Assessment

GOVERNMENT ONLINE
Self-Test
To test your understanding of key terms and main ideas, visit
PearsonSuccessNet.com

Directions: On a sheet of paper, write the answer to each question. Use complete sentences.

Section 1—The Nominating Process

1. What happens during the nomination process?

2. What are five ways in which nominations are made?

3. What are the two basic forms of the direct primary?

4. What is a petition?

5. How does the convention process begin?

6. **Critical Thinking** Why do you think a political party might not want a blanket primary? Explain your answer.

Section 2—Elections

7. Why were election laws passed?

8. What is a ballot?

9. Who sets the date for presidential and congressional elections?

10. When is absentee voting used?

11. What is a polling place? How does it differ from a precinct?

12. **Critical Thinking** Why do you think there is an interest in allowing people to vote online?

Section 3— Money and Elections

13. What factors determine how much will be spent on a campaign?

14. How do campaign contributions allow candidates to run for office?

15. Why might a person give money to a political campaign?

16. What is the difference between hard money and soft money?

17. **Critical Thinking** The Supreme Court has ruled that campaign contributions are a form of speech. Explain why you agree or disagree.

Apply What You've Learned

Exploring the Essential Question

Prepare an outline for a debate on the following topic: Money is essential to the electoral process. Answer Questions 18 and 19 below to help build your outline.

18. List the reasons why you do or do not think money is essential to the electoral process.

19. Think about what might happen if all money was removed from the political process.

Essential Questions Project

20. After you have written about the role of money in the electoral process, find a partner. Your partner should have chosen the opposite argument on the importance of money in the electoral process. Debate your stance against your partner with help from your teacher. The debate should help answer the Essential Question: **How fair and effective is the electoral process?**

Essential Questions
Journal

Go to your **Essential Questions Journal** to work on this chapter's Essential Question.

Test-Taking Tip

If you are unsure of an answer, put a check mark next to it. Once you have finished the test, go back to the items with check marks. Review and revise your answers as needed.

▲ Onlookers watch the news in Times Square, New York City.

Mass Media and Public Opinion

Essential Question
What is the place of the media and public opinion in a democracy?

Section 1: The Formation of Public Opinion

Section 2: Measuring Public Opinion

Section 3: The Mass Media

■ ■

Reading Strategy: Summarizing
When you summarize, you restate what you have read in your own words. As you read this chapter on the mass media and public opinion, ask yourself the following questions:
- What is the main idea of this chapter?
- What details are important to understanding the main idea?

When you can answer these questions, begin to write your summary.

ON THE GO

To study anywhere, anytime, download these online resources at PearsonSuccessNet.com
- Political Dictionary
- Audio Review
- Downloadable Interactivities

The Formation of Public Opinion

▲ Guests on *Meet the Press* discuss the 2008 presidential election.

What is public opinion, and what factors help to shape it? Use a concept web like the one below to show the factors that influence public opinion.

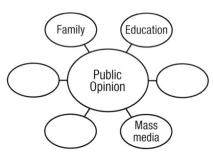

Objectives:

- Examine the term *public opinion* and understand why it is difficult to define.
- Analyze how family and education shape public opinion.
- Describe four additional factors that shape public opinion.

Public opinion is a major factor influencing our political leaders and their actions. The President, other elected leaders, and candidates running for office are all expected to act according to what the public wants.

What is public opinion?

The term *public opinion* is often used, but it is rarely fully understood. The term shows up in newspapers and magazines. It is discussed often on radio and television. To understand what public opinion is, you must first understand this important point: It is the attitudes about government and politics shared by many people. It reflects the most popular views of the people.

There are many publics in the United States. A public is a group of people who have the same ideas and views about a public issue. For example, people may belong to a public that believes in national health insurance. Education and the environment are other issues of concern for many people.

It is also important to note that public opinion is only concerned with **public affairs.** Public affairs are events and issues that concern a great many people. Politics, political parties, taxes, the economy, national defense, and healthcare are considered public affairs (**Figure 8.1**). People are also interested in many other things, such as music, entertainment, or sports. The opinions of people concerning these interests are usually not considered public opinion, however.

✔**Checkpoint**   What are two examples of public affairs?

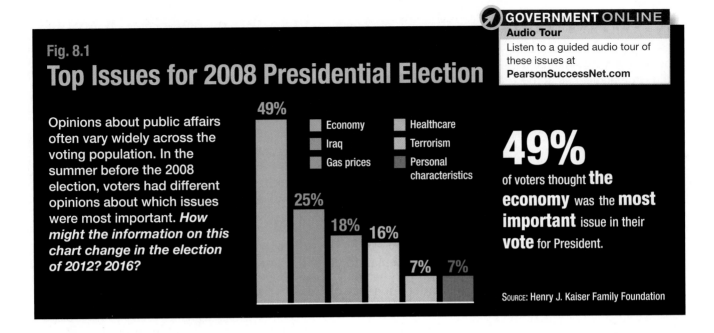

Fig. 8.1

Top Issues for 2008 Presidential Election

Opinions about public affairs often vary widely across the voting population. In the summer before the 2008 election, voters had different opinions about which issues were most important. *How might the information on this chart change in the election of 2012? 2016?*

49%

- Economy
- Iraq
- Gas prices
- Healthcare
- Terrorism
- Personal characteristics

49%
25%
18%
16%
7%
7%

49% of voters thought **the economy** was the **most important** issue in their **vote** for President.

Source: Henry J. Kaiser Family Foundation

Public opinion is difficult to define. It may be said that **public opinion** is the attitudes held by a large number of people concerning government and politics. The people must express these views in order for them to be considered public opinion. The attitudes and opinions can be spoken or written. They can also be displayed on billboards or expressed at demonstrations. Voting for a candidate with similar views is another way people express their opinions.

How does family and education influence public opinion?

Each person has his or her own political opinions. These opinions develop over time and are influenced by many factors. Chapter 6 described the political socialization process. The experiences a person has over a lifetime form that person's viewpoints and opinions.

Family and education have a huge influence on a person's political opinions. Children first learn attitudes about concepts like authority, property, and other people from the family. Later, children form political opinions based on these attitudes. Many tend to vote as their parents vote. Others form opinions of their own.

Although the family strongly influences the political development of a child, schools also play an important role. Schools teach American values. They stress good citizenship and patriotism. Children learn to salute the flag and say the Pledge of Allegiance. They are taught about the importance of government, its development, and its outstanding leaders.

Schools also provide a place for informal learning. At school, children must learn to make decisions and to get along with all types of people.

Public affairs
Events and issues that concern many people

Public opinion
The attitudes shared by many people about government and politics

Reading Strategy
Summarizing
Look through this section. What are two factors that influence public opinion?

Mass media
Types of communication that reach large audiences at the same time, especially television, radio, printed publications, and the Internet

Peer group
People with whom one regularly associates, including friends, classmates, neighbors, and co-workers

Family and education are not the only factors in the making of public opinion. They do, however, play a leading role.

✓ **Checkpoint** What are two major influences on a person's political opinions?

What other factors influence public opinion?

One important factor that influences public opinion is occupation. For example, national health insurance is a topic of great concern in America. Many working people are not given health insurance where they work. These people tend to support candidates who promise a plan to provide insurance.

Gender and place of residence also have influence on public opinion. Candidates who believe in equal pay for women or fight for programs that benefit all Americans are often supported by women and minority groups. Cleaning up a lake will often be of interest to people who live near that lake. These people may support the candidate or party that supports the environmental project.

Besides family, education, gender, race, and residence, there are four other main factors in the opinion-making process. Those four factors are the mass media, peer groups, opinion leaders, and historic events.

The **mass media** include all the ways information is communicated to large groups of people. Newspapers, magazines, radio, the Internet, and television are all forms of mass media. Television is the largest provider of information to the greatest number of people. The mass media often tries to shape public opinion (**Figure 8.2**).

Schoolchildren usually associate with the same classmates day to day. These classmates become a child's **peer group.** As a child grows into adulthood, the peer group expands to include friends, neighbors, and co-workers. A person's peer group has a strong influence on his or her attitudes and actions. Because trust usually develops within the peer group, the members of the group tend to share experiences and support each other's opinions.

Fig. 8.2

" WE DO WANT TO WARN YOU THAT THIS NEWS HAS YET TO BE SPUN, SO YOU MAY HAVE TO FORMULATE YOUR OWN OPINION. "

▲ Analyzing Cartoons An effort to shape the public's response is known as "spin." *What is the cartoonist implying about the media here?*

An **opinion leader** is a person who has a strong influence on others. Many opinion leaders hold public office. Others are writers, broadcasters, important businesspeople, and professionals. People listen to the ideas of these leaders, and so they often help to shape public opinion.

People's attitudes about public policy are greatly affected by historical events. The terrorist attacks of September 11, 2001, changed many people's views on national security and foreign policy. The Great Depression also changed many people's views about government. During that crisis, people began to expect the national government to take a bigger part in the economy.

The events of the 1960s and early 1970s also shaped public opinion about government. After World War II, most people felt optimistic about the place of the United States in the world. That attitude changed after several tragic events. In the 1960s, President John F. Kennedy and Martin Luther King, Jr., were both shot and killed. The civil rights movement that followed brought turmoil to the country. In 1974, the Watergate scandal brought about the resignation of President Richard Nixon. These years of unrest caused some people to distrust the government. This attitude still exists today among some groups of citizens.

Opinion leader
A person who has strong influence on others

Essential Questions Journal Go to your **Essential Questions Journal** to work on this chapter's Essential Question.

SECTION 1 ASSESSMENT

Quick Write

Using the Internet, other sources, and your textbook, identify a public issue. The issue may be about the environment, energy, or any other topics related to politics, public issues, or public policy. Write a brief summary of the issue. Make sure to discuss public opinion on the issue.

1. **Guiding Question** Use your completed concept web to answer this question: What is pubic opinion, and what factors help to shape it?

Key Terms and Comprehension

On a sheet of paper, write the answer to each question. Use complete sentences.

2. When a person is said to belong to a public, what does that mean?

3. To what kinds of issues and affairs is public opinion limited?

4. Name the main factors that influence public opinion.

5. How have historical events changed public opinion about government?

Critical Thinking

6. **Draw Conclusions** Why might people base their own opinions on those of leaders in their communities?

7. **Identifying Central Issues** What public issues might have been discussed after the terrorist attacks of September 11, 2001?

Measuring Public Opinion

▲ NBC News pollster conducts an election exit poll.

Guiding Question

How is public opinion measured and used? Use a table like the one below to take notes on the section.

Measuring Public Opinion	
Elections	Voting results can sometimes reflect public opinion.
Interest Groups	Interest groups present their views by different means.

Objectives:

- Describe the challenges involved in measuring public opinion.
- Explain why scientific opinion polls are the best measure of public opinion.
- Identify five steps in the polling process.
- Understand the difficulties involved in evaluating polls.
- Recognize the limits on the impact of public opinion in a democracy.

Polls are the most common way public opinion is measured. Before an important election, the phrase "According to the latest poll . . ." is often heard. The leaders who make public policy want to know what people think. In this section, you will read about how public opinion is measured.

How is public opinion measured?

There are many ways to measure public opinion. Voting statistics, editorial comments on television and radio, Internet blogs, and paid advertising are all ways to measure public opinion. The American political system depends on the effort to find an accurate idea of what people think and want. (See **Figure 8.3** on the next page.)

In a democracy, the voice of the people is expressed on election day. In this way, election results are important indicators of public opinion. The people who cast votes for a candidate often do so because they believe in the candidate's views. The votes may also show approval for the candidate's political party. After a successful election, the winning party may claim to have a **mandate.** This means the party believes the majority of the people want them to carry out their campaign promises. Election results, though, are often not the best measure of public opinion. Some voters are not sure of the candidate's or the party's views. The reasons for voting for a particular candidate are varied. Elections can be said to give only broad ideas about public opinion.

Interest groups are another important way to measure public opinion. Interest groups are private organizations whose members have the same views or opinions about what government should do about a particular matter. Sometimes these groups are called pressure groups or special-interest groups. Interest groups express their views through lobbyists, letters, telephone calls, e-mails, and other efforts. It is hard for political leaders to know just how many people belong to an interest group.

The media are another measure of public opinion. It is important to remember, however, that magazines, television commentators, and blogs are not only mirrors of public opinion. They are also shapers of opinion.

A final way to measure public opinion, besides polls, is through personal contact. Public officials spend a great deal of time connecting with the people in their districts. Congressmen stay in touch with the public through mail, phone calls, and e-mail. Other officials, such as governors, mayors, and legislators, also make direct contact with the public. They do this in their offices, public meetings, and social events. Some public officials are better than others at understanding what the people want. Unfortunately, they too often listen only to views that agree with their own.

✔ **Checkpoint** What are interest groups?

Mandate
The instructions or commands of the people given to their elected officials

Interest group
Group whose members share the same viewpoint and work to shape public policy on certain issues

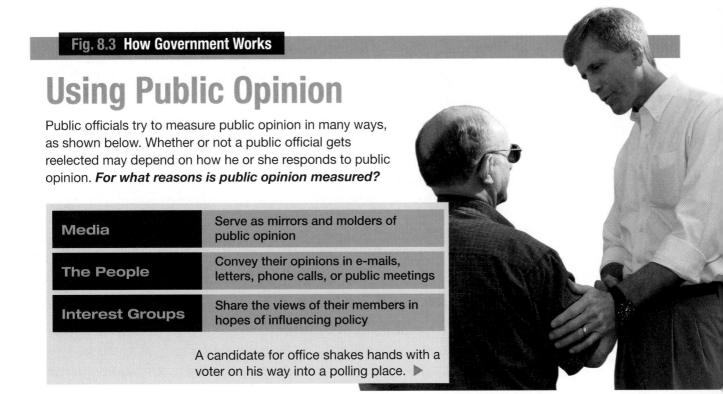

Fig. 8.3 How Government Works

Using Public Opinion

Public officials try to measure public opinion in many ways, as shown below. Whether or not a public official gets reelected may depend on how he or she responds to public opinion. *For what reasons is public opinion measured?*

Media	Serve as mirrors and molders of public opinion
The People	Convey their opinions in e-mails, letters, phone calls, or public meetings
Interest Groups	Share the views of their members in hopes of influencing policy

A candidate for office shakes hands with a voter on his way into a polling place. ▶

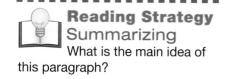

Reading Strategy
Summarizing
What is the main idea of
this paragraph?

Public opinion poll
Device that collects information by
asking people questions

Straw vote
Poll that seeks to read the public's
mind by asking the same question
of a large number of people

Universe
The entire population that a poll
wants to measure

What are public opinion polls?

Public opinion is best measured by **public opinion polls.** Opinion polls are taken in order to collect information by asking people questions. There are two major types of opinion polls: straw polls and scientific polls.

Early polling efforts relied on the straw vote. A **straw vote** is a poll that tries to measure public opinion by asking the same question to a large number of people. Straw polls are still used today. For example, radio talk-show hosts ask questions and listeners can call in with their responses. This type of polling is not reliable, however, because the people who respond to the poll do not accurately represent the total population. The straw vote may get a large number of responses, but those responses are only from a narrow segment of the population. They do not reflect the opinions of the majority of the people.

In 1936, the *Literary Digest* conducted a famous straw poll before the presidential election. The magazine sent out more than 10 million postcards. More than 2 million people responded. The people who were sent postcards were chosen from automobile registration lists and the phone book. As a result of this poll, the magazine predicted that Republican Alfred Landon would win the presidency. Instead, Franklin Roosevelt won. He was elected by a 60 percent majority of the popular vote. Many of the people who voted for Roosevelt in the election were poor. They did not own cars or have telephones, so they did not receive postcards. They were not represented in the poll.

A scientific poll is the other type of opinion poll. In America today, there are more than 1,000 groups that conduct these polls. Many of these polls are conducted to judge consumer likes and dislikes. More than 200 companies conduct scientific polls about politics. The best-known polling groups are the Gallop Organization and the Pew Research Center for the People and the Press. Scientific polls have developed over the decades and have become very sophisticated.

✔**Checkpoint**   What are the two different kinds of opinion polls?

What is the polling process?

Scientific poll-taking is a very difficult process. Analyzing the results of these polls also can be difficult (**Figure 8.4** on page 190). In general, however, the polling process can be described in five steps:

1. Define the universe to be surveyed. **Universe** means the whole group that a poll wants to measure. For example, all voters in California or every high school student in a state make up a universe.

2. Construct a sample. In most cases a universe is too large a group to be able to poll everyone in it. Instead, a **sample** of the universe is taken. A sample is a smaller group that represents the larger group. Many pollsters use a **random sample.** This is a certain number of people who are randomly picked. It is a sample in which each member of the universe and each geographic area within it has an equal chance of being included. As few as 1,500 people may be polled to reflect the views of the entire country. The law of probability says that this number (1,500) will accurately reflect the views of the nation within a margin of + or – 3 percent. This margin of error means a spread of 6 percentage points.

Other pollsters use a **quota sample.** For example, the exact ratio of males and females are picked to match the ratio in a universe. This kind of sample is less reliable than random samples.

3. Ask well-written questions. Questions used by pollsters must be easy to understand. They also must be carefully worded because the way a question is asked can affect how it is answered. Responsible pollsters try to avoid questions that lead the respondent to a particular answer. For example, if asked "Should taxes be reduced?" most people would probably answer "Yes." The same people would probably also answer "Yes" if asked "Should the police force be increased to fight rising crime?" Yet increasing the size of the police force would almost certainly require raising taxes.

Sample
A representative portion of the total universe

Random sample
A sample in which each member of the universe has an equal chance of being included

Quota sample
A sample constructed to reflect the major characteristics of a given population

Government in Your Life

Government on the Internet

The Internet has many Web sites that offer information about the federal government. For example, each department has a home page. The home page lists information you might want to know about the department. Internet users can click on a topic to find additional information.

The Web site for the White House is www.whitehouse.gov. People who are on the Internet can learn more about the federal government from the White House Web site. They can look at government documents and connect to other government departments and agencies. The House and Senate each have their own Web sites, as does the Supreme Court.

Fig. 8.4

Evaluating Polls

Questions to Ask About Polls

GOVERNMENT ONLINE
Audio Tour
To learn additional questions to ask about polls, visit
PearsonSuccessNet.com

Poll results are often published in newspapers, in magazines, or online. You should learn to analyze such results carefully. Use the following questions as a starting point. *Why is it important to read poll results critically?*

WHO?

Who is responsible for the poll?

Polls sponsored by political campaigns may aim to mislead as much as inform.

WHAT?

What is the poll's universe?

The universe is the population the poll seeks to measure. Knowing this allows you to judge whether the sample from it is truly representative.

HOW?

How was the sample chosen?

Samples should be selected randomly. How were questions written and asked? The method of creating and asking questions can alter the results.

WHY?

Why is the poll being conducted?

Polls meant to boost a candidate's approval ratings are not reliable.

WHEN?

When was the data collected?

Opinions change quickly during elections—so knowing when the data was collected is important.

4. Conduct interviews. For a long time, most polls were taken door-to-door. Today most polls are done by telephone, with a sample selected by random digital dialing. In random digit dialing, calls are made to randomly chosen numbers within randomly chosen area codes around the country. Most professional pollsters agree that only one method should be used in any given poll. Pollsters do not recommend in-person interviews and random digital dialing used together.

Whichever method is used, the way the interview is handled is very important. Tone of voice and choice of words will influence the answers given by the people questioned. Therefore, people who do the interviews are carefully chosen and trained by the polling groups.

5. Analyze and report the findings. Polling groups collect huge amounts of information. The results must be reported to the public. To do this, computers and other electronic hardware are used to analyze the information. Conclusions are then drawn and published.

✔ **Checkpoint** What are the five steps of the polling process?

How are polls evaluated?

Most polls are reliable but not perfect. People who conduct the polls know that there are limits to their accuracy. Some problems that are difficult to overcome concern the intensity, stability, and relevance of the opinions that polls report. Intensity has to do with the strength of a person's opinion. Is it strong or weak? Stability has to do with the permanence of the opinion. Is the person likely to change his or her mind? Relevance has to do with the importance of the opinion. Will the person continue to be guided by the opinion?

Even though scientific polls receive criticism, they are the best way we have to measure public opinion. They may not be precise. However, they do give a reasonable guide to public opinion. They also focus attention on issues and encourage people to discuss them.

Reading Strategy
Summarizing
What are some important details that help you understand this section?

What are the limits on the impact of public opinion?

Public opinion has a strong influence on the making of public policy. A number of other influences are working at the same time, however. The United States government works on a system of checks and balances. There is a separation of power among the three branches of government. These safeguards protect minority interests and allow them to be heard.

SECTION 2 ASSESSMENT

Essential Questions
Journal
Go to your **Essential Questions Journal** to work on this chapter's Essential Question.

1. **Guiding Question** Use your completed table to answer the question: How is public opinion measured and used?

Key Terms and Comprehension

On a sheet of paper, write the answer to each question. Use complete sentences.

2. What is a mandate?

3. Why is it hard to determine much about public opinion based on the actions of interest groups?

4. Why are straw votes not a reliable way to measure public opinion?

5. What is a random sample?

Critical Thinking

6. **Draw Conclusions** Why might a candidate running for office want to know the public's opinion on different issues?

7. **Make Inferences** What are some of the limits that make evaluating polls difficult? What could be done to decrease the effect of these factors?

Conducting a Poll

We live in a representative democracy. This means that voters elect representatives to act on their behalf. Your school's student government may operate the same way. One way a representative can find out how the people feel about an issue is to conduct a poll. Yet, putting together a good poll requires knowledge and skill.

Follow these five steps to conduct an effective poll.

1. **Define the universe.** In polling, the universe is the group of people whose opinions you are interested in learning about. For a presidential candidate, it may be all the voters in the country. For a candidate for student council, it may be all the students in a school.

2. **Construct your sample.** In some cases, you may be able to poll every person in the universe. If that is not possible, you must identify whom you will poll—your sample. Your sample should be a selection of people chosen randomly from the universe. The goal is to poll a group that represents the whole universe. NOTE: People who volunteer to be polled are not a random sample.

3. **Prepare valid questions.** Good poll questions do not lead people to an answer. They also do not convey a strong attitude about an issue. They provide enough information to frame the question properly. Before you conduct your poll, invite friends or classmates to review your questions.

4. **Conduct interviews carefully.** Remember, the goal is to get answers that truly reflect people's attitudes. An interviewer must be careful not to lead subjects to a particular answer.

5. **Interpret the results.** Polls are not perfect. If you have used a random sample, your results will have a margin of error. When you interpret your results, remember to consider the intensity, stability, and relevance of the opinions shared.

▶▶ What do you think?

1. What is the first step in conducting an effective poll?

2. Why are the people that volunteer to be polled not a random sample?

3. **You Try It** Design a public opinion poll about an issue in your school or community. Use the five steps mentioned above to conduct an effective poll.

GOVERNMENT ONLINE
Citizenship Activity Pack
For an activity to help you further explore public opinion polling, go to **PearsonSuccessNet.com**

▲ People get their news from various news sources, such as the Internet.

SECTION 3
The Mass Media

Guiding Question

How has the development of different media helped inform the public about politics? Use a flowchart like the one below to take notes on the development of different media.

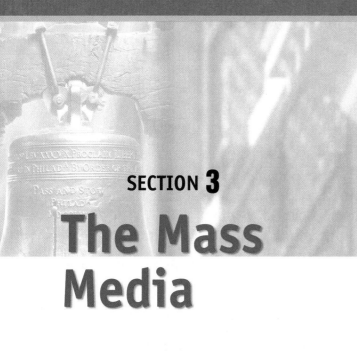

Newspapers	Magazines	Radio
■ Spread information about independence	■	■
■	■	■

Television	The Internet
■ New York World's Fair, 1939	■
■	■

Objectives:
- Examine the role of the mass media in providing the public with political information.
- Explain how the mass media influence politics.
- Understand the factors that limit the influence of the media.

How much television do you watch each day? One hour? Three hours? More? Studies show that by the time the average student graduates from high school today, he or she will have spent nearly 11,000 hours in classrooms. That same student will spend nearly 15,000 hours watching television—more than 20 hours of television each week. Television has a big impact on the lives of everyone in this country, as do all of the other kinds of mass media.

What is the role of the mass media?

Media is the plural of the word **medium.** A medium is a means of communication. Mass media are means of communication that can reach many people at the same time. In America, there are five types of mass media that are important in politics. They are television, newspapers, radio, magazines, and the Internet.

Mass media provide entertainment but also provide people with political information. News can be reported directly as it happens or given in radio and television programs, stories, and blogs. Public affairs are often covered in these ways. Most information people receive comes from the mass media.

Television

Television is the most widely used form of mass media. The first public use of television was seen at the New York World's Fair in 1939. Some people watched on small screens as President Franklin Roosevelt opened the fair. Since that time, television has played an important role in politics (**Figure 8.5**).

Television increased in popularity in the 1950s. By the 1960s, television was the major provider of news to most Americans. Today, there are more than 1,700 television stations. Three networks—CBS, ABC, and NBC— provide programming that accounts for nearly half of all television viewing time today.

In recent years, the dominance of these networks has been declining. There are now several independent broadcasting companies and cable broadcasters. The most popular are the Fox Network and the Cable News Network (CNN). The Public Broadcasting Service (PBS) also has more than 350 stations.

Television reaches millions of people. News programs and popular entertainment shows have up to 40 million viewers. Cable systems are now used by almost three fourths of our country's households.

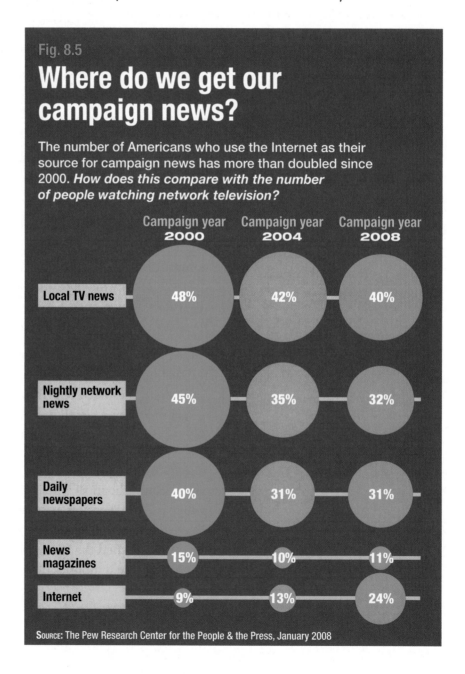

Fig. 8.5

Where do we get our campaign news?

The number of Americans who use the Internet as their source for campaign news has more than doubled since 2000. *How does this compare with the number of people watching network television?*

	Campaign year 2000	Campaign year 2004	Campaign year 2008
Local TV news	48%	42%	40%
Nightly network news	45%	35%	32%
Daily newspapers	40%	31%	31%
News magazines	15%	10%	11%
Internet	9%	13%	24%

Source: The Pew Research Center for the People & the Press, January 2008

Newspapers

Newspapers are another form of mass media. In 1704, the *Boston News-Letter* began publication. Soon, other newspapers appeared in the colonial cities of Boston, New York, and Philadelphia. Most were small weekly papers. Daily newspapers began to appear in 1783. During revolutionary days, papers spread information about the fight for independence and printed the text of the Declaration of Independence. When the Constitution was written, the 1st Amendment was added to guarantee freedom of the press. The Framers knew that this freedom was important to democracy.

Today, there are still thousands of newspapers in the United States. Daily and weekly papers in some foreign-languages are published. Almost half of the adults in the nation read a newspaper every day.

Radio, television, and the Internet have caused a decline in the number of daily newspapers. In 1920, more than 2,000 daily papers were printed. Today, that number has fallen to about 1,400.

Nevertheless, newspapers are still a major source of information about the government and politics for many people. Newspapers usually cover stories in greater detail than television does. Also, editorial sections of newspapers present different views concerning issues and candidates. Some influential newspapers today are the *New York Times*, the *Washington Post*, the *Wall Street Journal*, and *USA Today*. These papers are available around the country on the day they are published.

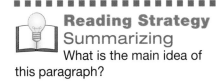

Reading Strategy
Summarizing
What is the main idea of this paragraph?

Radio

A third form of mass media, radio, began in 1920. Station KDKA broadcast the presidential election returns that year. By 1930, radio was a major medium of entertainment and news. President Franklin Roosevelt was the first President to make good use of radio. He broadcast weekly fireside chats with a strong, confident voice. Americans, for the first time, could hear a President in their own homes.

Some people thought that television would bring an end to radio. Radio has survived because it can be used anywhere—cars, outdoors, offices, and homes. Radio is still a major source of public information. The average person listens to about 15 hours of radio a week.

Magazines

The magazine is another type of mass media with its roots in colonial days. Most magazines published in the early days of our country, into the 1900s, were concerned with literature and social graces. Beginning in the mid-1800s, a few did cover political issues, including *Harpers Weekly* and *Atlantic Monthly*.

Today, there are more than 12,000 magazines published in the United States. Many cover topics such as trades or personal interests. The magazines with the highest circulation are *AARP the Magazine*, *Readers Digest*, and *National Geographic*. News magazines include *Time*, *Newsweek*, and *U.S. News and World Report*. They are important sources of political news and opinions.

The Internet

The Internet is quickly becoming the leading medium for news and information (Figure 8.6). The Internet can be traced back to a project of the Defense Department. During the Cold War era, the Defense Department established a four-computer network. Soon, it grew to connect computers at 15 locations across the country.

Fig. 8.6

The Transformation of Mass Media

As media have changed, so has the way that people participate. *What has been the impact of the Internet on political discussion?*

The "big three" networks, ABC, CBS, and NBC, dominated early television. Nightly news programs by respected anchors, such as Walter Cronkite (right), commanded large audiences and set the agenda for the nation.

Radio spread widely in the 1920s and 1930s, giving a national voice to elected officials and gifted speakers.

THEN... A Few Voices Imparting Information

From those beginnings, the Internet has expanded massively. By the 1990s, the Internet began to be used in the private sector. Today, it is a mass medium. The Internet is used as a source for political news and information more often than newspapers, radios, and magazines. Only television is more popular.

Other media have recognized the Internet's popularity. Nearly all newspapers now have Web sites. Magazines are also available online. Government agencies also use the Internet. Interest groups, political parties, elected officials, and campaign organizations all have Web pages as well.

The Internet has created **weblogs,** often called "blogs." Weblogs are Web site postings usually devoted to a specific subject. A single weblog author writes a series of posts. Many weblogs also allow visitors to post their own comments. Those blogs devoted to government usually have links to and commentaries from other sources.

✔ **Checkpoint** What are the five forms of mass media?

Weblog
A Web site posting, usually devoted to a specific subject

GOVERNMENT ONLINE
Audio Tour
For more information on the transformation of mass media, visit **PearsonSuccessNet.com**

Television and radio seek out and broadcast the opinions and questions of their audiences **The Internet** transforms the way people get political information. Instead of merely receiving information, people are e-mailing, podcasting, and creating videos to add their voices to political discussion. Television and the Internet joined forces (as shown here) when CNN partnered with YouTube to allow ordinary citizens to question presidential candidates in the 2008 primary debates.

NOW... *Millions of Conversations*

How do the media influence politics?

The media play an important role in American politics. This influence is seen mostly in the shaping of the **public agenda** and electoral politics. The public agenda includes the issues on which people's attention is focused.

The media help to shape the public agenda by focusing the public's attention on particular issues. Placing a political issue on the front page of a newspaper is one way of getting the public's attention. Mentioning an issue on a newscast is another tactic. People will discuss issues they hear about in the media even if they disagree with the opinion given. Most people rely on the media for political information on public issues. Even the President receives a daily report on all broadcasts and published news reports.

The media is important in electoral politics. Television, for example, allows political candidates to appeal directly to the people without the help of political parties. Campaign managers are aware that the impression the candidate displays on television is important. They carefully pick the location and other details before allowing the candidate to be televised. Newscasts of candidates are usually short and feature **sound bites.** Sound bites are short reports that are 30 or 40 seconds long.

What are the limits of media influence?

The impact of the media on American politics is limited for several reasons (Figure 8.7). First, few people follow political events very closely. Studies show that only about 15 percent of the people who vote are well-informed. In addition, the media carries content that deals more with entertainment than with politics. Finally, radio and television news shows do not usually report in depth. However, in-depth coverage is available in all media to those who want to find it.

Fig. 8.7 **The Mass Media's Impact on Public Opinion**

Benefits	Limits
• Help shape the public agenda • Influence electoral politics • In-depth media coverage is available to those who look for it, particularly on the Internet. • Changing nature of the media allows for more people to actively participate in discussions. • Publication of poll results allows media to show how public opinion is measured.	• Only a small number of people follow media very closely. • People tend to be selective in choosing political coverage. • Much media content is shallow and unrelated to political affairs. • Media such as radio and television tend to carry only short reports on general news and politics. • Newspapers and television depend on advertising revenue, which can sometimes dictate coverage.

Biography

Tom Brokaw (1940–)

Tom Brokaw is a television journalist. He was anchor and managing editor of NBC *Nightly News* from 1983 through 2004. Since 1962 he has reported on many national events. He covered the civil rights movement in Atlanta, Georgia, in the 1960s. He was White House correspondent during the Watergate era. In 1995, he reported on the Oklahoma City bombing.

Mr. Brokaw was born in Webster, South Dakota. He studied political science and graduated from the University of South Dakota. He married former Miss South Dakota and current author Meredith Auld. They have three daughters.

Tom Brokaw has written many books. He has received a number of honorary degrees. Although he stepped down from NBC *Nightly News* in 2004, he was asked to be the television host again after the death of his friend and colleague Tim Russert. He plans to work part time for NBC through 2014, serving as an analyst and documentary producer.

Essential Questions Journal Go to your **Essential Questions Journal** to work on this chapter's Essential Question.

SECTION 3 ASSESSMENT

1. **Guiding Question** Use your completed flowchart to answer the question: How has the development of different media helped inform the public about politics?

Key Terms and Comprehension

On a sheet of paper, write the answer to each question. Use complete sentences.

2. What are the five types of mass media that are important in American politics?

3. What is the media's role in shaping the public agenda?

4. What are sound bites?

5. What has caused the decline in the number of daily newspapers in the United States?

Critical Thinking

6. **Predict Consequences** What might happen if the mass media were not protected by the First Amendment?

7. **Draw Conclusions** Do you think the Internet will one day replace printed newspapers and magazines? Why or why not?

Chapter Summary

Section 1—The Formation of Public Opinion

- Public affairs are events and issues that concern a great many people.

- Public opinion is the attitudes of a large number of people concerning government and political matters.

- Family and education are the two biggest influences on a person's opinion.

- Occupation, race, gender, and place of residence also have an impact on a person's opinion.

- The mass media include all the ways information is communicated to large groups of people.

- An opinion leader is a person who has a strong influence on others and may shape public opinion.

- Historical events can play an important part in shaping public opinion.

Section 2—Measuring Public Opinion

- There are many ways to find out about public opinion on an issue. These include voting data, editorial comments in the media, and paid advertising.

- Interest groups let their views be known through lobbyists, letters, telephone calls, and other efforts.

- The mass media both reflect and shape public opinion.

- Public opinion is best measured by public opinion polls. There are two types of polls: straw polls and scientific polls.

- The scientific polling process has five steps: define the universe, construct the sample, ask well-written questions, conduct interviews carefully, and analyze the results.

Section 3—The Mass Media

- There are five types of mass media that are important in politics: television, newspapers, radio, magazines, and the Internet.

- The media play an important role in American politics. This influence is seen in the shaping of the public agenda and electoral politics.

- Most people rely on the media for political information on public issues.

- There are limits on the political influence the media has. Most of it provides more entertainment than in-depth coverage of political issues.

Guiding Question
Section 2 How is public opinion measured and used?

Guiding Question
Section 1 What is public opinion, and what factors help to shape it?

Guiding Question
Section 3 How has the development of different media helped inform the public about politics?

CHAPTER 8

Essential Question
What is the place of the media and public opinion in a democracy?

Document-Based Assessment

CAN-SPAM Act of 2003

In 2003, President George W. Bush signed a bill to target spam, or unsolicited e-mail. Unsolicited e-mail is any e-mail message received that was not requested by the person who received it. The law, called the CAN-SPAM Act of 2003, went into effect on January 1, 2004. The following passages from this law explain what spam is, why it is banned, and how people who send it may be punished.

Document at a Glance
- Bill to stop unsolicited e-mail
- Became law in 2004
- Sending spam is punishable by a fine or jail time.

Unsolicited commercial electronic mail is currently estimated to account for over half of all electronic mail traffic . . .

The receipt of unsolicited commercial electronic mail may result in costs to recipients [people receiving spam] who cannot refuse to accept such mail and who incur costs for the storage of such mail, or for the time spent accessing, reviewing, and discarding such mail, or for both . . .

Many senders of unsolicited commercial electronic mail purposefully include misleading information in the messages' subject lines in order to induce [encourage] the recipients to view the messages.

. . . Whoever . . . knowingly (1) accesses a protected computer without authorization . . . (2) uses a protected computer to relay or retransmit multiple commercial electronic mail messages, with the intent to deceive or mislead recipients, or any other Internet access service, as to the origin of such messages, (3) materially falsifies header information . . . (4) registers, using information that materially falsifies the identity of the actual registrant . . . (5) falsely represents oneself to be the registrant . . . shall be punished . . .

. . . PENALTIES—The punishment for an offense . . . is . . . a fine under this title, imprisonment [jail time,] . . . or both . . .

Document-Based Questions

1. What are the costs of spam to recipients?

2. Why would a sender use misleading information in a message's subject line?

3. Why do you think someone would send spam?

4. What information related to the registrant's identity is unlawful?

5. **Summarize** How does the CAN-SPAM Act protect people from spam?

SOURCE: Controlling the Assault of Non-Solicited Pornography and Marketing Act of 2003

Chapter Assessment

Directions: On a sheet of paper, write the answers to the
following questions. Use complete sentences.

Section 1—The Formation of Public Opinion

1. What are two examples of public affairs?

2. What makes up a "public" in the United States?

3. What is a peer group?

4. What are the two earliest influences on a person's opinions?

5. How do historical events play a part in shaping
   public opinion?

6. **Critical Thinking** What factors do you think give an opinion
   leader the ability to shape public opinion?

Section 2—Measuring Public Opinion

7. What are two ways to measure public opinion?

8. Why are scientific polls said to be the most accurate?

9. Why do political leaders spend time talking to the people
   they represent?

10. What is an example of a quota sample?

11. What are the three factors that even scientific polls have
    difficulty with?

12. **Critical Thinking** Why do you think polls sometimes fail to
    predict election results correctly? Explain your answer.

Section 3—The Mass Media

13. What type of media is the most widespread? Why is this
    the case?

14. What are the two ways that the media affect politics?

15. What are three limits of media?

16. How might someone interested in politics use a weblog?

17. Critical Thinking Only 15 percent of the voting population is well-informed. Why do you think the percentage is so low?

Apply What You've Learned

Exploring the Essential Question

For five days, keep track of all of the time you spend interacting with mass media. Write the amount of hours you spend watching television, listening to the radio, reading magazines, or browsing the Internet. After you have recorded your time, answer the following questions:

18. What programs did you watch or listen to, and what articles or other material did you read?

19. Did the programs, articles, or other materials discuss any type of public affairs? If so, what were they?

Essential Questions Project

20. Write a summary of your five-day mass media experience. Make sure to include the number of hours a day you interacted with mass media. Also include the programs you watched and articles you read and whether or not they included public affairs. If so, how did the programming change or impact your views of public affairs? Your summary should help to answer the Essential Question: **What is the place of the media and public opinion in a democracy?**

> **Essential Questions**
> **Journal**
>
> Go to your **Essential Questions Journal** to work on this chapter's Essential Question.

Test-Taking Tip

Do not wait until the night before a test to study. Plan your study time so that you can get a good night's sleep the night before a test.

▲ UNITE HERE, a powerful interest group, marches in New York City's Labor Day parade.

Interest Groups

Essential Question
To what extent do interest groups advance or harm democracy?

Section 1: The Nature of Interest Groups

Section 2: Types of Interest Groups

Section 3: Interest Groups at Work

Reading Strategy: Questioning
As you read about interest groups, ask yourself questions. This will help you understand the information better. Questioning the text will also help you be a more active reader. Ask yourself:
Before Reading:
• What do I want to learn about interest groups?
During Reading:
• What do the facts and details in this chapter tell me?
After Reading:
• Are there any interest groups or people in the chapter that connect with my life?

GOVERNMENT ONLINE
ON THE GO

To study anywhere, anytime, download these online resources at PearsonSuccessNet.com
• Political Dictionary
• Audio Review
• Downloadable Interactivities

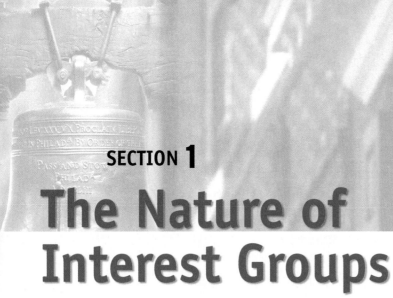

SECTION 1
The Nature of Interest Groups

▲ Members of an environmental group show their support for a "greener" city.

Guiding Question

What roles do interest groups play in our political system? Use the table to organize information about the positive and negative effects of interest groups.

Functions of Interest Groups	
Positive	Negative
■ Promote awareness of public affairs	■ May represent only a few
■	■
■	■

Objectives:

■ Describe how interest groups influence public policy.

■ Compare political parties and interest groups.

■ Explain why people see interest groups as both good and bad for American politics.

Interest groups are groups of people who share the same views on public matters and work to shape public policy. **Public policy** describes the laws and goals that a government follows or pursues. Some main areas of public policy include the economy, human services, public services, natural resources, and defense. Interest groups provide an effective way to get government to make public policy in response to the needs of the people.

What is the role of interest groups?

Interest groups, sometimes called "pressure groups," try to influence public policy. By doing so, they are much more powerful than a few people acting alone could ever be. Interest groups are known as leagues, associations, clubs, or unions. They are protected under the 1st Amendment of the Constitution, which protects people's right to assemble and to petition the government. See **Figure 9.1** on the next page.

Interest groups are found everywhere in America and are involved with every level of government. The United States is composed of many cultures, religions, and ethnic groups. Members of these diverse communities can shape public policy by joining or supporting an interest group. Joining an interest group can also be a way to take part in government.

✔ **Checkpoint**   Where are interest groups found?

Frederick Douglass, 1818–1895, former slave, American Anti-Slavery Society

Mary Church Terrell, 1863–1954, founder, National Association of Colored Women

Lewis Hine, 1874–1940 photographer, National Child Labor Committee

Oliver Hudson Kelly, 1826–1913, farmer, founder of current-day group known as "the Grange"

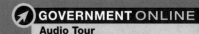
GOVERNMENT ONLINE
Audio Tour
To learn more about early interest groups, go to **PearsonSuccessNet.com**

Fig. 9.1

Early Interest Groups

Interest groups have always had a wide variety of goals. The people pictured here fought for equality, labor, and economic changes. *What tactics might the people and groups shown have used to accomplish their goals?*

"Congress shall make no law . . . abridging . . . the right of the people peaceably to assemble, and to petition the Government for a redress of grievances."

—1st Amendment

A Sioux Indian delegation traveled to Washington, D.C., in 1891 to protest the actions of the American cavalry at the battle of Wounded Knee, where almost 300 Native Americans were killed.

How are political parties and interest groups alike? How are they different?

Interest groups are like political parties because both types of groups join together for a political purpose. Even though they share this basic purpose, however, interest groups and political parties do differ in three main ways:

1. Parties nominate candidates, but interest groups do not, although they may support candidates.

2. Interest groups try to influence the policy of government no matter which candidate wins the office. Political parties are focused on winning elections.

3. Interest groups are private organizations. They focus on the concerns of their members. Political parties are expected to be interested in the concerns of all voters. They are judged by voters, while interest groups are judged only by their own members.

Interest group
Group of people who share the same views on public matters and work to shape public policy

Public policy
The laws and goals that a government follows or pursues

■ ■ ■ ■ ■ ■ ■ ■ ■ ■ ■ ■ ■ ■ ■ ■
Reading Strategy
Questioning
Think about the purpose
of this text. Ask yourself: "Am I
finding the information I expected
to when I began reading"?

■ ■ ■ ■ ■ ■ ■ ■ ■ ■ ■ ■ ■ ■ ■ ■
Public affairs
Issues and events that concern
the people at large

Fig. 9.2

▲ Analyzing Political Cartoons
AARP is a well-known interest
group for people over 50. *What is
this cartoon saying about that or
similar interest groups?*

Are interest groups good or bad?

Are interest groups important to our political system, or do they threaten that system? In the early days of the United States, interest groups were feared. In 1787, James Madison said that interest groups, or "factions," as he called them, could become too strong. Nearly 50 years later, Alexis de Tocqueville, from France, visited the United States. He was amazed at all of the different organizations in America. He noted that Americans of all ages and incomes joined together to advance their interests. He said, "Americans of all ages, all conditions, and all dispositions (natures), constantly form associations . . . not only commercial and manufacturing . . . but . . . of a thousand other kinds—religious, moral, serious, futile (useless), extensive or restricted, enormous or diminutive (small)."

Interest groups are believed to be valuable for the following reasons:

1. They either support or oppose public policies and inform people and raise awareness of **public affairs.**

2. They represent people with similar interests or needs no matter where they live. For example, the AARP is an interest group that responds to the needs of older Americans who live anywhere in the U.S. These common interests are often more important than where people live (Figure 9.2).

3. They provide the government with useful information.

4. They allow citizens to participate in government without running for office. Citizens share ideas and can unite with others to change public policy.

5. They are an informal part of the system of checks and balances. They keep track of officials and public agencies to be sure they are performing well.

6. Interest groups compete with one another. This competition creates a balance and a limit on the power of each group.

Interest groups are also criticized for several reasons. Sometimes there are concerns that certain interest groups only represent a few people and yet have enormous influence. In addition, those groups that are well organized and well financed get their way more often, which is not always good for the majority of the American people.

Sometimes a group's name may imply that the group has more members than it really has. For example, a group's title may start with "American Citizens for . . ." but really only represent a very few people. Groups do not always represent the views of everyone for whom they claim to speak.

Finally, some groups use unfair methods, such as bribery or threats, to influence others. Although these practices are not common, they do exist. If illegal practices were to become widespread in the groups, the whole political system might be damaged.

For a summary of the positive and negative features of interest groups, see Figure 9.3 below.

Fig. 9.3 Features of Interest Groups

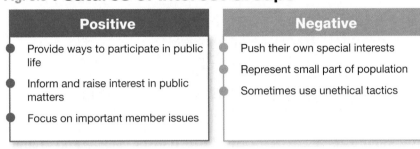

Positive	Negative
• Provide ways to participate in public life	• Push their own special interests
• Inform and raise interest in public matters	• Represent small part of population
• Focus on important member issues	• Sometimes use unethical tactics

✔ **Checkpoint** How do interest groups increase political participation?

Essential Questions Journal Go to your **Essential Questions Journal** to work on this chapter's Essential Question.

SECTION 1 ASSESSMENT

Quick Write

In this section, interest groups were seen as both good and bad. What do you think? Write a paragraph that answers this question. Remember to use complete sentences. Your opening sentence should clearly show whether you think interest groups are good or bad. The sentences that follow should explain why you feel that way.

1. **Guiding Question** Use your completed table to answer this question: What roles do interest groups play in our political system?

Key Terms and Comprehension

On a sheet of paper, write the answer to each question. Use complete sentences.

2. How do interest groups try to influence public policy?

3. How are political parties and interest groups different from each other?

4. What are two reasons interest groups may be good for Americans?

5. What are two reasons interest groups may be bad for Americans?

Critical Thinking

6. **Draw Conclusions** Why do you think a citizen would want to become involved in an interest group?

7. **Recognize Ideologies** What types of interest groups do you think would interest you, as a student? Why?

Types of Interest Groups

▲ Former AMA president Dr. J. Edward Hill discusses medical liability reform.

Guiding Question

What are the different types of interest groups at work in American society? Use the outline to record notes about the different types of interest groups.

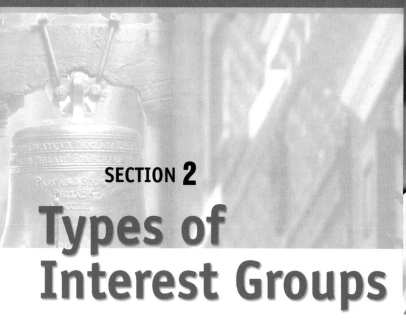

I. Types of Interest Groups
    A. Economic Interests
        1. _____
        2. _____
    B. Other Interest Groups
    C. Public-Interest Groups

Objectives:

■ Explain how the American tradition of joining organizations has resulted in many interest groups.

■ Describe four categories of groups based on economic interests.

■ Outline some reasons other interest groups have been created.

■ Identify the purpose of public-interest groups.

Interest groups in the United States allow all citizens to have a voice in government. They also keep people informed about public policy at every level of government. Work-related interest groups focus on wages, working conditions, and fair hiring practices. Other groups work with government on laws concerning the environment, religion, or taxes. Most citizens in the United States participate in interest groups at some time in their lives.

Why are interest groups an American tradition?

There are thousands of interest groups of all sizes in the United States today. Some have millions of members and are well-known, wealthy, and very well-organized. Others are small, with very little money and few members. Economic interests provide the basis for the largest number of interest groups. Others groups were formed to promote a cause, such as protection of the environment or gun control. Many interest groups form to help certain types of people, such as veterans, senior citizens, or people with disabilities. People may belong to any number of interest groups at the same time.

✔ **Checkpoint** What is one reason some interest groups form?

What are economic interest groups?

Most interest groups are based on economic interests. The most active of these groups represent business, labor, agriculture, and certain professionals. The next few pages will detail each kind of group.

Business Groups

Business groups have always depended on government to protect their interests. Some of the largest today are very organized and represent thousands of businesses. The National Association of Manufacturers (NAM) and the Chamber of Commerce of the United States are the best-known groups. NAM represents "big business." The Chamber of Commerce represents the nation's smaller businesses. There are thousands of chambers throughout the country with a total of more than 3 million members.

There are hundreds of **trade associations** that support most parts of the business community. Some of these are the American Trucking Association and the National Restaurant Association. The most powerful trade associations are those that represent pharmaceuticals, oil, and gas. These groups sometimes fight among themselves.

Labor Groups

A **labor union** is a group of workers who do the same job or work in the same industry. These workers push for government policies that will help their members. Automotive workers or steel workers are examples of people who may be in a labor union. The largest labor group is the AFL-CIO (American Federation of Labor–Congress of Industrial Organizations). It has 56 separate unions and 10 million members. Each member union is organized on a national, state, and local level.

In the past, labor unions were very powerful and obtained many benefits for their members. Today the strength of labor unions has declined, as has the number of members. (See Figure 9.4 on page 212.) As a result, the AFL-CIO is looking for new members. The AFL-CIO now includes migrant farmworkers and public employees in its union. Several unions have left the AFL-CIO because of disagreements. The Service Employees International Union (SEIU) and the International Brotherhood of Teamsters left it to form a new group, the Change to Win Coalition.

Labor unions usually work together on such issues as minimum wages, unemployment, and social welfare. Sometimes disagreements over issues divide union members. Blue-collar workers do not always agree with white-collar workers. Sections of the country may also have different concerns. In the transportation industry, the concerns and needs of truckers, railroad workers, and airplane workers may be different.

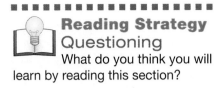

Reading Strategy
Questioning
What do you think you will learn by reading this section?

Trade association
Interest group within the business community

Labor union
A group of workers who join together to advance their wages, benefits, and safety

Fig. 9.4

The Changing State of Labor

GOVERNMENT ONLINE
Interactive Timeline
For an interactive timeline about labor unions, visit
PearsonSuccessNet.com

Union membership has declined as the economy has shifted from manufacturing to services. However, the voice of unions remains strong politically. Education, training, and library occupations have the highest rates of union membership. Unions have also become increasingly diverse demographically. *How have the interests of labor unions changed since the 1950s?*

Manufacturing
Half of all unionized workers in the 1950s were employed by factories.

Union Membership in 1955: **28%**

Service
Two in five public-sector employees, including teachers and other government employees, belong to a union.

Union Membership Today: **12%**

Agricultural Groups

For much of our history, most Americans lived on farms. The first census, taken in 1790, found that 94.9 percent of Americans lived in rural areas. Since then, the population has increased dramatically, but the farm population has dropped. Less than 2 percent of Americans now live on farms today.

Although the farm population has decreased over the years, farmers still have an influence on government's agricultural policies. There are many active agricultural groups. Some groups represent farmers who raise a certain crop, such as wheat or cotton.

The most well-known groups are the National Grange, the American Farm Bureau Federation, and the National Farmers Union. The Farm Bureau is the largest and favors the free market economy, but also supports government programs to promote agriculture. The National Farmers Union supports small farmers and calls itself the "champion of the dirt farmer."

Farm groups sometimes compete with each other to influence state and federal laws. Those who raise corn may disagree with dairy farmers, for example. Farmers in California may have different goals than those in Florida.

Professional Organizations

Members of professions, such as medicine, law, and teaching, have associations as well. These groups usually are not as organized or well-financed as some business or labor groups. Three of these professional organizations, though, are well-organized and successfully influence public policy. They are the National Education Association (NEA), the American Bar Association (ABA), and the American Medical Association (AMA). Other professional groups that are smaller and less well-known serve pharmacists, librarians, and people in other fields.

✔ **Checkpoint** How are professional organizations different from business or labor groups?

What other interest groups exist?

Many interest groups were formed to promote a cause or specific idea. One important group is the American Civil Liberties Union. It is concerned with civil and political rights. Common Cause was formed in 1970 to work for political reforms. The League of Women Voters helps promote participation in and knowledge of public affairs.

Conservation and protection of the environment is a popular cause of many interest groups. A few of the largest environmental groups are the National Wildlife Federation, the Sierra Club, and the Wilderness Society.

Other groups were formed to support opposing ideas. Among these groups is the National Right-to-Life Committee, which is opposed by the Planned Parenthood group. The National Rifle Association works against most forms of gun control. Other interest groups support gun control. Some groups even work to influence international events. (See Figure 9.5 on page 214.)

Research groups are also thought of as interest groups. Many are located in Washington, D.C. They are staffed by experts in their fields. Two of these research groups are the Heritage Foundation and the Brookings Institute. Most research groups print their views in books, newspapers, and journals. They may also promote their findings or issues on television.

Veterans, senior citizens, and ethnic communities all have interest groups devoted to their needs. The American Legion and the Veterans of Foreign Wars take interest in veterans. The AARP promotes the needs of senior citizens. Most ethnic groups in this country have interest groups that support their needs and encourage public policy in their favor.

Fig. 9.5

Influencing International Events

Can interest groups make a difference?

Locally, schools raise
awareness and funds.

There have been years of conflict in the Sudan between the government and rebel groups. Hundreds of thousands have died, and millions of people are without a home. Amnesty International and many other human rights groups provide resources to the refugees. They also ask for support from the United States and other nations to act on the situation. **What can interest groups do to persuade governments to respond to this problem?**

Refugees flee their villages in Darfur.

▪ ▪ ▪ ▪ ▪ ▪ ▪ ▪ ▪ ▪ ▪ ▪ ▪ ▪ ▪ ▪ ▪ ▪

Public-interest group
An interest group that works for the benefit of all citizens

Religious interest groups work to promote public policy for their members. The National Council of Churches includes many Protestant churches. The National Catholic Welfare Council represents the Roman Catholic Church. The American Jewish Congress and B'nai B'rith's Anti-Defamation League promote the interests of the Jewish population.

What are public-interest groups?

Interest groups usually represent a certain group of citizens. They try to influence public policy to serve the interests of their members. **Public-interest groups,** on the other hand, work for the benefit of all citizens, not just a certain group. Public-interest groups may be interested in issues such as consumer rights, voting practices, or product safety. They may also be interested in air and water quality or the protection of the environment. The best-known public-interest groups are Common Cause and all the groups that are part of Ralph Nader's Public Citizen, Inc. One of the oldest groups, the League of Women Voters, began by helping women earn the right to vote.

Biography

Al Gore: 1948–

Al Gore, the son of a United States congressman, served as a congressman (1977–1985) and as a senator (1985–1993). During his time in Congress, he was always active in issues related to the environment. President Clinton appointed him as his Vice President in 1993. He served two terms in this position. He ran for the U.S. presidency but lost to George W. Bush in the controversial election of 2000. Since his defeat, he has worked on problems related to global warming. His efforts related to the environment earned him a Nobel Peace Prize.

Essential Questions Journal Go to your **Essential Questions Journal** to work on this chapter's Essential Question.

SECTION 2 ASSESSMENT

1. **Guiding Question** Use your completed outline to answer this question: What are the different types of interest groups at work in American society?

Key Terms and Comprehension

On a sheet of paper, write the answer to each question. Use complete sentences.

2. What types of issues are work-related interest groups concerned with?

3. What is a labor union?

4. What is the goal of religious interest groups?

5. What is a public-interest group?

Critical Thinking

6. **Determine Cause and Effect** How have economic changes in the United States affected some of the labor unions in the country?

7. **Draw Conclusions** Economic interest groups are the most common type of interest group in the United States. Why do you think this is so?

ISSUES OF OUR TIME

Lobbying in the Federal Government

▶▶ Track the Issue

The 1st Amendment protects the right of interest groups to lobby government. The events below are important dates in the history of lobbying.

1876 The House passes a temporary measure requiring lobbyists to register with the clerk of the House.

1906 A series of articles in *Cosmopolitan* claim widespread corruption related to interest groups and Congress. The articles are titled "The Treason of the Senate."

1946 Congress passes the Federal Regulation of Lobbying Act.

1995 Congress adds to the 1946 law with the Lobbying Disclosure Act.

2007 Congress and the President respond to a major lobbying scandal. They pass the Honest Leadership and Open Government Act.

Rep. Rosa DeLauro (D., Conn.), left, greets a lobbyist at a conference.

▶▶ Perspectives

Lobbyists are people who try to convince public officials to do what interest groups want them to do. Recent problems with some lobbyists and members of Congress have raised questions. There have been charges that some lobbyists have improperly given gifts to or paid travel expenses for members of Congress. Lobbyists might do this to try to gain support in government. Because of these recent problems, the nation debated the benefits and drawbacks of lobbying and set new rules.

Benefits of Lobbying	Drawbacks of Lobbying
"Good lobbyists do their homework and help members of Congress understand the impact of legislation, the outcome of which citizens must live with every day. Good lobbyists understand the industry or organization that they are representing. Good lobbyists are great sources of information. Good lobbyists are factual. Good lobbyists are truthful." *—Lobbyist and former Rep. Bill Sarpalius*	"We want Congress to enact lobby reform legislation that sets new contribution and fundraising limits on lobbyists and lobbying firms; fundamentally changes the gift, travel, and employment relationships among members of Congress, lobbyists, and lobbying firms; and institutes new and effective enforcement mechanisms." *—League of Women Voters*

Connect to Your World

1. Read Bill Sarpalius's argument. How does he think lobbying helps the American system of government?
2. Read the League of Women Voters' argument. What are some specific arguments that concern the group?

In the News

For updates about the regulations for lobbyists, visit **PearsonSuccessNet.com**

SECTION 3

Interest Groups at Work

▲ Lobbyist Jack James of the AFL-CIO (right) speaks with Rep. Bennie Thompson (D., Miss.).

Guiding Question

In what ways do interest groups attempt to influence government and public opinion? Use the chart to record details of how interest groups work.

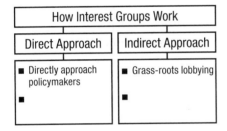

How Interest Groups Work	
Direct Approach	Indirect Approach
■ Directly approach policymakers ■	■ Grass-roots lobbying ■

Objectives:

- Understand the difference between direct and indirect approaches of interest groups.
- Describe how lobbyists influence the branches of government.
- Examine how interest groups use grass-roots lobbying.
- Identify the methods used to influence public opinion and policy.

Interest groups must have contact with the policymakers in Congress in order to influence policy. The members of interest groups can contact congressmen directly or indirectly. The direct method involves meeting congressmen in person. The indirect method is to send letters and e-mails or to make phone calls to congressmen. Members of the interest group or concerned citizens can easily make this indirect contact.

What is the direct approach?

Lobbying is the process of directly approaching policymakers to affect their decisions. **Lobbyists** are the people who contact public officials to let them know what the interest group wants. Wherever public policy is made lobbyists can be found, from Washington, D.C., to the smallest city hall. Lobbying is a big business, and most of the lobbyists are professionals. There are about 30,000 lobbyists in the country. They spend about $2 billion a year doing their jobs.

Larger companies and labor unions often have lobbyists. Many lobbyists work for law firms or public relation agencies. New rules about lobbyists have been in effect since 2007. Lobbyists must register with the clerk of the House and the secretary of the Senate. They must also report their income quarterly. Former senators and top-level executive branch officials must wait two years before they can become lobbyists. Former House members must wait one year. Members of Congress may not accept gifts from lobbyists or their clients.

✓ **Checkpoint**   How do lobbyists directly contact Congress?

■■■■■■■■■■■■■■■■■

Reading Strategy
Questioning
   What details are important
to understand what this paragraph
is about?

■■■■■■■■■■■■■■■■■

Lobbying
Trying to influence members of a
lawmaking group

Lobbyist
A person that tries to influence
members of a lawmaking group

***Amicus curiae* brief**
Latin for "friend of the court";
a brief that supports one of the
sides in a case being tried

How do lobbyists work with Congress?

Congress is the main place for the making of public policy in the
federal government. Because of this, lobbyists try to keep close ties
with members of Congress, especially the members of House and
Senate committees. You will study committees in Chapter 12.

Lobbyists testify before Congress when new legislation is being
considered. The lobbyists present the views of their organizations
and may also give Congress useful information on the subject of the
legislation. Often, many lobbyists representing different interests
attend if the proposed legislation will affect many groups.

Lobbyists will often help lawmakers by writing speeches, providing
information, or even writing legislation. The information is usually
accurate and the writing well done. Lobbyists need to be honest and
effective to earn the respect of the lawmakers. For a more detailed
look at the lobbying process, see Figure 9.6 on the next page.

How does lobbying work in the executive branch?

When the executive branch receives a law that Congress has
passed, there is still more work to be done. For example, the
executive department decides which manufacturer will be chosen
to supply military equipment. Lobbyists from manufacturing
companies may contact officials in the White House and the
executive agencies involved. By doing this, the lobbyists hope
to get contracts for their clients.

Lobbyists try to influence the President's selection of the top
officials in many agencies of the executive branch because this
may result in better treatment for their interest group in the future.
The very successful lobbyists have friends in many agencies. These
contacts are valuable for their clients.

✔**Checkpoint**   Why do lobbyists target the executive branch?

How is lobbying done in the courts?

Lobbyists can work through the courts to promote the ideas of their
client, the interest groups. The American Civil Liberties Union
and other interest groups often take legal action to promote their
interests. The lawsuits may involve issues that would not be likely to
succeed in Congress, but may win in the courts.

An interest group may file an *amicus curiae* ("friend of the court") **brief.** This type of brief is presented as support for one side of a case being tried. The interest group has not taken the legal action, but it does support one side in the case. Sometimes many interest groups will present briefs for the same case. Interest groups also try to influence the selection of federal judges.

What is the indirect approach?

The goal of indirect lobbying is the same as the goal of direct lobbying. Lobbyists want to influence public policy in favor of the interest group. There are three main indirect lobbying approaches: grass-roots lobbying, public-opinion shaping, and election-related activities.

Fig. 9.6 How Government Works

Lobbying in Action

GOVERNMENT ONLINE
Audio Tour
To learn more about how lobbying works, go to
PearsonSuccessNet.com

An electricity company recently announced plans to build a wind farm in a coastal location. There are a number of competing interest groups involved, and each is taking steps to make sure its influence is felt. At any step in the process, the project can be derailed. *What actions might these interest groups take to build public support for their views?*

Step 1 A Proposal
A project for building an electricity-generating wind farm in waters off the shores of a wealthy vacation area is announced. The plan promises a nonpolluting source of electricity.

Step 2 Debate Begins
Some environmental interest groups favor the project as a source of clean energy. But others oppose the project because it may harm birds or ocean life. Each side tries to build public support.

Step 3 Government Action
The project requires approval of several state and federal government agencies. These agencies consider everything from environmental impact to effects on the electricity industry. Interest groups mobilize to influence the views of the many agencies involved.

Step 4 Final Decision
Government agencies issue their rulings on the project and may sometimes pass legislation.

Fig. 9.7 How Government Works

Grass-Roots Organizing
Going Digital

GOVERNMENT ONLINE

Audio Tour

To learn more about grass-roots organizing, visit **PearsonSuccessNet.com**

Advances in technology have changed the way interest groups organize at the grass-roots level. Having access to Web sites and cell phones makes it easier to communicate. Using these tools, smaller groups can organize and raise money as quickly as can larger interest groups. *What might be some possible disadvantages of relying on technology to organize?*

Phones allow members to contact each other as well as their government officials about important issues.

Members can mobilize faster and easier with PDAs, as well as send important data to other members on the move.

Online Petitions are a way for groups to quickly garner a large number of signatures and increase interest.

AVAAZ.ORG
THE WORLD IN ACTION
SIGN UP | CAMPAIGNS | DONATE | BLOG | MEDIA |

HELP SUPPORT OUR WORK

Fundraising can be conducted more simply with online donation forms.

Organizers can set up Web sites based on their interests and connect with other members remotely.

What is grass-roots lobbying?

Grass-roots lobbying involves putting demands on government from the members of an interest group or regular citizens. This method is called **grass-roots pressure.** It can include phone calls, letters, faxes, and e-mails. This lobbying is often done on short notice. The AARP, with 35 million members is the group that is most effective at grass-roots lobbying. Members of Congress receive more contact from this group of citizens than any other group when pending legislation might effect retirees.

The Internet has helped interest groups promote their causes. Almost every organization has a Web site. Groups with low budgets may use the Internet to get started. At election time, the Internet is used to inform and encourage people to vote for the candidates that an interest group supports. For examples of grass-roots going digital, see Figure 9.7 on page 220.

Other popular methods of grass-roots lobbying are marches and demonstrations. Some are very organized and may take place near important public buildings. Many have been held in Washington, D.C. Interest groups may also keep records of how legislators vote on issues that are important to them. They use these records to change the voting behavior of the official or to defeat the official in future elections.

✔ **Checkpoint**   Why is the Internet an important tool for lobbyists?

How is public opinion shaped?

Organized groups use several means to shape public opinion. Most of these methods are expensive. They include television ads, newspaper reports, and magazine articles. The large, wealthy interest groups (such as oil, drug, and insurance companies) hope to become well-known, trusted, and supported by the general public. The American Medical Association (AMA) spent many years working against national health insurance proposals. The AMA asked doctors to post signs in waiting rooms and talk to patients about this issue. Because patients usually trust their doctors, the AMA knew they would be more willing to respect this viewpoint when it came from them.

Another method used to shape public opinion is the support of well-known people, especially from movies or television. The use of the mass media, however, is by far the most effective way of shaping public opinion. The public sometimes ignores paid ads, but coverage by the media lends importance to any event involving an interest group. Press releases, interviews, and studies are often produced by interest groups for media use.

Grass-roots pressure
Process of putting demands on government from all the members of a group

Reading Strategy
Questioning
What do you already know about grass-roots lobbying? How does this help you to better understand this section?

Propaganda is a method of persuasion used to influence individuals or groups. Propaganda often uses only evidence, true or false, that agrees with the ideas being presented. The media encourages the use of propaganda in its advertising and in politics. Two different types of propaganda are name-calling (putting a label on a person, such as "communist") and card stacking (presenting only one side of the issue). Propaganda is spread through the newspapers, radio, television, books, speeches, posters, and other outlets.

What is electioneering?

Electioneering is working to get someone elected to office. It is one of the many ways that interest groups try to influence the making of public policy (Figure 9.8). Groups help candidates through their political action committees (PACs). They make financial contributions and offer advice to candidates. PACs also help in campaign offices and on election day.

Fig. 9.8

How Lobbying Works

Lobbying occurs . . .
wherever public policy is made—at the national, state, and local levels of government all across the country.

Lobbyists are . . .
the representatives of a wide variety of interest groups.

Lobbying involves . . .
writing speeches, providing information to officeholders, making campaign contributions, drafting legislation, filing court briefs, and much more.

Lobbyists use . . .
a variety of techniques to shape opinions, including grass-roots pressures, propaganda, and election-related activities.

Government in Your Life

Labor Unions Sponsor a Bus Tour for the Jobless

On March 24, 2004, an eight-day bus tour began. It started in St. Louis, stopped in eighteen cities, and ended in Washington, D.C. It was sponsored by labor unions and a national organization for nonunion families. On the tour were 51 people who had no jobs or poor jobs.

One purpose of the tour was to show support for workers in areas of heavy job loss. Another purpose was to show the personal and economic effects of being jobless. The workers felt that legislation was needed to protect workers from outsourcing. Outsourcing is when businesses send jobs to other countries to avoid labor laws and taxes.

The group held rallies, and the media covered them. Some people on the tour recorded daily blogs. When the tour ended on April 1, a television advertising campaign began. The ads told viewers to let public officials know about the needs of the jobless and to work together to make a change in government policies.

Essential Questions Journal Go to your **Essential Questions Journal** to work on this chapter's Essential Question.

SECTION 3 ASSESSMENT

1. **Guiding Question** Use your completed table to answer this question: In what ways do interest groups attempt to influence government and public opinion?

Key Terms and Comprehension

On a sheet of paper, write the answer to each question. Use complete sentences.

2. What is an example of a direct approach to lobbying?

3. What is an example of an indirect approach to lobbying?

4. What is a lobbyist?

5. How do interest groups use the media to influence the public?

Critical Thinking

6. **Predict Consequences** What might happen if nothing was done to limit the role of lobbyists in government?

7. **Drawing Inferences** Why do interest groups want a positive public image?

Chapter Summary

Section 1—The Nature of Interest Groups

■ Interest groups are made up of people who work together to influence public policies at all levels of government.

■ Unlike political parties, interest groups do not elect candidates but do promote their own ideas no matter who is elected.

■ Interest groups are valued because they inform citizens and allow them to participate in government. They are criticized because some represent only a few citizens and others use unfair methods.

Section 2—Types of Interest Groups

■ The most active interest groups have economic interests, such as those related to business, labor, agriculture, or professional groups.

■ Labor groups or unions work together on minimum wage, unemployment, and social issues.

■ Agricultural groups serve farmers and companies in the farming industry.

■ Professional groups serve doctors, lawyers, teachers, and other professionals.

■ Other interest groups are issue oriented or serve groups in a specific community.

■ Public-interest groups work for the benefit of all citizens.

Section 3—Interest Groups at Work

■ Lobbying is the direct way of contacting public officials. Most lobbyists are professionals and must register in Congress.

■ Lobbyists try to work closely with members of Congress and the executive branch, supplying information and giving the views of their organizations.

■ In the courts, lobbyists may take legal action or support one side in a legal case.

■ Indirect lobbying may include phone calls, e-mails, or demonstrations to promote the cause of the interest group.

■ Interest groups shape public opinion through the mass media.

■ Electioneering involves trying to get a candidate elected. Political action committees make financial contributions to a candidate or work for the campaign.

Guiding Question
Section 2 What are the different types of interest groups at work in American society?

Guiding Question
Section 1 What roles do interest groups play in our political system?

Guiding Question
Section 3 In what ways do interest groups attempt to influence government and public opinion?

CHAPTER 9

Essential Question
To what extent do interest groups advance or harm democracy?

Document-Based Assessment

ASPCA Animal Watch (1996)

This article first appeared in the 1996 spring issue of the American Society for Prevention of Cruelty to Animals (ASPCA) publication, Animal Tracks. *ASPCA is an interest group that fights against the cruel treatment of animals. It also tries to get humane animal laws passed. The article below was written by the magazine's former managing editor, Pune Dracker.*

Document at a Glance
- Animal Protection Group
- Henry Bergh, Founder
- Supported Laws to Fight Animal Cruelty

A "Bergh's-eye view" of the 140 years at the ASPCA

Henry Bergh was born in New York City in 1813, the son of a prominent shipbuilder . . . In 1865 he was appointed to a diplomatic post at the Russian Court of Czar Alexander II . . . there he first took action against man's inhumanity toward animals . . .

In New York, Bergh pleaded on behalf of "the mute servants of mankind" at a . . . meeting at Clinton hall . . . Bergh detailed practices in America, including cockfighting and the horrors of the slaughterhouses . . .

Bergh's philosophy of protecting animals was an issue that crossed party lines. . . . To his audience . . . some of Manhattan's most powerful [leaders], he stressed, "This is a matter of conscience . . . It is a moral question . . ."

Bergh brought a charter for a proposed society to protect animals to the New York State Legislature . . . the charter incorporating the American Society for the Prevention of Cruelty to Animals was passed on April 10, 1888. Nine days later, an anti-cruelty law was passed and the ASPCA granted the right to enforce it . . . by 1888 . . . Humane Societies had sprung up throughout the nation. . . . Working for legislation continues to be one of [their] guiding principles . . .

Document-Based Questions

1. Where did Henry Bergh first take action against man's inhumanity toward animals?

2. What two American practices did Bergh describe to his audience at Clinton Hall?

3. When was the charter incorporating the ASPCA passed?

4. What continues to be one of the guiding principles of the resulting humane societies?

5. **Questioning** What other questions do you have after reading this article? Share your questions with the class.

SOURCE: Draker. "A 'Bergh's-eye View' of the 140 years at the ASPCA," *Animal Tracks,* Spring, 1996.

Chapter Assessment

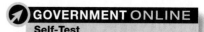

GOVERNMENT ONLINE
Self-Test
To test your understanding of
key terms and main ideas, visit
PearsonSuccessNet.com

Directions: Choose the letter of the best answer
or write the answer using complete sentences.

Section 1—The Nature of Interest Groups

1. What are interest groups sometimes called?

A. pressure groups   **C.** Congress

B. political parties   **D.** party politicians

2. How are interest groups part of the system of checks and balances?

A. They raise money for special interests.

B. They raise awareness of political issues.

C. They make sure officials and public agencies are performing well.

D. They compete with each other.

3. Where are interest groups found in the United States?

A. only in Washington, D.C.

B. all over the country, at every level of government

C. only in states with high populations

D. only in New York City and Washington, D.C.

4. In 1787, what did James Madison think of interest groups?

5. What are two unfair methods that interest groups might use to gain support?

6. **Critical Thinking** Why might politicians have feared interest groups in the early stages of the U.S. government?

Section 2—Types of Interest Groups

7. The American Medical Association (AMA) is an example of what type of interest group?

A. labor union   **C.** agricultural group

B. trade association   **D.** professional organization

8. An automotive worker might belong to what type of union?

A. environmental   **C.** agricultural

B. labor   **D.** international

9. Which group is an example of an environmental interest group?

A. Public Citizen, Inc.

B. The Sierra Club

C. American Civil Liberties Union

D. Brookings Institute

10. Why has the strength of labor unions declined in recent years?

11. On what concerns do interest groups concentrate?

12. Critical Thinking How might disagreement among interest groups affect their ability to influence policy?

Section 3—Interest Groups at Work

13. What is propaganda?

14. Why do interest groups want to work closely with the executive branch?

15. How are lobbyists involved in political campaigns?

16. What ways might a lobbyist use to influence Congress?

17. Critical Thinking Why might political action committees give politicians and political campaigns money? Do you think this practice is fair? Why or why not?

Apply What You've Learned

Exploring the Essential Question

18. Research an interest group discussed in this chapter. What are the goals of this group?

19. How does the group pursue its goals?

Essential Questions Project

20. Stage a press conference to talk about the interest group that you researched. Answer in your conference, **To what extent does the interest group you researched advance or harm democracy?** Be prepared for questions from the teacher or students about the interest group.

> **Essential Questions**
> **Journal**
>
> Go to your **Essential Questions Journal** to work on this chapter's Essential Question.

Test-Taking Tip

When you review your notes to prepare for an exam, use a marker to highlight key words and examples.

Essential Question

In what ways should people participate in public affairs?

Political parties, the media, voting, serving with interest groups—Americans today have unprecedented opportunities to take part in public affairs. How and why should we do so?

" ON THE FREE PRESS:

Freedom of expression—in particular, freedom of the press—guarantees popular participation in the decisions and actions of government, and popular participation is the essence of . . . democracy.

—Corazon Aquino, former President of the Philippines

ON A VOTER'S RESPONSIBILITIES:

"I'm undecided, but that doesn't mean I'm apathetic or uninformed."

" ON GOVERNMENT AND THE PEOPLE:

It is not the function of our Government to keep the citizen from falling into error; it is the function of the citizen to keep the Government from falling into error.

—Justice Robert Houghwout Jackson, *American Communications Association* v. *Douds*

Essential Question Warmup

Throughout this unit, you studied how people and government interact. Use what you have learned and the quotations and opinions above to answer the following questions. Then go to your **Essential Questions Journal.**

1. What responsibilities do the media have, if any?

2. Can citizens "keep the Government from falling into error" through voting alone?

3. Are interest groups democratic?

4. How successfully do political parties link citizens with the government?

| Essential Questions
Journal | To continue to build a response to the unit Essential Question, go to your **Essential Questions Journal.** |

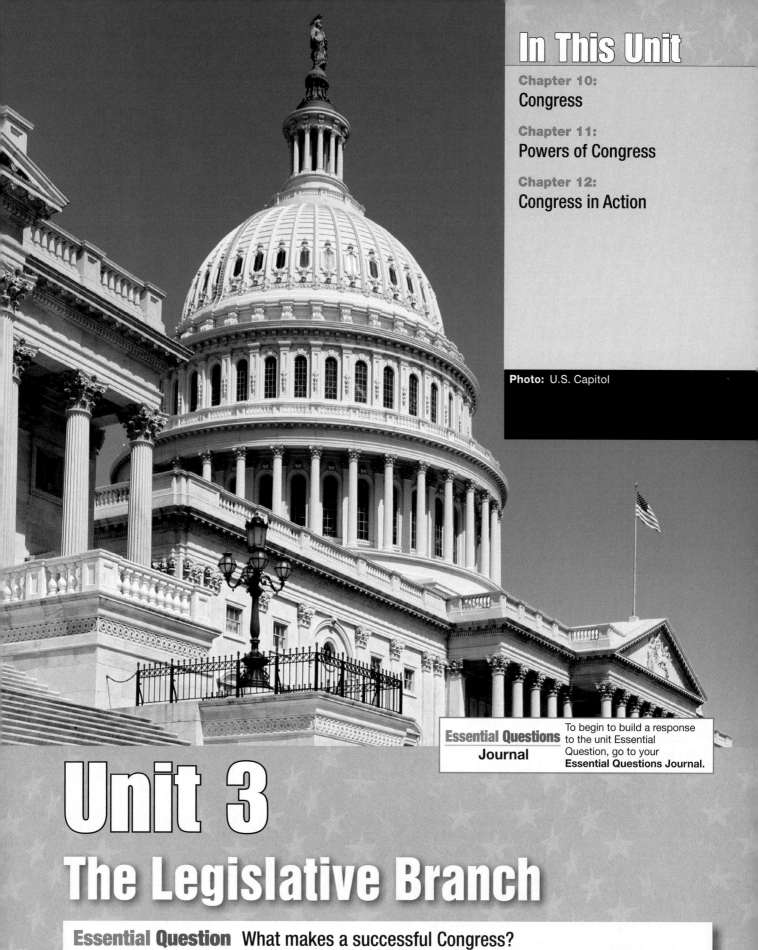

Photo: U.S. Capitol

Essential Questions Journal To begin to build a response to the unit Essential Question, go to your **Essential Questions Journal.**

Unit 3
The Legislative Branch

Essential Question What makes a successful Congress?

▲ Rep. Rahm Emanuel (D., Ill.) congratulates Nancy Pelosi (D., Calif.) on being elected Speaker of the House. Rep. James Clyburn (D., S.C.) looks on.

Congress

■ ■

Reading Strategy: Predicting
As you read about Congress, you can make predictions about what will happen next. It helps to preview the text and think about what you already know about the topic. As you make predictions, keep these ideas in mind.

- Make your best guess about what happens next.
- Use what you know to predict what will be next.
- Check your predictions. As you learn more information, you may find you need to change your predictions.

GOVERNMENT ONLINE
ON THE GO

To study anywhere, anytime, download these online resources at PearsonSuccessNet.com
- Political Dictionary
- Audio Review
- Downloadable Interactivities

▲ Senators Arlen Specter (R., Penn.) and Patrick Leahy (D., Vt.)

SECTION 1
The National Legislature

Guiding Question

Why does the Constitution establish a bicameral legislature? Use a chart to take notes on the reasons for a bicameral legislature.

Reason	Summary
Historical	
Practical	
Theoretical	Balance of power

Objectives:

- Explain why the Constitution provides for two houses of Congress.
- Describe a term of Congress.
- Explain when the President may interfere with the sessions of Congress.

Bicameral
A legislative body made of two chambers

Senate
A governing body that makes rules and laws

The federal government is divided into three separate branches. Each part has special powers granted by the Constitution. One branch is the legislative branch, which is Congress. In this section, you will learn about this national legislature.

What is a bicameral Congress?

The Framers of the Constitution decided on a **bicameral** legislature. Bicameral describes a legislative body made of two chambers. Congress is made up of two houses—the **Senate** and the House of Representatives. The Framers did this for three reasons:

- Past governments were set up this way. The British Parliament had two houses. Most Americans were familiar with the British Parliament, so the Framers followed the Parliament's example. Today in the United States all state legislatures are also bicameral, except for Nebraska's. It has only one legislative body.

- Having two houses settled a conflict during the Constitutional Convention. The large and small states could not agree on the size of the Congress. There was much debate. The Framers decided each state would have two representatives in the Senate. In the House of Representatives, each state would be represented according to its population.

- The two houses of Congress check each other. The Framers thought this would keep Congress from becoming too powerful. For example, both the Senate and the House must pass a new bill. Only then can the bill be sent to the President for approval.

✓ **Checkpoint** What are three reasons for a bicameral Congress?

What are the terms and sessions of Congress?

The Senate and House of Representatives begin their **sessions** in Washington, D.C., early in January. They work at the Capitol building (Figure 10.1). A session is a period of time each year when Congress meets to talk about laws. Each **term** of Congress has two sessions. The first session begins in January of odd-numbered years. For example, the first session of the 111th Congress began in January 2009.

Each session usually lasts until the work is completed. Sometimes Congress does not end the meeting, or **adjourn,** until late fall. Near the end of the session, Congress votes to adjourn. If a serious problem comes up after Congress has adjourned, the President may ask Congress to come back and hold a **special session.** A special session lasts until the problem is solved. For example, in 1933, President Franklin Roosevelt called a special session. Many people did not have jobs and needed help. The President wanted Congress to pass laws that would help these people.

✔ **Checkpoint**   How many sessions are there in each term of Congress?

Reading Strategy
Predicting
Read the title of this paragraph. What do you think are the terms and sessions of Congress?

Session
The period of time each year when Congress meets

Term
An assigned period of time for an elected official to serve

Adjourn
To bring a meeting to an end

Special session
A session called to deal with an emergency

Fig. 10.1

The Capitol Building

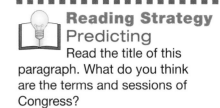

GOVERNMENT ONLINE
Interactive
For an animated, interactive version of the Capitol, visit **PearsonSuccessNet.com**

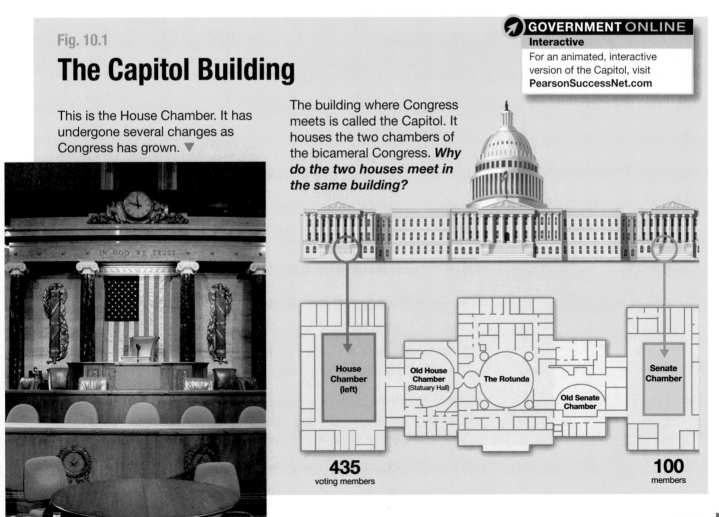

This is the House Chamber. It has undergone several changes as Congress has grown. ▼

The building where Congress meets is called the Capitol. It houses the two chambers of the bicameral Congress. *Why do the two houses meet in the same building?*

IN GOD WE TRUST

House Chamber (left)

Old House Chamber (Statuary Hall)

The Rotunda

Old Senate Chamber

Senate Chamber

435
voting members

100
members

Fig. 10.2 Representation in Congress

State	Population*	Senators	House Members
Wyoming	493,782	2	1
California	33,871,648	2	53

*Census of 2000   SOURCE: U.S. Census Bureau

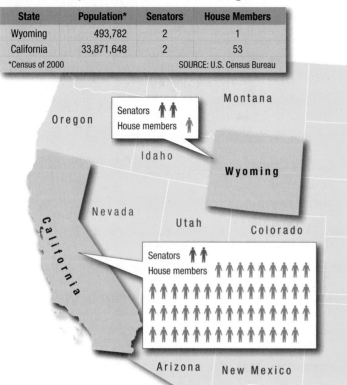

▲ California and Wyoming both elect two senators, even though they have a huge difference in population.

What is the representation of Congress?

Each state is represented both by senators and by House members. There are two senators for each state. The number of House members for each state is determined by its population. In the map on this page (Figure 10.2), California and Wyoming show how different each state's representation can be. Both states are represented by two senators. California has many more House members because of its large population. You will learn more about representation of Congress in Section 2 and Section 3 of this chapter.

✓ **Checkpoint** What determines the number of representatives in each state?

SECTION 1 ASSESSMENT

Word Bank

adjourn

bicameral

session

Senate

1. **Guiding Question** Use your completed chart to answer this question: Why does the Constitution establish a bicameral legislature?

Key Terms and Comprehension

On a sheet of paper, use the words from the Word Bank to complete each sentence correctly.

2. The Framers of the Constitution decided on a(n) _____ legislature.

3. Congress sometimes does not _____ until late fall.

4. The President may ask Congress to come back and hold a special _____.

5. The legislature is made up of the _____ and the House of Representatives.

Critical Thinking

6. **Draw Conclusions** Do you think the President should be able to call Congress for a special session? Explain your answer.

7. **Identify Alternatives** Do you think it is fair that the number of House members is determined by population? Why or why not?

Writing a Letter to a Public Official

Do you know how to communicate with your elected officials? Do you have an opinion about an issue that is being talked about in Congress? A letter or e-mail is a very effective way to let your representative and senators know about it. Members of Congress pay attention to the people who write to them.

When writing a letter or e-mail, here are some steps to follow:

1. Find out who represents you in Congress. Go to the Senate or House of Representatives Web site and type your zip code or state in the search box. Make sure you are using a government Web site. A Web address for a government site ends in *gov*. You can also use the blue (government) pages of your phone book to look up your representatives and their addresses.

2. Organize your thoughts. Think about the issue you care about the most. Before you write, make a list of reasons why you care about that issue. Put the reasons in order. The most important reason should be first. Include in your letter only the top two or three reasons why you are writing.

3. Clearly tell the representative what you want to happen. For example, you might say, "I want you to vote for Senate Bill 244, the bill that will continue funding for the Job Corps." Be very clear on what you want to happen.

4. Explain your reasons. Tell your representative why you think he or she should agree with you. Include details and personal experiences that have led you to your position: "My cousin was not doing well in school. He learned auto mechanics in the Job Corps and got a really good job. It turned his life around. He earned his GED and is going to college now. He is working part time and training as a

computer technician. I am writing to you to say that this is a great program. Please vote for funding to make sure this program continues. It gives people a chance at a better life."

5. Prepare your letter. Make sure to address your letter correctly. Also include your full name, phone number, and mailing address on the letter or e-mail.

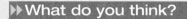

What do you think?

1. Why would an elected official want to hear about your experiences?
2. Why is it important to only list the top two or three reasons you care about an issue?

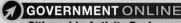
GOVERNMENT ONLINE
Citizenship Activity Pack
For an activity on expressing your opinion to an elected official, go to **PearsonSuccessNet.com**

▲ Members of the media follow Rep. John Conyers (D., Mich.), (front right), the chairman of the House Judiciary Committee.

The House of Representatives

Guiding Question

How are seats in the House distributed, and what qualifications must members have? Use a concept web to take notes on the House of Representatives.

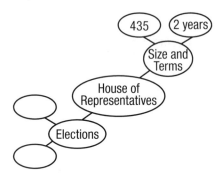

Objectives:

- Explain how House seats are won and describe the term of a representative.
- Explain how House seats are reapportioned after each census.
- Understand how Supreme Court decisions have changed the rules for reapportionment.
- Understand the qualifications for election to the House.

Every other autumn, all across the country, hundreds of people work to get elected to the House of Representatives. In this section, you will learn about the House of Representatives and the qualifications to be a candidate.

What are the terms and size of the House of Representatives?

The House of Representatives has 435 elected officials. Each representative is elected for a two-year term. The House of Representatives reflects the size of each state's population. States with more people living in them send more representatives to Congress than states with fewer people. Each state is divided into districts. Each district elects its own representative.

The leader of the House of Representatives is known as the Speaker of the House. The Speaker is elected by the majority party members in the House to serve for two years. The Speaker runs the House's business. The Speaker of the House becomes President of the United States if the President and Vice President cannot serve. The Speaker leads sessions, decides who may speak, calls for votes, and sees that rules are followed. The Speaker also places members of the House on committees. Because of this power, the Speaker can influence which laws the House passes.

✔ **Checkpoint** What are some of the responsibilities of the Speaker of the House?

What is reapportionment?

Every 10 years, according to the Constitution, a **census** is taken in the United States. As the population of the country grew, more seats were added to the House of Representatives. This practice continued until 1920, when the number of seats rose to 435. The House of Representatives had grown too large, and Congress decided not to add more seats. The **Reapportionment** Act of 1929 was passed. It set the number of seats at 435. After each census, the Census Bureau decides how to distribute the number of seats for each state. Congress must then approve this action of the Census Bureau. If Congress approves, the number of seats for each state is set (Figure 10.3).

The Constitution says that congressional elections are held on the same day in every state. Half of congressional elections happen in the years when there is no presidential election. These are called **off-year elections.**

What are congressional districts?

Each of the 435 members of the House of Representatives is elected from a district in a state. Seven states have only one district that covers the whole state. These states are allowed to elect their representatives **at-large.** *At-large* means that people can choose their representative from the whole state.

Census
A count of population

Reapportionment
To distribute differently

Off-year election
An election for Congress that takes place between Presidential election years

At-large
Describes an election of a candidate by the whole state rather than a single district

Reading Strategy
Predicting
Read the title of this paragraph. What do you think a congressional district is?

GOVERNMENT ONLINE
Audio Tour
Listen to a guided audio tour of this map at **PearsonSuccessNet.com**

Fig. 10.3 Congressional Apportionment 2003–2013

Source: Census 2000

▲ **Interpreting Maps** Every ten years the Census Bureau reapportions seats in the House according to the new population statistics. The number in the box tells how many House members are in each state. *What region has lost the most House members?*

Gerrymandering
The drawing of district lines to the advantage of a party or group

Reading Strategy
Predicting
How do you think the Court's ruling in *Westberry* v. *Sanders* affected candidates running for office?

What is gerrymandering?

By law, each district should have similar populations and district boundaries should touch one another. In the past, many states drew boundaries to put more voters in some districts than others. The Supreme Court ruled against this practice in *Westberry* v. *Sanders*. The Court said the population differences in Georgia's districts were too great and violated the Constitution. The Court said that one man's vote should be worth the same as another's. This decision changed the way many states drew district lines.

Many states still draw boundaries to favor one party or group over another. The term for this unfair districting is called **gerrymandering** (Figure 10.4). Gerrymandering is usually done to help one party elect a large number of representatives. Sometimes, states draw boundaries to help elected officials win reelection easily.

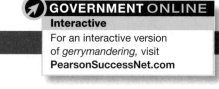

GOVERNMENT ONLINE
Interactive
For an interactive version of *gerrymandering*, visit **PearsonSuccessNet.com**

Fig. 10.4 How Government Works

Choosing Their Voters

Each dot on the pieces of paper represents 100 voters. Below are three ways that lawmakers try to keep in power by gerrymandering.
Why do you think some people want to outlaw gerrymandering?

Cracking
The party in power splits up voters from the opposing party.
Result: The orange party wins three districts.

Packing
State legislators "pack" as many opposing voters into a single district as possible.
Result: Two districts are safe for the orange party.

Kidnapping
The party in power redraws district lines to move a candidate into a different district. This is done because that district will probably not vote for that candidate.
Result: The orange party wins three districts.

What are qualifications for House members?

- Representatives must be at least 25 years of age.
- Representatives must have been citizens of the United States for at least seven years.
- Representatives must be residents of the state from which they are elected.

The Constitution allows the House to judge the qualifications and election results of its own members. In 1861, the House dismissed three members for "rebellion" against the country. As recently as 2003, the House dismissed a member convicted of a serious crime. Sometimes a member will resign to avoid punishment.

The informal qualifications of a representative may vary over time. A candidate that is able to get votes because of his name or political experience will often win the nomination of his party. For a summary of the House of Representatives, see Figure 10.5.

Fig. 10.5

House of Representatives

- Two-year term
- 435 voting members
- Smaller constituencies: elected from districts of approximately equal populations
- All elected every two years
- Modest prestige, less national media attention

SECTION 2 ASSESSMENT

Essential Questions Journal Go to your **Essential Questions Journal** to work on this chapter's Essential Question.

Quick Write

Do research online or at the library on the history of reapportionment in your state. How has your state changed over time? Has it gained representation? Lost representation? How many representatives does your state have? Write your findings using complete sentences. Share your information with the class.

1. **Guiding Question** Use your completed concept web to answer this question: How are seats in the House distributed, and what qualifications must members have?

Key Terms and Comprehension

On a sheet of paper, write the letter of the answer that correctly completes each question.

2. How many people make up the House of Representatives?
   A. 535   **B.** 435   **C.** 100   **D.** 50

3. As written in the Constitution, what takes place every 10 years?
   A. census   **B.** vote   **C.** secret ballot   **D.** poll

4. Where is each representative elected from in a state?
   A. city   **B.** county   **C.** district   **D.** suburb

5. When someone redraws district lines, what is it called?
   A. reappointment   **C.** gerrymandering
   B. appointing   **D.** at-large

Critical Thinking

6. **Identify Central Issues** Do you think politicians should be able to gerrymander? Explain your answer.

7. **Draw Conclusions** As population in the United States grows, should seats be added in the House of Representatives?

▲ Senator Edward Kennedy (D.) of Massachusetts

The Senate

How does the Senate differ from the House? Use a concept web to take notes on the Senate.

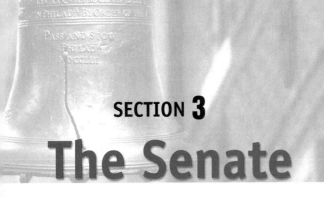

Objectives:

- Compare the size of the Senate to the size of the House of Representatives.
- Describe how senators are elected.
- Explain the differences between a senator's term and a representative's term.
- Understand the qualifications for election to the Senate.

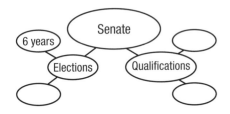

Reading Strategy
Predicting
Before you read the next page, predict what you think are some qualifications for senators.

Over a third of the Senate once served in the House of Representatives. None of the current members of the House ever served in the Senate. Many of the men and women who now serve in the House look forward to the day when, they hope, they will sit in the Senate. As you read this section, you will see why the Senate is often called the "upper house."

How many members are in the Senate?

The writers of the Constitution wanted to be sure that every state would be represented equally in the Senate. The First Federal Congress had 26 senators representing the 13 original states. Today, each of the 50 states elects two senators to serve in the Senate. Each state, no matter how large or how small its population, has the same number of votes in the Senate. There are 100 senators serving in the Senate today. Senators may serve for any number of terms.

The Framers of the Constitution hoped the smaller Senate would be a more responsible body than the House. They reinforced that hope by giving senators a longer term than the representatives. A representative's term is only two years. The six-year term of a senator is three times as long. The senators represent the entire state and need a range of knowledge to serve well. Senators are often concerned with issues that affect the entire country. They are interested in topics such as social security, national healthcare, and international issues.

✓ **Checkpoint**   Each state has how many senators?

What are the qualifications for senators?

Just like the House, there are qualifications to run for the Senate:

- Senators must be at least 30 years old.

- Senators must have been citizens of the United States for at least nine years.

- Senators must be residents of the state they represent.

A senator serves a six-year term. Only one-third of the Senate membership is elected at any one time. Only one senator from a state is elected to a full term in any given election. The Senate is a **continuous body.** A continuous body is one in which all the seats are never up for election at the same time.

Just as members of the House of Representatives have informal qualifications, so do the senators. They often need political experience and a familiar name, and they must appeal to a wide range of voters.

The Senate can judge the qualifications of its members just as the House does. In the past, 15 members of the Senate have been **expelled,** or forced to leave office. The first was in 1797. Later, during the Civil War, 14 senators from Confederate states were expelled. In 1995, Senator Bob Packwood resigned. He was one of the few senators ever to do so. For a summary of the Senate, see Figure 10.6.

■ ■ ■ ■ ■ ■ ■ ■ ■ ■ ■ ■ ■ ■ ■ ■ ■ ■ ■
Continuous body
A government body whose seats are never up for election all at the same time

Expelled
Forced to leave

Fig. 10.6

Senate
Six-year term
100 members; two from each state
Elected from entire state
One-third elected every two years
No term limit

✔ **Checkpoint** What are two qualifications for senators?

Essential Questions Journal Go to your **Essential Questions Journal** to work on this chapter's Essential Question.

SECTION 3 ASSESSMENT

Word Bank

citizens

expelled

six

two

1. **Guiding Question** Use your completed concept web to answer this question: How does the Senate differ from the House?

Key Terms and Comprehension

On a sheet of paper, use the words from the Word Bank to complete each sentence correctly.

2. Senators are elected for a term that lasts _____ years.

3. Representatives are elected for a term that lasts _____ years.

4. Senate candidates must be U.S. _____ for at least nine years.

5. In the past, 15 senators have been _____.

Critical Thinking

6. **Draw Conclusions** Why do you think representatives and senators must be residents of the states they represent?

7. **Make Generalizations** Do you think the informal qualifications of a candidate would be different in each state? Why?

▲ Republican senators

The Members of Congress

Guiding Question

What roles and functions do members of Congress perform?
Use a concept web to take notes on the roles and functions performed by members of Congress.

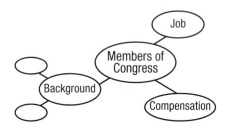

Objectives:

- Identify the backgrounds of members of Congress.
- Describe the jobs performed by those who serve in Congress.
- Understand the advantages of being a member of Congress.

Can you name your two senators? Your representative? Most Americans cannot—let alone tell much about their backgrounds, qualifications, or voting records. In this section, you will learn about the members of Congress.

What are the personal and political backgrounds?

The 535 members of Congress are all well-educated, and most have college degrees. Only a few members of Congress were born outside the country. Most were born in the states they represent. Members of the House of Representatives have an average age of 55. The average age of senators is 60.

Although men outnumber women in Congress, the number of women is growing. Many women are leaders in the Congress. Nancy Pelosi (D., California) is Speaker of the House. This position makes her third in line for the presidency. The number of African Americans, Hispanics, and Asians in Congress is also increasing. Representative David Wu (D., Oregon) is the first Chinese American to serve in Congress. Five African Americans have been elected to the Senate.

Most members of Congress are married and have families. Many different religions are represented by members of Congress. More than half of the senators are lawyers. Well over a third of the representatives are also lawyers. Members of Congress usually have many years of political experience. They have served as state officials, governors, Cabinet members, or important members of federal agencies.

Fig. 10.7

How Representative Is Congress?

COLLEGE DEGREES	WOMEN	AGE 60 AND OLDER	FOREIGN-BORN
27% of Americans	**51%** of Americans	**17%** of Americans	**13%** of Americans
93% of 110th Congress	**17%** of 110th Congress	**40%** of 110th Congress	**2%** of 110th Congress
In the First Congress, elected in 1789, only 48.4% of the members had college degrees. Today, 44% of senators and representatives have law degrees.	The first woman in Congress was Jeanette Rankin (R., Montana), a suffragist and peace activist elected in 1916.	The 110th Congress was, on average, the oldest that has ever served. The oldest member was 83, the youngest was 31.	Foreign-born members of Congress have come from Canada, Cuba, Hungary, Japan, Mexico, the Netherlands, Pakistan, Taiwan, and elsewhere.

Sources: U.S. Census Bureau; Congressional Research Service; Biographical Directory of the United States Congress; *Politics in the First Congress, 1789–1791*

▲ **Analyzing Charts** Over time, the membership of Congress has become more educated, older, and more diverse. *How much should the Congress reflect the backgrounds of the general population?*

In general, senators and representatives can be described as a group of well-educated, upper-middle-class Americans. They are experienced in politics and are asked to serve Americans they represent. For a look at the diversity in Congress, see Figure 10.7.

✔**Checkpoint** Describe the gender, ethnic, and religious diversity of members of Congress.

What is the job of a member of Congress?

Senators and representatives work for the people who elect them. They cast hundreds of votes for or against laws during each session of Congress. Voting is the most important job they do. When casting a vote, the members of Congress have four options. They can vote as delegates of the people of their state. They decide if they would vote for the **bill** or not. They can vote as **trustees** according to their personal opinion of the bill. Members of Congress can also vote as **partisans,** in line with the ideas of their party. The last option is to vote as a **politico** and combine their own views, the opinions of the people they represent, and their party's views.

Senators and representatives serve as committee members. Part of their job as committee members is to decide which bills go before Congress for **floor consideration.** Only when it is chosen for floor consideration can a bill be acted on by the full membership.

Bill
A suggested new law

Trustee
A person who is given power to act for others

Partisan
A person that votes by the party line

Politico
A person that tries to balance being a delegate, trustee, and partisan

Floor consideration
The consideration of and action on a bill by the full membership of the House or Senate

Reading Strategy
Predicting
Preview the title of this paragraph. Predict what you will learn about the benefits members of Congress receive.

Franking privilege
A benefit for members of Congress to mail letters and other materials for free

What benefits do members of Congress receive?

Members of Congress are paid $169,300 a year. The Speaker of the House and the majority and minority floor leaders receive even more. Salaries and benefits help members of Congress who must maintain two residences, one in their home state and one in Washington, D.C. Travel allowances, low insurance rates, and medical care are other benefits. Members of Congress are provided with offices and money for hiring a staff. The **franking privilege** allows them to mail letters and other materials for free. There are restaurants, gyms, swimming pools, and parking spaces available for members of Congress to use, free of charge.

The Constitution gives members of Congress a privilege that is not related to money. Article 1, Section 6, states, ". . . for any Speech or Debate in either House, they shall not be questioned in any other Place." This means that members of Congress cannot be questioned in the courts. This article applies to debates in Congress. However, it does not protect members of Congress if they attack another person verbally or in writing. The Supreme Court has ruled that members of Congress may be sued for statements made in public documents, such as newspapers.

✔**Checkpoint** What five benefits are offered to members of Congress?

Biography

Two People Who Served

Margaret Chase Smith and Barbara Jordan were two pioneers who worked toward equality and equal representation in the U.S. Congress.

Margaret Chase Smith was born in Maine in 1897. In 1940 she was elected to complete her husband's term when he died. She was reelected for four terms in the House of Representatives and later was elected to the Senate. She was the first woman elected to both houses of Congress. In 1964 Smith became the first woman to be placed in nomination for President at a major party convention. Smith served in the Senate until 1973.

Barbara Jordan was born in 1936. She became a lawyer and served as a state senator in Texas. In 1973 she became the first southern African American woman elected to the House. She served three terms. After she left Congress, Jordan taught courses in government and politics at the University of Texas at Austin.

Government in Your Life

Teens Testify Before Congress

Sometimes teens are asked to testify before congressional committees to share their views. Two teens who testified were Elisa Svenson and Danielle Shimotakahara.

In 1999, Svenson, a freshman in college, worked at the Institute for Youth Development. This organization provides information to help young people avoid smoking, alcohol, and other drugs. Svenson testified before the House Commerce Subcommittee on Health and the Environment. She spoke about teen smoking and addiction. Several of her family members had died due to smoking that began in their teen years. She wanted to prevent her peers from making the same mistake.

That same year, Shimotakahara, age 12, researched the effects of violence on children. She then started a campaign to prevent children from being exposed to violent video games. The next year, she testified before the United States Senate Commerce Committee. In 2001, the teen spoke before the Oregon state senate. She helped get an Oregon state resolution passed by the legislature. It strongly urged the video game industry to reduce violence in games for young people and to label video games for children under 17. Shimotakahara's written testimony was later sent to the United States Senate Committee on Science and Transportation.

Essential Questions **Journal**	Go to your **Essential Questions Journal** to work on this chapter's Essential Question.

SECTION 4 ASSESSMENT

1. **Guiding Question** Use your completed concept web to answer this question: What roles and functions do members of Congress perform?

Key Terms and Comprehension

On a sheet of paper, choose the letter of the best answer to each question.

2. What is an official who votes in line with a political party called?

    A. trustee   **C.** partisan

    B. delegate   **D.** representative

3. More than half of the senators and a third of representatives are what?

    A. college graduates   **C.** delegates

    B. doctors   **D.** lawyers

4. What is the salary of most senators and representatives?

    A. $100,600   **C.** $192,000

    B. $169,300   **D.** $535,000

5. What is happening to the number of minorities and women in Congress?

    A. growing   **C.** staying the same

    B. slowly declining   **D.** quickly declining

Critical Thinking

6. **Analyze Information** Do you think members of Congress get too many or too few benefits? Explain your answer.

7. **Draw Inferences** Why do you think members of Congress usually vote as partisans?

Chapter Summary

Section 1—The National Legislature

- Congress is bicameral. The two houses are the Senate and the House of Representatives.

- Every state has two representatives in the Senate. In the House of Representatives, each state is represented according to population.

- Each term of Congress is two years beginning in early January.

Section 2—The House of Representatives

- The House of Representatives has 435 members.

- Representatives are elected for two-year terms.

- A census is taken every ten years. The census decides the number of seats each state has in the House of Representatives.

- Members of the House of Representatives come from the congressional districts in each state.

Section 3—The Senate

- The Senate has 100 members. Senators serve six-year terms.

- Only one-third of the members of Senate are elected at one time. This means the Senate is a continuous body.

Section 4—The Members of Congress

- Members of Congress are well-educated, with years of political experience.

- Most members of Congress are married. Men outnumber women. The number of African Americans, Asians, and Hispanics is increasing.

- Members of Congress represent the people. They cast votes and pass laws. They work in committees.

- The salary of most members of Congress is $169,300, with other benefits allowed.

Guiding Question
Section 2 How are the seats in the House distributed, and what qualifications must members have?

Guiding Question
Section 3 How does the Senate differ from the House?

Guiding Question
Section 1 Why does the Consitution establish a bicameral legislature?

Guiding Question
Section 4 What roles and functions do members of Congress perform?

CHAPTER 10

Essential Question
Whose views should members of Congress represent when voting?

Document-Based Assessment

Term Limits for Members of Congress

There are no limits on the number of terms a member of Congress may serve. Some state legislatures want to change this. Many members of Congress have served four or more terms. In 1992, Arkansas added an amendment to its state constitution limiting the number of terms a member of Congress from that state could serve. The Arkansas legislature believed long-term officials ignored their duties in an effort to get reelected. Ray Thornton, in his fourth term in the House, filed a lawsuit. A national group, U.S. Term Limits, Inc., defended the Arkansas amendment. The case was heard in the Arkansas Supreme Court. Thornton thought the amendment violated the Constitution. The case went to the U.S. Supreme Court. Justice Stevens said the amendment went against the Constitution and must be removed. He delivered the opinion on the right.

Document at a Glance

- *U.S. Term Limits, Inc.* v. *Thornton*
- Justice Stevens Ruled Term Limits Unconstitutional
- No Term Limits for Members of Congress

Justice Stevens wrote, "The case today sets forth qualifications for membership in the Congress of the United States. . . . It presents a challenge to an amendment to the Arkansas State Constitution that prohibits the name of an otherwise-eligible candidate for Congress from appearing on the general election ballot if that candidate has already served three terms in the House of Representatives or two terms in the Senate. . . . Allowing individual states to adopt their own qualifications for Congressional service would be inconsistent with the Framers' vision of a uniform National Legislature. If the qualifications set forth in the text of the Constitution are to be changed, that text must be amended. . . .

"We are, however, firmly convinced that allowing the several states to adopt term limits for Congressional service would effect a fundamental change in the constitutional framework. . . ."

Document-Based Questions

1. Why did Arkansas want to change its constitution?

2. What limits did Arkansas want to put on the terms of a member of Congress?

3. Why did Arkansas want to limit the terms of members of Congress?

4. Why did Justice Stevens decide against limiting terms in Congress?

5. **Make a prediction** Do you think there will ever be term limits in Congress? Why or why not?

Source: *U.S. Term Limits, Inc.* v. *Thornton*, 1995

Chapter Assessment

GOVERNMENT ONLINE
Self-Test
To test your understanding of
key terms and main ideas, visit
PearsonSuccessNet.com

Directions: Choose the letter of the best answer
or write the answer using complete sentences.

Section 1—The National Legislature

1. When does Congress begin each session in Washington, D.C.?

   A. July   **B.** December   **C.** June   **D.** January

2. To send a new law to the President for approval, who must it be first approved by?

   A. Senate   **C.** Vice President

   B. House   **D.** Senate and House

3. What is the purpose of a special session?

4. **Critical Thinking** Does the two-house structure allow Congress to be more effective? Explain your answer.

Section 2—The House of Representatives

5. What is the leader of the House of Representatives known as?

   A. President   **C.** Speaker of the House

   B. Vice President   **D.** Governor

6. An election that takes place between presidential election years is called what?

   A. at-large   **C.** appointing

   B. off-year   **D.** open-ended

7. What is the purpose of gerrymandering?

8. **Critical Thinking** Why might a House member resign?

Section 3—The Senate

9. How many members did the first Senate have?

   A. 26   **B.** 50   **C.** 100   **D.** 435

10. How old must a candidate be to serve in the Senate?

    A. 25   **B.** 30   **C.** 35   **D.** 45

11. What is a government body called in which all seats are never up for reelection at the same time?

12. How is a senator's term different from the term of a member of the House of Representatives?

13. **Critical Thinking** What informal qualifications would you look for in a candidate for Congress?

Section 4—The Members of Congress

14. What is the current average age of a senator?

    A. 35   **B.** 50   **C.** 60   **D.** 100

15. A member of Congress mailing a letter or package for free is an example of what?

    A. delegate   **C.** franking privilege

    B. floor consideration   **D.** vote

16. What is a suggested new law called?

    A. delegate   **B.** bill   **C.** trustee   **D.** vote

17. Critical Thinking In your opinion, what is the most important job of a member of Congress?

Apply What You've Learned

Exploring the Essential Question

18. List the four voting options that members of Congress have as "representatives of the people." Make a graphic organizer of the advantages and disadvantages of these four options.

19. Which option would you want your members of Congress to use in deciding how to vote? Explain.

Essential Question Project

20. Research the three most recent votes by one of your representatives in Congress and the two senators from your state. Write a paragraph to explain how each person voted. Include an answer to the Essential Question: **Whose views should members of Congress represent when voting?**

Essential Questions
Journal

Go to your **Essential Questions Journal** to work on this chapter's Essential Question.

Test-Taking Tip

After you have completed a test, reread each question and answer. Ask yourself, Have I answered the question that I was asked? Have I answered it completely?

▲ Members of the House of Representatives are sworn in.

Powers of Congress

Essential Question
What should the limits be on the powers of Congress?

■ ■

Reading Strategy: Text Structure
Before you begin reading about the powers of
Congress, look at how the chapter is organized.
Look at the title, headings, boldfaced words,
photographs, and charts.

- Summarize the text according to its structure.
- Notice that the subject headings are in the form of
  questions. The answer to each question is provided in the
  paragraph(s). Therefore, the text is structured in a question-
  and-answer format.

GOVERNMENT ONLINE
ON THE GO

To study anywhere, anytime, download these online resources at
PearsonSuccessNet.com
- **Political Dictionary**
- **Audio Review**
- **Downloadable Interactivities**

The Expressed Powers of Money and Commerce

▲ Congress created the Coast Guard to protect coastal waters.

Guiding Question

What powers over money and commerce does the Constitution give to Congress, and what limits does it put on these powers? Use a table to keep track of the powers of Congress and their limits.

Money and Commerce	
Expressed Power	Limits on Power
■ Foreign trade	■ Cannot tax exports
■	■
■	■

Objectives:

- Identify the three types of congressional power.
- Analyze the commerce power of Congress.
- Summarize the congressional power to tax.
- Explain why the Framers gave Congress the power to issue currency.
- Explain the bankruptcy and borrowing powers.

Congress has a great many powers. At the same time, however, the Constitution places important limits on those powers. Those limits are based on two facts. One is that our government is a limited government. The other is that our government is federal in form. This means that the states also have important powers.

What are the delegated powers?

Sections 8 and 9 of Article I of the Constitution list many of the powers of Congress. These are the delegated powers. Delegated powers are those given to Congress by the Constitution. The Framers of the Constitution limited those powers in several ways. For example, Congress can pass a bill into law. The President does not have to sign the bill, however, and the Supreme Court can say that the law goes against the Constitution. These are two ways that the powers of Congress are limited.

The Constitution gives the states power over some issues. This means that the federal government has no power in these areas. They include such matters as creating a public school system or setting a minimum age for marriage licenses.

Even though the Constitution limits the powers of Congress, it also grants many powers. These powers are delegated in three different ways. The **expressed powers** are set out specifically in Article I. The **implied powers** are not stated specifically, but are based on the expressed powers. The **inherent powers** are those that all national governments have. For a summary of the powers, see Figure 11.1 on page 254.

What are the expressed powers?

Article I, Section 8 of the Constitution lists 27 of the expressed powers of Congress. The powers include collecting taxes, regulating trade, and raising an army. To find the real meaning of these powers, though, you must look at how Congress has used them over the years. Supreme Court rulings have also shaped the meaning of the expressed powers.

Many of the implied powers and much of what Congress does every day is based on two of the expressed powers: the commerce power and the taxing power.

✓ **Checkpoint** Which article of the Constitution grants Congress most of its expressed powers?

What is the commerce power?

Commerce is trade, or the buying and selling of goods. The Framers were concerned about trade when they wrote the Constitution. Because under the Articles of Confederation Congress had no power over interstate trade, the states had passed their own trade laws. These laws caused confusion. To solve this problem, the Framers added the Commerce Clause to the Constitution.

The **commerce power** is the power of Congress to regulate trade. Congress can regulate both interstate trade—trade between states— and foreign trade—trade with other countries. This power has been very important in the growth of this nation into a world leader.

The Supreme Court decided its first case involving the Commerce Clause in 1824. Aaron Ogden was running a steamboat line between New York City and New Jersey. Ogden had a contract from the State of New York. A man named Thomas Gibbons got a contract from the federal government and began running another steamboat line in the same area. Ogden sued Gibbons, and the case went to the Supreme Court.

The Court decided Gibbons could continue his steamboat business because the State of New York had no power over interstate commerce. As a result of this decision, many more steamboat companies began to do business. Railroads also developed. Soon, transportation in the United States was dramatically transformed. Over the years since the case was decided, the commerce power has allowed the federal government to become involved in many areas of life.

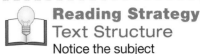

■■■■■■■■■■■■■■■■■■
Reading Strategy
Text Structure
Notice the subject headings are written as questions. After you read this page, answer the questions asked in the headings.

■■■■■■■■■■■■■■■■■■

Expressed powers
Powers of the national government that are found in the Constitution

Implied powers
Powers of the national government that are suggested by the expressed powers set out in the Constitution

Inherent powers
Powers the Constitution is presumed to have given to the national government because it is the government of a sovereign state within the world community

Commerce power
Exclusive power of Congress to regulate trade between states and foreign countries

Reading Strategy
Text Structure
Study the boldface word and the heading on this page. What do they tell you about what you will be learning?

Tax
A charge collected by government on persons or property to meet public needs

Fig. 11.1

Inherent powers are those that all sovereign nations have. An example is the power to control the nation's borders.

Expressed powers are stated in the Constitution. An example is that the Constitution grants Congress the power to regulate immigration.

Implied powers are not stated in the Constitution but drawn from the expressed powers. Based on the expressed power to regulate immigration, Congress established the U.S. Border Patrol to carry out that power.

▲ The Constitution creates a limited government. Therefore, some people dispute the existence of implied and inherent powers.

Some limits on the commerce power must be noted. Congress cannot tax exports. It cannot favor the port of one state over another or force vessels from one state to pay taxes to another state.

✔**Checkpoint**   What was the dispute in the case of *Gibbons* v. *Ogden*?

What is the power to tax?

The Articles of Confederation did not give Congress the power to tax. This caused major problems during the nation's early years. When the Framers wrote the Constitution, they made sure to include the taxing power.

A **tax** is an amount of money charged by the government on persons or property. The major purpose of taxes is to raise money for public needs, as shown in **Figure 11.2** on the next page. Taxes called protective tariffs can be imposed on foreign goods to protect industries in this country. Tariffs make the cost of foreign goods higher than that of goods made at home. Another purpose of taxes is to protect public health and safety. That is why the federal government requires a proper legal license to make or sell narcotics, for example. Licensing is a form of taxation.

The Constitution places the following limits on the power of Congress to impose taxes:

1. Congress may only tax for public purposes, such as defense or paying debts.

2. Congress cannot tax exports, which are goods sent out of the country. Imports (goods brought into the country) may be taxed.

3. Direct taxes must be equally divided among the states. Direct taxes are paid by a person directly to the government. Taxes on land or buildings are examples of direct taxes.

Income tax is another kind of direct tax. It does not have to be divided equally among the states. This is because wealth is not divided equally.

4. All indirect taxes must be collected at the same federal rate throughout the country. Examples of indirect taxes are those collected on gasoline, alcoholic beverages, and tobacco products. An indirect tax is one that is first paid by one person but then passed on to another in the cost of an item.

✔**Checkpoint**   What are two examples of taxes people pay directly to the government?

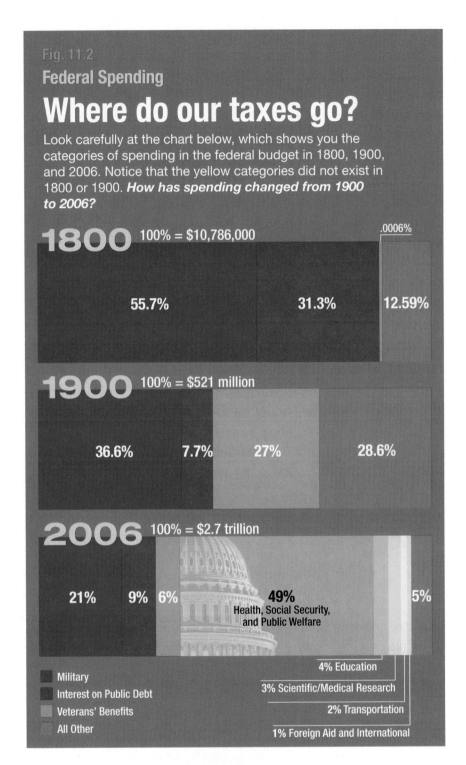

Fig. 11.2
Federal Spending
Where do our taxes go?

Look carefully at the chart below, which shows you the categories of spending in the federal budget in 1800, 1900, and 2006. Notice that the yellow categories did not exist in 1800 or 1900. *How has spending changed from 1900 to 2006?*

1800 100% = $10,786,000 .0006%

55.7% 31.3% 12.59%

1900 100% = $521 million

36.6% 7.7% 27% 28.6%

2006 100% = $2.7 trillion

21% 9% 6% **49%** Health, Social Security, and Public Welfare 5%

- Military
- Interest on Public Debt
- Veterans' Benefits
- All Other

4% Education
3% Scientific/Medical Research
2% Transportation
1% Foreign Aid and International

Public debt
All the money borrowed by the government and not yet repaid, plus the interest on that money

What is the borrowing power?

Article I of the Constitution allows Congress to borrow money for any purpose. The Constitution does not limit the amount of money that may be borrowed. Congress has, however, put a limit on the public debt. The **public debt** is all the money borrowed by the federal government, along with the interest on that money. Congress has had to raise that limit many times. The public debt now stands at over $9 trillion.

Deficit financing
Spending more money than is
taken in

Legal tender
Any kind of money that a creditor
must by law accept in payment for
debts

Bankruptcy
The legal procedure in which the
bankrupt's assets are paid to
those to whom a debt is owed

Over the years, the government has used **deficit financing.** This
means the government spends more than it takes in. To make up
the difference, the government borrows money. The government
has used deficit financing to deal with such matters as the Great
Depression, wars, and social programs. In all but seven years since
1930, the federal government has been in debt. Not until 1998 did
the government take in as much as it spent. The government was
only out of debt until 2002, however. Deficit spending returned in
that year.

What is the currency power?

Our country did not have a national money system in its early
years. English coins, Spanish money, paper money, and money
issued by several of the 13 states were all being used. The many
forms of money caused great confusion. In 1789, the Framers gave
Congress the currency power. Currency is money in any form used
as a medium of exchange. The states are denied the currency power.

At first, the United States issued coins made of gold, silver, and
other metals. The first Bank of the United States was created by
Congress in 1791. It had the power to issue bank notes (paper
money). These were not **legal tender,** which is any kind of money a
creditor must by law accept as payment.

It was not until 1862 that Congress created a national paper
currency. These bills were called Greenbacks. Private bank notes,
issued by state banks, competed with these new Greenbacks. After
Congress charged a tax on the private bank notes, they soon went
out of use.

There were several Supreme Court cases involving Greenbacks. In
1884, the Supreme Court decided that Greenbacks were constitutional.
The Court said that issuing paper money as legal tender was a proper
use of the currency power. The Court agreed that the currency power
could be implied from the borrowing and war powers.

What is the bankruptcy power?

If a person is bankrupt, that means that he or she does not have
enough money to pay his or her debts. **Bankruptcy** is a legal
procedure in which the bankrupt's assets, or everything the person
owns, are paid to those to whom a debt is owed. The person or
company is then free from all debts incurred before the bankruptcy.
See Figure 11.3. The Constitution gives Congress the power to
make laws about bankruptcy in the United States. The states and the
national government both have the power to regulate bankruptcy.
Because the federal bankruptcy law is very broad, however, the
federal district courts hear most of the bankruptcy cases.

Fig. 11.3

What Is Personal Bankruptcy?

Regulating bankruptcy is one of the expressed powers of Congress. The bankruptcy process can't be used for certain kinds of debts, such as mortgages and taxes. It can be used for credit cards, medical expenses, and other debts. ***Why is bankruptcy regulated by the federal government?***

Steps in Filing for Bankruptcy

1 A debtor must choose one of two kinds of bankruptcy:

The debtor agrees to give up most of his or her property, which is then sold to pay creditors, or people who are owed money.

▶ **Chapter 7** Liquidation Bankruptcy

The debtor works out a payment plan with creditors, who may accept a reduced amount in exchange for total repayment over time.

▶ **Chapter 13** Reorganization Bankruptcy

2 The application for bankruptcy requires detailed documentation of income, expenses, assets, liabilities, and all recent financial transactions.

Assets

Income

Liabilities

Expenses

3 When a bankruptcy application is filed, the court assumes responsibility for the debtor's finances. The court issues an order informing all creditors, stopping them from taking steps to collect their debts without court permission.

CREDITORS

4 With a court-appointed trustee, the debtor meets with creditors to negotiate and agree on how much each will be paid. The trustee's job is to recover as much money as possible for creditors.

5 At a hearing, a federal judge then declares the debt discharged, or dismissed.

Serving in the National Guard

Congress has extensive war powers, according to the Constitution. One of these is the power to call forth the militia in time of need. Today, the militia is called the National Guard or the Air National Guard. The Air National Guard was created in 1947. The National Guard began in colonial days when it was called the militia. It was used during the American Revolution.

Many high school students are interested in the military as a career. The regular military services require a complete commitment. The Guard services require members to work weekends and two weeks a year. The commitment is six to eight years. After three years, the member may become a reserve. There are hundreds of job opportunities in these two types of military services, including military police and public affairs. Guard members can serve while attending school or while holding a job. They receive a monthly paycheck and other benefits. Twenty Presidents have served their country in this way.

Both the state and the federal government can call up the National Guard. The Guard has been needed during natural disasters, such as hurricanes Katrina and Ike, and in time of war.

SECTION 1 ASSESSMENT

Essential Questions Journal Go to your **Essential Questions Journal** to work on this chapter's Essential Question.

1. **Guiding Question** Use your completed table to answer this question: What powers over money and commerce does the Constitution give to Congress, and what limits does it put on these powers?

Key Terms and Comprehension

On a sheet of paper, write the answer to each question. Use complete sentences.

2. What is the difference between expressed powers and implied powers?

3. What is the commerce power?

4. Why did the Framers give Congress the currency power?

5. What is bankruptcy?

Critical Thinking

6. **Drawing Inferences** Why did the Framers limit the power of Congress to collect taxes?

7. **Making Decisions** Do you think the bankruptcy process is fair to those in debt? Why or why not?

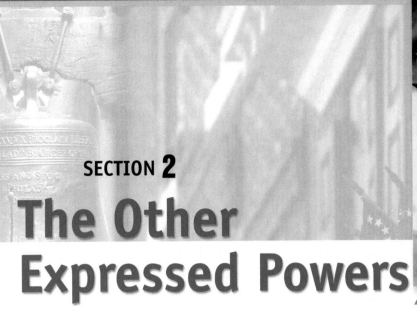

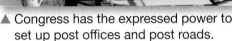

SECTION 2

The Other Expressed Powers

▲ Congress has the expressed power to set up post offices and post roads.

Guiding Question

How do the expressed powers reflect the Framers' commitment to creating a strong but limited national government? Use a table to organize information about the expressed powers of Congress.

Powers of Congress	
Foreign Policy	Domestic Policy
■	■ Naturalization laws
■	■

Objectives:

- Identify the foreign relations powers of Congress.
- Describe the relationship between Congress and the President on the issues of war and national defense.
- List the other key powers of Congress.

In Section 1 of this chapter, you reviewed the expressed powers of Congress related to commerce and money. The Constitution gives Congress a number of other expressed powers. In this section, you will learn about these expressed powers of Congress. See Figure 11.4 on page 260.

What are the foreign affairs powers of Congress?

The Constitution gives the President most of the responsibility for foreign policy, but Congress also plays an important part. The foreign affairs powers of Congress come from two sources. One is the expressed powers. The war powers and the power to control foreign commerce are especially important. The second is the lawmaking responsibility of Congress. This responsibility includes the power to act on matters that affect the nation's security. These matters include controlling immigration and fighting terrorism.

✔ **Checkpoint** What two expressed powers deal with foreign affairs?

What are the war powers?

The war powers of Congress are found in Section 8 of Article I of the Constitution. These powers are very important. Only Congress has the power to declare war. Congress can also raise and support armies and provide and maintain a navy. Congress can make rules for governing the nation's military forces. Congress can also call forth the militia (National Guard) and organize, arm, and discipline that force.

In Chapter 14 we will consider the President's power to make war. Throughout the years, most Presidents have used the armed forces in combat without a declaration of war by Congress. Many argue that this is unconstitutional. This use of the war powers raised serious concerns when Presidents Lyndon Johnson and Richard Nixon committed American troops to a long war in Vietnam (1964–1973). After the war, Congress passed the War Powers Resolution. It was meant to limit the President's war-making powers. The resolution states that Congress must declare war or at least approve the action in order for the President to commit American troops to combat abroad. However, if the United States or its armed forces have been attacked, the President can call troops into action. In this case, the President must report to Congress within 48 hours of the action. If American troops are deployed in this way, the commitment must end in 60 days, unless Congress authorizes a longer commitment. Congress can end a commitment at any time. The question of whether or not this resolution is constitutional has yet to be decided.

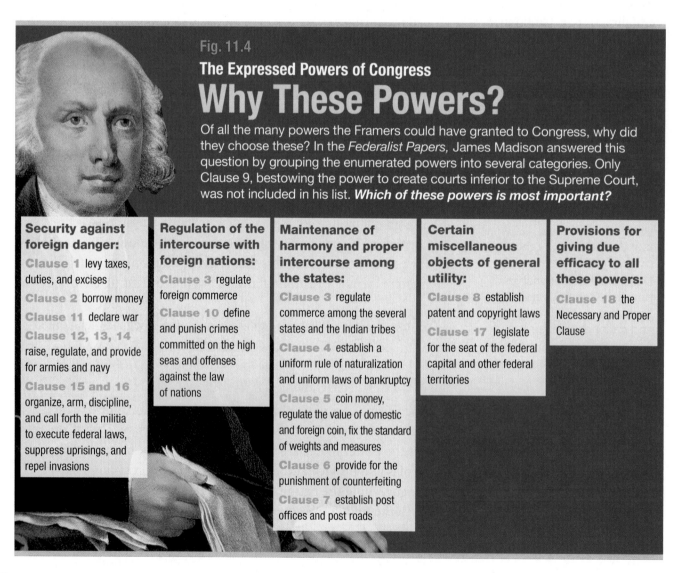

Fig. 11.4

The Expressed Powers of Congress

Why These Powers?

Of all the many powers the Framers could have granted to Congress, why did they choose these? In the *Federalist Papers,* James Madison answered this question by grouping the enumerated powers into several categories. Only Clause 9, bestowing the power to create courts inferior to the Supreme Court, was not included in his list. **Which of these powers is most important?**

Security against foreign danger:

Clause 1 levy taxes, duties, and excises

Clause 2 borrow money

Clause 11 declare war

Clause 12, 13, 14 raise, regulate, and provide for armies and navy

Clause 15 and 16 organize, arm, discipline, and call forth the militia to execute federal laws, suppress uprisings, and repel invasions

Regulation of the intercourse with foreign nations:

Clause 3 regulate foreign commerce

Clause 10 define and punish crimes committed on the high seas and offenses against the law of nations

Maintenance of harmony and proper intercourse among the states:

Clause 3 regulate commerce among the several states and the Indian tribes

Clause 4 establish a uniform rule of naturalization and uniform laws of bankruptcy

Clause 5 coin money, regulate the value of domestic and foreign coin, fix the standard of weights and measures

Clause 6 provide for the punishment of counterfeiting

Clause 7 establish post offices and post roads

Certain miscellaneous objects of general utility:

Clause 8 establish patent and copyright laws

Clause 17 legislate for the seat of the federal capital and other federal territories

Provisions for giving due efficacy to all these powers:

Clause 18 the Necessary and Proper Clause

What are the domestic powers?

The rest of the expressed powers in this section are domestic powers. Each one of these powers has a big effect on our daily lives.

Congress has the power to grant copyrights and patents. A **copyright** is the exclusive right of a person or company to reproduce, publish, and sell a creative work. Copyrights are registered by the Copyright Office in the Library of Congress. The copyright is good for the life of the artist plus 70 years. Copyrights cover many creative works, including books, music, paintings, maps, movies, and more. See Figure 11.5 on page 262. The federal courts, not the Copyright Office, hear cases involving copyright violations.

A **patent** gives a person or company the exclusive right to make and sell an invention. Patents cover art, machines, manufacturing processes, or new ways of doing things. A patent is good for up to 20 years. It is issued by the Patent and Trademark Office of the Department of Commerce.

The postal power (Article I, Section 8, Clause 7) gives Congress the power to set up post offices and postal routes. Postal routes include airlines, rail lines, and waterways within the United States. The United States Postal Service began in the colonial period. Today the country has over 33,000 post offices, and the Postal Service employs over 685,000 people.

Congress has made it a federal crime to obstruct the mail, or to use the mail to commit a criminal act. The law says that many items cannot be sent through the mail, including obscene materials, certain live animals, or dangerous goods. The states may not interfere with the mail. Also, states may not tax the post offices or other property of the Postal Service.

Congress also has the power to "fix the Standard of Weights and Measures" in the United States. In the 1800s, Congress made both the English and metric systems legal in this country. The National Institute of Standards and Technology keeps the original standard measures in our country. All other measures in the United States are tested and corrected against these standards.

✔ **Checkpoint** How long does a copyright last?

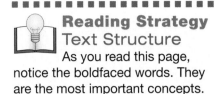

Reading Strategy
Text Structure
As you read this page, notice the boldfaced words. They are the most important concepts.

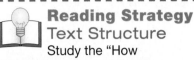

Reading Strategy
Text Structure
Study the "How Government Works" feature on the next page. How does it help you understand copyright infringement?

Copyright
The exclusive right of a person or company to reproduce, publish, and sell a creative work

Patent
A license issued to an inventor granting the exclusive right to use or sell the invention for a limited period of time

Fig. 11.5 **How Government Works**

How does copyright affect me?

Copyright infringement is a hot topic. The Internet makes sharing information easier than ever. However, Congress makes laws regulating what information can or cannot be shared freely. *How do copyright laws protect the rights of writers and artists?*

Alex, Ryan, and Chris form a band. They practice their favorite popular songs and sometimes play for their friends after school. They are asked to play at a school dance. **WARNING:** Although they are not earning money for their performance and they are not taking money away from the copyright holder, the band could be sued for using someone else's copyrighted work.

Ryan suggests they record an album of cover songs and distribute it for free. **WARNING:** The band would lose their case if they were sued for copyright infringement. If they record current songs, some people may download their version instead of buying the original CD. That would take money from the original artist or copyright holder.

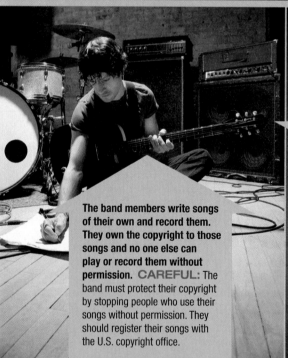

The band sells their songs over the Internet, but discover that some people are sharing the songs with friends who have not paid. **WHAT CAN THEY DO?** They can sue those who are illegally distributing and copying their songs. If they do not take action, they could forfeit their copyright.

The band members write songs of their own and record them. They own the copyright to those songs and no one else can play or record them without permission. **CAREFUL:** The band must protect their copyright by stopping people who use their songs without permission. They should register their songs with the U.S. copyright office.

A rival band records one of Ryan, Chris, and Alex's songs and sells the CDs at school. WHAT CAN THEY DO? They can sue the other band for copyright infringement. If they can prove that they wrote the song or recorded it first, they could win and force the other band to pay damages.

Fair Use Determining an infringement of copyright depends upon whether the test of "fair use" is met. The factors considered are (1) the purpose and character of the use, (2) the nature of the copyrighted work, (3) the amount and substance of the portion used, and (4) the effect of the use on the value of the copyrighted work. In addition, the U.S. Supreme Court has stated that the courts should focus on the extent that the new work is transformative—that is, does it alter the work with new expression, meaning, or message? The more transformative the new work is means that the other factors are less important.

In addition to the other domestic powers, the Constitution gives Congress the power to manage federal areas. This includes the District of Columbia, federal arsenals, dockyards, post offices, prisons, parks, and many other federal possessions. It also includes the federal **territories** of Puerto Rico, Guam, and the Virgin Islands. These territories are not states, but they are part of the United States. They have their own systems of government.

The power of **eminent domain** is the power of the federal government to take private property for public use. The 5th Amendment requires the government to pay the owner a fair price if his or her property is taken. The courts are often called in to decide in cases of eminent domain.

Congress also has the power to set the rules for naturalization. **Naturalization** is the process by which a citizen of one country becomes a citizen of another country. There are over 14 million naturalized citizens in the United States today.

Some of the domestic powers of Congress have to do with the courts. Most importantly, Congress can set up and organize all of the federal courts below the Supreme Court. You will learn more about the federal court system in Chapter 18.

Another judicial power of Congress is the power to define federal crimes and set the punishment for them. Three are mentioned in Article I of the Constitution: counterfeiting, piracies and felonies on the high seas, and the breaking of international law. Treason is listed in Article III. Congress has also decided on more than 100 other federal crimes using its implied powers.

Territory
A part of the United States not included in any state but organized with a separate system of government

Eminent domain
Power of a government to take private property for public use

Naturalization
The process of giving full citizenship to a person born in another country

✔**Checkpoint**   What is eminent domain?

Essential Questions Journal   Go to your **Essential Questions Journal** to work on this chapter's Essential Question.

SECTION **2** ASSESSMENT

1. **Guiding Question** Use your completed table to answer this question: How do the expressed powers reflect the Framers' commitment to creating a strong but limited national government?

Key Terms and Comprehension

On a sheet of paper, write the answer to each question. Use complete sentences.

2. What are the postal powers of Congress?

3. How is a copyright different from a patent?

4. How do the President and Congress share the foreign affairs powers?

5. What is naturalization?

Critical Thinking

6. **Predict Consequences** What might happen if musicians could not copyright their music?

7. **Identify Central Issues** Do you think eminent domain is fair to the landowner? Why or why not?

What Are the Limits on the Implied Powers of Congress?

In 1791, Congress established the Bank of the United States, despite objections from those who insisted that the Constitution did not give Congress such power. The Bank's charter expired in 1811. In 1816, Congress created the second Bank of the United States after another hard-fought battle. In both cases, those who favored a strong national government argued that a national bank was needed to stabilize the country's financial system. Those who opposed that view said Congress had no authority to establish a national bank.

In 1818, Maryland's state legislature placed a tax on all notes issued by any bank that was not chartered by the state legislature. James McCulloch, an officer of the Baltimore branch of the national bank, issued notes on which the tax had not been paid. The Maryland courts upheld the state's power to tax the Bank, but the United States, acting on McCulloch's behalf, appealed that decision to the Supreme Court.

Chief Justice John Marshall, knowing the great importance of the Court's decision, declared:

"The conflicting powers of the government of the Union . . . are to be discussed; and an opinion given, which may essentially influence the great operations of the government. No tribunal can approach such a question without a deep sense of its importance, and of the awful responsibility involved in its decision. But it must be decided peacefully . . ."

At the urging of Alexander Hamilton, Congress charters the First Bank of the United States, 1781.

The Department of the Treasury is officially established with Hamilton as Secretary, 1789.

Congress charters the second Bank of the United States, 1816.

In one of its most important decisions, the Court unanimously reversed the Maryland courts. It held that the Constitution did not need to expressly empower Congress to create a bank. The creation of the second Bank of the United States, said the Court, was "necessary and proper" to the execution of the taxing, borrowing, currency, and commerce powers.

As to the question of whether Maryland had the right to tax the Bank, the Court said, "The power to tax involves the power to destroy." If states had the power to tax the federal government, they could destroy it. This was not, the Court said, the intention of the people when they ratified the Constitution.

Arguments for Maryland

- The Constitution gives the federal government no right to establish a bank.
- The power to establish banks is therefore reserved to the states.
- States are sovereign and have the power to tax any bank within their borders.

Arguments for McCulloch and the National Bank

- The Necessary and Proper Clause gives Congress the right to do what is necessary to carry out its expressed powers.
- No state can lawfully tax any agency of the federal government.

Thinking Critically

1. What standard should be used to decide whether an act of Congress is "necessary and proper"?
2. **Constitutional Principles** How does the decision in *McCulloch* v. *Maryland* strengthen or weaken federalism?

President Andrew Jackson vetoes a bill to renew the charter of the second Bank of the United States, 1832.

The National Banking Act creates a uniform currency in the United States, 1863.

President Woodrow Wilson signs the Federal Reserve Act, creating the Federal Reserve system, December 23, 1913.

▲ Congress established the United States Border Patrol to guard the nation's borders.

SECTION 3
The Implied Powers

Guiding Question

How has the doctrine of implied powers increased the powers of Congress? Use a chart to record information about the implied powers.

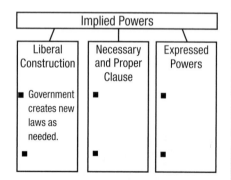

Implied Powers

Liberal Construction	Necessary and Proper Clause	Expressed Powers
■ Government creates new laws as needed. ■	■ ■	■ ■

Objectives:

- Explain the Necessary and Proper Clause.
- Compare strict construction and liberal construction.
- Summarize the key developments in the battle over the implied powers of Congress.

The Constitution says nothing about education. Yet Congress provides billions of dollars a year to the Department of Education for public schools. How can this be? The answer is the implied powers of Congress. In this section, you will learn about these implied powers.

What is the Necessary and Proper Clause?

The writers of the Constitution knew that issues would come up that were not covered in the Constitution. To handle these, they added the last part of Article I, Section 8. This part is called the **Necessary and Proper Clause.** The clause is also known as the Elastic Clause because it has been stretched so far over the years. It tells Congress that it can make all laws necessary to carry out its duties. See Figure 11.6.

For example, Congress was given the power to set up an army and navy to protect citizens. After a few years, Congress saw that military colleges were needed to train officers. However, the Constitution did not specifically give Congress the power to set up military schools. So Congress passed a law that gave money to states to set up and run military colleges. This is an example of how Congress used the power granted by this clause to provide better military defense for the United States. See Figure 11.7 on page 268 for more information about Congress and education.

✔ **Checkpoint** Why is the Necessary and Proper Clause also called the Elastic Clause?

What is strict versus liberal construction of the Constitution?

After the Constitution was approved, conflict still raged concerning the powers of Congress. The **strict constructionists** feared a strong national government. They wanted Congress to exercise only the expressed powers. They believed the government should be able to expand its powers only when needed. They wanted the states to be strong and powerful. The **liberal constructionists** believed in a strong national government. They believed government should be able to create new power as the country changes or as needed.

The Supreme Court has agreed with the use of the implied powers in many of its decisions. The most important case was *McCulloch v. Maryland* in 1819. Over the years, the power of the national government has grown. The liberal constructionists have won the argument about the powers of Congress.

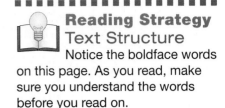

■ ■ ■ ■ ■ ■ ■ ■ ■ ■ ■ ■ ■ ■ ■ ■ ■

Reading Strategy

Text Structure

Notice the boldface words on this page. As you read, make sure you understand the words before you read on.

■ ■ ■ ■ ■ ■ ■ ■ ■ ■ ■ ■ ■ ■ ■ ■ ■

Necessary and Proper Clause
Gives Congress the power to make all laws "necessary and proper" for executing its powers

Strict constructionist
One who wants Congress to only use powers written in the Constitution

Liberal constructionist
One who believes government should be able to create new power when needed

---

Fig. 11.6

The Implied Powers of Congress

Many, if not most, of the laws Congress makes today are permitted because of the Necessary and Proper Clause. The Framers could not have predicted every situation that might arise in the modern world. ***Without its implied powers, how would Congress be able to address new situations?***

The expressed power to lay and collect taxes	Implies the power to: ■ Punish tax evaders ■ Regulate (license) some items (such as alcohol) and outlaw the use of others (such as narcotics) ■ Require states to meet certain conditions to qualify for federal funding
The expressed power to borrow money	■ Implies the power to establish the Federal Reserve System of banks
The expressed power to create naturalization law	■ Implies the power to regulate and limit immigration
The expressed power to raise armies and a navy	■ Implies the power to draft Americans into the military
The expressed power to regulate commerce	Implies the power to: ■ Establish a minimum wage ■ Ban discrimination in workplaces and public facilities ■ Pass laws protecting the disabled ■ Regulate banking
The expressed power to establish post offices	Implies the power to: ■ Prohibit mail fraud and obstruction of the mail ■ Bar the shipping of certain items through the mail

Fig. 11.7 **How Government Works**

Congress and Education

The Constitution does not mention education. The power to act in that major area of public policy is, instead, left to the states. Still, Congress has relied on several of its implied powers to establish important programs in the nation's public schools. *How has Congress involved itself in schools?*

14th Amendment

Section 1. No state shall . . . deprive any person of life, liberty, or property, without the due process of law; nor deny to any person . . . the equal protection of the laws.

Section 5. The Congress shall have power to enforce, by appropriate legislation, the provisions of this article.

The Civil Rights Act of 1964 directed the attorney general to bring court actions to eliminate race-based and other discrimination in the nation's public schools and colleges.

Civil Rights Act, 1964

Photo: Students attempt to attend Central High School in Little Rock, Arkansas, 1957, after a court order to desegregate the schools. Members of the U.S. armed forces stand ready to protect them.

Title IX of the Education Amendments to the Civil Rights Act forbids gender discrimination in federally funded education programs. Its most visible effect has been in girls' and women's athletics. Between 1970 and 2006, the number of female high school athletes increased from fewer than 300,000 to more than 3 million.

Title IX, 1972

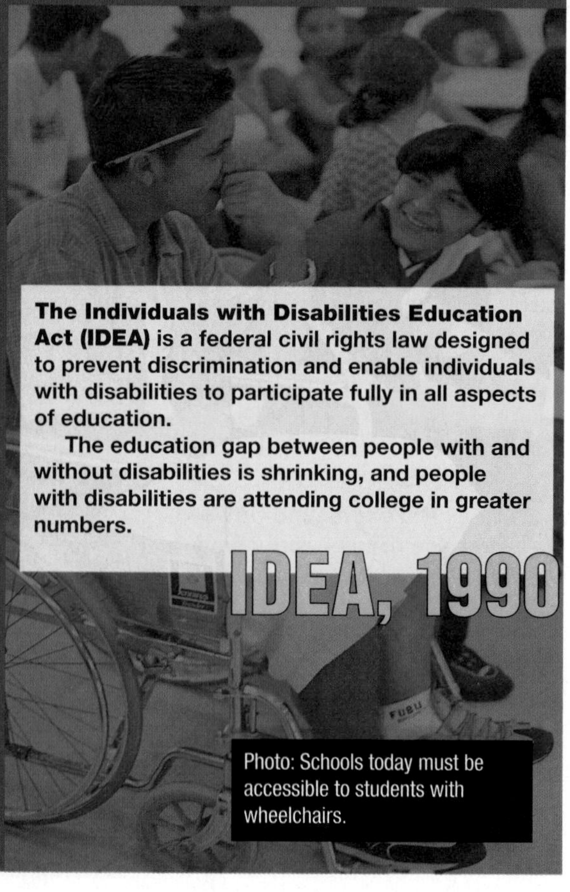

The Individuals with Disabilities Education Act (IDEA) is a federal civil rights law designed to prevent discrimination and enable individuals with disabilities to participate fully in all aspects of education.

The education gap between people with and without disabilities is shrinking, and people with disabilities are attending college in greater numbers.

IDEA, 1990

Photo: High school women's basketball team, Oakland, California, 1979.

Photo: Schools today must be accessible to students with wheelchairs.

Many factors have caused this growth of national power. They include wars, economic problems, and other national emergencies. Advances in technology, transportation, and social programs have required government involvement. Many Americans agree with the liberal constructionist view. Still, controversies exist about the proper limits of national government.

Reading Strategy
Text Structure
This section tells about a cause and effect. Ask yourself, What was the cause? What was the effect?

✔**Checkpoint** Why there has been a growth of national power? List two reasons.

How are the implied powers practiced today?

The Necessary and Proper Clause has allowed the government to meet the needs of the country through changing times. Every use of the implied powers must be based on one of the expressed powers. Most often, the use of an implied power is based on the commerce power, the power to tax and spend, and/or the war powers.

The Commerce Clause has been broadly defined to include all types of economic activity. Congress can now regulate manufacturing, foods and drugs, air travel, and more. The federal government builds highways, protects consumers, and protects the environment. In 1998 and again in 2007, Congress used its commerce power to stop a tax on Internet sales and other online activities. There are limits on the commerce power, however. A few of these constitutional limits were listed in Section 1 of this chapter. At times, the Supreme Court has also found that Congress has gone too far in using its implied powers.

The war powers give Congress the authority to protect the country. See **Figure 11.8.** In doing so, Congress cannot violate any part of the Constitution. Over the years, lawmakers have used the Elastic Clause to stretch these powers to include many things. For example, they have passed a law allowing the national government to draft men to serve in the military. The Supreme Court has upheld this use of the war powers.

✔**Checkpoint** How has Congress used the Commerce Clause?

Fig. 11.8

"I do want a war, but I'd like to be asked nicely."

▲ Analyzing Political Cartoons **Which implied power is the congressman in this cartoon referring to?**

Biography

Ada E. Deer (1935–)

Ada E. Deer headed the Bureau of Indian Affairs (BIA) from 1993 to 1997. She was the first woman to hold this office. She was born on the Menominee Indian Reservation in Wisconsin. She won a tribal scholarship to study at the University of Wisconsin at Madison and graduated from that school. She later received a Master of Social Work degree from Columbia University.

During her career, Ada Deer sought to restore sovereignty to Indian tribes. She thought they should be able to decide how to meet their own needs without government interference. This made necessary the doing away with the 1954 Termination Act, a federal government effort to assimilate Indians into the mainstream. Deer led the struggle to eliminate this act. In 1973, President Nixon signed the Menominee Restoration Act, which reversed the Termination Act. This is one of Deer's many accomplishments for social justice.

SECTION 3 ASSESSMENT

Essential Questions Journal Go to your **Essential Questions Journal** to work on this chapter's Essential Question.

Word Bank

strict constructionists

liberal constructionists

Necessary and Proper Clause

Commerce Clause

Quick Write

Do you think Congress has stretched the implied powers too far? Not far enough? Why do you think so? Work with a partner to write a persuasive paragraph. Share your argument with the class.

1. **Guiding Question** Use your completed concept web to answer this question: How has the doctrine of implied powers increased the powers of Congress?

Key Terms and Comprehension

On a sheet of paper, use the words from the Word Bank to complete each sentence correctly.

2. The _____ is also called the Elastic Clause. It allows Congress to stretch the expressed powers.

3. The _____ gives Congress the power to regulate foreign and interstate trade.

4. _____ fear a strong national government.

5. _____ believe in a strong national government.

Critical Thinking

6. **Drawing Inferences** How did war and economic problems increase the power of the national government?

7. **Predict Consequences** If implied powers were very limited, how might life be different in the United States today?

ISSUES OF OUR TIME

Congressional War Powers

▶▶ Track the Issue

The Constitution divides the war powers between Congress and the President. However, it remains unclear whether Congress can control the conduct of war.

1770s–1780s
Continental Congress acts as the civilian authority over the armed forces.

1860s
President Abraham Lincoln clashes with Congress over the conduct of the Civil War, the appointment of generals, and the freeing of slaves.

1898
Congress approves the use of force to secure Cuban independence but prohibits the nation's annexation.

1969
As the Vietnam War continues, Congress forbids military operations in Laos and Thailand.

2001
President George W. Bush requests military authority to prevent all terrorism; Congress approves force only against those involved in the 9/11 attacks.

General David Patraeus, former Commander of Armed Forces in Iraq

▶▶ Perspectives

Several years into the Iraq war, midterm elections returned Democratic majorities to both the House and the Senate. The Democrats pledged to use these majorities to end the increasingly unpopular war. The White House refused to consider withdrawal. It said that only the President has the power to make decisions about war.

Congressional War Power	Presidential War Power
"[Congressional war] powers are a clear and direct statement . . . that Congress has authority to declare, to define, and ultimately to end a war . . . By prohibiting funds . . . , Congress can force the President to bring our forces out of Iraq and out of harm's way . . . Since the President is adamant about pursuing his failed policies in Iraq, Congress has the duty to stand up and use its power to stop him." —*Senator Russell D. Feingold, D., Wisconsin*	"Congress does, of course, play a critical role in the defense of the nation and the conduct of a war. That role is defined and limited by the Constitution. After all, the military answers to one commander-in-chief in the White House, not 535 commanders-in-chief on Capitol Hill. Congress does have the purse strings . . . We expect the House and Senate to meet the needs of our military and the generals leading the troops in battle on time and in full measure." —*Vice President Richard B. Cheney*

Connect to Your World

1. **Understand** What reason did Senator Feingold give for his argument that Congress should end the war in Iraq?
2. **Compare and Contrast** How are the two views of congressional war powers alike and how are they different?

GOVERNMENT ONLINE
In the News
For updates about the power of the presidency visit **PearsonSuccessNet.com**

▲ Bill Gates testifies at a congressional hearing on technology innovation.

SECTION 4

The Nonlegislative Powers

Guiding Question

What nonlegislative powers does the Constitution delegate to Congress? Use a concept web to record the congressional powers described in this section.

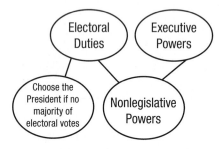

Electoral Duties

Executive Powers

Choose the President if no majority of electoral votes

Nonlegislative Powers

Objectives:

- Describe the role of Congress in amending the Constitution and in deciding elections.
- Describe Congress's power to impeach, and summarize presidential impeachment cases.
- Identify the executive powers of Congess.
- Describe the role of Congress to investigate.

The main function of Congress is to make laws (legislate). The Constitution does give Congress other functions as well, however. In this section, you will learn about the nonlegislative powers of Congress.

What is the constitutional amendment power?

According to Article V of the Constitution, Congress can propose amendments to the Constitution. Two thirds of the members of each house must vote in favor of an amendment. Amendments to the Constitution have been proposed 33 times. Article V also allows Congress to call a national convention to propose an amendment if it has the request from two thirds of the state legislatures. This has never happened.

Over recent years, a number of states have asked Congress for amendments to the Constitution. Among the proposals were to

- require the federal government to balance the budget every year;
- allow prayer in public schools;
- place term limits on members of Congress;
- prohibit flag burning;
- outlaw abortion; and
- prohibit same-sex marriages.

✔ **Checkpoint**   What types of amendments have states wanted Congress to add to the Constitution in recent years?

What are the electoral duties of Congress?

Congress has certain electoral duties. They are hardly ever used. The 12th Amendment states that if no one receives a majority of electoral votes in a presidential race, the House will choose the President. Congress chooses from among the top three winners in the electoral college. A majority of the states must vote, and each state gets one vote. See Figure 11.9. This has happened twice. In 1801, the House elected Thomas Jefferson. In 1825, the House chose John Quincy Adams.

The Senate is called on to choose the Vice President if no candidate receives a majority of the electoral votes. A full Senate is required. Each senator gets one vote. This happened in 1837 when Richard M. Johnson was chosen. If the office of Vice President becomes vacant, the 25th Amendment states that the President will pick a replacement. The Congress must approve this choice by a majority vote in both houses. This happened twice. Gerald Ford was approved in 1973, and Nelson Rockefeller was approved in 1974.

■ ■ ■ ■ ■ ■ ■ ■ ■ ■ ■ ■ ■ ■ ■ ■ ■ ■
Reading Strategy
Text Structure
Look at the chart at the bottom of the page. How does it help you understand the electoral duties of Congress?

Fig. 11.9 How Government Works

GOVERNMENT ONLINE
Update
For online updates about the electoral duties of Congress, go to **PearsonSuccessNet.com**

Electoral Duties of Congress

Who Wins?

No law says that only two people may run in the general election, but the Constitution does say that the winner must receive the majority of the Electoral College votes, which is now 270. ***What would happen if a minor-party candidate won enough votes to prevent any candidate from receiving the majority?***

STEP 1:
No candidate receives a majority of the **Electoral College votes**.

246   **25**   **267**

STEP 2:
Each state's members of the U.S. House of Representatives decide which of the top three candidates to support. They then **cast one vote** as a state. If they cannot agree, they do not vote.

STEP 3:
If a majority of the state delegations vote for the same candidate, that person becomes **the next President**. If no candidate wins a majority, or 26 votes, another vote is taken. The Vice President is selected by the Senate.

Winner!

Impeach
To bring formal charges against a public official

Acquit
Find not guilty of a charge

Perjury
The act of lying under oath

Censure
Issue a formal disapproval

What are the impeachment powers of Congress?

The President, Vice President, and all civil officers may be removed from office for committing a crime that is written in the Constitution in Article II, Section 4. Congress can cause them to be removed by using its power to **impeach.** The House is given the power to impeach, which means to accuse or charge an official with a crime. Impeachment requires a majority vote. If the person is impeached, the Senate will hold a trial, which may result in a conviction. Conviction requires a two-thirds vote in the Senate. The Chief Justice of the Supreme Court leads the Senate trial when a President is tried. A conviction results in removal from office. If there is a crime involved in the impeachment proceedings, this crime may be tried separately in a regular court. To this point, there have been 17 impeachments and 7 convictions. All 7 convictions were federal judges.

The House has impeached two Presidents: Andrew Johnson in 1868 and Bill Clinton in 1998. Both men were found not guilty in the Senate trials. Andrew Johnson became President after Abraham Lincoln was assassinated in 1865. President Johnson tried to carry out Lincoln's policies in the newly defeated Southern states. Radical Republicans wanted the states treated more harshly. President Johnson removed Edward Stanton, the Secretary of War, because he opposed Johnson's policies. This action went against the newly passed Tenure of Office Act. This Act required Senate approval for removing a person from office. The impeachment of Johnson was based on his violation of the Tenure of Office Act. The Senate **acquitted** Johnson by a one-vote margin.

The House impeached Bill Clinton in 1998. See Figure 11.10. President Clinton had admitted to an "inappropriate relationship" with a White House intern. The President was charged with **perjury**—obstruction of justice and lying under oath. The President refused to give information about his behavior with the intern. Some House members wanted his immediate removal from office. Others wanted only **censure,** which is a formal disapproval. The Senate received the articles of impeachment in 1999, and Clinton was acquitted.

Perhaps the biggest political scandal in our history was Watergate. In 1972, members of President Nixon's Republican Party attempted to break into the Democratic Party's national offices in the Watergate office complex in Washington, D.C. The media, especially the *Washington Post,* began an investigation. Many illegal acts were uncovered, including bribery, perjury, fraud, and illegal campaign contributions.

Fig. 11.10 **How Government Works**

The Impeachment Process
President Clinton's Impeachment

This timeline details the complex process of impeaching a President and shows how the process worked in the impeachment of President Clinton. *Why did the attempt to remove Clinton fail?*

1998

The House Judiciary Committee considers charges against the accused. It also votes on whether to send articles of impeachment to the full House. A simple majority vote is needed to start the process. ▼

December 11–12, 1998 After three months of hearings, the House Judiciary Committee approves four articles.

Acting much like a grand jury, the House considers the charge(s) brought by the Judiciary Committee. It can subpoena witnesses and evidence. It hears and debates arguments. ▼

December 18–19, 1998 The House holds 13 hours of bitter, partisan debate, in which more than 200 House members speak. Democrats briefly walk out to protest Republican leaders' refusal to consider the lesser punishment of censure.

Newspapers weighed in on the proceedings.

The House votes on each article. If any article is approved by a majority vote, the official is impeached, which is similar to being indicted. The House sends the article(s) of impeachment to the Senate. ▼

December 19, 1998 The House votes to impeach Clinton on two counts. The votes are 228–206 on one count of perjury and 221–212 on obstruction of justice. Voting is mostly along party lines.

1999

The Senate tries the case. If the President is to be tried, the Chief Justice of the United States presides. Selected members of the House act as managers (prosecutors). ▼

January 7, 1999 Chief Justice William Rehnquist opens a televised trial. Representative Henry Hyde of Illinois leads a team of 13 House managers. White House Counsel Charles Ruff leads Clinton's defense.

Republican leaders held a press conference.

Senators hear testimony and evidence. House prosecutors and lawyers for both sides present their cases. Additional witnesses may be called. Senators may also vote to curb testimony. ▼

January 7–February 11, 1999 With public distaste for impeachment growing, the Senate limits testimony to three witnesses, the intern among them. Closing arguments follow. For three days, the Senate deliberates in secret (despite Democrats' objections).

Protesters rallied outside the Capitol.

The Senate debates the articles, publicly or privately. It need not render a verdict. It could, for example, vote to drop the case and instead censure the official. A two-thirds vote is required for conviction. ▼

February 12, 1999 In a televised session, the Senate acquits Clinton on both charges, falling well short of the two-thirds vote needed for conviction. There are 55 Republicans and 45 Democrats in the Senate. On the perjury count, 45 Democrats and 10 Republicans vote not guilty. On the obstruction charge, 5 Republicans break with their party to vote with all of the Democrats against conviction.

Above right: Congress reviewed tapes of Clinton's testimony. Bottom: House Democrats walked out to protest the impeachment resolution.

Fig. 11.11 **How Government Works**

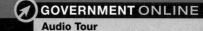

GOVERNMENT ONLINE
Audio Tour
Listen to a guided audio tour of this feature at
PearsonSuccessNet.com

Congressional Checks on the Presidential Treaty-Making Power

Congressional Influence

The Senate approves high-level appointments by the President. These include the Secretary of State, as well as ambassadors to foreign nations who often play a role in the treaty-making process.

The President consults with Congress during the negotiation of treaties. Here, Senate Foreign Relations Committee members former Sen. Joe Biden (D., Del.), left, and Sen. Richard Lugar (R., Ind.) talk to reporters. They discuss their meeting with President George W. Bush about a nuclear arms reduction treaty with Russia.

Presidents may need to make changes to a treaty when faced with significant opposition from Congress. This ensures that there is broad consensus for any such agreement among the American people.

Even after a treaty has been approved, Congress can abrogate (repeal) it. This is done by passing a law that is inconsistent with its terms, or by directing the President to abrogate. The Panama Canal Treaty of 1903 was abrogated for the new treaty in 1979, which returned the canal to Panama.

Subpoena
A legal order to appear or give evidence to the court

The House Judiciary Committee charged President Nixon with obstruction of justice, abuse of power, and failure to answer **subpoenas** (legal orders to appear or give evidence to the court). When it was certain that the House would impeach Nixon and the Senate would convict him, Nixon resigned. Many other officials involved in the scandal were convicted of crimes. Many went to jail.

✔**Checkpoint**   What was the Watergate scandal?

What are the executive powers of Congress?

The Constitution gives two executive powers to the Senate: the powers to make appointments and treaties.

Presidential appointments must be confirmed by a majority vote in the Senate. The Senate usually approves Cabinet officers and other top federal officials quickly. An unwritten rule known as "senatorial courtesy" can sometimes dictate appointments. According to this rule, the Senate will turn down an appointment by the President if it is opposed by a senator of the President's own party from the state involved. Senators who want to grant favors to their supporters can influence the President's selections. The President will sometimes honor the senator's choice by granting the appointment as a courtesy to the senator.

Reading Strategy
Text Structure
Notice the list of reasons that investigations are carried out. Rewrite each reason in your own words.

According to the Constitution, the President is allowed to make treaties with the advice and consent of the Senate. See Figure 11.11 on page 276. Two thirds of the senators must approve a treaty. In the past, the President consulted with the Senate when developing a treaty. Now, the Senate Foreign Relations Committee and other influential senators often advise the President.

What are the investigative powers of Congress?

The congressional power to investigate is implied in the Constitution in Article I, Section I. Both Senate and House committees and subcommittees investigate many matters involving the lawmaking power.

Investigations are carried out for five main reasons:

(1) to gather information when writing new laws;

(2) to oversee the executive agencies;

(3) to inform the public about certain matters;

(4) to expose the questionable actions of public officials, persons, or groups; and

(5) to promote the interests of some members of Congress.

In recent years, several new agencies were created to help Congress with investigations. They are the Congressional Budget Office, the Congressional Research Service, and the Government Accountability Office.

Essential Questions Journal Go to your **Essential Questions Journal** to work on this chapter's Essential Question.

SECTION 4 ASSESSMENT

1. **Guiding Question** Use your completed concept web to answer this question: What nonlegislative powers does the Constitution delegate to Congress?

Key Terms and Comprehension
On a sheet of paper, write the answer to each question. Use complete sentences.

2. What are the two executive powers of Congress?

3. What are the two ways that Congress can amend the Constitution?

4. Who advises the President in the development of treaties?

5. What is the process by which Congress approves or rejects presidential appointments?

Critical Thinking

6. **Draw Conclusions** Do you think the Framers made amending the Constitution too difficult? Explain.

7. **Determine Cause and Effect** What, if any, changes would you make to the impeachment process? Why?

Chapter Summary

Section 1—The Expressed Powers of Money and Commerce

- There are three types of congressional power: expressed, implied, and inherent.

- Commerce power gives Congress the power to control foreign trade and trade between states.

- The Commerce Clause has been the basis of many implied powers.

Section 2—The Other Expressed Powers

- Congress has many foreign relations powers. These powers include spending, regulating foreign trade, declaring war, and regulating immigration.

- The domestic powers of Congress include the postal, copyright and patent, weights and measures, naturalization, management of federal areas, and eminent domain powers.

Section 3—The Implied Powers

- The Necessary and Proper Clause gives Congress the power to make all laws that are necessary to carry out its duties.

- Strict constructionists want Congress to use only expressed powers. Liberal constructionists believe government should be able to create new powers.

- The Commerce Clause covers many types of economic activities.

Section 4—The Nonlegislative Powers

- Congress must have a two-thirds vote to amend the Constitution.

- Congress has electoral duties that are defined in the 12th Amendment.

- The House has impeached two Presidents: Andrew Johnson and Bill Clinton. Both were acquitted.

- President Richard Nixon avoided impeachment by resigning after the Watergate scandal.

- The Constitution gives two executive powers to Congress: appointments and treaties.

- Senate and House committees investigate matters involving the lawmaking process.

Guiding Question
Section 2 How do the expressed powers reflect the Framers' commitment to creating a strong but limited national government?

Guiding Question
Section 3 How has the doctrine of implied powers increased the powers of Congress?

Guiding Question
Section 1 What powers over money and commerce does the Constitution give to Congress, and what limits does it put on these powers?

Guiding Question
Section 4 What nonlegislative powers does the Constitution delegate to Congress?

CHAPTER 11

Essential Question
What should the limits be on the powers of Congress?

Document-Based Assessment

Article about Eminent Domain

This article was written by Thomas A. Garrett and Paul Rothstein. The title of the article is "The Taking of Prosperity? Kelo vs. New London and Economics of Eminent Domain." It argues that the taking of private property by eminent domain actually gets in the way of economic development.

Document at a Glance
- Article discussing eminent domain
- *Kelo* v. *New London* Supreme Court decision
- Action by House to limit eminent domain

The U.S. Supreme Court's decision in *Kelo* v. *New London* was an unlikely source of public outrage . . . the court didn't overturn anything in its June 2005 ruling; it . . . affirmed an earlier decision by the Supreme Court of Connecticut. That decision allowed the city of New London . . . designated as "distressed," to use the power of eminent domain to acquire 15 properties, one of which belonged to homeowner Susette Kelo . . . nothing in the court's decision altered the ability of state legislatures to limit the practice of eminent domain.

. . . reaction against both the court and its decision was swift and furious. . . . the House passed a bill that would withhold federal development funds from states and political subdivisions that use eminent domain in certain ways. Since the *Kelo* decision, 34 states have taken action to limit eminent domain . . . President Bush issued an executive order limiting . . . grounds on which the federal government can take private property . . . the Supreme Court of Ohio gave property owners the protection that was denied to Sussette Kelo in Connecticut.

Research has shown that without property rights, individuals will no longer face the incentive to make the best economic use of their property . . . Potential residents and businesses may avoid communities that have a record of taking private property . . . because of . . . uncertainty about losing their property to eminent domain.

Document-Based Questions

1. What was the Supreme Court decision in *Kelo* v. *New London*?

2. What did the U.S. House of Representatives do after the Court's decision?

3. What did President Bush do after the Court's decision?

4. What incentives will individuals lose if property rights are removed?

5. **Text structure** Is this document an example of compare and contrast, problem and solution, or cause and effect? Explain why.

SOURCE: *The Taking of Prosperity? Kelo vs. New London and Economics of Eminent Domain*, 2007

Chapter Assessment

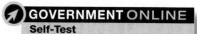

Directions: Choose the letter of the best answer or write the answer using complete sentences.

Section 1—The Expressed Powers of Money and Commerce

1. What are the three ways that the Constitution grants power to Congress?

2. What is the main purpose of taxation?

3. Why was Congress given the ability to regulate trade between states?

4. Critical Thinking Do you think Congress should have a firm limit on how much money it can borrow? Why or why not?

Section 2—The Other Expressed Powers

5. What are the postal powers of Congress?

6. What are the judicial powers of Congress?

7. What is eminent domain?

8. Critical Thinking Why do you think the Framers gave only Congress the power to declare war?

Section 3—The Implied Powers

9. What is the Necessary and Proper Clause?

10. What was important about the *McCulloch* v. *Maryland* case in 1819?

11. What is the main difference between strict constructionists and liberal constructionists?

12. Critical Thinking Imagine that you are a strict constructionist. What would you say to liberal constructionists to convince them to agree with you?

Section 4—The Nonlegislative Powers

13. What is perjury?

14. Which two amendments cover electoral duties of Congress?

15. Why are investigations carried out by Congress? List two reasons.

16. According to Article V, what action needs a two-thirds vote in Congress?

17. Critical Thinking Do you think President Clinton should have been impeached? Why or why not?

Apply What You've Learned

Exploring the Essential Question

18. How does the Constitution limit the powers of Congress? List at least two ways.

19. Do you think the "Elastic Clause" has been stretched too far? Why or why not?

Essential Question Project

20. Based on the content of the chapter and your answers to the two questions above, explain how current congressional activity might be different if the Constitution was strictly interpreted. Write your answer in a paragraph. In your paragraph, answer the Essential Question: **What should the limits be on the powers of Congress?**

> **Essential Questions**
> **Journal**
>
> Go to your **Essential Questions Journal** to work on this chapter's Essential Question.

Test-Taking Tip

When studying for a test, review the topics in the chapter. Then make up a practice test for yourself. Check your answers in the book.

▲ Members of the press take photographs at a Senate Select Committee on Intelligence session.

Congress in Action

Essential Question
Can and should the lawmaking process be improved?

▪ ▪

Reading Strategy: Summarizing
As you read the text in this chapter, think back to what you you have learned about Congress in the previous two chapters. Summarizing the facts you know will help you understand the new text. As you read, ask yourself these questions:

- Who or what is this about?
- What details are important to the main idea?
- What jobs of Congress are pointed out in this chapter?

ON THE GO

To study anywhere, anytime, download these online resources at PearsonSuccessNet.com.
- Political Dictionary
- Audio Review
- Downloadable Interactivities

Congress Organizes

▲ John Boehner (R., Ohio) hands the Speaker's gavel to Nancy Pelosi (D., Calif.).

How do constitutional and party officers keep Congress organized? Use a table like the one below to keep track of the officers in each house and what duties they perform.

Congressional Leaders and Their Duties	
House	Senate
Speaker of the House ■ Presides and keeps order ■	President of the Senate ■ ■

Objectives:

- Describe how and when Congress comes together.
- Compare the roles of the head officers in the Senate and the House.
- Identify the duties of the party officers in Congress.
- Describe how committee chairmen are chosen and explain their role.

Congress is the legislative branch of the United States government. It is divided into two chambers: the Senate and the House of Representatives. There are 100 senators and 435 voting members of the House. The main job of the Congress is to pass laws.

The duties of the members of Congress are complex. They require help from agencies. In fact, more than 30,000 people work for the legislative branch.

When does Congress come together?

Congress comes together every two years on January 3 of every odd-numbered year. On this day, they start a new term. The clerk of the House calls the members to order. Next, the **Speaker of the House** is chosen. The Speaker is always a member of the majority party, according to custom. The Speaker swears in the members of the House.

The House then elects a clerk, sergeant-at-arms, chief administrative officer, and chaplain. After members have been assigned to committees, the House of Representatives can begin its work.

In the Senate, only one third of the seats are open to election every two years. The Senate is a continuous body from one term to another. On opening day, new and reelected senators are sworn in, committees are filled, and other details are discussed.

Once Congress is organized, the President gives a speech to both houses. It is called the State of the Union address. The President describes the country's condition and the administration's policies.

Who are the presiding officers?

The presiding officers of the House of Representatives and the Senate are chosen according to Article I of the Constitution. The Speaker is the leader of the House, and the Vice President of the United States is the **president of the Senate.** To better understand the structure of leadership in Congress, see Figure 12.1.

The House has always elected one of its own members as Speaker. The Speaker is the leader of the majority party but is expected to act fairly to both parties. He or she is the most important leader in both houses of Congress. The duties include keeping order during discussions on the floor and presiding over each House session. The Speaker sends bills (proposed laws) to committees. If there is a tie in the voting, he or she may be called on to break the tie. After the Vice President, the Speaker is next in line to become President of the United States.

✔**Checkpoint** Who chooses the Speaker of the House?

Speaker of the House
The leading officer of the House of Representatives, chosen by and from the majority party in the House

President of the Senate
The leading officer of the Senate; the Vice President of the United States

Reading Strategy
Summarizing
Summarize the different responsibilities of the Speaker of the House.

GOVERNMENT ONLINE
Update
Check out who holds these offices today at
PearsonSuccessNet.com

Fig. 12.1

Leadership in the 111th Congress

HOUSE

Presiding Officer and Party Leader

Speaker of the House
NANCY PELOSI
(D., California)

Party Officers

Majority Floor Leader
STENY HOYER
(D., Maryland)

Minority Floor Leader
JOHN BOEHNER
(R., Ohio)

Majority Whip
JAMES CLYBURN
(D., South Carolina)

Minority Whip
ERIC CANTOR
(R., Virginia)

SENATE

Presiding Officers

President of the Senate
JOE BIDEN
(Vice President)

President Pro Tempore
ROBERT C. BYRD
(D., West Virginia)

Party Officers

Majority Floor Leader
HARRY REID
(D., Nevada)

Minority Floor Leader
MITCH McCONNELL
(R., Kentucky)

Majority Whip
DICK DURBIN
(D., Illinois)

Minority Whip
JON KYL
(R., Arizona)

▲ **Interpreting Charts** Party and constitutional leadership roles are very important in both houses of Congress. *How can you tell which party holds power in the House? The Senate?*

President *pro tempore*
The member of the Senate chosen to take the place of the Vice President when he or she is absent

Party caucus
A closed meeting of a party's House or Senate members

Floor leaders
Political party leaders in Congress

Majority leader
The floor leader of the party that holds the majority of seats in each house of Congress

Minority leader
The floor leader of the party that holds the minority of the seats in each house of Congress

The Senate does not pick its own presiding officer. According to the Constitution, the Vice President of the United States is the president of the Senate, but is not a member of the Senate. The president of the Senate may not even be a member of the controlling party in the Senate. The position has less power than the Speaker. The president of the Senate may not debate issues in Congress and may only vote to break a tie. If the Vice President cannot be present, the **president *pro tempore,*** who is elected by the Senate, takes the Vice President's place. The president *pro tempore* follows the Speaker as next in succession for the presidency.

Who are the party officers?

Both the House and the Senate have important leaders from the Republican and Democratic parties. They are chosen at the **party caucus** meeting held before Congress organizes. The party caucus is a closed meeting of the members of each party in each house. These party officers are the majority and minority **floor leaders.** The **majority leader** is powerful because his or her political party has more seats. The floor leader of the party that has the smaller number of seats in each house is the **minority leader.** Figure 12.2 below shows how many times each party has been the majority.

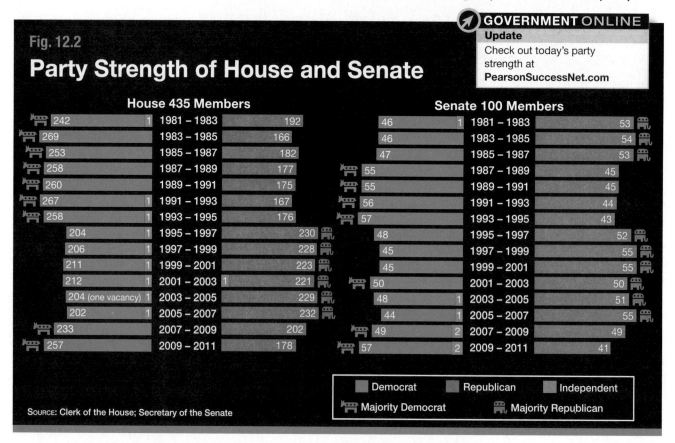

Fig. 12.2

Party Strength of House and Senate

SOURCE: Clerk of the House; Secretary of the Senate

▲ **Analyzing Charts** This chart shows the strength of each party at the start of the past fifteen terms of Congress. Independents are placed with their caucus party. *What is the largest majority that each party has held in each house?*

The assistants to the floor leaders are the party **whips.** The floor leaders depend on the party whips to encourage party members to be present for voting and to vote with the party leaders.

The party officers come from all different parts of the United States. For instance, the Speaker of the House (Nancy Pelosi, D.) is from California. The minority floor leader (Mitch McConnell, R.) is from Kentucky. **Figure 12.3** below shows how each state is represented in Congress.

Whips
Assistants to the floor leaders in the House and the Senate

✔**Checkpoint** What leaders are chosen during the party caucus meetings?

Fig. 12.3
Representation by State, 111th Congress

GOVERNMENT ONLINE
Update
Check out updated representation by state at **PearsonSuccessNet.com**

Analyzing Maps The maps below show how each state is represented in the House and the Senate. For instance, Ohio has 18 seats in the House. There are 8 Republicans and 10 Democrats. In the Senate, Ohio is represented by 1 Democrat and 1 Republican. *Which states are represented by the same party majority in both the House and the Senate?*

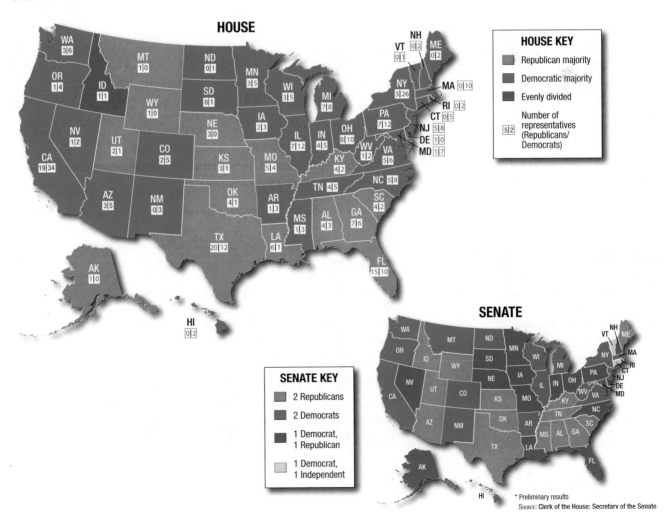

Committee chairman
Congress member who leads a standing committee

Seniority rule
A custom that gives the most important jobs in Congress to the members who have served the longest

Reading Strategy
Summarizing
List one positive and one negative of the seniority rule.

Who are the committee chairmen?

The **committee chairmen** are the leaders of the standing committees in both houses of Congress. The standing committees do most of the work in Congress. The committee chairmen hold much power. They schedule meetings, decide on bills to consider, and lead all discussions of the bills. The title *chairman*, rather than *chairperson,* is used in both houses of Congress today. Only 20 women have ever chaired a standing committee.

The **seniority rule** is a custom that gives the most important jobs in Congress to the members who have served the longest. Some people do not like this custom. They say it does not allow new ideas and leaves out the younger, newer members. People in favor of seniority say it ensures that members of Congress with the most experience become the committee chairmen.

✓**Checkpoint**   What does the seniority rule ensure?

SECTION 1 ASSESSMENT

Essential Questions Journal   Go to your **Essential Questions Journal** to work on this chapter's Essential Question.

Word Bank

committee chairmen

Congress

president *pro tempore*

whips

Quick Write

Pretend you are a newspaper reporter. Your job is to write about the opening day of Congress. Gather details from this section on all of the different events that happen that day. Include activities from both the House and the Senate. If needed, work with a partner or the teacher for additional help.

1. **Guiding Question** Use your completed table to answer this question: How do constitutional and party officers keep Congress organized?

Key Terms and Comprehension

On a sheet of paper, use the words from the Word Bank to complete each sentence correctly.

2. _____ convenes on January 3 of every odd-numbered year.

3. The _____ lead the standing committees in both houses of Congress.

4. The assistants to the floor leaders are called _____.

5. The _____ takes the Vice President's place in the Senate if the Vice President is not there.

Critical Thinking

6. **Understand Point of View** When Senator Howard Baker was the majority leader, he said the job was like "herding cats." What do you think he meant when he said this?

7. **Draw Conclusions** How important are committee chairmen in Congress? Why do you think so?

Committees in Congress

▲ Former Secretary of Defense Donald Rumsfeld testifies at a defense appropriations hearing.

Guiding **Question**

How do committees help Congress do its work? Use a table to keep track of the purpose and characteristics of each type of congressional committee.

Standing Committee	Select Committee	Joint Committee	Conference Committee
■Study the bills	■Usually temporary	■	■Settle differences in a bill
■Has sub-committees	■	■	■
■	■	■	■

Objectives:

- Explain how standing committees and their subcommittees work.
- Describe the duties and responsibilities of the House Rules Committee.
- Describe the role of select committees.
- Compare the functions of joint committees and conference committees.
- Explain the work of subcommittees within standing committees

Each house of Congress has a number of congressional committees. Some congressional committees are permanent and some are temporary. There are five types of congressional committees standing, subcommittees, select, joint and conference. Each type of committee will be discussed in this section.

What are standing committees?

Committees were first used in Congress in 1789. Soon permanent groups called **standing committees** were used. Similar bills were all sent to the same standing committee. Each standing committee considers a certain topic, such as how the United States gets along with foreign countries. One standing committee takes care of the needs of the armed services. Another committee, called the Ways and Means Committee, decides how to raise money for the federal government. Today there are 20 standing committees in the House and 17 in the Senate. (See Figures 12.4 and 12.5 on pages 290 and 291.) House of Representative members usually serve on one or two standing committees and senators on three or four.

Standing committees carefully study the bills assigned to them. Sometimes more than one committee will study a bill. If the committee accepts the bill, it is presented to the entire House or Senate for discussion. After the discussion, there is a vote.

■ ■ ■ ■ ■ ■ ■ ■ ■ ■ ■ ■ ■ ■ ■ ■ ■
Standing committee
Permanent committee that
considers certain topics

Fig. 12.4

House Standing Committee Chairs

Committee	Name, Party, State, Year Elected
Agriculture	Collin C. Peterson (D., Minn.), 1990
Appropriations	David Obey (D., Wis.), 1969
Armed Services	Ike Skelton (D., Mo.), 1976
Budget	John M. Spratt, Jr. (D., S.C.), 1982
Education and Labor	George Miller (D., Calif.), 1974
Energy and Commerce	Henry A. Waxman (D., Calif.), 1974
Financial Services	Barney Frank (D., Mass.), 1980
Foreign Affairs	Howard Berman (D., Calif.), 1982
Homeland Security	Bennie G. Thompson (D., Miss.), 1993
House Administration	Robert A. Brady (D., Penn.), 1998
Judiciary	John Conyers, Jr. (D., Mich.), 1964
Natural Resources	Nick J. Rahall II (D., W. Va.), 1976
Oversight and Government Reform	Edolphus Towns (D., N.Y.), 1982
Rules	Louise M. Slaughter (D., N.Y.), 1986
Science and Technology	Bart Gordon (D., Tenn.), 1984
Small Business	Nydia M. Velazquez (D., N.Y.), 1992
Standards of Official Conduct	Vacant
Transportation and Infrastructure	James L. Oberstar (D., Minn.), 1974
Veterans' Affairs	Bob Filner (D., Calif.), 1992
Ways and Means	Charles B. Rangel (D., N.Y.), 1970

SOURCE: *Congressional Directory* and Clerk of the House

▲ Analyzing Charts *What predictions can you make about the committees' jurisdictions based on their names?*

GOVERNMENT ONLINE
Update
To check out who holds these positions today, go to **PearsonSuccessNet.com**

Some standing committees have more influence than others. Members of both houses try to serve on important committees such as Rules, Ways and Means, Armed Services, Foreign Affairs, or Judiciary.

Members of committees are chosen according to the seniority rule. The majority party always holds the most seats on a standing committee. The committee chair is the leader of a committee.

■ ■ ■ ■ ■ ■ ■ ■ ■ ■ ■ ■ ■ ■ ■ ■ ■
Reading Strategy
Summarizing
What are some of the important standing committees?

✔**Checkpoint**   How many standing committees are in the House? The Senate?

What are subcommittees?

Most standing committees have a number of subcommittees. **Subcommittees** do much of the work of the standing committees. Each subcommittee has a name. The Judiciary Committee has three subcommittees: Crime and Drugs, Human Rights, and The Constitution. Members of the standing committee may serve on more than one subcommittee. Subcommittees may hold hearings, write bills, and handle legislation of the Senate or the House.

✔ **Checkpoint** What types of jobs do subcommittees do?

■■■■■■■■■■■■■■■■■■■
Subcommittee
A smaller part of a standing committee

What is the House Rules Committee?

Many bills are introduced in the House each term and then discussed in committees. Made up of only 13 members, the House Rules Committee is a very powerful standing committee. It decides what new bills are brought to the floor to be reviewed by the full House. Only a few new bills are chosen for full review.

Fig. 12.5

Senate Standing Committee Chairs

Committee	Name, Party, State, Year Elected
Agriculture, Nutrition, and Forestry	Tom Harkin (D., Iowa), 1984
Appropriations	Daniel K. Inouye (D., Hawaii), 1962
Armed Services	Carl Levin (D., Mich.), 1978
Banking, Housing, and Urban Affairs	Christopher C. Dodd (D., Conn.),1980
Budget	Kent Conrad, (D., N.D.), 1986
Commerce, Science, and Transportation	Jay Rockefeller (D., W.V.), 1984
Energy and Natural Resources	Jeff Bingaman (D., N.M.), 1982
Environment and Public Works	Barbara Boxer (D., Calif.), 1992
Finance	Max Baucus (D., Mont.), 1978
Foreign Relations	John F. Kerry (D., Mass.), 1984
Health, Education, Labor, and Pensions	Edward M. Kennedy (D., Mass.), 1962
Homeland Security and Governmental Affairs	Joseph L. Lieberman (I., Conn.), 1988
Indian Affairs	Byron L. Dorgan (D., N.D.), 1992
Judiciary	Patrick T. Leahy (D., Vt.), 1974
Rules and Administration	Dianne Feinstein (D., Calif.), 1992
Small Business and Entrepreneurship	Mary Landrieu (D., La.), 1996
Veterans' Affairs	Daniel K. Akaka (D., Hawaii), 1990

SOURCE: *Congressional Directory* and Secretary of the Senate

▲ **Analyzing Charts** *Why do you think the Senate has fewer committees than the House?*

GOVERNMENT ONLINE
Update
To check out who holds these positions today, go to **PearsonSuccessNet.com**

Select committee
A House or Senate committee that is set up for a limited time

Joint committee
A committee made up of members of both parts of Congress

Conference committee
A committee that settles Senate and House differences in bills

What are select committees?

Select committees can be formed in either the House or the Senate. The committees are set up for a limited time. They handle issues of national importance. The Senate Watergate Committee was a select committee. The committee investigated the Watergate scandal involving President Nixon's administration. It found evidence of illegal activities. These findings led to the resignation of President Nixon in 1974. In another investigation, the House and Senate select committees worked together. The combined committee was known as the Iran-Contra Committee. It investigated actions of President Reagan's administration in both Iran and Nicaragua that were prohibited by an act of Congress.

✔**Checkpoint** What kinds of issues do select committees handle?

Fig. 12.6

Joint Committees of Congress

The **Joint Economic Committee** addresses matters related to the U.S. economy.
Chair: Sen. Charles Schumer (D., N.Y.)

The **Joint Committee on the Library** addresses matters related to the Library of Congress.
Chair: Sen. Dianne Feinstein (D., Calif.)

The **Joint Committee on Printing** oversees the Government Printing Office and other printing by the federal government.
Chair: Rep. Robert A. Brady (D., Penn.)

The **Joint Committee on Taxation** is involved in legislation about taxes. The chair position rotates between the chairs of the House Ways and Means Committee and of the Senate Finance Committee.

▲ Analyzing Charts The Joint Committees of Congress include members from both houses. *Why do you think the matters listed are dealt with by joint committees?*

What are joint committees and conference committees?

A few committees are made up of members of both the Senate and the House. These **joint committees** can be temporary or permanent. Joint committees deal with matters best handled by the two houses working together, such as government printing or the Library of Congress. For a list of the joint committees, see **Figure 12.6**.

For a bill to be sent to the President, it must be passed in the same form in both the Senate and the House. A special committee known as a **conference committee** settles any differences in a bill. Leaders of the Senate and the House choose the members of this committee. After a bill is worked on by the conference committee, it goes back to both houses for approval. No changes may be made to the bill at this time. If both houses pass the bill, it is sent to the President for approval.

✔**Checkpoint** What is the difference between a conference committee and a joint committee?

Government in Your Life

Government on Cable TV

C-SPAN stands for Cable Satellite Public Affairs Network. This television network shows only political events and meetings. C-SPAN started in 1979 by televising sessions in the House of Representatives. C-SPAN2, a second channel, televises Senate sessions and political news. C-SPAN3 covers national events such as Senate and House hearings, political conventions, news conferences, and history programs. C-SPAN also has viewer call-in programs so viewers can talk with policymakers.

C-SPAN channels provide "gavel-to-gavel" coverage of the House and Senate sessions. Meetings begin with the knocking of a wooden hammer, called a gavel, on a table. The television coverage begins and ends when the gavel is used. Employees of both houses control the cameras. No reporters and no commercials are allowed.

Every two years, at the beginning of each new session of Congress, the leaders of both houses call for a vote from the members. The members vote to allow C-SPAN cameras to broadcast live from the floors of the House and Senate.

Essential Questions Journal Go to your **Essential Questions Journal** to work on this chapter's Essential Question.

SECTION 2 ASSESSMENT

1. **Guiding Question** Use your completed table to answer this question: How do committees help Congress do its work?

Key Terms and Comprehension
On a sheet of paper, write the answer to each question. Use complete sentences.

2. What are standing committees?

3. What is the job of a joint committee?

4. What is the job of a conference committee?

5. Why is the House Rules Committee important?

Critical Thinking

6. **Predict Consequences** What might happen if all proposed bills were sent straight to the full House for a vote?

7. **Analyze Information** Why do you think subcommittees do most of the work in Congress?

Making Law: The House

▲ Representative Greg Walden (R., Oregon) waves a bill during a committee meeting.

Guiding Question

What are the steps of a successful bill as it moves through the House? Use a flowchart to keep track of the progress of a bill through the House.

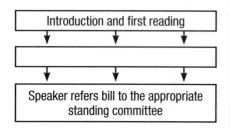

Introduction and first reading
↓ ↓ ↓
↓ ↓ ↓
Speaker refers bill to the appropriate standing committee

Objectives:

- List the first steps in the introduction of a bill to the House.
- Describe what happens to a bill once it is brought to a committee.
- Explain how the House leaders schedule a debate on a bill.
- Explain what happens to a bill on the House floor and identify the final step in the passage of a bill in the House.

Congress considers thousands of new bills and resolutions during each session. The House and the Senate follow certain steps when considering these measures. Very few bills become laws. Those that do must first be approved by the President. The process of turning a bill into a law is very complicated and involves many steps.

What are the first steps?

A **bill** is an idea for a new law or for a change in an old law. An idea for a bill can come from citizens who write to their senators or representatives. Ideas for bills can also come from various groups, such as businesspeople, veterans, or parents. Senators, representatives, and the President of the United States can also suggest ideas for bills. Often, before a member introduces a bill, he or she will send around a letter telling the other members about it. The person introducing the bill hopes to gain support for it before he or she introduces it. Once members have read the bill, they may sign on with their support. Some members become cosponsors of the bill.

✓ **Checkpoint** What is a bill?

What are the types of bills and resolutions?

The two types of bills are public and private. Public bills apply to the whole country. Public bills could include such matters as tax increases or war policy. These bills may involve a change in a law or creation of a new law. Private bills apply to certain places or people.

▲ The Democratic House leadership held a rally before an all-night debate on a bill that would withdraw U.S. troops from Iraq. *Why might members of Congress hold a public rally before holding a debate on a bill?*

Bill
A proposed law

Joint resolution
A proposal for action that has the force of law when passed

Concurrent resolution
Explains the government's position; requires the House and Senate to act together

Resolution
A measure dealing with some matter in one house; does not have the force of law and does not require the President's signature

Rider
Unrelated provision added to an important bill so that it will "ride" through the legislative process

A **joint resolution,** when passed, has the same power as a law. It may deal with a temporary matter, such as granting money for a special presidential event.

Concurrent resolutions require the House and Senate to act together. They are not as strong as law. They are often used by Congress to explain the government's position on matters such as foreign affairs.

The Senate and the House each use **resolutions** to manage rules within one house of Congress. Resolutions do not have the force of a law that is signed by the President. (See Figure 12.7.)

A bill or resolution may include a **rider.** This is an addition to the measure and may be unrelated to the content of the bill or resolution. A rider is included because it would not pass on its own. Riders are often added to bills involving money. They get accepted if Congress and the President want the main bill or resolution passed.

Fig. 12.7

Types of Bills and Resolutions	
Bill	A proposed law
Joint Resolution	A proposal for action that has the force of law when passed; usually is for a temporary matter
Concurrent Resolution	Explains the government's position; requires the House and Senate to act together
Resolution	A measure dealing with some matter in one house; does not have the force of law, and does not require the President's signature

What happens at introduction and first reading?

The clerk of the House numbers each bill as it is introduced and gives it a short title. A record is kept of every bill in the House *Journal* and in the *Congressional Record.* When this numbering is done, the bill receives its first reading. The bill is then printed and given to the members.

■ ■ ■ ■ ■ ■ ■ ■ ■ ■ ■ ■ ■ ■ ■ ■ ■

Pigeonhole
To set aside a bill that is no longer
being considered

Discharge petition
A petition that releases a bill from
being pigeonholed

■ ■ ■ ■ ■ ■ ■ ■ ■ ■ ■ ■ ■ ■ ■ ■ ■

Reading Strategy
Summarizing
In your own words, write a
summary of this paragraph.

As the bill is considered in the House, it receives a total of three readings to be sure the bill is considered carefully. After the first reading, the next step is to send the bill to a standing committee that deals with all bills of the same subject. The second reading occurs during discussion on the floor and the third during voting.

✔ **Checkpoint** How many times is a bill read in the House?

What happens to bills in committee?

Standing committees decide which bills are important enough to send to the House or Senate for all members to consider. Most bills are rejected by committees and are **pigeonholed.** (See Figure 12.8.) Pigeonholed means that the bill is set aside and no longer considered. Sometimes these bills are held by a committee and then released when a member files a **discharge petition.** The petition has to be signed by a majority of the House.

Fig. 12.8

The Number of Bills That Become Laws*

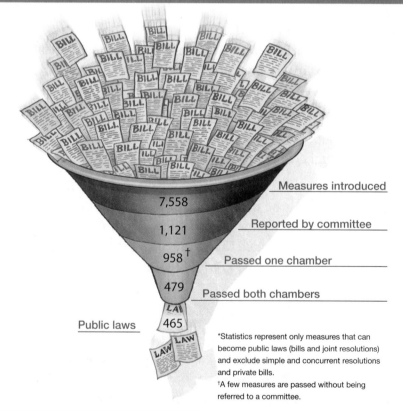

Measures introduced — 7,558
Reported by committee — 1,121
Passed one chamber — 958 †
Passed both chambers — 479
Public laws — 465

*Statistics represent only measures that can
become public laws (bills and joint resolutions)
and exclude simple and concurrent resolutions
and private bills.
†A few measures are passed without being
referred to a committee.

Source: Library of Congress. Figures are for the 109th Congress.

▲ **Interpreting Charts** This chart shows the many steps a bill must pass through before it becomes law. *After which step do most bills stop in the process?*

Fig. 12.9

Congressional Committee Staffers

What Are Their Duties?

There are more than 2,500 staffers on the congressional committees. These people are experts in the subjects that their committees cover. They are also experts on political action. Their hard work makes Congress more effective. *How might staffers add to the effectiveness of committees?*

Committee staffers deliver press copies of a Select Committee report on China's theft of U.S. nuclear weapons secrets.

A committee staffer presents information about the possible impact of oil exploration on Alaska's polar bears.

The committees do most of their work through their subcommittees. In addition to the members of Congress, many other people are involved (Figure 12.9). Sometimes an important bill receives a public hearing. The hearing allows important people who come to speak to the committee to present more information about the bill. After a subcommittee works on a bill, the full committee goes into action. It does one of the following:

(1) recommends passing the bill;

(2) pigeonholes the bill;

(3) presents the bill with changes or amendments;

(4) makes unfavorable comments about the bill (not done often); or

(5) presents an entirely new bill as a replacement.

How are floor debates scheduled?

Bills are scheduled for discussion after being placed on one of the five House calendars. There is the Calendar of the Committee of the Whole for money or property bills. There is also the House Calendar for public bills, the Private Calendar, the Corrections Calendar, and the Discharge Calendar. The House has a very exact schedule of when bills are to be considered. For example, bills from the Corrections Calendar are heard on Tuesdays. Wednesdays are used for bills from the Union Calendar or the House Calendar.

Reading Strategy
Summarizing
What are the five actions that committees may take on a bill?

■ ■ ■ ■ ■ ■ ■ ■ ■ ■ ■ ■ ■ ■ ■ ■

Quorum
A majority

■ ■ ■ ■ ■ ■ ■ ■ ■ ■ ■ ■ ■ ■ ■ ■

Reading Strategy
Summarizing
In your own words, describe the difference between the House and the Committee of the Whole.

The Rules Committee sets a day when a bill is taken from the calendar and discussed on the floor. Some bills are special and can be called at any time ahead of other bills.

The rules of the House may also be suspended for important measures that need to be considered right away. All of the rules used by the House have developed over time. The House is very large and hears a great many measures. The rules and calendars help the House of Representatives organize and complete its work.

What happens to bills on the floor?

Bills that reach the floor of the House are read for a second time. If they are minor bills, they may be passed quickly. The more important bills are considered by the Committee of the Whole, which helps bills to pass quickly. The entire House acts as one large committee, not as the House itself. It is normally led by a member, not the Speaker. Sections of the bill are read and voted on. Normally, for a vote in the House, there needs to be a **quorum** (majority) of the House members present. In contrast, only 100 people need to be present in the Committee of the Whole. After the vote, the Committee of the Whole disbands and the House resumes its business with the Speaker in charge.

Fig. 12.10

"The only solution I can see is to hold a series of long and costly hearings in order to put off finding a solution."

▲ **Analyzing Political Cartoons** This cartoon makes fun of the lawmaking process. ***Does this cartoon show how Congress actually works or how the general public thinks it works?***

Debate on bills has limits imposed by rule. A member may speak for one hour unless all agree he or she may go on. A member may demand a vote on the issue to stop the debate. Another rule says a bill may be voted on several times if it has amendments. Votes also may be called to table the bill (put it aside). The process can take time, but it is necessary and effective. The public does not always think so. (See Figure 12.10.)

The House has several ways of taking votes. In 1973, the House began using a computer voting system to replace roll call by the clerk. Members have cards and use them in the 48 computers at stations in the House. They push buttons to record the vote—"Yea," "Nay," or "Present." The "Present" button is mostly used if a quorum of members is present in the House. Otherwise, it is used when a member does not wish to vote on a question but still wants to be recorded as present.

A bill is printed in its final form after it is approved at the second reading. Then a third reading is done and the final vote taken. If the bill is approved at this third reading, the bill is sent to the desk of the president of the Senate.

✔ **Checkpoint** What is the purpose of the Committee of the Whole?

Biography

Honorable Samuel Rayburn (1882–1961)

Samuel (Sam) Rayburn was born in 1882. He grew up on a farm in Texas. After working his way through East Texas Normal College, he taught school and then became a lawyer.

He was first elected to the United States House of Representatives in 1912. He served in the House for 48 years. He served on important committees and coauthored six important laws.

In 1940, he became Speaker of the House. He held that position for 17 years. Rayburn described himself as a Democrat and was often called "Mr. Democrat."

Essential Questions Journal Go to your **Essential Questions Journal** to work on this chapter's Essential Question.

SECTION 3 ASSESSMENT

1. **Guiding Question** Use your completed table to answer this question: What are the steps of a successful bill as it moves through the House?

Key Terms and Comprehension

On a sheet of paper, write the answer to each question. Use complete sentences.

2. What is a concurrent resolution?

3. What happens to most bills in committee?

4. What is a rider?

5. What happens after a bill passes in the House?

Critical Thinking

6. **Draw Conclusions** Why do you think committees pigeonhole most bills?

7. **Compare and Contrast** How are the House and the Committee of the Whole similar? How are they different?

ISSUES OF OUR TIME

Minority Rights

▶▶ Track the Issue

The Senate minority party has used strategies such as filibusters to make sure its voice is heard.

1790 Southern senators use the first filibuster. They want to keep the First Congress from being located in Philadelphia.

Early 1800s Congress admits states into the Union as pairs. They admit one slave state and one free state at the same time to ensure balance in the Senate.

1960s The Senate introduces a "two-track" option. The option allows the Senate to continue to work during a filibuster.

1975 The Senate lowers the number of votes needed for cloture.

2000s The Senate today is often known as the 60-vote Senate. Sixty votes is the number needed to make cloture, or the number of votes needed to end a debate.

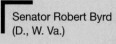

Senator Robert Byrd
(D., W. Va.)

▶▶ Perspectives

The term *filibuster* is a Dutch word that means "pirate." It is used to describe the tactic of talking about a bill to death. In 2005, Democratic filibusters had prevented President Bush from confirming judicial appointments. The Republican majority leader threatened to try to outlaw judicial filibusters. Democrats threatened back and said they would bring the Senate to a stop. A group of moderate Republicans and Democrats compromised. You will read more about filibusters on pages 301 and 302.

Against Judicial Filibusters	For Judicial Filibusters
"[The filibuster] presents a serious challenge to . . . the principle so essential to our general liberty—the separation of powers. . . .[T]he Framers concluded that the President should have the power to appoint. . . . But the Minority's filibuster prevents the Senate from giving 'advice and consent.' They deny the Senate the right to carry out its Constitutional duty. . . . This filibuster is . . . a formula for tyranny by the minority." —*Former Senate Majority Leader Bill Frist (R., Tennessee)*	"If senators are denied their right to free speech on judicial nominations, an attack on extended debate on all other matters cannot be far behind. This would mean no leverage for the minority to effect compromise, and no bargaining power for individual senators as they strive to represent the people of their states. . . . Let the Senate continue to be the one in which a minority can have the freedom to protect a majority from its own folly." —*Senator Robert Byrd (D., West Virginia)*

Connect to Your World

1. According to Bill Frist, what basic principle does the filibuster challenge?
2. Do you agree with Bill Frist or Robert Byrd? Why?

GOVERNMENT ONLINE
In the News
For updates about minority rights visit **PearsonSuccessNet.com**

SECTION 4

Making Law: The Senate

▲ Senate pages carry copies of a bill to the Senate floor.

Guiding Question

What are the major differences between House and Senate procedures for passing legislation? Use a Venn diagram to keep track of ways the House and Senate procedures compare and contrast.

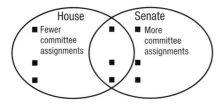

House — Senate
■ Fewer committee assignments
■ More committee assignments

Objectives:

- Explain how a bill is introduced in the Senate.
- Compare the Senate's rules for debate with those of the House.
- Describe the role of conference committees in the legislative process.
- Describe the actions the President can take after both houses have passed a bill.

The Senate receives bills from the House and also introduces its own bills. Both houses of Congress must approve a bill before it can be sent to the President. The steps for handling bills are similar in both houses of Congress. There are, however, some important differences in the lawmaking process in the Senate.

What happens on the Senate floor?

Senators may introduce bills only in the Senate. The bills are given a number, read twice, and then sent to a standing committee. The steps a bill follows after this are much the same as in the House. The Senate, however, has only one calendar for bills after they come out of committee. The House has five calendars. The majority leader handles the bills on the Senate floor. Sometimes the minority leader will also help with the bills.

What are the rules for debate?

Rules for debate are not limited in the Senate as they are in the House. Senators may speak as long as they like and on any topic. At times, all Senate members may agree on important bills that come to the Senate floor. Floor time given to one of these bills is short, if no senator objects to the bill or any of its amendments.

Senators are limited by the "two-speech rule" that allows only two speeches on a topic on a legislative day. By recessing at night (only interrupting for a time) instead of ending a session, the rule can extend for much longer than an actual day. This practice prevents senators from making too many speeches. Senators are given more freedom to debate than members of the House. This debate may result in a **filibuster.**

▲ Strom Thurmond held up the Civil Rights Act of 1957 with the longest filibuster in history.

■ ■ ■ ■ ■ ■ ■ ■ ■ ■ ■ ■ ■ ■ ■ ■

Reading Strategy
Summarizing
What is the main point being made about filibusters in this paragraph?

■ ■ ■ ■ ■ ■ ■ ■ ■ ■ ■ ■ ■ ■ ■ ■

Filibuster
An effort to keep talking long enough to prevent a vote on a bill

Cloture
Limiting debate

A filibuster is an effort to keep talking long enough to prevent the Senate from voting on a bill. This is usually only done by a few senators. The Senate may run out of time or change the bill to please the minority. There have been a few famous filibusters in the country's history. One filibuster lasted over 24 hours. Senator Strom Thurmond was trying to prevent measures that eventually led to the passage of the Civil Rights Act of 1957. Over 200 measures have been defeated in the Senate by filibusters.

The Senate adopted the Cloture Rule in 1917. The rule provides for **cloture** (limiting debate). This rule is not always in force. It must be voted in by three fifths of the Senate. Once voted in, only 30 hours of floor time are allowed for discussion of each measure on the floor. The measure then must be voted on. Many senators do not like the Cloture Rule. They think it takes away the Senate tradition of free debate and the effective use of the filibuster.

In recent years, filibusters have been used when one party has a large minority. For example, the Senate was evenly split with 49 Democrats and 49 Republicans during the 110th Congress. The two Independent members supported the Democrats. Filibusters have been successful because they can protect the minority. On the other hand, they can prevent any action by the Senate, a delay that is not popular with the public. (See "Issues of Our Time" on page 300.)

✔ **Checkpoint**   What is the Cloture Rule?

What happens in conference committees?

Both houses of Congress must pass the exact same bill. If the House and Senate pass different versions, often the first house will agree to the other's changes. Sometimes this agreement does not happen and the measure is given to a conference committee. This is a temporary committee made up of important members of both houses. This committee is usually able to settle the differences. The committee cannot add new material to the bill. After the conference committee completes its work, both houses vote on the bill again. The bill usually passes then. Many important decisions and compromises are made in conference committees.

✔ **Checkpoint**   When does a bill go to a conference committee?

What actions can the President take on a bill?

The Constitution requires that every bill, order, and resolution be presented to the President. Then the Constitution states four things the President may do:

- The President may sign the bill into law.

- The President may **veto** the bill. It is then returned to the house where it was introduced. Congress can still pass the bill by a two-thirds majority vote in both houses. Congress rarely does this.

- The President may allow the bill to become a law by not signing it within ten days of receiving it. Sundays are not counted.

- The President may use the **pocket veto.** This means if Congress adjourns its session within 10 days of submitting a bill to the President, and the President does not act on it within that time, the measure dies.

Congress rarely has enough votes to override a presidential veto. If the Congress thinks the President may veto a bill they are considering, they may change the provisions of the bill.

Congress added the Line Item Veto in 1996. It allowed the President to reject single items in appropriation bills. In 1998, the Supreme Court declared that law unconstitutional in *Clinton* v. *New York.*

The next page shows the whole process of how a bill becomes a law. (See Figure 12.11.) There are many steps that go into the process. And even if the President vetoes a bill, Congress can still make it law.

Veto
The power of a person or group of people to reject or forbid a rule of law

Pocket veto
An indirect veto of a bill by the President not acting on it

◀ President George W. Bush signs the Voting Rights Act of 2006 during a ceremony on the South Lawn of the White House.

Fig. 12.11 How Government Works

How a Bill Becomes a Law

GOVERNMENT ONLINE
Self-Test
For an interactive version of
How a Bill Becomes a Law, visit
PearsonSuccessNet.com

A bill may be introduced in either chamber. The path to the right is that of a bill that begins in the House (H.R. 1). If a bill were to start in the Senate (S.1), steps 5, 6, and 7 would precede steps 1, 2, 3, and 4. *In what ways does the lawmaking process in the House differ from the one in the Senate?*

1 **H.R. 1 INTRODUCED IN HOUSE**

2 **COMMITTEE ACTION**
H.R. 1 referred to standing committee for study, hearings, revisions, and approval

3 **RULES COMMITTEE**
The Rules Committee sets conditions for debate and amendment on the floor.

5 **S. 1 INTRODUCED IN SENATE**

4 **FLOOR ACTION**
H.R. 1 debated, then passed or defeated. If passed, it goes to the Senate.

6 **COMMITTEE ACTION**
S. 1 referred to standing committee for study, hearings, revisions, and approval

7 **FLOOR ACTION**
S. 1 debated, then passed or defeated

8 **CONFERENCE COMMITTEE**
Conference Committee resolves differences between House and Senate versions of bill.

9 **CONGRESSIONAL APPROVAL**
House and Senate vote on final passage. Approved bill is sent to the President.

10 **PRESIDENTIAL ACTION**
The President signs, vetoes, or allows bill to become law without signing. A vetoed bill returns to Congress and the veto may be overridden.

As you have read, the House and the Senate both act to make law, but they do so in different ways. Figure 12.12 below lists the major differences between the two houses of Congress.

■ ■ ■ ■ ■ ■ ■ ■ ■ ■ ■ ■ ■ ■ ■ ■ ■ ■
Reading Strategy
Summarizing
Figure 12.12 lists the major differences between the House and Senate. What other differences can you think of from reading Chapters 10 and 11?

Fig. 12.12

Comparing the House and the Senate

House of Representatives	Senate
Smaller personal staffs	Larger personal staffs
Fewer committee assignments	More committee assignments
More formal, less flexible rules	Fewer, more flexible rules
Committee work usually more important than floor debate in shaping outcome of legislation	Floor debate often more important than committee work in shaping outcome of legislation
Floor debate strictly limited	Floor debate largely unlimited, but subject to cloture vote by 60 senators to end debate

Essential Questions Journal — Go to your **Essential Questions Journal** to work on this chapter's Essential Question.

SECTION 4 ASSESSMENT

Word Bank

cloture

filibuster

pocket veto

veto

1. **Guiding Question** Use your completed table to answer this question: What are the major differences between House and Senate procedures for passing legislation?

Key Terms and Comprehension

On a sheet of paper, use the words from the Word Bank to complete each sentence correctly.

2. Talking for a long time to prevent the Senate from voting is called a _____.

3. The _____ Rule limits debates to 30 hours.

4. A _____ is the power of a person or group to reject or forbid a rule of law.

5. A _____ is an indirect rejection of a bill by the President not acting on it.

Critical Thinking

6. **Draw Inferences** Why do you think that filibusters are an important part of the Senate tradition?

7. **Understand Point of View** Why might some Presidents have used vetoes a lot, while others have used them very little?

Chapter Summary

Section 1—Congress Organizes

■ Congress convenes every two years starting in January.

■ The presiding officer of the House is the Speaker, the most powerful member of Congress.

■ The presiding officer of the Senate is the Vice President of the United States.

■ Party officers in both houses are the majority and minority leaders and the party whips.

■ Committee chairmen lead the standing committees and are chosen by seniority rule.

Section 2—Committees in Congress

■ The standing committees of Congress are permanent. They do most of the work through the many subcommittees.

■ The Rules Committee is very powerful and controls which bills the House discusses.

■ Select committees of Congress handle issues of national importance.

■ Joint committees are made up of members of both houses.

Section 3—Making Law: The House

■ A bill is a proposed law and can only be introduced by a member of Congress.

■ Joint resolutions have the force of law.

■ Standing committees refer bills to subcommittees for consideration.

■ The Rules Committee schedules bills for discussion on the floor of the House.

■ Bills that are approved by the House are sent to the Senate.

Section 4—Making Law: The Senate

■ The Senate follows the same steps as the House in considering bills, with a few exceptions.

■ Senate debate is limited by the "two-speech rule," but senators may use the filibuster.

■ Both houses must pass the bill in the same form before it can be sent to the President.

■ The President may veto or sign a bill, or allow it to become a law without signing it.

Guiding Question
Section 1 How do constitutional and party officers keep Congress organized?

Guiding Question
Section 2 How do committees help Congress do its work?

Guiding Question
Section 3 What are the steps of a successful bill as it moves through the House?

Guiding Question
Section 4 What are the major differences between House and Senate procedures for passing legislation?

CHAPTER 12

Essential Question
Can and should the lawmaking process be improved?

Document-Based Assessment

Roger Sherman's Speech Against the "Right to Instruct"

Roger Sherman of Connecticut, a member of the Constitutional Convention, argued against the "right to instruct." Many people wanted the Bill of Rights to include this provision. It would have required the people's representatives in Congress to vote according to the citizens' views. Sherman was strong in his argument to the convention. Because of his words and the words of others, the provision was not added to the Bill of Rights.

Document at a Glance

- Sherman's speech during the Constitutional Convention
- Argued against "right to instruct"

In his speech, Roger Sherman said the following:

"It appears to me that the words are calculated to mislead the people by conveying an idea that they have a right to control the debates of the legislature. This can not be admitted to be just, because it would destroy the object of their meeting. I think when the people have chosen a representative it is his duty to meet others from different parts of the Union, and consult and agree with them to such acts as are for the general benefit of the whole community. If they are to be guided by instructions there would be no use in deliberation; all that a man would have to do would be to produce his instructions and lay them on the table and let them speak for him."

The "right to instruct" amendment was voted on. It lost by a vote of 10–41. Although representatives are very interested in knowing what the citizens feel and think, they are not required by law to vote how the people would vote.

Document-Based Questions

1. Where would the "right to instruct" be added in the Constitution?

2. Who would be affected by the provision?

3. What did Sherman say was the duty of a representative?

4. How would the "right to instruct" interfere with this duty?

5. **Summarize** In your own words, rewrite the main ideas of Roger Sherman's speech. Do you agree with him? Why or why not?

Source: http://www.econlib.org/Library/YPDBooks/Lalor/llCy579.html

Chapter Assessment

GOVERNMENT ONLINE
Self-Test
To test your understanding of
key terms and main ideas, visit
PearsonSuccessNet.com

Directions: On a sheet of paper, write the answer to each question. Use complete sentences.

Section 1—Congress Organizes

1. How often does a new term begin in Congress?

2. Who is the presiding officer in the House? Who is the presiding officer in the Senate?

3. How are committee chairmen chosen in standing committees?

4. **Critical Thinking** Can you think of a better way to choose committee chairmen instead of by seniority? Explain your answer.

Section 2—Committees in Congress

5. Which committee decides the bills that the House discusses?

6. Which committee decides how to raise money for the federal government?

7. What is a subcommittee?

8. If both the House and the Senate pass a bill, what happens next?

9. **Critical Thinking** Why are some committees more influential than others? Why might members of Congress want to join those committees?

Section 3—Making Law: The House

10. What do joint resolutions have that other resolutions do not?

11. Which committee schedules bills for discussion on the floor of the House?

12. Once bills are passed by the House, where do they go next?

13. **Critical Thinking** Before the computer voting system was used in the House, how do you think the House members voted? Explain your answer.

Section 4—Making Law: The Senate

14. How does a filibuster prevent a bill from being passed?

15. What are the four actions that a President can take with a bill?

16. How can a bill still become law even if it is vetoed by the President?

17. Critical Thinking Why might a President let a bill become law by not signing it instead of just signing it right away? Explain your answer.

Apply What You've Learned

Exploring the Essential Question
Write a summary paragraph for each question.

18. What is the process of making laws in the House?

19. What is the process of making laws in the Senate?

Essential Questions Project

20. Outside of class, find two or three adults that you can interview. The adult could be a parent, neighbor, or teacher. Read each adult your two summary paragraphs on the process of making laws in Congress. Then ask them the essential question: **Can and should the lawmaking process be improved?** Write their answers. Share the answers with the class.

Essential Questions
Journal

Go to your **Essential Questions Journal** to work on this chapter's Essential Question.

Test-Taking Tip

When studying for a test, use the titles and subtitles in the chapter to help you recall information.

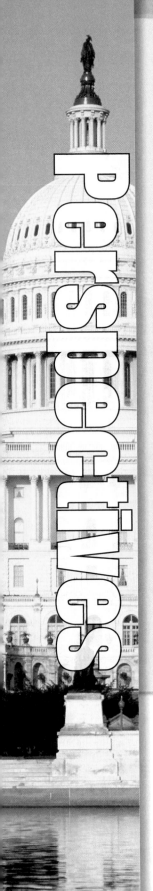

Essential Question

What makes a successful Congress?

There are many ways to define a successful Congress. The following examples offer perspectives on different qualities.

" ON SETTING PRIORITIES:

Congress should pass laws that reflect the will of the people; that is, Congress should be responsive to popular majorities. Congress should pass laws that deal promptly and effectively with pressing national problems. . . . Only in a perfect world would what the majority wants always accord with what policy experts deem most likely to be effective. When a conflict exists, which should take priority?

—Barbara Sinclair, *An Effective Congress and Effective Members: What Does It Take?*

ON COMPROMISE:

" ON EFFICIENCY:

. . . Congress simply isn't set up to be efficient. . . . Its job is to understand [issues] thoroughly, weigh the beliefs and interests of an astounding variety of Americans, and consider carefully how to move forward.

— Rep. Lee Hamilton (D., Indiana)

Essential Question Warmup

Throughout this unit, you studied the powers and functions of Congress. Use what you have learned and the quotations and opinions above to answer the following questions. Then go to your **Essential Questions Journal.**

1. How should members of Congress balance their roles as representatives of what voters want and as trustees who protect the best interests of the nation as a whole?

2. How should members of Congress balance their roles as party members with the need to compromise?

3. What should be the role of debate in Congress?

Essential Questions Journal — To continue to build a response to the unit Essential Question, go to your **Essential Questions Journal.**

Photo: Members of the executive branch gather in front of the White House.

Essential Questions Journal

To begin to build a response to the unit Essential Question, go to your **Essential Questions Journal.**

Unit 4
The Executive Branch

Essential Question What makes a good President?

311

▲ Citizens of Ohio meet presidential candidate Barack Obama in 2008.

The Presidency

Essential Question
Does the current electoral process result in the best candidates for President?

Section 1: The President's Job Description

Section 2: Presidential Succession and the Vice Presidency

Section 3: Presidential Selection: The Framers' Plan

Section 4: Presidential Nominations

Section 5: The Presidential Election

- -

Reading Strategy: Visualizing

Visualizing is another strategy that helps readers to understand what they are reading. It is like creating a movie in your mind. Use the following ways to visualize the text in Chapter 13.

- Look at the photographs, graphs, cartoon, and figures. Think about what these reveal about the topic.
- Think about experiences in your own life that may help you understand the presidency.

GOVERNMENT ONLINE
ON THE GO

To study anywhere, anytime, download these online resources at PearsonSuccessNet.com
- Political Dictionary
- Audio Review
- Downloadable Interactivities

The President's Job Description

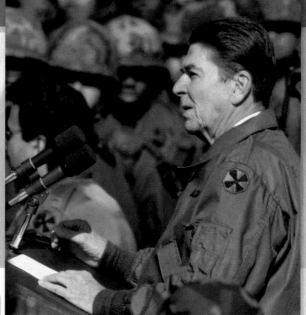

▲ President Ronald Reagan talks to U.S. troops in South Korea in 1983.

Guiding Question

What are the roles and qualifications of the office of the President? Use an outline like the one below to keep track of presidential roles and qualifications.

I. The President's Roles
   A. Chief of state
      1. Symbol of the nation
      2. _____
   B. Chief executive
      1. _____
      2. _____

Objectives:

- Describe the President's many roles.
- Understand the formal qualifications necessary to become President.
- Explain how the President's term of office has changed over time.
- Describe the President's pay and benefits.

Do you know who the youngest person ever to be President of the United States was? The oldest? Who held the presidency for the longest time? The shortest? Can a person born in a different country become President? In this section, you will find the answers to these questions and much more.

What are the presidential roles?

There is only one President of the United States. This one person must fill a number of different roles at the same time. These roles are: (1) chief of state, (2) chief executive, (3) chief administrator, (4) chief diplomat, (5) commander in chief, (6) chief legislator, (7) party chief, and (8) chief citizen.

Chief of state refers to the President as the head of the government. He is the symbol of all the people. In the United States, the President also rules over the government. In many countries, the chief of state reigns over government but does not rule. Examples of this can be found in England, Denmark, Japan, Italy, and Germany.

The President is also **chief executive,** vested by the Constitution with broad executive powers. This power is used at home on domestic issues and also extends to foreign affairs. The executive power is limited, however, by our government's system of checks and balances.

As **chief administrator,** the President is in charge of the executive branch of the federal government. This branch employs more than 2.7 million civilians.

The President is also the nation's **chief diplomat,** the main author of American foreign policy. Everything the President says and does is closely followed, both at home and in other countries.

In addition, the Constitution makes the President the **commander in chief** of the armed forces. This power gives the President direct and immediate control of the military.

As **chief legislator,** the President shapes public policy. The President may suggest, request, and insist that Congress enact laws he believes are needed. Sometimes, Congress does not agree with the President and decides against legislation. Working with Congress takes up a major part of the President's time.

The six presidential roles you just read about are written in the Constitution. The President must also fill two other roles—chief of party and chief citizen.

The President is automatically the **chief of party**—the leader of the political party that controls the executive branch. Political parties are not mentioned in the Constitution, but they are an important part of government.

Finally, the President is **chief citizen.** This means the President should represent all of the people of the United States. Citizens expect the President to work for their interests and provide moral leadership.

The President must carry out each of these roles at the same time. Sometimes, the failure to perform one duty can lead to failure in another area. For example, President Richard Nixon was forced to resign from office in 1974 because of the Watergate scandal. The people who had elected and trusted him were unhappy with the way he chose to fulfill the roles of party leader and chief citizen.

Chief of state
The President as ceremonial head of the United States

Chief executive
The President as the holder of the executive power of the United States

Chief administrator
The President as the leader of the executive branch of the federal government

Chief diplomat
The President as the main architect of American foreign policy and the nation's chief spokesperson to other countries

Commander in chief
The President as the commander of the nation's armed forces

Chief legislator
The President as the main author of public policy

Chief of party
The President as the leader of his or her political party

Chief citizen
The President as the representative of all the people

✓ **Checkpoint** What are the President's responsibilities as the nation's chief of state?

President Bill Clinton meets with Israeli and Palestinian leaders at Camp David in 2000 to conduct peace talks. *What role is President Clinton fulfilling here?* ▶

What are the formal qualifications?

The Constitution says that a candidate for President must meet certain formal qualifications. The President must:

- be a natural born American citizen
- be least 35 years old
- have been a resident of the United States for at least 14 years.

Most Presidents have been in their 50s when they entered the White House. John F. Kennedy was the youngest at age 43 to be elected President. Theodore Roosevelt succeeded to the office at the age of 42 after President William McKinley was assassinated. Ronald Reagan was elected at age 69. He left office at age 77, the oldest person ever to hold the presidency.

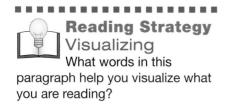

Reading Strategy
Visualizing
What words in this paragraph help you visualize what you are reading?

✔ **Checkpoint**   What are the three qualifications a person must meet to be eligible for the presidency?

How long can a President serve?

At first, the Framers debated between a single term for the President, lasting six or seven years, and a four-year term, with the possibility of reelection. They finally chose the second option. The Framers did not set a limit on the number of times a President could be reelected.

During the 1940s, Franklin Roosevelt served four terms, or 16 years, as President. To make sure this would not happen again, Congress passed the 22nd Amendment. The states ratified this amendment, which limits the President to two full terms in office. If the Vice President succeeds to the presidency and then is elected twice, he or she can serve up to ten years in office.

Many people criticize the 22nd Amendment. Presidents Truman, Eisenhower, and Reagan each called for its repeal. They claimed it should be left to the people to decide how long a President should serve. Others say it weakens the President's authority at the end of the second term. Those in favor of the 22nd Amendment claim it prevents one person from having too much power.

What are the pay and benefits?

Congress sets the President's salary, and it cannot change during a President's term. Since 2001, the President has been paid $400,000 a year. The President also has a $50,000 expense account to spend any way he or she chooses each year. The President is also given many benefits. One benefit is living in the 132-room White House in the center of Washington, D.C. The President also has use of a fleet of cars, Air Force One, and several other planes and helicopters.

Biography

Ronald Reagan (1911–2004)

Ronald Reagan was born in Tampico, Illinois, on February 6, 1911. He graduated from Eureka College in Illinois and became a radio sports announcer. This led to a career in the movies. He also served in the army from 1942 to 1945. After his wartime service, Reagan became president of the Screen Actors' Guild. This was the beginning of his political career. When he was first elected governor of California in 1966, he fought for lower taxes and reduction in government spending. In 1981 he was elected President of the United States and served two terms. President Reagan became known for his grace and wit. His economic policies were called "Reaganomics."

Ronald Reagan and his wife, Nancy, returned to their ranch in California at the end of his second term. He suffered from Alzheimer's disease the last ten years of his life. He died in 2004.

Essential Questions Journal Go to your **Essential Questions Journal** to work on this chapter's Essential Question.

SECTION 1 ASSESSMENT

Quick Write

Research one President that is talked about in this section. Write a paragraph on your findings. Make sure to include the President's full name, years in office, and number of terms. Also include any interesting facts you find about the President.

1. **Guiding Question** Use your completed outline to answer this question: What are the roles and qualifications of the office of the President?

Key Terms and Comprehension

On a sheet of paper, write the answer to each question. Use complete sentences.

2. What is the President's role as chief of state?

3. Which two presidential roles did not come from the Constitution?

4. What is the purpose of the 22nd Amendment?

5. What are two of the benefits of being President of the United States?

Critical Thinking

6. **Draw Conclusions** Why do you think the Framers set formal qualifications for the presidency?

7. **Demonstrate Reasoned Judgment** Some people think that the President is paid too little. Others believe the President is paid too much. What do you think? Why?

Evaluating Leadership

"Tuesday's election for the State Assembly seat in Gloucester County is going to be a close one. Recent polls show that Jane Arbino is leading among voters who think lowering taxes is important. Voters who favor a national health insurance program are much more likely to vote for her opponent, Keith James."

What qualities are important to you when you choose whom to vote for in an election? Many different factors can make someone the right candidate for you. Your criteria might not be the same ones that matter to someone else. It is important to decide what is important to you before you vote.

1. Decide what factors are most important to you. Before you start thinking about the candidates, you should determine what leadership qualities you care about the most. Do you want a leader who has been in office for a long time? Past behavior can be a good indication of how someone will perform in the future. You may want to evaluate candidates based on their personalities or characters. Does the candidate

have the ability to motivate or inspire others? Does the candidate share your beliefs and values?

2. Match the skills to the job. Your evaluation of the candidates may depend on the position that is being filled. A town mayor may need different skills than a town clerk. The qualities of a good senator might be different than those of a good Board of Education member. For some positions, it is important to have a strong vision and an ability to unite people. For others, someone who can stand up to opposition is ideal. It is important to match the specific requirements

of the job with the abilities of the candidate.

3. Compare qualifications. Once you have done Steps 1 and 2, you will need to compare candidates against those factors. Who meets most of your requirements? Does your list of requirements reduce your options to one candidate? If not, you will have to compare the candidates to determine who you think will be the best choice for the position.

▶▶ What do you think?

1. What do you think is the most important leadership quality for a United States senator? What about for a high school principal?

2. Do you think it is a good idea for a leader to admit when he or she has made a mistake?

3. **You Try It** Make a list of the qualities that you think make a good leader. Then, choose someone in a leadership position, such as a member of Congress or the President. Evaluate this person based on the criteria on your list.

GOVERNMENT ONLINE
Citizenship Activity Pack
For activities on evaluating leadership, go to
PearsonSuccessNet.com

Presidential Succession and the Vice Presidency

▲ Service men read of President Franklin Roosevelt's death, April 12, 1945.

Guiding Question

What occurs when the President is unable to perform the duties of the office? Use a chart like the one below to keep track of the main ideas about presidential succession.

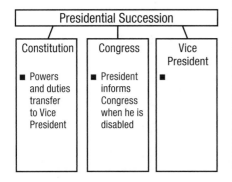

Presidential Succession		
Constitution	**Congress**	**Vice President**
■ Powers and duties transfer to Vice President	■ President informs Congress when he is disabled	■

Objectives:

■ Explain how the Constitution provides for presidential succession.

■ Understand the constitutional provisions related to presidential disability.

■ Describe the role of the Vice President.

In the history of the United States, there have been 47 Vice Presidents. Fourteen of these men have gone on to become President. Some succeeded to the presidency because the President was assassinated, died, or resigned. Other former Vice Presidents were elected on their own.

What does the Constitution say about presidential succession?

Presidential succession is the plan to fill a vacancy in the presidency. If the President dies, resigns, or is impeached, the Vice President becomes President.

The Constitution did not originally have a way to fill the office of President if it became vacant. It stated only that the "powers and duties" of the President were to be transferred to the Vice President, not the office itself. In 1841, President William Henry Harrison died and Vice President John Tyler succeeded him as President. This became the practice for filling a presidential vacancy. This practice became part of the Constitution when the 25th Amendment was adopted in 1967. It said that the Vice President would become President if the President died, resigned, or was removed from office.

The **Presidential Succession Act of 1947** set the order of succession following the Vice President. If the Vice President is unable to take the office, the Speaker of the House is next in line for the presidency. The complete line of succession appears on the next page (**Figure 13.1**).

✔ **Checkpoint** What happened in 1967?

Presidential succession
Scheme by which a presidential vacancy is filled

Presidential Succession Act of 1947
Law specifying the order of presidential succession following the Vice President

What happens if the President becomes disabled?

Before 1967 and the passage of the 25th Amendment, no guidelines existed in the Constitution for deciding what to do when a President was disabled. The 25th Amendment filled this gap in the Constitution. It says that the Vice President will become Acting President if the President informs Congress that he or she cannot carry out the duties of the office. Or, the Vice President and a majority of the members of the Cabinet can inform Congress that the President is disabled. The President decides when to go back to the duties and informs Congress. The Vice President and a majority of the Cabinet may challenge this decision. In that case, Congress has 21 days to decide the matter.

✓ **Checkpoint**   What happens if the President becomes disabled?

What are the duties of the Vice President?

The Vice President has only two formal duties according to the Constitution. The first duty is to preside over the Senate. The second is to help decide if the President is disabled. Through the years, the office of Vice President has been considered unimportant.

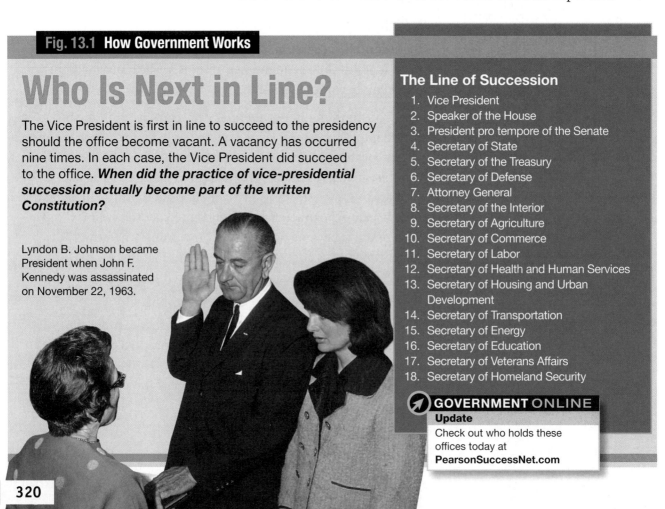

Fig. 13.1 How Government Works

Who Is Next in Line?

The Vice President is first in line to succeed to the presidency should the office become vacant. A vacancy has occurred nine times. In each case, the Vice President did succeed to the office. *When did the practice of vice-presidential succession actually become part of the written Constitution?*

Lyndon B. Johnson became President when John F. Kennedy was assassinated on November 22, 1963.

The Line of Succession
1. Vice President
2. Speaker of the House
3. President pro tempore of the Senate
4. Secretary of State
5. Secretary of the Treasury
6. Secretary of Defense
7. Attorney General
8. Secretary of the Interior
9. Secretary of Agriculture
10. Secretary of Commerce
11. Secretary of Labor
12. Secretary of Health and Human Services
13. Secretary of Housing and Urban Development
14. Secretary of Transportation
15. Secretary of Energy
16. Secretary of Education
17. Secretary of Veterans Affairs
18. Secretary of Homeland Security

GOVERNMENT ONLINE
Update
Check out who holds these offices today at
PearsonSuccessNet.com

Vice Presidents themselves have described the office that way. In fact, however, the office is very important, because the Vice President is "only a heart beat away" from the presidency.

The low opinion of the vice presidency is partly due to the way candidates for the office are chosen. The President is carefully selected based on his or her qualifications, but the Vice President is chosen mostly to **balance the ticket.** This means the choice of the vice-presidential candidate is meant to attract voters, perhaps from a particular geographic region. Political parties do not usually consider the possibility of succession to the presidency when choosing a vice-presidential candidate.

What is the vice presidency like today?

The vice presidency has taken on more importance in recent years. Vice President Dick Cheney was considered the most influential Vice President in the country's history to that point. Vice President Joe Biden had a 36-year Senate career and significant foreign relations experience before becoming Vice President.

Even though the Vice President has risen in importance, none has yet become a true assistant to the President. One reason for this may be that the Vice President is not subject to removal from office by the President. The President can never fire the Vice President. If the office of Vice President becomes vacant, the 25th Amendment says that the President must nominate a Vice President. Both houses of Congress must confirm this nomination by a majority vote. This is written into the 25th Amendment (1967).

Balance the ticket
The practice of choosing a presidential running mate who can strengthen a presidential candidate's chance of being elected

Reading Strategy
Visualizing
How could this paragraph be written differently to create a stronger picture in your mind?

Essential Questions Journal Go to your **Essential Questions Journal** to work on this chapter's Essential Question.

SECTION 2 ASSESSMENT

1. **Guiding Question** Use your completed chart to answer this question: What occurs when the President is unable to perform the duties of the office?

Key Terms and Comprehension
On a sheet of paper, write the answer to each question. Use complete sentences.

2. What is presidential succession?

3. What two official duties does the Constitution assign to the Vice President?

4. Which amendment deals with presidential disability?

5. What does it mean to balance the ticket?

Critical Thinking

6. **Demonstrate Reasoned Judgment** Do you think the attempt to "balance the ticket" is a good way of selecting a Vice President? Why or why not?

7. **Synthesize Information** How can the past experiences of a Vice President help the position rise in importance?

▲ The presidential candidates in 1800: Aaron Burr (left) and Thomas Jefferson.

SECTION 3
Presidential Selection: The Framers' Plan

The President is chosen according to terms listed in the Constitution, state and federal laws, and tradition. This complicated mix is not what the Framers originally intended. In this section, you will read about the Framers' plan and why it changed.

Guiding Question

How did the process of choosing a President change over time? Use a flowchart like the one below to keep track of the main ideas about selecting the President.

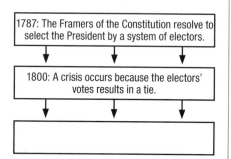

1787: The Framers of the Constitution resolve to select the President by a system of electors.

1800: A crisis occurs because the electors' votes results in a tie.

Objectives:

- Explain the Framers' original plan for choosing the President.
- Understand how political parties changed the original process for choosing a President.

What were the original provisions for choosing a President?

The Framers considered many methods for selecting a President. At first, many delegates favored the idea of Congress choosing the President. Those against this plan argued that the choice of President should be controlled by the people, not the legislature. Only a few delegates favored choosing the President by popular vote, however. Most felt that the country was too large and spread out for voters to be able to learn enough about the candidates to make a wise decision.

Finally, after weeks of talking, the Framers chose a plan suggested by Alexander Hamilton. According to this plan, the President and Vice President were to be chosen by a special body of **presidential electors.** These electors would be chosen in each state. Each state would have as many electors as it has senators and representatives in Congress. These electors would each cast two **electoral votes,** each for a different candidate. The person with the most votes would be President. The person the second largest number of votes would become Vice President. The Framers believed the electors chosen by each state would be informed and respected citizens.

✔ **Checkpoint** Whose plan did the Framers pick for choosing the President and Vice President?

How did the rise of political parties affect the process of choosing a President?

The **electoral college** is the group of people chosen from each state and the District of Columbia to formally select the President and Vice President. The original version of the Framers' plan only worked until 1796. By that time, two political parties existed: Federalists and Democratic-Republicans. The electors chose John Adams (a Federalist) as President. His rival from the Democratic Republican Party, Thomas Jefferson, was elected Vice President. He had received the second largest number of votes. This meant Jefferson had to serve under Adams. In our government today, the President and Vice President are always from the same party.

In the election of 1800, the electoral system completely failed (Figure 13.2). Political parties were now well-established. Each party nominated presidential and vice presidential candidates. The electoral college voting produced a tie for the presidency. Therefore, the election was thrown into the House of Representatives. In the House, all the states had to vote 36 separate times before Thomas Jefferson was finally chosen as President.

Presidential elector
A person elected by the voters to represent them in making a formal selection of the Vice President and President

Electoral vote
Vote cast by electors in the electoral college

Electoral College
Group of persons chosen in each state and the District of Columbia every four years who make a formal selection of the President and Vice President

Reading Strategy
Visualizing
How does this illustration on the page help you better understand what you are reading?

Fig. 13.2
The Electoral College
Crisis Causes Change

The Framers saw the electoral college as an appropriate way to select the President and Vice President. They did not foresee the development of political parties, however, and the parties' participation in the election of 1800 caused a serious breakdown in the Framers' plan. *What did the Framers hope to accomplish by designing the electoral college system as they did?*

The 12th Amendment

Separate elections

President Vice President

1787
The Framers' Original Plan

- Each elector casts two electoral votes, each for a different person for President.
- The person receiving a majority of the electoral votes becomes President.
- The person with the second highest number of electoral votes becomes Vice President.

1800
The Crisis

In accord with the Framers' original plan, the electors cast their two votes for two different persons. Each of the 73 Democratic-Republican electors votes for that party's two nominees, producing a tie. In the end, it takes 36 separate votes in the House of Representatives to finally select the President and, by default, the Vice President.

1804
Changes to the Original Plan

- The 12th Amendment to the Constitution separates the presidential and vice-presidential elections.
- Each presidential elector now casts one vote for President and one vote for Vice President.

Fig. 13.3
The Election of 1800

▼ **Interpreting Maps** Differing attitudes about the role of the government and the interpretation of the Constitution gave rise to political parties in the United States. How do the map and chart below illustrate these political divisions?

Election of 1800

Federalist 47%
Democratic-Republican 53%

Candidate and Party	Electoral Votes
Thomas Jefferson Democratic-Republican	73
Aaron Burr Democratic-Republican	73
John Adams Federalist	65
Charles C. Pinckney Federalist	64
John Jay Federalist	1

SOURCE: National Archives and Records Administration

After the election of 1800, (Figure 13.3) the 12th Amendment was added to the Constitution. The amendment made one major change in the electoral college. It separated the presidential and vice-presidential elections. The 12th Amendment says, "The Electors . . . shall name in their ballots the person voted for as President, and in distinct ballots the person voted for as Vice–President."

The rise of political parties, the election of 1800, and the 12th Amendment laid the foundation for the presidential selection system we use today.

✔ **Checkpoint** Who was elected President in 1800?

Essential Questions Journal Go to your **Essential Questions Journal** to work on this chapter's Essential Question.

SECTION **3** ASSESSMENT

1. **Guiding Question** Use your completed flowchart to answer this question: How did the process of choosing a President change over time?

Key Terms and Comprehension

On a sheet of paper, write the answer to each question. Use complete sentences.

2. What is the electoral college?

3. How many delegates does each state have in the electoral college?

4. What happened in 1800 that led to a change in the electoral process?

5. What amendment was added to the Constitution following the election of 1800?

Critical Thinking

6. **Recognize Bias** The Framers believed that the presidential electors would be the smartest and most respectable citizens in each state. How did this reflect the voting population at the time?

7. **Determine Relevance** How did the loyalty to one political party complicate the election of 1800?

▲ Delegates cheer on a speaker at the 2008 Democratic National Convention.

SECTION 4
Presidential Nominations

Guiding Question

Does the nominating system allow Americans to choose the best candidates for President?
Use a chart like the one below to keep track of the main ideas about the nomination process.

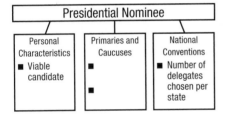

Objectives:

- Explain the role of conventions in the nominating process.
- Evaluate the importance of presidential primaries.
- Understand the caucus-convention process.
- List the important events that happen during a national convention.
- Consider the typical characteristics of most presidential candidates.

The Constitution does not describe how presidential candidates should be chosen. Instead, the Framers designed the electoral college system. When political parties arose and affected the outcome of the election of 1800, however, that system changed forever. In this section, you will read about the way that presidential candidates are chosen today.

How does the national convention work?

Political parties first used congressional caucuses to nominate their presidential candidates. That arrangement ended because it represented the views of too few people. By 1832, both major parties had begun to use national conventions to nominate presidential candidates. The national convention is still used today.

The convention was developed by the two major parties rather than federal or state law. In both parties, a committee decides on the place and date of the convention. The conventions are very large. In 2008, the Republicans had 2,380 delegates and the Democrats had 4,233.

Delegates from each state are chosen by the parties to attend the convention. The number of delegates from each state is based on that state's electoral vote. Both parties now award bonus delegates to some states. These are the states that have supported a party's candidate in the past.

The selection of delegates to the convention produces a struggle in each party. State laws and/or party rules set the procedures for picking delegates in each state. The Republican Party allows the individual state organizations to choose its delegates. The Democratic Party process is governed by national rules to include more people in the selection process.

What is a presidential primary?

Many states use a **presidential primary** to select delegates for the national convention and/or to express a preference for their party's presidential nominee. The media play close attention to these primaries. Any candidate who hopes to have a chance at his or her party's nomination must do well in the primaries.

The presidential primary began in the early 1900s. Corrupt party bosses had dominated the convention system. The process needed to be reformed. Primaries allowed more input from party members. Wisconsin passed the first law providing for the popular election of delegates to the national convention. By 1916, about half of the states had similar laws. Today, some form of the presidential primary is used in most states. For 2008, 40 states used the presidential primary system.

What are primaries like today?

Primaries today are difficult to describe. Each state has a different way to choose its delegates. In addition, the Democratic Party has reformed its rules many times since 1968. Even the dates of the state primaries are confusing. New Hampshire holds its primaries first and has done so since 1920. It has a state law that says its primary is to be held at least a week before that of any other state. Most states want an early date for their primary. As a result, 16 states hold their primaries on "Super Tuesday" (February 5th). Three fourths of the primaries are held by mid-March.

In the recent past, primaries were used both to select delegates and to show preference for a presidential candidate. Several primaries were **winner-take-all** contests. Candidates who won the preference vote also won the support of all the delegates chosen at that primary. These winner-take-all contests have almost all disappeared. The Democrats now have a **proportional representation** rule (Figure 13.4). A candidate who wins at least 15 percent of the primary votes gets the number of that state's delegates that matches his or her share of that primary vote. Most states had to change their primary laws to account for the Democrats proportional representation rule.

✔️ **Checkpoint** What is proportional representation?

Presidential primary
An election in which a party's voters (1) choose the delegates to their national convention, and/or (2) vote for their party's presidential candidate

Winner-take-all
A type of primary that is no longer used in which a winning presidential candidate automatically won the support of all the party's delegates

Proportional representation
Rule applied in Democratic primaries that awards delegates based on the number of votes the candidate wins in the primary

---

Fig. 13.4

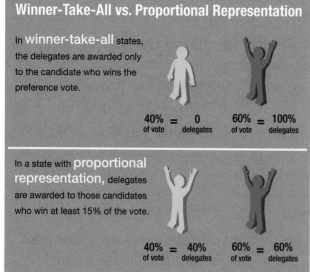

Winner-Take-All vs. Proportional Representation

In winner-take-all states, the delegates are awarded only to the candidate who wins the preference vote.

40% of vote = 0 delegates   60% of vote = 100% delegates

In a state with proportional representation, delegates are awarded to those candidates who win at least 15% of the vote.

40% of vote = 40% delegates   60% of vote = 60% delegates

▲ Analyzing Charts As political parties' rules have changed, so has the manner in which primaries have been conducted. *Why do you think candidates who receive less than 15% of the vote are not assigned delegates?*

The presidential primary is very confusing, but also very important in our system of government. Presidential primaries allow the people to decide on candidates for President. In addition, they force potential nominees to test their abilities in real political action. In this way, the less capable candidates are eliminated. This does not often happen in the party in power, however, because that party may have the President running for reelection or giving his backing to someone he favors.

Some people believe the presidential primary process should be reformed again. One idea is for each of the major parties to hold one nationwide primary just to choose their presidential candidate. National conventions would be done away with. Others suggest a series of regional primaries, held by groups of states every two or three weeks. Hope for any of the plans is uncertain because both houses of Congress would have to work with the states and the major political parties. Neither party seems to have much interest in reform. They see the national convention as a way to promote party unity and strengthen party influence.

What is a caucus?

Some states do not hold primaries. In these states, the delegates to the national convention are chosen in a system of local caucuses and district and/or state conventions. A caucus is a closed meeting of members of a political party who gather to select delegates to the national convention. Caucuses are meetings held locally, usually in a precinct (a local polling district). At this meeting, they choose delegates to a local convention. At this local convention, delegates to a state convention are chosen. At this state convention, delegates to the national convention are finally selected.

The caucus method is very old and has declined over the years. In 2008, less than one fourth of all delegates to both major party conventions were selected by the caucus-convention method.

The Iowa caucuses have been the first delegate-selection event in every presidential election since 1972. In the election of 2008, the Iowa caucus was held five days before the New Hampshire primary (Figure 13.5).

Fig. 13.5

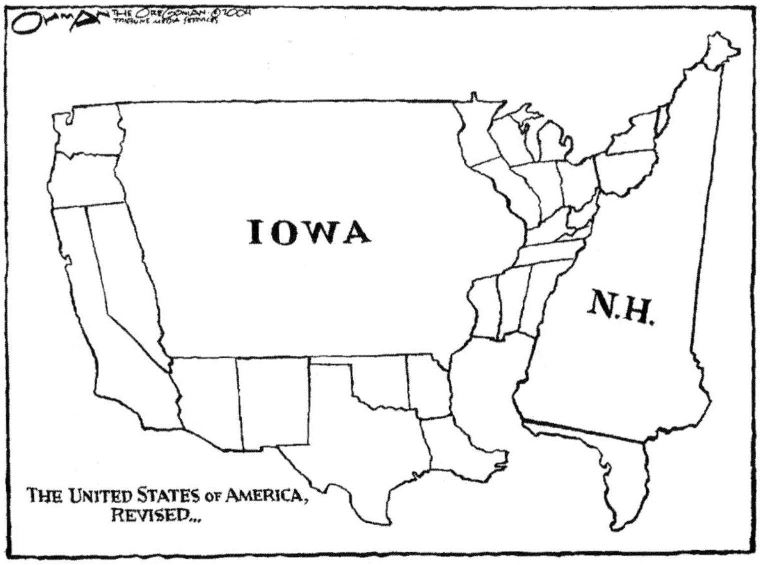

▲ Analyzing Political Cartoons The first delegate-selection event in a presidential election by caucus is held in Iowa, followed afterward by the first scheduled primary in New Hampshire. *How does this cartoon illustrate the emphasis placed on the elections held in these two states?*

Fig. 13.6 **How Government Works**

The Race for the Presidency

The race begins as presidential contenders compete to become their party's nominee. As the pace intensifies, the field dwindles to a contest between two contenders for the ultimate prize—the presidency. *How does the contest for the White House reflect the American democratic ideal?*

1-4 Years Before Election The first steps for potential candidates include broadening their visibility, testing their appeal nationwide, and developing committees to explore their viability as a candidate. If the results are encouraging, the contender will officially announce his or her candidacy.

1-4 Years Before Election The costs of running for office are huge and raising funds is an ongoing effort throughout the campaign. Lack of funds often caues contenders to drop out of the race.

January–June of the Election Year Primaries and caucuses help determine the party's nominee. At this stage, voters choose their party's frontrunner and many candidates concede defeat.

Start the Race   **Fundraising**   **Primaries and Caucuses**

National convention
Meeting at which a party's delegates pick the presidential and vice-presidential candidates

Platform
A political party's formal statement of basic principles, stands on major issues, and objectives

Keynote address
Speech given at a party convention to set the tone for the convention and the campaign to come

How is the presidential candidate chosen at the national convention?

After all the primaries and caucuses are over, it is time for each major party to hold its **national convention.** The convention is just one step in the very long race to the presidency (**Figure 13.6**). The convention has three main goals: 1) naming the party's presidential and vice presidential candidates, 2) promoting party unity, and 3) adopting the party's **platform.**

During the first days of the convention, many important party leaders make speeches. The most important is the **keynote address.** The keynote address is a speech given to set the tone for the convention and campaign to come. It prompts loud demonstrations and an enthusiastic show of support for the party.

August–September of the Election Year Delegates to each party's convention adopt the party platform, nominate their party's presidential candidate, and ratify his or her choice of vice-presidential running mate.

September–November of the Election Year Following the conventions, each candidate focuses on his or her opponent. Debates provide opportunities to compare and contrast each candidate's qualifications and plans for the future.

November on the Tuesday after the first Monday in November, the voters cast their ballots and the president-elect is determined.

National Conventions   **Debates**   **Election Day**

On the last two days of the convention, delegates choose the party's vice presidential and presidential candidates. Delegates first choose the vice presidential candidate. The nominee then gives an acceptance speech meant to get the party ready for the next big event: The vote for the presidential candidate. As the convention chairperson calls the states in alphabetical order, each state announces its choice. Each complete roll call of states is called a ballot. Usually a candidate wins the party's nomination on the first ballot. If no candidate receives a majority of votes on the first ballot, the chairperson calls for a second ballot.

All of the excitement at the convention leads up to the presidential candidate's acceptance speech. This speech, and the convention that precedes it, are meant to inspire voters and win support for the party. The convention ends and the party's general election campaign is launched.

✔**Checkpoint** What is the keynote address?

Reading Strategy
Visualizing
How does the illustration on these pages help you better understand the race for the presidency?

Who is nominated for President?

A President who has only served one term usually runs for a second term. In this case the nomination is easy for the party in power. When a President is not eligible to run again, as in the 2008 election, many people may try for the nomination. Usually only two or three become serious candidates at convention time.

The candidate nominated by a party is usually someone who the party believes can win. This person has usually held other elective office and has won elections in the past. The person is often well known, with a good public record free of controversy. Governors of larger states are often chosen. In the past, candidates were usually from the more populated states. Television and the Internet have allowed several personalities from smaller states to win nominations in recent years, however.

In 2008, Senator Hillary Clinton of New York became the first woman to be seriously considered for nomination as the Democratic Party's presidential candidate. She competed against the Democratic Party's chosen candidate, Barack Obama, who was born to a white mother from Kansas and an African father from Kenya. When he was elected, the racial barrier to the presidency was broken. The Republicans also broke a historical record. John McCain, at 72, was the oldest candidate ever to run for President.

Essential Questions Journal Go to your **Essential Questions Journal** to work on this chapter's Essential Question.

SECTION 4 ASSESSMENT

1. **Guiding Question** Use your completed chart to answer this question: Does the nominating system allow Americans to choose the best candidates for President?

Key Terms and Comprehension

On a sheet of paper, write the answer to each question. Use complete sentences.

2. What is a caucus?

3. What is one of the goals of the national convention?

4. What is a platform?

5. What happens on "Super Tuesday"?

Critical Thinking

6. **Draw Conclusions** Why do you think there is such a desire for a state to hold its primary as early as possible?

7. **Demonstrate Reasoned Judgment** What characteristics would you like to see in a presidential candidate? Explain.

▲ Young volunteers encourage voter participation.

SECTION 5

The Presidential Election

Guiding Question

Does the election process serve the goals of American democracy today? Use a table like the one below to keep track of the main ideas about the election process.

Electoral College	
Defects	Significance
■ Winner-take-all system	■ Winner of the popular vote not guaranteed presidency
■	■
■	■

Objectives:

- Describe the features of the presidential campaign.
- Explain how the electoral college works.
- Identify the problems with the electoral college system.
- Outline the advantages and disadvantages of proposed reforms of the electoral college.

In America, a presidential election is held every four years. Wars and other crises have never prevented an election. This remarkable fact is not true in any other country in the world.

In this section, you will read about running a presidential campaign and how the electoral college works.

What is a presidential campaign?

The presidential campaign is an all-out effort to win the election. The candidate must convince the voters that he or she will be the best President. Voters learn about the candidate on television, the radio, the Internet and in newspapers and magazines. Candidates travel to many states and attend rallies and parties in an attempt to become well known.

At the start of the campaign, about one third of voters have not yet decided which candidate they will support. These **swing voters** attract much attention as each candidate tries to swing them to their side. Presidential candidates are also interested in the states that are too close to call. These states are called the **battleground states.** Any major candidate could win these states.

Presidential debates are now very important factors in deciding a campaign. In 1960, Vice President Richard Nixon and Democrat John F. Kennedy held the first televised debate. Kennedy performed well and went on to win the election. Since then, debates have taken place in every campaign.

✔ **Checkpoint** What is a battleground state?

■ ■ ■ ■ ■ ■ ■ ■ ■ ■ ■ ■ ■ ■ ■ ■ ■ ■ ■

Swing voter
Those voters who have not yet decided which candidate they will support at the start of the campaign and who are open to persuasion by either side

Battleground states
States in which any major candidate could win and the outcome is too close to call

■ ■ ■ ■ ■ ■ ■ ■ ■ ■ ■ ■ ■ ■ ■ ■

Reading Strategy
Visualizing
What clues on this page help you visualize the number of flaws in the electoral college?

When people vote in the presidential election, they are really voting for presidential electors. According to the Constitution, the electoral college elects the President. Each state has as many electors as it has members of Congress. The Framers expected the electors to choose whichever candidate they believed most qualified. Today, however, that does not happen. Instead, the electors are expected to vote for their party's candidates for President and Vice President.

Electors are chosen by popular vote in each state. They are chosen on a winner-take-all basis. The presidential candidate who receives the largest number of popular votes wins all of that state's electoral votes.

Voters usually know which candidate has won a majority of electoral votes by midnight of election day. But it is not until the electors from each state meet the Monday after the second Wednesday in December that the formal election of the President and Vice President actually takes place. On that date, the electors cast their votes and the signed and sealed ballots are sent to the President of the Senate in Washington, D.C. In early January, the sealed votes are opened and counted before a joint session of Congress. The President and Vice President are then declared elected.

If no candidate wins a majority of electoral votes (270 out of 538), the election is decided in the House of Representatives. Each state has one vote and it takes a majority of 26 to elect. If the House fails to choose a President by January 20, the 20th Amendment says that the Vice President shall act as President until a decision is made.

What are the flaws in the electoral college?

There are three major flaws, or defects, in the electoral college system. First, there is always the danger that the winner of the popular vote will not win the presidency. This has happened four times, most recently in 2000. The winner-take-all factor means that any votes won by the loser of the popular vote are not reflected in the electoral vote. For example, in 2008, Barack Obama won only 51 percent of the popular vote in Ohio. Still, he won all of Ohio's 20 electoral votes, even though 2.5 million Ohioans voted for John McCain.

The second flaw is that the Constitution does not require the electors to vote for the candidate who wins the popular vote. Electors do not usually refuse to vote for their party's presidential nominee. It has happened only eleven times. In none of these contests did this action change the outcome of the election.

Third, if neither candidate wins a majority in the electoral college, the election would have to be decided in the House of Representatives. This is a problem because each state would then have one vote. States with smaller populations would count as much as larger states. Plus, if a state could not decide on a candidate, it would lose its vote. Finally, if a strong third party candidate were involved in an election, it is possible that the House could not make a decision by Inauguration Day.

✔ **Checkpoint**   What are the three flaws with the electoral college?

What reforms have been proposed?

Through the years, several plans have been suggested to reform, or fix, the electoral college. Under the first, the **district plan,** two electors would be chosen from each state. They would be required to vote in line with their state's popular vote. Other electors for each state would come from that state's congressional districts. These electors would cast their votes to match the popular vote in their districts.

Under the **proportional plan,** each candidate would get a share of the electoral vote. This share would equal his or her share of the popular vote. Neither of these two plans would require a change to the Constitution. But neither plan would ensure that the winner of the popular vote would become President.

The **direct popular election** would do away with the electoral college. Each vote in the nation would count equally. The winner would always be the majority choice.

Many Americans favor this plan but obstacles stand in its way. For one, the small states do not like this change because they would lose their advantage in the electoral college. Other people feel it would weaken the federal system by taking away the states' role in the choice of President. Still other critics feel that candidates would be stretched too thin as they tried to campaign in every state. Voter fraud could also be a factor in a direct popular election.

✔ **Checkpoint**   What is the proportional plan?

District plan
Proposal for choosing presidential electors by which two electors would be selected in each state according to the statewide popular vote and the other electors would be selected separately in each of the state's congressional districts

Proportional plan
Proposal by which each presidential candidate would receive the same share of a state's electoral vote as he or she received in the state's popular vote

Direct popular election
Proposal to do away with the electoral college and allow the people to vote directly for President and Vice President

National popular vote plan
Proposal for electing the President whereby each state's election laws would provide for all of the state's electoral vote and enter into an interstate compact agreeing to elect the President by national popular vote

The proposed **national popular vote plan** is a fairly new plan that would not call for a change in the Constitution. This plan calls for the states to amend their election laws. The new state laws would provide that all of a state's electoral votes are to be awarded to the winner of the national popular vote. This change has been passed in four states to date: Hawaii, Illinois, Maryland, and New Jersey. The plan has gotten national attention and has been considered by at least 20 states. This new plan answers all the major objections about the electoral college without a need to amend the Constitution.

What are the benefits of the electoral college?

Some people do defend the electoral college system. They say critics often exaggerate the dangers of the system. Only two elections have been sent to the House and none in the last 180 years. Another point defenders of the system make is that the winner of the popular vote has lost the election only four times in 56 presidential elections. Defenders of the electoral college list these three strengths: the electoral college is a known process, it identifies the President quickly and certainly, and it helps promote the nation's two-party system.

Reading Strategy
Visualizing
How does the map on this page help you better understand what you are reading?

Fig. 13.7

The 2008 Presidential Election

McCain vs Obama

GOVERNMENT ONLINE
Update
To learn more about the results of recent elections, visit
PearsonSuccessNet.com

▼ Interpreting Maps Although John McCain won 46 percent of the popular vote in the 2008 election, he received only 32 percent of the electoral vote. *How do these results illustrate the significance of the winner-take-all factor in state contests?*

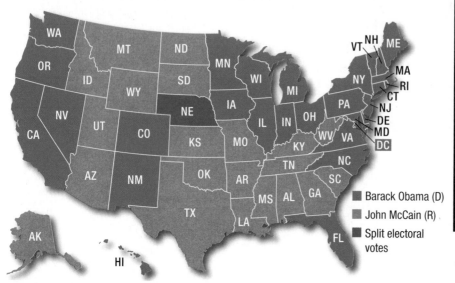

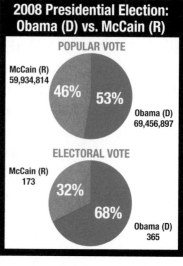

2008 Presidential Election: Obama (D) vs. McCain (R)

POPULAR VOTE
McCain (R) 59,934,814 — 46% / 53% — Obama (D) 69,456,897

ELECTORAL VOTE
McCain (R) 173 — 32% / 68% — Obama (D) 365

■ Barack Obama (D)
■ John McCain (R)
■ Split electoral votes

SOURCE: Federal Election Commission

Government in Your Life

Political Campaigns and Propaganda

During a political campaign, candidates use the media to convince citizens to vote for them. They present their beliefs and ideas as the best answer to the country's problems. They also attack other candidates' views.

A *"get on the bandwagon" approach* tries to convince you that everyone else will vote for the candidate, so you should too. Name-calling happens when a candidate attacks another candidate with names, such as *unpatriotic* or *fiscally irresponsible.* This promotes fear of what would happen if the other candidate gets elected. Card stacking is when a candidate presents only the facts that support his or her point of view.

The *plain folks approach* is used by candidates who are trying to convince voters that they are just ordinary people. Candidates dress in working clothes and are seen visiting farms, talking with people, and holding babies.

Misleading messages such as these appeal to people's emotions rather than their reason. It is best, instead, to focus on facts such as experience and stands on the major issues when casting a ballot.

Essential Questions Journal Go to your **Essential Questions Journal** to work on this chapter's Essential Question.

SECTION 5 ASSESSMENT

1. **Guiding Question** Use your table to answer this question: Does the election process serve the goals of American democracy today?

Key Terms and Comprehension
On a sheet of paper, write the answer to each question. Use complete sentences.

2. What is a swing voter?

3. What is a battleground state?

4. What is one flaw in the electoral college?

5. What is one defense of the electoral college?

Critical Thinking

6. **Summarize** What four options are suggested as alternatives to the electoral college?

7. **Demonstrate Reasoned Judgment** Which of the four options to reform or replace the electoral college do you feel is most democratic? Explain.

Chapter Summary

Section 1—The President's Job Description

- The President fills eight different roles at the same time.

- There are three formal qualifications for President.

- The President may be elected to a maximum of two full terms.

Section 2—Presidential Succession and the Vice Presidency

- The 25th Amendment says that the Vice President succeeds to the presidency if the President cannot serve.

- The Presidential Succession Act of 1947 fixes the order of succession following the Vice President.

- The Vice President has two formal duties.

Section 3—Presidential Selection: The Framers' Plan

- In the Framers' plan, the President would be selected by electors chosen in each state.

- The rise of political parties and the election of 1800 caused the breakdown of the system devised by the Framers.

- The 12th Amendment was added to the Constitution to separate the presidential and vice presidential elections.

Section 4—Presidential Nominations

- By 1832, both major political parties used national conventions to nominate candidates.

- At their national conventions, the Democrats and Republicans name their candidates for President and Vice President.

- Presidential candidates usually have a strong public record.

Section 5—The Presidential Election

- The presidential candidate who wins the largest number of popular votes in each state wins all of that state's electoral votes.

- Among other flaws in the electoral college, it is possible that the winner of the popular vote will not win the presidency.

- Over the years, several plans have been proposed to reform the electoral college, but defenders say it is a known process that quickly defines the President-to-be.

Guiding Question
Section 2 What occurs when the President is unable to perform the duties of the office?

Guiding Question
Section 3 How did the process of choosing a President change over time?

Guiding Question
Section 4 Does the nominating system allow Americans to choose the best candidates for President?

Guiding Question
Section 1 What are the roles and qualifications of the office of the President?

CHAPTER 13

Essential Question
Does the current electoral process result in the best candidates for President?

Guiding Question
Section 5 Does the election process serve the goals of American democracy today?

Document-Based Assessment

The Eisenhower/Nixon Agreement (1953)

In 1953, President Dwight Eisenhower and Vice President Richard Nixon signed an agreement dealing with presidential succession. Later, President John F. Kennedy and Vice President Lyndon Johnson did the same. This agreement was the forerunner of the 3rd and 4th Sections of the 25th Amendment of the Constitution.

Document at a Glance

- Agreement on presidential succession
- Eisenhower and Nixon
- Precursor to 25th Amendment

The President and the Vice President have agreed that the following procedures are in accord [agree with] with the purposes and provisions of Article 2, Section 1 of the Constitution, dealing with presidential inability. They believe that these procedures, which are intended to apply to themselves only are in no sense outside or contrary to the Constitution but are consistent with its present provisions and implement its clear intent.

(1) In the event of inability the President would—if possible—so inform the Vice President, and the Vice President would serve as Acting President exercising the powers and duties of the office until the inability had ended.

(2) In the event of an inability which would prevent the President from so communicating with the Vice President, the Vice President, after such consultation as seems to him appropriate under the circumstances, would decide upon the devolution of the powers and duties of the Office and would serve as Acting President until the inability had ended.

(3) The President, in either event, would determine when the inability had ended and at that time would resume the full exercise of the powers and duties of the Office.

Document-Based Questions

1. Who serves as President if the President is unable to serve?

2. Which sections of the 25th Amendment did this agreement produce?

3. If the President should become unable to serve, who would first inform the Vice President?

4. Who determines when the President's inability has ended?

5. **Visualize** Think about a situation in which the President became unable to serve. What words in this agreement help you visualize what would happen next?

SOURCE: http://www.amendment25.com/eisenhowernixon.html

Chapter Assessment

Directions: On a sheet of paper, write the answer to each question. Use complete sentences.

Section 1—The President's Job Description

1. What are two of the President's eight roles?

2. What are the formal qualifications for the presidency?

3. How many full terms may a President serve?

4. **Critical Thinking** Which presidential role do you think is the most important? Explain.

Section 2—Presidential Succession and the Vice Presidency

5. What are the Vice President's two formal duties?

6. What happens if the President becomes disabled?

7. **Critical Thinking** Why do you think the Vice President's duties have changed over time?

Section 3—Presidential Selection: The Framers' Plan

8. What is a presidential elector?

9. What was the Framers' original plan for the selection of the President?

10. **Critical Thinking** How did the election of 1800 change the method of selecting a President?

Section 4—The Presidential Campaign and Elections

11. What is a presidential primary?

12. What is the purpose of a national convention?

13. **Critical Thinking** As the presidential race progresses, what happens to the number of presidential candidates? Why?

Section 5—The Presidential Election

14. What determines the number of electors for each state?

15. What is one flaw of the electoral college?

16. What is a battleground state?

17. **Critical Thinking** How can a presidential candidate receive the largest number of popular votes in an election and still not win the presidency?

Apply What You've Learned

Exploring the Essential Question

With a partner, conduct research on either the Republican or Democratic primary/caucus results in your state for the most recent presidential election. Research the following:

18. How many candidates were in the race?

19. What percentage of your state's population voted in the primary/caucus? In the presidential election? Did your state's electoral college vote reflect the results of its popular vote?

Essential Questions Project

20. Based on your research, create a chart that illustrates your findings about the presidential election results in your state. The research should help you answer the Essential Question: Does the current electoral process result in the best candidates for President?

> **Essential Questions**
> **Journal**
>
> Go to your **Essential Questions Journal** to work on this chapter's Essential Question.

Test-Taking Tip

If you do not know the meaning of a word in a question, read the question to yourself, leaving out the word. Then see if you can figure out the meaning of the word from its context in the sentence.

▲ President Lyndon B. Johnson at work in the Oval Office

The Presidency in Action

Essential Question
How much power should the President have?

■ ■

Reading Strategy: Metacognition
Metacognition means being aware of the way you learn. Use metacognition to become a better reader.

- Write the main idea, details, and any questions you have.
- Make predictions and ask yourself what you already know about the presidency.
- Visualize what is happening in the text. If something does not make sense, go back and read it again.
- Summarize what you have read and make inferences about the meaning.

GOVERNMENT ONLINE
ON THE GO

To study anywhere, anytime, download these online resources at PearsonSuccessNet.com
- Political Dictionary
- Audio Review
- Downloadable Interactivities

▲ President George Washington

SECTION **1**

The Growth of Presidential Power

Guiding **Question**

What factors have contributed to the growth of presidential power? Use a concept web like the one below to keep track of the main ideas on the growth of presidential power.

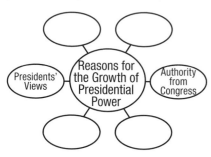

Objectives:

- Explain why Article II of the Constitution can be described as "an outline."
- Understand the reasons for the growth of presidential power.
- Explain how the Presidents' own views affected the power of the office.

The President of the United States is one of the most powerful people in the world. To make sure that the President does not become too powerful, the Framers of the Constitution limited his powers. Yet, over time, the President's power has grown. In this section, you will learn about the growth of presidential power.

What is Article II?

Article II, Section 1 of the Constitution set up the office of President. It states that "the executive power shall be vested in a President of the United States." The Constitution goes on to explain the duties and responsibilities of the President. The President is responsible for the executive branch. The President's main duty is to see that laws are carried out.

Although Article II lists most of the presidential powers, it describes them in broad, sketchy terms. For this reason, it has been used as an outline of the powers. Over the years, different meanings have been given to some of the powers. For example, civil rights issues, transportation needs, and safety concerns have changed. The President must take action to solve problems in those areas, with the approval of Congress.

✓ **Checkpoint** Why is Article II called an "outline of the powers"?

Why has presidential power grown?

Many of the current powers of the President are not written in the Constitution. As the country developed and grew, the power of the President grew. The federal government now plays a larger role in such issues as health, education, and welfare.

The President has to act quickly during times of war. As commander in chief, the President can send troops anywhere in the world if there is danger to the United States. President Harry Truman used his power to help end World War II. He made the decision to drop the atomic bomb in 1945. Throughout the nation's history, Presidents have used military force more than 200 times. Three Presidents sent troops to Vietnam, although Congress had not declared war. After the Vietnam War ended, Congress passed the War Powers Act. The War Powers Act limits the military actions a President can take. President George W. Bush sent troops to Afghanistan and Iraq with the agreement of Congress.

Sometimes the Supreme Court prevents the President from acting. In 1952, a labor problem almost shut down the country's steel mills. The war in Korea would have been affected. President Harry Truman ordered the Secretary of Commerce to continue to run the steel mills. The Supreme Court did not allow the President's order to be carried out. The Court said only Congress could make the decision to keep the mills going. In 2006, the Supreme Court did not allow President George W. Bush to set up military **tribunals** to bring captured fighters to trial. A tribunal is a court or forum of justice. He wanted to use these tribunals against people captured in the war against terrorism. The Supreme Court ruled that only Congress could create these courts.

✓**Checkpoint**   Why has presidential power grown? List two reasons.

What is the presidential view?

The President is the most powerful elected official in the country. The Constitution gave the President many powers. At certain times when the country was in trouble, Presidents wanted to take quick action. They wanted to expand presidential power. For example, when Franklin Roosevelt was elected, the country was in an economic depression. Millions of Americans were without jobs. Roosevelt quickly set up programs to help farmers and businesses. He created hundreds of new agencies that Congress quickly approved.

Other Presidents have had the opposite view. They believed the President should act only as directed by the Constitution. President William Howard Taft put these views in writing in 1916 when he wrote "the true view of the Executive function is, as I conceive it, that the President can exercise no power which cannot be fairly and reasonably traced . . . in the Federal Constitution or in an act of Congress. . . ."

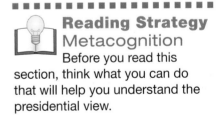

People sometimes worry that the President will make decisions in secret. Many people fear the President will make decisions illegally. In 1973, President Nixon was investigated for illegal acts he may have encouraged. He tried to keep recordings of his conversations a secret from Congress.

Government in Your Life

No Child Left Behind

Most students in the United States have been affected by the No Child Left Behind Act (NCLB). It was endorsed by the President and passed by Congress in 2002. The NCLB Act greatly expanded the educational power of the President. This law was enacted to improve the performance of schools in the United States. Requirements were set for all schools, but each state set its own testing program.

Federal funds were not given to states that had failing schools according to NCLB standards. In 2007, the President and the administration suggested changes to the law. More freedom would be given to schools that use federal money.

The NCLB Act has been criticized by educators. They claim there is too much interference by the federal government. In 2007, some members of Congress introduced legislation to change some parts of the NCLB Act.

| **Essential Questions** Journal | Go to your **Essential Questions** **Journal** to work on this chapter's Essential Question. |

SECTION 1 ASSESSMENT

Word Bank

Article II

powers

tribunal

War Powers Act

Quick Write

Pretend you are the President of the United States. Write a speech to the American people to explain three problems the nation faces and some ways to solve them. Include an introduction, body, and conclusion. Share your speech with the class.

1. **Guiding Question** Use your completed concept web to answer this question: What factors have contributed to the growth of presidential power?

Key Terms and Comprehension

On a sheet of paper, use the words from the Word Bank to complete each sentence correctly.

2. Section 1 of _____ set up the office of the President.

3. Many of the current _____ of the President are not written in the Constitution.

4. The _____ limits the military action of the President.

5. A(n) _____ is a court or forum of justice.

Critical Thinking

6. **Draw Conclusions** Why do you think some people are worried that the President has become too powerful?

7. **Compare Point of View** Do you agree with Franklin Roosevelt or William Howard Taft on presidential power? Why?

ISSUES OF OUR TIME

Expanding Presidential Powers

▶▶ Track the Issue

Article II of the Constitution provides only an outline of the duties and powers of the presidency. Most Presidents have tried to extend their powers in order to do their job more effectively.

1787 The U.S. Constitution calls for a strong national government with an independent President.

1930 President Franklin D. Roosevelt expands the executive branch to fight the Great Depression.

1950 President Eisenhower claims to have special rights to keep conversations private from the courts and Congress.

1970 The Nixon administration tries to ignore and mislead Congress.

2006 President George W. Bush claims the power as commander in chief to do whatever is necessary to defend the United States.

President George W. Bush speaks with Secretary of Homeland Security Michael Chertoff.

▶▶ Perspectives

Following the 9/11 terrorist attacks, President George W. Bush privately ordered the National Security Agency (NSA) to secretly record communications. He wanted them to record conversations without a warrant between American citizens and suspected terrorists. Current law bans the NSA from spying within the United States unless the President first gets a warrant. The President defended his actions as necessary to protect people from harm.

Defending the President	Against the President
"What we're trying to do is learn of communications, back and forth, from within the United States to overseas with members of Al Qaeda. . . . We also believe the President has the inherent authority under the Constitution, as Commander-in-Chief, to engage in this kind of activity. . . . The operators out at NSA tell me that we don't have the speed and the agility that we need, in all circumstances, to deal with this new kind of enemy." *—Attorney General Alberto Gonzales*	"The Government appears to argue here that . . . [the President] has been granted the inherent power to violate not only the laws of the Congress but the First and Fourth Amendments of the Constitution, itself. . . . the Office of the Chief Executive has itself been created, with its powers, by the Constitution. There are . . . no powers not created by the Constitution. So all 'inherent powers' must derive from that Constitution." *—Judge Anna Diggs Taylor*

Connect to Your World

1. How did President Bush expand the power of the presidency?
2. Describe the Attorney General's comments. Describe the judge's comments. Which person do you agree with? Why?

GOVERNMENT ONLINE
In the News
For updates on the expansion of presidential powers, visit **PearsonSuccessNet.com**

▲ President-Elect Ronald Reagan takes the oath of office.

SECTION 2
The Executive Powers

Guiding Question

What are the executive powers and how were they established?
Use a flowchart like the one below to keep track of the supporting details of the President's executive powers.

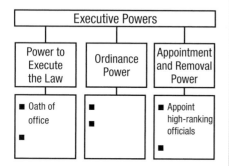

Executive Powers

Power to Execute the Law	Ordinance Power	Appointment and Removal Power
■ Oath of office ■	■ ■	■ Appoint high-ranking officials ■

Objectives:

- Examine how the President executes the law.
- Understand the ordinance power.
- Explain how the appointment power works and the debate over the removal power.
- Understand the power of executive privilege.

The President has many roles and responsibilities. One of the chief executive's responsibilities is to execute the law. Executing the law gives the President a lot of power. In this section, you will learn about the President's executive powers.

How does the President execute the law?

The President carries out the laws. This is only one of his duties. When the President is elected, the U.S. Chief Justice swears the President into office. In this **oath of office,** the President swears to "faithfully execute the office of President . . . ." The Constitution in Article II, Section 3 states, "He shall take care that all the laws be faithfully executed." This power includes all federal laws. Even if the President does not agree with a law, the President must still make sure all laws are followed.

Sometimes the President and the executive department need to interpret the details of a law. For example, Congress passes tax laws and the executive department may have to decide to whom the tax applies and the amount of the tax. During wartime the President may have to set up programs because of the needs of the military. President Roosevelt began a program of gasoline rationing during World War II. In 2002, the Homeland Security Act was passed. The President was called on to make decisions about border and transportation security, especially at airports.

The executive branch is made up of many departments, bureaus, boards, and other agencies. There are over two million men and women who work in the executive branch. The President is in charge of these groups.

What is the ordinance power?

The President has the power to make an **executive order.** An executive order is an order the President gives based on the authority of the Constitution or that given by Congress. This power is known as the **ordinance power.** The President also has the power to allow other members of the executive department to issue orders. Over the years, Congress has given more power to the executive department to carry out the many programs needed to run the country.

What is the appointment power?

The Constitution states that the President "shall **appoint** Ambassadors, other public Ministers and Consuls, Judges of the Supreme Court, and all other Officers . . ."

The President appoints most of the top-ranking officers of the federal government. This means the President names or chooses a person for an office, but not by election. The Senate must approve these appointments. Sometimes the officers are accused of "parroting" (copying) the President's views to get appointed (Figure 14.1). Among these officials are ambassadors, Cabinet members, the heads of the independent agencies, federal judges, U.S. marshals, and attorneys. For more on the presidential nomination process, see Figure 14.2 on page 348.

There is an unwritten rule that applies to federal officers who serve within a state. If the senators from that state are members of the President's party and approve the President's choice, then the Senate usually confirms the appointment. This is a custom that has been followed for years. Only some officials are appointed. Civil service tests are used to select more than half of all federal civilian workers. The Office of Personnel Management hires these workers.

✔**Checkpoint** Whom does the President appoint?

What is the removal power?

The President has the power to remove any official he has appointed, except for federal judges. The first Congress debated this issue before granting the power. Some members wanted the President to get approval of Congress before removing an official. Other members of Congress said the President should have the power to remove anyone appointed.

Reading Strategy
Metacognition
Remember to ask yourself questions as you read. This will help you make sure that you understand the President's executive powers.

Oath of office
Oath taken by the President on the day he takes office

Executive order
An order the President gives based on the authority of the Constitution or that given by Congress

Ordinance power
Power of the President to issue executive orders

Appoint
To name or choose a person for an office, but not by election

Fig. 14.1

▲ Analyzing Political Cartoons
Although the President's first choice may be rejected, a nominee with the type of qualities the President desires usually gets Senate approval. *How does this cartoon make this point?*

Congress has tried to stop the President from removing officials. In 1867, Congress passed the Tenure of Office Act. This act held that a person holding office by presidential appointment could not be removed until the Senate confirmed someone to take his or her place. President Andrew Johnson vetoed the bill, but his veto was overridden. Ignoring the law, Johnson removed several top officers. This led to an impeachment trial, but Johnson was acquitted. The law was finally repealed in 1887.

The power to remove officials and the other powers of the President are shown in Figure 14.3 on the next page.

GOVERNMENT ONLINE
Interactive
For an interactive version of actual confirmation hearings, visit **PearsonSuccessNet.com**

Fig. 14.2 How Government Works

Who Gets the Job?

Some high-level positions, such as Supreme Court justice, require Senate approval. The multistep process can be long and drawn out. *Why is this multistep process necessary?*

The President Nominates a Candidate

- The White House staff conducts a search for the candidate.
- Experts provide the White House with information.
- The President selects a nominee and submits the choice to the Senate.

The Senate Committee Examines the Candidate

- The nominee talks in front of the Senate committee.
- The Senate committee takes a vote. A majority is needed to recommend the nominee to the full Senate.

The Senate Debates the Candidate

- The full Senate debates the nomination.
- Senators debate the nominee's qualifications.
- If the Senate really does not like the candidate, the President may withdraw the nomination.
- A floor vote is taken.

The Nominee Is Confirmed or Rejected

- If a majority of the Senate approves the nominee, the nominee is confirmed.
- If the Senate does not approve, the process of choosing a candidate starts again.

In 1926, the President's removal power was tested again. President Woodrow Wilson removed Frank Meyers, a postmaster. Meyers sued for the salary for the rest of his term based on a law passed in 1876. The Court said the law was unconstitutional and President Wilson had a right to remove Meyers.

✔ **Checkpoint** Does the President still have removal power?

What is executive privilege?

At times the executive department and the President need to keep information private. President Eisenhower and his advisors referred to this as "executive privilege." During a Senate investigation of communism, questions were asked about the loyalty of members of the executive department. Eisenhower, using his executive power, refused to release information to the committee.

Vice President Dick Cheney kept information secret during meetings about energy policy. He wanted advice of experts in the energy field. The Sierra Club sued to have information from the meetings released. The Supreme Court accepted Cheney's executive privilege. It said the information did not have to be made public.

✔ **Checkpoint** What is executive privilege?

Fig. 14.3

The Powers of the President
Executive Powers

- Execute the law
- Direct the administration
- Appoint key officials
- Remove officials

Essential Questions Journal Go to your **Essential Questions Journal** to work on this chapter's Essential Question.

SECTION 2 ASSESSMENT

1. **Guiding Question** Use your completed flowchart to answer this question: What are the executive powers and how were they established?

Key Terms and Comprehension

On a sheet of paper, write the letter of the choice that correctly answers each question.

2. What kind of order is given by the President based on the authority of the Constitution or that given by Congress?

   A. executive order
   B. oath of office
   C. office act
   D. appointment

3. What can be used if a President wants to keep information private?

   A. appointment
   B. executive order
   C. executive privilege
   D. impeachment trial

4. How does a President pick high-ranking federal officials?

   A. impeachment
   B. appointment
   C. confirmation
   D. votes in

5. If the Senate does not approve a President's nominee, what happens next?

   A. process starts over
   B. Senate debates more
   C. nominee goes back to committee
   D. nominee is approved with executive privilege

Critical Thinking

6. **Draw Conclusions** Why are the appointments made by the President so important to the success of the President's time in office?

7. **Predict Consequences** Do you think a President should be able to keep information secret during a national crisis or war? Why?

What Are the Limits of Executive Privilege?

Many chief executives think that the Constitution gives the President the power to keep information private. They even think that the President can keep information from Congress or the federal courts. This authority is known as "executive privilege." Executive privilege was first recognized in the historic case *United States* v. *Nixon*, in 1974. That same year, Nixon resigned from the office of President. This was the first time in United States history that a President left the position.

What could possibly have happened to force Nixon to resign? It all started when five burglars broke into the Watergate apartments in 1972. The apartments were a part of the Democratic National Committee headquarters. The burglars were members of President Nixon's Republican reelection campaign. Over the next two years, the Nixon administration denied any involvement in the Watergate break-in. However, an investigation into the break-in began. In the end, criminal charges were brought against several of the President's top advisors. They were accused of trying to get in the way of justice.

During the investigation, a White House staff member talked about a secret the President was keeping. Nixon had taped most of his telephone calls and conversations in the Oval Office. When Mr. Nixon was ordered to release the tapes, he refused. He said that executive privilege gave him the right to keep the tapes private.

Burglars break into the Watergate complex, June 1972.

President Nixon denies any knowledge of the break-in, April 1973.

Executive privilege is not part of the details of the Constitution. The idea, however, was founded on the principle of separation of powers.

The case was taken to the Supreme Court. The justices decided that Nixon did not have a right to hold on to the tapes. The Court agreed that the secrecy between the President and his close advisors is important, but should be limited. If the President had total executive privilege, the executive branch would be unchecked. President Nixon resigned shortly after the tapes were released.

Arguments for Nixon

- Under the principle of separation of powers, no court has the power to question executive privilege.

- The President must have the power to keep various communications secret.

- Forcing the President to release communications could threaten the nation's security.

Arguments for the Supreme Court

- Separation of powers does not mean that the three branches of government are totally independent of one another.

- The privacy of the President's communications is important. However, it should be limited to military and diplomatic matters.

Thinking Critically

1. Should the executive branch have the right to keep all discussions with advisors private? Why or why not?

2. **Constitutional Principles** How does this case relate to the principle of separation of powers?

President Nixon refuses to turn over the White House audio tapes, July 1973.

Nixon announces he will resign from the office of the presidency, August 1974.

▲ President Jimmy Carter meeting with Chinese leader Deng Xiaoping in 1981.

SECTION 3
Diplomatic and Military Powers

Guiding Question

What tools are available to the President to implement foreign policy? Use a concept web like the one below to keep track of the main ideas and supporting details on foreign policy tools.

Objectives:

- Explain how treaties are made and approved.
- Explain why and how executive agreements are made.
- Understand the power of recognition.
- Understand the powers that the President has in the role of commander in chief.

The President has diplomatic and military power. As the diplomatic leader, the President works with other nations to maintain peace and trade. As the military leader, the President works to make sure the United States is safe. In this section, you will learn about these two powers. For a quick summary of these two powers, see Figure 14.4 on the next page.

What is the power to make treaties?

The President of the United States is the country's chief **diplomat.** The President deals with heads of foreign governments and helps prepare **treaties.** A treaty is a formal agreement between two or more countries. The President attends summit meetings with heads of other governments and suggests peace agreements. Summit meetings with leaders of the G8, or Group of Eight major industrial nations, have become a regular event.

When preparing a treaty, the President usually works with the secretary of state. Treaties are made with other countries and involve issues such as regulating trade or maintaining peace.

The Senate must approve treaties by a two-thirds majority. The President ratifies the treaties with the country involved. The terms of a treaty cannot go against the Constitution. The Supreme Court has never declared a treaty unconstitutional.

What is the power to make executive agreements?

An **executive agreement** is a pact between the President and the head of a foreign country. These pacts do not require the approval of Congress. Some of the agreements follow after a treaty is made.

Although agreements do not have to be approved by Congress, they are legally binding. When a new President takes office, the executive agreements expire and need to be agreed upon by the new President.

What is the power of recognition?

The power of **recognition** means the President will accept the legal existence of another country. When the leader or representative of another country visits the United States, the President greets him or her. By this action of recognition the President shows that the United States accepts the country as a nation in the world community. This does not mean the President approves all of the actions of the country. If a serious problem arises with a foreign country, the President may ask for their ambassador to be removed from our country. In this instance, the ambassador is called *persona non grata,* an unwelcome person. The President may also recall an American ambassador from a foreign country. This act would show that the United States disapproves of the actions of that country. Often this is the first step to a war.

✔**Checkpoint** What does it mean when the President recognizes another country?

What are the President's duties as commander in chief?

The President is **commander** in chief of the armed forces. The President does not lead forces into battle but can send military forces anywhere in the world. The President is always in close contact with the country's military leaders.

The President must report to Congress in writing within 48 hours after sending troops to a foreign country. The troops can only remain for 60 days, unless Congress approves a longer time. If Congress does not approve, the troops must return.

In 2002, Congress agreed with President George W. Bush that the United States military should take steps to eliminate the threat posed by Saddam Hussein in Iraq. By 2003, Saddam Hussein and his government were removed from power. American troops stayed in Iraq to keep order.

✔**Checkpoint** How might a President exercise the role of commander in chief?

Reading Strategy
Metacognition
Before you read this paragraph, make a prediction about the power of recognition. Check your prediction as you continue reading.

Diplomat
A person whose work is to manage relations between nations

Treaty
A formal agreement between two or more countries

Executive agreement
A pact between the President and the head of a foreign country

Recognition
To accept the legal existence of another country

Persona non grata
An unwelcome person

Commander
A person who has full control of a group

Fig. 14.4

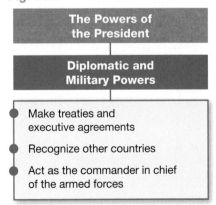

The Powers of the President

Diplomatic and Military Powers

- Make treaties and executive agreements
- Recognize other countries
- Act as the commander in chief of the armed forces

Biography

Franklin Delano Roosevelt: 1882–1945

Born in Hyde Park, New York, Roosevelt attended Harvard University and Columbia Law School. He married Anna Eleanor Roosevelt in 1905. Roosevelt was elected to the New York Senate in 1910. President Wilson appointed him Assistant Secretary of the Navy, and he was a nominee for Vice President in 1920.

At age 39, Roosevelt developed polio, a disease that causes muscles to shrink and deform. In 1928 he became governor of New York. Then, in 1932, Roosevelt was elected President of the United States, the first of four terms. At this time, the United States and many other countries were in a deep economic depression. Millions of Americans were without jobs. Roosevelt set up programs to bring recovery to business and farming and to create many new jobs. He greatly expanded the power of the presidency by taking strong actions to help the American people during hard times.

Roosevelt tried to keep the United States out of World War II, but he did send aid to Great Britain. The United States entered the war when Japan attacked Pearl Harbor in Hawaii on December 7, 1941. During the war, Roosevelt planned the creation of the United Nations, an organization to help keep international peace in the future.

SECTION 3 ASSESSMENT

Essential Questions Journal Go to your **Essential Questions Journal** to work on this chapter's Essential Question.

1. **Guiding Question** Use your completed concept web to answer this question: What tools are available to the President to implement foreign policy?

Key Terms and Comprehension
On a sheet of paper, write the answer to each question. Use complete sentences.

2. What is a **diplomat?**

3. How does the Senate approve a **treaty?**

4. What is the power of **recognition?**

5. What is the difference between an **executive agreement** and a treaty?

Critical Thinking

6. **Draw Conclusions** Why might the President ask for an ambassador to be removed?

7. **Analyze Information** Which presidential power (diplomat or commander in chief) do you think is more important? Explain your answer.

▲ President George W. Bush gives the State of the Union address.

SECTION 4

Legislative and Judicial Powers

Guiding Question

How can the President check the actions of the legislative and judicial branches? Use a flowchart like the one below to keep track of the checks the President has on the other branches.

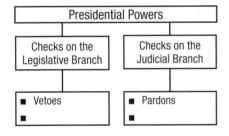

Presidential Powers	
Checks on the Legislative Branch	Checks on the Judicial Branch
■ Vetoes ■	■ Pardons ■

Objectives:
- Understand the President's two major legislative powers.
- Examine the President's judicial powers.

In addition to diplomatic and military powers, the President also has legislative and judicial powers. These powers are given to the President as written in the Constitution. This authority makes it possible to check the actions of Congress and the federal courts. In this section you will learn about the President's legislative and judicial powers. For a quick summary of these powers, see **Figure 14.6** on page 357.

What are the legislative powers?

The President is the nation's chief legislator. All bills passed by Congress must be sent to the President to be signed or vetoed. The President can also suggest laws to Congress.

The Constitution directs the President to "give to the Congress Information of the State of the Union, and recommend to their Consideration such Measures as he shall judge necessary . . ." Once each year, the President makes a speech to Congress. This is called a State of the Union address. In this message, the President tells Congress and the nation about the condition of the country. Soon after the State of the Union address, the President prepares a budget. The President then presents it to Congress for approval. This is followed by the annual Economic Report.

The veto power, which gives the President the power to reject a new bill, is written in the Constitution. Congress must present every order and resolution to the President, according to the Constitution. If the President vetoes a bill passed by Congress, it can still become law. It goes back to Congress, and if the bill is passed by a two-thirds majority vote in each house, it becomes law. In the past, Congress has had trouble getting a two-thirds majority after a presidential veto.

■■■■■■■■■■■■■■
Reading Strategy
Metacognition
Before you read this page,
think about what you can do that
will help you understand the text.

■■■■■■■■■■■■■■

Pocket veto
An indirect veto of a bill by the
President not acting on it

Signing statements
Statements used to point out
problems in a new law

Line-item veto
A President's cancellation of
specific dollar amounts (line items)
from a congressional spending bill

If the President does not sign or veto a bill, the bill will become law in 10 working days. If the President does nothing and Congress adjourns before the 10-day period, the bill does not become law. This is called a **pocket veto.** This veto has been used often because Congress passes many bills in the last days of a session. For more on the power of the veto, see Figure 14.5.

When the President signs a bill into law, the President may still write additional information about the bill. The information might include criticisms of the new law or how he plans to enforce the law. These written issues are called **signing statements.** Andrew Jackson issued signing statements in the 1830s. In recent times, President George W. Bush used these statements in place of a veto. In the statements, he said how he thought the law should be applied and used.

In 1996 Congress passed The Line Item Veto Act, but the Supreme Court struck it down. A **line-item veto** means the President can cancel some parts of a new law. Most Presidents are in favor of being allowed to do this as part of the veto process. People who favor line-item vetoes say it would cut down on federal spending. Some people say line-item vetoes would give too much power to the executive branch. According to the Supreme Court decision, an amendment to the Constitution would have to be passed to allow a line-item veto.

Fig. 14.5

The Power of the Veto

The veto power is used when the President opposes a piece of legislation. When the President and the majority of Congress belong to the same party, opposition is rare. However, under a divided government, a struggle over legislation is more likely. ***Does the veto give the President too much power?***

GOVERNMENT ONLINE
Online Update
Check out the history of
presidential vetoes at
PearsonSuccessNet.com

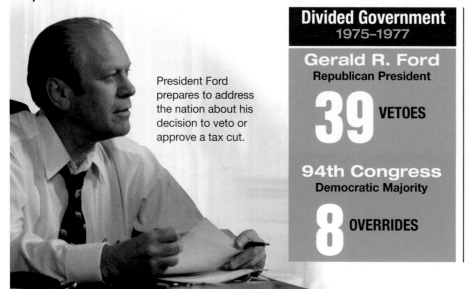

President Ford
prepares to address
the nation about his
decision to veto or
approve a tax cut.

Divided Government 1975–1977	United Government 2005–2007
Gerald R. Ford Republican President	**George W. Bush** Republican President
39 VETOES	**1** VETO
94th Congress Democratic Majority	**109th Congress** Republican Majority
8 OVERRIDES	**0** OVERRIDES

Other legislative powers of the President include the power to call Congress into special session. This was done after World War II to discuss economic actions. The President can also adjourn Congress whenever the two houses cannot agree on a date. This has never happened.

What are the President's judicial powers?

The President gets judicial powers from the Constitution. The Constitution states that the President can "grant Reprieves and Pardons for Offenses against the United States, except in Cases of Impeachment." A **reprieve** is the delay in carrying out a sentence. A **pardon** is the legal forgiveness of a crime. These are powers of **clemency.** Clemency is mercy granted to an offender. The President may pardon a federal offender before the person is tried or charged. There has been some debate about the accused person accepting pardons. Some feel it is an admission of guilt. The Supreme Court finally ruled a pardon must be accepted for it to be effective. The President also has **amnesty** power. Amnesty is a pardon that affects many people. In 1977, President Jimmy Carter granted amnesty to Vietnam War draft evaders.

✔**Checkpoint** What are the judicial powers of the President? List three.

Reprieve
Delay in carrying out

Pardon
Legal forgiveness of a crime

Clemency
Mercy granted to an offender

Amnesty
A pardon that affects many people

Fig. 14.6

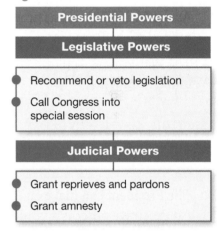

Presidential Powers
Legislative Powers

- Recommend or veto legislation
- Call Congress into special session

Judicial Powers

- Grant reprieves and pardons
- Grant amnesty

Essential Questions Journal Go to your **Essential Questions Journal** to work on this chapter's Essential Question.

SECTION 4 ASSESSMENT

Word Bank

amnesty

clemency

pardon

pocket veto

1. **Guiding Question** Use your completed flowchart to answer this question: How can the President check the actions of the legislative and judicial branches?

Key Terms and Comprehension

On a sheet of paper, use the words from the Word Bank to complete each sentence correctly.

2. A pardon that affects many people is called _____.

3. A(n) _____ is a legal forgiveness of a crime.

4. _____ is mercy given to an offender.

5. If the President does not act on a bill and it does not become a law, it is called a(n) _____.

Critical Thinking

6. **Summarize** Why might the President use a pocket veto?

7. **Predict Consequences** Would you accept a pardon from a President if you knew you were not guilty of the crime? Why or why not?

Chapter Summary

Section 1—The Growth of Presidential Power

- Section 1 of Article II in the Constitution lists the "outline" of the powers of the President.

- As the United States has grown, so have the powers of the President.

- The War Powers Act limits the military power of the President.

Section 2—The Executive Powers

- The President makes sure that all federal laws are executed.

- The President can make an executive order. An executive order is an order given by the President based on the authority of the Constitution or Congress.

- The President appoints most of the top-ranking officers of the federal government.

- The President has the power to remove any official he has appointed, except for federal judges.

- Executive privilege may be used when the President needs to keep information private.

Section 3—Diplomatic and Military Powers

- The President makes treaties with other nations. The Senate must approve the treaties by a two-thirds majority.

- The power of recognition means the President can accept the legal existence of another country.

- The President is commander in chief of the armed forces.

Section 4—Legislative and Judicial Powers

- All bills Congress passes must be sent to the President for approval or veto.

- The President can give pardons and reprieves, commute sentences, and give amnesty.

Guiding Question
Section 2 What are the executive powers and how were they established?

Guiding Question
Section 3 What tools are available to the President to implement foreign policy?

Guiding Question
Section 1 What factors have contributed to the growth of presidential power?

Guiding Question
Section 4 How can the President check the actions of the legislative and judicial branches?

CHAPTER 14

Essential Question
How much power should the President have?

Document-Based Assessment

John F. Kennedy's Inaugural Address

On January 20, 1961, John Fitzgerald Kennedy became the 35th President of the United States.

As President, Kennedy wanted to gather support for his plans for the country, especially in foreign affairs. The following passages are from his Inaugural Address.

Document at a Glance
- Kennedy's first speech as President
- Promoted liberty and citizenship

We observe today not a victory of party, but a celebration of freedom—symbolizing an end, as well as a beginning—signifying renewal as well as change . . .

Let the word go forth from this time and place, to friend and foe alike, that the torch has been passed to a new generation of Americans—born in this century, tempered by war, disciplined by a hard and bitter peace, proud of our ancient heritage—and unwilling to witness or permit the slow undoing of those human rights to which this nation has always been committed, and to which we are committed today at home and around the world.

Let every nation know, whether it wishes us well or ill, that we shall pay any price, bear any burden, meet any hardship, support any friend, oppose any foe, in order to assure the survival and success of liberty. This much we pledge—and more . . .

Finally, to those nations who would make themselves our adversary [enemy], we offer not a pledge but a request: that both sides begin anew the quest for peace . . .

And so, my fellow Americans: ask not what your country can do for you—ask what you can do for your country.

My fellow citizens of the world: ask not what America will do for you, but what together we can do for the freedom of man.

Finally, whether you are citizens of America or citizens of the world, ask of us here the same high standards of strength and sacrifice which we ask of you. With a good conscience our only sure reward, with history the final judge of our deeds, let us go forth to lead the land we love . . .

Document-Based Questions

1. What did President Kennedy mean when he said that "the torch has been passed to a new generation"?

2. What did Kennedy pledge Americans would do on behalf of liberty?

3. What did the President offer to enemies?

4. What did Kennedy ask Americans and world citizens to ask themselves?

5. **Use Metacognition** What other questions do you have about this speech? Brainstorm ideas with the class.

SOURCE: President John F. Kennedy's Inaugural Address, 1961

Chapter Assessment

Directions: On a sheet of paper, write the answer to each
question. Use complete sentences.

Section 1—The Growth of Presidential Power

1. As the nation's chief executive, what is the President's
main duty?

2. What is the War Powers Act?

3. What was William Taft's opinion of presidential view?

4. Critical Thinking Why might the Framers have created
Article II only as "an outline" of presidential power?
Explain your answer.

Section 2—The Executive Powers

5. When the President is elected, what does the U.S. Chief
Justice do?

6. About how many people work in the executive branch of the
U.S. government?

7. What was the Tenure of Office Act? When was it repealed?

8. If the Senate rejects a presidential nomination, what
happens next?

9. Critical Thinking Do you think the President should be able
to appoint top-ranking officials without Senate approval? Why
or why not?

Section 3—Diplomatic and Military Powers

10. What are two kinds of agreements the President can make
with other countries?

11. What presidential action is often the first step to a war?

12. How long can troops remain in a country without the approval
of Congress?

13. Critical Thinking Why might the Senate not approve of a
treaty between a President and another country? List at
least two possibilities.

Section 4—Legislative and Judicial Powers

14. What are the President's two major legislative powers?

15. Why is the pocket veto the most often used type of veto?

16. What is a reprieve?

17. Critical Thinking Do you think the President should have amnesty power? Why or why not?

Apply What You've Learned

Exploring the Essential Question

18. Should the President have so much control over the appointment of high-ranking officials? Why or why not?

19. Does the President have too much power as commander in chief? Why or why not?

Essential Question Project

20. Use the content of this chapter to answer the Essential Question: **How much power should the President have?** Write a paragraph describing the powers. Share your paragraph with the class. After you listen to your classmates' paragraphs, think about your opinion again. If you find your opinion has changed, rewrite your paragraph.

Essential Questions
Journal

Go to your **Essential Questions Journal** to work on this chapter's Essential Question.

Test-Taking Tip

For open-book tests, write short summaries of every chapter or section.

▲ More than half of all income tax returns are filed electronically. Still, the IRS must deal with millions of pages of paperwork.

Government at Work: The Bureaucracy

Essential Question
Does the federal bureaucracy result in good government?

▪ ▪

Reading Strategy: Summarizing
When you summarize, you focus on the big ideas. One way to summarize is to ask questions about what you are reading. This is also a way to review content. As you read about the federal bureaucracy in this chapter, ask yourself these questions:

- What is the main point of each section?
- What details are most important about the federal bureaucracy?
- What departments and agencies are discussed?

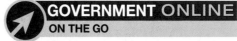

GOVERNMENT ONLINE
ON THE GO

To study anywhere, anytime, download these online resources at PearsonSuccessNet.com
- **Political Dictionary**
- **Audio Review**
- **Downloadable Interactivities**

▲ A Customs and Border Protection officer screens a passenger entering the United States.

SECTION 1

The Federal Bureaucracy

Guiding Question

What is the structure and purpose of the federal bureaucracy? Use a flowchart like the one below to keep track of the main ideas of the federal bureaucracy.

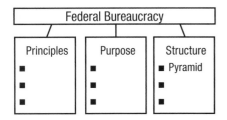

Federal Bureaucracy

Principles	Purpose	Structure
■	■	■ Pyramid
■	■	■
■	■	■

Objectives:

- Define a bureaucracy.
- Identify the major elements of the federal bureaucracy.
- Explain how groups within the federal bureaucracy are named.
- Describe the difference between a staff agency and a line agency.

The federal government is the largest organization in the country. Federal employees deliver the mail, collect taxes, defend the nation, and provide hundreds of other services. In fact, you usually cannot go a single day without coming in contact with the federal government in some way.

What is a bureaucracy?

A **bureaucracy** is a large, complex structure that handles the everyday business of an organization. Bureaucracies have three main features: structure, job specialization, and formal rules.

A bureaucracy is organized like a pyramid with several levels. Each level reports to the level above it. This structure is often referred to as a hierarchy. Officials or units at the top have control over the units in the middle. Officials at the middle levels direct those at the bottom. Each person working in the bureaucracy is called a **bureaucrat.** Each worker has specific duties.

A bureaucracy is an effective way to get work done for several reasons. First, the hierarchical structure helps speed action by reducing conflicts over who has power. The higher a person's rank in the organization, the greater the decision-making power he or she has. Two other features of the bureaucracy help it to run efficiently: job specialization and formalized rules. Job specialization means that each person in the organization is required to focus on one particular job. Therefore, the worker gains a set of specialized skills and knowledge. Formalized rules mean that decisions are based on a set of known standards, not on someone's likes and dislikes. These rules help everyone in the organization understand what is expected.

What are the major elements of the federal bureaucracy?

The federal bureaucracy is made up of all the agencies through which the government operates. Almost all of the federal bureaucracy is found in the executive branch. The executive branch is made up of three broad groups of agencies. (See Figure 15.1 on page 366.) They are the Executive Office of the President, the 15 Cabinet departments, and a large number of independent agencies. Congress and the federal court system are examples of bureaucracies not in the executive branch.

At the top of the pyramid is the President. The President has the highest position in the country. The President is responsible for seeing that all parts of the executive branch operate as they should. At the next level is the Executive Office of the President. The individuals and agencies in this office directly assist the President. Below the Executive Office are the executive departments. Their department heads and the attorney general make up the President's Cabinet. The bottom part of the pyramid, or base, is made up of many agencies. This level is the largest part of the federal government.

✓ **Checkpoint** What are the three broad groups of agencies that make up the executive branch?

What are the names given to the executive branch units?

The name *department* is reserved for agencies that make up the Cabinet. Many other titles are used for the other units in the executive branch. These include *agency, administration, commission, corporation,* and *authority.* Agencies that regulate business are usually called commissions, such as the Federal Trade Commission. Agencies that carry on business may be called corporations or authorities, such as the Tennessee Valley Authority. *Bureau* is the name given to a section of a department. For example, under the Department of Justice is the Federal Bureau of Investigation.

Many federal agencies are known by their initials or a nickname. Some examples are the FBI, IRS, FCC, and CIA. The Government National Mortgage association is called Ginnie Mae. Amtrak is the nickname for the National Railroad Passenger Corporation.

■ ■ ■ ■ ■ ■ ■ ■ ■ ■ ■ ■ ■ ■ ■ ■ ■

Bureaucracy
A large, complex structure that handles the everyday business of an organization

Bureaucrat
A person who works for a bureaucratic organization

■ ■ ■ ■ ■ ■ ■ ■ ■ ■ ■ ■ ■ ■ ■ ■ ■

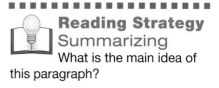

Reading Strategy
Summarizing
What is the main idea of this paragraph?

Fig. 15.1 **How Government Works**

The Executive Branch

The executive branch is comprised of a large number of agencies created by Congress to carry out the laws of the country. ***Why do you think the executive branch makes up the majority of the federal bureaucracy?***

GOVERNMENT ONLINE

Update

Check out these agencies of the executive branch at **PearsonSuccessNet.com**

EXECUTIVE OFFICE
of the President

The Executive Office of the President contains agencies staffed by the President's closest advisors and assistants.

- White House Office
- Office of the Vice President
- Council of Economic Advisors
- Council on Environmental Quality
- National Security Council
- Office of Administration
- Office of Management and Budget
- Office of National Drug Control Policy
- Office of Policy Development
- Office of Science and Technology Policy
- Office of the United States Trade Representative

EXECUTIVE
Departments

Often called the Cabinet departments, the executive departments and their subunits carry out much of the work of the federal government.

- Department of State
- Department of the Treasury
- Department of Defense
- Department of Justice
- Department of the Interior
- Department of Agriculture
- Department of Commerce
- Department of Labor
- Department of Health and Human Services
- Department of Housing and Urban Development
- Department of Transportation
- Department of Energy
- Department of Education
- Department of Veterans Affairs
- Department of Homeland Security

INDEPENDENT
Agencies*

Independent agencies are responsible for the wide variety of tasks necessary to carry out government business as well as serve the public.

- Amtrak
- Central Intelligence Agency
- Consumer Product Safety Commission
- Environmental Protection Agency
- Farm Credit Administration
- Federal Communications Commission
- Federal Deposit Insurance Corporation
- Federal Election Commission
- Federal Reserve System
- Federal Trade Commission
- National Aeronautics and Space Administration
- National Endowment for the Arts
- National Labor Relations Board
- National Science Foundation
- National Transportation Safety Board
- Nuclear Regulatory Commission
- Office of Government Ethics
- Office of Personnel Management
- Peace Corps
- Securities and Exchange Commission
- Small Business Administration
- Social Security Administration
- Tennessee Valley Authority
- United States Postal Service

*The agencies listed are just a sampling of the independent agencies.

What are staff and line agencies?

The agencies that make up the administration are called either **staff agencies** or **line agencies.** Staff agencies give support. For example, the agencies that make up the Executive Office of the President are staff agencies. Each exists to support the President. Line agencies are given goals to meet, and actually carry out public policy. For example, the Environmental Protection Agency (EPA) is a line agency. It is responsible for seeing that the antipollution laws are followed. Staff agencies help line agencies meet their goals by advising, budgeting, planning, and managing. See Figure 15.2 below.

Staff agency
An agency that supports the chief executive and other administrators

Line agency
An agency that performs tasks to meet its goals

Reading Strategy
Summarizing
What were some of the important details that helped you understand this section?

Fig. 15.2

Staff Agencies
- Serve in support capacity
- Offer advice and management assistance

- Form the federal administrative organizations
- Work together to meet goals

Line Agencies
- Perform specific tasks
- Meet goals set by Congress and the President
- Administer public policy

Essential Questions Journal — Go to your **Essential Questions Journal** to work on this chapter's Essential Question.

SECTION 1 ASSESSMENT

Word Bank

bureaucrat

department

line agency

staff agency

1. **Guiding Question** Use your completed flowchart to answer this question: What is the structure and purpose of the federal bureaucracy?

Key Terms and Comprehension

On a sheet of paper, use the words from the Word Bank to complete each sentence correctly.

2. A _____ gives support to the administration.

3. A _____ makes sure that goals are met in the administration.

4. Each person working in a bureaucracy is called a_____.

5. The name _____ is used for agencies that make up the Cabinet.

Critical Thinking

6. **Summarize** Why are many different governmental departments and organizations needed?

7. **Analyze Information** Is the federal bureaucracy too large? Explain.

▲ President Bush works on his State of the Union address with speechwriter Michael Gerson.

SECTION 2

Executive Office of the President

Guiding Question

What agencies and advisors are part of the Executive Office of the President, and what are their functions? Use a table like the one below to keep track of the units and functions within the Executive Office of the President.

Executive Office of the President	
Agency	Function
■ NSC	■ Advises about security
■	■
■	■

Objectives:

- Describe the Executive Office of the President.
- Explain the duties of the White House Office, the National Security Council, and the Office of Management and Budget.
- Identify additional agencies in the Executive Office of the President.

Thomas Jefferson had two workers to help him with his presidential duties. One was a messenger and one was a secretary. In all, only 2,100 people worked in the executive branch under President Jefferson. Today, there are 2.7 million men and women in the administration.

What is the Executive Office of the President?

The **Executive Office of the President** (EOP) is the group of agencies that work most closely with the President. These agencies are made up of many advisors and aides. These individuals help the President carry out the duties of the presidency. They manage his day-to-day work. Most of the people in the executive office work in the White House or in nearby buildings. The Executive Office of the President now is staffed by 900 of the President's closest advisors and assistants. President Franklin D. Roosevelt persuaded Congress to set up the EOP in 1939.

Who works in the White House Office?

The people who are closest to the President work in the White House Office. This is part of the EOP. Its workers often are longtime supporters of the President. The White House Office includes key officials, such as the press secretary. The press secretary supplies White House news to the press. Another assistant helps write the President's speeches. The President also has a personal doctor.

The President's chief of staff has the most influence and leads the White House Office. The White House advisors give the President legal advice about policy decisions. Other assistants and deputy assistants keep the President informed about such subjects as foreign policy, the economy, Congress, and the public. Most of these people work in the West Wing of the White House. See Figure 15.3.

Fig. 15.3

The West Wing

The White House is a large structure that includes two office buildings and the President's home. The East and West wings extend from the residence and host key presidential aides and advisors. The President's closest advisors are located in the West Wing, only steps away from the Oval Office. *Why is it important that these advisors be so close to the President's office?*

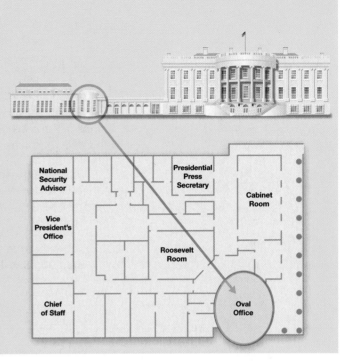

What is the National Security Council?

The National Security Council (NSC) advises the President about security, or the safety, of the country. The NSC is concerned with military and foreign policy. It often meets on short notice to deal with situations as they arise. The President, Vice President, and secretaries of state and defense are all on the National Security Council. The Director of National Intelligence, the President's chief advisor on national security, attends meetings of the NSC. The NSC is a staff agency. This means its job is only to advise the President, not to carry out any policies.

✔ **Checkpoint** Who is on the National Security Council?

Executive Office of the President
An organization of several agencies staffed by the President's closest advisors

What is the Office of Management and Budget?

The Office of Management and Budget (OMB) is in charge of preparing the federal budget. This budget is prepared yearly and lists all the income (money) that is expected and the ways it will be spent by the government. When the budget is ready, the President presents it to Congress. The OMB also studies how the executive branch is run. It makes suggestions to the President for improvements and changes.

Fig. 15.4 **How Government Works**

Federal Budget

How is the President's budget created?

The Office of Management and Budget must consider a variety of factors before it creates the President's final budget proposal. *Based on the information below, what challenge does the OMB face when creating the budget?*

What can the government spend?
Taxes are the government's main source of income. This revenue may be affected by the economy. The OMB estimates how much will be received in taxes, then reduces that estimate by how much is paid out to mandatory programs and the federal debt.

What do Americans want?
Citizens expect the government to provide continued public services. The OMB must decide how to distribute the remaining funds without harming any agency's ability to function. Budgets of underperforming programs may be reduced or cut completely.

What does the President want?
Some programs have a higher priority than others because they are important to the President. The OMB must take this into account and may modify the budget to ensure that these priorities are met.

The federal budget is very detailed. Each federal agency submits an estimate of the money it will need that year. The OMB holds hearings to decide how much money to give to each federal agency. The OMB also watches over the spending of federal money after Congress authorizes that spending. In addition, the OMB helps write executive orders and the President's veto messages. See Figure 15.4.

✓**Checkpoint** What is the main role of the OMB?

Reading Strategy
Summarizing
What office was talked about in this section?

What are some of the other offices in the EOP?

The Office of National Drug Control Policy was set up in 1989. It prepares an annual plan to help with the country's war on drugs. The goals of this plan are to reduce illegal drug use and crime. The director of this office also helps the other federal agencies involved in drug control.

The Council of Economic Advisors gives the President information and advice about the nation's economy. The President uses this information to prepare the annual Economic Report to Congress.

The Office of Policy Development advises the President on **domestic affairs.** Domestic affairs are all matters not directly connected to foreign affairs.

The Council on Environmental Quality seeks to maintain clean water and air, and fosters careful use of natural resources. It sees to it that federal agencies comply with the nation's environmental laws.

The Office of the Vice President is made up of more than 50 employees who help the Vice President with the duties of the office. Over the years, the duties of the Vice President have grown, and so has the size of this office.

The Office of United States Trade Representative advises the President on everything related to foreign trade. The agency has more than 200 people who are experts on trade issues. They travel to all regions of the world for the President to arrange trade agreements and settle problems. The head of this office is an ambassador and may represent the President at foreign trade meetings.

Domestic affairs
All matters not directly connected to foreign affairs

Reading Strategy
Summarizing
What are some important details that help you understand these paragraphs?

Biography

Two Former Peace Corps Volunteers

Lillian Gordy Carter, mother of former President James Carter, was 68 when she volunteered for the Peace Corps. Her great-grandson Jason Carter also volunteered for the Peace Corps 32 years later.

Lillian Gordy Carter was born in 1889. As a nurse, she cared for many poor neighbors in Plains, Georgia, without pay. Later, Lillian joined the Peace Corps and served in India for two years. She worked as a nurse in Godrej Colony, about 30 miles from Bombay. Here she saw extremes of poverty and disease. Communication was difficult because she did not know the language. She was often cold and her diet was poor. Lillian Carter died of cancer in 1983.

After graduating from Duke University, **Jason Carter** joined the Peace Corps in 1998. He served two years in the South African village of Lochiel near the border of Swaziland. His assignment was to help teachers with more difficult subjects. He spoke the Zulu language, which helped him be accepted by the villagers. The village had no running water or electricity. After returning to the United States, Jason Carter entered the University of Georgia Law School.

Fig. 15.5

Executive Office of the President

- White House Office comprised of the President's key personal and political staff

- National Security Council advises on matters relating to national security.

- OMB prepares the federal budget and assists in executive branch management.

- Other units provide advice on issues ranging from the economy to domestic affairs.

The Office of Science and Technology Policy advises the President on the development of scientific and technological policies. This office also works with private groups to improve the environment, national security, and education in the field of science and engineering.

The Office of Administration provides clerks, data processors, librarians, financial managers, drivers, messengers, and other support people. These people assist the other units of the Executive Office of the President.

For a summary of EOP offices, see Figure 15.5.

✓ **Checkpoint** How does the Office of National Drug Control Policy help with the country's war on drugs?

SECTION 2 ASSESSMENT

Essential Questions Journal Go to your **Essential Questions Journal** to work on this chapter's Essential Question.

1. **Guiding Question** Use your completed table to answer this question: What agencies and advisors are part of the Executive Office of the President, and what are their functions?

Key Terms and Comprehension

Choose the letter of the best answer or write the answer using complete sentences.

2. Which office is staffed by 900 of the President's advisors and assistants?
   A. Office of Science and Technology
   B. Executive Office of the President
   C. Office of Policy Development
   D. Office of Management and Budget

3. Which office provides support staff to assist the EOP?

4. What is the function of the National Security Council?

5. What is the role of the Office of Policy Development?

Critical Thinking

6. **Summarize** How does the White House Office help the President fulfill the role of chief administrator?

7. **Demonstrate Reasoned Judgment** Do you think there are too many agencies within the EOP? Explain.

SECTION 3

The Cabinet Departments

▲ Secretary of Agriculture Charles Kuperus (left) meets with a farmer in New Jersey.

Guiding Question

What is the Cabinet and what does it do? Use a concept web like the one below to keep track of the supporting details about the Cabinet.

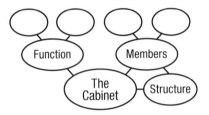

Function

Members

The Cabinet

Structure

Objectives:

- Describe the origin and work of the executive departments.
- Explain how the members of the Cabinet are chosen.
- Identify the role of the Cabinet in the President's decisions.

Reading Strategy Summarizing What are some important details that help you understand this section?

The executive branch has grown over time to meet the changing needs of the country. In this section, you will learn about one part of the executive branch: the Cabinet or executive departments.

What are the executive departments?

There are 15 **executive departments** that carry out much of the work of the federal government. (See Figures 15.6 and 15.7.) Two thirds of the federal government's **civilian** workforce is employed by the executive departments. A **secretary,** aided by a deputy secretary, leads each department, except the Department of Justice. The **Attorney General** leads this department.

The executive departments are made up of smaller units called bureaus, offices, services, or divisions. These units carry out the day-to-day work of the department. These offices are not all in Washington, D.C. They are found throughout the country wherever they are needed to serve the people. The Department of Agriculture, for example, has offices in every state to help farmers and consumers. The Food and Nutrition Service provides food stamps and maintains the school lunch program. These programs make food available to those in need.

The departments vary in size. The Department of Defense is the largest. It has more than 700,000 civilian workers and more than 1.4 million men and women in uniform. The Department of Homeland Security is the newest. It was created in 2002.

✔**Checkpoint** What is the job of the executive departments?

Fig. 15.6 How Government Works

The Executive Departments

The executive departments were actually established over time. The responsibilities of each reflect the conditions of the period and the issues that the nation faced when each department was created by Congress. *What new departments might be created in the 21st century?*

Federalist Era

While the new republic develops its system of government, it quickly establishes the four key departments necessary to govern a nation.

State 1789
- Advises the President on foreign policy
- Negotiates agreements with foreign countries
- Represents the United States abroad and in international organizations

Defense 1789
- Provides military forces to deter war and protect the nation's security

Justice 1789*
- Prosecutes those accused of violating federal law
- Provides legal advice to the President
- Represents the United States in court
- Enforces federal laws
- Operates federal prisons

Treasury 1789
- Produces coins and bills
- Borrows money and manages public debt
- Enforces alcohol, tobacco, and firearms laws
- Collects taxes

* Called the Office of the Attorney General until 1870

Expansion Era

As the United States expands to the West, two new departments are established to manage these lands and their use.

Interior 1849
- Manages public lands, wildlife refuges, and national parks
- Operates hydroelectric power plants
- Helps Native Americans manage their affairs

Agriculture 1889
- Assists farmers and ranchers
- Administers food stamp and school lunch programs
- Inspects food and ensures quality standards
- Manages national forests

Industrial Era

Congress creates two executive departments to address issues arising from industrialization and a growing economy.

Commerce 1903*
- Promotes international trade, economic growth, and technological development
- Grants patents and registers trademarks
- Conducts census

Labor 1913
- Enforces federal laws on minimum wages, maximum hours, and safe working conditions
- Operates job training programs
- Administers unemployment insurance and workers' compensation programs

* Called the Department of Commerce and Labor until 1913, when the Department of Labor was created

---

Executive departments
Often called the Cabinet departments, they are traditional units of federal administration

Civilian
A person not on active duty in a military, police, or firefighting force

Secretary
An official in charge of a department of government

Attorney General
The head of the Department of Justice

What is the Cabinet?

The President has a group of advisors called the Cabinet. The Cabinet is not mentioned in the Constitution. It came about to fill a need and has grown over time. Cabinet members meet with the President as a group to make top-level decisions.

The Cabinet is made up of the heads of the 15 executive departments. These department heads, or secretaries, are appointed by the President. However, the Senate must approve each secretary. Since 1789, the Senate has only rejected 12 choices of Presidents.

How are Cabinet members chosen?

A member of the President's Cabinet must have knowledge and experience. The Secretary of Agriculture, for example, may be a farmer or have a background in farming. The Secretary of the Treasury should have experience in the world of finance.

Postwar Era

Following World War II, the Cabinet expands to match the federal government's larger role in the economy and public services. The Cabinet also address technological challenges.

Health and Human Services 1953
- Funds healthcare research programs
- Conducts programs to prevent and control disease
- Enforces pure food and drug laws
- Administers Medicare and Medicaid

Housing and Urban Development 1965
- Operates home-financing and public housing programs
- Enforces fair housing laws

Transportation 1967
- Administers programs to promote or regulate highways, mass transit, railroads, waterways, air travel, and oil and gas pipelines
- Works with state and local levels on land, energy, resource, and technology programs

Energy 1977
- Promotes production of renewable energy, fossil fuels, and nuclear energy
- Transmits and sells hydroelectric power
- Conducts nuclear weapons research and production

Education 1979
- Administers federal aid to schools
- Ensures equal access to education
- Conducts educational research

Veterans Affairs 1989
- Administers benefits, pensions, and medical programs for veterans of the armed forces
- Oversees military cemeteries

21st Century

The 9/11 attacks bring a new focus on national security, and the newest executive department is established.

Homeland Security 2002
- Ensures border and transportation security
- Develops emergency preparedness and response programs
- Safeguards national infrastructure and information systems

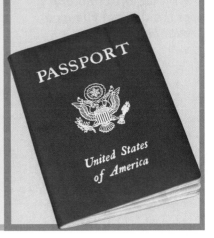

Most of the members of the Cabinet come from the President's party. The President selects members from all across the country. For example, the Secretary of Agriculture usually comes from the Midwest. Interest groups also influence the President's choices.

The President considers abilities, experience, race, and gender in selecting the heads of departments. In the past, Presidents did not consider race, ethnicity, or gender in making selections. It was not until 1933 that Frances T. Perkins became the first female Cabinet member. She was the Secretary of Labor. Robert C. Weaver was the first African American appointed to the Cabinet. He was selected by Lyndon Johnson in 1966. Both George W. Bush and Bill Clinton appointed several women and people of different cultural backgrounds to the Cabinet.

Fig. 15.7

Executive Departments
- Traditional units of the federal administration
- Built around broad field of authority
- Headed by a department secretary, serving as link between presidential policy and the department
- Structured geographically and much work done through regional offices

✔ **Checkpoint** What does the President consider when choosing a department head?

▲ President George W. Bush's first Cabinet (above) was very different from that of President George Washington in 1790 (right). **Why has the structure of the Cabinet changed over time?**

What is the role of the Cabinet?

The members of the Cabinet have two main responsibilities. Each member is the leader of an executive department. Each member is also an advisor to the President. In the past, the Cabinet was the main source of advice for the President, although the President can choose whether or not to follow that advice. With the growth of the Executive Office of the President, the importance of the Cabinet has decreased. The EOP has many advisors who help the President. Presidents still call Cabinet meetings today. Often these meetings seek support for policies rather than asking for help in forming these policies.

SECTION 3 ASSESSMENT

Essential Questions Journal Go to your **Essential Questions Journal** to work on this chapter's Essential Question.

1. **Guiding Question** Use your completed concept web to answer this question: What is the Cabinet and what does it do?

Key Terms and Comprehension
On a sheet of paper, write the answer to each question. Use complete sentences.

2. Which part of the executive branch has evolved over time to meet the changing needs of the country?

3. What is the President's group of advisors called?

4. Who must approve the President's Cabinet appointments?

5. What is the leader of the Department of Justice called?

Critical Thinking

6. **Make Comparisons** Compare the Cabinet of today with the Cabinet under President Washington. How are they the same? How are they different?

7. **Analyze Information** Why do you think it is important that the President rather than Congress select the Cabinet?

▲ A U.S. Post Office employee sorts through the day's mail.

SECTION 4

Independent Agencies

Guiding Question

What are the roles and structures of the independent agencies? Use a table like the one below to keep track of the types of independent agencies.

Federal Independent Agencies		
Executive	Regulatory	Corporation
▪	▪ Ensures economic stability	▪
▪	▪	▪
▪	▪	▪

Objectives:

- Explain why Congress has created independent agencies.
- Identify the characteristics of independent executive agencies.
- Describe the history and formation of NASA, the OPM, and Selective Service.
- Explain the structure and function of the independent regulatory commissions.
- Describe the structure of government corporations.

In the 1880s, Congress began to create **independent agencies.** These agencies handle many specific concerns of the government including exploring outer space, protecting the environment, and maintaining peaceful relations with other countries. Today, there are more than 100 independent agencies. In this section you will learn about the independent agencies and how they function.

Why are there independent agencies?

Independent agencies work outside the Cabinet departments. Many of them were set up because they did not fit within the Cabinet departments. Others were formed to provide services for government agencies. For example, the General Services Administration (GSA) takes care of the construction and operation of public buildings. The GSA also provides supplies and equipment to agencies. Some agencies are independent to protect them from the influence of political parties and interest groups. Other independent agencies came about as the need arose or to take care of sensitive and high-security matters. The independent agencies are divided into three groups: (1) independent executive agencies, (2) independent regulatory commissions, and (3) government corporations.

What are independent executive agencies?

Independent executive agencies handle specific concerns of the government. One person heads each independent agency. Some agencies have many employees and are run like large businesses. Other agencies have only a few employees and small budgets. Some agencies provide services to the public and do not have power to enforce rules or regulations.

Independent agencies
Agencies created by Congress located outside of the Cabinet departments

Civil service
Civilian employees whose hiring and pay are regulated by Congress

Patronage system
The practice of giving jobs to supporters and friends

Spoils system
The practice of giving jobs to supporters and friends

Reading Strategy
Summarizing
What important functions has NASA performed during its existence?

What are NASA and OPM?

Congress established the National Aeronautics and Space Administration (NASA) in 1958 to help develop peaceful uses for the exploration of outer space. NASA has put satellites and astronauts into space and made it possible to walk on the moon. This agency researched the creation of Spacelab. Scientists used Spacelab for experiments as it traveled high above the earth. NASA's space shuttle program has allowed people to go into space several times in the same vehicle. The shuttle missions are used to explore outer space, to repair damaged satellites, and to perform experiments for industry and medicine. NASA has also led efforts to build a permanent space station with Canada, Japan, Russia, and many European countries.

The Office of Personnel Management is a government agency that hires, promotes, and pays the employees of all the government agencies. Nearly three million people work for the federal government. These civilians hold all types of jobs needed to run the agencies. There are secretaries, computer programmers, lawyers, engineers, truck drivers, FBI agents, and many more. Most of these workers are part of the **civil service.** The civil service is the group of career government employees whose hiring and pay are regulated by Congress. See Figure 15.8.

✔**Checkpoint** What role does NASA perform?

What is the history of the civil service?

In the early years of the country, government jobs were given to friends of the government leaders. This is known as the **patronage system.** It is also called the **spoils system.** This system led to corruption in government. In 1881, a person who did not get a government position assassinated President Garfield. The new President, Chester Arthur, convinced Congress to pass the Pendelton Act. The new act made the quality of a person's work the basis for hiring and awarding promotions.

The Pendelton Act set up two categories of employment. The two categories are classified and unclassified. All of the classified jobs are based on merit determined by examinations given by the Civil Service Commission (now the OPM). At first, only about 10 percent of the federal government's jobs were classified. By 1909, President Theodore Roosevelt had extended the coverage to two thirds. Today, nearly 90 percent of government workers are classified.

✔**Checkpoint** What is the patronage system?

Fig. 15.8
Careers in the Civil Service

The civil service has a great variety of career opportunities in a range of diverse fields. **What is the main purpose of the civil service system?**

The chief veterinarian of the National Zoo treats a baby panda. ▶

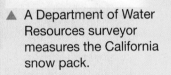
▲ A Department of Water Resources surveyor measures the California snow pack.

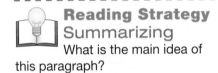
▲ A diver from the National Oceanic and Atmospheric Administration marks a marine sanctuary.

What is the civil service like today?

The civil service system was created to recruit the best possible employees to work for the federal government. Today most of these employees are hired through the merit system set up by the civil service. Another agency, the Merit Systems Protection Board, was created to enforce the merit system. It is made up of members of both political parties appointed by the President and Senate. This board reviews problems reported to it by federal workers. These problems often involve firings, salaries, or promotions.

✔ **Checkpoint** Why was the civil service created?

Reading Strategy
Summarizing
What is the main idea of this paragraph?

Draft
Choosing individuals from a group; required military service

What is the Selective Service System?

The military in the United States has usually depended on volunteers. However, from 1940 to 1973, the **draft** was used. A draft is a way of choosing individuals from a group. In this instance, the draft was for selecting young men for required military service. Before 1940, the draft was used in a limited way during the Civil War. In 1917, almost half of the men who served in World War I were drafted under the terms of the Selective Service Act.

World War II, before the United States was involved, brought the nation's first peacetime draft. The Selective Training and Service Act of 1940 was passed. More than 10 million Americans entered military service under this law. The draft ended after the war but was quickly brought back in 1948. It lasted until 1973.

Fig. 15.9 **How Government Works**

GOVERNMENT ONLINE
Update
Check out the regulatory
commissions at
PearsonSuccessNet.com

Regulatory Commissions

The focus of the independent regulatory commissions is to ensure the stability of the nation's economy. Eleven federal agencies have been established to set and enforce standards on financial markets, employment, business practices, and public safety. *Should the government regulate these industries?*

Protecting
Financial Security

Federal Reserve System (The FED) est. 1913 Formulates and administers the nation's credit and monetary policy by regulating the money supply, influencing the availability of credit, and supervising banking system practices.

The Fed regulates the amount of money in circulation.

Securities and Exchange Commission (SEC) 1934 Regulates securities and other financial markets, investment companies, and brokers to ensure fair and honest transactions.

Commodity Futures Trading Commission 1974 Protects investors from fraud and improper practices related to the sale of commodity futures. Its regulations encourage sound markets and competition as well as ensure market integrity.

Disagreements in the workplace are remedied by the NLRB.

Equality in the workplace is enforced by the EEOC.

Ensuring
Workplace Equality

National Labor Relations Board (NLRB) 1935 Administers federal laws on labor-management and is responsible for the prevention or remedy of unfair labor practices by employers and unions.

Equal Employment Opportunity Commission (EEOC) 1964 Enforces laws prohibiting discrimination based on race, color, religion, sex, national origin, disability, or age in employment.

Securing
Business Integrity

Federal Trade Commission (FTC) 1914 Ensures consumer welfare and protects competition by regulating pricing, preventing monopolies and false advertising, stopping fraud, and protecting consumers from unfair business practices.

Federal Communication Commission (FCC) 1934 Regulates interstate and foreign communications by radio, television, wire, satellite, and cable while ensuring reasonable rates.

Federal Maritime Commission 1936 Regulates the foreign and domestic ocean-borne commerce by monitoring shipping companies, tariffs, and services to ensure compliance and fairness.

Federal Energy Regulatory Commission 1977 Regulates the transport and sale of electricity, natural gas, and oil by pipeline, licenses hydroelectric power projects, and oversees environmental issues related to energy resources.

Guarding
Public Safety

The NRC regulates the means used to store nuclear waste.

Consumer Product Safety Commission 1972 Regulates consumer products in order to protect the public from risks of injury from those products by requiring corrective action to items already on the market, establishing labeling standards, and advising the public of product recalls.

Nuclear Regulatory Commission (NRC) 1974 Licenses, regulates the use of nuclear energy to protect public health, safety, and the environment; sets rules and standards for nuclear reactors, facilities, and waste materials.

During the years that the draft law was used, it required all males between the ages of 18 and 26 to register for military service. The local selective service boards picked the people who would serve. In 1980, President Jimmy Carter issued an executive order to start the draft registration again. It required men to register soon after their eighteenth birthday.

What are the independent regulatory commissions?

Eleven agencies are **independent regulatory commissions.** They make rules for activities that are important to the country's economy. They are mostly beyond the President's control. A board or commission of five to seven members leads each agency. The President appoints the members, and the Senate must approve them. These agencies have executive, legislative, and judicial powers. All of the regulatory commissions are explained in Figure 15.9 on page 380.

What are the government corporations?

Government corporations are under the control of the executive branch. Unlike the other agencies, they were set up by Congress to carry out business activities. The first one created was the Bank of the United States in 1791. Government corporations are said to have more flexibility than the typical government agency.

During World War I and the Depression, Congress created more corporations to carry out emergency programs. The Federal Deposit Insurance Corporation insures bank deposits. The Export-Import Bank of the United States makes loans to help in the sale of American goods. Both of these corporations still exist today.

■■■■■■■■■■■■■■■■■■■
Independent regulatory commissions
Independent agencies created by Congress to regulate important aspects of the nation's economy

■■■■■■■■■■■■■■■■■■■
Reading Strategy
Summarizing
In your own words, summarize the history of government corporations.

Government in Your Life

The Civil Service Program

Early in American history, government jobs were given to people from the President's party. Sometimes these people did not have the skills for the job. This practice changed in 1883 when Congress passed the Civil Service Act. This law, which is still in effect, sets rules for how the government hires its workers. Citizens take a civil service exam to see if they have the skills for a government job. If they pass the exam, their name goes on a list.

According to the law, an agency can only hire from this list.

Most federal workers are hired through the Civil Service System. These workers are called classified employees because they are hired on the basis of ability. Another group of workers are unclassified employees. They are usually appointed to their jobs. For example, members of the President's Cabinet are unclassified employees.

Fig. 15.10

▲ Analyzing Political Cartoons **What does this cartoon imply about bureaucracy? Do you agree? Why or why not?**

There are now more than 50 government corporations. Some of these are well-known. Two of the best known are the U.S. Postal Service and the National Railroad Passenger Corporation.

Most government corporations operate like private corporations. They have a board of directors, and the income earned goes back into the business. The difference is that Congress decides on the purpose of the government corporations, and the President selects most of the top officers.

✓ **Checkpoint** Why were government corporations set up by Congress?

Essential Questions Journal Go to your **Essential Questions Journal** to work on this chapter's Essential Question.

SECTION 4 ASSESSMENT

Quick Write

Choose an independent agency to research. Write a paragraph explaining why you think the agency is doing a good job or a bad job. Back up your opinions with facts.

1. **Guiding Question** Use your completed table to answer this question: What are the roles and structures of the independent agencies?

Key Terms and Comprehension

On a sheet of paper, write the answer to each question. Use complete sentences.

2. Why did Congress create independent agencies?

3. What function does the Office of Personnel Management perform?

4. What role does a regulatory commission carry out?

5. How are government businesses like private businesses?

Critical Thinking

6. **Compare Points of View** During times of need, is the draft a good way to pick people for the military? Why or why not?

7. **Draw Conclusions** Why might special interest groups become involved in the function of independent agencies?

ISSUES OF OUR TIME

The Size of Government

▶▶ Track the Issue

The Constitution makes no provisions for federal involvement in education. Over the last few decades, however, the federal government has taken an increasingly larger role in funding and supervising local schools.

1787 Thomas Jefferson argues that a democratic state must educate its citizens in order to survive.

1865 Congress establishes the Freedmen's Bureau that builds over 1,000 schools for newly freed African Americans.

1958 In response to the Soviet Union's successful launch of the Sputnik satellite, the National Defense Education Act funds math and science education in local public schools.

1979 Congress creates the Department of Education to oversee federal funding of educational programs.

2002 The No Child Left Behind Act gives the federal government unprecedented influence over local schools.

President George W. Bush promotes his education reforms.

▶▶ Perspectives

The question of federal involvement in local schools is closely related to the larger question of the size and purpose of the federal government. People who favor a smaller government often point to agencies like the Department of Education as a sign of unnecessary "big government" policies. Others believe that the federal government has an important role to play in improving the quality of education for all Americans.

Against the Department of Education	For the Department of Education
"Our goal is nothing less than a renaissance in American education, begun by returning its control to parents, teachers, [and] local school boards. . . . The federal government has no constitutional authority to be involved in school curricula. . . . That is why we will abolish the Department of Education [and] end federal meddling in our schools. . . . We further urge that federal attempts to impose outcome- or performance-based education on local schools be ended." —*1996 Republican Party platform*	"The quality of our public schools directly affects us all. . . . Yet too many children in America are segregated by low expectations, illiteracy, and self-doubt. . . . The federal government is partly at fault for tolerating these abysmal results. The federal government currently does not do enough to reward success and sanction failure in our education system. [These reforms] address a general vision for . . . linking federal dollars to specific performance goals to ensure improved results." —*President George W. Bush on the No Child Left Behind Act*

Connect to Your World

1. In 1996, what role did the Republican Party suggest the federal government should play in education?
2. Why did President Bush want government more involved in education?

GOVERNMENT ONLINE
In the News
For updates about education and the federal government visit **PearsonSuccessNet.com**

Chapter Summary

Section 1—The Federal Bureaucracy

- A bureaucracy is a large, complex structure that handles the everyday business of an organization.

- The federal bureaucracy is made up of all the agencies through which the government operates.

- A staff agency supports; a line agency carries out public policy.

Section 2—The Executive Office of the President

- The EOP is an organization of several agencies staffed by the President's closest advisors.

- The White House staff is made up of advisors and assistants to the President.

- The National Security Council advises the President about the safety of the country.

- The Office of Management and Budget is in charge of preparing the federal budget.

- There are many agencies in the EOP. Each agency provides important help to the President.

Section 3—The Cabinet Departments

- The executive branch has been built up over time.

- There are 15 executive departments. They do much of the work of the federal government.

- The President appoints the heads of the departments, who make up the Cabinet. The Senate approves the selections.

- The President calls Cabinet meetings to seek support for policies.

Section 4—Independent Agencies

- Independent agencies were set up by Congress to handle specific concerns of the government.

- NASA and the OPM are two examples of independent agencies.

- Independent regulatory commissions make rules for activities that are important to the country's economy. They are beyond the President's control.

- Government corporations were set up by Congress to carry out business activities.

Guiding Question
Section 2 What agencies and advisors are part of the Executive Office of the President, and what are their functions?

Guiding Question
Section 3 What is the Cabinet and what does it do?

Guiding Question
Section 1 What is the structure and purpose of the federal bureaucracy?

Guiding Question
Section 4 What are the roles and structures of the independent agencies?

CHAPTER 15

Essential Question
Does the federal bureaucracy result in good government?

Document-Based Assessment

The National Science Foundation

The National Science Foundation (NSF) educates and trains scientists and engineers, advances research engineering, and provides the tools to accomplish both. Below is more information about the NSF.

Document at a Glance
- Independent Agency
- Promotes Science
- Advances Technology

The National Science Foundation (NSF) is an independent agency of the U.S. government, established by the National Science Foundation Act of 1950. . . .

The Act established the NSF's mission:
To promote the progress of science; to advance the national health, prosperity, and welfare; and to secure the national defense.

The Foundation's legislation authorizes it to engage in the following activities:
Initiate and support, through grants and contracts, scientific and engineering research and programs to strengthen scientific and engineering research potential, and education programs at all levels, and

appraise or determine the impact of research upon industrial development and the general welfare. . . .

Foster or encourage the interchange of scientific information among scientists and engineers in the United States and foreign countries.

Foster and support the development and use of computers and other scientific methods and technologies, primarily for research and education in the sciences. . . .

Initiate and support specific scientific and engineering activities in connection with matters relating to international cooperation, national security, and the effects of scientific and technological applications upon society. . . .

Document-Based Questions

1. What act established the NSF?

2. Who is on the National Science Board?

3. What are three activities the NSF authorizes?

4. What does the NSF foster among scientists and engineers?

5. Summarize What is the mission of the NSF?

SOURCE: www.nsf.gov/home/about/creation.htm

Chapter Assessment

Directions: On a sheet of paper, write the answer to each question. Use complete sentences.

Section 1—The Federal Bureaucracy

1. What is a bureaucracy?

2. What is the President's role in the federal bureaucracy?

3. Why are different names used for agencies that make up the executive branch?

4. **Critical Thinking** Do you think the organization of the government makes it more effective or less effective? Why?

Section 2—The Executive Office of the President

5. What is the function of the Executive Office of the President?

6. Why might the Executive Office sometimes be called the President's "right arm"?

7. What are domestic affairs?

8. Why has the Office of the Vice President grown over the years?

9. **Critical Thinking** Which activity of the Executive Office has the most impact on the lives of Americans? Why?

Section 3—The Cabinet Departments

10. What is a civilian?

11. What is the process for selecting the heads of the Cabinet departments?

12. What are the two responsibilities of the Cabinet?

13. **Critical Thinking** Why might the Senate reject a President's Cabinet choice?

Section 4—Independent Agencies

14. What is a draft?

15. What is the purpose of the civil service?

16. What are three types of independent agencies?

17. Critical Thinking How do regulatory commissions differ from agencies that provide services to the public?

Apply What You've Learned

Exploring the Essential Question

18. What is the purpose of the federal bureaucracy?

19. Why does the government create new agencies over time?

Essential Question Project

20. Use the content of this chapter to answer the Essential Question: **Does the federal bureaucracy result in good government?** Write a paragraph to explain your opinion. Use your answers to the questions above to help guide your writing. Share your paragraph with classmates. After you listen to your classmates' paragraphs, think about your opinion again. If you find your opinion has changed, revise your paragraph.

Essential Questions
Journal

Go to your **Essential Questions Journal** to work on this chapter's Essential Question.

Test-Taking Tip

If you do not know a word in a question, read the question again but leave out the word. Then see if you can figure out the meaning of the word from its use in the sentence.

▲ A U.S. Mint engraver works on a plaster image of President John Adams. The image is for the presidential coin series.

Financing Government

Essential Question
How should the federal budget reflect Americans' priorities?

Section 1: Taxes and Other Revenue

Section 2: Borrowing and the Public Debt

Section 3: Spending and the Budget

Section 4: Fiscal and Monetary Policy

Reading Strategy: Questioning
As you read about financing government, ask yourself questions. This will help you to be a more active reader. Ask yourself:

- What do I want to learn about financing government?
- What do the facts and details in this chapter tell me?
- Do any facts about money, borrowing, or spending connect with my life?

GOVERNMENT ONLINE
ON THE GO

To study anywhere, anytime, download these online resources at PearsonSuccessNet.com
- Political Dictionary
- Audio Review
- Downloadable Interactivities

SECTION 1

Taxes and Other Revenue

▲ Taxpayers work on their income tax forms.

Guiding Question

How is the federal government financed? Use a chart like the one below to keep track of the main ideas about financing government.

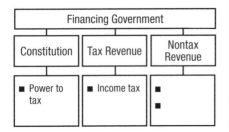

Objectives:

- Explain how the Constitution gives Congress the power to tax and places limits on that power.
- Describe the most important federal taxes collected today.
- Identify nontax sources of revenue.

If government is to work, it must have ways to raise and spend money. The **fiscal policy** of the government consists of all the ways money is acquired and then used. The nation's economy depends on good fiscal policy.

What is the taxing power of Congress?

The Constitution lists the power to tax first before all other powers given to Congress. Taxes are the main source of money for the government. Sometimes the power to tax is used to regulate or even prevent an activity that the government believes is dangerous to its citizens. For example, licensing certain activities, such as the buying and selling of firearms, is a form of taxation.

Congress can also force change by levying a tax. In 1861, for example, Congress created a national paper money system. Some banks printed bank notes that also were used as money. To stop this, Congress levied a 10 percent tax on the notes. Very soon, the private banks stopped printing their bank notes.

What are the limits on the taxing power?

As Congress uses its taxing power, it must follow the Constitution. Four limits are clearly stated in the Constitution.

1) Taxes may be levied only for public purposes, not private interests.

2) Taxes may not be placed on exports.

3) Direct taxes must be evenly collected from the states according to population. Congress has not imposed a direct tax since 1861.

4) Indirect taxes levied by the federal government must be set at the same rate in all parts of the country.

What are the current federal taxes?

The federal government collects several different types of taxes.

Income Tax. The federal government gets most of its money from the income tax. The income tax is flexible. This means its rates may be changed depending on how much money the government needs. It is also a **progressive tax.** The higher a person's income, the higher the tax paid. Both individuals and corporations pay income tax. The individual income tax produces the largest amount of revenue for the government (Figure 16.1). A tax return must be filed (sent to the government) each year. A tax return tells how much a person earned in the last calendar year. Employers must withhold a certain amount of money from the paychecks of their employees. This money is sent to the government for income taxes. When the employee files a tax return, he or she will be told if the money withheld was enough. If it was not, the person must pay the difference. If the employer withheld too much, the person will receive a refund.

Corporation Income Tax. A corporation pays taxes on its net income. Net income is the amount of money the corporation earns after paying all the costs of running the business.

Social Insurance Tax. The federal government has three major social welfare programs: Social Security, Medicare, and the unemployment compensation program. These programs are supported by **payroll taxes.** They are called payroll taxes because the amount owed by employees is withheld from their paychecks. Employees pay a certain percentage of their income to each program. Social insurance taxes are **regressive taxes.** This means they are collected at a flat rate, not according to a person's income.

Excise Tax. Another name for the **excise tax** is "luxury tax" because the goods taxed are not necessities. Food, clothing, and medicine are not subject to the excise tax. Federal excise taxes are imposed on items such as gasoline, tobacco, liquor, firearms, and more.

Estate and Gift Tax. An **estate tax** is a levy imposed on the assets (the estate) of a person who dies. Only estates worth more than 3.5 million are subject to the federal estate tax. A **gift tax** is one imposed on a gift from one living person to another. Gifts of more than $12,000 are taxed.

Fiscal policy
All the ways money is acquired and then used by the government

Progressive tax
A tax that is laid in proportion to a person's income

Payroll tax
A tax withheld from an employee's paycheck

Regressive tax
Tax that is collected at a flat rate without regard to income

Excise tax
Tax on the manufacture, sale, or use of goods and services

Estate tax
A levy imposed on the assets (the estate) of a person who dies

Gift tax
A tax on a gift from one living person to another

Fig. 16.1

"GIBBS, I SUBTRACTED YOUR FEDERAL, STATE AND SOCIAL SECURITY TAXES AND MEDICAL FROM YOUR PAYCHECK, AND YOU OWE THE FIRM $50."

▲ **Analyzing Political Cartoons** Many people complain about high taxes, but are unwilling to give up the government programs and services they pay for. *How does this cartoon illustrate this issue?*

■■■■■■■■■■■■■■■■■■■

Customs duties
Taxes levied on goods brought into the United States from other countries

Interest
A fee charged for borrowing money

■■■■■■■■■■■■■■■■■■■

Reading Strategy
Questioning
There are many types of taxes discussed in this section. Which taxes, if any, have you paid?

Customs Duties. These are taxes levied on goods brought into the United States from other countries. They are also called tariffs or duties. Congress decides which imports will be taxed. In the past, customs duties were the major source of income for the government. Today, they account for only one percent of all the money the government takes in.

What are sources of nontax revenue?

Nearly $50 billion a year is taken in by the federal government from nontax sources. A large portion is the **interest** charges of the Federal Reserve System. Interest is a charge for borrowing money. Other sources of nontax revenue are canal tolls and fees for passports, copyrights, patents, and trademarks. Sale of coins and fines collected by the courts are two other sources. The United States Postal Service also creates revenue by selling stamps to collectors.

Essential Questions Go to your **Essential Questions Journal** to work on this chapter's Essential Question.
Journal

SECTION **1** ASSESSMENT

Quick Write
There are many ways that the government is financed. Write a summary on the different taxes used to collect money. Remember to write in complete sentences.

1. **Guiding Question** Use your completed chart to answer this question: How is the federal government financed?

Key Terms and Comprehension
On a sheet of paper, write the answers to the following questions. Use complete sentences.

2. What are two limits on the taxing power of Congress?

3. What are two important features of the income tax?

4. Which social programs are supported by payroll taxes?

5. What is an example of a nontax source of revenue for the federal government?

Critical Thinking

6. **Demonstrate Reasoned Judgment** Why do you think the power to tax was one of the first powers given to Congress? Explain your answer.

7. **Identify Central Issues** Why do you think the federal government has employers withhold money from each paycheck instead of letting taxpayers pay their taxes in one payment at the end of the year?

▲ Work Projects Administration (WPA) workers build sidewalks during the Great Depression.

SECTION 2

Borrowing and the Public Debt

Guiding Question

What effect does borrowing have on the federal budget and the nation's economy? Use a concept web like the one below to keep track of the main ideas about the government's influence on the economy.

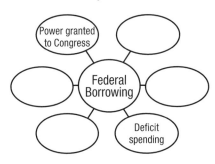

Objectives:

- Describe federal borrowing.
- Explain how the federal government's actions can affect the economy.
- Analyze the causes and effects of the public debt.

The United States government has been in operation for more than 200 years. During that time, the government has been both a borrower and a lender. In this section, you will read about how the government borrows money and how that borrowing creates the public debt.

What is federal government borrowing?

The Constitution gives Congress the power to borrow money. Congress first used that power in 1790. Since then, it has borrowed money hundreds of times. At first, the government borrowed only to fund wars or to pay for large projects. In the 1930s, the government began borrowing for another reason: deficit financing. A **deficit** occurs when the government's income is not enough to cover its spending. In the last 80 years, the government has almost always had a deficit. The government has not seen a **surplus** in most of those years. A surplus means the government takes in more money than it spends.

✔**Checkpoint** When did Congress first borrow money?

What is Keynesian economics?

During the Great Depression of the 1930s, President Franklin Roosevelt and the Democrats began a program of job creation and government spending. These ideas were based on the theories of John Maynard Keynes. Keynes was a British economist who believed that government should spend large amounts of money in times of high unemployment. He believed this would result in higher employment. Higher employment would bring in more taxes. This theory is sometimes called **demand-side economics.**

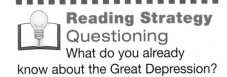

Reading Strategy
Questioning
What do you already
know about the Great Depression?

Deficit
The shortfall between money
taken in and money spent

Surplus
An amount over what is needed;
extra

Demand-side economics
Part of Keynesian economics;
belief that government should
spend more in times of high
unemployment to bring in more
jobs, and thus, more in taxes

Supply-side economics
A belief that lowering taxes will
result in a stronger economy

Public debt
All the money borrowed by the
government and not yet repaid
plus the interest owed on that
money; also called the national
debt or the federal debt

Demand-side economics still influences federal fiscal policy.
Some Presidents, however, such as Ronald Reagan and George
W. Bush did not follow Keynes's ideas. They thought lower
taxes would result in a stronger economy. This theory is
called **supply-side economics.**

✓**Checkpoint**   According to Keynes, what is the result of huge
government spending?

How does borrowing occur?

Congress must approve all borrowing by the federal government. The
Treasury Department issues securities to investors. The investors are
individuals, banks, investment companies, and other financial groups.
The securities are in the form of Treasury notes and bonds. Bonds are
used for long-term borrowing. These securities are promissory notes
that the government promises to repay. The federal government is
able to borrow money at a lower rate than private borrowers. This is
because the federal government securities are considered safe.

✓**Checkpoint**   How does the federal government borrow money?

Biography

John Maynard Keynes
(1883–1946)

John Maynard Keynes was a British economist from a
rich family. His theories are known as Keynesian economics.
He was educated at Eton and King's College, Cambridge.
Later, he lectured at Cambridge University. He served in
England on many money-related matters, including working
for the Chancellor of the Exchequer. This job is similar to the
secretary of the treasury in the United States. He wrote many
books on economics. He was a member of England's House
of Lords. Toward the end of World War II, he led a British
delegation that helped establish the Bretton Woods system.
This was a plan to restore world trade after the war.

Keynes died at his vacation home in Tilton, East Sussex, on
April 21, 1946.

What is the public debt?

The **public debt** is all the money the federal government has borrowed over the years (Figure 16.2). This money has not yet been repaid. The public debt also includes the interest charged on this borrowed money. The federal government has borrowed steadily over the years. In 2008, the government owed over $10 trillion. The amount of the public debt has climbed rapidly. For example, in 1981 the public debt was $1 trillion. The Constitution has not placed a limit on the amount of money the government can borrow. There is much worry and criticism concerning the rapid increase in the public debt. The main worry is the effect of this huge debt on America's future taxpayers. The federal government now spends one in every ten dollars to just pay the interest on the debt.

✓ **Checkpoint** How much money did the government owe in 2008?

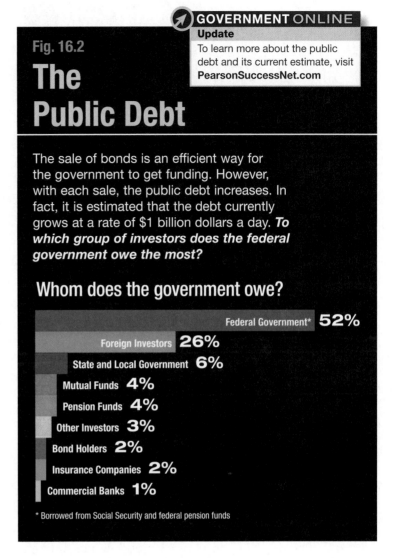

Fig. 16.2

The Public Debt

The sale of bonds is an efficient way for the government to get funding. However, with each sale, the public debt increases. In fact, it is estimated that the debt currently grows at a rate of $1 billion dollars a day. *To which group of investors does the federal government owe the most?*

Whom does the government owe?

Federal Government* **52%**
Foreign Investors **26%**
State and Local Government **6%**
Mutual Funds **4%**
Pension Funds **4%**
Other Investors **3%**
Bond Holders **2%**
Insurance Companies **2%**
Commercial Banks **1%**

* Borrowed from Social Security and federal pension funds

Essential Questions Journal   Go to your **Essential Questions Journal** to work on this chapter's Essential Question.

SECTION 2 ASSESSMENT

1. **Guiding Question** Use your completed concept web to answer this question: What effect does borrowing have on the federal budget and the nation's economy?

Key Terms and Comprehension

On a sheet of paper, write the answers to the following questions. Use complete sentences.

2. What is a deficit?

3. What is John Maynard Keynes's economic theory?

4. How does the federal government borrow money?

5. What is the public debt?

Critical Thinking

6. **Draw Conclusions** What might be the long-term consequences of deficit spending?

7. **Analyze Information** Why do you think Congress and the President borrow money rather than balance the budget?

Spending and the Budget

▲ An elderly patient receives medical care through federally funded Medicare.

How is federal spending determined? Use a concept web like the one below to keep track of how the federal budget is determined.

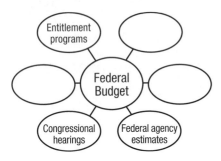

Objectives:

■ Identify the key elements of federal spending.

■ Define controllable and uncontrollable spending.

■ Explain how the President and Congress work together to create the federal budget.

Federal spending has a huge effect on the American economy. The federal government takes in and then spends billions of dollars each year. The President and Congress decide how the money is used. In this section, you will learn how the government spends all that money and how it plans for that.

How are federal funds spent?

The Department of Health and Human Services is one of the many departments of the federal government. It spends more money than any other federal agency. This money pays for Medicare, Medicaid, food stamps, veterans' benefits, and other **entitlement** programs. Entitlements are benefits that must be paid to those people who meet the requirements. People who receive these entitlements must meet certain age or income requirements. If they do, they are entitled to (have a right to) these benefits. OASDI (the Old Age, Survivors, and Disability Insurance program) is the "social security" program. It is the largest entitlement program in America today.

Defense spending also takes a large share of the budget. It has grown since the war on terrorism began. The Department of Defense is not the only department that spends money on defense. The Department of Energy does so as it conducts research and development on nuclear weapons. The Department of Homeland Security, too, spends a lot of money protecting and defending the nation.

Interest on the public debt also costs more and more money. It is the fourth largest category of federal spending.

✔ **Checkpoint** What are two examples of federal spending?

What is controllable spending and uncontrollable spending?

Much of the spending done by the federal government is **controllable spending.** Controllable spending is spending that the President and Congress can control. Controllable items in the federal budget include things like the highways, national parks, and civil service payroll.

Much of the money the government spends is **uncontrollable spending.** Uncontrollable spending means that the President and Congress cannot change the amount of money spent on a program. The funds are part of the program and increase as the needs of the program increase. For example, the public debt is uncontrollable. The government must borrow money and the interest must be paid when due. Two other examples of uncontrollable spending programs are Social Security benefits and food stamps. Congress cannot control how many people will become eligible for these programs each year. Uncontrollable spending has increased greatly in recent years.

✔**Checkpoint**   What are two examples of uncontrollable spending?

How is the federal budget made?

The President submits a federal budget to Congress each year. Congress then reviews that budget, makes changes, and arrives at a final document that controls how much and on what the government can spend money.

The budget is a long, important document. It is a very detailed financial statement. It is also a public policy statement because it shows the priorities and goals of the federal government. Creating the budget each year is a long process. First, each federal agency sends its money requests to the Office of Management and Budget (OMB). After reviewing the requests, the OMB submits a spending plan for all the government agencies. Hearings are often held to decide on funding for a certain agency. The final amounts granted to each agency by the OMB may be lower than requested. The President sends the final documents to Congress.

✔**Checkpoint**   What is the role of the OMB?

Entitlement
A benefit that federal law says must be paid to all who meet the requirements

Controllable spending
An amount determined by Congress and the President to be spent on many individual government costs

Uncontrollable spending
Spending that Congress and the President have no power to change directly

Continuing resolution
An emergency spending bill that allows agencies to continue working based on the previous year's appropriations

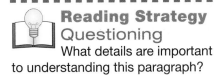

Reading Strategy
Questioning
What details are important to understanding this paragraph?

What is the budget process in Congress?

Congress does all of its work on the federal budget through committees. The President's budget is studied by the Budget Committee in each house. The Congressional Budget Office (CBO) helps these committees study the budget requests. The CBO provides both houses of Congress with basic budget information. The President's budget is also sent to the House and Senate appropriations committees. These committees look at all the requests and listen to testimony from interested citizens. The two appropriations committees then create the bills to appropriate (set aside) the funds for the agencies. These measures are reported to each house of Congress.

The two Budget Committees in Congress then set overall spending and income targets to guide the committees in Congress. They do this first in May and then again in September. This second budget resolution sets the final, binding spending limits for the federal agencies.

The President must approve the budget by October 1—the beginning of the fiscal year. (Congress usually does not make the deadline.) If Congress fails to complete the budget by October 1, it must pass an emergency spending bill. This is called a **continuing resolution.** It must be signed by the President in order for the agencies to continue to operate. Otherwise, the government would have to shut down to avoid spending any more money.

Essential Questions
Journal
Go to your **Essential Questions Journal** to work on this chapter's Essential Question.

SECTION 3 ASSESSMENT

1. **Guiding Question** Use your completed concept web to answer this question: How is federal spending determined?

Key Terms and Comprehension
On a sheet of paper, write the answers to the following questions. Use complete sentences.

2. What are entitlement programs?

3. How is controllable spending different from uncontrollable spending?

4. What is a continuing resolution?

5. Who begins the federal budget process each year? Who reviews the budget in Congress?

Critical Thinking

6. **Identify Central Issues** The federal budget is more than a financial statement. Explain why this is true.

7. **Predict Consequences** What might happen if the OMB gave each agency all the money it wanted each year? Explain.

Analyzing Television News Programs

"Welcome to the Channel Four Evening News. Tonight's top story is the cutting of interest rates again by the Fed. They are trying to address the nation's economic problems. But first, some early speculation about the Academy Awards. . . ."

Television news programs are one of the major ways Americans keep up with local, national, and world events. These news programs are a good resource for people who want to stay informed. These programs can change public opinion.

When you watch a news program, think about how the information is presented.

1. **Think about the choice of stories.** There are more news events that happen each day than a news program could cover. The producers of the programs have to choose which stories to report. By keeping track of the choice of stories, you can get a sense of the priorities of the program.

2. **Pay attention to headlines and pictures.** Television news programs often use pictures and headline graphics. This is done to shape viewer reaction. For each story, look closely at the graphics. Which words are the biggest? Are any parts added just for entertainment or shock value?

3. **Compare with news coverage on other stations.** It can be very interesting to watch multiple television news programs on the same day. The stations may handle a story differently. They might not be doing the same stories or describing them the same way.

4. **Look for signs of bias.** You will often hear people talk about "liberal bias" or "conservative bias" in television news programs. All news programs have to make choices about what stories to report and how to report them. Sometimes these choices might be informed by political opinions.

▶▶ What do you think?

1. What does it mean when one television news program spends more time on a story than another news program?

2. Other than lack of time, why might a news program leave out information from a story?

3. **You Try It** Watch one local news program and one national news program. Compare the coverage of the same day's news. Then write a summary comparing the two programs. Which program did you think had more useful information? Why?

GOVERNMENT ONLINE
Citizenship Activity Pack
For activities on analyzing television news programs, go to **PearsonSuccessNet.com**

Fiscal and Monetary Policy

▲ Federal Reserve Chairman Ben Bernanke testifies at a congressional hearing.

Guiding Question

How does the federal government achieve its economic goals? Use a table like the one below to keep track of the methods used by the government to meet its broad economic goals.

Types of Economic Policy		
Goal	Fiscal Policy	Monetary Policy
■ Full employment	■ Increase government spending	■ Increase money supply
■	■	■

Objectives:

■ Describe the overall goals of the federal government in the economy.

■ Understand fiscal policy.

■ Understand monetary policy.

Most citizens in the United States are interested in the economy and how it affects their lives. The President is in charge of managing the economy. Because of this, the success of the President's political party often depends on how well the economy is doing. In this section you will read how the federal government manages the economy and sets goals for economic growth.

What are the government's economic goals?

The American economy is very large and complicated. The goods and services that are produced in the country each year total more than $14 trillion. This amount is known as the nation's **gross domestic product** (GDP). As the federal government works to control the American economy, it tries to meet three goals:

Full employment. This means there are enough jobs for all citizens who want to work.

Stable prices. The government tries to make sure that prices do not rise too much (**inflation**) or drop too much (**deflation**).

Economic growth. A growing economy means the GDP increases at a steady rate. This means better living conditions for more Americans. When economic growth slows, a **recession** occurs.

What is fiscal policy?

The federal government's **fiscal policy** is the way it decides to use the power to tax and spend to influence the economy. Spending decisions by government affect all phases of the economy. More spending increases economic activity. Tax increases slow economic growth because people have less money to spend.

For many years, the government did not try to influence the economy. Then, during the Great Depression, the government began to involve itself in economic matters to end the misery of those years. This government involvement continues today. Fiscal policy does have limits, however. Its effects take time, and deciding when to cut taxes or increase spending is tricky.

What is monetary policy?

Monetary policy involves the money supply (how much currency is in circulation) and how much credit is available. Monetary policy is another way the federal government can affect the nation's economy. It is executed by the Federal Reserve Board (the Fed), which acts as the nation's central bank. By controlling the money supply, the Fed can boost or slow down the economy.

The Fed has three major tools when controlling the money supply. **Open market operations** are the buying and selling of government securities from and to the nation's banks. This can increase or decrease the money supply. The banks can then loan more money. The **reserve requirement** is the amount of money banks must keep on hand. This money is kept in their vaults or with one of the 12 Federal Reserve Banks in the country. The amount of the reserve requirement can be changed by the Fed. The **discount rate** is the rate of interest a bank must pay when it borrows money from a Federal Reserve Bank. Raising the discount rate means banks cannot borrow as much money. Banks then raise their interest rate to customers. If the Fed cuts the discount rate, banks can lower their interest rate to customers.

Gross domestic product
The total value of goods and services in one year

Inflation
A general increase in prices

Deflation
A general decrease in prices

Recession
A time of no economic growth and a shrinking economy

Fiscal policy
The federal government's powers to tax and spend as a way to control the economy

Monetary policy
Policy that involves the money supply and how much credit is available in the economy

Open market operations
The buying or selling of government securities (such as bonds) by the Fed from banks

Reserve requirement
Amount of money that a bank must keep on hand

Discount rate
Rate of interest a bank must pay when it borrows money from a Federal Reserve Bank

Essential Questions Journal Go to your **Essential Questions Journal** to work on this chapter's Essential Question.

SECTION 4 ASSESSMENT

1. **Guiding Question** Use your completed table to answer this question: How does the federal government achieve its economic goals?

Key Terms and Comprehension
On a sheet of paper, write the answers to the following questions. Use complete sentences.

2. What is the gross domestic product?

3. What is the difference between inflation and deflation?

4. What are two ways that the Fed can change the money supply in the country?

5. What is a discount rate?

Critical Thinking

6. **Identify Central Issues** What are the three economic goals the government tries to achieve? Why are these goals important?

7. **Drawing Conclusions** Do you think the federal government should have the power to control the nation's economy? Why or why not?

Chapter Summary

Section 1—Taxes and Other Revenue

- The Constitution gives Congress the power to tax. There are limits on the use of this power.

- Federal income taxes are the largest source of income for the country.

- Nontax revenue includes interest charges, tolls, and fees, and the sale of federal bonds.

Section 2—Borrowing and the Public Debt

- The Constitution gives Congress the power to borrow money.

- The federal government borrows money to help the economy. This was first done during the Great Depression.

- Federal fiscal policy has been and continues to be influenced by the theories of John Maynard Keynes.

- The public debt is all the money borrowed by the government and not yet repaid, plus the interest on that money.

Section 3—Spending and the Budget

- The most expensive items in the federal budget are entitlements, defense, and interest on the public debt.

- Much spending by the federal government is controllable. Congress and the President decide how much each agency will receive.

- Some federal spending is uncontrollable because neither Congress nor the President can change the amount of funding directly.

- The President prepares the budget each year. Congress reviews it and acts on it before sending it back to the President to be approved.

Section 4—Monetary and Fiscal Policy

- The federal government has three economic goals: full employment, stable prices, and economic growth.

- Fiscal policy is the power to tax and spend as a way to control the economy. Monetary policy involves the money supply and available credit.

- The Fed can change the money supply in three ways: open market operations, reserve requirements, and the discount rate.

Guiding Question
Section 1 How is the federal government financed?

Guiding Question
Section 2 What effect does borrowing have on the federal budget and the nation's economy?

Guiding Question
Section 3 How is federal spending determined?

Guiding Question
Section 4 How does the federal government achieve its economic goals?

CHAPTER 16

Essential Question
How should the federal budget reflect Americans' priorities?

Document-Based Assessment

President Barack Obama's Inaugural Address

On January 20, 2009, Barack Obama was sworn in as the 44th President of the United States. In his inaugural address in Washington, D.C., President Obama spoke frankly about the nation's economic crisis. He faced a situation similar to that of Franklin D. Roosevelt in 1933. President Obama confronted rising unemployment rates, an enormous budget deficit, and a plunging stock market. He called for all citizens and the government to work together to solve tough problems.

Document at a Glance
- Obama's Inaugural Address
- Acknowledges economic hardship
- Calls for Americans to work together to solve problems

That we are in the midst of crisis is now well understood. . . . Our economy is badly weakened. . . . Homes have been lost; jobs shed; businesses shuttered. . . .

In reaffirming the greatness of our nation, we understand that greatness is never a given. It must be earned. Our journey . . . has not been . . . for those who prefer leisure over work, or seek only the pleasures of riches and fame. Rather, it has been the risk-takers, the doers, the makers of things—some celebrated but more often men and women obscured in their labor, who have carried us up the long, rugged path towards prosperity and freedom.

This is the journey we continue today. . . . Starting today, we must pick ourselves up, dust ourselves off, and begin again the work of remaking America.

For everywhere we look, there is work to be done. The state of the economy calls for action, bold and swift, and we will act—not only to create new jobs, but to lay a new foundation for growth. We will build the roads and bridges, the electric grids and digital lines that feed our commerce and bind us together. . . . We will harness the sun and the winds and the soil to fuel our cars and run our factories. And we will transform our schools and colleges and universities to meet the demands of a new age. All this we can do. All this we will do.

Document-Based Questions

1. What crisis did President Obama say the nation was experiencing?

2. What specific problems did he mention?

3. According to President Obama, what kind of people built the nation?

4. What work did President Obama say must be done to strengthen the nation's economy?

5. **Ask Questions** What other questions do you have about this speech? Brainstorm ideas with the class.

SOURCE: http://www.cnn.com/2009/POLITICS/01/20/obama.politics/index.html

Chapter Assessment

Directions: On a sheet of paper, write the answers to the
following questions. Use complete sentences.

Section 1—Taxes and Other Revenue

1. What document gives Congress the power to tax?

2. What four limits are placed on the taxing power?

3. What are regressive taxes?

4. What are two examples of nontax revenue?

5. Critical Thinking Do you think the current tax system is fair?
Why or why not?

Section 2—Borrowing and the Public Debt

6. How did the federal government help end the
Great Depression?

7. How does the government borrow money?

8. How much did the public debt grow between 1981
and 2008?

9. Critical Thinking Why do many people worry that the public
debt is too high?

Section 3—Spending and the Budget

10. What is the difference between controllable and
uncontrollable spending?

11. How does the President begin the budget-making process?

12. What is Congress's role in the budget-making process?

13. Critical Thinking Do you think the Constitution should be
amended to make sure that the budget is balanced each
year? Why or why not?

Section 4—Fiscal and Monetary Policy

14. What are the three economic goals of the federal government?

15. What is a recession?

16. What tools does the Fed use to control the money supply?

17. Critical Thinking Do you think the government should be involved in the economy? Why or why not?

Apply What You've Learned

Exploring the Essential Question

Take a poll of 10 to 15 people in your community. Remember, a poll is a way to measure public opinion by interviewing a random sample of people.
Ask the following questions:

18. What issues are priorities for Americans today? Which issue is most important to you?

19. Do you think the federal government is responsive to the priorities of Americans? Why or why not?

Essential Questions Project

20. Using the results of your poll, create a chart that shows the top priorities for Americans today. Also include the answers to Question 19 in your chart. The chart should help answer the Essential Question: **How should the federal budget reflect Americans' priorities?**

Essential Questions
Journal

Go to your **Essential Questions Journal** to work on this chapter's Essential Question.

Test-Taking Tip

After you have completed a test, reread each question and your answer. Ask yourself: Have I answered the question that was asked? Have I answered it completely?

▲ President Ronald Reagan walks with British Prime Minister Margaret Thatcher as she reviews the honor guard at the White House.

Foreign Policy and National Defense

Essential Question
How should the United States interact with other countries?

Section 1: Foreign Affairs and Diplomacy

Section 2: National Security

Section 3: American Foreign Policy Overview

Section 4: Foreign Aid and Alliances

Reading Strategy: Predicting
Preview the text. Think about what you already know about foreign policy or national defense. Look for new information. This process will help you predict what will happen next. Check your predictions as you read. As you learn more information, you may find you need to change your predictions.

GOVERNMENT ONLINE
ON THE GO

To study anywhere, anytime, download these online resources at PearsonSuccessNet.com.
• **Political Dictionary**
• **Audio Review**
• **Downloadable Interactivities**

SECTION 1

Foreign Affairs and Diplomacy

▲ Former Secretary of State John Foster Dulles meets with General Chiang Kai-Shek in 1955.

Guiding Question

How is foreign policy made and conducted? Use a chart like the one below to keep track of the main themes in the conduct of American foreign policy.

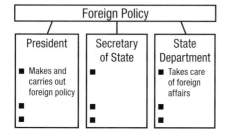

Foreign Policy		
President	**Secretary of State**	**State Department**
■ Makes and carries out foreign policy	■	■ Takes care of foreign affairs
■	■	■
■		■

Objectives:

- Understand the differences between isolationism and internationalism.
- Understand that a nation's foreign policy is all the actions it takes in dealing with other countries.
- Explain the functions, components, and organization of the State Department.

Foreign affairs and diplomacy in the United States are carried out by the State Department. Crafting foreign policy is a complex process and includes many activities. Diplomacy, trade agreements, foreign aid, and peacekeeping actions are all part of United States foreign policy.

Why did the United States go from isolationism to internationalism?

The first 150 years of United States history was a busy time for the American people. After winning independence from England, the country needed to take care of **domestic affairs.** Domestic affairs are events that happen at home. **Foreign affairs** were not a concern at that time. Foreign affairs are the nation's relationships with other nations. During this time, the United States practiced **isolationism.** Isolationism is a refusal to be involved with other countries**.** This policy changed when the country became involved in World War II. American troops were sent overseas to protect America and help other countries, and isolationism ended.

The security and safety of America depends on good relations with other countries. If there are conflicts with other countries, the United States tries to find solutions. Solutions are not always possible, however. The United States has fought five major wars over the past century. Terrorism continues to threaten the security of the United States.

Economic conditions worldwide affect the United States economy. The American economy has become global. American corporations and other businesses operate in many countries of the world. Because the world is so interconnected, the United States now practices internationalism, realizing that the well-being of everyone in this country is affected by events everywhere around the world. For a summary of U.S. foreign policy, see Figure 17.1.

✔ **Checkpoint** What is isolationism?

What is foreign policy?

Foreign policy is all the actions a nation takes in dealing with other countries of the world. American foreign policy is carried out by the federal government. The government makes treaties and trade alliances with other countries. The government also provides economic aid to countries and participates in cultural exchange programs. To aid foreign policy efforts, the United States belongs to the United Nations. Within this country, the government is concerned with immigration, space exploration, and other matters.

The President has always been responsible for making and carrying out foreign policy (Figure 17.2). To do this huge job, the President gets help from many officials and agencies, including the State Department and the Department of Defense.

Domestic affairs
All matters not directly connected to foreign affairs; events that happen at home

Foreign affairs
A nation's relationship with other countries

Isolationism
A refusal to be involved with other countries

Foreign policy
The plan a country follows in dealing with other countries

Fig. 17.1

U.S. Foreign Policy Positions

American Foreign Policy Until World War II
- Purposeful detachment from world affairs
- Domestic affairs are primary focus
- Allows for some ties with foreign nations

American Foreign Policy Since World War II
- Economic and political involvement in international affairs
- Focus on collective security
- Acknowledges impact of global events on the United States

Fig. 17.2

NOW SHAKE HANDS.....

GENTLY.

▲ **Analyzing Political Cartoons** Several Presidents have tried to make peace between Palestine and Israel. The Presidents have brought the country's leaders together to help them settle their disagreements. *According to this cartoon, how successful have these efforts been in creating peace?*

What is the State Department?

The State Department is one of the 15 executive departments. President George Washington created the department in 1789. It handles foreign affairs for the country. The President works closely with the State Department when dealing with foreign countries. The State Department has four goals for its foreign policy (Figure 17.3). These four goals are protecting America, advancing democracy, promoting American values, and protecting and supporting diplomatic officials abroad.

Fig. 17.3 How Government Works

GOVERNMENT ONLINE
Audio Tour
To learn more about implementing foreign policy, visit
PearsonSuccessNet.com

The State Department

Carrying Out Foreign Policy

The State Department aims to achieve four major goals as it carries out America's foreign polices. It uses the methods outlined below. *How might achieving one of these goals relate to achieving the others?*

Protecting America

- Maintaining and strengthening diplomatic ties with other nations
- Managing domestic and international travel and trade policies
- Promoting global stability

Secretary of State Colin Powell arrives in Lebanon in 2002 to help ease the Arab-Israeli conflict.

Advancing Democracy

- Supporting newly established democracies
- Promoting fair voting practices and just legal systems
- Monitoring human rights issues globally

An Afghan voter reviews the ballot in an election in her country.

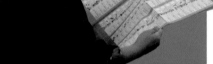

Promoting American Values

- Using government-supported and other media to provide information on American values to other peoples
- Supporting cultural exchange programs

A Voice of America radio journalist provides news and information on human rights to refugees in Burundi.

Supporting Diplomatic Officials

- Sending diplomats abroad to implement American foreign policy
- Protecting American diplomats and others abroad

Following terrorist threats, the U.S. embassy in Indonesia increased security with the support of local police.

▲ An architect's drawing of the new U.S. embassy in Beijing, China. **Why do you think the embassy is set back and surrounded by water in the drawing?**

The secretary of state is the head of the State Department. The President names the secretary of state and the Senate must approve that choice. Thomas Jefferson was the first secretary of state. The duties of the office are now concerned mostly with foreign affairs. The secretary of state is one of the President's top advisors and the most important member of the President's Cabinet.

There are many agencies in the State Department. Some of these agencies focus on different areas of the world. For example, the Bureau of African Affairs deals with issues in Africa. Other agencies handle special issues, such as narcotics or law enforcement. An assistant secretary is in charge of each agency.

Who are the overseas representatives?

The Foreign Service has about 12,000 men and women, most of whom are serving in other countries. The **right of legation,** a part of international law, states that countries have the right to send and receive diplomats. International law is a set of rules followed by all countries.

An **ambassador** is a person appointed by the President to represent the United States in a foreign country. Ambassadors are stationed at the capital of each nation recognized by the United States. American embassies are located in more than 180 countries around the world. Consular offices are also located abroad. These offices encourage trade, gather information about other countries, and help American citizens who are abroad.

Right of legation
The right to send and receive diplomatic representatives

Ambassador
A person appointed by the President to represent the United States in a foreign country

Reading Strategy
Predicting
Before you read this section, predict what those serving overseas do.

Reading Strategy
Predicting
What purpose do you think passports and visas might serve?

Diplomatic immunity
Rule that says an ambassador is not bound by the laws of the country where he or she is serving

Passport
A legal document issued by a state that identifies a person as a citizen of that state

Ambassadors are granted **diplomatic immunity.** This means they are not bound by the laws of the country where they are serving. They cannot be arrested, sued, or taxed by that country. Diplomats' houses cannot be searched, and diplomats' property is protected. Most countries follow the rules of diplomatic immunity. There are exceptions, however. An extreme case happened in Iran on November 4, 1979. Radical Iranian students took over the American embassy in an angry protest against United States support of the existing government. They took 52 Americans hostage and held them for 444 days. The hostages were released when Ronald Reagan became President on January 20, 1981 (Figure 17.4).

Governments give **passports** to citizens who want to leave the country. A passport identifies a person as a legal citizen of a country. Most countries require a person to have a passport to enter their borders. The United States issues over 10 million passports to citizens each year.

Fig. 17.4
The Iran Hostage Crisis

An American hostage is paraded in front of the reporters by Iranian militants in 1979.

The Iran Hostage Crisis was an unusual assault against both a nation and international diplomatic law.
Why does the United States send diplomats to posts where political conditions are unstable?

For the first time, yellow ribbons were tied to trees to symbolize public support for the hostages.

A **visa** is a permit that allows a person to enter another country. It is issued by the country one wishes to enter. Visas to enter the United States are usually issued at American consulates in foreign countries. For more on passports and visas, see Figure 17.5.

Visa
A permit to enter another country; must be obtained from the country the person wants to enter

Fig. 17.5

Travel Documents

Years ago, a valid passport was all one needed to travel abroad. Today most countries also require a visa. *Why do you think this is now the case?*

Passports	Visas
• Identifies the person carrying the passport as a citizen or national of the issuing country	• Issued by the country the person requests permission to enter
• Entitles the person carrying the passport to protection while abroad and to return to his or her country of citizenship	• Permit the traveler to remain in a country for a specified period of time, but do not guarantee entry
• Valid for ten years	• Valid only for the time period stated
• Three types: diplomatic, official, tourist	• Includes transit, tourist, business, and student

Essential Questions Journal Go to your **Essential Questions Journal** to work on this chapter's Essential Question.

SECTION **1** ASSESSMENT

1. **Guiding Question** Use your completed chart to answer this question: How is foreign policy made and conducted?

Key Terms and Comprehension

On a sheet of paper, write the answers to the following questions. Use complete sentences.

2. What is foreign policy?

3. Which event changed U.S. foreign policy from isolationism to internationalism?

4. What is an ambassador?

5. What is the major difference between a passport and a visa?

Critical Thinking

6. **Demonstrate Reasonable Judgment** Do you think the United States could ever return to isolationism? Why or why not?

7. **Draw Conclusions** Why do you think the United States sends ambassadors to other countries? Explain your answer.

▲ Two members of the Joint Service Color Guard present the colors at a military ceremony.

SECTION 2

National Security

Guiding Question

How does the federal government safeguard this nation's security? Use a table like the one below to keep track of the methods used to protect national security.

Protecting National Security	
Secretary of Defense	■ Advises the President on defense policies
	■
	■
	■

Objectives:

- Summarize the functions, components, and organization of the Department of Defense and the military departments.
- Explain how the Office of the Director of National Intelligence and the Department of Homeland Security contribute to the nation's security.

Security means freedom from danger, fear, or worry. National security in the United States is achieved through many federal agencies. The largest of these are the State Department and the Defense Department. The newest agency is the Department of Homeland Security. In this section, you will learn about the many ways the federal government safeguards the nation's security.

What is the Department of Defense?

Congress created the Department of Defense in 1947, when it combined the Department of War and the Department of the Navy. All of the country's armed forces are under the control of this department. Today more than 1.4 million men and women serve in the armed forces. More than 1 million serve in the National Guard and Reserves, and some work in the Defense Department.

The Framers knew that defense was vital to the success of the nation. They mentioned defense in the Preamble to the Constitution and throughout the Constitution itself. These men also saw the possible danger if the nation's military power was abused. To keep this from happening, they gave some of this power to civilians. The power to declare war was given to Congress, the people's elected representatives. The President was named commander in chief of the armed forces.

✔ **Checkpoint** Who is the commander in chief of the armed forces?

What is civilian control of the military?

The principle of civilian control has always been a major factor in the making of defense policy. It has also played an important role in the creation and staffing of the various agencies responsible for executing the defense policy. The importance of civilian control is clearly illustrated by this fact: The National Security Act of 1947 provides that the secretary of defense cannot have served on active duty in the armed forces for at least 10 years before being named to that post. In **Figure 17.6** below, civilian control of the military is further explained. Notice the civilians and military work together to take action.

■ ■ ■ ■ ■ ■ ■ ■ ■ ■ ■ ■ ■ ■ ■ ■
Reading Strategy
Predicting
Before you read this section, predict which other departments and agencies might help to carry out national security.

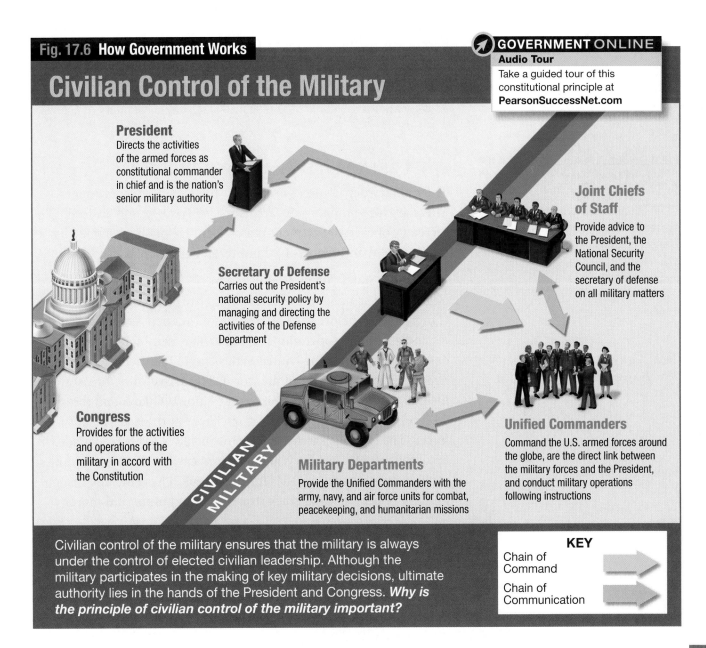

Fig. 17.6 How Government Works

GOVERNMENT ONLINE
Audio Tour
Take a guided tour of this constitutional principle at **PearsonSuccessNet.com**

Civilian Control of the Military

President
Directs the activities of the armed forces as constitutional commander in chief and is the nation's senior military authority

Joint Chiefs of Staff
Provide advice to the President, the National Security Council, and the secretary of defense on all military matters

Secretary of Defense
Carries out the President's national security policy by managing and directing the activities of the Defense Department

Congress
Provides for the activities and operations of the military in accord with the Constitution

CIVILIAN
MILITARY

Military Departments
Provide the Unified Commanders with the army, navy, and air force units for combat, peacekeeping, and humanitarian missions

Unified Commanders
Command the U.S. armed forces around the globe, are the direct link between the military forces and the President, and conduct military operations following instructions

Civilian control of the military ensures that the military is always under the control of elected civilian leadership. Although the military participates in the making of key military decisions, ultimate authority lies in the hands of the President and Congress. *Why is the principle of civilian control of the military important?*

KEY
Chain of Command
Chain of Communication

The secretary of defense is appointed by the President and must be confirmed by the Senate. He or she leads the Defense Department and advises the President on defense policies. The Department of Defense headquarters is called the Pentagon. This massive five-sided building is located in Virginia, across the Potomac River from the Capitol. The work of the Defense Department takes about one fourth of all federal spending. It has increased greatly since the September 11 terrorist attacks. In 2009, spending for the Department of Defense is expected to reach $600 billion.

The Joint Chiefs of Staff is made up of six members. It is led by the chairman of the Joint Chiefs. The other members are the army chief of staff, the chief of naval operations, the commander of the Marine Corps, and the air force chief of staff. All are appointed by the President and approved by the Senate. They are the main military advisors to the secretary of defense. They also advise the President and the National Security Council (NSC). The NSC is part of the executive office and advises the President about the safety of the country.

✓ **Checkpoint**   What are the responsibilities of the secretary of defense?

■ ■ ■ ■ ■ ■ ■ ■ ■ ■ ■ ■ ■ ■ ■ ■
Reading Strategy
Predicting
   What do you think are the current military departments of the United States?

What are the military departments?

The military departments are part of the Defense Department. There are three military departments: army, navy, and air force. The secretary of each department is a civilian. He or she is named by the President and reports to the secretary of defense.

The United States Army, established in 1775, is the largest and oldest of the armed forces. It was set up by the Second Continental Congress even before the Declaration of Independence was written. It handles military operations on land. The army stands ready to defeat any attack on the United States and to take action to protect American interests around the world. The active-duty forces include the Regular Army, the Army National Guard, and the army reserve. The army chief of staff is in charge of these active-duty forces. The Regular Army, which now includes women, is made up of the infantry, artillery, and armored cavalry. Many other units provide services and supplies for the troops. These include the military police, medical corps, transportation units, and more.

Fig. 17.7
The Armed Forces Overseas

Major Military Deployments

GOVERNMENT ONLINE
Update
Find out where American troops are currently deployed at **PearsonSuccessNet.com**

Protecting the nation's security does not end at the nation's borders. In fact, nearly one fourth of the armed forces of the United States is now stationed abroad. Today, the top five areas to which the men and women of the American military are deployed are in East Asia, Southwest Asia, and Europe. *Why is it necessary to post the armed forces overseas in order to protect national security?*

	Total	Army	Navy	Marine Corps	Air Force
East Asia					
Japan	33,164	2,483	3,734	14,226	12,721
South Korea	26,076	17,798	227	108	7,943
Europe					
Germany	57,155	42,023	277	319	14,536
Southwest Asia					
Afghanistan	25,700	19,700	800	400	4,800
Iraq	196,600	125,800	21,300	26,900	22,600

SOURCE: Department of Defense, Personnel and Procurement Statistics, 2007

An American soldier attends a farewell event before he leaves for Iraq.

The United States Navy takes care of sea warfare and defense. It was also created by the Second Continental Congress. The chief of naval operations is in charge of the navy. The chief is responsible for keeping the officers and enlisted members ready for combat. (See Figure 17.7 above.)

The United States Marine Corps is a separate service within the Navy Department. It was created in November 1775. The leader of the marines is the commandant, who reports directly to the secretary of the navy. The marines carry out land and air operations for the navy.

The United States Air Force was not established as a separate branch of the military until 1947. Today, the air force takes care of military air and aerospace missions. During peacetime and wartime, it is the country's first line of defense. The air force will attack enemy targets, defend the United States, and provide transportation for all troops.

✔**Checkpoint** Which military department includes the marine corps?

What is the Office of the Director of National Intelligence?

The director of national intelligence is the head of the Office of the Director of National Intelligence (DNI). This agency was created in 2005 to collect and share information following the September 11 attacks. The DNI is now the President's chief advisor for national intelligence. Intelligence is the gathering of information about other countries to help defend the nation. The duties of the DNI include overseeing those who gather information needed to defend the country. This information comes from all parts of the world.

Some agencies now under the control of the DNI have been operating for a long time. These agencies include the FBI, the DEA (Drug Enforcement Agency), and the CIA. Other agencies are less well-known. For example, the world's largest spy agency, the National Security Agency, is involved in **espionage.** Sometimes even Congress does not know about all the activities of the NSA. Most Americans think that these agencies are very important to keeping them safe. Both government leaders and citizens must also recognize that too much government secrecy can be dangerous to a democratic society.

✔**Checkpoint**   What are three agencies that are under the control of the DNI?

What is the Department of Homeland Security?

The Department of Homeland Security (DHS) protects the American homeland and citizens from **terrorism.** Terrorists are people who use violence or force to achieve political goals.

Congress created the Department of Homeland Security in November 2002. The DHS became operational in 2003. Before the DHS was formed, many different government groups handled homeland protection. Now, the DHS is responsible for the coordination and the direction of the antiterrorist activities of all public agencies that participate in national security. These agencies include thousands of police departments, fire departments, emergency medical and search-and-rescue units, and other disaster response agencies across the country. On the next page, Figure 17.8 shows the different responsibilities of the DHS: prevention, protection, and response.

Fig. 17.8 How Government Works

Department of Homeland Security
Safeguarding the Nation's Security

GOVERNMENT ONLINE
Update
To learn more about the
Department of Homeland Security,
visit **PearsonSuccessNet.com**

The September 11, 2001, attacks showed that the United States and its people were not well-protected from terrorist attacks. After those tragic events, the Department of Homeland Security was created. The department is now in charge of protecting the security of the country. To best do this, the DHS gets help from several agencies, state and local governments, and the American people. *Why do you think coordinating the efforts of all levels of government is important to safeguarding the nation's security?*

San Francisco's Golden Gate Bridge

Prevention

To detect and deter threats to the United States, the department

- Secures the nation's borders against terrorists, means of terrorism, illegal drugs, and other illegal activity
- Develops technology to detect and prevent the illegal possession and use of chemical, biological, radiological, and nuclear materials
- Coordinates the collection and sharing of information
- Strengthens the security of the nation's transportation system
- Enforces the nation's immigration laws

Protection

To safeguard the nation's infrastructure, economy, and citizens from acts of terrorism or other emergencies, the department

- Implements a plan to protect both the nation's physical infrastructure and cyber infrastructure
- Combats financial and electronic crimes and identity theft
- Protects the President and other key government officials
- Works with other agencies to protect governmental activities
- Administers a preparedness strategy affecting all levels of government and the private sector

Response

To lead, manage, and coordinate the national response to acts of terrorism or other emergencies, the department

- Maintains response plans focusing on communities that are most likely to need help
- Promotes response readiness to meet such crises as health and medical emergencies or acts of terrorism
- Provides emergency housing following major disasters
- Partners with other agencies and the private sector to assist mariners in distress and to protect property

A U.S. Border Patrol agent examines borders in New Mexico.

Secret Service agents ensure the President's safety.

A U.S. Coast Guard officer searches for survivors of Hurricane Katrina.

As you have read, the Department of Homeland Security has a huge responsibility. It keeps United States citizens safe. This job involves trying to secure over 600,000 bridges; 170,000 water systems; and 5,000 power plants; as well as roads, airports, harbors, and much more. The Department of Homeland Security provides, in all, five main services:

- protects the necessary infrastructure of communities, including water, roads, and bridges;

- provides safeguards from terrorist weapons;

- makes the country's borders and ports secure;

- works with local governments to prepare citizens for possible emergencies; and

- studies intelligence (information about an enemy) from all government agencies.

Given the huge job facing the DHS, the best it can do is to stop most terrorist attacks and bring those responsible for them to justice.

✔ **Checkpoint**   Why was the DHS created by Congress?

Essential Questions Journal	Go to your **Essential Questions Journal** to work on this chapter's Essential Question.

SECTION 2 ASSESSMENT

Quick Write

There are many problems around the world today. For instance, political unrest in many countries is a world concern. Can you think of other issues that the world struggles with today? Write a list of the world's problems. Then work with a group to try and find a solution to one of the issues.

1. Guiding Question   Use your completed table to answer this question: How does the federal government safeguard this nation's security?

Key Terms and Comprehension

On a sheet of paper, write the answers to the following questions. Use complete sentences.

2. Who are the key advisors to the President on issues of defense?

3. What are the three military departments?

4. What is espionage?

5. What is terrorism?

Critical Thinking

6. Identify Central Issues   Why do you think the Framers gave civilians control of the military? Explain your answer.

7. Summarize   What are the five main services that the Department of Homeland Security provides?

American Foreign Policy Overview

▲ American diplomat Benjamin Franklin is received at the French court in Versailles in 1778.

Guiding **Question**

How has American foreign policy changed over time? Use a timeline to keep track of the major changes in American foreign policy.

Policy of Isolationism begins | Open Door Policy

1789   1899

Objectives:

- Summarize American foreign policy from independence through World War I.
- Show how the two world wars affected America's policy of isolationism.
- Define the principles of collective security and deterrence and their use during the Cold War.
- Describe American foreign policy since the end of the Cold War.
- Explain why the world remains a dangerous place.

American foreign policy is carried out for many reasons. But the main reason is that Americans want security and freedom from fear. The country grew, and the government needed to become more involved with foreign countries. Today the United States is a world power. One of the goals of today's foreign policy is to help countries remain at peace.

What was American foreign policy before World War I?

Isolationism was a foreign policy goal that lasted for the first 150 years of American history. In his Farewell Address in 1796, George Washington advised the nation to stay away from involvement with other countries. During this time, the United States was just beginning as a new nation and was busy with matters at home. Of course, the country was not completely cut off from the rest of the world. The government sent diplomats abroad, made treaties, and built up trade with other countries. These activities were confined mostly to the Western Hemisphere.

The Monroe Doctrine, delivered to Congress by President James Monroe in 1823, encouraged isolationism. The President wanted America to stay out of European affairs. He also warned Europe to stay out of the affairs of North America and South America. Countries in Latin America had begun breaking away from Spain and Portugal. The United States feared that European countries would come to help. This could have threatened the security and economy of America.

The Monroe Doctrine was first put to the test in 1867, when France invaded Mexico. The United States helped Mexico defeat the French.

Later, many Latin Americans criticized the Monroe Doctrine. They claimed the United States was looking out only for its own interests and not really concerned with the independence of Latin American countries.

After the Revolutionary War, the United States had made two purchases of land that greatly increased the size of the country. To the west, the Louisiana Purchase in 1803 doubled the size of the country. The Florida Purchase Treaty in 1819 expanded the country to the south. Most Americans believed it was this nation's mission to expand its boundaries. They called this the nation's "Manifest Destiny." By 1900, the United States had acquired all the land west to the Pacific Ocean. During this time, the United States also had become a world power.

Problems in Central America and South America threatened the United States in the late 1800s. There were many revolutions in South America. Dangerous conditions existed in the countries involved. During President Theodore Roosevelt's administration, the United States began to help countries such as Haiti and Cuba. The United States became involved in Cuba's fight for independence from Spain in 1898. Its victory in that war gave the United States colonies of its own (Figure 17.9).

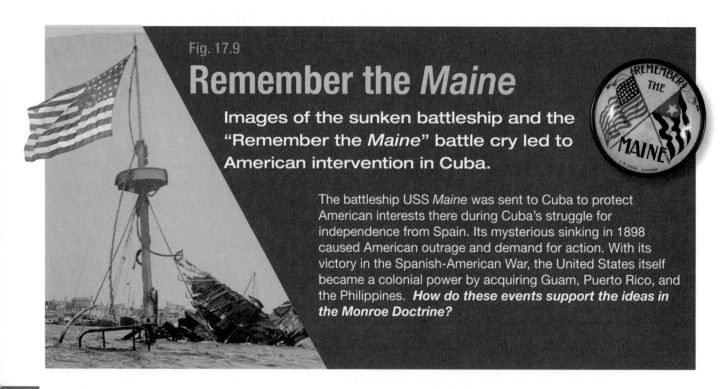

Fig. 17.9

Remember the *Maine*

Images of the sunken battleship and the "Remember the *Maine*" battle cry led to American intervention in Cuba.

The battleship USS *Maine* was sent to Cuba to protect American interests there during Cuba's struggle for independence from Spain. Its mysterious sinking in 1898 caused American outrage and demand for action. With its victory in the Spanish-American War, the United States itself became a colonial power by acquiring Guam, Puerto Rico, and the Philippines. *How do these events support the ideas in the Monroe Doctrine?*

Panama revolted against Columbia in 1903 and became an independent country. The new country agreed to let the United States buy rights from Panama to build a canal across the Isthmus of Panama. The United States bought the Virgin Islands from Denmark to protect the canal. Many countries in Latin America began to resent the involvement of the United States in their region.

When Franklin Roosevelt became President, he made a major change in foreign policy. He believed in reducing the amount of military involvement with Latin America. This was called the Good Neighbor Policy. President Roosevelt wanted to win friends in the region.

Today, the United States is the strongest power in the Western Hemisphere. The Monroe Doctrine is still an important part of American foreign policy.

The United States also had dealings in Asia, beginning in the mid-1800s. Secretary of State John Hay began the Open Door policy with China in 1899. America had always traded in Asia. This trade, especially with China, had become threatened. Other countries, such as France and Germany, were claiming parts of China for their own trade. The Open Door policy insisted on equal trade opportunities for all countries. It also insisted that China be allowed to govern itself. As a result of this policy, America and China became allies. This alliance ended in 1949 when China became a Communist country.

✔ **Checkpoint** What is the Open Door policy?

How did foreign policy change during the two World Wars?

The United States was forced to enter World War I in 1917. American ships had been attacked by Germany in the North Atlantic. This ended American isolationism. The country had to be protected. After Germany and the Central Powers were defeated, however, the United States returned to its isolationism. Congress refused to have the United States join the League of Nations, which was formed after the war. Many Americans, including the government, still believed the concerns of Europe were not important to the United States.

■■■■■■■■■■■■■■■■■■■
Reading Strategy
Predicting
Preview the red heading on this page. Ask yourself, What do I think this section will be about?

Collective security
Principle that calls for countries to act together to promote peace and security

Fig. 17.10

Key American Foreign Policies

Monroe Doctrine	Isolates the U.S. from international affairs unless North or South America is threatened
Roosevelt Corollary	Extends the Monroe Doctrine by giving the U.S. the authority to intervene in the affairs of Latin America
Good Neighbor Policy	Reduces American political and military interference in Latin America
Deterrence	Maintains that superior military strength will deter hostile powers from attacking the nation
Truman Doctrine	Affirms that the U.S. will oppose any aggressor's attempt to control another nation and its people
Containment	Prevents the spread of communism by assisting threatened nations
Détente	Reduces tensions between the United States and other countries
Collective Security	Unifies nations against any nation that threatens the peace

Isolationism finally ended when the United States entered World War II. After the attack on Pearl Harbor in 1941, the country was completely involved in the war. The United States and its allies—Great Britain, Russia, and China—defeated the Axis Powers. The countries that made up the Axis Powers were Germany, Italy, and Japan. After the war, the United States became the strongest military power in the world.

✔ **Checkpoint** When did isolationism end?

What two new principles emerged after World War II?

The United States and other countries were determined to keep the peace after World War II. Many countries looked to the principle of **collective security.** Collective security means countries act together to promote peace and security. The United Nations was formed in 1945. It was created to promote peace in the world. It soon became clear, however, that the relationship between the United States and the Soviet Union was a key factor in world peace. That relationship was tense for 40 years. Then the Soviet Union broke apart, and the United States was the only remaining superpower in the world. In that role, this country has built a network of security alliances.

Another principle of United States foreign policy since World War II is known as **deterrance.** Deterrence is the strategy of building a very strong military. This military must be able to deter (prevent) any country from attacking the United States. Hostile countries will not attack if they know the United States will strike back with great force. President Truman began this strategy. It is still followed today. See **Figure 17.10** on the previous page for descriptions of this and other foreign policies of the United States.

What was the Cold War?

The **Cold War** refers to the 40 years in which the United States and the Soviet Union were unfriendly toward each other. There was no actual war, but both sides made many threats. After World War II ended in 1945, the Soviets had promised to set up democratic governments in Europe. The Soviet Union broke its promise and set up dictatorships in those countries. These actions led to the beginning of the Cold War (**Figure 17.11**).

Deterrence
Building a strong military to discourage any attacks against the country

Cold War
A period of 40 years during which the United States and Soviet Union were unfriendly toward each other

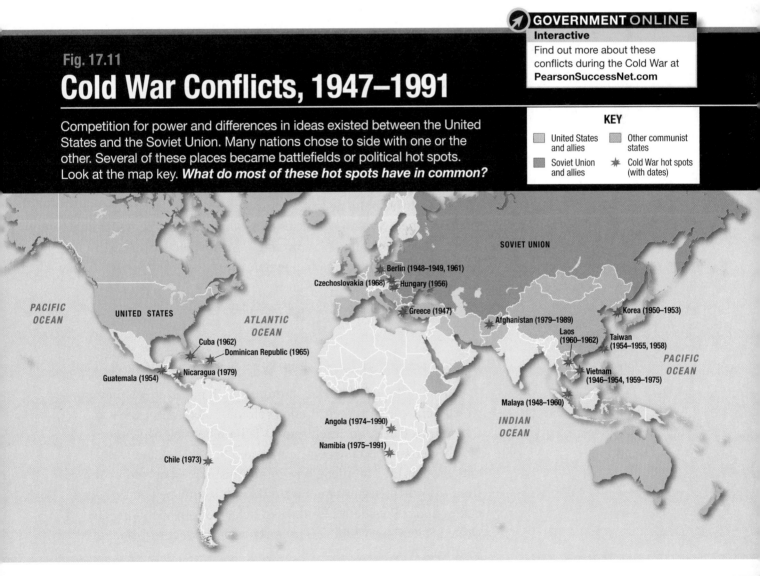

GOVERNMENT ONLINE
Interactive
Find out more about these conflicts during the Cold War at **PearsonSuccessNet.com**

Fig. 17.11
Cold War Conflicts, 1947–1991

Competition for power and differences in ideas existed between the United States and the Soviet Union. Many nations chose to side with one or the other. Several of these places became battlefields or political hot spots. Look at the map key. *What do most of these hot spots have in common?*

KEY
- United States and allies
- Soviet Union and allies
- Other communist states
- ✳ Cold War hot spots (with dates)

PACIFIC OCEAN
UNITED STATES
ATLANTIC OCEAN
SOVIET UNION

Berlin (1948–1949, 1961)
Czechoslovakia (1968)   Hungary (1956)
Greece (1947)
Afghanistan (1979–1989)
Korea (1950–1953)
Cuba (1962)
Dominican Republic (1965)
Laos (1960–1962)
Taiwan (1954–1955, 1958)
Guatemala (1954)   Nicaragua (1979)
PACIFIC OCEAN
Vietnam (1946–1954, 1959–1975)
Malaya (1948–1960)
Angola (1974–1990)
INDIAN OCEAN
Namibia (1975–1991)
Chile (1973)

■ ■ ■ ■ ■ ■ ■ ■ ■ ■ ■ ■ ■ ■ ■ ■ ■

Reading Strategy
Predicting
Predict what you might learn about the Korean War and the Vietnam War. After you have read these pages, check your prediction.

■ ■ ■ ■ ■ ■ ■ ■ ■ ■ ■ ■ ■ ■ ■ ■ ■

Containment
A policy based on the belief that if communism could be kept within its existing boundaries, it would collapse

Congress approved the Truman Doctrine in 1947. It was a program of economic and military aid to countries threatened by the Soviet Union. It became part of the policy of **containment** (holding in) of communism in countries where it already existed. This was a key American foreign policy. The policy of containment was followed from 1947 to the end of the 1980s. Containment was based on the belief that if communism could be kept within its existing boundaries, it would collapse.

Twice during the Cold War, war almost broke out. During 1948 and 1949, the Soviets tried to overrun the German city of West Berlin. In 1962, the Soviet Union placed missiles on the island of Cuba. They were within striking distance of the United States. The United States threatened to attack Cuba unless the missiles were removed. The Soviets backed down in both West Berlin and Cuba. The United States did fight in two wars in Asia, however: the Korean War and the Vietnam War.

✔ **Checkpoint**   What two countries were involved in the Cold War?

What was the Korean War?

The Korean War began in 1950 when communist North Korea invaded democratic South Korea. The United Nations asked all members to help South Korea. The United Nations Command fought against the North Koreans and the communist Chinese troops helping them. The war lasted more than three years. In the end, the Republic of South Korea remained a democratic country. Although it was not a definite victory for the UN, the aggression was contained. Several countries had joined forces with the United States under the United Nations flag. This was the first time in history a united effort had happened.

✔ **Checkpoint**   Why was there a war in Korea?

What was the Vietnam War?

Shortly after World War II, communist nationalists in Vietnam won a long war with their French colonial rulers. After the war, they signed truce agreements and Vietnam became two zones: North Vietnam became communist, and South Vietnam was anticommunist. The Viet Cong communist forces, helped by those from the north, began a civil war in South Vietnam. The United States, under President Eisenhower, helped South Vietnam. The United States believed it was important for the security of all of Southeast Asia.

When John F. Kennedy became President, he supported the Vietnam War. It became a full-scale war in 1965 under President Lyndon Johnson. Thousands of Americans were killed in Vietnam. As the war was being fought, many Americans opposed it. Then President Richard Nixon gradually pulled troops out of Vietnam. In 1973, a cease-fire was reached and the United States troops left Vietnam.

✔ **Checkpoint** Which President pulled American troops out of Vietnam?

■ ■ ■ ■ ■ ■ ■ ■ ■ ■ ■ ■ ■ ■ ■ ■ ■ ■

Détente
A relaxation of tensions

How did American policies succeed?

After the Vietnam War, the Nixon administration began a program of **détente.** *Détente* means a "relaxation of tensions." The program was an attempt to improve relations with the Soviet Union and China. In 1972, President Nixon visited China. This visit led to diplomatic ties with the country. Soon after, Nixon went to Moscow to meet with Soviet Premier Leonid Brezhnev. The two leaders signed SALT I (Strategic Arms Limitation Talks), an agreement to control nuclear weapons in both countries. The Soviets continued, at this time, to help revolutionary actions in other countries. They tried to set up a communist regime in Afghanistan, but failed. The United States helped Afghanistan.

The Cold War ended soon after Mikhail Gorbachev came to power in the Soviet Union in 1985. President Ronald Reagan met with Gorbachev and they talked about limiting weapons stockpiles. The two leaders had more meetings and were able to come to other agreements. These meetings and other events led to the end of the Cold War. During this time, Eastern Europe and the Soviet Union were in turmoil. The Soviet Union fell in 1991 when the communists lost power. The United States policies of deterrence and containment contributed to the fall of some communist countries.

▲ President Nixon's meetings with Chinese diplomats in 1972 begin the process of improving relations between the United States and China.

What dangers remain in the world?

The end of the Cold War brought some international peace in some regions. Today, however, conflicts continue in the world, making it a dangerous place. Terrorist groups, especially al Qaeda, worry most people in democratic countries. Countries such as Iran and North Korea are interested in becoming nuclear powers. Civil wars in parts of Africa and trouble between India and Pakistan threaten those countries. Closer to the United States, Venezuela's president Hugo Chavez has criticized America. Many other countries in South America support Chavez.

Middle Eastern oil is vital to the United States, and so is the United States' relationship with Israel. Soon after Israel was created as an independent state in 1948 by the United Nations, other countries in the area invaded it. The United States has remained Israel's friend and supporter. The United States also tries to maintain friendly relations with the other countries in the Middle East. In 1979, President Carter helped Israel and Egypt forge a peace treaty called the Camp David Accord. Israel has also made treaties with Jordan and the Palestine Liberation Organization (PLO). The Israeli-Palestinian relationship is, however, still filled with problems and, at times, violence.

The Soviets invaded Afghanistan in 1979. They controlled the country for nine long years. Groups within Afghanistan tried to gain control. Civil war broke out. The Taliban, an Islamic group, gained power in the country. In 2001, after the terrorist attacks of September 11, the United States fought against the Taliban. The Taliban had protected Osama bin Laden and the terrorists who had carried out the attacks. NATO helped a new democratic government take control in Afghanistan. The Taliban had not been destroyed, however. Since 2002, the Taliban has begun activities again in Afghanistan.

The United States defeated Saddam Hussein and Iraq in the first Gulf War in 1991. That war was fought because Iraq had invaded the country of Kuwait. Afterward, Saddam Hussein agreed to destroy Iraq's chemical and biological weapons.

Government in Your Life

Helping to Ease the Oil Crisis

In 2008, oil prices reached an all-time high. During the crisis, the U.S. government looked for ways to help ease the oil crisis in the country. Some government officials wanted to end our need for foreign oil and to expand domestic production of oil. Many wanted legal barriers lifted that prevent the greater use of nuclear energy. Some encouraged the production and use of methanol and ethanol. People contributed to the effort to offset the rising cost of oil and gas. For example, some began to use public transportation, drive less, or drive more fuel-efficient vehicles.

In 2003, President George W. Bush believed Saddam Hussein had not kept his promise and was a threat to the security of the United States and the world. President Bush tried to persuade the United Nations Security Council to take action. This attempt was unsuccessful. The President then proposed a plan to Congress. Despite the controversy of the issue, Congress passed a joint resolution. This resolution allowed the President to take the necessary actions to remove Iraq's threat to the world.

Operation Iraqi Freedom began in March 2003. This second war against Iraq was more successful, and Saddam Hussein was defeated in six weeks. Since that time, Iraq has been in a state of unrest and violence. The United States will most likely be involved in the rebuilding of Iraq for many more years.

✔ **Checkpoint** Who helped Israel and Egypt forge the Camp David Accord?

Reading Strategy
Predicting
Based on what you have just read, what do you think the next paragraph will be about?

SECTION **3** ASSESSMENT

Essential Questions Journal Go to your **Essential Questions Journal** to work on this chapter's Essential Question.

Word Bank

Cold War

collective security

détente

deterrence

1. **Guiding Question** Use your completed timeline to answer this question: How has American foreign policy changed over time?

Key Terms and Comprehension

On a sheet of paper, use the words from the Word Bank to complete each sentence correctly.

2. When countries act together to promote peace and security, they are practicing _____.

3. When the Soviets broke their promise to not spread communism, it led to the _____.

4. _____ is the strategy of building a very strong military to discourage any attacks on the country.

5. In the early 1970s, the Nixon administration began a program of _____.

Critical Thinking

6. **Formulate Opinions** Do you think the United States should have gone to war in Iraq in 2003? Why or why not?

7. **Summarize** What was the reason for the Vietnam War? How did it end?

America's Role in the World

▶▶ Track the Issue

United States foreign policy deals with military conflicts. It also deals with humanitarian and economic matters.

1796 George Washington argues against significant involvement in foreign affairs.

1899 The Open Door policy is created. The United States wants China to be free to establish economic relationships with other countries.

1933 Franklin D. Roosevelt begins the Good Neighbor policy. The policy results in diplomatic involvement in Latin America.

1948 Through the Marshall Plan, the United States takes an active role in rebuilding Europe.

2001 The United States provides humanitarian aid to different regions of the world.

The head of USAID delivers aid to cyclone-struck Myanmar.

▶▶ Perspectives

For the most part, American foreign aid has one main goal. That goal is to better serve our foreign policy interests and ensure national security. Some people believe we spend too much money on international aid. And they say, as we do so, we place our own domestic issues and concerns at risk. Below, Condoleezza Rice argues for foreign aid programs. John J. Duncan argues that there must be limits to our generosity.

For Foreign Aid	Limit Foreign Aid
In today's world, America's security is linked to the capacity of foreign states to govern justly and effectively. . . . We have begun an effort to relieve the poorest countries of the crushing burden of debt and we have doubled our overseas development assistance. . . . America's taxpayers must know that we are using their hard-earned dollars efficiently and effectively to improve our own security, but also to improve people's lives around the world. —Secretary of State Condoleezza Rice, 2006	[N]o country has ever done as much for another country as the United States has done for Iraq. We have spent hundreds of billions rebuilding their infrastructure, providing police protection, giving free medical care. . . . [T]here needs to be some limit to our generosity. . . . We need to start putting our own people first. If we do not, we are soon not going to be able to pay all the Social Security and . . . other things we have promised our own people. . . . —Rep. John J. Duncan, Jr. (R., Tenn.), 2007

Connect to Your World

1. How does Secretary Rice justify the costs of foreign aid?
2. How does Representative Duncan justify cutting foreign aid? Whom do you agree with? Why?

GOVERNMENT ONLINE
In the News
For updates about American foreign aid, visit **PearsonSuccessNet.com**

▲ Marshall Plan funding helps in the rebuilding of West Berlin.

SECTION 4

Foreign Aid and Defense Alliances

Guiding Question

In what ways does the United States cooperate with other nations? Use a chart like the one below to keep track of the methods used in international cooperation.

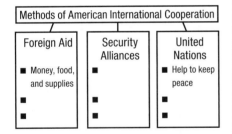

Methods of American International Cooperation		
Foreign Aid	**Security Alliances**	**United Nations**
■ Money, food, and supplies	■	■ Help to keep peace
■	■	■
■	■	■

Objectives:

- Identify the two types of foreign aid and describe United States foreign aid policy.
- Describe the major security alliances developed by the United States.
- Examine the role and structure of the United Nations and the problems it faces.

American foreign policy has two basic parts: foreign aid and security alliances. In this section, you will learn about both and how they shape American foreign policy today.

What is foreign aid?

The United States has long helped other countries with money, food, and other supplies. This **foreign aid** began before the United States entered World War II. President Franklin Roosevelt started the Lend-Lease program to help Great Britain. Great Britain needed war supplies to fight Nazi Germany but had no money. In return for the supplies, Britain leased land to the United States. This land was to be used for air and naval bases abroad. As the war went on, Lend-Lease was extended to other countries. The United States has sent more than $500 billion in aid to foreign countries since World War II.

The United States also helped European allies rebuild after World War II. Under the Marshall Plan, named after Secretary of State George C. Marshall, the United States gave $12.5 billion in foreign aid. This money helped people in 16 nations in Western Europe from 1948 to 1952.

Today, the United States gives more military aid to foreign countries. Since the 1950s, the largest amount of aid has gone to Asia, the Middle East, and Latin America. Most aid is given to countries that are critical to United States foreign policy. The United States Agency for International Development (USAID) works with the Department of State and the Department of Agriculture to handle aid programs.

✓ **Checkpoint** What was the Marshall Plan?

Foreign aid
Economic and military aid given to other countries

Regional security alliance
Agreement among nations to act together to meet any attack against any member

NATO
North Atlantic Treaty Organization

What are security alliances?

Since World War II, the United States has built many **regional security alliances.** One security alliance is the North Atlantic Treaty Organization (NATO). **NATO** promotes peace and provides a common defense against military attacks. After the fall of the Soviet Union, the countries of Eastern Europe joined NATO. NATO now has 26 members (Figure 17.12). The members have agreed that an attack against one or more of them will be considered an attack against them all. In 2001, the United Nations created a military force made up of many nations. This military is called the International Security Assistance Force (ISAF). NATO now commands the ISAF. Today, the ISAF has over 40,000 troops from 37 nations.

Fig. 17.12

The Expansion of NATO

GOVERNMENT ONLINE
Audio Tour
To find out more about the members of NATO, visit
PearsonSuccessNet.com

Analyzing Maps Membership in the North Atlantic Treaty Organization has extended beyond Western Europe with the addition of several nations that were once part of the Soviet-dominated Eastern Bloc. *Why might an invitation to join NATO be extended to Russia?* ▼

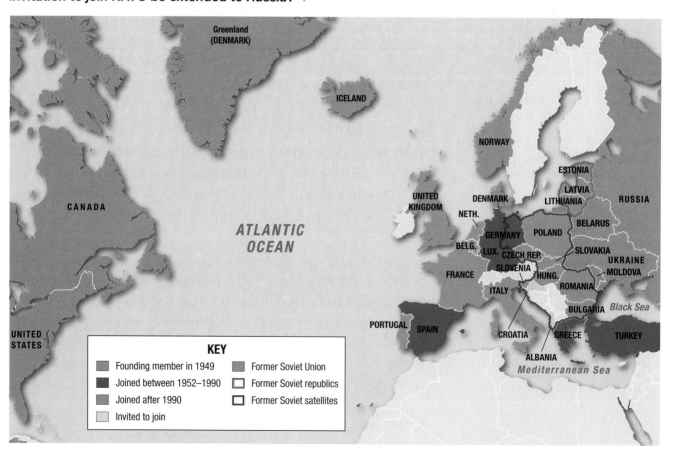

KEY
- Founding member in 1949
- Joined between 1952–1990
- Joined after 1990
- Invited to join
- Former Soviet Union
- Former Soviet republics
- Former Soviet satellites

The United States is a partner in many other security alliances around the world. The Organization of American States is a group of nations from North, Central, and South America. It tries to promote policies that improve economic and social development in the Americas. The United States, Canada, and 32 Latin American countries signed the Rio Pact in 1947. The treaty commits those nations to defending one another against attacks and settling their arguments peacefully. Cuba is not part of this agreement. The United States also has alliances with Japan and Korea. The Japanese Pact of 1951 commits the United States to protecting Japan. In return, the Japanese allow the United States to keep military forces in and around its territory.

Another treaty, the ANZUS pact, was signed in 1951. It joined the United States, Australia, and New Zealand in an alliance that covered the South Pacific.

What is the United Nations?

The **United Nations** (UN) is an international organization that was established in 1945. After World War II ended, the Allies wanted to help ensure that no such war could ever happen again. Fifty countries met in California to write a charter that listed the basic principles of the United Nations. The United States was the first to ratify the charter. The document said that the United Nations would help keep peace in the world. It would help develop friendly relations among nations and protect human rights. Today, it has 192 member nations.

How is the United Nations organized?

The United Nations has six main divisions. The first is the General Assembly. The General Assembly has been called "the town meeting of the world." Every UN member has a seat and a vote in the Assembly. It meets once a year in New York City.

The second part of the UN is the **Security Council.** It has 15 members and is responsible for keeping peace around the world. It often provides forces to keep violence from breaking out in trouble spots.

The Economic and Security Council is made up of 54 members elected by the General Assembly. It carries out the UN's economic, cultural, educational, and health activities.

The Trusteeship Council was formed to oversee the world's trust territories. All eleven trust territories are now able to govern themselves, so this council is no longer needed. The council exists in name only.

United Nations
An international organization of 180 member nations created to develop peace and friendly relations and to protect human rights worldwide

Security Council
A 15-member panel that has the major responsibility for keeping international peace

Reading Strategy
Predicting
Go back to your prediction of the meaning of a *security alliance*. Were you correct in your prediction?

The last two UN divisions are the International Court of Justice (ICJ) and the Secretariat. The ICJ acts as the World Court. It has 15 judges and handles cases brought by both members and nonmembers. The Secretariat is headed by the secretary-general. This person manages the staff of 9,000 people who do the daily work of the UN.

✓ **Checkpoint**   What are the six divisions of the United Nations?

How does the United Nations work?

The United Nations acts as a mediator between countries and groups within countries that are having disagreements. The UN can place sanctions, or trade limits, on countries that break rules. The United Nations can call on member countries to send troops to act as peacekeepers in troubled areas. The Security Council must vote on these actions. Nine of the 15 member countries of the Security Council must agree before an action is taken.

The UN also tries to help poor nations, improve world health and the environment, and address issues related to human rights. The UN has many agencies that help to achieve its goals.

- The Food and Agriculture Organization of the United Nations is concerned with ending hunger in countries around the world.

- The goal of the Educational, Scientific, and Cultural Organization (UNESCO) is to end extreme poverty.

- The World Bank Group supports programs that fight poverty and improve living conditions in developing nations.

- The United Nations Children's Fund (UNICEF) was created after World War II to provide food, clothing, and healthcare to children in Europe.

- The World Health Organization (WHO) supports health around the world.

How is the United States working with the United Nations?

The United States holds a permanent seat in the Security Council. Although there are 192 members of the UN, the United States pays more than 20 percent of the UN budget. At times, the United States has criticized some decisions of the UN and has withheld money. Even so, the United States still works closely with the UN to aid needy countries.

Biography

Carol Bellamy (1942–)

Carol Bellamy has a long history of helping others. In 1995, she was named executive director of UNICEF. As director, she challenges world leaders to use national resources for the benefit of children. Before joining UNICEF, Bellamy was the director of the Peace Corps, another group that helps developing countries. She was the first former Peace Corps volunteer to head UNICEF. She has worked as a banker and a lawyer on Wall Street. She was the first woman elected head of the New York City Council. Bellamy also served in the New York state senate from 1973 to 1977.

SECTION 4 ASSESSMENT

Essential Questions Journal Go to your **Essential Questions Journal** to work on this chapter's Essential Question.

1. **Guiding Question** Use your completed table to answer this question: In what ways does the United States cooperate with other nations?

Key Terms and Comprehension

On a sheet of paper, write the answers to the following questions. Use complete sentences.

2. What is foreign aid?

3. What is NATO?

4. What is a regional security alliance?

5. What does the Security Council have to do before the UN can take action?

Critical Thinking

6. **Identify Central Issues** Why do you think countries have formed regional security alliances around the world?

7. **Formulate Opinions** Do you think the United States should aid nations in a conflict? Explain your answer.

Chapter Summary

Section 1—Foreign Affairs and Diplomacy

- The United States went from a policy of isolationism to one of full involvement with other countries after World War II.

- Foreign policy is all the actions a country takes in dealing with other countries.

- The State Department handles foreign affairs and advises the President. The secretary of state heads the State Department.

- The State Department is made up of many agencies.

Section 2—National Security

- The Department of Defense handles the country's armed forces and advises the President. The secretary of defense is the head of the Defense Department.

- The Joint Chiefs of Staff advise the secretary of defense, the President, and the National Security Council.

- The Office of the Director of National Intelligence was created in 2005 to gather intelligence to defend the country.

- The Department of Homeland Security protects the country from terrorism.

Section 3—American Foreign Policy Overview

- America followed a policy of isolationism for 150 years.

- After World War II, many countries practiced collective security and deterrence.

- The Cold War was a time of hostility between the United States and the Soviet Union.

- The United States fought two wars in Asia: the Korean War and the Vietnam War.

- The Cold War came to an end in 1991.

Section 4—Foreign Aid and Alliances

- Foreign aid and security alliances are the basic parts of American foreign policy.

- The North Atlantic Treaty Organization (NATO) and the United Nations were formed to promote peace after World War II.

- The UN Security Council, made up of fifteen member countries, decides what actions the UN takes.

Guiding Question
Section 2 How does the federal government safeguard the nation's security?

Guiding Question
Section 3 How has American foreign policy changed over time?

Guiding Question
Section 1 How is foreign policy made and conducted?

CHAPTER 17

Essential Question
How should the United States interact with other countries?

Guiding Question
Section 4 In what ways does the United States cooperate with other nations?

Document-Based Assessment

Colin Powell's Remarks About NATO

Following a meeting of the North Atlantic Council at North Atlantic Treaty Organization (NATO) headquarters in Brussels, Belgium, in December of 2001, Secretary of State Colin Powell made the following remarks. He spoke about how NATO provided security and stability. He referred to Article V, which states that NATO members must consider coming to the aid of an ally under attack.

Document at a Glance

- Colin Powell speaking about NATO
- Praises NATO for response after September 11 attacks
- NATO continues work towards peace.

Immediately after the September 11 attacks, NATO was the first to offer its support, invoking Article V for the first time in its history . . .

It has meant a great deal to us in the United States to have this immediate response on the part of this great alliance we have proudly served within over the last . . . fifty-two years . . . the critical assistance this alliance has provided has sent a clear message to our enemies about the depth of our common purpose . . .

Our resolve is shown by the NATO AWACS [military aircraft] flying over the skies of North America and by NATO naval forces deployed in support of Operation Enduring Freedom. Allied nations sent forces to the field to fight side by side alongside our forces, and more are standing by should they be needed . . .

Today . . . we agreed to move rapidly to defend against terrorism and other emerging threats . . .

NATO will continue to anchor the continent's new democracies firmly in the transatlantic community and to ensure the success of democratic institutions and the democratic transition process . . .

NATO and the transatlantic community continue to form the indispensable foundation for the peace and prosperity of all our nations and those who are friends of NATO as well . . . together we will conquer today's challenges as well.

Document-Based Questions

1. What did Powell say was invoked for the first time in history?

2. What message did NATO's response to the September 11 attacks send to our enemies?

3. What operation did Powell mention NATO naval forces supported?

4. What did Powell say we need to move rapidly to defend today?

5. **Make a Prediction** Based on this document, do you think NATO will continue to work toward world peace in the future? Explain your answer.

SOURCE: Remarks by Colin Powell following the meeting of the North Atlantic Council, December 6, 2001

Chapter Assessment

Directions: On a sheet of paper, write the answer to each
question. Use complete sentences.

Section 1—Foreign Affairs and Diplomacy

1. What is the difference between domestic affairs and
foreign affairs?

2. What is the difference between isolationism and
internationalism?

3. What is diplomatic immunity?

4. What is the right of legation?

5. **Critical Thinking** What is one benefit of being an
ambassador of the United States in a different country?
What is one risk?

Section 2—National Security

6. When was the Department of Defense created?

7. What does "civilian control" of the military mean?

8. Why was the Office of Director of National Intelligence created?

9. **Critical Thinking** Why do you think it is so difficult to
completely protect the United States against terrorist attacks?

Section 3—American Foreign Policy Overview

10. What is the policy of deterrence?

11. What is the policy of containment?

12. Which event led to the Cold War?

13. **Critical Thinking** How has American foreign policy in the
Middle East succeeded? How has it failed?

Section 4—Foreign Aid and Alliances

14. What is UNICEF?

15. What is the main function of the UN Security Council?

16. Why were NATO and the UN formed?

17. Critical Thinking Why do you think the United States has paid so much (20 percent) of the United Nations budget?

Apply What You've Learned

Exploring the Essential Question

Select a country to which the United States has provided aid in the last 20 years. Research the country to answer the following questions:

18. Why did the United States provide aid to the country? For how long did the United States provide support?

19. What kind of aid was given by the United States? What was the result?

Essential Questions Project

20. Use the results of your research to write a paper that helps express your opinion on the Essential Question: **How should the United States interact with other countries?** If needed, have your teacher help you get started. Your paragraph should be well thought out and should include facts that support your view.

**Essential Questions
Journal**

Go to your **Essential Questions Journal** to work on this chapter's Essential Question.

Test-Taking Tip

Pace yourself. If you are unsure about a question, put a check next to it and move on. If you have time, go back and try to answer the checked questions.

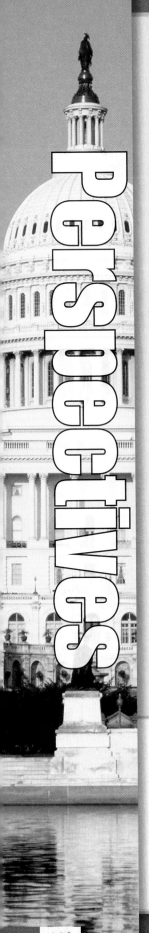

Perspectives

Essential Question
What makes a good President?

Familiarizing yourself with the variety of viewpoints on the success of a presidency can help you identify the factors that define a good President.

" ON THE QUALITIES OF A GREAT PRESIDENT:

. . . [R]esearch indicate[s] that great presidents, besides being stubborn and disagreeable, are more extraverted, open to experience, assertive, achievement striving, excitement seeking and more open to fantasy, aesthetics, feelings, actions, ideas and values. Historically great presidents were low on straightforwardness, vulnerability and order.
—American Psychological Association, August 2000

ON HISTORY'S JUDGMENT OF THE PRESIDENT:

In a pun on the names of cars and Presidents, Gerald Ford joked during his presidency that he was "a Ford, not a Lincoln."

" ON THE OPPORTUNITY TO BECOME A GREAT PRESIDENT:

All our great presidents were leaders of thought at times when certain ideas in the life of the nation had to be clarified.
—Franklin D. Roosevelt

Essential Question Warmup

Throughout this unit, you studied the job and the office of the President. Use what you have learned and the quotations and opinions above to answer the following questions. Then go to your **Essential Questions Journal.**

1. How do voters judge candidates?
2. Why does history often judge Presidents differently from how they were judged in their own time?
3. Should a President strive to be popular or strive to be effective?
4. Can a President be great if there is no clear opportunity to show greatness?

Essential Questions Journal
To continue to build a response to the unit Essential Question, go to your **Essential Questions Journal.**

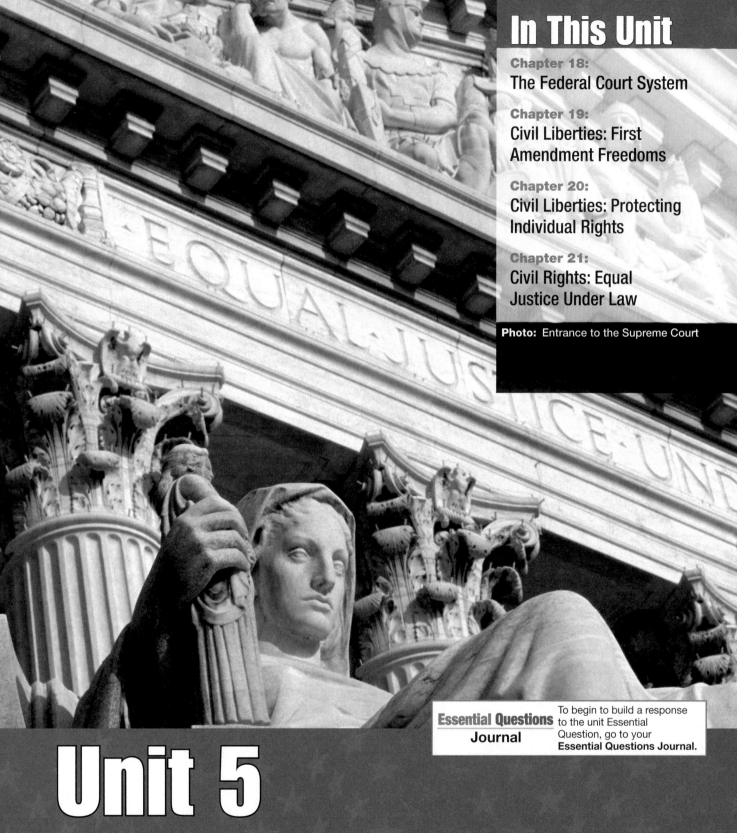

Photo: Entrance to the Supreme Court

Essential Questions Journal To begin to build a response to the unit Essential Question, go to your **Essential Questions Journal.**

Unit 5
The Judicial Branch

Essential Question What should be the role of the judicial branch?

▲ Attorney Frank Dunham holds a news conference in front of the U.S. Supreme Court building.

The Federal Court System

Essential Question
Does the structure of the federal court system allow it to administer justice effectively?

Reading Strategy: Text Structure
Understanding how the text is organized helps you decide which information is most important. Before you begin reading about the federal court system, do the following.

- Look at the title, headings, boldfaced words, and photographs.
- Summarize the text by thinking about its structure.

GOVERNMENT ONLINE
ON THE GO

To study anywhere, anytime, download these online resources at PearsonSuccessNet.com
- Political Dictionary
- Audio Review
- Downloadable Interactivities

The National Judiciary

▲ Judge Maryanne Trump Barry, U.S. Court of Appeals, Third Circuit

Guiding Question

What are the structure and function of the national judiciary? Use a table like the one below to take notes on the section.

The National Judiciary	
Structure	Types of Jurisdiction
■ Dual court system ■	■ Exclusive jurisdiction ■ Original jurisdiction

Objectives:

- Explain why the Constitution created a national judiciary, and describe its structure.
- List the types of cases heard in federal courts and compare the types of federal court jurisdiction.
- Understand the appointment process for federal judges and list their terms of office.
- Understand the impact of judicial philosophy.
- Examine the roles of federal court officers.

The United States government is made up of three parts. They are called the legislative, executive, and judicial branches. In this chapter, we will look at the judicial branch.

The judicial branch includes all federal courts. The Supreme Court is the highest federal court. The courts below the Supreme Court are called the inferior courts. The inferior courts include the constitutional courts and the special courts.

The federal courts were set up to interpret and apply the Constitution and the laws of the land. Cases that involve federal law are always heard in federal courts. In this section, you will learn about the national judiciary, or court system.

Why was a national judiciary created?

Under the Articles of Confederation, there was no national judiciary and no national courts. Each state decided how to interpret the laws of the United States. This system did not work because each state ignored the rulings of the other states. There was a need for a national court system to the laws. When the Framers met in Philadelphia in 1787, they created a national judiciary. They did so in Article III of the Constitution.

What is the dual court system?

The United States has *two* separate court systems. The Constitution created a national system of courts. These federal courts are located in all 50 states. The second court system is the state courts. Every state has its own system of courts. The state courts hear most of the cases in the country.

What are the two kinds of federal courts?

The two types of federal courts are constitutional courts and special courts. Congress created these **inferior courts** based on Article III of the Constitution. The constitutional courts include the courts of appeals, the district courts, and the United States Court of International Trade.

The special courts handle cases that arise from the expressed powers of Congress described in Article I of the Constitution. There are many types of special courts. Each court hears a very narrow range of cases. Special courts are covered in detail in Section 4 of this chapter. For a summary of the federal courts, see Figure 18.1.

✓**Checkpoint** What courts make up the constitutional courts?

Reading Strategy
Text Structure
Preview this page. Notice the headings, features, and checkpoint questions.

Inferior courts
The lower federal courts, beneath the Supreme Court

What is the jurisdiction of the federal courts?

The Constitution gives federal courts the authority to hear cases that involve the following:

- a person or group who violates any part of the Constitution
- a person or group who breaks a federal law

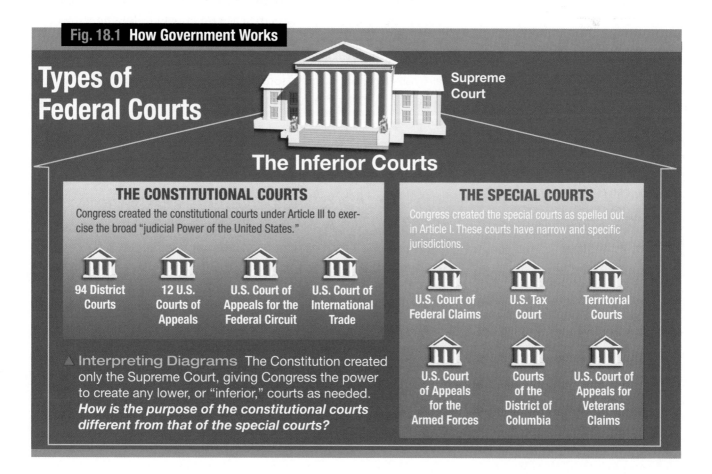

Fig. 18.1 How Government Works

Types of Federal Courts

Supreme Court

The Inferior Courts

THE CONSTITUTIONAL COURTS

Congress created the constitutional courts under Article III to exercise the broad "judicial Power of the United States."

- 94 District Courts
- 12 U.S. Courts of Appeals
- U.S. Court of Appeals for the Federal Circuit
- U.S. Court of International Trade

THE SPECIAL COURTS

Congress created the special courts as spelled out in Article I. These courts have narrow and specific jurisdictions.

- U.S. Court of Federal Claims
- U.S. Tax Court
- Territorial Courts
- U.S. Court of Appeals for the Armed Forces
- Courts of the District of Columbia
- U.S. Court of Appeals for Veterans Claims

▲ **Interpreting Diagrams** The Constitution created only the Supreme Court, giving Congress the power to create any lower, or "inferior," courts as needed. *How is the purpose of the constitutional courts different from that of the special courts?*

Exclusive jurisdiction
The power of the federal courts alone to hear certain cases

Concurrent jurisdiction
The power shared by federal and state courts to hear certain cases

Plaintiff
In civil law, the party who brings a suit or some other legal action against another (the defendant) in court

Defendant
The person against whom a complaint is made

Original jurisdiction
The power of a court to hear a case first, before any other court

Appellate jurisdiction
The authority of a court to review decisions of inferior (lower) courts

Reading Strategy
Text Structure
As you read, write the steps taken to appoint a federal judge.

The federal courts also hear those cases in which:

- a foreign nation or ambassador sues the U.S. or a U.S. citizen
- an American citizen sues a foreign government or person
- a crime occurs on a U.S. ship at sea or on federal property
- a disagreement arises between states or between citizens of different states.

What are the types of jurisdiction?

There are many types of jurisdiction. **Exclusive jurisdiction** means that only a federal court may try certain cases. For example, if a person commits a crime on an American ship, that person must be tried in a federal court. Cases involving federal taxes are always tried in a federal court.

Some cases may be tried in either a federal or a state court. The courts then have **concurrent jurisdiction.** Many of these cases involve money disagreements between citizens of different states. The person who files the cases is called the **plaintiff.** The plaintiff may choose whether to be heard in a state or a federal court. The **defendant** is the person about whom the complaint is made. The defendant can have the trial moved under certain circumstances.

A court has **original jurisdiction** if the case must be heard in that court first. A court that hears the case on appeal following a lower court ruling has **appellate jurisdiction.** This court can change the decision of the lower court or uphold that decision. District courts have only original jurisdiction. Appeals courts have only appellate jurisdiction. Only the Supreme Court has both types of jurisdiction.

✔**Checkpoint** What are the four types of jurisdictions discussed in this section?

How are federal judges appointed?

The Constitution gave the President the power to appoint Supreme Court justices. The President needs the approval of the Senate. The Senate also has a part in the appointment of all other federal judges. The Constitution does not set any qualifications for federal judges. When choosing judges, the President often takes advice from the senators from the State where the judge will serve. This practice is called senatorial courtesy. The President also asks for advice from the Attorney General and political advisors.

Federal judges are often former attorneys, professors of law, members of Congress, or state judges. Presidents will often choose judges from their own political party.

What is judicial philosophy?

A President may consider the judicial philosophy of candidates for judge. A judge may practice either **judicial activism** and **judicial restraint.** Judicial restraint means a judge will consider **precedent** (what was decided in other cases) when making decisions about a case. The judge will also consider the Constitution and what the law originally intended. Judicial activism means the judge tends to be more aware of changes since the law was made. The judge might interpret the law according to newer values in the country. A judge's belief in either judicial activism or judicial restraint is called judicial philosophy. For more on judicial philosophy, see Figure 18.2.

What is the term and pay of judges?

Supreme Court justices are appointed for life and can only be removed by impeachment. This is stated in the Constitution. The Framers wanted judges to be independent and did not want them to worry about whether or not they would be reappointed. Special court judges are not appointed for life. They are named to terms of 8 to 15 years, depending on the court.

Congress sets the salaries of all federal judges. Federal judges may retire at age 70 and receive full salary for the rest of their lives, if they have served 10 years.

Judicial activism
A belief that the courts should take an active role in deciding cases related to politics and social issues

Judicial restraint
A belief that the courts should decide cases based on the original intent of a law and on precedent.

Precedent
A court decision that stands as an example to be followed in the future

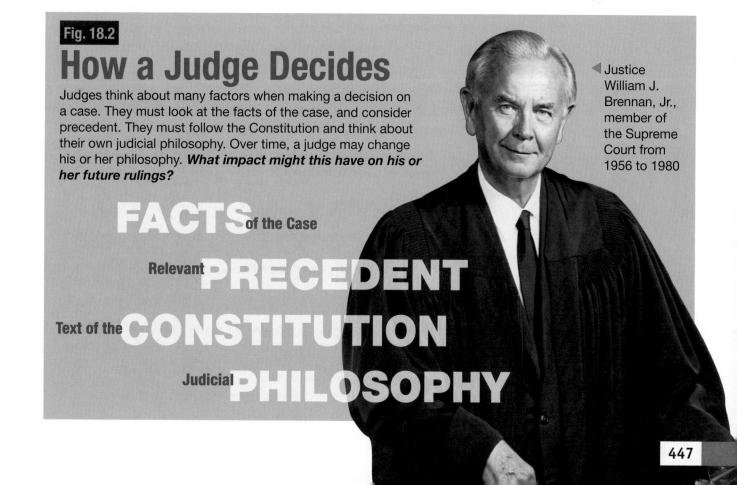

Fig. 18.2

How a Judge Decides

Judges think about many factors when making a decision on a case. They must look at the facts of the case, and consider precedent. They must follow the Constitution and think about their own judicial philosophy. Over time, a judge may change his or her philosophy. *What impact might this have on his or her future rulings?*

FACTS of the Case

Relevant PRECEDENT

Text of the CONSTITUTION

Judicial PHILOSOPHY

◄ Justice William J. Brennan, Jr., member of the Supreme Court from 1956 to 1980

Who are the court officers?

There are many people who work in the federal courts and support federal judges. There are clerks, bailiffs, court reporters, probation officers, and others.

Federal judges also appoint U.S. magistrates to help run the district courts. Magistrates are justices who handle minor civil complaints and misdemeanor cases. There are more than 400 magistrates in the court system.

Bankruptcy judges are assigned to each federal judicial district. They are appointed for a 14-year term by judges of a federal court of appeals. There are about 300 bankruptcy judges.

The President and the Senate appoint a U.S. attorney for each federal judicial district. These U.S. district attorneys assist law enforcement agencies. They also help in all civil actions against the federal government.

United States marshals also serve in each of the district courts. Their duties include making arrests, choosing people to serve on juries, and responding to emergencies, including possible terrorist attacks.

Essential Questions Journal Go to your **Essential Questions Journal** to work on this chapter's Essential Question.

SECTION 1 ASSESSMENT

1. **Guiding Question** Use your completed table to answer this question: What are the structure and function of the national judiciary?

Key Terms and Comprehension

On a sheet of paper, write the answer to each question. Use complete sentences.

2. What is the difference between **original jurisdiction** and **appellate jurisdiction?**

3. What is **precedent?**

4. Over what types of cases do federal courts have jurisdiction?

5. Name the two types of federal courts.

Critical Thinking

6. **Draw Conclusions** Why do you think the President needs Senate approval to appoint Supreme Court justices? Do you think this system is fair? Why or why not?

7. **Identify Alternatives** Do you think that judges should be appointed for life? Why or why not?

ISSUES OF OUR TIME

Judicial Restraint vs. Activism

▶▶ Track the Issue

The Court's power of judicial review is an important part of the governing of this country. Throughout the Court's history, it has used both judicial restraint and judicial activism in different cases. A few examples are highlighted below.

1819 In *McCulloch* v. *Maryland,* Chief Justice John Marshall used judicial activism. He expanded constitutional provisions without giving precedent.

1849 The Court's decision in *Luther* v. *Borden* is one of the earliest cases of judicial restraint.

1954 The decision in *Brown* v. *Board of Education* provides an example of judicial activism.

2005 Newly appointed Chief Justice John Roberts promises judicial restraint.

Chief Justice
John Roberts

▶▶ Perspectives

There are two different thoughts on judicial decision making. One side supports judicial restraint—the belief that judges should strictly follow the law and apply precedent. The other side supports judicial activism—the belief that judges should consider precedent, but also be able to freely interpret the Constitution and shape public policy.

Judicial Restraint	Judicial Activism
"In our democratic system, responsibility for policy making properly rests with those branches that are responsible . . . to the people. It was . . . because the Framers intended the judiciary to be insulated from popular political pressures that the Constitution accords judges tenure during good behavior. . . . To the extent the term 'judicial activism' is used to describe unjustified intrusions by the judiciary into the realm of policy making, the criticism is well-founded. . . . It is not part of the judicial function to make the law . . . or to execute the law." *—John Roberts, Chief Justice of the United States, 2005–*	"We are under a Constitution, but the Constitution is what the judges say it is, and the judiciary is the safeguard of our liberty and of our property under the Constitution." *—Charles Evan Hughes, Chief Justice of the United States, 1930–1941*

Connect to Your World

1. What reasons does Justice Roberts give for supporting judicial restraint? What reason does Hughes provide in favor of judicial activism?
2. What do you think the role of the courts should be? Should the courts show judicial restraint or judicial activism? Why?

GOVERNMENT ONLINE
In the News
To find out more about judicial decision making, visit
PearsonSuccessNet.com

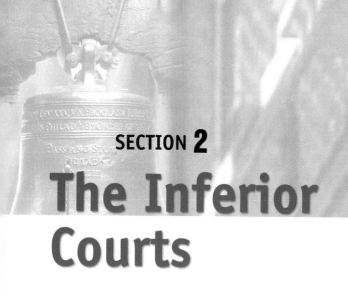

SECTION 2
The Inferior Courts

▲ An attorney for an online music firm speaks outside of the 9th Circuit Court of Appeals.

Guiding Question

What are the structure and jurisdiction of the inferior courts? Use a table like the one below to take notes on the structure and jurisdiction of the inferior courts.

The Inferior Courts	
Structure	Jurisdiction
■ District courts	■ Original jurisdiction
■ Appellate courts	■
■	■

Objectives:

- Describe the structure and jurisdiction of the federal district courts.
- Describe the structure and jurisdiction of the federal courts of appeals.
- Describe the structure and jurisdiction of the two other constitutional courts.

The inferior courts are the lower federal courts. They were created by Congress. They hear about 80 percent of all federal cases. They are referred to as inferior courts because they are below the Supreme Court.

What are the district courts?

Federal cases are heard in the district courts. Each state has at least one district court. Some larger states are divided into two or more districts. There are a total of 94 district courts with more than 650 judges. Several judges are assigned to each district court. District courts are the only federal courts that use a jury. In most other federal courts, judges make decisions without a jury. For more on judicial districts, see Figure 18.3 on the next page.

What is district court jurisdiction?

District courts are the main trial courts in the federal court system. Because of this, they are known as the "courts of first instance." They have original jurisdiction over most federal criminal and civil cases. A **criminal case** is one in which a defendant is tried for breaking a law, such as kidnapping. A **civil case** is one that involves a noncriminal matter. This may be an argument over the terms of a contract, for example.

Most of the decisions from the 94 district courts are final. Occasionally, those decisions are appealed to the courts of appeals or the Supreme Court.

✓**Checkpoint** What are the main courts in the federal court system?

What are the court of appeals?

The courts of appeals were created by Congress in 1891. They were needed because the Supreme Court had so many cases to hear that the justices could not keep up. They were three years behind in hearing these cases. People accused of crimes who feel that their trial was unfair in the district court may appeal. They may ask a higher court to review their cases. These reviews take place in courts of appeals. These are sometimes called appellate courts. Courts of Appeals have only appellate jurisdiction. They only hear cases on appeal from the lower courts in their districts. Some cases do come from the U.S. Tax Court and territorial courts. Sometimes the courts of appeals hear cases from a federal regulatory agency.

There are now 13 Courts of Appeals in the federal judicial system. One of these is the Court of Appeals for the Federal Circuit, located in the District of Columbia. Unlike the other courts of appeals, it hears cases from all over the United States. It is mostly concerned with appeals of decisions in patent, copyright, and international trade cases.

■ ■ ■ ■ ■ ■ ■ ■ ■ ■ ■ ■ ■ ■ ■

Reading Strategy
Text Structure
Notice the paragraph headings are written as questions. After you read each paragraph, try to answer the question asked in the heading.

■ ■ ■ ■ ■ ■ ■ ■ ■ ■ ■ ■ ■ ■ ■

Criminal case
A case in which a defendant is tried for breaking the law

Civil case
A case involving a noncriminal matter

Fig. 18.3
Federal Court Circuits and Districts

Interpreting Maps Each state comprises at least one United States judicial district. The nation is divided into 13 judicial circuits as shown on the map. The 13 circuits include the Court of Appeals for the District of Columbia and the Court of Appeals for the Federal Circuit. *Which states are in the fifth circuit?* ▼

GOVERNMENT ONLINE
Audio Tour
Listen to a guided audio tour of the judicial circuit map at
PearsonSuccessNet.com

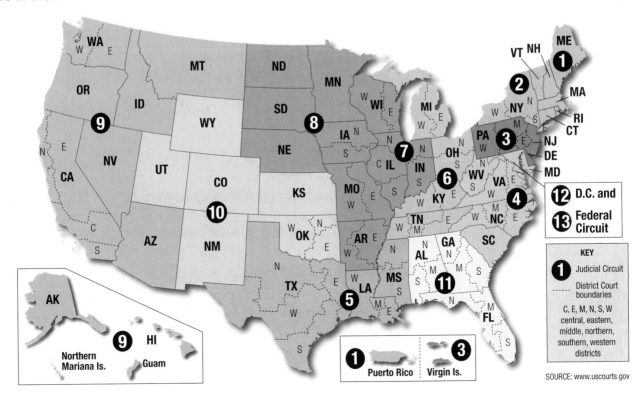

KEY
1 Judicial Circuit
- - - District Court boundaries
C, E, M, N, S, W
central, eastern, middle, northern, southern, western districts

SOURCE: www.uscourts.gov

Fig. 18.4

Constitutional Courts

- District Courts
- U.S. Courts of Appeals
- U.S. Court of Appeals for the Federal Circuit
- U.S. Court of International Trade

There are 179 judges in Courts of Appeals. One Supreme Court justice is also assigned to each court. Figure 18.5 on the next page shows the path that cases take in appellate courts.

When a court of appeals receives a case to review, the judges study the history of the case. The judges cannot ask for new facts to be presented. Instead, they review the original trial record and carefully consider the arguments for each side. If the judges decide the trial was unfair, they will reverse the district court's decision. They also may send the case back to the district court for a new trial. If the judges decide that the original trial was fair and the verdict justified, the district court judgment stands. Very few of their decisions are appealed to the Supreme Court.

✔ **Checkpoint**   How does a case get to the Court of Appeals?

What is the Court of International Trade?

Congress has established one other constitutional court. It is called the Court of International Trade. It hears civil cases related to taxes on imported goods collected by customs officials and other trade-related issues. It is also called the Trade Court. (Figure 18.4) The Trade Court has nine judges. During court trials, the judges sit in panels of three. They often hold trials at such major ports as San Francisco, New Orleans, Boston, and New York.

Government in Your Life

Jury Trial

The 6th Amendment gives an accused person the right to a speedy public trial by a jury in the state where the crime took place. A defendant must be told what the charges are and is entitled to have a lawyer.

A trial jury is usually made up of 12 persons. Jurors typically live in the community in which the crime took place. The jury members are chosen at random from lists of voters or taxpayers. They must decide, after hearing both sides of the case, whether a person is guilty or innocent. If a jury cannot agree on a verdict, a new trial may be held, or the charges may be dropped.

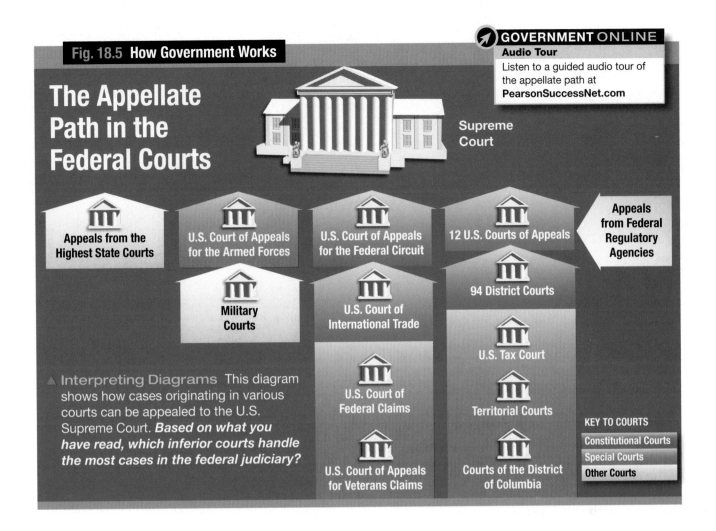

Fig. 18.5 How Government Works

GOVERNMENT ONLINE
Audio Tour
Listen to a guided audio tour of the appellate path at **PearsonSuccessNet.com**

The Appellate Path in the Federal Courts

Supreme Court

Appeals from the Highest State Courts

U.S. Court of Appeals for the Armed Forces

U.S. Court of Appeals for the Federal Circuit

12 U.S. Courts of Appeals

Appeals from Federal Regulatory Agencies

Military Courts

U.S. Court of International Trade

94 District Courts

U.S. Tax Court

U.S. Court of Federal Claims

Territorial Courts

U.S. Court of Appeals for Veterans Claims

Courts of the District of Columbia

KEY TO COURTS
Constitutional Courts
Special Courts
Other Courts

▲ **Interpreting Diagrams** This diagram shows how cases originating in various courts can be appealed to the U.S. Supreme Court. *Based on what you have read, which inferior courts handle the most cases in the federal judiciary?*

SECTION 2 ASSESSMENT

Essential Questions
Journal
Go to your **Essential Questions Journal** to work on this chapter's Essential Question.

1. **Guiding Question** Use your completed table to answer this question: What are the structure and jurisdiction of the inferior courts?

Key Terms and Comprehension
On a sheet of paper, write the answer to each question. Use complete sentences.

2. Why are the lower federal courts called inferior courts?

3. What are the main courts in the federal court system?

4. If people feel their trials were unfair in a federal district court, what might they do next?

5. What types of cases does the Court of International Trade hear?

Critical Thinking

6. **Analyze Information** Why do you think so many of the courts in the federal judiciary are appellate courts?

7. **Draw Inferences** Why do you think judges cannot ask for new facts in a court of appeals hearing?

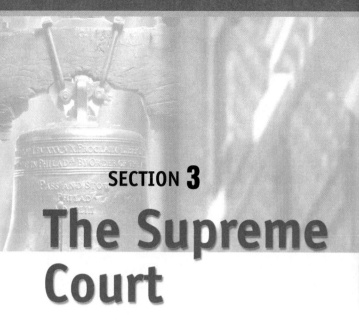

SECTION 3

The Supreme Court

▲ Chief Justice John Marshall, 1801–1835

Guiding Question

What is the Supreme Court's jurisdiction, and how does the court operate? Use an outline like the one below to take notes on the Supreme Court.

I. The Supreme Court
   A. Judicial review
      1. Established in *Marbury* v. *Madison*, 1803
      2. _____
   B. Jurisdiction
      1. _____
      2. _____

Objectives:

- Understand the concept of judicial review.
- Describe the jurisdiction of the Supreme Court.
- Understand how cases get to the Supreme Court.
- Examine the way the Court works.

In Article III, Section 1, the Framers created the Supreme Court of the United States. It is the only court created in the Constitution and is the highest court in the nation. Its decisions are final and cannot be appealed. The Framers intended the Supreme Court to be as powerful as Congress and the President.

The Supreme Court is headed by a Chief Justice, who works with eight associate justiºces. Congress first set the number of associate justices at five. In 1869, Congress changed this number to eight. It has remained at eight since that date. Justices are appointed for life, but may resign at any time.

Justices are appointed by the President. Those appointments must be approved by the Senate. The Senate Judiciary Committee holds hearings to decide whether the person whom the President appointed would be a good justice.

✓ **Checkpoint** Where in the Constitution is the Supreme Court created?

What is judicial review?

As both federal and state courts settle cases involving constitutional questions, they interpret the meaning of the Constitution. This is known as the power of judicial review. The Constitution does not list this power, but it is certain that the Framers intended that the federal courts, and especially the Supreme Court, should have it.

The Supreme Court is the final authority on the meaning of the Constitution. Using the power of judicial review, the Court can declare laws and actions of local, state, or national governments to be unconstitutional.

Why was *Marbury* v. *Madison* important?

The Supreme Court established its power of judicial review in the case of *Marbury* v. *Madison* in 1803. William Marbury was appointed a justice of the peace on the last day of John Adams's term as President. The commission confirming the appointment was not delivered before Thomas Jefferson took office.

When Jefferson became President the next day, he would not allow his new secretary of state, James Madison, to make the appointment. Marbury sued Madison. Marbury cited the Judiciary Act of 1789. It stated he could take his case to the Supreme Court. The Supreme Court decided this part of the Judiciary Act went against Article III of the Constitution. The Court refused Marbury's request. By doing so, it claimed the power of judicial review. Since that time, many laws passed by Congress have gone to the Supreme Court. The Court then decides whether or not they are Constitutional and how they should be interpreted.

✔ **Checkpoint** How did this case establish judicial review?

What is the Supreme Court's jurisdiction?

Figure 18.6 shows the jurisdiction of the Supreme Court. The Court has both original and appellate jurisdiction. It hears most cases under its appellate jurisdiction, from the lower federal courts and the highest state courts. Someone has to challenge, or question, the law involved in a case before it can go to the Supreme Court. **Figure 18.7** on page 456 shows the route cases can take to the Supreme Court.

In a small number of cases, the Supreme Court has original jurisdiction. This happens when a state is a party in a case. The Court also has original jurisdiction when an ambassador, minister, or consul is involved. The Court hears only one or two cases each year under its original jurisdiction.

✔ **Checkpoint** When does the Supreme Court have original jurisdiction?

How does the Supreme Court operate?

The Supreme Court is in session from October to about July. When the High Court hears a case, the justices listen to oral, or spoken, arguments from both sides. The justices usually ask questions of each attorney during oral arguments. The justices also review the written statements, or briefs, provided by each side.

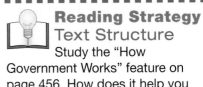

Reading Strategy
Text Structure
Study the "How Government Works" feature on page 456. How does it help you understand how a case reaches the Supreme Court?

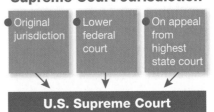

Fig. 18.6

Supreme Court Jurisdiction

Original jurisdiction	Lower federal court	On appeal from highest state court

U.S. Supreme Court

Fig. 18.7 How Government Works

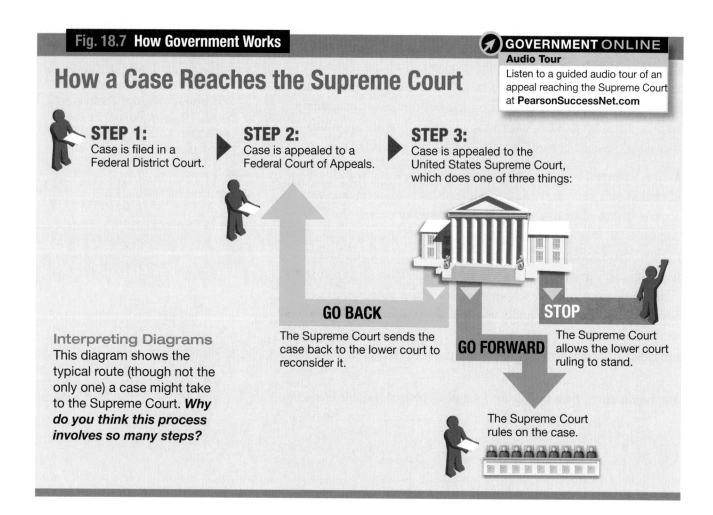

How a Case Reaches the Supreme Court

GOVERNMENT ONLINE
Audio Tour
Listen to a guided audio tour of an appeal reaching the Supreme Court at **PearsonSuccessNet.com**

STEP 1:
Case is filed in a Federal District Court.

STEP 2:
Case is appealed to a Federal Court of Appeals.

STEP 3:
Case is appealed to the United States Supreme Court, which does one of three things:

GO BACK
The Supreme Court sends the case back to the lower court to reconsider it.

GO FORWARD

STOP
The Supreme Court allows the lower court ruling to stand.

The Supreme Court rules on the case.

Interpreting Diagrams
This diagram shows the typical route (though not the only one) a case might take to the Supreme Court. *Why do you think this process involves so many steps?*

Majority opinion
Officially called the Opinion of the Court; announces the Court's decision and sets out the reasoning upon which it is based

Concurring opinion
Written explanation of the views of one or more judges who support the majority of the Court

Dissenting opinion
Written explanation of the views of one or more judges who disagree with a decision reached by the majority of the Court

More than 8,000 cases are appealed to the Supreme Court each year. The Court considers only a few hundred of those. This is because the Court usually agrees with the lower court's decision or because the case doesn't raise any important constitutional issues. Of the cases the Court agrees to consider, less than 100 involve a full hearing.

What are Court opinions?

The decisions made in the Supreme Court are reached by a majority vote of the nine justices. For a look at the current Court, see **Figure 18.8** on the next page. Six justices must be present to call for a vote. After the Court votes, the Chief Justice or one of the associate justices writes the **majority opinion.** This is a carefully worded statement that explains why the decision was made.

The Court's opinions are very important. They are used as precedents in similar cases. Sometimes, a justice may write a **concurring opinion** to add facts to the majority opinion. Other times, the justice might write a concurring opinion to state different reasons for reaching the decision. Those justices who did not agree with the majority opinion often write a **dissenting opinion.** Dissenting opinions cannot become precedent in the lower courts.

Fig. 18.8
Who Is on the Court Today?

GOVERNMENT ONLINE
Online Update/Interactive
For online updates and to choose your own Court, go to
PearsonSuccessNet.com

Justice	Age When Appointed	Appointed by (Year)	Previous Years as a Judge
Chief Justice John G. Roberts, Jr.	50	G.W. Bush (2005)	2
John Paul Stevens	55	Ford (1975)	5
Antonin Scalia	50	Reagan (1986)	4
Anthony M. Kennedy	51	Reagan (1988)	13
David H. Souter	51	G.H.W. Bush (1990)	13
Clarence Thomas	43	G.H.W. Bush (1991)	2
Ruth Bader Ginsburg	60	Clinton (1993)	13
Stephen G. Breyer	55	Clinton (1994)	14
Samuel A. Alito, Jr.	55	G.W. Bush (2006)	16

A President often appoints justices who share his or her views. Today's Supreme Court is often divided in its decisions, likely due to the controversial nature of the cases that it hears. The Court has recently made 5–4 decisions on topics such as protection for wetlands and capital punishment for juvenile offenders. *What might be the impact on society when a justice changes his or her viewpoint?*

Front row: Anthony Kennedy, John Paul Stevens, Chief Justice John Roberts, Antonin Scalia, David Souter. Back row: Stephen Breyer, Clarence Thomas, Ruth Bader Ginsburg, Samuel Alito

Essential Questions Journal
Go to your **Essential Questions Journal** to work on this chapter's Essential Question.

SECTION 3 ASSESSMENT

Quick Write

Do research online or at the library to choose one of the following Supreme Court cases: *Marbury* v. *Madison, Brandenburg* v. *Ohio,* or *City of Boerne* v. *Flores.* Then write two or three paragraphs on the case you chose. Include details such as who, what, when, where, and why.

1. **Guiding Question** Use your completed outline to answer this question: What is the scope of the Supreme Court's jurisdiction, and how does the Court operate?

Key Terms and Comprehension

On a sheet of paper, write the answers to each question. Use complete sentences.

2. What is judicial review?

3. What has to happen before a case can get to the Supreme Court?

4. When is the Supreme Court in session?

5. What is a majority opinion?

Critical Thinking

6. **Draw Conclusions** Why is it important that there is an odd number of Supreme Court justices?

7. **Analyze Information** Why was the *Marbury* v. *Madison* case so important?

▲ U.S. Army attorney before a court-martial

SECTION 4
The Special Courts

Guiding Question

What are the special courts, and what is the jurisdiction of each?
Use a concept web to take notes on the special courts.

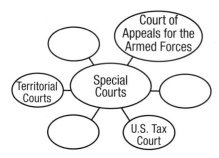

Objectives:

- Understand the difference in jurisdiction between the Court of Appeals for the Armed Forces and the Court of Appeals for Veterans Claims.
- Explain how a citizen may sue the government in the Court of Federal Claims.
- Examine the roles of the territorial courts and the District of Columbia courts.
- Explain the types of cases heard in the Tax Court.

The national court system is made up of the constitutional courts, which are covered in Section 2, and the special courts. In this section, you will learn about the special courts. These courts were created by Congress to hear cases that arise as it exercises its powers. They each have a very narrow jurisdiction and focus. Unlike the constitutional courts, judges in the special courts are not appointed for life. Instead, they serve for a term of four, eight, or fifteen years, depending on the court.

What is the Court of Appeals for the Armed Forces?

Congress began setting up a system of military courts in 1789. These courts are called **courts-martial.** These military courts take care of the needs of the armed forces. They are not a part of the federal court system. The judges and other persons who work in these courts are members of the military. Usually they are officers. A trial in a court-martial is similar to a trial held in any other court.

Congress set up the Court of Military Appeals in 1950. It is now called the Court of Appeals for the Armed Forces. This court is a **civilian tribunal** and reviews serious court-martial convictions. As a civilian tribunal, it is separate from the military. Sometimes, but not often, cases heard in it are appealed to the Supreme Court. Most often it is the court of last resort for cases involving military law.

✔**Checkpoint** When is a civilian tribunal used?

What is the Court of Appeals for Veterans Claims?

Congress created the Court of Appeals for Veterans Claims in 1988. This court hears appeals from decisions made by the Board of Veterans Appeals in the Department of Veterans Affairs, known as the VA. Cases involve claims for benefits that the VA has denied. If the case loses in this court, it may be appealed to the Court of Appeals for the Federal Circuit.

What are military commissions?

Military commissions are boards of five commissioned officers. They are not part of the courts-martial system. Instead, they are separate groups set up to try suspected terrorists captured in Afghanistan and Iraq. Most of these suspects are in prison in Guantanamo Bay, Cuba.

George W. Bush created these military commissions by executive order in 2001. He was acting as commander in chief. In the past, military tribunals had been set up during wars such as the Mexican-American War, Civil War, and World War II. In 2006, however, the Supreme Court decided that the President could not set up these commissions without an act of Congress. The Court told the President to work with Congress to resolve this issue. (Figure 18.9)

■ ■ ■ ■ ■ ■ ■ ■ ■ ■ ■ ■ ■ ■ ■
Reading Strategy
Text Structure
As you read this section, make a list of features of each court for your concept web.

■ ■ ■ ■ ■ ■ ■ ■ ■ ■ ■ ■ ■ ■ ■

Court-martial
A court composed of military personnel, for the trial of those accused of violating military law

Civilian tribunal
A court operating as part of the judicial branch, separate from the military establishment

Fig. 18.9

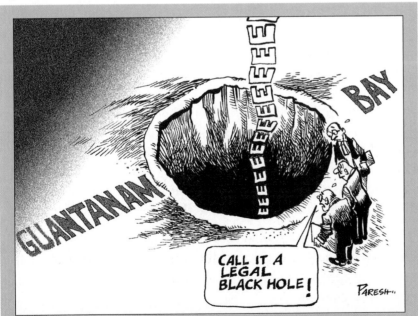

▲ **Analyzing Political Cartoons** Military tribunals have been established at various times in America's past—during the Mexican-American War, the Civil War, and World War II. The people in this cartoon believe that the military commissions at Guantanamo Bay are like a black hole. *Why do you think they feel that way?*

Appropriate
To assign to a particular use

Fig. 18.10

Special Courts
U.S. Court of Appeals for the Armed Forces
U.S. Court of Appeals for Veterans Claims
U.S. Court of Federal Claims
Territorial Courts
Courts of the District of Columbia
U.S. Tax Court

What is the Court of Federal Claims?

The United States cannot be sued unless it agrees to that suit. When Congress declares the government open to suit on a particular matter, the case goes to the Court of Federal Claims. This court hears cases involving money claims against the federal government from all across the country. A decision in favor of the person bringing the suit usually results in money being paid to that person. Congress **appropriates** the money. Cases heard in this court may be appealed to the Court of Appeal for the Federal Circuit.

Sometimes, those who lose in the Claims Court may still win some money. Several years ago, a Puget Sound mink rancher had claimed that low-flying Navy planes scared his animals and the females stopped reproducing. He was asking for $100 per mink. He lost. Then his congressman introduced a bill that eventually paid him $10 for each animal.

What are the territorial courts and the District of Columbia courts?

The territorial courts were created for the country's territories. These territories are Guam, the Virgin Islands, and the Northern Marianas. They serve the same function as the local courts in the 50 states.

The District of Columbia has a judicial system that includes a district court and court of appeals for the district. Congress has also set up two local courts for the District of Columbia: a superior court and a Court of Appeals.

What is the United States Tax Court?

Congress set up the United States Tax Court in 1969. The United States Tax Court hears appeals concerning payment of federal taxes. This court does not hear criminal cases. It settles disagreements about the amount or type of tax. The cases come from the Internal Revenue Service and other agencies. The decisions of the United States Tax Court may be appealed to the federal courts of appeal.

Figure 18.10 lists the special courts in the federal court system. Remember that the Tax Court really is not a part of this system. It is included here because its cases are generated by agencies in the federal government.

✔ **Checkpoint**   What is the purpose of the United States Tax Court?

Biography

Justice Sandra Day O'Connor: 1930–

In 1981, Sandra Day O'Connor was the first woman to become a Supreme Court justice. She was born in El Paso, Texas, and grew up on her family's ranch. After attending Stanford University, she graduated from Stanford University Law School in 1952. She practiced law for several years, and then became assistant attorney general in Arizona. Later, O'Connor served as a state senator in Arizona. She was voted Senate majority leader in 1973, becoming the first woman in the United States to hold that position.

Sandra O'Connor was nominated to the Supreme Court by President Ronald Reagan. She was considered conservative because she believed that the Court should interfere with laws only when necessary. Over the years, Sandra Day O'Connor supported more liberal policies. Liberal policies favor change and support individual rights. For example, she voted in favor of policies that promote equality for women and minorities in the workplace. Sandra Day O'Connor resigned from the Court in 2006.

Essential Questions Journal Go to your **Essential Questions Journal** to work on this chapter's Essential Question.

SECTION 4 ASSESSMENT

Word Bank

Court of Appeals for Veterans Claims

civilian tribunal

courts-martial

Court of Federal Claims

1. **Guiding Question** Use your completed concept web to answer this question: What are the special courts, and what is the jurisdiction of each?

Key Terms and Comprehension

On a sheet of paper, use the words from the Word Bank to complete each sentence correctly.

2. A court of military personnel is called a(n) _____.

3. A court operating separate from the military is called a(n) _____.

4. The _____ hears cases involving money claims against the federal government.

5. The _____ hears cases involving claims for benefits the VA has denied.

Critical Thinking

6. **Draw Conclusions** Why do you think there is a need for special courts?

7. **Identify Alternatives** Why do you think civilians rather than other military officers review serious offenses by military people?

Chapter Summary

Section 1—The National Judiciary

- The need for a uniform interpretation of the laws led the Framers to create a national judiciary.

- The two types of federal courts are the constitutional courts and the special courts.

- There are several types of jurisdiction, depending on which court has the authority to hear a case. Federal courts might have exclusive, concurrent, original, or appellate jurisdiction.

- Judges may practice either judicial activism or judicial restraint when deciding a case.

Section 2—The Inferior Courts

- Inferior courts are lower federal courts that act below the Supreme Court.

- There are 94 district courts. Some larger states have two or more districts.

- Accused people who feel that their trials were unfair in a district court may ask a Court of Appeals to review the case.

Section 3—The Supreme Court

- The Supreme Court is the highest court in the nation. Its decisions are final.

- The Supreme Court uses judicial review to interpret the Constitution.

- In *Marbury* v. *Madison*, the Supreme Court established its power of judicial review.

- There are nine justices (or judges) on the Supreme Court, including a Chief Justice.

Section 4 —The Special Courts

- The special courts have a very narrow focus.

- The Court of Appeals for the Armed Forces uses a civilian tribunal to review serious court-martial cases. The Court of Appeals for Veterans Claims hears cases involving veterans' benefits.

- Military commissions were set up to try suspected terrorists.

- The Court of Federal Claims hears money claims against the government.

- The United States Tax Court hears cases concerning payment of federal taxes.

Guiding Question
Section 2 What are the structure and jurisdiction of the inferior courts?

Guiding Question
Section 3 What is the Supreme Court's jurisdiction, and how does the Court operate?

Guiding Question
Section 1 What are the structure and function of the national judiciary?

Guiding Question
Section 4 What are the special courts, and what is the jurisdiction of each?

CHAPTER 18

Essential Question
Does the structure of the federal court system allow it to administer justice effectively?

Document-Based Assessment

Westside Community Schools v. Mergens (1990)

Bridget Mergens, a senior at Westside High School, wanted to start an after-school Christian club. The principal denied her request, saying the club would be illegal in a public school. Bridget challenged the principal's decision.

The Equal Access Act of 1984 addresses this issue. This law requires a public school to allow religious or political clubs if the school allows other clubs not related to the curriculum. Bridget's school already had a chess club and a scuba diving club, which weren't related to her school's curriculum.

This case went to the Supreme Court and became a test case for deciding if the Equal Access Act was constitutional. The Supreme Court held in favor of Bridget and allowed the Christian club.

Document at a Glance

- Supreme Court case
- Test of Equal Access Act
- Christian Club allowed

The Court said, "We think that secondary school students are mature enough and are likely to understand that a school does not endorse or support student speech—that it merely permits it."

Justice Sandra Day O'Connor said the Equal Access Act was violated because, ". . . Westside's existing clubs include one or more non-curriculum related groups. . . . Westside's denial of . . . religious groups constitutes a denial of equal access to the school's limited open forum . . . although the school apparently permits respondents to meet informally after school . . . they seek equal access in the form of official recognition . . . denial is based on the religious content of the meetings . . . it violates the [Equal Access] Act . . . there is little, if any, risk of government endorsement . . . where no formal classroom activities are involved . . . and no school officials actively participate. . . . . Westside does not risk entanglement between government and religion by complying with the Act.

Document-Based Questions

1. Why did the principal deny Bridget Mergens's request to start an after-school club?

2. What does the Equal Access Act allow?

3. How did the Supreme Court rule in this case?

4. What did the Court say about high-school students?

5. **Text structure** Is this document an example of compare and contrast or problem and solution? Explain why.

Chapter Assessment

GOVERNMENT ONLINE
Self-Test
To test your understanding of
key terms and main ideas, visit
PearsonSuccessNet.com

Directions: Choose the letter of the best answer
or write the answer using complete sentences.

Section 1—The National Judiciary

1. Which court is NOT a part of the federal court system?

    A. district court

    B. state court

    C. court of appeals

    D. Supreme Court

2. What is appellate jurisdiction?

3. Which court has both appellate and original jurisdiction?

4. What is judicial activism?

5. **Critical Thinking** Why do you think the President takes advice from political advisors when appointing federal judges?

Section 2—The Inferior Courts

6. How many district courts are in the United States?

7. If appellate court judges decide a district court trial was fair, what happens next?

    A. The case goes to the Supreme Court.

    B. The judges send the case back for a new trial.

    C. The judges reverse the court's decision.

    D. The district court verdict stands.

8. When a court of appeals reviews a case, which of the following may its judges not do?

    A. review the original trial record

    B. ask for new facts to be presented

    C. consider the arguments for each side

    D. decide whether the lower court decision was constitutional

9. **Critical Thinking** Why were the appellate courts added to the judicial system process? Do you think they are necessary?

Section 3—The Supreme Court

10. How many justices sit on the Supreme Court, including the Chief Justice?

    A. 6   **B.** 7   **C.** 8   **D.** 9

11. Why might a judge write a dissenting opinion?

12. When does the Supreme Court have original jurisdiction?

13. Critical Thinking Why are the Court's opinions so important?

Section 4—The Special Courts

14. What are territorial courts?

15. Which court hears cases from the Internal Revenue Service and other Treasury Department agencies?
   A. Court of Federal Claims
   B. District of Columbia court
   C. Tax Court
   D. Court of Appeals for the Armed Forces

16. Why did George W. Bush create military commissions in 2001?

17. Critical Thinking If you were a plaintiff in a case, would you want a judge or a jury to decide your outcome? Why?

Apply What You've Learned

Exploring the Essential Question

18. What is the structure of the federal court system?

19. What might happen if the federal court system did not exist?

Essential Questions Project

20. Work with a group of students to write an opinion paragraph. Decide if the structure of the federal court system allows it to administer justice effectively. Share your opinion with the class.

Essential Questions
Journal

Go to your **Essential Questions Journal** to work on this chapter's Essential Question.

Test-Taking Tip

Pace yourself. If you are unsure about a question, put a checkmark next to it and move on. If you have time left, go back and try to answer the checked questions.

▲ Peaceful protest is a First Amendment right.

Civil Liberties: First Amendment Freedoms

Section 1: The Unalienable Rights

Section 2: Freedom of Religion

Section 3: Freedom of Speech and Press

Section 4: Freedom of Assembly and Petition

■ ■

Reading Strategy: Visualizing

When readers create pictures in their heads about what they are reading, they are using visualization. This is a strategy that helps readers understand what they are reading. Use the following ways to visualize the text:

• Look at the photographs, illustrations, and descriptive words.
• Think about the experiences in your life that may add to the images.
• Notice the order in which things are happening and what you think might happen next.

GOVERNMENT ONLINE
ON THE GO

To study anywhere, anytime, download these online resources at PearsonSuccessNet.com.
• Political Dictionary
• Audio Review
• Downloadable Interactivities

▲ James Madison drafted the Bill of Rights.

The Unalienable Rights

Guiding **Question**

How does the Constitution protect the rights of individuals against government? Use a concept web to identify three parts of the Constitution that protect individual rights.

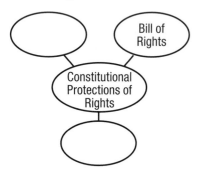

Objectives:

- Explain the actions of Americans that led to the Bill of Rights.
- Understand that the rights guaranteed in the Constitution are limited.
- Understand how federalism affects individual rights.
- Describe how the 9th Amendment helps protect individual rights.

The Declaration of Independence and the Constitution of the United States both talk about **unalienable** rights. Unalienable rights are rights that are absolute. They cannot be surrendered. It is written in the Declaration of Independence "that all men are created equal, that they are **endowed** [given] by their Creator with certain unalienable rights, that among these are Life, Liberty, and the pursuit of Happiness. . . ." The Constitution also included unalienable rights for the people. More rights were added to the Constitution in the form of amendments. The first ten amendments are called the Bill of Rights.

Why do Americans believe in personal freedom?

The commitment to personal freedom in this country reaches back before colonial days. The people of England had struggled to win individual rights for many years. Later, the colonists brought the idea of freedom with them to America. After the Revolutionary War was fought and won, a Constitution was written and approved. This new plan for government guaranteed freedom for all Americans. At first, the Constitution did not include a list of the rights for the people. Before all the States would ratify the Constitution, the Bill of Rights had to be added. It became part of the Constitution in 1791. The later amendments, especially the 13th and 14th, added more personal freedoms to the Constitution.

The Constitution guarantees both **civil liberties** and **civil rights** to the American people. Civil liberties are the freedoms that the government may not take away. They include freedom of religion, press, speech, **assembly, petition,** and the right to a fair trial.

Civil rights are the protections granted by government. For example, the Constitution protects us against **discrimination** on the basis of race, sex, religious belief, or national origin.

What is limited government?

Limited government is a basic principle of the U.S. government. The Constitution sets limits on the power of government. By contrast, in a government ruled by a dictator, the rights of the citizens are often ignored. Although our government has the authority to rule, it may never take away a person's basic freedoms. These freedoms are listed in the Bill of Rights and the Constitution.

The many rights granted to citizens in our government are limited, or relative to the rights of others. No person can prevent another from exercising a right. In addition, when exercising his or her own rights, no person can infringe on the rights of others. For example, everyone has a right to free speech. That freedom, however, does not allow a person to use speech to spread false statements about another person. Also, the press may not print or broadcast material that damages a person's reputation or gives away security or military secrets.

Different rights sometimes conflict with one another. One example of this is when freedom of the press collides with a person's right to a fair trial. Some famous trials have been appealed in the courts because publicity may influence people who might serve on a jury.

The rights listed in the Constitution are guaranteed to all citizens, as well as **aliens.** An alien is a person who lives in a country but is a citizen of another country. Aliens are denied some rights at times, such as the right to vote and to travel freely throughout the country.

Unalienable
Unable to be surrendered

Endowed
Given as a gift

Civil liberties
Guarantees of personal freedoms against possible threats from government

Civil rights
Acts of government that make the constitutional guarantees of freedom a reality

Assembly
A coming together for a common purpose

Petition
Written requests to the government

Discrimination
Treating people unfairly because of their race, sex, age, religion, or physical condition

Alien
A person who lives in a country but is a citizen of another country

Loud music late at night is not a right, because it interferes with the rights of others. ▶

Due Process Clause
Part of the 14th Amendment that guarantees that no state may deny basic rights to its people

Reading Strategy
Visualizing
Look at the chart on this page. What does this chart explain to you?

After the Japanese bombed Pearl Harbor in World War II, all persons of Japanese descent living on the Pacific Coast of the United States were moved from their homes. This action caused hardship. It was criticized because many were American citizens. In 1988, the U.S. government agreed it had been wrong. Money was paid to each living person who had been forcibly relocated by the government.

How does federalism affect individual rights?

The U.S. government is based on the principle of federalism. This means the power of government is divided between national and state governments. The Bill of Rights was added to the Constitution to make the national government less powerful.

The power of the states is discussed in part of the 14th Amendment. This part of the Amendment is called the **Due Process Clause.** The Due Process Clause guarantees that no state may deny basic rights to its people. The Supreme Court has used the 14th Amendment often to uphold basic rights. The Court has held that most of the guarantees in the Bill of Rights are also covered in the 14th Amendment (Figure 9.1).

Fig. 19.1
The 14th Amendment's Due Process Clause: Incorporation of Rights

GOVERNMENT ONLINE
Audio Tour
Listen to a guided audio tour of these rights at
PearsonSuccessNet.com

- Provisions of the Bill of Rights INCORPORATED into the 14th Amendment's Due Process Clause

1st AMENDMENT
- Freedom of speech
- Freedom of press
- Freedom of assembly, petition
- Free Exercise Clause
- Establishment Clause

4th AMENDMENT
- No unreasonable searches, seizures

5th AMENDMENT
- No self-incrimination
- No double jeopardy

6th AMENDMENT
- Right to counsel
- Right to confront and obtain witnesses
- Right to speedy trial
- Right to trial by jury in criminal cases

8th AMENDMENT
- No cruel, unusual punishments

- Provisions of the Bill of Rights NOT INCORPORATED into the 14th Amendment's Due Process Clause

2nd AMENDMENT
- Right to keep, bear arms

3rd AMENDMENT
- No quartering of troops

5th AMENDMENT
- Grand jury

7th AMENDMENT
- Trial by jury in civil cases

▲ **Interpreting Charts** This chart shows which rights the Supreme Court has incorporated into the Due Process Clause of the 14th Amendment. *Why do you think some, but not all, rights are incorporated?*

This has become known as the **process of incorporation.** It guarantees that most freedoms listed in the Bill of Rights are covered in the Due Process Clause. The Supreme Court first decided this in 1925 in *Gitlow* v. *New York*. Gitlow had been convicted in New York of a criminal act. He had made speeches calling for the violent overthrow of the United States. Gitlow appealed his case to the Supreme Court.

The Supreme Court upheld the conviction. The important part of this decision was not Gitlow's guilt or innocence. Instead, it was important because the Court decided that freedom of speech and press are protected by the Due Process Clause of the 14th Amendment. This was the first time the Court had ruled that a right guaranteed in the Bill of Rights must also be guaranteed by the states. Thirteen more cases were decided the same way.

✔ **Checkpoint** What is the process of incorporation?

Process of incorporation
The process of incorporating, or including, most of the guarantees in the Bill of Rights into the 14th Amendment's Due Process Clause

What is the 9th Amendment?

The Constitution contains most of the rights and freedoms granted to citizens. The 9th Amendment says that there are other rights, even though they are not written in the Constitution. The Supreme Court has decided many cases using the 9th Amendment. They include the guarantee that an accused person cannot be tried using evidence gained illegally.

✔ **Checkpoint** Why is the 9th Amendment important?

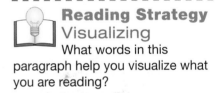
Reading Strategy
Visualizing
What words in this paragraph help you visualize what you are reading?

Essential Questions Journal Go to your **Essential Questions Journal** to work on this chapter's Essential Question.

SECTION **1** ASSESSMENT

1. **Guiding Question** Use your completed graphic organizer to answer this question: How does the Constitution protect the rights of individuals against government?

Key Terms and Comprehension
On a sheet of paper, write the answer to each question. Use complete sentences.

2. What was needed before the States would approve the Constitution?

3. What are civil liberties?

4. What is the Due Process Clause?

5. What has the process of incorporation guaranteed?

Critical Thinking

6. **Draw Inferences** Why do you think there is a limit to freedom of speech?

7. **Identify Central Issues** Why do you think certain rights are denied to aliens at times?

▲ Americans are free to practice religion as they please.

Freedom of Religion

Guiding Question

How does the 1st Amendment protect the freedom of religion? Use a chart like the one below to take notes on three Supreme Court cases that protect the freedom of religion.

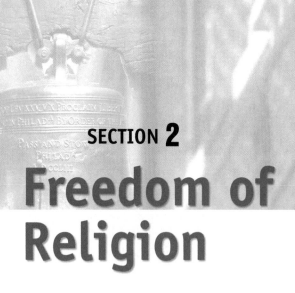

Freedom of Religion	
Case	Ruling
■ *Stone* v. *Graham,* 1980 ■ ■	■ ■ ■

Objectives:

- Examine why the freedom of religion is protected in the Bill of Rights.
- Describe the separation of church and state.
- Summarize the Supreme Court rulings on religion and education, as well as other Establishment Clause cases.
- Explain how the Supreme Court has limited the Free Exercise Clause.

Alexis de Tocqueville, a French political writer, came to America in the early 1800s. He believed in freedom and wanted to see how the people of America lived in the new democracy. His book, *Democracy in America,* described the freedoms enjoyed by all Americans.

What is religious liberty?

The 1st Amendment guarantees that Americans may worship as they choose, or not worship at all. The first guarantee separates church and state, and is called the **Establishment Clause.** It prohibits an establishment of an official religion in the United States. The second guarantee is called the **Free Exercise Clause.** It guarantees the right to each person to believe whatever he or she chooses about religion. This religious liberty is also protected by the 14th Amendment's Due Process Clause. It prevents the states and local governments from interfering with the people's right to worship.

✔ **Checkpoint** What are the two guarantees of religious liberty?

Why is there separation of church and state?

The Establishment Clause of the 1st Amendment does not allow the government to set up or support any one religion. Although the church and government (state) are separated by the Constitution, religion is encouraged. Many public officials use the name of God in taking the oath of office. Sessions of Congress open with prayer. The nation's anthem and money both use the name of God. On the Washington Monument there is an aluminum cap at the very top that says "Lau Deo." This means "praise be to God" in Latin.

Which cases established separation of religion and education?

The Court's first ruling on the Establishment Clause occurred in 1947. The case of *Everson* v. *Board of Education* is often called the New Jersey School Bus case. The Court upheld a state law that provided busing for all students attending schools in New Jersey, including **parochial** (church-related) schools. The Court said the law was not a support of religion. Instead, they said, it was needed to keep all students safe. Since then, the Court has heard many cases involving religion and education. See Figure 19.2.

Some public schools allow "released time" during school hours. This means public school students may leave school to attend religious classes. In *McCollum* v. *Board of Education*, 1948, the Supreme Court struck down the released time program because the religious classes were held in public facilities. A few years later the Court upheld New York City's released time program in *Zorach* v. *Clauson*, 1952. In that case, the classes were held in private places, such as homes.

Reciting prayers and using the Bible in public schools have been challenged many times and have been declared unconstitutional at least seven times by the Supreme Court. For example, in the case of *Stone* v. *Graham*, 1980, a law that ordered the posting of the Ten Commandments in public school classrooms was struck down by the Court.

Establishment Clause
Separates church and state

Free Exercise Clause
Guarantees the right to each person to believe whatever he or she chooses about religion

Parochial
Church-related, as in a *parochial school*

Reading Strategy
Visualizing
Study the photo in Figure 19.2. Are the football players violating the separation of church and state?

Fig. 19.2

1st Amendment

Congress shall make no law respecting an establishment of religion, or prohibiting the free exercise thereof; or abridging the freedom of speech, or of the press; or the right of the people peaceably to assemble, and to petition the Government for a redress of grievances.

FROM THE CONSTITUTION

Ruling on Religion The Court has held that public schools cannot support religious exercises. It has not ruled, however, individuals that cannot pray when and as they choose in schools or in any other place. Nor has it held that students cannot study the Bible in a literary or historical context in school. The Court's rulings have nevertheless been widely criticized. Many critics have proposed that the Constitution be amended to allow voluntary group prayer in public schools. Despite the Court's decisions, both organized prayer and Bible readings are found in many public school classrooms today. ***How does the separation of church and state reflect the principle of limited government?***

▲ Public schools cannot support prayer at school-related events.

In Rhode Island, a prayer used as part of a graduation program was declared unconstitutional. In a Texas school district, students led prayers before football games. The Supreme Court ruled in 2000 that this should no longer be allowed.

According to the Equal Access Act of 1984, student religious groups are allowed to meet in schools in the same way as other student groups. When the law was challenged, the Supreme Court found in favor of the Act. The Court said that not allowing the meetings violated the students' 1st and 14th amendment rights.

Over the years, the Court has also ruled against laws that forbid the teaching of the scientific theory of evolution. Such a case was decided in Arkansas in 1968. There, the Court said the state should have no interest in protecting any or all religions from views they do not agree with.

There have been many cases on aid to parochial schools. In these cases, the Supreme Court must decide what types of aid are constitutional. Aid may be given in the form of books, transportation, testing, and equipment. Supporters of this aid by the state claim that parochial schools save the state money. Opponents of aid argue that parents chose the parochial school and must accept the cost.

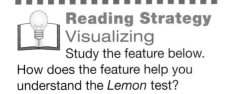

Reading Strategy
Visualizing
Study the feature below. How does the feature help you understand the *Lemon* test?

After the case of *Lemon* v. *Kurtzman,* 1971, the Court decided the Establishment Clause was written to prevent three things when aiding private or parochial schools (Figure 19.3).

(1) The purpose of the aid must not be religious.

(2) The aid must not advance or inhibit religion.

(3) The aid must avoid "excessive entanglement of government with religion"—or too much mixing of government and religion.

Over the years, many aid programs have passed the *Lemon* test.

Fig. 19.3 How Government Works

GOVERNMENT ONLINE
Interactive
To apply the *Lemon* test to various scenarios, visit
PearsonSuccessNet.com

The Lemon Test

The courts determine whether state aid to parochial schools is constitutional by applying the *Lemon* test. **How does the Lemon *test* uphold the separation of church and state?**

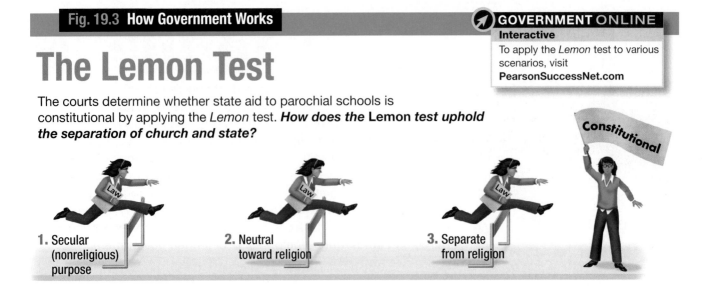

1. Secular (nonreligious) purpose

2. Neutral toward religion

3. Separate from religion

Constitutional

What are other cases that involve the Establishment Clause?

Other church and state cases have involved seasonal displays, chaplains, and the Ten Commandments.

In Rhode Island, the Supreme Court decided the city of Pawtucket could display a nativity scene. The display featured other seasonal items, such as Santa's sleigh and candy canes. In 1989, in *County of Allegheny* v. *ACLU,* the Supreme Court ruled against a large display in the county courthouse. That display included only a religious celebration of the birth of Jesus. The Court said it violated the 1st and 14th amendments.

Chaplains (people that lead religious meetings) offer prayers in Congress and in state legislatures. The Supreme Court has ruled that this is constitutional. The Court said prayers have been offered since colonial times. Also, the Court said legislators are not influenced by religious teaching the way schoolchildren are.

Displays of the Ten Commandments have been challenged several times, twice in 2005. The Supreme Court ruled that a monument displaying the Ten Commandments at the Texas State Capitol did not violate the Constitution. The reason given was that the monument had been put up 40 years earlier, and it was part of a large historical and cultural display. Then the Supreme Court ruled on a case in Kentucky. The Court said the display of the Ten Commandments at the county courthouse was clearly meant to support religion. It was therefore unconstitutional.

▲ A tablet of the Ten Commandments is removed from a public building.

✔ **Checkpoint** Why does the Court allow prayer in Congress and state legislatures?

What is the Free Exercise Clause?

The Free Exercise Clause, part of the 1st Amendment, allows people to believe what they choose in matters of religion. **(Figure 19.4)** It does not give people the right to violate the law or the safety of others. It also does not give people the right to force their beliefs on others.

Fig. 19.4

Freedom of Religion
● Creates a separation of church and state (Establishment Clause)
● Protects people's right to believe what they wish in matters of religion (Free Exercise Clause)

Indeed, there are limits on what people may do. The Supreme Court has heard many cases concerning free exercise and has agreed with the laws that were challenged. For example, the Supreme Court agreed with laws that require schoolchildren to be vaccinated. The Court also agreed with a law that requires businesses to be closed on Sundays in some areas. The Court also decided that people who have religious objections to serving in the military could be drafted.

Sometimes the Supreme Court has struck down government laws. For example, Amish children do not have to attend school past the eighth grade. The Amish hold that their lifestyle as farmers and their religious faith are harmed by modern education.

Other religious groups, such as Jehovah's Witnesses, have refused to salute the flag. In 1940, the Supreme Court upheld a school rule that children salute the flag in *Minersville School District* v. *Gobitis*. The Court felt saluting the flag did not interfere with a religious belief. Three years later in *West Virginia Board of Education* v. *Barnette,* the Supreme Court reversed that decision and said a flag-salute law was unconstitutional.

✔ **Checkpoint**   What does the Free Exercise Clause allow?

SECTION 2 ASSESSMENT

Essential Questions Journal   Go to your **Essential Questions Journal** to work on this chapter's Essential Question.

Quick Write

In this section, you read about many Supreme Court cases. Many cases involved the separation of church and state. Write a paragraph on the issue that was the most interesting to you.

1. **Guiding Question** Use your completed graphic organizer to answer this question: How does the 1st Amendment protect the freedom of religion?

Key Terms and Comprehension

On a sheet of paper, write the answer to each question. Use complete sentences.

2. Which amendments protect religious liberties?

3. What is the Establishment Clause?

4. What does the *Lemon* test evaluate?

5. What does the Free Exercise Clause NOT allow?

Critical Thinking

6. **Draw Inferences** Why do you think the relationship between church and state is a continuing issue?

7. **Compare Points of View** Do you think there should be state aid for parochial schools? Why or why not?

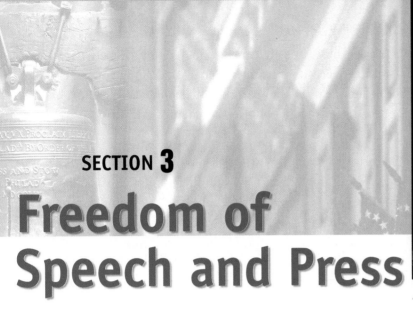

SECTION 3

Freedom of Speech and Press

▲ Network television news anchor Katie Couric

Guiding Question

What are the limits on the guarantees of free speech and free press? Use a table like the one below to take notes on how freedom of expression is limited in the various types of speech and media.

Type of Expression	Limitation
Seditious speech	

Objectives:

- Explain the guarantees of free expression.
- Summarize how the Supreme Court has limited seditious speech and obscenity.
- Examine the limits the Supreme Court has placed on the media.
- Understand symbolic and commercial speech; describe the limits of their exercise.

The Constitution gives all Americans the freedom to speak or write what they want. These words can be about anything, including the government or its leaders. This freedom of expression does have some restrictions. False statements that may harm others are not allowed. Also, Americans may not prevent others from expressing themselves.

What is free expression?

The 1st Amendment guarantees all people the right to express themselves in speech or in writing. The amendment guarantees this expression even if the words offend others. This freedom is meant to allow everyone to hear the opinions and ideas of others. In our democracy, the people must have as much information and discussion as possible in order to make the best choices on public issues.

Freedom of the press is another guarantee of the 1st Amendment. This means that people can speak freely and write their opinions. These opinions can then be published in newspapers, magazines, and pamphlets. The opinions can also be presented online, on television, or on the radio.

In the United States, the government does not own the press. Private individuals or groups of persons own the press. The press can print what it believes to be true and fair. It cannot print or broadcast material that damages someone's reputation or reveals national security secrets.

The restrictions on free expression also include **libel** and **slander.** Libel is the use of false or unjust statements in writing. These statements are called slander if they are spoken. There are also laws restricting material that encourages people to commit a crime or overthrow the government by force.

Libel
False or unjust statements in writing

Slander
False or unjust statements in speech

Sedition
An effort of people or groups to overthrow or harm the government using violence

Seditious speech
Speech that encourages an effort of people or groups to overthrow or harm the government using violence

Espionage
Spying

Obscenity
Disgusting to the senses; offensive

What are seditious speech and obscenity?

Sedition is a crime. It is an effort of people or groups to overthrow or harm the government using violence. **Seditious speech** is used to influence people to commit the crime of sedition. This type of speech is not protected by the 1st amendment. Congress has passed laws against sedition.

The **Espionage** Act of 1917 was passed during World War I. Among other things, this act made it illegal to encourage disloyalty in the military. It also made it illegal to speak or print disloyal statements about the government. Many people were found guilty of violating the Espionage Act. In *Schenck* v. *United States,* 1919, the Supreme Court heard the appeal of Charles Schenck, who was convicted of harming the war effort. He encouraged men to resist the draft in leaflets that he wrote. Justice Oliver Wendell Holmes, Jr. wrote the opinion of the Court in this case, which upheld the conviction of Schenck. In his opinion, Justice Holmes established the "clear and present danger" rule. He said that words can be weapons and can create a clear and present danger. He felt that Congress should have a right to prevent that danger.

Obscenity is something that is disgusting and offensive. The Court has had many discussions about what materials should be considered obscene. The difficulty of the matter lies in the fact that moral standards differ among people. In 1973, the Court set up a three-part test to decide whether material is obscene. These rules have generally been followed ever since.

✔ **Checkpoint**   What is the difference between sedition and seditious speech?

Government in Your Life

Students' Rights

Students have most of the same rights as adults. They have the right of free speech. They are protected from unreasonable searches. They may refuse to be questioned by the police in a criminal case.

Certain rights are restricted when students are at school. Schools are permitted to have certain rules.

Schools can limit the type of articles published in a school newspaper. They may limit the use of offensive speech. They can set a dress code. The police and school staff cannot search students' possessions or lockers without a search warrant or a good reason.

Schools are required to have, and distribute to students, a policy manual outlining their rules.

Biography

Oliver Wendell Holmes, Jr.

Prior restraint
Placing a ban on written or spoken words before they are expressed

Justice Holmes was born in Boston, Massachusetts, in 1841. His father was the famous writer and physician Oliver Wendell Holmes. Justice Holmes graduated from Harvard College and Harvard Law School. Holmes was a Civil War veteran and a professor of law at Harvard. Appointed by Theodore Roosevelt, he served on the United States Supreme Court for 30 years. He retired from the Court at age 90.

Justice Holmes is one of the most quoted members of the Supreme Court. He was known for his opinions on many Bill of Rights cases. He declared that the "due process of law" was the basic principle of freedom. In *Schenck* v. *United States,* Justice Holmes declared that expressions that represented a clear and present danger should be punished. In this same case, he said the 1st Amendment would not protect a person that was causing panic by falsely shouting "Fire!" in a crowded theater.

What is prior restraint?

Prior restraint means placing a ban on written or spoken words before they are expressed. The 1st Amendment does not allow the government to practice prior restraint. The Supreme Court heard the leading case, *Near* v. *Minnesota*, concerning prior restraint in 1931. The state of Minnesota passed a law outlawing the publication of any magazine or article that intended to cause harm. On the basis of that law, a local court forbade the publication of the *Saturday Press* newspaper. That paper had printed several articles attacking public officials for corruption.

The justices ruled in favor of the *Saturday Press*. The Court said the paper's publication could not be stopped just because the state thought it would print a malicious, or mean, article.

In the case *New York Times* v. *United States,* 1971, concerning the Vietnam War and the Pentagon Papers, the Court ruled against the government. The Pentagon Papers were stolen and leaked to the press. The government claimed these papers were classified, or secret, documents. The Court ruled that the government had not proved that printing these documents would threaten national security.

Shield laws
Laws that give reporters some protection against having to reveal their sources

The Supreme Court has approved some prior restraints. The CIA rule that agents must never publish information about the CIA without the agency's permission was found to be constitutional. Also, the Court has ruled that school newspapers may be censored or edited by school authorities.

✔ **Checkpoint** Why did the Court find for the paper in *Near* v. *Minnesota*?

What are the Supreme Court's limits on the media?

News reporters demand the right to keep the sources of their information private. If not, people might not feel comfortable revealing information the public needs to know. Reporters have gone to jail rather than reveal a source. The Supreme Court has heard appeals from reporters in several cases. The Court has said reporters must answer questions in a grand jury investigation or criminal trial. Some states, on the suggestion of the Court, have passed **shield laws.** These laws give some protection to news reporters.

Fig. 19.5 How Government Works

GOVERNMENT ONLINE
Interactive
For an interactivity on the freedoms of speech and press visit **PearsonSuccessNet.com**

Freedoms of Speech and Press:

Rules of the Road

The 1st Amendment stands as a monument to the central importance of free speech and the media in a free society. Various forms of speech, however, are regulated by government. *Why are radio stations and network television subject to federal regulation?*

The Supreme Court has ruled that school administrators can exercise "editorial control over the style and content of student speech in school-sponsored expressive activities. . . ."

The Federal Communications Act, administered by the FCC, bans the use of indecent language on the radio and on television. It may also deny violators a renewal of their operating licenses.

The Children's Internet Protection Act (CIPA) requires public libraries that receive federal money to use filters to block their computers' access to adult entertainment sites on the Internet.

Except in the most extreme situations, government cannot place any prior restraint on newspapers and other print media.

In 1915, the Supreme Court ruled that the showing of motion pictures is a business. It is not part of the press. As a result of this decision, movie review boards were set up. The Court later reversed this decision, but it has never given the film industry the same level freedom from prior restraint that it gives newspapers. The Supreme Court upheld a rule that a group of people (called censors) may review films before they are released. These reviews are very uncommon now. Today, most people rely on the rating system set up by the film industry.

The Federal Communications Act of 1934 regulates both radio and television broadcasting. The companies that use public airwaves must have a license. Congress does not allow the Federal Communications Commission (FCC) to censor programs before they are broadcast. The FCC can ban the use of obscene language and refuse to renew a station's license.

The Supreme Court has given the cable television industry more 1st Amendment freedoms than network television. The Court struck down an attempt by Congress to limit certain programs to late-night hours. The Court said this violated the 1st Amendment rights of adults.

The Internet has created only a handful of Supreme Court cases. Each of these cases has involved attempts by Congress to regulate access to pornography on the Web. The goal of Congress was to protect minors from obscene material. The Communications Decency Act of 1996 made it a crime to purposely send obscene speech and images to people under the age of 18. The Court promptly declared the law unconstitutional. It said the language in the law was too vague. It also said that the law denied adults access to material that is protected by the 1st Amendment. See Figure 19.5 on page 480.

In recent cases, the Supreme Court has upheld laws concerning public libraries and the Internet. Libraries must place filters on their computers to block access to obscene Internet sites.

What is symbolic and commercial speech?

Symbolic speech is a way to communicate without words. For example, carrying a sign can be a type of symbolic speech. Facial expressions can also send a message. **Picketing,** when groups of striking workers come together at a business site, is another example of symbolic speech. Picketing, done peacefully, is allowed by the 1st and 14th amendments. Picketers are trying to show they do not like what a company or business is doing. The Supreme Court has protected the right to picket several times. In 1940, the Court struck down a state law that said it was a crime to picket a place of business.

■ ■ ■ ■ ■ ■ ■ ■ ■ ■ ■ ■ ■ ■ ■ ■
Symbolic speech
Communicating ideas through facial expressions, body language, or by carrying a sign or wearing an arm band

Picketing
The gathering of striking workers at a business site as a sign of protest

■ ■ ■ ■ ■ ■ ■ ■ ■ ■ ■ ■ ■ ■ ■ ■
Reading Strategy
Visualizing
How could this paragraph be written differently to create a stronger picture in your mind?

Commercial Speech

Speech for business purposes, most often for advertising

Fig. 19.6

Freedom of Speech and Press
● Guarantee the right to speak, write, and symbolically communicate most ideas
● Ensure people's right to hear those ideas

The Supreme Court has censored some types of symbolic speech. (Figure 19.6) It upheld a state law in Virginia that banned the burning of crosses. The Court said burning crosses was done only to scare people. Cross burning at rallies or parades is not a crime. The Court also ruled in favor of symbolic speech in a case in 1969. Students in an Iowa school district had worn black armbands to protest the Vietnam War. The school suspended them. The Court ruled the school officials had violated the students' rights.

The Supreme Court has also struck down flag-burning laws. This form of political protest is protected by law in the 1st and 14th amendments.

Commercial speech is speech for business purposes, most often for advertising. This type of speech was not protected by the Constitution until *Bigelow* v. *Virginia,* 1975. In this case, the Supreme Court struck down a state law banning advertising for abortions. The next year, the Court struck down a law that forbade the advertisement of prescription drug prices. There are some cases in which the government can ban commercial speech. False advertising is not allowed. Cigarette ads were banned in 1970. Chewing tobacco and snuff ads were banned in 1986.

SECTION 3 ASSESSMENT

Essential Questions Journal — Go to your **Essential Questions Journal** to work on this chapter's Essential Question.

Word Bank

libel

picketing

seditious speech

slander

1. Guiding Question Use your completed graphic organizer to answer this question: What are the limits on the guarantees of free speech and free press?

Key Terms and Comprehension

On a sheet of paper, use the words from the Word Bank to complete each sentence correctly.

2. A group of striking workers coming together to protest is called _____.

3. Telling friends to harm the government is an example of _____.

4. _____ is false or unjust statements in writing.

5. _____ is false or unjust statements in speech.

Critical Thinking

6. **Draw Inferences** What are the advantages and disadvantages of a free press?

7. **Predict Consequences** Why do you think the Supreme Court has censored some types of symbolic speech?

Participating in Public Debate

Dear Student,

Our State Department of Education has set up new requirements for the current school year. Effective immediately, the school year will be lengthened from 180 days to 200 days. In addition, each school day will be extended one additional hour. The DOE feels strongly that this decision is necessary in order to remain competitive in the global economy. Statistics show that schools in China and India are in session 225–250 days a year. Students in those countries are well on their way to outperforming American students.

Thank you for your cooperation,

George Carruthers, Principal

Your right to participate in public debate is central to the founding principles of our country. If you received a letter from your school like the one above, you would probably have strong feelings about it. One way to express your views is by participating in public debate. You might speak at a city council or town hall meeting, or address your local school board. Use these opportunities to voice your opinions by following these steps:

1. **Choose an issue of concern to you and then find out whom to contact.** Your opinion counts most when you express it to those people who have some authority or influence in the matter. That could be city council members, a school board, or a media outlet.

2. **Organize your arguments.** Decide on the best way to get your ideas across. Create an outline or a list of talking points to organize your thoughts. Think of supporting details for each point. Then identify the most important points that you will emphasize.

To more strongly influence your audience, you might want to make these points in the first few lines of your speech. Most important, rehearse what you will say.

3. **Present your ideas.** Speak in a loud, clear voice when you present your ideas. Keep your speech lively and exciting, and be particular with the words you use. If you are civil and respectful, you may persuade other citizens to take up your cause.

▶▶ What do you think?

1. Whom might you contact to express your views in the situation presented here?
2. What short-term and long-term goals might you seek through participating in public debate?

🔺 GOVERNMENT ONLINE
Government Activity Pack
For activities on participating in public debate, go to **PearsonSuccessNet.com**

Freedom of Assembly and Petition

▲ The 1st Amendment protects the people's right to protest peaceably.

Guiding Question

How has the Supreme Court ruled on assembly and petition cases? Use a table like the one below to take notes on important Supreme Court cases involving freedom of assembly.

Case	Issue	Ruling
Cox v. Louisiana		No parades near courthouses

Objectives:

- Explain the freedoms of assembly and petition.
- Summarize how the government can limit assembly.
- Compare and contrast assembly issues on public versus private property.
- Explain how the Supreme Court interprets freedom of association.

The right to assemble and petition the government has always existed in America. People assemble, or gather together, for many reasons, including political rallies, parades, and marches. The protestors are not allowed to interfere with the rights of others or to cause riots. Assemblies must be peaceful. Citizens can use petitions (written requests to the government) for any reason.

What does the Constitution guarantee?

Assembling in a peaceful way and for peaceful purposes is protected by the 1st Amendment. In some countries this is not allowed. Any group in the United States has the right to hold meetings. It does not matter if the group's ideas are popular. Outdoor or indoor meetings and protests are allowed.

The Supreme Court has ruled that people can assemble in public places. These assemblies can be stopped only if there is a danger to citizens. State and local officials can make rules for such gatherings, but they cannot stop the gatherings. A city usually requires people to get a permit for these gatherings.

Another guarantee in the 1st Amendment is the right to petition. People can ask government officials to do something or to stop doing something. These petitions, or requests, can come from individuals or from groups. The petitions may be letters, e-mails, or formal written requests. Group petitions can also be prepared and signed by many people and sent to government officials. For example, people may send petitions to ask that the building of a highway or a shopping center be stopped.

What are rules on time, place, and manner?

The government can make rules about the time, place, and manner of assemblies. For example, people may not gather near schools. In *Cox* v. *Louisiana,* 1965, the Court upheld a state law that prohibits parades near a courthouse. The people involved in this case were attempting to influence the court.

The government's rules must be **content neutral.** This means assemblies may not be stopped because of what might be said. (Figure 19.7) In *Forsyth County* v. *Nationalist Movement,* 1992, the Court stopped a law that charged a $1,000 fee for public demonstrations. A group that challenged the law had gathered to protest the creation of a national holiday for Martin Luther King, Jr. The Court found that the law was not content neutral.

Can people assemble on public property?

Most demonstrations are held in protest. They are usually held in public places to gain attention for a cause. These protests may threaten the peace, or put people in danger. Because of this, a license is often required for a demonstration or parade. The Supreme Court has upheld laws that require prior notice or permits for assemblies in public places.

How much regulation can authorities use to control demonstrators? Can police order them to stop if they are causing a safety problem? In *Gregory* v. *Chicago,* 1969, Dick Gregory and a group marched five miles. They walked through a neighborhood to the mayor's house. This group was demanding an end to segregation in Chicago's schools. When the crowd watching the march became unruly, the police ordered the marchers to leave. Gregory and the marchers were arrested because they would not leave. The Court overturned the convictions, saying the crowd became unruly not the marchers.

Can people assemble on private property?

The Supreme Court has held that the rights of assembly and petition do not give people the right to trespass on private property. This means that no one has the right to hand out leaflets or to ask people to sign petitions in privately owned shopping centers. However, a state can require the owners of shopping centers to allow the right of petition on their property. See Figure 19.8 on page 486.

Content neutral
The government may not regulate assemblies on a basis of what might be said

Fig. 19.7

Freedom of Assembly and Petition
● Protect people's right to assemble peaceably to express their views
● Ensure people's right to bring their views to public attention

Reading Strategy
Visualizing
Create a graphic organizer outlining the rules that government can make for assemblies.

Fig. 19.8

PUBLIC PROPERTY

The right to demonstrate peacefully in public is constitutionally guaranteed. In some situations, however, preventing a protest from becoming violent can be used as an excuse to prevent speech. The line between crowd control and thought control can be very narrow.

PRIVATE PROPERTY

Demonstrations on private property are not constitutionally guaranteed. Still, many state constitutions encourage businesses to allow petition. In that event, there is no violation of the property owners' rights, *PruneYard Shopping Center* v. *Robins*. **Why has the Court ruled differently on public and private property demonstrations?**

■ ■ ■ ■ ■ ■ ■ ■ ■ ■ ■ ■ ■ ■ ■ ■ ■ ■ ■

Reading Strategy
Visualizing
How do these photos help you understand the difference between public and private assembly?

■ ■ ■ ■ ■ ■ ■ ■ ■ ■ ■ ■ ■ ■ ■ ■ ■ ■ ■

Right of association
Citizens may freely associate with others to promote a cause.

What is freedom of association?

The **right of association** means citizens may freely associate with, or join with, others to promote a cause. The Constitution does not set out this right. Still, the Court has ruled in favor of this freedom because it is an important freedom of expression. An example is *National Association for the Advancement of Colored People* v. *Alabama*, 1958. This case is one of the earliest right-to-associate cases. A state law required the Alabama branch of the NAACP to provide a list of all its members in the state. The Supreme Court overturned the decision. It said there was no acceptable reason why the state should have the NAACP's membership list.

There is no absolute right of association, however. See **Figure 19.9** on the next page. In New Jersey, the Boy Scouts of America banned a homosexual boy from a troop. The state supreme court ordered the New Jersey troop to readmit James Dale, an eagle scout.

The case, *Boy Scouts of America* v. *Dale,* 2000, went to the Supreme Court. The Court overturned the ruling by the New Jersey supreme court. The Court ruled that a state cannot force an organization to accept members when doing so goes against the organization's beliefs.

Fig. 19.9

◀ Analyzing Political Cartoons *Do you think the Supreme Court would rule in favor of the boys (freedom of association) or in favor of the girl (antidiscrimination)? Explain your answer.*

Essential Questions Journal Go to your **Essential Questions Journal** to work on this chapter's Essential Question.

SECTION 4 ASSESSMENT

1. **Guiding Question** Use your completed graphic organizer to answer this question: How has the Supreme Court ruled on assembly and petition cases?

Key Terms and Comprehension

On a sheet of paper, write the letter of the answer that correctly answers each question.

2. Which of the following best illustrates the use of a petition?

    A. A newspaper publishes an opinion piece that urges people to recycle.

    B. A mother writes a letter to the President asking him to stop the war.

    C. A girl obtains a permit to keep her pet ferrets.

    D. Teachers gather to protest the latest school budget cuts.

3. A local hunting club meets at a state's capitol to protest the latest weapons bill. What freedom is this an example of?

    A. assembly   **C.** association

    B. petition   **D.** parade

4. Demonstrations on public property usually require which of the following?

    A. a court order   **C.** a permit

    B. a petition   **D.** a guarantee

5. When can government limit assembly?

    A. when it disagrees with what is being said

    B. when public property is being used

    C. when time, place, and manner are a concern

    D. when safety is a concern

Critical Thinking

6. **Draw Conclusions** What might happen if people were not allowed to assemble peacefully?

7. **Determine Relevance** Which freedom do you think will be most relevant in your life, assembly or petition? Explain your answer.

Chapter Summary

Section 1—The Unalienable Rights

- Unalienable rights are rights that are absolute.

- Before the states ratified the Constitution, the Bill of Rights had to be added.

- The Constitution guarantees both civil liberties and civil rights to the American people.

- Limited government sets limits on the power of government.

- The Due Process Clause guarantees that no state may deny basic rights to its people.

- The 9th Amendment says that there are other rights, even though they are not written in the Constitution.

Section 2—Freedom of Religion

- The Establishment Clause separates church and state in the United States. The Supreme Court has ruled on many Establishment Clause cases involving education.

- The Free Exercise Clause guarantees the right of each person to believe whatever he or she chooses about religion.

Section 3—Freedom of Speech and Press

- The 1st Amendment guarantees all people the right to express themselves in speech or in writing. It does not protect seditious speech, and does not allow the government to practice prior restraint.

- Shield laws give some protection to news reporters.

- Symbolic speech is a way to communicate without words. Commercial speech most often means advertising. These types of speech are not always protected.

Section 4—Freedom of Assembly and Petition

- The Supreme Court has ruled that people can assemble in public places. Still, the government can make rules about the time, place, and manner of assemblies.

- Freedom of association means citizens may freely associate with others to promote a cause.

Guiding Question
Section 1 How does the Constitution protect the rights of individuals against government?

Guiding Question
Section 2 How does the 1st Amendment protect the freedom of religion?

Guiding Question
Section 3 What are the limits on the guarantees of free speech and free press?

Guiding Question
Section 4 How has the Supreme Court ruled on assembly and petition cases?

CHAPTER 19

Essential Question
How can the judiciary balance individual rights with the common good?

Document-Based Assessment

The Declaration of Sentiments and Resolutions

The Declaration of Sentiments and Resolutions was the first document in the United States to express the need for equal rights for women. At the time it was written, women had very few rights. The Declaration was adopted on July 19, 1848, at a meeting of more than 300 women and men in Seneca Falls, New York.

Feminists Elizabeth Cady Stanton and Lucretia Mott were the driving forces behind this meeting. They thought women should have the same rights and freedoms that men had. Stanton wrote the Declaration to express the lack of women's rights. She used the Declaration of Independence, the American symbol of liberty, as a pattern. This passage is from the Declaration of Sentiments and Resolutions.

Document at a Glance

- July 19, 1848
- Equal rights for women
- Modeled after the Declaration of Independence

We hold these truths to be self evident: that all men and women are created equal; that they are endowed by their creator with certain inalienable rights; that among these are life, liberty, and the pursuit of happiness . . .

. . . The history of mankind is a history of repeated injuries . . . of man toward woman. . . .

He has never permitted her to exercise her inalienable right to . . . [the vote].

He has taken from her all right in property, even to the wages she earns.

. . . He has denied her the facilities for obtaining a thorough education. . . .

. . . Now, in view of the . . . [denial of legal rights] of one-half the people of this country . . . we insist that they have immediate admission to all the rights and privileges which belong to them as citizens. . . .

Resolved, that woman is man's equal . . .

Resolved, that it is the duty of the women of this country to secure to themselves their sacred right to [the vote].

Document-Based Questions

1. Why did Elizabeth Cady Stanton use the Declaration of Independence as a pattern for the Declaration of Sentiments?

2. What words in the first line of the Declaration of Sentiments are not in the Declaration of Independence?

3. Name three rights the document claimed women were denied.

4. Do you think that women today receive the treatment demanded in the declaration? Explain.

5. **Visualize** What is the order of rights requested in the declaration?

Source: Declaration of Sentiments and Resolutions, Elizabeth Cady Stanton, 1848

Chapter Assessment

Directions: Choose the letter of the best answer or write the answer using complete sentences.

Section 1—The Unalienable Rights

1. Besides the Bill of Rights, what other amendments add more personal freedoms to the Constitution?

A. 11th and 12th   **C.** 9th and 14th

B. 13th and 14th   **D.** 11th and 13th

2. A city passes a law that forbids people with green eyes to use the library. What basic principle of U.S. government does this law go against?

3. What is the process of incorporation?

4. **Critical Thinking** Why do you think the 9th Amendment was included in the Bill of Rights?

Section 2—Freedom of Religion

5. Why are student religious groups allowed to meet in schools?

6. Which of the following is NOT protected under the Free Exercise Clause?

A. A group of people worshipping many gods.

B. An employer giving an employee a day off because it is a holiday.

C. A family going to church on Sunday.

D. A state requiring a public official to take an oath to practice a particular religion.

7. How does the government encourage religion in the United States? List two examples.

8. **Critical Thinking** Why do you think the Court allows organized prayer in Congress but not in schools?

Section 3—Freedom of Speech and Press

9. Which of the following allows people to express themselves in speech or writing?

A. slander   **C.** libel

B. free expression   **D.** commercial speech

10. The "clear and present danger" rule was established as a result of what Supreme Court case?

11. Why has the Court limited some forms of symbolic speech?

12. What measures have some states taken to protect news reporters?

13. Critical Thinking Do you agree with laws that prohibit the advertisement of certain legal goods? Why or why not?

Section 4—Freedom of Assembly and Petition

14. What is usually required for a demonstration on public property?

15. What right is not in the Constitution but has been upheld by the Supreme Court?

16. What are two ways a person can petition the government?

17. Critical Thinking Why might the state capitol or national monuments be popular places to protest?

Apply What You've Learned

Exploring the Essential Question

18. What individual rights does the 1st Amendment protect?

19. When are your individual rights not protected by the 1st Amendment?

Essential Question Project

20. Create a brochure for your classmates to help answer the Essential Question: **How can the judiciary balance individual rights with the common good?** Consider the freedoms of speech, press, and assembly. Include examples from the chapter of how individual rights are protected by the courts without compromising the good of society.

Essential Questions
Journal

Go to your **Essential Questions Journal** to work on this chapter's Essential Question.

Test-Taking Tip

If you do not know a word in a question, read the question again but leave out the word. Then, see if you can figure out the word from its use in the sentence.

▲ Statue of Lady Justice

Civil Liberties: Protecting Individual Rights

Essential Question
To what extent has the judiciary protected the rights of privacy, security, and personal freedom?

Section 1: Due Process of Law

Section 2: Freedom and Security of the Person

Section 3: Rights of the Accused

Section 4: Punishment

Reading Strategy: Summarizing

When readers summarize, they restate in their own words what they read. As you read this chapter on civil liberties, ask yourself the following questions:

- What is this chapter about?
- What is the main point being made about civil liberties?
- What details about civil liberties are important?

When you can answer these questions, begin to write your summary.

To study anywhere, anytime, download these online resources at PearsonSuccessNet.com.
- **Political Dictionary**
- **Online Review**
- **Downloadable Interactivities**

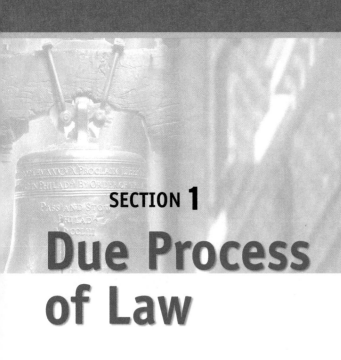

▲ Due process includes the forensic testing of evidence.

Due Process of Law

Guiding Question

Why is the concept of due process important to a free society? Use a chart like the one below to take notes on due process.

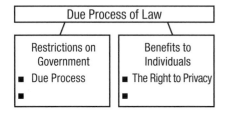

Objectives:

- Explain the meaning of due process as set out in the 5th and 14th amendments.
- Define police power and understand its relationship to civil rights.
- Describe the right of privacy and its origins in constitutional law.

Due process of law is guaranteed to every American citizen. If a person is accused of a crime, the actions taken by the government to investigate the crime must be fair. If a trial is held, the rules and procedures followed must be allowed by the 5th and 14th amendments of the United States Constitution. In this section you will learn about the meaning of due process and about the rights of citizens in the United States.

What is the meaning of due process?

Due process refers to the fact that the government must act fairly and follow established rules. The 5th Amendment introduced due process. The Amendment prevents the federal government from depriving a person of life, liberty, or property unless all the rules of due process are followed. The 14th Amendment extends the due process rules to state and local government. The Supreme Court has refused to give an exact definition of due process. Because due process is not clearly defined, the Court makes decisions about it on a case-by-case basis. The Court will decide if the government's methods are fair (**procedural due process**) and if the law involved in a case is fair (**substantive due process**). For more on due process, see Figure 20.1.

In one case where procedural due process was involved (*Rochin* v. *California*, 1952), extreme methods were used to obtain evidence. A person's home was broken into illegally. His stomach was pumped to search for drugs. In this case, the Court decided the 14th Amendment was violated and the suspect could not be tried.

In another case where substantive due process was involved (*Pierce* v. *Society of Sisters,* 1925), the State of Oregon had passed a law requiring all children to attend public school. The Roman Catholic Church challenged the law. When the Court heard the case, it decided the law was unconstitutional. The Court said the law interfered with the parents' right to control their children's upbringing.

✔**Checkpoint** What is procedural due process? What is substantive due process?

■ ■ ■ ■ ■ ■ ■ ■ ■ ■ ■ ■ ■ ■ ■ ■
Reading Strategy
Summarizing
What is the main idea of this paragraph?

■ ■ ■ ■ ■ ■ ■ ■ ■ ■ ■ ■ ■ ■ ■ ■

Due process
The government must act fairly and follow established rules.

Procedural due process
The government must use fair procedures and methods.

Substantive due process
The government must create fair policies and laws.

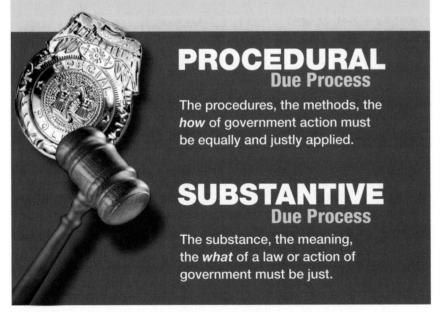

Fig. 20.1

Due Process

The following limit is placed on the federal government in the **5th Amendment,** and on state and local governments in the **14th Amendment:**

> Government cannot deprive any person of life, liberty, or property without following due process of law.

Both the **procedures** and the **laws** of government must be in accord with due process.

PROCEDURAL Due Process
The procedures, the methods, the *how* of government action must be equally and justly applied.

SUBSTANTIVE Due Process
The substance, the meaning, the *what* of a law or action of government must be just.

▲ Rulers have often made unfair judgments throughout history instead of practicing justice. *Why are procedural and substantive due process both necessary in a just society?*

Police power
The authority of each state to guard the safety, health, and welfare of its citizens

Search warrant
A court order authorizing a search

What is police power?

Police power allows each state, along with its local governments, to guard the safety, health, and welfare of citizens. In other words, it is the power of each state to keep its people safe.

This police power often involves problems with civil rights and other rights of individuals. The right of privacy, for example, may be violated if a driver is stopped for reckless or drunken driving. The tests used on the suspected driver must be fair. If the procedure is challenged in court, the safety of the public usually wins out over the right of the individual. This has happened often in the state and federal courts. The leading case to test police power over drunk drivers is *Schmerber* v. *California,* 1966. The Court found no objection to the police ordering a doctor to draw blood from the suspect. The Court gave three reasons for its decision:

- The blood was drawn in a safe way.
- The officer had reasonable grounds to believe the suspect was drunk.
- The officer had no time to secure a **search warrant** because the evidence would have disappeared from the suspect's system. A search warrant is a court order authorizing a search.

States take the following actions to safeguard the health, welfare, and morals of its citizens:

- limit the sale of alcoholic beverages and tobacco
- require vaccination of school children
- regulate gambling and outlaw obscene material or prostitution
- make education laws
- help the medically needy
- limit the profits of public utilities

Reading Strategy
Summarizing
In your own words, summarize how the states keep citizens safe.

✔ **Checkpoint** When might a person's right to privacy be overridden by the police? Give one example.

What is the right to privacy?

The guarantees in the due process clauses imply a right to privacy. This means a person has the right to be free from government invasion. The Constitution does not mention this right of privacy in so many words. The Supreme Court has, however, ruled on the right of privacy many times. In a very controversial case, *Roe* v. *Wade* (1973), the Court struck down a Texas law that made abortion a crime. The Court said the 14th Amendment's right to privacy includes a woman's right to control her pregnancy, especially in the first 12 weeks.

In later cases, the Court rejected several challenges to *Roe* v. *Wade*. Over the years, the Court has shifted to permit more state restrictions on abortions. For example, in Missouri, a law strictly limiting abortions in public hospitals after 20 weeks of pregnancy was upheld. In Ohio, a law was allowed that says a minor must inform a parent before an abortion.

Essential Questions Journal Go to your **Essential Questions Journal** to work on this chapter's Essential Question.

SECTION 1 ASSESSMENT

Quick Write

Pick a Supreme Court case from this section. Select the case that most interests you. Research the case online. Write a summary paragraph on what you find.

1. **Guiding Question** Use your completed chart to answer this question: Why is the concept of due process important to a free society?

Key Terms and Comprehension

On a sheet of paper, write the answer to each question. Use complete sentences.

2. What is the meaning of due process?

3. What is the difference between **substantive due process** and **procedural due process?**

4. What is an example of a state using **police power** to keep its citizens safe?

5. What right of privacy is argued in the controversial case, *Roe* v. *Wade?*

Critical Thinking

6. **Identifying Central Issues** Why do you think the Supreme Court has not given an exact definition of due process?

7. **Drawing Conclusions** Do you think the police ordering a blood sample of a suspected drunk driver is an abuse of police power? Why or why not?

Freedom and Security of the Person

▲ Police must have probable cause when they stop a vehicle.

Guiding Question

How does the Constitution protect the freedom and security of the person? Use a concept web like the one below to take notes on the section.

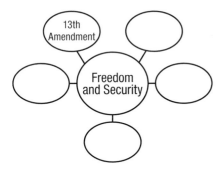

Objectives:

- Outline Supreme Court decisions regarding slavery and forced labor.
- Explain the intent and use of the 2nd Amendment's protection to the right to keep and bear arms.
- Summarize constitutional provisions used to guarantee security of home and person.

The 1st Amendment of the Bill of Rights guarantees basic freedoms of expression and religion to American citizens. The Framers of the Constitution also felt many other rights were important. The Constitution guarantees that Americans can live in freedom. This means that Americans have freedom from physical restraints. It also means that people have the right to be secure in person and at home.

How does the 13th Amendment address slavery and forced labor?

The protection of civil rights was left mostly to the individual states until the Civil War of 1861–1865. Both in 1863 and at the end of the Civil War, the federal government declared that the slaves were free people. The document that gave slaves freedom in 1863 is called the Emancipation Proclamation. However, the proclamation applied only to parts of states that had left the United States and formed a new country.

After the Civil War ended, Congress passed the 13th Amendment to end slavery and **involuntary servitude.** Involuntary servitude means forced labor. The issue of slavery had been one of the causes of trouble between the North and the South. There had always been an antislavery movement. See Figure 20.2 on the next page. There were also many who wanted to keep slavery legal. The Civil War finally ended the dispute. In 1867, it also became illegal to force someone to work to fulfill a contract or pay off a debt. The Supreme Court has ruled that the military draft and imprisonment, however, do not violate the 13th Amendment.

Section 2 of the 13th Amendment gives Congress the power to enforce the amendment by passing laws. Congress passed several civil rights laws after the Civil War. When one of these laws was challenged, the Supreme Court held that **discrimination** (unfairness) against African Americans by private persons was permitted because it was not slavery. The Court changed its mind in 1968. Congress upheld an old civil rights law from 1866. That law said citizens of any race or color could hold, buy, or sell property. In the case of *Jones* v. *Mayer*, 1968, Mayer refused to sell property to Jones, who was African American. The Court ruled in favor of Jones and decided the law of 1866 was constitutional.

✔**Checkpoint** What was the decision in the *Jones* v. *Mayer* case?

What is the right to keep and bear arms?

During the Revolutionary War, the British tried to take weapons away from the American colonists. Colonists believed they needed the guns to serve in their state militias and to defend themselves. The 2nd Amendment was added to the Constitution to protect the right of each state to keep a militia. The amendment's aim was to preserve the concept of the citizen-soldier. The amendment states "A well-regulated Militia, being necessary to the security of a free State, the right of the people to keep and bear Arms, shall not be infringed [violated]."

One interpretation of the 2nd Amendment is that it grants individuals the right to keep and bear arms. The Supreme Court has heard two cases involving this interpretation. First, in *United States* v. *Miller*, 1939, the Court rejected the individual right argument. It upheld a section of the National Firearms Act of 1934. This act made it a crime to ship a sawed-off shotgun or submachine gun across state lines without a license. The Court said that it could find no link between the shotgun involved in the case and "the preservation of a well-regulated militia."

In 2008, however, the ruling in *Miller* was basically overturned in *District of Columbia* v. *Heller*. In this case, the Court found the *District's* very strict gun control law unconstitutional. It ruled, for the first time, that the 2nd Amendment forbids "the absolute prohibition of handguns held and used for self-defense in the home." The Court's decision in this case did not overrule other restrictions on firearms. For example, it is still prohibited to carry firearms in certain places, such as schools and government buildings. It is also illegal for felons or the mentally ill to possess firearms.

■■■■■■■■■■■■■■■■■

Involuntary servitude
Forced labor

Discrimination
Treating people unfairly because of their race, sex, age, religion, or physical condition

Fig. 20.2

▲ The 13th Amendment ended slavery in 1865. *What types of involuntary servitude are permitted today?*

■■■■■■■■■■■■■■■■■

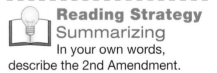

Reading Strategy
Summarizing
In your own words, describe the 2nd Amendment.

■ ■ ■ ■ ■ ■ ■ ■ ■ ■ ■ ■ ■ ■ ■ ■ ■
Reading Strategy
Summarizing
What is the main topic
discussed in this paragraph?

Over the next several years, many cases will challenge the state and federal laws that limit the right to keep and bear arms. The Supreme Court has never found that the 14th Amendment's Due Process Clause covers the 2nd Amendment. Today, many people hold that the right to bear arms is as important as the rights given in the 1st Amendment, such as free speech and religion.

✔**Checkpoint**   Why was the 2nd Amendment added to the Constitution?

What is the security of home and person?

The security of home and person dates back to the colonial days. The British forced many colonists to allow soldiers to stay in their homes. This resulted in the 3rd Amendment, which protects people from having to let soldiers stay in their homes. This amendment has never been challenged in the Supreme Court and has little importance today.

The 4th Amendment makes it illegal, in most cases, for the government to search a home without good reason. In colonial days, people in authority felt free to enter and search private homes. Sometimes the people searching were looking for stolen goods. At other times they had no reason to search a home. In 1967, the Supreme Court extended the scope of the amendment and ruled that it protects people from listening devices. It is illegal to install a hidden listening device in telephone lines or offices without a special court order.

◀ This statue, called *The Minuteman,* honors the colonial militia. **Why was the 2nd Amendment added to the Constitution?**

The 4th Amendment says, in part, that warrants are needed to search for evidence. The warrants can only be given if there is **probable cause,** which means there is a real suspicion of a crime. If the police take evidence or search anywhere without a warrant, the evidence may not be allowed in court.

Police officers can arrest a person if they have probable cause. They must believe a crime has been committed or is about to be committed. For example, a person runs away when he sees a police officer. The court may decide the act of fleeing was probable cause for the arrest. Police may also search the arrest site for a weapon or evidence.

Automobiles are often searched without a warrant. The Court has upheld this practice many times. In 1991, the Court set a rule about automobile searches. The Court said that when police officers stop a car, they do not need a warrant to search anything in the vehicle. But they need to have reason to believe the car holds evidence of a crime. There needs to be probable cause for the search. This rule also protects any passengers and their belongings from unlawful searches.

What is the exclusionary rule?

The 4th Amendment protects against unlawful searches and seizures. To make sure that the amendment protects citizens, the Supreme Court adopted the **exclusionary rule.** This rule states that if police find evidence as the result of an illegal search, this evidence cannot be used in court. The rule was first used in a court case in 1914. Then, for many years, the Court let the states decide the issue of illegal evidence. In 1961, the exclusionary rule was finally extended to cover state courts. State officials now must also follow the exclusionary rule.

Some people have criticized the exclusionary rule. For various reasons, the Supreme Court has limited the rule's use in a few cases. For example, the Court found in one case that "good faith" changed the rule. The officials thought they had a legal warrant but discovered later the warrant was illegal. The Court ruled in the officials' favor because they had acted in "good faith." Drug tests may also be done without warrants or probable cause. The Court decided this in several cases. The cases have involved armed drug enforcement officers, railroad workers, and student athletes.

A recent law that allows exceptions to the exclusionary rule is the USA PATRIOT Act. Also known as the Patriot Act, this law was passed by Congress and signed by President George W. Bush six weeks after the terrorist attacks of September 11, 2001. The law was renewed in 2006. It allows the federal government increased powers to guard against terrorism in the United States, as well as in foreign countries.

■ ■ ■ ■ ■ ■ ■ ■ ■ ■ ■ ■ ■ ■ ■ ■ ■ ■ ■
Probable cause
Reasonable suspicion of a crime

Exclusionary rule
A rule that states that if police find evidence as the result of an illegal act, this evidence cannot be used in court.

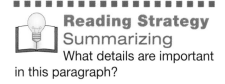

Reading Strategy
Summarizing
What details are important in this paragraph?

The Patriot Act allows the government to use new provisions to investigate suspected terrorists and control immigration. One new provision allows investigators to enter a home or place of business when no one is there and conduct a search. The person being investigated does not have to be told. Searches may continue to occur for months without being discovered.

Wiretapping, electronic eavesdropping, and videotaping are now covered by the 14th Amendment. They are the newest forms of "searches" and "seizures." No one has to enter a building to obtain evidence with these new methods. In the first case heard by the Court involving wiretapping, the conviction was upheld. The Court said the home was not invaded and therefore the 4th Amendment was not violated. Years later, this ruling was changed in *Katz* v. *United States,* 1967. The evidence against Katz came from a "bugging" device outside of a phone booth. The Court said the evidence could not be used because Katz was entitled to make a private phone call. The Court also said listening devices may only be used with a search warrant. As a result, Congress passed laws requiring the use of warrants in wiretapping in the United States.

There are many protections of freedom and security in the Constitution that were covered in this section. For a summary, see Figure 20.3 on the next page.

Biography

Andrea Davis Pinkney 1963–

Andrea Davis Pinkney was born in Washington, D.C., on September 25, 1963. She was born into a family dedicated to the civil rights movement. She often attended National Urban League conferences with her parents. She became a writer. In her book, *LET IT SHINE: Black Women Freedom Fighters,* she makes this statement: "Black empowerment was more than a slogan in our home. It was a deeply held belief that my parents, through their example, instilled in their three children. To brand myself a product of the Civil Rights Movement is no overstatement." As the author of children's books, she expresses to young people her dedication to civil liberties.

Fig. 20.3

Protections of Freedom and Security

13th Amendment:
"Neither slavery nor involuntary servitude, . . . shall exist within the United States, or any place subject to their jurisdiction."

2nd Amendment:
"A well regulated Militia, being necessary to the security of a free State, the right of the people to keep and bear Arms, shall not be infringed."

4th Amendment:
"The right of the people to be secure in their persons, houses, papers, and effects, against unreasonable searches and seizures, shall not be violated, and no Warrants shall issue, but upon probable cause, supported by Oath or affirmation, and particularly describing the place to be searched, and the persons or things to be seized."

4th Amendment's Due Process Clause:
"No State shall . . . deprive any person of life, liberty, or property, without due process of law . . ."

Essential Questions Journal Go to your **Essential Questions Journal** to work on this chapter's Essential Question.

SECTION 2 ASSESSMENT

1. **Guiding Question** Use your completed graphic organizer to answer this question: How does the Constitution protect the freedom and security of the person?

Key Terms and Comprehension

On a sheet of paper, write the answer to each question. Use complete sentences.

2. What does the 13th Amendment guarantee?

3. How does the 4th Amendment limit government?

4. What is probable cause?

5. What is the exclusionary rule?

Critical Thinking

6. **Draw Conclusions** Do you think the police should need probable cause to search a home? Why or why not?

7. **Draw Inferences** Why might people find the right to bear arms just as important as the right to free speech or to religion?

ISSUES OF OUR TIME

Balancing Security and Liberty

▶▶ Track the Issue

As international contact grew in the 20th century, so did the government surveillance.

1908 The Bureau of Investigation is formed (BOI). It becomes the Federal Bureau of Investigation (FBI) in 1935.

1947 The National Security Act establishes the Central Intelligence Agency (CIA) to coordinate intelligence about national security.

1978 The Foreign Intelligence Surveillance Act (FISA) is passed. The FISA Court must issue warrants for government to secretly use surveillance on suspected terrorists in the U.S.

2001 The Patriot Act is passed. The National Security Agency (NSA) secretly monitors international calls and e-mails of Americans with suspected ties to terrorists without a court-approved warrant.

2008 The Protect America Act revises FISA warrant requirements granting amnesty to telecommunication companies that eavesdropped on Americans without warrants.

▶▶ Perspectives

The 4th Amendment protects people from unreasonable search and seizure without probable cause. This amendment is always tested during times of war. The government argues that getting a search warrant takes too much time. And with the speed of modern technology, terrorists have an advantage. Should government be able to ignore the 4th Amendment during times of war? Justice Sandra Day O'Connor says no in her argument below. In contrast, President Bush's press secretary argues the government must move quickly to keep people safe.

Keep Due Process	Probable Cause Not Always Needed
"It is during our most challenging . . . moments that our Nation's commitment to due process is most severely tested . . . . We have . . . made clear that a state of war is not a blank check for the President when it comes to the rights of the Nation's citizens. Whatever power the . . . Constitution envisions for the Executive in its exchanges with other nations or with enemy organizations in times of conflict, it most assuredly envisions a role for all three branches when individual liberties are at stake. . . ." —*Former Justice Sandra Day O'Connor, 2004*	"FISA requires the intelligence community to make a finding of probable cause. . . . [which] was never intended to be expanded to protect the rights of foreign terrorists overseas. Showing probable cause often takes time, is sometimes impossible, and makes intelligence officers spend valuable time convincing lawyers that this standard is met, rather than doing their most important task—hunting down terrorists and other foreign threats." —*Dana Perino, White House Press Secretary, 2008*

Connect to Your World

1. Why does the press secretary think that there should not be due process during times of war?
2. Which argument do you agree with most? Why?

⟶ GOVERNMENT ONLINE
In the News
To find out more about balancing security and liberty, visit
PearsonSuccessNet.com

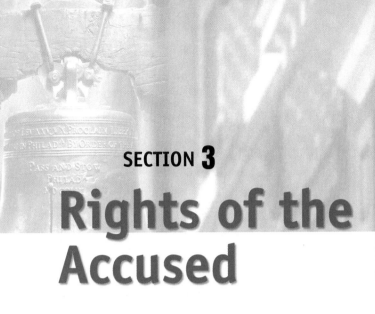

▲ A suspect must be brought before the court and informed of the charges against him.

SECTION 3
Rights of the Accused

Guiding Question

What protections does the Constitution set out for persons accused of crimes? Use a table to take notes on the section.

Rights of the Accused	
5th Amendment	6th Amendment
■ Double jeopardy	■ Speedy and public trial
■	■
■	■

Objectives:

- Define the writ of habeas corpus, bills of attainder, and ex post facto laws.
- Outline the ways the right to a grand jury and the guarantee against double jeopardy help ensure rights of the accused.
- Describe issues that arise from the guarantee of a speedy and public trial.
- Determine what makes up a fair trial by jury.
- Examine the right to an adequate defense and guarantee against self-incrimination.

Think about this statement: "It is better that ten guilty persons go free than that one innocent person be punished." This statement is one of the keys to the American legal system. Of course, society must punish criminals. However, the law intends that every person is innocent until proven guilty.

What is the writ of habeas corpus?

A **writ of habeas corpus** is a court order telling an officer to bring his or her prisoner to the court. The officer must explain to the court why the prisoner is being held. According to the Constitution, a writ of habeas corpus can be taken away only if public safety is in jeopardy. Only Congress and the President may suspend a writ and only if there is war. The governor of Hawaii tried to take away the writ during the attack on Pearl Harbor. The Supreme Court later ruled that the governor did not have the power to take that action.

What is the bill of attainder?

A **bill of attainder** is a legislative act that inflicts punishment on a person without a court trial. There is a ban on bills of attainder written into the Constitution by the Framers. They knew that the colonial legislatures and the English parliament had passed many bills of attainder. In the United States, a legislative body cannot pass a law that says a person is guilty of a crime and set the punishment of the person. However, laws can be passed that define a crime and explain the penalties if the crime is committed. In only a few rare cases has the Supreme Court struck down a law as a bill of attainder.

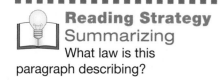
Writ of habeas corpus
A court order telling an officer to
bring his or her prisoner to the
court

Bill of attainder
A legislative act that inflicts
punishment on a person without a
court trial

Ex post facto law
"After the fact" law; a criminal law
that applies to a crime committed
before the law was passed

Grand jury
A group of persons from a federal
district court

Indictment
A formal complaint before a grand
jury which charges the accused of
one or more crimes

Information
A formal charge filed by the
prosecutor without the action of a
grand jury

Double jeopardy
Being tried twice for the same
crime

What are ex post facto laws?

An **ex post facto law** (Latin for "after the fact") is a criminal law that applies to a crime committed before the law was passed. For example, a law may be passed changing the punishment for murder from a life sentence to the death penalty. This law could not then apply to a person who committed murder before the law was passed. Ex post facto law does not happen very often in our country. Neither Congress nor the states may pass ex post facto laws.

✓ **Checkpoint**   What does *ex post facto* mean?

What is the right to a grand jury?

The 5th Amendment says a person cannot be accused of a serious crime without going before a grand jury. A **grand jury** is a group of citizens from the area of a federal district court. The grand jurors hear the evidence in a case. If at least 12 jurors decide there is enough evidence for a trial, the grand jury makes an **indictment.** The 14th Amendment's Due Process Clause does not extend the grand jury indictment procedure to the states. The states use an **information** to bring criminal cases to trial. In this document, the prosecutor swears that there is enough evidence to hold a trial.

✓ **Checkpoint**   How is an indictment made in a federal district court?

What is double jeopardy?

The 5th Amendment also guarantees against **double jeopardy,** which means that a person cannot be tried twice for the same crime. Many common situations are not double jeopardy. A person may violate both a state and a federal law with one crime. He or she can be tried for the federal crime in a federal court and also tried in a state court for the state crime. If a jury cannot come to a verdict in a trial, there is no jeopardy. It is the same as not having a trial. The accused criminal may be tried again for the same crime. Also, if the case is appealed to a higher court, that situation is not considered double jeopardy.

✓ **Checkpoint**   Which amendment guarantees against double jeopardy?

What is the right to a speedy and public trial?

The Supreme Court has decided that a reasonable time frame for a speedy trial is different in each case. In 1972, the Court listed these four considerations for deciding if the speedy trial guarantee in the Constitution is violated: length of delay, reasons for delay, harm caused by the delay, and whether the accused asked for a speedy trial. The Speedy Trial Act of 1974 decided on 100 days as the time between arrest and the beginning of a trial.

The 6th Amendment also says a trial must be public. A judge can, however, limit or ban people from a courtroom. A judge can also order the courtroom to be cleared if the information about to be heard may embarrass a witness or others in the courtroom. A public trial open to the general public is usually open to the media. There can even be television cameras in the courtroom.

The 6th Amendment also guarantees that a fair and impartial jury must be used to try those accused of a federal crime. The trial jury is usually a petit jury, from the French word for "small." The jury members must come from the state and district where the crime took place. If the defendant thinks the jurors are prejudiced, he or she may ask that the trial be moved to another location. The defendant can also waive (give up) the right to have a jury trial. The defendant would then have a **bench trial,** which is heard by a judge without a jury. If the defendant pleads guilty, there is usually no trial.

Juries in federal courts must have 12 members. Most states follow this rule. Some states have juries of only six members. The Supreme Court has ruled that no person can be kept from serving on a jury because of race, religion, national origin, or sex.

What is the right to adequate defense?

According to the 6th Amendment, a defendant in a federal court has certain rights. See Figure 20.4 on page 508. The defendant must be told the reasons for the charge and allowed to question the witnesses against him. The defendant can also call witnesses to court that will help in his defense. These favorable witnesses can be **subpoenaed,** or forced to appear in court. The last guarantee of the 6th Amendment states that the defendant has the right "to have the Assistance of Counsel for his Defense," or help of a lawyer. In 1963, the Supreme Court said that a defendant must be provided with a lawyer if he cannot afford one.

Bench trial
A trial that is heard by a judge without a jury

Subpoenaed
Forced to appear in court

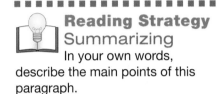

Reading Strategy
Summarizing
In your own words, describe the main points of this paragraph.

Fig. 20.4 **How Government Works**

Rights of the Accused

Steps of Justice

Any person accused of a crime is presumed to be innocent until proven guilty. *What protection does the Constitution give to those accused of a crime?*

Arrest

- Officers must have a warrant or act on probable cause.
- No unreasonable search or seizure
- Accused may request writ of habeas corpus to challenge detention.

Interrogation

- Accused must be informed of rights to counsel and to remain silent.
- No third-degree methods or coerced confession

Grand Jury Proceeding

- Grand jury weighs evidence provided by prosecutor.
- Accused may be charged by indictment or presentation.
- Bail, if required, cannot be excessive.

Self-incrimination
A person forced to be a witness against him- or herself

Miranda Rule
Rule that states that a person must be told of his or her rights before being questioned

What is the guarantee against self-incrimination?

A rule against **self-incrimination** is one of the protections written into the 5th Amendment. It means that no person can be forced to be a witness against him- or herself. The prosecution must prove the defendant's guilt in a criminal case. The guarantee can be used in any government proceeding where a person must answer a question. The defendant still may be fingerprinted or appear in a line-up. He or she must also give evidence that may incriminate others. A defendant cannot be tortured or questioned for an exceedingly long period of time to get a confession. In 1944, the Court overturned a conviction of a man who was questioned continually for 36 hours.

The **Miranda Rule** states that a person must be told of his or her rights before being questioned. The rule is based on the case of a man, Ernesto Miranda, who confessed to a crime after two hours of questioning. He had not been told of his constitutional rights. When the case (*Miranda* v. *Arizona*) went to the Supreme Court in 1966, Miranda's conviction was overturned.

Trial

- Public trial by an impartial jury must be within 100 days of arrest.
- Accused may request a change of venue.
- Assistance of counsel guaranteed
- No self-incrimination
- Favorable witnesses may be subpoenaed, opposing witnesses confronted.
- Jury's verdict to convict must be unanimous.
- No double jeopardy

Punishment
(if found guilty)

- No excessive fine
- No cruel and unusual punishment

Appeals

- Either side may appeal a verdict against it.

GOVERNMENT ONLINE
Audio Tour
To learn more about the rights of the accused, visit
PearsonSuccessNet.com

Essential Questions
Journal
Go to your **Essential Questions Journal** to work on this chapter's Essential Question.

SECTION 3 ASSESSMENT

1. **Guiding Question** Use your completed graphic organizer to answer this question: What protections does the Constitution set out for persons accused of crimes?

Key Terms and Comprehension

On a sheet of paper, write the answer to each question. Use complete sentences.

2. What is a writ of habeas corpus?

3. What is an ex post facto law?

4. Who has the burden of proof in a criminal case?

5. What is the Miranda Rule?

Critical Thinking

6. **Express Problems Clearly** Do you think television cameras should be allowed in courtrooms? Why or why not?

7. **Draw Conclusions** Do you agree with a person's right to not be tried twice for the same crime? Why or why not?

What Are the Rights of the Accused?

- You have the right to remain silent.
- Anything you say can and will be used against you in a court of law.
- You have the right to an attorney.
- If you cannot afford an attorney, one will be appointed for you.

You have probably heard these words before on television dramas. The words come from the 5th and 6th Amendments. They are called the Miranda rights. These words must be spoken to suspects before police question them.

In 1963, Ernesto Miranda was arrested in his home in Phoenix, Arizona. He was accused of robbery, kidnapping, and rape. He was questioned at the police station by two police officers. After two hours of questions, he signed a confession that he had done the crime. The confession was used at his trial. Miranda was found guilty and sentenced to 20 to 30 years in prison. Miranda's attorney appealed to the Supreme Court in Arizona. He argued that Miranda was not told he had the right to remain silent. He was also not told he had the right to an attorney. The Arizona Court upheld the conviction. That Court wrote that Miranda had never asked for an attorney. The case then went to the United States Supreme Court.

The Supreme Court overturned the conviction of Miranda (right). He was retried without his confession. There were witnesses and other evidence. He was found guilty and served 11 years.

Judge Harlan did not agree with the decision. He thought that the cost of crime was too great to call in new rules.

In a 5 to 4 decision, the Supreme Court overturned the conviction in 1966. The Court argued that the 5th Amendment should protect people in all settings. And, the accused people should not be forced to incriminate themselves. The Court concluded that the setting of a police station would pressure people to speak when they normally would not speak. In order to combat this pressure, the accused must know his rights. And those rights must be honored.

Arguments for Miranda

- Miranda was poor and uneducated. He did not know his 5th Amendment right to remain silent. He also did not know his 6th Amendment right to an attorney.

- Arizona ignored rules and got evidence illegally and did not tell Miranda he had the right to an attorney.

- Miranda's confession was illegally obtained.

- Miranda's conviction was unfair. He deserved a new trial.

Arguments for Arizona

- Miranda was not a stranger to police proceedings. He negotiated with police using intelligence and understanding.

- Miranda signed the confession voluntarily.

- The prosecution was proper. The conviction was based on Arizona law, and the prison sentence was fair.

- The Arizona Supreme Court agreed with the lower court.

Thinking Critically

1. Does Miranda's first confession mean that he was guilty? Why do you think so?

2. If you were on the Supreme Court, would you decide for Miranda or Arizona? Why?

The Miranda ruling made it less likely that police would bully the accused.

The Miranda rights must be read as soon as the suspect has been controlled.

The Miranda rule has become "part of our national culture," *Dickerson* v. *United States*, 2000.

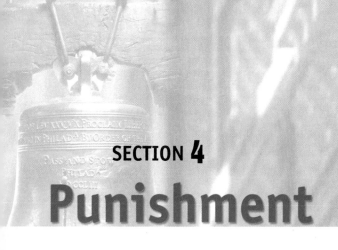

Punishment

▲ A bar advocate reviews her client's paperwork before a bail hearing.

How does the Constitution set limits on punishments for crime?
Use a table like the one below to take notes on this section.

Punishment
8th Amendment Limits
■ No cruel or unusual punishment
■

Objectives:

- Explain the purpose of bail and preventative detention.
- Describe cruel and unusual punishment.
- Outline the history of the Court's decision on capital punishment.
- Define the crime of treason.

In our country, a person found guilty of a crime in a court of law is usually punished. The form of punishment used must follow the rules of the 8th Amendment of the Constitution. Even people convicted of crimes can expect fair and equal treatment in the United States. In this section, you will learn about the protections of the 8th Amendment.

What is bail and preventative detention?

Bail is an amount of money paid to the court by an accused person to be released from prison temporarily. The bail acts as a guarantee that the accused person will show up for the trial. Once released on bail, the defendant can prepare for his or her trial. The 8th Amendment states that bail may not be "excessive" (too much). If the defendant cannot afford the bail, the court may still release him or her on their honor.

Some people accused of federal crimes are held in jail without the option of bail. This action is called **preventative detention.** The judge may decide the accused will commit another crime if released. Some believe this is really punishment for a crime before the trial. Congress made preventative detention a law in 1984. The Supreme Court upheld this law in *United States* v. *Salerno,* 1987. Every state has now passed preventative detention laws to better protect their communities.

✔ **Checkpoint**   What is preventative detention?

What is cruel and unusual punishment?

The 8th Amendment forbids "cruel and unusual punishment." The amendment was written to prevent barbaric punishments such as crucifixion and burning at the stake. Most cases that have been heard have involved being punished by death. Issues such as the overcrowding of jails have also been discussed. See Figure 20.5. In both matters, the Supreme Court usually rejects the "cruel and unusual" argument. In one case (*Robinson* v. *California*, 1962), the Court did reverse a conviction of a person jailed for narcotics addiction. California had a state law making narcotics addiction a crime. The Court said this was a cruel and unusual punishment because narcotics addiction is a disease, not a crime. The addiction needed to be treated and not punished. The Court said that only the buying, selling, and possession of narcotics is classified as a crime. For a summary of the protections of the 8th Amendment, see Figure 20.6.

✔ **Checkpoint**   What does the 8th Amendment forbid?

Bail
Money paid to the court by an accused person to guarantee that the person will show up for trial

Preventative detention
A law that allows judges to order an accused person to stay in jail without bail when there is good reason to believe that the person will commit another serious crime before trial

Fig. 20.6

Limits on Punishment

8th Amendment
• "Excessive bail shall not be required, nor excessive fines imposed. . . ."
• Forbids "cruel and unusual punishment"

Fig. 20.5

"OVERCROWDED–I'll say it's OVERCROWDED!"

▲ **Analyzing Political Cartoons** The 8th Amendment forbids cruel and unusual punishment. *What point is the cartoonist making here?*

What is capital punishment?

Capital punishment is punishment for a crime by death. Some people believe this is cruel and unusual. For many years, the Supreme Court did not hear many cases about capital punishment. Then, in 1972 *(Furman* v. *Georgia),* the Court struck down all state laws allowing the death penalty. The Court argued that the judges and juries had too much power to decide the ultimate punishment. The Court also found that the death penalty was chosen over imprisonment too randomly or without good reason.

Congress and the states then quickly passed new capital punishment laws. Some states required the death penalty for certain crimes. Other states passed laws requiring two steps in a capital punishment case. First, a trial is held to decide on the guilt or innocence of the accused. Second, a hearing is held to decide if the punishment should be death. The Supreme Court found the mandatory laws unconstitutional. The two-step method in capital cases was allowed. The Court also decided the death penalty can only be used in crimes resulting in death. The death penalty cannot be used on mentally retarded criminals or those who were under 18 when the crime was committed. The Supreme Court has decided in many cases that the death penalty is constitutional if applied fairly.

■■■■■■■■■■■■■■■■■■

Reading Strategy
Summarizing
In your own words, describe the two-step method for capital punishment cases.

GOVERNMENT ONLINE
Audio Tour
For additional information on capital punishment, visit
PearsonSuccessNet.com

Fig. 20.7

Capital Punishment Debate

Capital punishment has a long history, and so does the controversy around it. The punishment has been a part of American law since the colonial period. Many States allow capital punishment. Nearly 1,100 people have been killed in the United States since the Supreme Court allowed capital punishment again in 1976. Only about 3 of 100 death sentences are ever carried out. Forty-two persons were killed in 2007. More than 3,200 persons are in prisons today waiting for the death penalty. *Do you think the maximum penalty for murder should be death? Or do you think life in jail without parole is a better option? Why do you think so?*

47%
prefer **death penalty**

Public Opinion

48%
prefer **life without parole**

SOURCE: Gallup poll, 2006

Capital punishment continues to be a hot topic today. See Figure 20.7 on page 514. Public opinion polls, like the one on page 514, show that there is support for capital punishment. The people that support capital punishment also realize that it needs to be applied fairly. The Death Penalty Information Center reports that over the last 30 years, 125 people that were sentenced to death have been released from prisons. They were found to be not guilty. As retired Supreme Court Justice Sandra Day O'Connor noted, "If statistics are any indication, the system may well be allowing some innocent defendants to be executed."

What is treason?

Treason is the only crime defined in the Constitution. According to Article III, Section 3, treason is either making war against the United States or giving aid to the enemies of the United States. Treason is a federal crime. It can only be committed during times of war. Treason applies to all citizens, even if they live outside of the United States. No one has ever been executed for treason against the United States.

Congress has defined other crimes against the government. It is a crime to attempt to overthrow the government by force, to spy on or sabotage the government, or to join together with others to do these things.

Treason
Betrayal of one's country; making war against the United States or giving aid to enemies of the United States

✔ **Checkpoint** What are two examples of crimes against the United States?

Essential Questions Journal Go to your **Essential Questions Journal** to work on this chapter's Essential Question.

SECTION 4 ASSESSMENT

1. **Guiding Question** Use your completed table to answer this question: How does the Constitution set limits on punishments for crime?

Key Terms and Comprehension
On a sheet of paper, write the answer to each question. Use complete sentences.

2. What is the purpose of bail?

3. Which punishments were considered cruel and unusual when the 8th Amendment was written?

4. What is capital punishment?

5. What is treason?

Critical Thinking

6. **Identify Point of View** Why do you think some people disapprove of preventative detention?

7. **Draw Inferences** Why do you think some people strongly oppose the death penalty?

Chapter Summary

Section 1—Due Process of Law

- The 5th Amendment says the federal government may not take away a person's right to life, liberty, or property unless due process rules are followed.

- Procedural due process involves government actions; substantive due process involves the laws used by government. The right to privacy is guaranteed in the due process clauses.

Section 2—Freedom and Security of the Person

- The 13th Amendment ended slavery and involuntary servitude.

- The 2nd Amendment allows people to own guns and allows states to organize militia.

- The 4th amendment states that warrants are needed to search for or to seize evidence or persons.

- The Patriot Act allows the government increased powers to guard against terrorism.

- Wiretapping and other devices for eavesdropping may be used only after a warrant is obtained.

Section 3—Rights of the Accused

- The writ of habeas corpus is a court order telling an officer to bring his prisoner to court and show cause for his arrest.

- A bill of attainder is a legislative act that inflicts punishment without a trial.

- The 5th Amendment says a person cannot be accused of a serious crime without a grand jury.

- The 5th Amendment says no person can be forced to testify against himself. The Miranda rule states a person must be told of his or her rights before the police question them.

Section 4—Punishment

- Bail is money paid to the court by the accused to be released from prison until the trial.

- The 8th Amendment forbids cruel and unusual punishment.

- Capital punishment is punishment by death for a crime that involves murder.

- Treason is a federal crime committed only in wartime.

Guiding Question
Section 1 Why is the concept of due process important to a free society?

Guiding Question
Section 2 How does the Constitution protect the freedom and security of the person?

Guiding Question
Section 3 What protections does the Constitution set out for persons accused of crimes?

Guiding Question
Section 4 How does the Constitution set limits on punishments for crime?

CHAPTER 20

Essential Question
To what extent has the judiciary protected the rights of privacy, security, and personal freedom?

Document-Based Assessment

Book Review by George C. Leef

In 2006, George C. Leef wrote a review of a book written by Geoffrey R. Stone. The book, PERILOUS TIMES—Free Speech in Wartime, *talks about how civil liberties are compromised during times of war. George C. Leef is the book review editor for* The Freeman *and has written essays for* The Wall Street Journal, *the* Detroit Free Press, *and the* Detroit News.

Document at a Glance
- Book review by George C. Leef
- Explores free speech during wartime
- Civil liberties taken away during times of war

In *PERILOUS TIMES, Free Speech in Wartime* . . . law school professor Geoffrey Stone writes: "Time and again, Americans have allowed fear and fury to get the better of them. Time and again, Americans have suppressed dissent [disagreement], imprisoned and deported dissenters [people that disagree], and then—later—regretted their actions."

Stone begins with a discussion of the importance of freedom of speech. Woodrow Wilson [said] in his speech calling for a declaration of war in 1917, "If there should be disloyalty, it will be dealt with . . . [by] a hand of stern repression". . . .

Franklin D. Roosevelt was little interested in protecting civil liberties. . . . He [Stone] writes:

"Nothing compares with the massive internment [imprisonment] of Americans of Japanese ancestry . . . a Court Justice wrote, 'No adequate reason is given for failure to treat these Japanese Americans on an individual basis. . . .'

" . . . The aspiration of Americans to be fair, tolerant of others, and respectful of constitutional liberties may be more deeply embedded in American culture today than at any time in the nation's history."

Document-Based Questions

1. What have Americans done "time and again" to people that dissent (disagree) during times of war?

2. What was Woodrow Wilson's attitude toward people who disagreed?

3. What happened to Americans of Japanese ancestry during WWII?

4. According to Stone, how is American culture different today than say, during WWII.

5. **Summarize** In your own words, rewrite the book review. If necessary, work with a partner. Share your own words with the class.

SOURCE: http://www.fff.org/freedom/fd0512g.asp

Directions: On a sheet of paper, write the answer to each
question. Use complete sentences.

Section 1—Due Process of Law

1. What did the Supreme Court decide in *Rochin* v.
   California, 1952?

2. Which amendment states that the federal government may
   not take away a person's right to life, liberty, or property
   unless due process rules are followed?

3. What is police power?

4. What area of the right to privacy has been the most
   controversial?

5. **Critical Thinking** How do procedural due process and
   substantive due process work together to guarantee justice?

Section 2—Freedom and Security of the Person

6. What is involuntary servitude?

7. What is probable cause?

8. Can a vehicle be searched by the police during a routine
   traffic stop? Why?

9. **Critical Thinking** How does the exclusionary rule support
   procedural due process?

Section 3—Rights of the Accused

10. What is a bill of attainder?

11. What is self-incrimination?

12. What rights do defendants in a federal court have? Name two
    or more.

13. **Critical Thinking** Do you think you would like to serve on a
    grand jury for an important case? Why or why not?

Section 4—Punishment

14. Which Amendment forbids cruel and unusual punishment?

15. How does the Supreme Court view capital punishment?

16. What did the Supreme Court case *Furman* v. *Georgia* decide?

17. Critical Thinking In what ways have states responded to objections to the death penalty?

Apply What You've Learned

Exploring the Essential Question

18. How has the judiciary protected the right to privacy? List one example.

19. How has the judiciary protected the rights to security and personal freedom? List at least one example for each.

Essential Questions Project

20. Based on the questions you answered above, create a poster that answers the Essential Question: **To what extent has the judiciary protected the rights of privacy, security, and personal freedoms?** Your poster should list the rights of privacy, security, and personal freedom. The freedoms should relate to your life. For example, the freedoms could include privacy in your home, car, on your computer, and/or on your phone.

Essential Questions Journal

Go to your **Essential Questions Journal** to work on this chapter's Essential Question.

Test-Taking Tip

Read test questions carefully to identify those that require more than one answer.

▲ March on Washington, August 28, 1963

Civil Rights: Equal Justice Under Law

Essential Question
Why are there ongoing struggles for civil rights?

Section 1: Diversity and Discrimination

Section 2: Equality Before the Law

Section 3: Federal Civil Rights Laws

Section 4: American Citizenship

■■■■■■■■■■■■■■■■■■■■■■■■■■■■■■■■■■■

Reading Strategy: Metacognition
Metacognition means being aware of the way you learn. This awareness will help you become a better reader.

- Preview the text, noting the main idea, details, and any questions you have.
- If you do not understand something, go back and read it again.
- Summarize what you have read. Make inferences about the meaning.

GOVERNMENT ONLINE
ON THE GO

To study anywhere, anytime, download these online resources at PearsonSuccessNet.com
- **Political Dictionary**
- **Audio Review**
- **Downloadable Interactivities**

SECTION 1

Diversity and Discrimination

▲ The United States takes pride in its diversity.

Guiding Question

How have various minority groups in American society been discriminated against? Use a table like the one below to take notes on the section.

African Americans	Native Americans	Hispanic Americans	Asian Americans
■ Slaves	■ Forced onto poor land	■	■ Chinese Exclusion Act
■	■	■	■
■	■	■	■

Objectives:

- Understand what it means to live in a diverse society.
- Summarize the history of race-based discrimination in the United States.
- Examine discrimination against women in the past and present.

Have you ever read George Orwell's classic book, *Animal Farm*? Even if you have not read the book, you may have heard this line before: "All animals are created equal, but some animals are more equal than others." Keep this line in mind while you read this chapter.

What is a heterogeneous society?

Heterogeneous means "different kinds." *Hetero* is Greek for "different." *Genos* is Greek for "kind." A heterogeneous society is made up of different kinds of people.

The United States is a heterogeneous society. It is made of many different races and has become more diverse over time. In 1790, more than 80 percent of Americans were white. About 20 percent of the population were African American. The government did not count Native Americans. At the present time the white population is still the largest group. Since the 1960s, though, other ethnic populations have grown faster than the white population. Minority groups include African Americans, Native Americans, Hispanic Americans, and Asian Americans. **Immigrants** from around the world have arrived in the country in large numbers. Immigrants are **aliens**—people from other countries—admitted to the United States as legal residents. Women are not a minority. They represent about 51 percent of the population and have for the last fifty years.

✔ **Checkpoint** What does it mean to live in a heterogeneous society?

What is race-based discrimination?

Race-based discrimination is not giving people of different races a full and equal place in social, economic, and political life. The groups that have been affected the most by race-based discrimination are African Americans, Native Americans, Hispanic Americans, and Asian Americans.

African Americans

The ancestors of most African Americans were brought to this country as slaves. The slaves were freed after the Civil War when the 13th Amendment abolished slavery. Although free, African Americans continued to be discriminated against in jobs, housing, voting, and other areas. Dr. Martin Luther King, Jr., led the effort to get equal rights for African Americans. The Civil Rights Act of 1964 was a result of his work. Another result was the Voting Rights Act of 1965. Today, more than 40 million African Americans make up the second-largest minority group in the United States.

Native Americans

Large numbers of white settlers came to America beginning in the 1600s. At that time, about a million Native Americans already lived here. By 1900, their number was much smaller. Many natives died from diseases brought from Europe. As the settlers moved west, many Native Americans were victims of war. Their land was taken by white settlers, and Native Americans were forced to move to poor lands. At the present time, there are approximately 2.8 million Native Americans in the United States. A third of the them live on **reservations.** A reservation is public land reserved for their use by the federal government. Some of the problems facing Native Americans are lack of jobs, poverty, and alcoholism.

Hispanic Americans

Hispanic Americans share a Spanish-speaking background. Since 2000, Hispanic Americans have been the largest minority group in the United States. The Hispanic population is made up mostly of the following main groups: Mexican Americans, Puerto Ricans, Cuban Americans, and Central and South Americans. Some of the Hispanic Americans who came from Central and South America were **refugees.** A refugee is a person who wants protection from dangers such as war or persecution. Over the last 30 years, refugees have come to the United States from Nicaragua, El Salvador, Guatemala, Colombia, and Chile. Many immigrants have also come from the Dominican Republic, which is an island country in the Caribbean.

Heterogeneous
Made up of different races or genders; from the Greek meaning "different kinds"

Immigrant
An alien admitted to the United States as a legal resident

Alien
A person who lives in one country but is a citizen of another country

Reservation
Public land set aside by the government for use by Native American tribes

Refugee
A person who flees from a different country to a safer place

Reading Strategy
Metacognition
Before you read this section, think about what you already know about discrimination against Native Americans.

Fig. 21.1

Diversity in the United States

The U.S. Census Bureau divides the American population into many groups. It measures race and Hispanic origin separately. The separate categories acknowledge that persons of Hispanic origin may be of any race. The Hispanic population, therefore, is provided next to the pie graphs.

Population by Race and Hispanic Origin

Race
- White alone
- African American alone
- Asian alone
- All other races[1]

1790
- 19.3%
- 80.7%

2010*
- 4.6%
- 3.0%
- 13.1%
- 79.3%

Hispanic (of any race)** **15.5%** of total population

Assimilation
The process by which people of one culture become a part of another culture

Reading Strategy
Metacognition
Remember to ask yourself questions as you read. This strategy will help you make sure you understand the different minority populations.

Asian Americans

Many Asian Americans first came to this country in the 19th century as laborers. The first Asian Americans were Chinese workers who came to work on railroads and in mines. White laborers did not like this competition. In response, Congress passed the Chinese Exclusion Act in 1882. This law banned Chinese immigration.

For the next 80 years, only a small number of Asians were permitted into the country. This number included the Japanese and people from other countries. During WWII, the United States government arrested people of Japanese descent and moved them to camps. Many of these were native-born American citizens. In time, the United States expressed its regret that this had happened. In 1965, Congress changed immigration laws. Many more Asians were permitted to enter the country. (See Figure 21.1.) They include a diverse population from the Philippines, China, Korea, Vietnam, and India.

For any immigrant group, **assimilation** into American culture can be difficult. Assimilation is the process by which people of one culture become part of another culture.

✔ **Checkpoint** Why did Congress pass the Chinese Exclusion Act in 1882?

GOVERNMENT ONLINE
Audio Tour
Listen to a guided audio tour of these graphs at
PearsonSuccessNet.com

Although the population of the United States remains predominantly white, minority populations are growing at a faster rate than the majority population. *What is the rate of growth for Asian Americans? What are the benefits of diversity in a community?*

Population Increase, 2000–2010*

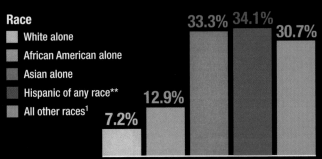

Race
- White alone
- African American alone
- Asian alone
- Hispanic of any race**
- All other races[1]

7.2%   12.9%   33.3%   34.1%   30.7%

For both charts:
*Projected **The U.S. Census Bureau added its classification of Hispanic Origin to better reflect the growing diversity of the nation's population.

[1]Includes American Indian and Alaska Native alone, Native Hawaiian and other Pacific Islander alone, and two or more races. SOURCE: U.S. Census Bureau

How are women discriminated against?

Women represent 51 percent of the United States population. Even though they are a majority, women have not had equal rights in education and the workplace. In the past, women could not vote and had limited rights to own property. Although much has changed, women are still paid less, on average, than men in similar jobs. Men hold more high-paying jobs and government positions. Many low-paying service jobs are held mostly by women. (See Figure 21.2 on page 526.)

It is illegal to pay women less than men for the same work. The Equal Pay Act of 1963 requires employers to pay men and women the same wages for the same job in the same place and working conditions. The Civil Rights Act of 1964 also prohibits job discrimination based on gender. Yet, more than 45 years after Congress passed those laws, working women earn about 80 cents for every dollar men earn.

There are a number of reasons women earn less. First, it is a fact that the male workforce is overall, better educated and has more job experience. Some blame the "Mommy track," in which women put their careers on hold to have children. Others claim that there is a "glass ceiling" of discrimination. This means that women are blocked from getting the highest positions in the corporate world.

Fig. 21.2

Gender Discrimination

Disparity in Pay

Studies show that women earn less than 80 cents for every dollar arned by men.
What do the cartoon and graph say about equality in the workplace?

'Another day, another eighty cents.'

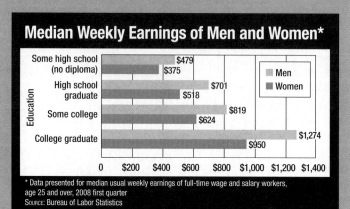

Median Weekly Earnings of Men and Women*

* Data presented for median usual weekly earnings of full-time wage and salary workers,
age 25 and over, 2008 first quarter
Source: Bureau of Labor Statistics

It is true that until recently, women were limited to a narrow range of jobs. In many cases, women were encouraged not to work outside the home once they were married. Even now, many jobs held by women are in low-paying clerical and service jobs.

Efforts on behalf of equal rights for women have gained ground. But, that ground has not included an Equal Rights Amendment to the Constitution.

Essential Questions Journal Go to your **Essential Questions Journal** to work on this chapter's Essential Question.

SECTION 1 ASSESSMENT

1. **Guiding Question** Use your completed graphic organizer to answer this question: How have various minority groups in American society been discriminated against?

Key Terms and Comprehension

On a sheet of paper, write the answer to each question. Use complete sentences.

2. Who are immigrants?

3. What event and which amendment ended slavery in the United States?

4. How are refugees different from other immigrants?

5. What is assimilation?

Critical Thinking

6. **Formulate Opinions** Should there be a limit on the number of immigrants who can come from one country? Give reasons for your answer.

7. **Draw Conclusions** How has the history of Native Americans differed from that of other minority groups? Why do you think this is so?

Equality Before the Law

▲ The statue *Freedom,* atop the nation's Capitol

Guiding Question

How has the interpretation of the guarantee of equal rights changed over time? Use a flowchart like the one below to take notes on this section.

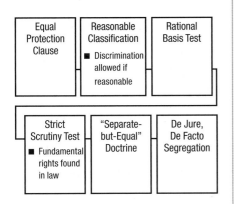

Equal Protection Clause	Reasonable Classification ■ Discrimination allowed if reasonable	Rational Basis Test

Strict Scrutiny Test ■ Fundamental rights found in law	"Separate-but-Equal" Doctrine	De Jure, De Facto Segregation

Objectives:

■ Explain the importance of the Equal Protection Clause.

■ Describe the history of segregation in America.

■ Examine how classification by gender relates to discrimination.

Democratic governments promise to treat all people the same. The Constitution and laws passed by Congress guarantee equal protection for citizens in America. In this section you will read about the 14th Amendment, which guarantees equal rights before the law. You will also read about laws passed by the states that treated people differently because of their race.

What is the Equal Protection Clause?

The Declaration of Independence was the first document of the United States government to declare that all persons were equal. The Constitution followed with the addition of the 14th Amendment in 1868. It was passed after the slaves were freed and states refused to give African Americans equal rights.

The Equal Protection Clause is part of the 14th Amendment. It says, in part, "… nor shall any state deprive any person of life, liberty, or property, without due process of law; nor deny to any person within its jurisdiction the equal protection of the law."

Today, the 14th Amendment and the 5th Amendment do not allow discrimination that is considered unreasonable. However, government has the power to classify, or group, people in a reasonable way. Otherwise, the government could not regulate human behavior. For example, convicted criminals are treated differently than ordinary citizens. This type of discrimination is allowed because it is reasonable.

Reading Strategy
Metacognition
Think about all of the things you know about equal rights. Use that information as you read about segregation in the United States.

■ ■ ■ ■ ■ ■ ■ ■ ■ ■ ■ ■ ■ ■ ■ ■ ■ ■

Rational basis test
A test that measures if the action of the government achieves a fair purpose

Strict scrutiny test
The requirement that a law must show a "compelling government interest" for treating groups of people differently

Segregation
To separate or set apart from others

Jim Crow law
A law that separates people on the basis of race

"Separate but equal" doctrine
A constitutional basis for laws that separate one group from another on the basis of race

The Supreme Court has decided many cases that challenged discrimination. The decisions have often been made using a standard known as the **rational basis test.** The test asks this question: Does the government's discrimination achieve a fair purpose? For example, states discriminate by age when they do not allow children to vote. These laws are thought to be rational because children are not mature enough to vote. But it is not rational to deny a group of adult people the right to vote simply because of race or ethnic background.

In some equal protection cases the government uses a higher test: the **strict scrutiny test.** It applies to laws that touch on the basic rights of a "suspect class." A suspect class is a group defined by race or national origin. These laws must show that the government has a "compelling government interest" for treating these people differently. This means that the government must prove it has a very strong reason for the law.

What is segregation by race?

Segregation means the separation of one group of people from another. Racial segregation laws were passed in this country in the late 1800s. They were known as **Jim Crow laws.** These laws separated African Americans from white people in many public and private places. Schools, parks, hotels, restaurants, buses, and even drinking fountains were segregated. In *Plessy* v. *Ferguson,* the Supreme Court upheld a Louisiana law requiring segregation in rail coaches. Using a **"separate but equal" doctrine,** the Court declared this law constitutional. The Court said that African Americans could be forced to use separate rail coaches if all rail coaches were equal. The court found the law did not go against the Equal Protection Clause. However, the schools and services set aside for African Americans were usually much worse than those used by white people.

It was not until the 1930s that the government began looking closely at the separate places provided for African Americans. In 1938, an African American student named Lloyd Gaines was denied admission to University of Missouri law school. He was qualified, but the school would not accept African Americans. The Supreme Court decided that Gaines must be admitted to the law school because the state of Missouri did not have a separate law school for Gaines to attend.

In 1954, in *Brown* v. *Board of Education of Topeka,* the Court overturned laws requiring separate public schools for white students and African American students. The Court said that separate schools could never be equal. This important decision affected schools in several states. In 1955, the Supreme Court told the states to end segregation as quickly as possible. Many states in the South resisted. Some passed more laws to block **integration.** Integration is the process of bringing a group of people into the mainstream of society. The Civil Rights Act of 1964 denied federal money to states that continued to practice segregation. It allowed the federal government to sue to integrate schools and other places. States began to integrate their schools more quickly. By 1969, the Supreme Court declared, "Continued operation of segregated schools . . . is no longer constitutionally permissible."

Integration
The process of bringing a group of people into the mainstream of society

✔ **Checkpoint**   What is segregation?

Biography

Two Famous Children of Immigrants

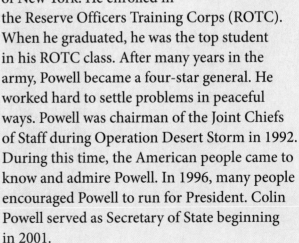

Cesar Chavez was born in 1927 in Arizona. His parents were born in Mexico and had come to the United States. When Cesar was a boy, he and his family became migrant farm workers in California. Migrant farm workers pick crops and move from place to place as crops need picking.

Chavez later dedicated his life to helping underpaid farm workers. Using peaceful means, he helped them get better pay and better working conditions. Chavez led the United Farm Workers. Under Chavez's leadership, grape pickers refused to work for almost five years. Finally the farm owners agreed to give the workers higher pay. After Chavez died in 1993, President Clinton awarded him the Presidential Medal of Freedom in 1994. His family and others carry on the work he did for migrant farm workers.

Colin Powell was born in 1937 in the Harlem area of New York City. His parents were immigrants from Jamaica and had little education. Powell attended the City College of New York. He enrolled in the Reserve Officers Training Corps (ROTC). When he graduated, he was the top student in his ROTC class. After many years in the army, Powell became a four-star general. He worked hard to settle problems in peaceful ways. Powell was chairman of the Joint Chiefs of Staff during Operation Desert Storm in 1992. During this time, the American people came to know and admire Powell. In 1996, many people encouraged Powell to run for President. Colin Powell served as Secretary of State beginning in 2001.

Fig. 21.3
De Jure Segregation

In 1896, the *Plessy* decision made "separate but equal" facilities constitutional. Jim Crow laws limited voting rights and required separate facilities for African Americans. Similar laws legalized Mexican American segregation in parts of the Southwest. *What federal law quickened the pace of desegregation?*

WE SERVE WHITE'S only NO SPANISH or MEXICANS

PARAMOUNT THEATRE
COLORED ENTRANCE
Enjoy Good Shows in Comfort

WHITE ONLY

OPEN 7 A.M. CLOSE 11:30 PM

Separate but equal

De jure segregation
Segregation by law

De facto segregation
Segregation even if no law requires it

What are de jure and de facto segregation?

De jure segregation is segregation by law (See Figure 21.3). By 1970, school systems that were segregated by law were all integrated. However, some schools remained segregated because parents and groups created new private schools. **De facto segregation** is segregation that exists even though it is not required by law. It may happen in a city when people of the same races live in certain areas. In order to desegregate these areas, communities have sometimes changed school district boundaries. Busing is another method of desegregating. In this method, students are brought out of racially segregated areas to attend integrated schools elsewhere. The Supreme Court has ruled in favor of busing. The first case about this strategy was heard in 1971 in North Carolina.

✔ **Checkpoint** What are two ways that communities have desegregated?

What is classification by gender?

Classification by gender means giving separate treatment to men and women. Classification by gender is not in the Constitution where it explains civil rights. Guarantees of civil rights are given to citizens, not just to men or to women. The only reference to gender in the Constitution is in the 19th Amendment. It forbids the denial of the right to vote "on account of sex" (gender). Before this amendment, only men were allowed to vote. In the past, laws were passed to protect women because they were considered weaker than men. The Supreme Court used to uphold many such laws that limited the rights of women in government and business. The Supreme Court did not declare any gender-based classification to be unconstitutional until 1971.

Recently, the Supreme Court has struck down many laws that discriminate against women. For example, the Court said the practice of barring women from state-run military schools was unconstitutional. In California, a law was struck down that prevented women from joining community service clubs. Sometimes, however, the Court agreed with a law that discriminated against women. For example, the Court upheld the military draft, which requires men but not women to serve in the military.

✔ **Checkpoint** What does the Constitution say about gender?

SECTION 2 ASSESSMENT

Essential Questions Journal Go to your **Essential Questions Journal** to work on this chapter's Essential Question.

1. **Guiding Question** Use your completed graphic organizer to answer this question: How has the interpretation of the guarantee of equal rights changed over time?

Key Terms and Comprehension

On a sheet of paper, write the answer to each question. Use complete sentences.

2. What is the Equal Protection Clause?

3. What is integration?

4. What is the difference between de jure segregation and de facto segregation?

5. What was the issue argued in *Plessy* v. *Ferguson*?

Critical Thinking

6. **Recognize Ideologies** Do you think it is OK to have certain laws that discriminate against women? For instance, consider the law preventing women from becoming prison guards in male prisons. Explain your answer.

7. **Summarize** How did *Brown* v. *Board of Education* begin the process of ending segregation in schools?

Is Segregation in Schools Constitutional?

The Supreme Court ruled that it was not. A third-grader named Linda Brown lived in Topeka, Kansas. Each day, she had to walk a mile through a dangerous railroad yard and then take a bus to get to school. There was another school much closer to home. School officials would not let her go to that school because it was for white students. Separate elementary schools for whites and nonwhites were maintained by Topeka's Board of Education.

Linda's father, Oliver Brown, turned to the National Association for the Advancement of Colored People (NAACP) for help. The NAACP believed it had a strong case. The NAACP used Brown's complaint, along with 13 other African Americans' complaints, to make the case for school desegregation. The case was brought to the United States District Court for the District of Kansas. The district court ruled in favor of *Board of Education*. It ruled that way because of *Plessy* v. *Ferguson.* As you recall, that case allowed for "separate but equal" facilities. The NAACP appealed the case to the Supreme Court.

In a 9–0 decision, the Supreme Court overturned the "separate but equal" doctrine. Chief Justice Earl Warren delivered the opinion of the Court: "We come to the question presented: Does segregation of children in public schools solely on the basis of race, even though the physical facilities and other 'tangible' factors may be equal, deprive the children of the minority group of equal

Before *Brown*, schools designated for African Americans were separate. But the schools were definitely not equal. The buildings, library resources, and teachers' pay was much worse.

Linda Brown was the subject of the landmark case. The case involved many people. Oliver Brown was named plaintiff because he was a male.

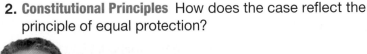

GOVERNMENT ONLINE

In the News

To learn more about the relevance of the case today, go to **PearsonSuccessNet.com**

educational opportunities? We believe that it does. . . . To separate them from others of similar age and qualifications solely because of their race generates a feeling of inferiority as to their status in the community that may affect their hearts and minds in a way unlikely ever to be undone. . . . We conclude that in the field of public education the doctrine of 'separate but equal' has no place. Separate education facilities are inherently unequal."

Arguments for Brown

- Segregating African American students from white students made them feel inferior.

- A sense of inferiority affects a child's motivation to learn.

- Segregation results in the fundamentally unequal education of minority students.

Arguments for Board of Education of Topeka

- Minority schools in Topeka are equal in every way to, and sometimes have better programs than, schools for whites.

- There is no solid evidence that segregation by race affects the education of children.

- Segregated schools prepare black children for the segregated society they will face in adulthood.

Thinking Critically

1. On what basis did the district court reach its decision? On what basis did the Supreme Court reach its decision?

2. **Constitutional Principles** How does the case reflect the principle of equal protection?

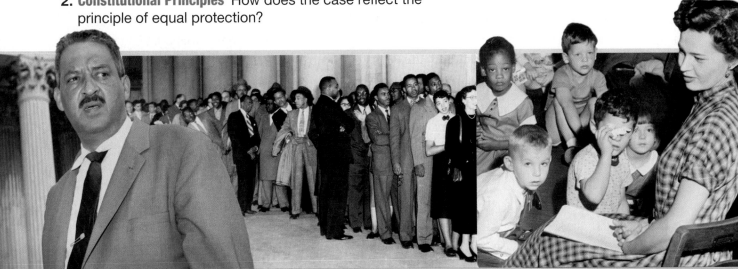

Thurgood Marshall was the lead attorney for Brown. In 1967, he became the first African American Supreme Court justice.

People waited in long lines outside of the Supreme Court building. The people wanted to hear the Court's decision.

Because of the *Brown* ruling, classrooms across the country were required to desegregate.

▲ Dr. Martin Luther King, Jr., acknowledges the crowd at his "I Have a Dream" speech, August 28, 1963.

SECTION 3

Federal Civil Rights Laws

Guiding Question

What is the history of civil rights legislation from Reconstruction to today? Use a timeline like the one below to take notes on the section.

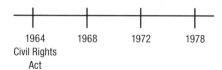

1964
Civil Rights
Act

1968   1972   1978

Objectives:

- Outline the history of civil rights legislation from Reconstruction to today.
- Explain the issues of affirmative action.

The federal government did not pass civil rights laws until the late 1950s. From the 1870s until the 1950s, few people in the federal government were concerned about the rights of African Americans, Native Americans, or other nonwhite people. Then the civil rights movement led by Dr. Martin Luther King, Jr., brought change to America. People became aware of unfair treatment of minority groups by government, especially local government. Encouraged by Dr. King's work, Congress passed new laws on civil rights, voting rights, and education.

What is the history of civil rights?

The Civil Rights Act of 1964 was one of the most important civil rights laws passed by Congress. The law banned discrimination by race in government and business. It included provisions for voting. It outlawed discrimination in many areas, such as hotels, motels, theaters, restaurants, parks, playgrounds, sports arenas, and swimming pools. The law was later amended and more provisions were added.

Today, the 1964 law prohibits discrimination in public places, or any places that provide services. In the workplace, employers and labor unions may not discriminate because of race, color, religion, national origin, gender, physical disability, or age. The 1964 law also prohibits discrimination in programs that receive federal money.

Another big victory of the civil rights movement was the Civil Rights Act of 1968. This act is sometimes called the Open Housing Act. The act forbids anyone to refuse to sell or rent houses on the basis of race, religion, national origin, gender, or disability. Homeowners cannot refuse to sell or rent their houses to families just because they have children. Today, the law has been strengthened. The Justice Department may now bring criminal charges against those who violate this act.

Title IX, a part of the Education Amendment of 1972, forbids discrimination on the basis of gender. Title IX affects any educational program receiving federal money. School athletic programs, especially at the college level, were most affected by Title IX. Women's athletic programs in public schools now receive the same amount of money as men's programs.

✔ **Checkpoint** What does the Civil Rights Act of 1968 forbid?

What is affirmative action?

Affirmative action is a policy begun by the federal government. The program was developed in 1965. It is an attempt to make up for past discrimination policies. Affirmative action requires companies and employers with few women and minority workers to try to hire more. This affirmative action policy applies to all federal agencies and state governments. It also applies to companies who sell to the federal government. Rules for hiring a set number of people from a minority group are called **quotas.**

Some people feel affirmative action is **reverse discrimination** (discrimination against the majority). These critics also believe affirmative action goes against the Constitution. For a timeline on affirmative action and equal rights policies, see Figure 21.4 on the next page.

Affirmative action has been challenged many times over the years. In a famous case, Allan Bakke, a white male, sued the University of California because he was denied admission to its medical school. There were 100 openings at the school, and 16 had been reserved for nonwhite students. Bakke claimed reverse discrimination and a violation of the Equal Protection Clause. The Supreme Court said Bakke must be admitted to the school. However, the Court also said that the school had the right to consider race as a factor when admitting students although it may not be the only factor.

✔ **Checkpoint** Why did Allan Bakke sue the University of California?

Affirmative action
A policy that requires most employers to take positive steps to make better the effects of past discrimination

Quota
A rule requiring set numbers of jobs or promotions for members of a certain group

Reverse discrimination
Discrimination against the majority group

Reading Strategy
Metacognition
There were many important dates in the history of civil rights. Think about strategies you use in your daily life to remember important dates. The same stategies might work here.

Fig. 21.4

Equal Rights and Affirmative Action

1800s

1868 States ratify the 14th Amendment, which includes the Equal Protection Clause.

1896 The Supreme Court decision in *Plessy* v. *Ferguson* establishes the "separate but equal" doctrine.

1900s

1954 In *Brown* v. *Board of Education,* the Court overrules *Plessy,* holding that "separate but equal" public schools are unconstitutional.

1964 Civil Rights Act of 1964 overturns all Jim Crow laws.

African Americans sit in protest at a whites-only lunch counter in North Carolina in 1960. ▷

▲ **Analyzing Timelines** Affirmative action programs arose in the 1960s to help rectify the harm suffered by minorities as a result of discrimination. ***What act was passed in 1990?***

What other affirmative action cases went to the Supreme Court?

The Supreme Court heard in favor of affirmative action in some cases involving industries, especially construction. These industries had a history of discrimination in hiring, and few are owned by minorities. In 1987, the Court upheld the promotion of a woman over a man who had scored higher on an interview. The Court upheld the company's affirmative action policy to hire and promote more women and minorities.

Later, in *Adarand Constructors* v. *Pena,* 1995, the Court set limits on such affirmative action cases. Adarand Constructors challenged an affirmative action policy of the Federal Highway Administration (FHWA). Under that policy, FHWA gave bonuses to contractors who hired companies owned by racial minorities and other "disadvantaged" businesses to do ten percent or more of the work.

▲ Title IX increased opportunities for women to participate in sports.

1978 In *Regents of the University of California* v. *Bakke,* the Court rules that affirmative action is acceptable, but strict quotas are not.

1990 Americans with Disabilities Act prohibits discrimination on the basis of disability.

1972 Title IX of the Education Amendment forbids gender discrimination in all federally funded educational programs.

1995 In *Adarand Constructors* v. *Pena,* the Court finds that affirmative action programs will be upheld only if shown to serve some "compelling government interest."

2000s

2003 The Court finds that a state university may take race into account in admitting students *(Grutter* v. *Bollinger)* but it may not blindly give extra weight to race in that process *(Gratz* v. *Bollinger).*

2007 In *Parents Involved* v. *Seattle School District* and *Meredith* v. *Jefferson County Board of Education,* the Court overturns school integration policies that rely too heavily on race.

Until *Adarand,* the Court usually upheld affirmative action programs. This time, the Court held that all affirmative action cases will be reviewed under strict scrutiny and must show that the programs serve some "compelling governmental interest."

In 1997, two students were denied admission to the University of Michigan. Jennifer Gratz was trying to enter as a freshman, and Barbara Grutter wanted to enter the law school. Both were white women who were denied admission. Gratz and Grutter both had higher test scores than minority students who were admitted. Both women sued the chief admissions officer because he had used race to make his admission decisions.

The Supreme Court held in favor of Jennifer Gratz. The Court said the quota policy used by the school went against the Equal Protection Clause of the 14th Amendment of the Constitution. In the case of *Grutter,* the rejection of her admission to law school was upheld. The Court decided the states have a right to use race as one factor to diversify their schools. The law school at the University of Michigan had a low number of minority students, and the state government had a compelling interest in creating a diverse class of students.

Fig. 21.5 Affirmative Action

Causes		Effects
• Discriminatory practices based on such factors as race, color, national origin, or gender • Difficult for the underprivileged to obtain a quality education • Difficult for minorities to find fair opportunities in the workforce	Affirmative Action Policies and Legislation	• More companies hire women and minorities. • Reverse discrimination • Controversy and many court cases over the constitutionality and/or proper administration of affirmative action

■ ■ ■ ■ ■ ■ ■ ■ ■ ■ ■ ■ ■ ■ ■ ■ ■ ■

Reading Strategy
Metacognition
Summarize all that you have read in this section. If you do not understand something, go back and read it again.

In 2007, the Supreme Court heard its most recent affirmative action cases. Two school districts, one in Seattle and the other in Louisville, were assigning students to public schools based on race. The districts were trying to balance their schools' population racially even though the schools' neighborhoods were largely either white or minority. The Supreme Court decided in both cases that the school districts were relying too much on race in their plans. The Court said this policy went against the 14th Amendment's Equal Protection Clause. Figure 21.5 shows the many effects that affirmative action has had.

✓ **Checkpoint**   Why did the Supreme Court vote in favor of Jennifer Gratz?

Essential Questions
Journal
Go to your **Essential Questions Journal** to work on this chapter's Essential Question.

SECTION 3 ASSESSMENT

Quick Write

Write a summary paragraph about a problem or challenge that a minority group is facing. Include why you think this is a problem for the minority group. Look at all of society as you consider this matter.

1. **Guiding Question** Use your completed timeline to answer this question: What is the history of civil rights legislation from Reconstruction to today?

Key Terms and Comprehension

On a sheet of paper, write the answer to each question. Use complete sentences.

2. What is affirmative action?

3. Who must follow the affirmative action policy?

4. What is reverse discrimination?

5. When has the Supreme Court upheld the use of affirmative action?

Critical Thinking

6. **Demonstrate Reasoned Judgment** What does Title IX provide? Do you agree with Title IX? Why or why not?

7. **Synthesize Information** Do you think the United States government should support affirmative action? Why or why not?

Writing a Letter to the Editor

Editor:

I read the article about additional budget cuts to public education. The article was "Governor Proposes Slashing School Funding." It was written on May 9. I think there should not be any more budget cuts. The money spent on public education is an investment in our community. I am a junior at Westfield High School. I know these cuts would place students' futures in jeopardy. Last year, there were cuts in the number of teachers and elective courses. The cuts were because of the reduction in funding. These cuts impact our education. Our education should not be a sacrifice this town should make again.

—Thomas Grey, St. Clairsville

The Constitution guarantees all people the right to express their views. Writing a letter to the newspaper editor is your chance to share your opinion. You can let the newspaper know how you feel about important issues that affect you and your community. Follow these steps to write a good letter:

1. **Summarize the issue.** A good letter to the editor should be short and to the point. Begin your letter by clearly stating the issue. You may be responding to an article previously written in the newspaper. If so, make sure to mention the article by title and date in your first sentence. State your opinion right away.

2. **Explain your position.** You should explain why you feel the way you do about the issue. Support your explanation with at least one or two specific examples. If you feel really strongly about it, let your emotions come out. But never use name-calling or vulgar language. If you do, people will not take your letter seriously.

3. **Make a suggestion.** The main idea of your letter might be your opinion. In addition to your opinion, you could also suggest future actions. If you were writing about problems in the community, explain how you would fix the problems.

4. **Identify yourself.** Sign your letter with your real name. If you don't want to provide your name, provide contact information. Most editors will not print a letter without knowing the name of the person who wrote it. The editor must be able to verify your identity. You can also mention any experiences you have had regarding this issue.

▶▶ What do you think?

1. Why do you think a letter to the editor should be short and to the point?

2. Why would adding suggestions for action make your letter better?

3. **You Try It** Choose an issue that interests you. Write a letter to the editor of your local newspaper.

GOVERNMENT ONLINE
Citizenship Activity Pack
For activities on writing a letter to the editor, go to **PearsonSuccessNet.com**

▲ New citizens take the oath during a naturalization ceremony in Miami, Florida.

SECTION 4
American Citizenship

Guiding Question

How can American citizenship be attained, and how has immigration policy changed over the years? Use an outline like the one below to take notes on this section.

```
I. Citizenship
    A. By Birth
        1. _____
        2. _____
    B. _____
    C. By Naturalization
II. Immigration
```

Objectives:

■ Describe how people become American citizens.

■ Explain how an American can lose citizenship.

■ Understand how the United States is a nation of immigrants.

■ Compare and contrast the status of undocumented aliens and legal immigrants.

Most people who live in the United States are **citizens.** In America's history there was some confusion about citizenship. The 13th Amendment banned slavery in the United States. But the amendment did not say the freed slaves were citizens. The 14th Amendment cleared up this confusion. This amendment declared that all persons born or naturalized in the United States were citizens.

What is citizenship by birth?

Two basic rules determine citizenship at birth. The first rule is **jus soli**—the law of the soil. A person who is born in the United States or in one of its territories becomes a citizen when he or she is born. The second rule is **jus sanguinis**—the law of the blood. A person born to American parents is also a citizen at birth.

What is citizenship by naturalization?

Many people hope to become citizens of the United States. They can do this by a process called **naturalization.** Naturalization is the legal process by which a person can become a citizen of another country. Most often, naturalization is an individual process. The U.S. Citizenship and Immigration Services in the Department of Homeland Security looks at each application for citizenship. The department reports its findings to a court. If the judge is satisfied with the findings, the alien is made a citizen. There is also collective naturalization. Collective naturalization is when an entire group of people become citizens of the United States. This has happened most often when the United States acquired a new territory.

How is citizenship lost?

It is possible for naturalized citizens to lose their citizenship. This may happen only because the person lied when he or she applied for citizenship. Citizenship is then taken away by court order. This process is called **denaturalization.** Citizens can also give up their citizenship if they choose. **Expatriation** is the legal process of giving up citizenship. The Supreme Court does not allow Congress to take away citizenship automatically.

✔**Checkpoint**　How do naturalized citizens lose their citizenship?

In what ways is the United States a nation of immigrants?

Since 1820, more than 70 million people have immigrated to America. Congress did not put any rules on immigration for a long time. Most early immigrants came from northern and western Europe. The first major restriction was the Chinese Exclusion Act of 1882. By 1920, more than 30 groups of people were refused entry to the United States.

Congress tried to cut immigration. It passed the Immigration Acts of 1921 and 1924, along with the National Origins Act of 1929. Each country was given a quota. The largest quotas were given to countries in northern Europe. The quota system did not apply in the Western Hemisphere. The Immigration Act of 1965 finally eliminated the country-based quota system. Immigrants were allowed to enter without regard to race, nationality, or country of origin. Special preference was given to relatives of citizens and legal aliens.

✔**Checkpoint**　Which act eliminated the quota system for immigration?

What are the immigration policies today?

Today, the Immigration Act of 1990 determines who may enter the United States. This law increased the number of aliens who may enter the United States each year to about 675,000 (See Figure 21.6 on the next page). Families and highly skilled workers are given preference. Criminals, suspected terrorists, and people with contagious diseases, among others, are banned from the United States. Sometimes aliens are ordered out of the country. **Deportation** is a legal process by which aliens are removed from the country.

■ ■ ■ ■ ■ ■ ■ ■ ■ ■ ■ ■ ■ ■ ■ ■

Citizen
A person given certain rights, duties, and privileges because he or she was born in or chooses to live in a certain place

Jus soli
The law of soil, which determines citizenship based on where a person is born

Jus sanguinis
The law of blood, which determines citizenship based on one's parents' citizenship

Naturalization
The act of giving full citizenship to a person born in another country

Denaturalization
Citizenship taken away by court order

Expatriation
The legal process of giving up citizenship

Deportation
A legal process by which aliens are removed from the country

■ ■ ■ ■ ■ ■ ■ ■ ■ ■ ■ ■ ■ ■ ■ ■

Reading Strategy
Metacognition
　Remember to ask yourself questions as you read. This strategy will help you make sure that you understand what you are reading.

Fig. 21.6

Immigrants in the United States

Analyzing Maps The Immigration Act of 1990 allows 675,000 immigrants to enter the United States each year. The percentage of foreign-born people living in each state in 2006 ranged from less than 2 percent to more than 25 percent. *Which states have the largest immigrant populations?* ▼

GOVERNMENT ONLINE
Audio Tour
Listen to a guided audio tour of the map at
PearsonSuccessNet.com

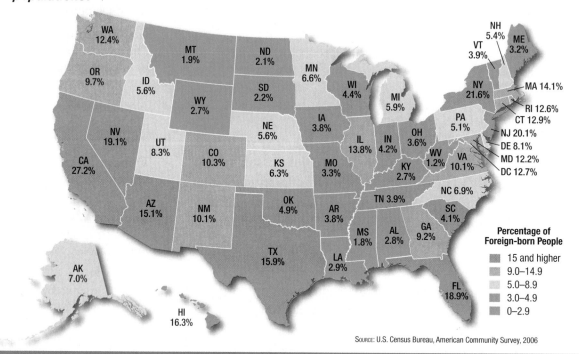

WA 12.4%
MT 1.9%
ND 2.1%
MN 6.6%
NH 5.4%
VT 3.9%
ME 3.2%
OR 9.7%
ID 5.6%
WY 2.7%
SD 2.2%
WI 4.4%
MI 5.9%
NY 21.6%
MA 14.1%
RI 12.6%
CT 12.9%
NV 19.1%
UT 8.3%
CO 10.3%
NE 5.6%
IA 3.8%
IL 13.8%
IN 4.2%
OH 3.6%
PA 5.1%
NJ 20.1%
DE 8.1%
MD 12.2%
DC 12.7%
CA 27.2%
KS 6.3%
MO 3.3%
KY 2.7%
WV 1.2%
VA 10.1%
AZ 15.1%
NM 10.1%
OK 4.9%
AR 3.8%
TN 3.9%
NC 6.9%
SC 4.1%
MS 1.8%
AL 2.8%
GA 9.2%
TX 15.9%
LA 2.9%
AK 7.0%
HI 16.3%
FL 18.9%

Percentage of Foreign-born People
- 15 and higher
- 9.0–14.9
- 5.0–8.9
- 3.0–4.9
- 0–2.9

SOURCE: U.S. Census Bureau, American Community Survey, 2006

Who are undocumented aliens?

Undocumented aliens are people who are living in the United States illegally. Most enter by crossing the Mexican or Canadian borders. Others are aliens who entered legally but have stayed past the time allowed for their visits. Undocumented aliens are most common in California, Arizona, Texas, and Florida. Many people in the United States feel the government should work harder to reduce illegal immigration. Other people want to make it easier for the undocumented aliens already in the country to apply for citizenship.

✓ **Checkpoint** How do most undocumented aliens enter the United States?

Government in Your Life

Political Asylum

The United States may offer political asylum to aliens. The word *asylum* refers to "a place of safety." Political asylum means a place where a person is safe from dangerous actions. This danger may come from the person's own government or country.

Political asylum may be given to visitors, athletes, artists, or sailors from another country, or workers from another government. It is given to people who believe they are being mistreated in their own countries. The United States offers this protection until it is clear why they want to leave their native land. If the reason is strong enough, the aliens are allowed to stay.

SECTION **4** ASSESSMENT

Essential Questions Journal Go to your **Essential Questions Journal** to work on this chapter's Essential Question.

Word Bank

deportation

naturalization

jus soli

jus sanguinis

1. **Guiding Question** Use your completed outline to answer this question: How can American citizenship be attained, and how has immigration policy changed over time?

Key Terms and Comprehension

On a sheet of paper, use the words from the Word Bank to complete each sentence correctly.

2. The _____ rule applies if a person is born in the United States.

3. The _____ rule applies if a person has parents that are American citizens.

4. _____ is the legal process by which aliens are admitted to the country.

5. _____ is the legal process by which aliens are removed from the country.

Critical Thinking

6. **Demonstrate Reasoned Judgment** Why do you suppose people who have relatives in the United States are given preference over those who don't?

7. **Compare and Contrast** What is the difference between undocumented aliens and other aliens?

Quick Study Guide

Chapter Summary

Section 1—Diversity and Discrimination

- Minority groups include African Americans, Native Americans, Hispanic Americans, and Asian Americans.

- Minority groups and women have suffered discrimination in the United States.

- Since the 1960s, immigration has made the United States much more diverse.

Section 2—Equality Before the Law

- The 14th Amendment's Equal Protection Clause and the 5th Amendment do not allow unreasonable discrimination.

- Segregation is the separation of one group of people from another.

- In *Plessy* v. *Ferguson*, 1896, the Supreme Court allowed "separate but equal" services for whites and African Americans.

- Jim Crow laws, passed by the states, segregated people by race in all areas of life.

- In 1954, the Supreme Court struck down laws requiring separate schools for African Americans and whites.

Section 3— Federal Civil Rights Laws

- The Civil Rights Act of 1964 prohibits discrimination in public places, the workplace, and federally funded programs.

- The Civil Rights Act of 1968 prohibits discrimination in selling or renting housing.

- Affirmative action encourages organizations to hire women and minorities to make up for past discrimination.

Section 4— American Citizenship

- All people born in the United States or born to American parents are citizens.

- Many people become citizens by a process of naturalization. This is a legal process that includes rules for citizenship.

- The United States is a nation of immigrants. Congress once set limits, or quotas, on the number of immigrants from each country.

- Today, the Immigration Act of 1990 decides who may enter the country.

- Undocumented aliens are people living illegally in the United States.

Guiding Question
Section 1 How have various minority groups in American society been discriminated against?

Guiding Question
Section 2 How has the interpretation of the guarantee of equal rights changed over time?

Guiding Question
Section 3 What is the history of civil rights legislation from Reconstruction to today?

Guiding Question
Section 4 How can American citizenship be attained, and how has immigration policy changed over the years?

CHAPTER 21

Essential Question
Why are there ongoing struggles for civil rights?

Document-Based Assessment

Equal Rights for Women

Representative Shirley Chisholm addressed the United States House of Representatives on May 21, 1969. She represented New York in Congress from 1969 to 1983. In her remarks, she speaks in favor of the Equal Rights Amendment (ERA) for women.

Document at a Glance

- Speech by Shirley Chisholm
- In favor of ERA
- House of Representatives, 1969

Mr. Speaker, when a young woman . . . starts looking for a job . . . she will be asked, "Do you type?" The unspoken assumption is that women do not have executive ability . . .

As a black person, I am no stranger to race prejudice . . . in the political world I have been far more often discriminated against because I am a woman than because I am black . . . there is very little understanding . . . of the immorality involved in double pay scale and the classification of most of the better jobs "for men only." . . . [As] there are 3 1/2 million more women in the United States than men . . . this is outrageous.

It is for this reason I wish to introduce today a proposal that has been before every Congress for the last forty years . . . the Equal Rights Amendment.

[One of the two] . . . commonest arguments against this amendment . . . is that women are already protected under the law . . . A second argument . . . is that it would eliminate legislation that many states and the Federal Government have enacted giving special protection to women . . . Women need no protection that men do not need. What we need are laws that protect working people . . .

Document-Based Questions

1. What does Representative Chisholm say a young, job-seeking woman might first be asked?

2. What does she say are the arguments against the Equal Rights Amendment?

3. At the time of this speech, how many more women were there than men?

4. How many times had the ERA been proposed before Congress?

5. **Use Metacognition** What did you learn about discrimination against women by reading this selection? What do you still want to know about this topic?

SOURCE: scriptorium.lib.duke.edu/wlm/equal/

Chapter Assessment

Directions: On a sheet of paper, write the answer to each question. Use complete sentences.

Section 1—Diversity and Discrimination

1. What does it mean to say that the population of the United States is heterogeneous?

2. What is a reservation?

3. Why did the first Asian immigrants come to the United States?

4. What type of discrimination do women face?

5. **Critical Thinking** Why do you think the United States government ordered Asian Americans into camps during World War II?

Section 2—Equality Before the Law

6. What is one example of reasonable government discrimination?

7. What is segregation?

8. What did the Civil Rights Act of 1964 force states to do?

9. **Critical Thinking** How did the Supreme Court's ruling in *Brown* overturn the "separate but equal" doctrine?

Section 3—Federal Civil Rights Laws

10. What do the Civil Rights Acts of 1964 and 1968 prohibit?

11. What is affirmative action?

12. How did the Supreme Court rule in *University of California* v. *Bakke*?

13. **Critical Thinking** Why might people claim that affirmative action is unconstitutional?

Section 4—American Citizenship

14. How might a child born outside of the United States become an American citizen at birth?

15. What is denaturalization?

16. What did the Immigration Act of 1990 decide?

17. Critical Thinking Why do you think undocumented aliens are most common in California and Texas? Explain your answer.

Apply What You've Learned

Exploring the Essential Question

Research a civil rights leader in the United States. You can pick a leader from this chapter or with help from the teacher. Find out the following about the civil rights leader:

18. What struggles did the civil rights leader have?

19. What successes did the civil rights leader have?

Essential Questions Project

20. Based on your research of the civil rights leader and your knowledge from this chapter, create a timeline. Partner with a classmate for help. The timeline should include civil rights legislation and court cases that the civil rights leader influenced. Use the timeline to help answer the Essential Question: **Why are there ongoing struggles for civil rights?**

Essential Questions
Journal

Go to your **Essential Questions Journal** to work on this chapter's Essential Question.

Test-Taking Tip

When studying for a test, review the topics in the chapter. Then make up a practice test for yourself.

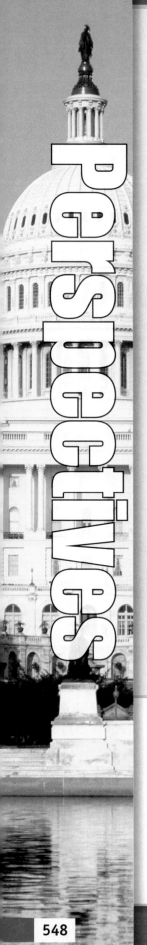
Essential Question

What should be the role of the judicial branch?

Whether the role of the judicial branch should be to make law, apply law, or explain the law has been debated throughout history. The following examples each offer a perspective on the answer.

" ON JUDICIAL ACTIVISM:

We want courts to settle the question of whether someone has exceeded the limits set by the law. And we want judges to be free of essential dependence upon the wielders of power so that they can do what they are supposed to do without being intimidated.

—**Joseph Tussman,** *Judicial Activism and the Rule of Law—Toward a Theory of Selective Intervention*

" ON THE IMPLICATIONS OF LAWS WITHOUT COURTS:

Laws are dead letters without courts to expound and define their true meaning and operation.

—**Alexander Hamilton,** *The Federalist* No. 78

ON HOW JUSTICES RULE:

Frank and Ernest

Essential Question Warmup

Throughout this unit, you studied the judicial branch. Use what you have learned and the quotations and opinions above to answer the following questions. Then go to your **Essential Questions Journal.**

1. What did Hamilton think should be the role of the judicial branch?

2. Are all laws completely constitutional or unconstitutional?

3. Should the role of the judicial branch change to adapt to changing times? Explain.

4. Should judges allow their personal views to guide their decisions? Why or why not?

Essential Questions Journal

To continue to build a response to the unit Essential Question, go to your **Essential Questions Journal.**

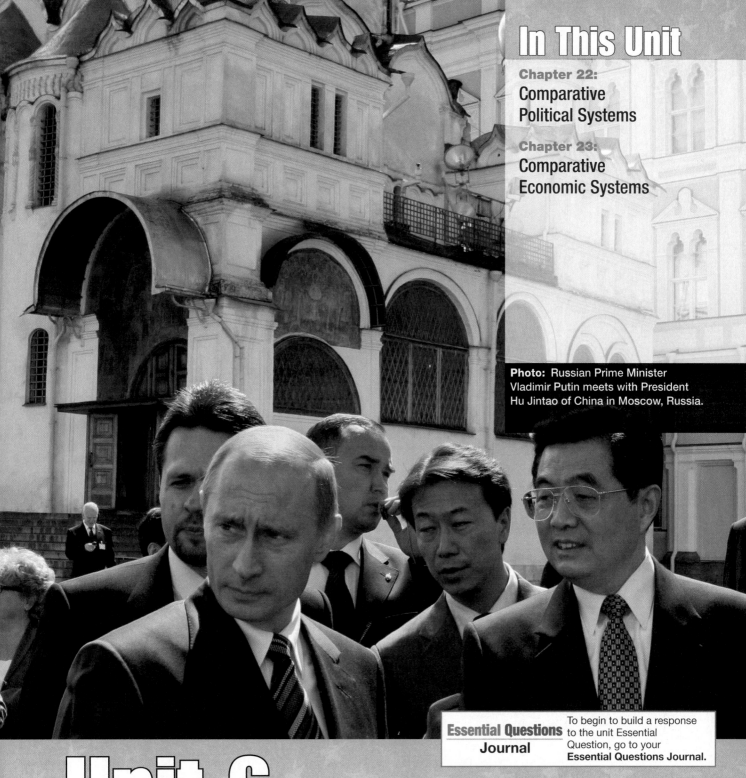

Photo: Russian Prime Minister Vladimir Putin meets with President Hu Jintao of China in Moscow, Russia.

Essential Questions Journal To begin to build a response to the unit Essential Question, go to your **Essential Questions Journal.**

Unit 6
Political and Economic Systems

Essential Question How should a government meet the needs of its people?

▲ China's Premier Wen Jiabao opens the National People's Congress in Beijing.

CHAPTER

22

Comparative Political Systems

Essential Question
How should you measure different governments?

Section 1: Origins of the Modern State

Section 2: Ideas and Revolutions

Section 3: Transitions to Democracy

Section 4: Case Studies in Democracy

Reading Strategy: Summarizing
When you summarize, you ask questions about what you are reading. That way you can determine the most important information. As you read this chapter, ask yourself these questions:

- What details are most important about the political systems?
- What is the main point of each section?
- What political systems are talked about in this chapter?

GOVERNMENT ONLINE
ON THE GO

To study anywhere, anytime, download these online resources at PearsonSuccessNet.com
- Political Dictionary
- Audio Review
- Downloadable Interactivities

Chapter 22   **551**

▲ The *agora,* a large public space, was the ancient home of Athenian democracy.

SECTION 1

Origins of the Modern State

Guiding Question

On what early political ideas and traditions was modern government founded? Use an outline to take notes on the roots of modern American democracy.

```
I. Ancient Foundations
    A. Athens: The First Democracy
        1. _____
        2. _____
    B. The Roman Republic
        1. _____
        2. _____
```

Objectives:

- Identify the ancient foundations of the state in Athens, in Rome, and in the feudal system.
- Analyze the rise of sovereign states.
- Explain how governments may achieve legitimacy.
- Understand why European nations turned to colonialism.

All people that live together in groups share a need for rules and laws. Governments were formed to help people survive. Early groups of people lived simply. As life became more complicated, governments grew in size and power.

What were the ancient foundations of government in the United States?

The government of the United States was formed after the colonists broke away from English rule. Many ideas for the new government came from ancient Greece and Rome. Ideas from newer European governments also became part of the new government.

Greece was home to the first democracy, beginning around 700 B.C. Greece was made up of city-states with large amounts of land around each of them. Athens, the most famous city-state, began as a monarchy. By the sixth century B.C., the people of Athens revolted and formed a democracy, or "rule by the people." Only free men were members of the ruling body, called the Assembly. The members of the Assembly ran the government and took turns holding office. Wars in Greece caused the city-states to weaken. Rome, another great power at the time, soon took over the Greek city-states.

Rome had a large population. The citizens elected representatives to speak and act for them. This system of government was called a republic. This republic had two classes of citizens. The upper-class landowners were the **patricians.** The common people were known as **plebeians.** The elected representatives formed the Senate. The 300 members of the Senate appointed two consuls, who were very powerful. The Roman Empire came to an end in the fifth century A.D. The next thousand years are known as the Middle Ages.

What was feudalism?

Feudalism began to slowly develop in Europe in the ninth century. In the feudal system, powerful feudal lords owned large amounts of land. These powerful lords gave land to lesser lords known as vassals. The vassals served their lords by taking care of the lands. The basic unit of the feudal system was the lord's manor, or the land a lord owned. The lords protected the people who lived and worked on the manors. Most of the population during this time were known as serfs. They were peasants who were bound to the land. They never left the land they farmed without permission. Serfs led very harsh lives.

The Roman Catholic Church, along with feudalism, gave some form of government to parts of Europe during the Middle Ages. Most of Europe was Christian and the Roman Catholic Church became powerful. The Church owned large amounts of land. The Pope, along with monarchs and lords, ruled most people's lives. See **Figure 22.1.**

Reading Strategy
Summarizing
What is the main idea of this paragraph?

Patricians
The rich, upper-class, landowning people of the Roman Republic

Plebeians
The common people of the Roman Republic

Feudalism
A system in which a feudal lord gave protection to the people who lived and worked on his land in return for their services

---

Fig. 22.1
Roots of the Sovereign State

The defining elements of sovereign states developed over time and in different lands. *What characteristics define the United States as a sovereign state?*

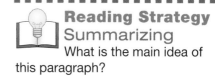
GOVERNMENT ONLINE
Interactivity
For an interactive exploration of this timeline, visit
PearsonSuccessNet.com

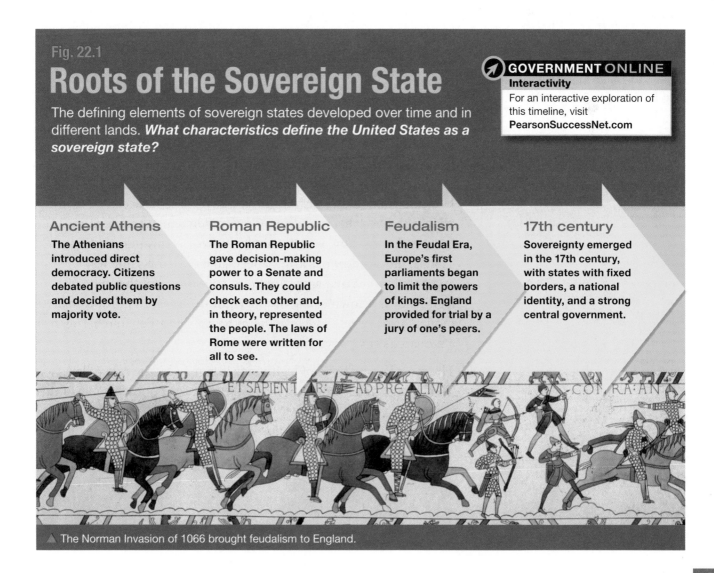

Ancient Athens
The Athenians introduced direct democracy. Citizens debated public questions and decided them by majority vote.

Roman Republic
The Roman Republic gave decision-making power to a Senate and consuls. They could check each other and, in theory, represented the people. The laws of Rome were written for all to see.

Feudalism
In the Feudal Era, Europe's first parliaments began to limit the powers of kings. England provided for trial by a jury of one's peers.

17th century
Sovereignty emerged in the 17th century, with states with fixed borders, a national identity, and a strong central government.

▲ The Norman Invasion of 1066 brought feudalism to England.

Why did the sovereign state begin to rise?

In the 1300s, new developments in economics and politics changed how people lived and were governed. Towns began to develop across Europe, where merchants and skilled tradesmen lived and worked. New trade routes introduced new goods and spread the use of money, which was rare in the feudal system. Merchants still had to pay lords for protection and to use roads and bridges, but they enjoyed more freedom than the serfs. In the 1340s, the Black Plague arrived in Europe and killed one third of the population. The survivors found their labor was worth more because there were fewer people to work for the lords. They demanded more freedom and better rewards for their work.

✓ **Checkpoint**   What caused feudalism to end?

Even during feudalism, monarchs ruled in Europe. They were weak and needed the lords to govern their lands. As the lords grew weaker, and towns became more important, merchants turned to monarchs for leadership. In England, Spain, and France, monarchs built strong central governments. Because they had always reigned in some form, they had sovereignty. **Sovereignty** is the sole authority to make decisions and keep peace within a country.

How did governments gain legitimacy?

All governments must have legitimacy to rule. **Legitimacy** is the belief of a people that a government has the right to make decisions for the people. The sovereign states controlled and ruled the people. Now they had to establish legitimate governments accepted by the people and by other countries. Governments may gain legitimacy in several ways. One way to gain legitimacy is through tradition. That is, the country has always been governed the same way and people want that government to continue. Another type of legitimacy is known as the **divine right of kings.** In Europe, many monarchs believed God gave them the right to rule. To rebel against a monarch's rule was a sin.

The most lasting form of legitimacy is gained by the rule of law. The United States, under the Constitution, is a good example of this type of legitimacy.

What are colonialism and mercantilism?

Colonialism is control of foreign lands by one nation. This began in Europe in the late 1400s. People from European countries settled in other parts of the world. There was great rivalry among European nations to settle and claim these foreign lands in the Americas, Africa, and Asia.

Merchants became wealthy during this time. **Mercantilism** was adopted. Mercantilism is the belief that money is the chief source of a nation's wealth. Countries tried to obtain gold and silver and build new industries. They did this by colonizing other lands, which had resources such as gold, lumber, or rich farmland. The colonies were allowed to trade only with the colonizing country. The colonies sold raw materials cheaply and bought goods made in Europe. In the 1500s through 1700s, Europeans colonized lands in the Western Hemisphere. Monarchs set up companies to control trade with these new lands, bringing them wealth and power. Britain, France, Spain, and Portugal were the leading countries to colonize the Americas.

Colonialism
Control of foreign lands by one nation

Mercantilism
The belief that money is the chief source of wealth

SECTION **1** ASSESSMENT

Essential Questions Journal Go to your **Essential Questions Journal** to work on this chapter's Essential Question.

Quick Write

Based on what you have read in this section, write a paragraph about how the United States gained legitimacy. Remember to use complete sentences. Summarize the events that occurred that lead to the legitimacy of the government.

1. **Guiding Question** Use your completed outline to answer this question: On what early political ideas and traditions was modern government founded?

Key Terms and Comprehension

On a sheet of paper, write the answer to each question. Use complete sentences.

2. What is feudalism?

3. What were the two classes of people in the Roman Republic?

4. What are two different ways a government can gain legitimacy?

5. What is colonialism?

Critical Thinking

6. **Understanding Cause and Effect** How did the rise of towns contribute to the fall of the feudal system?

7. **Drawing Inferences** Why is it important for governments to gain legitimacy?

Using the Internet as a News Source

Imagine that your teacher gave you an assignment in your government class. The assignment is to write a report on the recent visit of Japan's prime minister to the United States. Include places where the prime minister spoke and report on meetings the prime minister had with the U.S. President.

When researching current events, Internet news sources are very helpful. You must be very careful about which sites you choose. Major television networks, newspapers, and magazines have Web sites. These sites are usually good resources that can be trusted. Examples include CNN, the BBC, National Public Radio, and *The Wall Street Journal.* Government Web sites are also excellent places to find news.

To use the Internet as a news source, follow these steps:

1. **Determine specific search term(s).** There is a lot of information on the Internet. To search the Internet most

effectively, you need to figure out a specific term or topic. Searching for a general subject can give you too many results. For example, if you type in "Japan's prime minister" you will get thousands of results. Typing the name of the prime minister, along with "U.S. visit" would be a better choice. You would be more likely to get the information you are looking for.

2. **Use a search engine to find information on your topic or to locate specific news sources.** Type the search term for your topic. You can also use a specific news organization, such as *Newsweek.* A different method to use would be to type "news" into

the search engine. News sources that are local to the event may provide the best coverage.

3. **Be sure that your sources have a good reputation.** Some news organizations have better reputations for accuracy than others. When you find a fact on a Web site, be sure to confirm it on a different site.

▶▶ What do you think?

1. Why is it important to determine specific search terms?
2. Which news sources are the most reliable?
3. **You Try It** Choose a recent topic about government that you saw on the news. Determine your search term, and then type it into the search engine. Follow the links that you think are good news sources. Take notes on the information you find. Go to at least one other reliable Web site to confirm the facts you found.

GOVERNMENT ONLINE
Citizenship Activity Pack
For an activity to help you use the Internet for research, go to
PearsonSuccessNet.com

▲ Simón Bolívar led many South American nations to independence from Spain.

Ideas and Revolutions

Guiding Question

How have some nations expanded popular sovereignty?
Use a flowchart similar to the one below to record information about how different nations have expanded popular sovereignty.

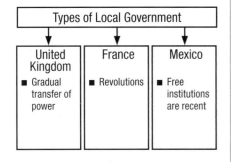

Types of Local Government		
United Kingdom	France	Mexico
■ Gradual transfer of power	■ Revolutions	■ Free institutions are recent

Objectives:

- Understand how Enlightenment ideas influenced the growth of popular sovereignty.
- Analyze the role of popular sovereignty in Great Britain, France, and the rest of the world.
- Describe events in Latin America, Asia, and Africa that expanded popular sovereignty.
- Examine how fascism and communism distort the idea of popular sovereignty.

Stable governments usually remain in power for a long time. Other governments may fail because of revolutions or problems with the leaders. If citizens do not support the government or show their approval, the government may lack legitimacy and fail.

What is the Enlightenment?

The Enlightenment was a time in the 18th century when new ideas developed. Many scientific discoveries were made. People began to discuss government, economics, and other ideas about how people should live. Some important political thinkers during this time had ideas about the natural rights of people. John Locke believed people had a right to life, liberty, and to own property. Thomas Hobbes said that people needed strong responsible leaders to keep them safe. Adam Smith and David Ricardo criticized economic policies that made monarchs rich while their subjects suffered in poverty.

In France, Voltaire believed in freedom of religion and the importance of scientific study. Montesquieu wrote about ideas of the government, especially the separation of power, that were later written into the Constitution of the United States.

These ideas from important theorists began to replace religious ideas. People rejected monarchs who abused their power. Popular sovereignty became important. Popular sovereignty remains the basic principle for many republics and democracies today.

✔**Checkpoint** Who were three important figures of the Enlightenment?

How did Great Britain and France establish popular sovereignty?

Great Britain and France both have popular sovereignty. (Figure 22.2) Great Britain was one of the first countries to allow people to directly participate in government. This happened slowly over time. France, on the other hand, suffered through a revolution to achieve popular sovereignty.

Great Britain is a constitutional monarchy. The monarch leads the country but has few real powers. The people elect and support a leader as we do in the United States. Britain is a democracy run by a parliament and a prime minister.

Powerful monarchs once ruled the country. The Magna Carta, written in 1215, gave the English people rights for the first time. During the 1600s, the British monarchy began to lose power to Parliament. Parliament was a national legislature with the power to collect taxes. The Petition of Right of 1628 and the English Bill of Rights in 1689 gave Parliament more control of the government. Parliament was not truly democratic. Many members were unelected. Only male property owners in some towns had the right to vote. In addition, only members of official Protestant churches could hold government office.

Fig. 22.2

Two Revolutions

Monarchies in Great Britain and France adapted to popular sovereignty—one nation peacefully, the other violently. Each country's transition began with a revolutionary moment that shaped future events. *What were the effects of each form of revolution?*

The French Revolution

1789–1794 The French revolutionary government violently overthrew King Louis XVI, the nobility, and the Church. This created a new republic with new institutions that did not last very long.

Britain's Glorious Revolution

1688 Parliament invited William and Mary (above) to peacefully replace King James II on condition that they recognize the authority of Parliament and the rights of individuals.

New laws were passed in Great Britain in the 1800s and early 1900s. All adult citizens, both men and women, could now vote and run for office. Through all these changes, Great Britain still protected the monarchy and kept this link to the past.

France followed a different path to popular sovereignty. The French monarchy was most powerful under Louis XIV (1643–1715). In 1789, the French people revolted against the monarchy. This was followed by a period of terror and the destruction of the monarchy, the Catholic Church, and traditional laws. Many revolutions and changes in government took place in France after the revolution of 1789. Kings and emperors took power again, followed by new revolutions. Today, France is a constitutional democracy like the United States.

✓ **Checkpoint** How did France achieve popular sovereignty?

How did Latin America gain independence?

Spain controlled lands in North America, South America, and the Caribbean. The Spanish government began a system called the **encomienda.** This system gave the settlers control over the Indians living in their areas. The settlers forced the Indians to work for them in mines and on farms in return for protection. They also taught the Indians Christianity. This system did not work and was replaced with *haciendas.* These were large estates with many workers. The haciendas were powerful centers of politics and money in Latin America.

In 1821, Mexico was able to gain independence from Spain. See Figure 22.3 on the next page. Spain had been conquered by Napoleon. In the turmoil that followed, Agustin de Iturbide declared independence for Mexico and crowned himself emperor.

Many other countries in Latin America also became independent from Spain in the 19th century. Bolívar led revolutions in many countries in South America. Simón Bolívar began to create a new political order in Latin America. The new order was based on popular sovereignty. Brazil also gained its independence from Portugal during this time.

■■■■■■■■■■■■■■■■■■■
Encomienda
A system used by the Spanish government to force the Indian population to work in the mines and on farms

■■■■■■■■■■■■■■■■■■■
Reading Strategy
Summarizing
Read this paragraph. Summarize the purpose of the encomiendas and haciendas.

Fig. 22.3
Latin American Independence

Interpreting Maps Most of the countries in Latin America won their independence from Spain or Portugal. These countries had a different type of government than the United States. *What country ruled Brazil?* ▼

BRITISH NORTH AMERICA (Br.)

UNITED STATES 1776

ATLANTIC OCEAN

TEXAS 1836

MEXICO 1821

Bahamas (Br.)

Cuba (Sp.)

HAITI 1804

DOMINICAN REPUBLIC 1844

Puerto Rico (Sp.)

British Honduras

Jamaica (Br.)

GUATEMALA 1838

EL SALVADOR 1838

Mosquito Coast (Br.)

HONDURAS 1838

NICARAGUA 1838

COSTA RICA 1838

VENEZUELA 1830

British Guiana

Dutch Guiana

French Guiana

COLOMBIA 1819

ECUADOR 1822

PACIFIC OCEAN

PERU 1824

BRAZIL 1822

BOLIVIA 1825

PARAGUAY 1811

CHILE 1818

ARGENTINA 1816

URUGUAY 1828

KEY
- ▪ former British colony
- ▪ former French colony
- ▪ former Portuguese colony
- ▫ former Spanish colony
- ▨ British colony
- ▨ Dutch colony
- ▨ French colony
- ▨ Spanish colony

Dates shown are dates of independence

● GOVERNMENT ONLINE
Audio Tour
Listen to a guided audio tour of this map at
PearsonSuccessNet.com

There were many obstacles to the formation of stable governments in Latin America. In Spain and Portugal, powerful monarchs ruled these countries, and the people had no control. There was no tradition of popular sovereignty. The hacienda landowners were powerful, wealthy, and did not want change. The Catholic Church also had control and influence and did not favor change. New countries had no history of self-government. The new governments were weak and inexperienced. Often, powerful landowners did not accept or support these governments and civil wars broke out.

In contrast, the British colonies had a tradition of limited representation of the people. The American colonists shared a belief in their government and their rights. Countries in Latin America did not grow and prosper. The governments were too unstable and divided to govern well.

✔ Checkpoint When did Mexico gain independence?

What was the Mexican Revolution?

Under President Porfirio Diaz, Mexico had a long period of peace and economic growth from 1876 to 1910. Most Mexican citizens did not benefit from this wealth and remained very poor. Finally the people revolted. A long civil war followed. By 1917, the civil war had ended. A new constitution was written, and the National Revolutionary Party (PRI) was formed. By controlling elections and providing a stable government, the party became very strong and ran Mexico until 2000.

What is Latin America like today?

Latin America experienced many revolutions during the 19th and 20th centuries. Military leaders and dictators tried to take over in several countries. The Cuban revolution in 1959 brought communist control to Cuba. **Guerrilla warfare** was often used in these revolutions. Guerrilla warfare is conducted by small bands of rebels using hit-and-run methods.

In some Latin American countries, military leaders claimed to be trying to restore democracy. The United States accepted military rule in other countries because communists might take control and ally with the Soviet Union. That threat passed in the 1980s when the Cold War ended. Some Latin American countries are now developing more democratic governments with the support of the United States.

✔**Checkpoint**   What led to communist control in Cuba?

Guerilla warfare
Fighting that is carried out by small groups in hit-and-run raids

Reading Strategy
Summarizing
What are some important details that help you understand this paragraph?

What happened when Asian and African countries became independent?

Many countries in Asia and Africa were under colonial control until the mid-20th century. European nations divided nearly all of Africa into colonies (**Figure 22.4**). Often ethnic groups were split among different states or combined in countries with other nations. This "divide and rule" method caused tension and fighting even after the African countries became independent. Rwanda experienced terrible mass killings in the 1990s between the Hutu and Tutsi peoples.

Most colonies of Africa and Asia won their independence during the Cold War in the 1950s and 1960s. These countries were caught in Cold War struggles between the United States and the Soviet Union. Vietnam was a French colony that split in two, north and south, when it won independence. In the Vietnam War, the United States defended South Vietnam from a Communist-led invasion by North Vietnam. The Soviet Union and China supported North Vietnam.

Some countries in Asia and Africa found it difficult to form democratic governments. There were many different ethnic groups, which led to conflicts and mistrust. The new governments that formed were not able to provide for their peoples' needs. The people did not trust the governments. Most people were poor, there was no middle class, and there were only a few wealthy people. The strongest, most organized group in these new countries was the military, which often had control of the government.

Reading Strategy
Summarizing
In your own words, tell what this paragraph is about.

Fig. 22.4

▲ **Interpreting Political Cartoons** The borders of many modern African nations were drawn by European colonizing powers. *Why is Africa (spelled Afrique in French) shown as a cake in this picture?*

Fascism
A political system based on a strong racist government

Communism
A political and economic system based on state control of the economy

What are fascism and communism?

Fascism and **communism** are two ideas that dictatorships in many countries followed. Fascism is based on a strong central government with racist and aggressive policies. In a fascist state, individual rights and beliefs are less important than the state's needs. Communism is both an economic system and a political system. The government controls all businesses and the use of all resources. Both fascist and communist governments may hold elections. However, only the ruling party's candidates win.

Some examples of fascist governments are Germany under Adolf Hitler, Italy under Benito Mussolini, and Spain under Francisco Franco. These governments began during a worldwide economic depression in the early 1900s. The powerful leaders and their governments were militaristic. People who disagreed with them were arrested, attacked, or killed. In these fascist governments, the state controlled all social and economic policy.

Communist ideas were based on the theories of Karl Marx. He believed workers would revolt and overthrow the government. Then the free market system would disappear and the workers, "the people," would rule. In a communist state, an all-powerful central government owns all property and runs the economy. The government claims to rule on behalf of workers. The Soviet Union and People's Republic China are examples of communist states. You will read more about communism in Chapter 23. Figure 22.5 provides a summary of each type of government system. Figure 22.6 on the next page compares and contrasts fascism and communism.

Fig. 22.5

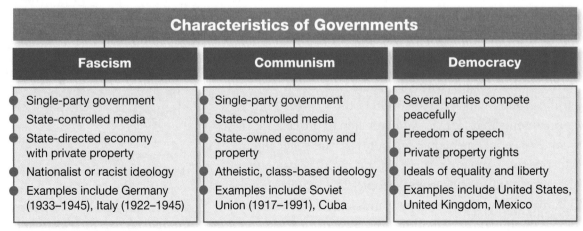

Characteristics of Governments		
Fascism	**Communism**	**Democracy**
• Single-party government	• Single-party government	• Several parties compete peacefully
• State-controlled media	• State-controlled media	• Freedom of speech
• State-directed economy with private property	• State-owned economy and property	• Private property rights
• Nationalist or racist ideology	• Atheistic, class-based ideology	• Ideals of equality and liberty
• Examples include Germany (1933–1945), Italy (1922–1945)	• Examples include Soviet Union (1917–1991), Cuba	• Examples include United States, United Kingdom, Mexico

Fig. 22.6

Fascism and Communism

Fascism and communism are political systems, in which the state has complete control. However, they have different goals and economic policies. *How did fascist and communist governments benefit from identifying and attacking an "enemy of the people"?*

Similarities

- One-party states with no free elections or fair courts
- People gathered into a mass movement against an enemy
- A strong military and militarized society
- Government-controlled media broadcasting propaganda and censored news

Nazi youth parade in Germany ▶

Differences

Fascist state

- Nation defined on racial or ethnic terms
- Foreign powers and minorities are the enemy
- State-directed economy with private enterprise
- Some religions tolerated but controlled

Adolf Hitler,
Fascist dictator
Germany, 1933–1945

Communist state

- State embodies the working class
- Global capitalism is the enemy
- State-controlled economy
- Religion discouraged or outlawed

Josef Stalin,
Communist dictator
Soviet Union, 1924–1953

Essential Questions
Journal
Go to your **Essential Questions Journal** to work on this chapter's Essential Question.

SECTION 2 ASSESSMENT

1. **Guiding Question** Use your completed flowchart to answer this question: How have some nations expanded popular sovereignty?

Key Terms and Comprehension

On a sheet of paper, write the answer to each question. Use complete sentences.

2. In which century was the age of Enlightenment?

3. What was the encomienda system? What system replaced it?

4. What is guerilla warfare?

5. What is fascism?

Critical Thinking

6. **Compare and Contrast** How were Great Britain's and France's paths to popular sovereignty different?

7. **Understand Cause and Effect** Why do you think fascism and communism began during an economic depression in the early 1900s?

▲ Germans celebrate the fall of the Berlin Wall in November 1989.

Transitions to Democracy

Guiding Question

How successfully have some nations achieved democratic governments? Use a table similar to the one below to record information about modern transitions to democracy.

Russia	Iraq	Yugoslavia
▪ 1985—softliner Gorbachev becomes general secretary	▪	▪ Country split apart
▪	▪	▪

Objectives:

- Understand how governments changed from dictatorship to democracy.
- Describe the fall of the Soviet Union.
- Explain the factors necessary for democratic consolidation to take place.
- Analyze why some countries experience setbacks or failed transitions to democracy.

Many countries want to become democracies. Some are not able to form a stable government. Other countries do succeed, although it takes many years.

What factors lead to democracy?

Certain factors can lead to democracy. For example, a dictatorship may change to a democracy if groups within the government disagree, the economy fails, or there is unrest among the citizens. Influential individuals can propel governments to become democratic. Lech Walesa, a shipyard worker in Poland, helped bring an end to communism. Pope John Paul II also helped Poland and other countries of Eastern Europe move toward democracy. Soviet author Alexander Solzhenitsyn wrote about Russian prison camps to show the need for human rights.

What events led to the fall of the Soviet Union?

The Communist Party ran the Soviet Union from 1917 until 1990. It was the only political party in the country. Mikhail Gorbachev became general secretary of the Soviet Union in 1985. He was a **soft liner,** or a leader who is willing to reform the government in order to stay in power. This brought about political and economic changes. It also allowed the government more openness and tolerance. Gorbachev was opposed by **hard-liners** in the Soviet government. Hard-liners oppose all democratic changes within a dictatorship. Several hard-liners tried to overthrow Gorbachev in 1991 and failed. After their attempt, three Baltic states left the Soviet Union, followed by the other twelve Soviet republics. Gorbachev resigned and the Soviet Union dissolved as a nation.

What has occurred in Russia since independence?

The Russian Federation was the largest Soviet republic. At independence, it became "a democratic, federal, legally-based state with a republican form of government." Under a new constitution, individual rights and freedoms were put in place. Boris Yeltsin served as president. He was reelected in 1996. When the economy began to fail in 1999, Yeltsin resigned. Vladimir Putin became president. He was reelected in 2000 and 2004. He concentrated much power in the presidency. In 2007, he stepped down as president. He chose a successor, Dmitry Medvedev, to lead his party. Medvedev was elected president and chose Putin to be his prime minister. Putin reversed many democratic reforms and increased government control of elections, television, and large businesses.

✔**Checkpoint** What happened in the Russian parliament in 2007?

Soft-liners
Group that fights to have government change or be open to policy reform

Hard-liners
Group that fights to keep government the same

Democratization
The change from a dictatorship to a democracy

Democratic consolidation
The process where all the factors necessary for a democracy are put in place

What is democratic consolidation?

Democratization is the change from a dictatorship to a democracy. It must include free and fair elections. Then, the essentials of democracy must be put into place so that democracy will survive. This is called **democratic consolidation.** These essential factors are a free press, a multiparty system, civilian control of the military, and a fair economic system.

Biography

Vladmir Putin (1952–)

Prime Minister Vladimir Putin is credited with helping Russia regain stability and world power. He was born in Leningrad (now St. Petersburg) on October 7, 1952. In 1983, he married Lyudmila Shkrebneva and they have two daughters. Putin became a KGB intelligence officer stationed in East Germany and then served as Boris Yeltsin's prime minister. He became acting president when Yeltsin resigned in 1999. Due to term limits, Putin ended his presidency in 2008. He picked a successor who then made him Russia's prime minister.

Genocide
An attempt to eliminate an entire race of people

Failed state
A country that does not have government control

The United States is trying to establish a democracy in Iraq. The dictatorship there, led by Saddam Hussein, fell in 2003. Since that time the country has been in turmoil. There are many ethnic and religious groups. It is difficult to unify these groups and establish peace. However, the Iraqis were able to elect a parliament and write a constitution in 2005.

✔ **Checkpoint**   What is democratization?

Reading Strategy
Summarizing
What are some important details that help you understand this section?

Why have some countries failed to become democracies?

Although some countries have successfully become democratic, others have failed. This happened in Yugoslavia, a country with many ethnic groups. The Communist Party began to weaken, ethnic differences flared, and the country split apart. In some provinces there was heavy fighting, and the Bosnians suffered genocide. **Genocide** is an attempt to eliminate an entire race of people.

Some countries have a government that controls only a small part of the country or nothing at all. In the 1990s, Afghanistan was divided by civil war. Somalia, in East Africa, does not have a government and is ruled by warlords. These countries are known as **failed states.** Failed states often become home to terrorists and outlaws who threaten other countries.

Essential Questions Journal   Go to your **Essential Questions Journal** to work on this chapter's Essential Question.

SECTION **3** ASSESSMENT

1. **Guiding Question** Use your completed table to answer this question: How successfully have some nations achieved democratic governments?

Key Terms and Comprehension
On a sheet of paper, write the answer to each question. Use complete sentences.

2. What is the main difference between a hard-liner and a softliner?

3. What is democratic consolidation?

4. How did the Soviet Union come to an end?

5. What is a failed state?

Critical Thinking

6. **Summarize** Why has Iraq had difficulties becoming a democracy?

7. **Drawing Conclusions** How might the United States help other countries build strong, independent democratic institutions?

Case Studies in Democracy

▲ Felipe Calderon, President of Mexico.

Guiding Question

What form does democratic government take in the United Kingdom and in Mexico?

Use a Venn diagram to record information about the modern governments of the UK and Mexico.

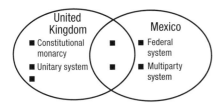

United Kingdom
- Constitutional monarcy
- Unitary system
- ■

Mexico
- Federal system
- Multiparty system

Objectives:

- Examine the United Kingdom's parliamentary democracy.
- Describe regional and local government in the United Kingdom.
- Analyze the federal government of Mexico.

The United Kingdom and Mexico both have democratic governments. Each country has a different approach to democracy. In this section, you will read about the similarities and differences between the countries.

What makes the United Kingdom a constitutional monarchy?

The United Kingdom, or UK, is a democracy. All power is given to one elected group, the Parliament. The constitution is different from the United States Constitution because only part of it is written. The written part includes sections of historic documents such as the Magna Carta and the English Bill of Rights. Acts of Parliament also are included in the written constitution. The unwritten parts of the constitution consist of customs and practices of British politics. These are known as "the conventions of the constitution."

Queen Elizabeth II has been the monarch in the UK since 1952. All acts of government are performed in the name of the monarch, according to tradition. The prime minister and other high officials hold the real power of government. The monarch appoints the prime minister. The prime minister is the leader of the majority party in the House of Commons. The members of that house must approve the choice. The monarch has very little power and again, reigns over the government by tradition.

What is the structure and function of the British government?

The British government has one central institution, the Parliament. It is made up of two houses: the House of Lords and the House of Commons.

The House of Commons

The House of Commons has 646 elected members known as MPs (members of Parliament).The House of Commons approves the monarch's choice for the prime minister and the prime minister's cabinet. It also introduces most new laws or measures. There are several committees who study the new bills and present them to all members for a vote.

The House of Lords

The House of Lords has limited power. They approve or reject bills passed by the House of Commons. If they reject a bill, it can still become law if the House of Commons approves it again.

The prime minister

The prime minister is the chief executive of Great Britain. The majority party in the House of Commons appoints him. If there is no majority party, a **coalition** is formed. A coalition is a temporary union of parties. There is no time limit on how long the prime minister may serve. The prime minister makes the final decisions on important issues of British politics.

The cabinet

The prime minister selects the cabinet members, called **ministers.** Individual cabinet ministers serve as heads of the executive departments. The opposition party also names people who will lead those departments if their party wins a majority in Parliament. They are known as the **shadow cabinet** and have no official powers.

The United Kingdom's court system

There are three separate court systems in the United Kingdom. England and Wales, Northern Ireland, and Scotland each have their own systems. England and Wales have county courts, the Crown Court for criminal cases, and magistrates' courts. Northern Ireland's courts are similar. Scotland has a simple court system and its own code of law. The House of Lords acts as the final court of appeals in the UK; the Law Lords can never overrule Parliament.

The United Kingdom's election process

The House of Commons does not have a specific date for general elections. An election must be held within five years of the previous election. All seats in the House of Commons are up for election. The prime minister may call an election earlier if he thinks his party may win. Sometimes the government falls because it loses the support of the House of Commons. The prime minister must then ask the monarch to dissolve Parliament. This happens when a majority of MPs refuses to support the prime minister. A general election is held and the government may change at this time. If this happens, a new prime minister is named.

■■■■■■■■■■■■■■■■

Reading Strategy
Summarizing
In your own words, tell what this paragraph is about.

Political parties in British government

The Conservative Party and the Labour Party are the two largest parties. Middle- and upper-class Britons tend to prefer less government involvement in business and usually vote Conservative. The Labour Party gets most of its support from the working class, who support government spending, unions, and government involvement in the economy.

Great Britain's regional and local governments

Great Britain has a unitary government. All power belongs to the central government. Local governments exist because the central government has created them. The central government also provides the local governments with the money to operate and provide services for the people. In the 1990s, the UK gave many powers to regional governments in Scotland and Wales.

✔ **Checkpoint**   What are the two major parties in British government?

What is the structure and function of Mexico's government?

Mexico's political system has much in common with the United States. There are three branches of government and an elected president. The three branches of government are the executive, the legislature, and the judiciary.

■■■■■■■■■■■■■■■■

Reading Strategy
Summarizing
What are some important details that help you understand this section?

The executive branch is the most powerful branch. The president of Mexico is elected by the people and serves only one six-year term. His duties include choosing ministers for the cabinet, officers in the military, and federal judges. The president can also propose amendments to the constitution and make certain laws on economic issues.

The legislature in Mexico is called the General Congress. It is made up of a Senate and a Chamber of Deputies. There are 64 senators and 500 members of the Chamber. All the senators serve six-year terms. Only 300 Chamber members are directly elected and they serve for three years. They cannot be reelected. The other 200 members come from political parties according to their party's share of the vote in national elections. The General Congress meets for only a short time each year. The term limits and the low pay that members receive causes the General Congress to be weak.

The independent judicial system of Mexico uses judges, not juries, to try a case. There are both state and federal courts in Mexico's federal system. The federal courts have district and circuit courts. There are also 31 state court systems. These have trial and appellate courts and a state Supreme Court of Justice.

Mexico's regional and local governments

Mexico is divided into 31 states and a Federal District. The capital, Mexico City, is in the Federal District and is run by a governor. Each state has a governor, a legislature, and state courts. Governors serve for six years and appoint judges. State legislators serve for three years.

✔ **Checkpoint**   Where is the capital city of Mexico located?

What is Mexico's political process?

The Institutional Revolutionary Party (PRI) held power in Mexico from 1929 to 2000 by winning elections dishonestly. For this reason, Mexico was not thought of as a democracy. Finally, in 1990, candidates from two other parties, the National Action Party (PAN) and the Democratic Revolutionary Party (PRD) first won seats in federal, state, and local governments.

In the presidential election of 2000, the PAN candidate, Vincente Fox, was elected. He was very popular at first but then his approval rating dropped. Economic conditions in Mexico had not improved. The PRI seemed to be gaining popularity again. Then in the election of 2006, another PAN candidate, Felipe Calderon, was elected president. PAN also won the largest number of seats in both houses of Congress.

✔ **Checkpoint**   When was a multiparty system established in Mexico?

Government in Your Life

Local Government in Action

The UK and Mexico both have local governments with similarities to those in the United States. Local government is the level of government closest to everyday life. Yet many citizens do not know much about their local government. Although people can attend city council meetings, few people go to them. Cable television channels often show these local government meetings. Citizens can learn about local issues that will affect them by watching these meetings on television. People who watch the meetings can let the mayor or city council members know how they feel about the issues discussed.

> **Essential Questions Journal** Go to your **Essential Questions Journal** to work on this chapter's Essential Question.

SECTION 4 ASSESSMENT

1. **Guiding Question** Use your completed Venn diagram to answer this question: What form does democratic government take in the United Kingdom and in Mexico?

Key Terms and Comprehension

On a sheet of paper, write the answer to each question. Use complete sentences.

2. Under what circumstances would a coalition government be formed in the United Kingdom?

3. What is a shadow cabinet?

4. What are the two houses called that make up the British Parliament?

5. What is the Mexican legislature called?

Critical Thinking

6. **Making Comparisons** What is one difference between the office of prime minister of Great Britain and the office of President of the United States?

7. **Drawing Inferences** What might be one disadvantage to having judges, not juries, decide cases in Mexico's courts?

Chapter Summary

Section 1—The Roots of Modern Political Systems

- Modern democracies draw on ideas from Ancient Greece, Rome, the feudal era, and later.

- Feudalism was a system in which lords protected the people who lived and worked on their manors.

- Sovereign states formed after the feudal system failed.

Section 2—Ideas and Revolutions

- The Enlightenment was a time in the 18th century when political thinkers emphasized the importance of popular sovereignty in governments.

- Governments in Great Britain and France followed different paths to gain popular sovereignty.

- Colonial governments in Latin America, Africa, and Asia did not prepare those colonies well for independence and democracy.

- Fascism and communism are systems of government that glorify the state over the rights of individuals.

Section 3—Transitions to Democracy

- Dictatorships can become democracies when economies weaken or there is civil unrest.

- The Communist Soviet Union peacefully broke up into many republics.

- Russia, the largest republic, is not a full democracy.

- Democratic consolidation is when all the factors necessary for a successful democracy are put in place.

- Some countries that fail to become democracies may experience violence or civil war.

Section 4 –Case Studies in Democracy

- The United Kingdom is a constitutional democracy. It has one central institution, the elected Parliament.

- The leader of the majority party of the House of Commons leads the country as prime minister.

- The Conservative Party and the Labour Party are the two largest parties in Britain.

- Mexico has three branches of government: the executive, the legislative, and the judiciary.

- Until 2000, the PRI was the ruling political party in the country. There is now a multiparty system in Mexico.

Guiding Question
Section 1 On what early political ideas and traditions was modern government founded?

Guiding Question
Section 2 How have some nations expanded popular sovereignty?

Guiding Question
Section 3 How successfully have some nations achieved democratic governments?

Guiding Question
Section 4 What form does democratic government take in the United Kingdom and in Mexico?

CHAPTER 22
Essential Question
How should you measure different governments?

Document-Based Assessment

Voltaire on Politics

Voltaire was a great French writer. He was born in 1694. He was an Enlightenment writer, essayist, and philosopher. He also attacked the political and social institutions of his time. The following are excerpts from his writings entitled, Philosophical Letters on the English. *This was the eighth letter in the series and talked negatively about Parliament. It was written in 1733.*

Document at a Glance

- Famous French writer in the 1700s
- Published letters against Parliament
- Differences between Rome and England

The Members of the English Parliament are fond of comparing themselves, on all occasions, to the old Romans.

The two nations [Rome and England] appear to me quite opposite in character, with regard both to good and evil . . . here follows a more essential difference between Rome and England. . . . The civil wars of Rome ended in slavery, those of England in liberty. The English . . . have been able to prescribe limits to the powers of kings by resisting them . . . at last established that wise government where the prince is all powerful to do good and . . . is restrained from doing evil; nobles are great . . . though there are no vassals . . . where the people share in government without confusion. . . . The greatest defect in the government of the Romans raised them to be conquerors. . . . The English are not fired with the splendid folly of making conquests but would only prevent their neighbors from conquering. They are not only jealous of their own liberty, but even that of other nations.

Document-Based Questions

1. What two nations did Voltaire say appeared to be quite different in character?

2. How did Voltaire say the civil wars of Rome ended?

3. Whose civil wars ended in liberty?

4. What was the greatest defect in the government of the Romans?

5. **Summarize** What is the main idea of this letter?

SOURCE: http://oll.libertyfund.org/?option=com_staticxt&staticfile=show.php%3Ftitle=666&chapter=81876&layout=html&Itemid=27

CHAPTER

22

Chapter Assessment

GOVERNMENT ONLINE
Self-Test
To test your understanding of
key terms and main ideas, visit
PearsonSuccessNet.com

Directions: Choose the letter of the best answer or write the answer using complete sentences.

Section 1—Origins of the Modern State

1. What did the monarchs have that gave them the authority to make decisions and keep peace?
   - **A.** right to assembly
   - **B.** plebeian rule
   - **C.** feudalism
   - **D.** sovereignty

2. What is the divine right of kings?

3. What is legitimacy? Why is it important?

4. How did merchants help end feudalism?

5. **Critical Thinking** There are many ways for a government to gain legitimacy. What do you think is the best way? Why?

Section 2—Ideas and Revolutions

6. In which century was the Enlightenment?
   - **A.** 17th century
   - **B.** 18th century
   - **C.** 19th century
   - **D.** 20th century

7. How did France gain popular sovereignty?

8. How did Mexico gain independence?

9. **Critical Thinking** Do you think governments need goals to be successful? Why or why not?

Section 3—Transitions to Democracy

10. In what year did the Soviet Union fall?
    - **A.** 1992
    - **B.** 1984
    - **C.** 1980
    - **D.** 1990

11. What is genocide?

12. What is democratic consolidation?

13. **Critical Thinking** Why do democracies need multiple parties in order to survive?

Section 4—Case Studies in Democracy

14. Who has the real power to name the prime minister of the UK?

    A. the House of Lords

    B. the majority party in the House of Commons

    C. the minority party in the House of Commons

    D. former prime ministers

15. How is the United Kingdom's government similar to the United States?

16. What are Mexico's three branches of government?

17. Critical Thinking What was significant about the 2000 election in Mexico? Explain your answer.

Apply What You've Learned

Exploring the Essential Question

Speak with an immigrant of the United States. Or, if you do not know a U.S. immigrant, find someone who knows an immigrant well. Find answers to these questions.

18. What was the government like in your native country?

19. How do you view the United States government compared to your native country?

Essential Questions Project

20. Based on what you learned about democracy from this chapter and from your interview, write an immigration guide. The guide should include information about the United States government. It should help immigrants learn about its basic function and structure. Your guide should help you answer the Essential Question: *How should you measure different governments?*

Essential Questions
Journal

Go to your **Essential Questions Journal** to work on this chapter's Essential Question.

Test-Taking Tip

Before you begin a test, look over it quickly. Try to set aside enough time to complete each section.

▲ Traders buy and sell at the Chicago Mercantile Exchange.

Comparative Economic Systems

Essential Question
To what extent should governments participate in the economy?

Reading Strategy: Questioning
What do you know about economic systems? What might you want to learn in this chapter? Asking questions as you read will help you to find answers and remember more of the information. Ask yourself:

- What do I hope to learn about economic systems?
- What do the facts and details in this text tell me?
- How does information about economic systems connect to my life?

GOVERNMENT ONLINE
ON THE GO

To study anywhere, anytime, download these online resources at PearsonSuccessNet.com
- **Political Dictionary**
- **Audio Review**
- **Downloadable Interactivities**

▲ Small businesses are an important part of the free enterprise system.

SECTION 1
Capitalism

Guiding Question

What is the role of the government in the U.S. economy? Create a chart like the one below to record information.

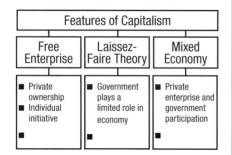

Features of Capitalism		
Free Enterprise	Laissez-Faire Theory	Mixed Economy
■ Private ownership ■ Individual initiative ■	■ Government plays a limited role in economy ■	■ Private enterprise and government participation ■

Objectives:

- Identify the factors of production.
- Describe the free enterprise system and laissez-faire theory.
- Analyze the role of government in a mixed economy.
- Compare and contrast business organizations.
- Explain the role of profit and loss in a free enterprise system.

The United States has an economy based on **capitalism.** Capitalism is an economic system in which people and businesses own and control production. The economy of the United States is the largest and most powerful in the world. In capitalist countries, the government is involved in the economic activity to an extent. Businesses operate according to laws made by the government. These laws protect consumers and workers.

What are factors of production?

The economy needs basic resources to produce all goods and services. These resources are the **factors of production.** Resources are needed to produce goods and services. The United States has a good but limited supply of resources. The three types of resources needed for the production of goods and services are land, capital, and labor. Land includes all natural resources, such as forests, oil, coal, and water. Land has many economic uses, including agriculture and mining. The government encourages businesses and citizens to conserve natural resources.

Capital includes all the human-made resources. Physical capital, for example, includes buildings, tools, machinery, factories, trucks, and highways. The capital produced is then reinvested in the economy. **Labor** is the work people do. Men and women work in all types of places. People's various skills are needed in our economy. Both skilled and unskilled labor are needed for the production of goods and services.

✔ **Checkpoint** What are the three factors of production?

578 Capitalism

What is the role of the entrepreneur?

Someone who owns capital and puts it to good use is called a capitalist. Capitalists are people who own large businesses or factories, as well as investors and the owners of small businesses. The economy of our country depends on the success of capitalists. **Entrepreneurs** are people who bring the factors of production together to produce goods and services. Entrepreneurs and their businesses help the economy grow. They do this by creating jobs and providing the goods and services that contribute to a high standard of living (Figure 23.1).

What is the free enterprise system?

The **free enterprise system** is the system used in the United States. Goods and services are bought and sold in a **free market.** A free market is a market in which buyers and sellers are free to buy and sell what they want. People, not the government, make most of the economic decisions in the free enterprise system of the United States. The free enterprise system is based on four factors: private ownership, individual initiative, profit, and competition. See Figure 23.2 on page 580.

Capitalism
An economic system in which people and businesses own and control production

Factors of production
Basic resources that are used to make all goods and services

Capital
Human-made resource: buildings, machines, money

Labor
Human activity that provides goods or services

Entrepreneur
An individual who combines land, labor, and capital resources to produce goods or services

Free enterprise system
Freedom of private businesses to operate with few government rules

Free market
Buyers and sellers are free to buy and sell what they want

Fig. 23.1
Factors of Production

Land, labor, and capital make up the factors of production. The entrepreneur brings these factors together to create something consumers will buy. Look up *land* and *capital* in the dictionary. *How do the definitions differ from the definitions used in this book?*

Land includes property and the resources found in nature.

Labor describes the work of individuals.

Capital includes the tools, money, and human expertise that turn labor and land into goods and services.

Entrepreneurs are risk-taking individuals who have the skill and drive to create new products or services for the market.

Goods and Services are the items people buy and the things they need others to do for them.

Reading Strategy
Questioning
Think about the purpose of this text. Ask yourself, "Am I finding out the information I expected to when I began reading?"

Fig. 23.2

- Private ownership of land, labor, and capital
- Limited government
- **Free Enterprise**
- Free markets and prices
- Competition among entrepreneurs

Private Ownership: Companies or individuals own most of the resources used to produce goods or services. For example, people own the right to their own labor. Companies also make the decisions concerning production. This private ownership and control is part of the free enterprise system in the United States. Rights are protected by the 5th and 14th amendments of the Constitution. A person may not be deprived of life, liberty, or property.

Individual Initiative: An important part of our economic system is the right of individuals to start businesses. They may run the businesses as they choose according to the law. Not all countries allow this individual initiative.

Profit: An individual or company is entitled to the earnings of the business. There are risks involved in starting a business. The ability to earn profits encourages entrepreneurs to take these risks.

Competition: Competition is the last of the four factors of the free enterprise system (Figure 23.3). Competition happens when a number of companies offer a similar product or service. Consumers will usually buy the best product or service with the best price. Companies try to keep the cost of production low. That way they can offer the product to the consumer at the lowest price. This process helps keep prices down in the free enterprise system of our country.

✓ **Checkpoint** What are the four factors of free enterprise?

Fig. 23.3
Elements of Free Enterprise

Free markets cannot succeed without four basic elements: private ownership, individual initiative, profit, and competition. These factors allow for the many transactions that define a free market economy. *What is the role of government in the free enterprise system?*

Private ownership

Profit

Competition

Individual initiative

Fig. 23.4

Supply and Demand:

How are prices set in a free market?

GOVERNMENT ONLINE
Audio Tour
Listen to a guided audio tour of Supply and Demand at **PearsonSuccessNet.com**

In general, suppliers will produce more goods when prices are high and fewer goods when prices fall. Consumers usually seek to purchase (demand) more of a commodity at low prices and less at high prices. Where people enjoy the freedom to trade, they will find the market price that suits both sides. *What is a market signal that a price is too high?*

Price	Suppliers produce	Consumers want	What happens?
$5.00	5,000	20,000	• Not enough for sale • Empty shelves
$15.00	10,000	10,000	• Market price • Both sides happy
$30.00	20,000	5,000	• Too many goods • Too few buyers

The **law of supply and demand** determines the market price for goods and services (Figure 23.4). Supply is the amount of a product offered for sale. Demand is the amount of a product that consumers want to buy. The law of supply and demand tells us that when goods are plentiful, prices will go lower. If goods become limited, prices will go higher. If demand drops, the sellers may lower their prices to encourage more people to buy. Sellers can also adjust their prices higher if demand suddenly rises.

A **monopoly** is the control by one company of the production of a specific good and service. Monopolies can be very powerful and can control prices. In the late 1800s, several companies in the same business merged (joined together). This was known as a **trust.** Some of the trusts controlled businesses such as oil, steel, and beef. The government decided trusts were unfair and passed the Sherman Anti-Trust Act in 1890 to end the trusts.

The Department of Justice has an Anti-Trust division to watch business activities. If a merger or sale threatens competition, the government can stop the sale or merger. Fair competition among businesses must be allowed for the free enterprise system to work.

Law of supply and demand
When goods are plentiful, prices are lower. When goods become limited, prices are higher.

Monopoly
One company controls the production of a specific good or service

Trust
Several corporations in the same business working to eliminate competition and regulate prices

✔ **Checkpoint** What is a trust?

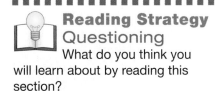
Reading Strategy
Questioning
What do you think you will learn about by reading this section?

What is the laissez-faire theory?

The **laissez-faire theory** says that government should take a very limited part in society. Adam Smith, an early capitalist philosopher, introduced the theory in his book, *The Wealth of Nations. Laissez faire* is a French term meaning "to let alone." This theory says that the main purpose of government should be to run foreign affairs and defense. Government may also maintain the police and courts, and encourage competition in business. Although the laissez faire theory has not been applied in the United States, it has had an influence on our economic policies.

What is a mixed economy?

Economists describe the American economy as a mixed economy because both government and private enterprise are involved.

Private Enterprise + Government Participation = Mixed Economy

Government regulates and promotes all parts of the American economy. For example, the government passes laws to prevent trusts and protect the environment. The government constructs highways, provides services, operates the Social Security system, and offers loans to businesses. At times, the government takes over some private businesses that are losing money.

What are the types of business organizations?

There are three types of business organizations: sole proprietorships, partnerships, and corporations. A sole proprietorship is a business owned by one person. The advantages of a sole proprietorship are that it is easy to organize and the owner has total control. One disadvantage is that the owner alone is liable for all debts and improvement costs.

A partnership is a business owned by two or more people. Partners usually share the cost of starting and improving the business. An advantage of a partnership is that it brings together people with different business skills. These differences may also cause conflicts.

A corporation may be a small business or a large national company. Corporations have many owners, called shareholders. People who want to invest buy a small share of the company. The corporation may have thousands of shareholders. They provide money for improvements and special projects. If the company fails, shareholders can only lose the amount of money they have invested.

What is profit and loss?

Profit is the amount of money left in a business after all production costs are paid. The costs may include machinery, fuel, salaries, and more. Sometimes the money earned by a business is less than the production costs. The business then takes a loss.

Government in Your Life

Identity Theft

Identity theft happens when someone takes another person's identity. This is a crime. The thief may take money from bank accounts, make credit card purchases, or run up large phone bills. These crimes are called identity fraud.

Identity thieves may look through trash or mailboxes to find banking or credit card account numbers. At times, they gain personal information by telephone or during Internet sessions. You can decrease the likelihood of identity theft in the following ways.

- Shred old credit cards and banking materials before throwing them into the trash.
- Never give out personal information over the telephone unless you know the other person well.
- Make Internet purchases only through secure payment sites and pay by credit card.
- Review monthly credit card and bank statements.

Recovering from identify theft can be a very long, difficult process. In 1998, the U.S. Congress passed laws that made identity theft a federal crime.

Essential Questions Journal Go to your **Essential Questions Journal** to work on this chapter's Essential Question.

SECTION 1 ASSESSMENT

Word Bank

entrepreneurs

factors of production

free enterprise system

mixed economy

1. **Guiding Question** Use your completed graphic organizer to answer this question: What is the role of the government in the U.S. economy?

Key Terms and Comprehension

On a sheet of paper, use the words from the Word Bank to complete each sentence correctly.

2. Land, labor, and capital are the _____.

3. The _____ is the system used in the United States.

4. _____ combine resources to start businesses of their own.

5. Private enterprise + government participation = _____

Critical Thinking

6. **Compare and Contrast** How are trusts and monopolies the same? How are they different?

7. **Draw Conclusions** What advantage does a mixed economy offer consumers? What advantages does it offer businesses?

SECTION 2
Socialism and Communism

▲ Communist artwork often celebrated workers in industry and agriculture.

Guiding Question

What is the role of the government under socialism and communism? Create a table like the one below. Use it to record information about the role of government under socialism and communism.

Role of Government	
Socialism	Communism
■ State owns largest industries	■ No private property or businesses
■	■
■	■

Objectives:

- Summarize the ideas of Karl Marx.
- Identify important parts of socialist economics.
- Outline the parts of communist economics.
- Describe socialism and communism in today's nations.
- Evaluate the pros and cons of socialism and communism.

Capitalism gives all citizens the same political and economic opportunities. Some people are able to gain more wealth than others. In socialist and communist countries, the government controls most parts of the economic system. The government tries to give everyone the same amount of wealth.

What is Karl Marx's theory?

Karl Marx was a critic of capitalism. Capitalism spread during the Industrial Revolution in the nineteenth century. Working conditions were very bad during this time. Marx, together with Friedrich Engels, wrote **The Communist Manifesto** in 1848. It criticized working conditions and told workers they were enslaved and should free themselves.

The Communist Manifesto and *Das Kapital,* Marx's later work, contained the same ideas. Marx believed that working people would revolt if governments allowed capitalists to keep power. He also believed that as a result of this revolution, social classes would go away and property would be owned by all. Marx believed that, in the future, **communism** would bring an end to nationalism, a major cause of European wars.

During the nineteenth century many people accepted the ideas of Karl Marx. Some people thought change would come peacefully in a democratic way. The term **socialism** is used to describe this idea. Others, like Marx, thought a new and more equal society would only happen after a revolution.

✔**Checkpoint** Why is Karl Marx important? According to Karl Marx, what would happen if capitalists kept power?

What are the characteristics of socialist economies?

The governments of socialist countries typically use four public policies to achieve socialism:

1. Nationalization: Government controls some, if not all, industries. Usually these industries have many workers or new technology, or they are important to the country's economy.

2. Public Welfare: Government provides services such as pensions, healthcare, education, and housing. Countries that offer all of these services, and more, are called **welfare states** (Figure 23.5). In these countries, many benefits are provided to people. Payments are often made for new mothers, vacations, and job loss for any reason.

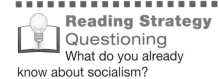

Reading Strategy
Questioning
What do you already know about socialism?

The Communist Manifesto
A document written by Karl Marx and Friedrich Engels that criticized the Industrial Revolution

Communism
An economic system in which government owns all property and business

Socialism
An economic system in which government owns large industries and provides many benefits

Welfare state
A country whose government provides many services, including pensions, healthcare, education, and housing

National Healthcare:

What Is the Cost of Free Healthcare?

The United Kingdom's National Health Service provides free healthcare for all. The healthcare is paid for by the national government. While the ideal of national healthcare is very popular (top), many people complain about the long waits for treatment (bottom). *What might happen if healthcare were free, according to the law of supply and demand?*

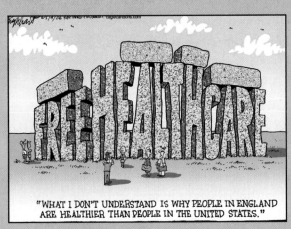

"WHAT I DON'T UNDERSTAND IS WHY PEOPLE IN ENGLAND ARE HEALTHIER THAN PEOPLE IN THE UNITED STATES."

YOUR INJURY IS IMPORTANT TO US. ALL OUR DOCTORS ARE BUSY HELPING OTHER CUSTOMERS. PLEASE WAIT, YOU ARE ADVANCING IN THE QUEUE AND YOU WILL BE SEEN AS SOON AS A DOCTOR BECOMES AVAILABLE.

BILL PROUD

Command economy
An economy in which the government plans what to produce and how much money to invest

3. Taxation: Taxes are high in socialist countries. The money is needed to provide for the many services. Some taxes are as high as 60 percent. These taxes are paid mostly by the middle and upper classes.

4. Command Economy: In socialist countries, and even more in communist countries, government leaders make economic decisions. In a **command economy,** the government plans what to produce and how much money to invest. In contrast, under capitalism, private individuals and companies make the economic decisions; the government does not.

✔**Checkpoint**   What are the four characteristics of a socialist economy?

What is socialism like today?

Today in Europe, socialist programs continue with the support of democratic ideas. Nationalization, or government control of industries, is no longer popular. In some countries, such as Britain, France, and Germany, socialists have been out of power recently. Programs were too costly and became unpopular with the citizens.

In the developing countries of Africa and Latin America, socialism is popular. Governments there took control of many industries from foreign owners. Leaders promised services and land to the people, making the leaders popular and powerful. This happened in Venezuela after 1999. President Hugo Chavez nationalized the country's industries. He then used the profits to create services such as healthcare, housing, and education.

What are the characteristics of communist economies?

Communism has been less successful than socialism. Communism is different than socialism in many ways (**Figure 23.6**). During the twentieth century, violence was often used to promote communist ideas.

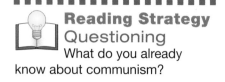

Reading Strategy
Questioning
What do you already know about communism?

Fig. 23.6

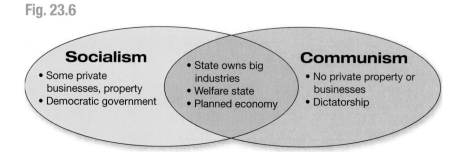

Socialism
• Some private businesses, property
• Democratic government

• State owns big industries
• Welfare state
• Planned economy

Communism
• No private property or businesses
• Dictatorship

The following are the common characteristics of communism:

1. Dominant Role of the Communist Party: In communist countries, the Communist Party has all the power. The party runs both the government and the economy. Many aspects of the lives of citizens are under strict party control.

2. Central Planning: A **five-year plan** is used by Communist countries to set economic goals. The development of industry and agriculture is decided for this time period by the government. Prices, along with the distribution of goods and services, are also planned.

3. Collectivization: **Collectivization** means the joining together of small private farms into a large government-controlled agricultural enterprise. Farmers have resisted doing this.

4. State Ownership: Parts of the economy, such as factories and transportation, are state owned. In some countries, such as China, local governments, instead of the central government, own industries.

As you have read, there are many similarities and differences between socialism and communism. Figure 23.7 compares and contrasts the two economic systems.

Five-year plan
A plan that projects economic development over the next five years

Collectivization
Collective or state ownership of the means of production; refers largely to agriculture

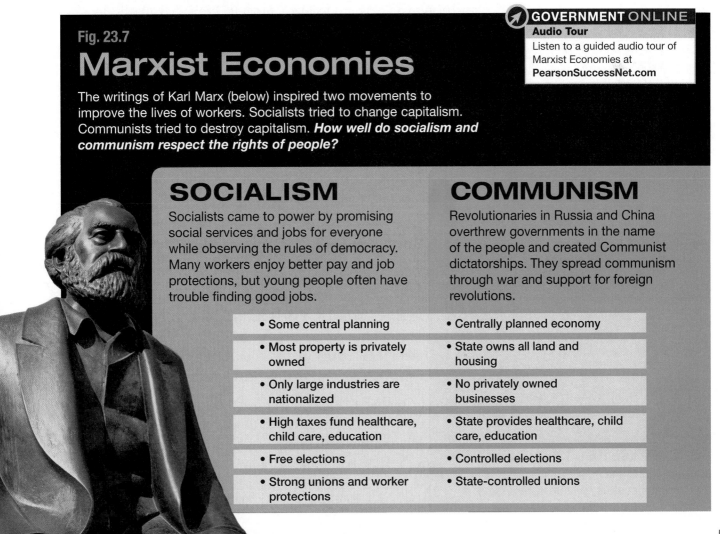

GOVERNMENT ONLINE
Audio Tour
Listen to a guided audio tour of Marxist Economies at **PearsonSuccessNet.com**

Fig. 23.7
Marxist Economies

The writings of Karl Marx (below) inspired two movements to improve the lives of workers. Socialists tried to change capitalism. Communists tried to destroy capitalism. *How well do socialism and communism respect the rights of people?*

SOCIALISM

Socialists came to power by promising social services and jobs for everyone while observing the rules of democracy. Many workers enjoy better pay and job protections, but young people often have trouble finding good jobs.

COMMUNISM

Revolutionaries in Russia and China overthrew governments in the name of the people and created Communist dictatorships. They spread communism through war and support for foreign revolutions.

SOCIALISM	COMMUNISM
• Some central planning	• Centrally planned economy
• Most property is privately owned	• State owns all land and housing
• Only large industries are nationalized	• No privately owned businesses
• High taxes fund healthcare, child care, education	• State provides healthcare, child care, education
• Free elections	• Controlled elections
• Strong unions and worker protections	• State-controlled unions

What was the Soviet Union's economic system?

In 1917, V.I. Lenin and his followers began to create a one-party state in the Soviet Union. Josef Stalin took over after Lenin's death and continued the effort to strengthen the one-party state. Stalin started the First Five-Year Plan (1928–1933). Industries were increased and farms were joined together. The plan did not work well, and many people died.

In the 1980s, under Mikhail Gorbachev, communism in the Soviet Union was failing. In 1991, the Soviet Union divided into 15 independent countries. Russia was the largest independent country. Many industries became privatized in Russia. **Privatization** is the process of returning nationalized enterprises to private ownership.

What was China's economic system?

The founder of the People's Republic of China was Mao Zedong. He took control in 1949. China developed a command economy of its own. The government improved education and took complete control of the labor market. People were not allowed to choose where they worked. The **Great Leap Forward** of 1958 was a five-year plan to quickly modernize China. It eliminated all private industry. Large collective farms were joined together in communes run by the Communist Party. There were no incentives to work hard. As a result, this plan was a failure and caused a famine.

In 1977, Deng Xiapong came to power and changed the economy. He modernized industry, agriculture, science, and defense. He began a market economy and allowed foreign investment. Today, China encourages private enterprise, although there are still state-owned industries. China is showing strong economic growth.

What are some other communist countries?

Today, there are only a few communist countries in the world. Cuba, led by Fidel Castro from 1959 to 2008, began a Communist government with help from the Soviet Union. After the fall of the Soviet Union, Cuba suffered an economic crisis. The economy of Cuba is still state controlled.

In Southeast Asia, Vietnam and Laos are communist countries. The central government plans their economies. Since the late 1980s, both countries have tried to become free market economies. Communist North Korea is under complete control of Kim Jong-Il. The country has food shortages and has not improved its economy.

▲ Although China still identifies itself as a Communist state, private enterprise and investment have grown.

What are the results of socialism and communism?

Free market and command economies have both strengths and weaknesses. Critics say socialist countries have too many officials and decisions are difficult to make. Individual initiative is not encouraged. Command economies are criticized because of the high taxes. There is no reason to work harder and earn more money. Critics of socialism and communism claim the economy is too complicated to be run by central planners.

Defenders of socialism and communism reply that everyone's needs are met. They claim their systems give citizens control and security in their jobs. Factories do not close suddenly as they may in capitalist countries. Workers and leaders work together for common needs and not just for investors.

✔ **Checkpoint** What claims do defenders of socialism and communism make?

| Essential Questions Journal | Go to your **Essential Questions Journal** to work on this chapter's Essential Question. |

SECTION **2** ASSESSMENT

Quick Write

In the first two sections of this chapter, you have learned about capitalism, socialism, and communism. Based on your reading, which economic policy do you prefer? Try to recall the positive and negative aspects of each type of government. Give at least two arguments for your answer. Use complete sentences.

1. **Guiding Question** Use your completed chart to answer this question: What is the role of government under socialism and communism?

Key Terms and Comprehension

On a sheet of paper, write the answer to each question. Use complete sentences.

2. How did Karl Marx's theories lead to socialism and communism?

3. What role does the government play in a command economy?

4. In your own words, describe how communism is supposed to work.

5. What was the Great Leap Forward?

Critical Thinking

6. **Make Decisions** Do you think the government should make sure that every citizen has a job? Why or why not?

7. **Draw Conclusions** Why do you think some socialist and communist economies are allowing citizens more economic freedoms?

ISSUES OF OUR TIME

Globalization and Free Trade

▶▶ Track the Issue

Until the 1940s, the United States did not conduct much free trade.

1789 Congress passes the first Tariff Act, giving the new federal government its main source of revenue.

1832 South Carolina, a rural state, threatens the unity of the country. The state does not like the federal tariffs that protect northern manufacturers.

1947 The General Agreement on Tariffs and Trade (GATT) is signed. GATT makes it possible to lower tariffs.

1994 The North American Free Trade Agreement (NAFTA) removes trade barriers among the United States, Canada, and Mexico.

1995 The World Trade Organization is created to expand global trade and resolve disputes.

President Bill Clinton promoted farm exports through NAFTA.

▶▶ Perspectives

The growth of free trade has been good and bad for Americans. Trade has grown in some areas of the United States. The United States is the world's largest exporter, but it has also had many job losses. What issues do government leaders need to consider when thinking about free trade agreements?

Danger of Increased Trade	Benefit of Increased Trade
Today, the global economy is enriching corporate profiteers, wealthy families and dictators, but it isn't working for working families. In the United States, we're losing high-paying, full-benefit manufacturing jobs and more and more family members are having to join the workforce to maintain living standards. Our trade deficit is eating away at economic stability and our basic industries are being hammered by . . . unfair trade practices. Around the world . . . inequality is rising, both among and within nations. —AFL-CIO, Campaign for Global Fairness	With our strong institutions, deep capital markets, flexible labor markets, technological leadership, and penchant [like] for entrepreneurship and innovation, no country is better placed than the United States to benefit from increased participation in the global economy. If we resist protectionism and isolationism while working to increase the skills and adaptability of our labor force, the forces of globalization and trade will continue to make our economy stronger and our citizens more prosperous. —Federal Reserve Chairman Ben S. Bernanke

Connect to Your World
1. What does the AFL-CIO think about free trade? What does Bernanke think about free trade?
2. Whom do you agree with? Why?

GOVERNMENT ONLINE
In the News
To find out about how free trade affects you, visit
PearsonSuccessNet.com

SECTION 3
The United States in a Global Economy

▲ Traders signal an offer on an exchange floor.

Guiding Question

How does the federal government support economic growth at home and abroad?
Use an outline to take notes on the ways in which the government takes part in both domestic and global economies.

```
I. The Domestic Economy
   A. Supports free enterprise
      1. Federal Reserve System
      2. _____
   B. _____
```

Objectives:

- Describe the role of government in the domestic economy.
- Understand why nations participate in trade.
- Describe the role of the federal government in the global economy.
- Explain the cause of globalization and its effects on the American economy.

The federal government works to protect and regulate the economy. Today, the economy includes worldwide markets connected by free trade agreements. Large companies have locations in several countries. Americans buy goods made around the world.

What is the role of the federal government in the domestic economy?

At first, the federal government did not interfere in the economic concerns of the country. There were no welfare programs or income taxes. Today, the government supports the country's economic system. Laws protect consumers, workers, and businesses. Government agencies work to oversee the economic activities in the United States. Two of the most important economic agencies are the Federal Reserve System and the Securities and Exchange Commission.

The Federal Reserve System, often called the Fed, was founded in 1913. It is the central banking system of the United States. In the beginning it limited the amount of paper money that could be printed. Today, it includes 12 regional banks and many other member banks. (See **Figure 23.8** on the next page.) Banks are allowed to borrow from other banks. The Fed controls the interest rate. This is the federal funds rate that is charged to banks that want to borrow money. By controlling this rate, the Fed controls the amount of money in the economy and how fast the economy grows.

The Securities and Exchange Commission (SEC) was created in 1934 after the stock market crash. The job of the SEC is to oversee trading in the stock market. The SEC also makes sure companies truthfully report finances and do not give false information.

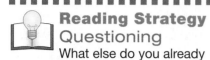
Globalization
The act of making something worldwide

The Department of Labor offers many services to protect American workers. It sees that federal laws are carried out. The department has many agencies and divisions. The Employment Standards Administration makes sure rules about wages, benefits, and contracts are followed. It also enforces fair hiring practices that protect minorities, women, veterans, and disabled people.

✔**Checkpoint** What is the role of the SEC?

What is a global economy?

The countries of the world now depend on one another for trade. This practice is known as **globalization.** Communication has been made easier by new technology. Transportation of goods has also improved.

Increasing international trade is a goal of the United States government. In fact, trade is necessary for most countries. Most countries cannot produce all that they need. Trade allows a country to buy what it needs from other countries. Some countries have special resources, such as petroleum, that other countries need.

Fig. 23.8 How Government Works

The Federal Reserve System

Twelve regional banks make up the Federal Reserve System, known as the Fed. The leaders at each bank make important decisions that affect the national and global economy. *Why do you think the Board of Governors is in Washington D.C.?*

GOVERNMENT ONLINE
Audio Tour
Listen to a guided audio tour of the Federal Reserve System at **PearsonSuccessNet.com**

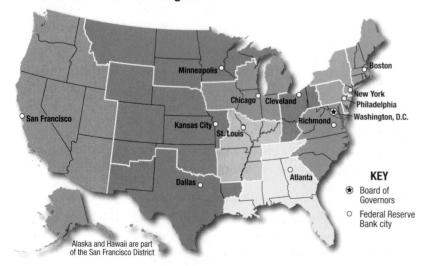

Alaska and Hawaii are part of the San Francisco District

KEY
⊛ Board of Governors
○ Federal Reserve Bank city

The Fed's Responsibility: Set interest rates to encourage steady economic growth

If the Fed sets interest rates too High
• businesses will not borrow and invest
• the economy slows
• people lose jobs

If the Fed sets interest rates too Low
• too much money is borrowed
• businesses make risky investments
• prices rise quickly

The federal government supports trade and also protects producers and consumers in the United States. Canada, China, and Mexico are the main trading partners of the United States, with the volume of the trade in that order. China became a major trading partner after its government made changes in its communist economic system. The United States imports and exports more goods and services than any other country in the world.

✔ **Checkpoint**   Why is trade necessary for most countries?

What are the U.S. trade policies?

One goal of the federal government has been to protect American producers and workers by keeping prices high. Another goal is to minimize competition from imports. Most national governments try to control imports to protect their own industries from foreign competition. This practice is known as **protectionism.**

The main way a government protects the country's industries is through trade barriers. These trade barriers are tariffs, import quotas, and trade embargoes. **Tariffs** are fees on imported goods. The fee raises the selling price. **Import quotas** set limits on the number of goods a foreign country may sell in another country. Many countries use import quotas to protect their own economies. A **trade embargo** completely stops trade with a country.

Protectionism
The effort of countries to protect their industries from foreign competition

Tariff
Tax charged by a country on goods coming into a country; sometimes called a duty

Import quota
A set limit on the number of goods a foreign country may sell in another country

Trade embargo
Stopping trade with a country

Biography

Dr. Benjamin S. Bernanke (1953–)

Benjamin S. Bernanke became chairman and member of the Board of Governors of the Federal Reserve System in 2006. In this powerful position, he controls the lending rates used by banks. The economy of the United States is greatly affected by the decisions of Chairman Bernanke and the Federal Reserve Board.

Dr. Bernanke was born in December 1953 in Augusta, Georgia. He attended Harvard and received his Ph.D. in economics from the Massachusetts Institute of Technology. He has written articles and books in the field of economics.

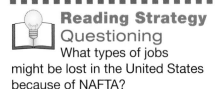

NAFTA
An agreement of free trade among the United States, Canada, and Mexico

World Trade Organization
An organization that oversees international trade and helps settle trade disagreements between countries; created in 1995

Reading Strategy
Questioning
What types of jobs might be lost in the United States because of NAFTA?

What is NAFTA?

NAFTA is the North American Free Trade Agreement. It took effect in 1994. NAFTA is an important part of the U.S. economy (Figure 23.9). With NAFTA, there are no longer trade barriers among the United States, Canada, and Mexico. Some people in the United States had objections to NAFTA. They were afraid of job losses in this country. People in favor of NAFTA thought more exports would increase jobs. Actually NAFTA has resulted in the loss of some jobs in the United States. But NAFTA has also increased trade and increased exports.

What are some international economic organizations?

The United States has formed several free trade agreements and alliances to increase American economic activity. The General Agreement on Tariffs and Trade (GATT) was signed in 1947 to encourage world trade and help countries recover from World War II. The **World Trade Organization** (WTO) was formed in 1995. It oversees international trade and helps settle trade disagreements between countries. The World Bank and the International Monetary Fund (IMF) help countries in financial trouble. The World Bank lends money for development. The IMF helps countries with their banking systems.

The eight major industrial nations (G8) meet each year. The leaders meet to discuss problems and world affairs. The European Union (EU) began to develop when six European nations joined together to trade. In 2002, a single form of European money, the euro, was introduced. Twelve countries now use the euro. The EU is now made up of 27 nations. There are a number of regional trade organizations in different parts of the world.

✔**Checkpoint**   Why has the United States formed free trade agreements?

Fig. 23.9

Major Economic Institutions		
U.S. Government	**International Groups**	**Trade Agreements**
Federal Reserve Securities and Exchange Commission Department of Labor	World Bank International Monetary Fund G8 European Union	GATT and World Trade Organization North American Free Trade Agreement

What is the impact of global trade?

Globalization has brought products from every country to American consumers. As developing countries improve their economies, more American products are sold in them. As countries trade and depend on one another, fewer conflicts may occur.

Global trade also has problems. The United States is losing manufacturing jobs to workers in other nations. These foreign workers are paid much less. Trade deficits with China and Japan have occurred. The United States buys much more from these countries than they buy from the United States. China and Japan have also loaned money to the United States and bought assets in the country. They own a portion of the American economy.

What is the future of the world economy?

As you have read, the trend in the world economy is toward greater interdependence among nations. The good news is that there is a demand around the world for American services. The downside is that some people of the United States will continue to lose jobs to people in other countries that will do the same work for less pay.

Essential Questions Journal Go to your **Essential Questions Journal** to work on this chapter's Essential Question.

SECTION 3 ASSESSMENT

1. **Guiding Question** Use your completed outline to answer this question: How does the federal government support economic growth at home and abroad?

Key Terms and Comprehension

On a sheet of paper, write the answer to each question. Use complete sentences.

2. What is one role of the Federal Reserve System?

3. What is protectionism?

4. What is NAFTA's main purpose?

5. What is one role of the World Trade Organization?

Critical Thinking

6. **Summarize** How has NAFTA affected different people in different ways?

7. **Draw Inferences** Why do you think the euro was introduced in some countries in the European Union?

Chapter Summary

Section 1—Capitalism

- Capitalism is the basis of the free market economy of the United States and other countries.

- The resources needed for the production of goods are land, capital, and labor.

- The free enterprise system is based on private ownership, individual initiative, profit, and competition.

- The United States has a mixed economy. The government is involved in all parts of the economy.

- The types of business organizations are sole proprietorships, partnerships, and corporations.

Section 2—Socialism and Communism

- Karl Marx and Friedrich Engels wrote books that led to socialism and communism.

- In socialist economies the government controls most of the industries. High taxes pay for many services. Today the socialists have lost some power.

- In communist countries the Communist Party holds all the power.

- Communism failed in the Soviet Union in 1991. Fifteen independent countries formed. The biggest in size and population is Russia.

- China has a Communist government. Today, China encourages private enterprise and has shown economic growth.

Section 3—The United States in a Global Economy

- The federal government supports the country's economic system through agencies such as the Federal Reserve System.

- Countries depend on one another for trade to buy all the goods they need.

- The United States is the largest importer of goods. Its main trading partners are Canada, China, and Mexico.

- Trade policies used by the United States are tariffs, import quotas, and trade embargoes.

- The United States has formed trade agreements to help the economy, including NAFTA.

- Globalization allows countries to buy what they cannot produce.

Guiding Question
Section 2 What is the role of the government under socialism and communism?

Guiding Question
Section 3 How does the federal government support economic growth at home and abroad?

Guiding Question
Section 1 What is the role of the government in the U.S. economy?

CHAPTER 23

Essential Question
To what extent should governments participate in the economy?

Document-Based Assessment

Wealth of Nations

Adam Smith is known as the father of modern economics. In 1776, he wrote a book called An Inquiry into the Nature and Causes of the Wealth of Nations. *Smith's book was written over two centuries ago, but many economists still think it is the best statement about capitalism. In this reading, Smith discusses the value of money and the price of labor.*

Document at a Glance

■ Adam Smith's book, *Wealth of Nations*

■ Influenced capitalism in the United States

Every man is rich or poor according to the degree in which he can afford to enjoy the necessaries, conveniences, and amusements of human life. But after the division of labour has once thoroughly taken place, it is but a very small part of these with which a man's own labour can supply him. The far greater part of them he must derive [gain] from the labour of other people, and he must be rich or poor according to the quantity of that labour which he can command, or which he can afford to purchase. The value of any commodity [product], therefore, to the person who possesses it, and who means not to use or consume it himself, but to exchange it for other commodities, is equal to the quantity of labour which it enables him to purchase or command. Labour, therefore, is the real measure of the exchangeable value of all commodities.

The real price of everything, what everything really costs to the man who wants to acquire it, is the toil and trouble of acquiring it. . . . Labour was the first price, the original purchase-money that was paid for all things. It was not by gold or by silver, but by labour, that all the wealth of the world was originally purchased; and its value, to those who possess it, and who want to exchange it for some new productions, is precisely equal to the quantity of labour which it can enable them to purchase or command.

Document-Based Questions

1. According to Smith, what determines a person's wealth?

2. How is labor related to wealth?

3. How does the author define labor in this reading? What is the real price of everything?

4. How was wealth purchased before gold and silver were used?

5. Questioning Are Smith's ideas still true today? Why or why not?

SOURCE: *An Inquiry into the Nature and Causes of the Wealth of Nations,* by Adam Smith, 1776

23

Chapter Assessment

GOVERNMENT ONLINE
Self-Test
To test your understanding of
key terms and main ideas, visit
PearsonSuccessNet.com

Directions: On a sheet of paper, write the answer using complete sentences.

Section 1—Capitalism

1. What is the law of supply and demand?

2. What are the three factors of production?

3. What is a monopoly?

4. What is the laissez-faire theory?

5. What are the three types of business organizations?

6. Critical Thinking What might happen in a market without competition? Why do you think so?

Section 2—Socialism and Communism

7. What did Karl Marx think about capitalism?

8. In communist countries, who holds all the power?

9. What are two features of socialism?

10. What are two features of communism?

11. What are two current communist countries?

12. Critical Thinking Many people say that socialism and communism discourage people from taking initiative. Do you agree? Why or why not?

Section 3—The U.S. in a Global Economy

13. What are tariffs?

14. What is a trade embargo?

15. What is globalization?

16. What is one trade agreement that the United States has formed?

17. Critical Thinking Many people protest when international organizations come together to meet. Why do you think this is? Explain your answer.

Apply What You've Learned

Exploring the Essential Question

In a small group, meet with a business owner in your community. Think of questions that you want to learn about the business. Have someone in the group take notes on the answers. While there, also ask the following questions:

18. In what ways would your life and business be different in a socialist or communist country?

19. Do you think the federal government should be more or less involved in the economy? Why?

Essential Questions Project

20. With your small group, write a summary of the discussion with the business owner in your community. Use complete sentences. Make sure to include the answers the business owner gave to the two questions above. At the end of the summary, write how you think the business owner would answer the essential question: **To what extent should governments participate in the economy?** Do you agree with the owner's response? Explain your answer.

Essential Questions Journal

Go to your **Essential Questions Journal** to work on this chapter's Essential Question.

Test-Taking Tip

Read multiple-choice questions completely before reading the answer choices.

Perspectives

Essential Question
How should a government meet the needs of its people?

The hundreds of sovereign states in the world today identify the needs of their people in different ways and disagree on how or to what extent governments should attempt to meet them.

" ON THE LIMITS OF GOVERNMENT:

Conservatives know that governments don't have all the answers. But if they govern with the right values, they can make a real difference.

—UK Conservative Party Manifesto, 2005

ON MEASURING THE IMPROVEMENT IN LIVES:

Prosperity Indicators, U.S.

	1950	2007
Life Expectancy at Birth (years)	68.2	78.0
Per Capita Gross Domestic Product (constant 2000 dollars)	$11,720*	$38,020
Population with Bachelor's Degrees, age 25 and up	6.2%	28.7%

*approximate

By most measures, Americans are healthier, better educated, and more affluent today than in the past.

" ON THE RESPONSIBILITIES OF A COMMUNIST PARTY:

Without the efforts of the Chinese Communist Party . . . as the mainstay of the Chinese people, China can never achieve independence and liberation, or industrialization and the modernization of her agriculture.

—Mao Zedong, 1945

Essential Question Warmup

Throughout this unit, you studied the history and ideas behind political systems and economic systems around the world. Use what you have learned and the quotations, data, and opinions above to answer the following questions. Then go to your **Essential Questions Journal.**

1. How would you define "the needs of the people"?

2. How might other nations, and specific leaders in history, define "the needs of the people" differently?

3. Can a country led by a single party or person successfully represent a country's people?

4. How does a free market economy help meet people's needs?

Essential Questions Journal To continue to build a response to the unit Essential Question, go to your **Essential Questions Journal.**

Photo: Voters express their views at a town meeting in Hardwick, Vermont.

Essential Questions Journal To begin to build a response to the unit Essential Question, go to your **Essential Questions Journal.**

Unit 7 Participating in State and Local Government

Essential Question What is the right balance of local, state, and federal government?

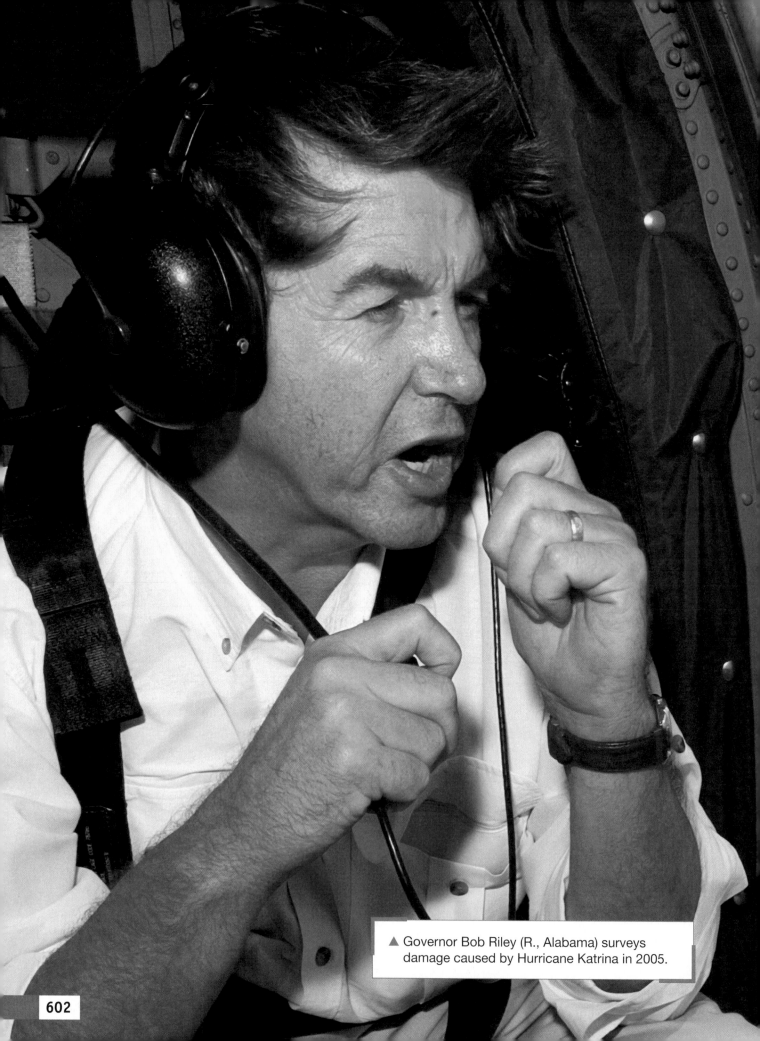

▲ Governor Bob Riley (R., Alabama) surveys damage caused by Hurricane Katrina in 2005.

Governing the States

Essential Question
How much power should state government have?

■ ■

Reading Strategy: Predicting
Previewing a text helps prepare readers to look for new information—to predict what will follow. A prediction is your best guess about what might happen next.

- As you read the text, notice details that could help you make a prediction.
- While you read, check your prediction.
- You may have to change your prediction as you learn more about how state governments work.

GOVERNMENT ONLINE
ON THE GO

To study anywhere, anytime, download these online resources at PearsonSuccessNet.com
- Political Dictionary
- Audio Review
- Downloadable Interactivities

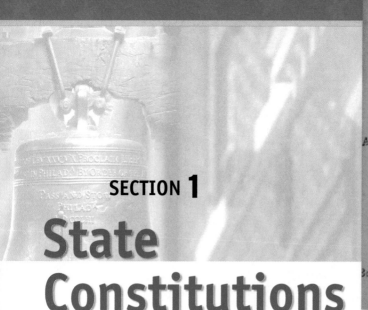

CONSTITUTION

OR

FRAME OF GOVERNMENT,

Agreed upon by the DELEGATES of the People of the State of
MASSACHUSETTS-BAY,

IN

CONVENTION,

Begun and held at *Cambridge* on the First of *September*, 1779.

▲ The Constitution of the State of Massachusetts (1779)

SECTION 1

State Constitutions

Guiding Question

What are the defining features of state constitutions? Use an outline to take notes on the defining qualities of state constitutions.

I. The First State Constitutions
  A. Independence
    1. _____
    2. _____
  B. Basic Principles
    1. _____
    2. Limited government

Objectives:

- Understand state constitutions.
- Describe the basic principles and the terms common to all state constitutions today.
- Explain how state constitutions are changed.
- Examine why state constitutions are in need of change.

In 1788 the United States was made up of 13 states. Today, 50 states are joined by the authority of the federal government in Washington, D.C. Each state flies its own flag. Each state follows its own constitution, based on the same principles of government found in the United States Constitution. Although state governments are alike in many ways, each state makes its own rules and laws. Each state also gives smaller areas within its borders the power to govern themselves.

What were the first constitutions like?

Under English rule, the original 13 colonies used **charters** to rule. Charters were documents given by England that allowed each colony to govern itself. After the Declaration of Independence was written, each colony wrote its own constitution. Later, each new state wrote its own constitution. Today, each state's government receives its power from a constitution.

In colonial times, some people in Massachusetts decided that the religious rule there was too strict. They moved and settled in the Connecticut area. The group leader was Thomas Hooker. He believed in a more democratic government that would give more control to the people. Hooker and his followers drew up a plan of government. In this plan, they agreed to create an assembly with elected representatives. The group agreed to elect a governor and judges.

This first plan set an example. After the colonies declared independence in 1776, they wrote their own constitutions. Massachusetts' constitution set up a public school system paid for with tax money. Years later, in 1787, the writers of the United States Constitution took many ideas from these early colonial constitutions.

The state constitutions and the United States Constitution follow the same basic principles.

- Popular sovereignty—People control their government because they elect the leaders.

- Separation of powers—Each of the three branches of state government has separate and definite powers. This keeps any one branch from becoming too powerful.

- Checks and balances—Each branch can check the work of another branch. Other branches must approve certain actions and decisions. For example, the legislative branch must approve judges appointed by the executive branch.

- Limited government—State and federal officials must obey the law and the Constitution. The government must never do anything to take away an individual's basic freedoms as explained in the Bill of Rights.

✔ **Checkpoint** What ideas were included in the early colonial constitutions?

What are state constitutions like today?

Today, each state constitution follows the same basic principles of popular sovereignty and separation of powers. They rely on a system of checks and balances to control each branch. Most constitutions have provisions that guarantee civil rights and other freedoms, just as the United States Constitution does.

Each constitution is important for many reasons. (See Figure 24.1.) State constitutions explain how both the state and local governments should be set up. The powers given to the branches of government are explained. Local issues, such as education, taxes, and elections, are important to the states. These issues are usually part of the constitution.

Fundamental law describes the basic laws that make up a constitution. Each state constitution explains how it may be changed or added to. This is more difficult than changing a simple ordinance or law.

✔ **Checkpoint** What principles do state constitutions follow today?

■ ■ ■ ■ ■ ■ ■ ■ ■ ■ ■ ■ ■ ■ ■ ■ ■ ■

Reading Strategy
Predicting
Preview the subheadings in this section. Predict what you think you will learn about in this section and the sections to follow.

■ ■ ■ ■ ■ ■ ■ ■ ■ ■ ■ ■ ■ ■ ■ ■ ■ ■

Charter
A document that states a group's purpose and plan

Fundamental law
Law of basic and lasting importance which may not easily be changed

Fig. 24.1

From the *Rotarian*, June 1972. By permission of the publisher.
"Now you try to get a fire started while I draft a constitution."

▲ Analyzing Political Cartoons
What does this cartoon tell you about the importance of a constitution?

Revision
A change that affects a written plan

Initiative
The process of proposing a law through a petition and then voting on it

What are the two kinds of constitutional change?

There are two kinds of changes that can be made to state constitutions. Amendments are changes made to add a few provisions. **Revisions** are changes that affect the basic constitution and may cover a wide range of issues. Most revisions to older constitutions have been made at constitutional conventions.

Most amendments are suggested by the legislature. In some states, citizens can suggest constitutional amendments through an **initiative.** A petition showing the proposed law must be signed by a certain number of people. This initiative is then placed on the ballot for voter approval. For more on the amending process, see Figure 24.2.

Ratification means the proposed amendment is accepted. The amendment is then added to the state constitution. The approval is usually a simple majority. However, some states call for a larger margin; for example, a two-thirds majority.

✓**Checkpoint**   What types of changes can be made to state constitutions?

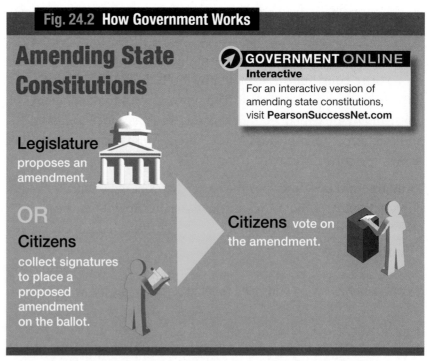

▲ Analyzing Diagrams No matter where an amendment comes from, citizens must vote to approve the amendment. This is true in most states. ***How does this process reflect the idea of popular sovereignty?***

Why is there a need for reform?

There are many reasons why state constitutions need reform or change. Many of the constitutions are quite long. They have been revised and added to many times. New laws and provisions were added to these constitutions as the states grew. Some of these additions are outdated and unnecessary. For example, many constitutions contain **statutory law.** Statutory law is the name for ordinary regulations by legislators. They do not need to be in the constitution and add to its length. Initiatives, which have become very popular, are proposed and passed by voters. These add to the length of constitutions.

Another problem is that many state constitutions are outdated. They were written for another time and need major revision. However, changes often add to the length. States have tried to reform and shorten their constitutions. Most states are still using constitutions more than 100 years old.

Statutory law
Ordinary regulations passed by the legislature

Reading Strategy
Predicting
Think about your prediction. What details can you now add to make your prediction more specific?

✔ **Checkpoint**   What are the two main problems of state constitutions today?

Essential Questions
Journal
Go to your **Essential Questions Journal** to work on this chapter's Essential Question.

SECTION **1** ASSESSMENT

1. **Guiding Question** Use your completed outline to answer this question: What are the defining features of state constitutions?

Key Terms and Comprehension
On a sheet of paper, write the answer for each question. Use complete sentences.

2. What are checks and balances?

3. What is the difference between amendments and revisions?

4. How can citizens suggest an amendment to their state constitution?

5. What are statutory laws?

Critical Thinking

6. **Predict Consequences** The experiences of the American Revolution shaped the way early state governments were set up. How might state governments be different today had they not grown from these experiences?

7. **Draw Inferences** Why do you think some states have not tried to shorten their constitutions?

▲ Virginia's House of Delegates

SECTION 2
State Legislatures

Guiding Question

What are the defining traits and purpose of state legislatures?
Use a table similar to the one below to record the main facts about state legislatures.

Purpose/ Structure	Powers	Legislation
■ Purpose is to make the law	■ Pass laws	■ Referendum
■ 49 have two houses	■	■
■	■	■

Objectives:
- Understand state legislatures.
- Explain the election process, terms, and pay of state legislators.
- Examine the powers and organization of state legislatures.
- Understand the legislative processes at the state level.

The legislative branch of each state is a lawmaking body that works nearly the same as the United States Congress. The main duty of this lawmaking body is to pass laws. In most states, the name for this group is the *legislature*. Some states call this group the *general assembly* or *legislative assembly*. New Hampshire and Massachusetts use the name *general court*.

What are the structure and size of state legislatures?

Like Congress, most state legislatures have two houses—a senate and house of representatives. Only Nebraska has one house in its legislature. While no state has a legislature as large as Congress, the state legislatures differ in size. The house of representatives is always larger than the senate.

The voters in each state elect the members of the state senate and house. The states are divided into voting districts. A voting district is an area where a certain number of people live and vote for their government leaders. The house has smaller districts and the senate has larger districts. In most states, the senators serve a four-year term, and the representatives serve for two years.

Who are the state legislators?

Most state legislators are elected from the Democratic or Republican parties. In most states, senators must be at least 25 years old, and representatives must be at least 21. These qualifications are written in most state constitutions. Legislators also need other characteristics to secure votes. Name recognition, religion, or occupation will attract voters.

Legislators are nominated at the Democratic and Republican party primaries. They are elected in November of even-numbered years, in most states. Four states hold elections in odd-numbered years. They are Mississippi, New Jersey, Virginia, and Louisiana.

Compensation, or payment, for serving in state legislatures is low. Legislators receive a basic salary. In addition, they get an expense allowance for each day the legislature is in session. When the legislature is not in session, they receive a monthly allowance. The pay is less than $30,000 per year in most states.

Most state legislatures now hold annual sessions because of the increased workload. The governor or the legislature can call a special session if an emergency or special need arises.

When the legislature's regular session begins, the members form committees. Each of these small groups has a special task or job to do. These committees handle matters such as education, highways, courts, and local government needs. Bills, or ideas for new laws, are first discussed in committees.

✔ **Checkpoint**   Why are states divided into voting districts?

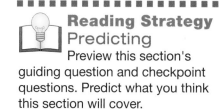

Reading Strategy
Predicting
Preview this section's guiding question and checkpoint questions. Predict what you think this section will cover.

From left: State representatives Alisha Thomas Morgan of Georgia (left) and Justin Davis of South Dakota (right) were in their early 20s when first elected. *What changes might young legislators bring to government?*

■ ■ ■ ■ ■ ■ ■ ■ ■ ■ ■ ■ ■ ■ ■ ■ ■ ■

Police power
The authority of each state to act to protect and promote its laws and citizens

Impeachment
A charge of wrongful conduct of a public official

Constituent power
The nonlegislative power to revise or amend the state constitution

Presiding
Acting as a leader or official

What are the powers of the legislature?

State legislatures have the power to pass laws. These laws cannot go against any federal law or any provision in the state constitution. The state legislature passes laws because it has **police power.** This is the power to protect the health and safety of the state's citizens.

Legislatures also have the power to tax, take care of finances, maintain public schools, and regulate trade. The legislatures set up a system of courts and maintain a system of justice. Each state maintains a police force that enforces the laws and provides protection to citizens.

What are nonlegislative powers?

All 50 states have nonlegislative powers. These powers are not involved with the lawmaking process. The legislature exercises *executive* power when it approves a state official or judge appointed by the governor. Sometimes the legislature itself appoints state officials, although this does not happen in all states.

The legislature has certain *judicial* powers. The most important judicial power is the power of **impeachment.** The legislature can remove any state judge or officer through the impeachment process, which involves a trial. The legislature also has **constituent power.** This is the power to revise or amend the state constitution. All state legislatures have this power.

How are state legislatures organized?

Each house of the state legislature has a **presiding** officer. This person is usually an important political figure. The presiding officer is elected by the members of either the senate or the house. This leader appoints committee members and their leaders.

The house of representatives elects a leader called the speaker. In most states, the senators choose their own leader. In other states, the lieutenant governor of the state acts as the president of the senate. If the lieutenant governor cannot be present, members of the senate choose a temporary president for the time being.

When the legislature begins its session, the members form committees. Committees do most of the work of the legislature. They decide which bills all members will discuss. Standing committees are set up by the work they do. They handle matters such as education, roads, or elections. A judiciary committee decides if bills are constitutional and should be discussed. Sometimes bills stay in one of these standing committees. This is done to prevent the bill from being discussed and voted on.

✔ **Checkpoint**   Where is most of the work of the legislature done?

What is the legislative process?

As you may recall, a bill is an idea for a new law or for a change in an old law. Only a member of the legislature may formally introduce a bill. Ideas for bills can come from citizens who write their senators or representatives with suggestions. The President of the United States, governors, senators, and representatives also can suggest ideas for bills.

Many states allow citizens to take a direct part in proposing new legislation. They can do this through the initiative or the referendum. For more information on initiatives and referendums, see Figure 24.3.

Some states allow citizens to suggest new laws through the initiative process. This is similar to the process of amending the constitution that was discussed in Section 1. With the initiative, a certain number of people must sign a petition. Once the petition has enough signatures, the proposed law is put on the ballot. In some states, the legislature must approve it first. If the initiative receives a majority of votes, it can become a law.

Another way citizens can change legislation is through a **referendum.** A referendum is a process in which certain bills are voted on at the polls. It takes place at the state level. There are three different kinds of referendums: popular, optional, and mandatory.

■ ■ ■ ■ ■ ■ ■ ■ ■ ■ ■ ■ ■ ■ ■ ■ ■

Referendum
The act of submitting a matter to direct vote

Fig. 24.3 How Government Works

Initiative and Referendum:

Voters in many states can write new laws or stop them from passing through initiative and referendum. *Why do you think many legislators are against the initiative process?*

GOVERNMENT ONLINE
Audio Tour
Listen to a guided audio tour of this diagram at
PearsonSuccessNet.com

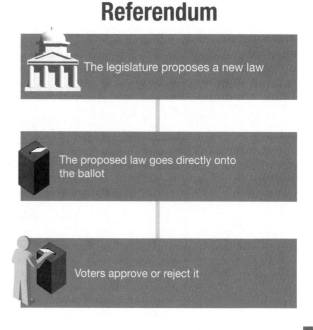

Initiative

1 Voters write a new law and gather signatures in support

2 The proposed law goes directly onto the ballot

The proposed law goes to the legislature

3 Voters approve or reject it

Legislature approves law or sends to voters

Referendum

1 The legislature proposes a new law

2 The proposed law goes directly onto the ballot

3 Voters approve or reject it

■■■■■■■■■■■■■■■■■■■

Reading Strategy
Prediction
      Think about your earlier
prediction. How accurate was it?
Did your prediction help guide
your reading?

■■■■■■■■■■■■■■■■■■■

Petition
A written document or legal paper
asking for a right or benefit from
those in power

After the state legislature passes a law, citizens may use a **petition** to protest the law. Someone who objects to the law may create a petition and have people sign it. If enough people sign the petition, a *popular referendum* will be placed on the ballot. Voters can vote for or against the law at the polls. If enough votes are cast against the law, the law will be rejected.

In some states, the legislature may refer a proposed law to the public for acceptance or rejection. This is called an *optional referendum.* In this case, the legislature is not forced by law to refer the law to the voters, but it does so willingly. Usually the issues referred to the voters are ones that have caused many disputes.

Some state laws require that certain issues be sent to the voters for their approval or rejection. In these cases, a *mandatory referendum* is used. For example, a state may use a mandatory referendum to get voter approval to change the state constitution. Delaware is the only state that may change its constitution without public approval.

✔ **Checkpoint**   What are the differences between the three types of referendums?

Essential Questions
Journal

Go to your **Essential Questions Journal** to work on this chapter's Essential Question.

SECTION 2 ASSESSMENT

Quick Write

Use the Internet to find your state legislature's Web site. Identify a government official, such as a senator or a member of the house of representatives. Choose one official in the legislative branch and write a brief biography on him or her. You can use online or library resources to create your report.

1. **Guiding Question** Use your completed table to answer this question: What are the defining traits and purpose of state legislatures?

Key Terms and Comprehension

On a sheet of paper, write the answer for each question. Use complete sentences.

2. How many houses make up the legislature in most states?

3. How are legislators chosen?

4. What are three powers of state legislatures?

5. What are two ways a citizen can take part in the legislative process?

Critical Thinking

6. **Draw Conclusions** What are some reasons a governor or legislature might call a special session?

7. **Analyze Information** Would you support an amendment to your state's constitution that called for a unicameral legislature? (A unicameral legislature is a legislature with one house.) Explain your answer.

The Governor and State Administration

▲ Governor M. Jodi Rell (R., Connecticut) signs a bill into law.

Guiding Question

What are the roles and powers of a governor? Use a chart to identify the roles and responsibilities of a governor.

Roles and Responsibilities		
Executive	Legislative	Judicial
■ Carry out laws ■ ■	■ Make suggestions ■ ■	■ Appoint judges ■ ■

Objectives:

- Describe the main features of the office of governor.
- Understand a governor's roles, powers, duties, and the limitations of the office.
- Describe the other executive offices at the state level.

Every state has a governor. As the principal executive officer, the governor plays a key role in state politics. In this section, you will learn about the importance of these state leaders.

What are the qualifications for governor?

The state constitution lists the qualifications for a person seeking the office of governor. The minimum age in most states is between 25 and 30. The candidate for governor must be an American citizen and have lived in the state for a certain period of time. In most states it is at least five years. These are the formal qualifications. It also helps the candidate for governor if he or she has experience and is known to voters. Candidates may appeal to some voters because of their religion, race, or sex.

How is a governor selected?

Every state chooses the governor by popular vote. Sometimes, however, there is not a clear majority. A clear majority means the candidate receives more than half of all votes. In Arizona, Georgia, and Louisiana, the top two candidates then face one another in a runoff election to decide the winner. In Mississippi, the legislature picks the new governor if there is no clear majority. In Vermont, both houses of the legislature choose the new governor if there is no majority.

In most states, candidates for governor from each party are chosen in primary elections. About half of the states have a joint election for the governor and lieutenant governor. The two candidates run as a team, and the voters cast only one vote. In other states, the two positions are filled by separate votes.

■ ■ ■ ■ ■ ■ ■ ■ ■ ■ ■ ■ ■ ■ ■ ■
Recall
The process of removing a public official from office by a vote

How long is a governor's term of office?

In 48 states, governors are elected for a four-year term. Only New Hampshire and Vermont limit their governors' terms to two years. More than half of the states allow the governor to serve only two terms. Some governors have served four and even six terms, in states that have no term limits.

How is a governor succeeded?

If a governor dies in office or is no longer able to serve, the states have provided for a replacement. This is written in each state constitution. In 44 states, the lieutenant governor assumes the role. In three states—Maine, New Hampshire, and West Virginia—it is the president of the senate. In three other states—Arizona, Oregon, and Wyoming—the replacement is the secretary of state.

✔ **Checkpoint**   Where can you find information on how a governor is succeeded?

How can a governor be removed from office?

A governor can be removed from office by impeachment in every state except Oregon. An impeachment trial is held for a crime or serious misconduct. Only five governors have been impeached over the years—four immediately after the Civil War and one in 1988 in Arizona.

Sometimes people wish to remove an elected official from office before his or her term ends. Usually this happens when the official has done something wrong while in office. For example, an official might be accused of a crime, such as using public funds for the official's personal life. To remove the official, citizens in 18 states may use the **recall** process. They draw up a petition, get a large number of signatures, and meet certain legal requirements.

Government in Your Life

Licenses

Every state has a department that deals with licensing. Licensing allows state governments to be sure that people who perform specific activities meet certain requirements. For public safety, anyone who drives a motor vehicle must have a license. To get a driver's license, usually one must complete a driver education course and pass a written test and a road test. Other licenses control activities that could be harmful. Hunting and fishing licenses, for example, protect wildlife. Certain professions require licenses. For example, doctors and teachers are licensed. Most licenses require a fee and are renewed regularly. Licensing also raises money for the state.

Then the recall issue is placed on the ballot. If a majority of the voters are in favor of the recall, the elected person must leave office. Only two governors have ever been recalled—in 1921 in North Dakota and in 2003 in California.

■ ■ ■ ■ ■ ■ ■ ■ ■ ■ ■ ■ ■ ■ ■ ■ ■
Reading Strategy
Predicting
Think about what you predicted earlier. Does your prediction still work, or do you need to revise your prediction?

How is a governor paid?

Governors are paid a salary ranging from $70,000 in Maine to more than $200,000 in California. In most states, the governor lives in a governor's mansion that belongs to the state. The state may pay part of the governor's living expenses in the form of an expense account.

Governors are important people, usually well-respected by the citizens of their states. Some have become President, such as Franklin Roosevelt, Jimmy Carter, Ronald Reagan, Bill Clinton, and George W. Bush.

What are a governor's roles?

The governor of a state is the leader of his or her political party. In this role, the governor performs many duties, including appearing at ceremonies and making speeches. As party leader, the governor can suggest laws to the legislature and influence the passage of laws. Citizens of a state often respect the governor's opinion on political matters. Many governors bring positive changes to their states during their terms of office.

What are a governor's executive powers?

The governor heads the executive branch of state government. The executive branch is made up of departments and agencies. Other government officials assist with operating the state.

As the chief executive, or leader, the governor has considerable power. A governor's duties are much like the duties of the President of the United States.

The governor appoints the heads of the departments and agencies needed to run a state. Sometimes, if required by the state constitution, the state senate must approve these appointments. Another duty of the governor is to prepare the state budget proposal. Also, the governor is commander in chief of the state militia, part of which is the National Guard. The National Guard can be called up in an emergency such as a flood, fire, or hurricane, including war.

✔ **Checkpoint** What are a governor's executive powers?

Biography

Sarah Palin: 1964–

Sarah Palin was born in Sandpoint, Idaho, in 1964. Her parents brought her to Alaska that same year. After graduating from the University of Idaho in 1987, she worked in the media and utility industries. Not long after, she began her career in public service. Beginning in 1992, Palin served two terms in the city council of Wasilla, Alaska. Then, in 1996, she began two terms as mayor of the same city. Palin made history in December 2006 when she was elected Alaska's 11th—and first female—governor. In her first legislative session as governor, Palin passed two major laws.

The first law dealt with improving the state's ethics. The legislation was intended to lead to more openness in government. The second piece of legislation attempted to manage the development of Alaska's resources. It set up a process to construct a gas pipeline. A hunter and fisher, Governor Palin enjoys taking part in all that Alaska has to offer.

In August 2008, Republican presidential nominee John McCain announced Palin as his vice presidential running mate. The McCain/Palin ticket lost the election to Democrats, Barack Obama and Joe Biden.

Item veto
The power to eliminate or remove certain parts of a bill

What are a governor's legislative powers?

The governor is the state's chief legislator. In a State of the State address, the governor outlines his or her programs and makes suggestions for new legislation. The governor works closely with legislators throughout the entire session. In this way, the governor has a strong voice in running the state. Governors have the power to call special sessions of the legislature when needed. A special session is a way to get important legislation passed before the legislature adjourns.

The governor of each state has the power to veto laws passed by the legislature. But most governors do not have the pocket veto as the President does. With a pocket veto, a bill does not become a law if the President does not sign it and the federal legislature has adjourned. However, most states include the **item veto** in the governor's veto power. With an item veto, the governor can veto certain parts of a bill. The item veto is often used to restrict spending in bills. In most states, two-thirds of the membership in each house is needed to override a governor's veto. Governors veto only a small percentage of laws passed by their legislatures.

✔ **Checkpoint**   What is a governor's role in the legislature?

What are a governor's judicial powers?

Governors have several judicial powers, including appointing some judges and dealing with people convicted of a crime. In every state, the governor may use his or her powers of clemency. Clemency is showing mercy toward a person convicted of a crime.

There are several ways a governor can use the power of clemency.
1.) The power of **commutation** allows the governor to reduce the sentence given by the court.
2.) The power to pardon releases a person from the punishment given by the court. The pardon may be full or conditional, but must be given after a person is convicted of a crime.
3.) The power to **parole** allows the release of a prisoner before his or her sentence is fully served.
4.) Finally, the power to reprieve delays the execution of a sentence. Sometimes the governor may share these powers with a parole board or a board of pardons.

■ ■

Commutation
Reducing the sentence given by the court for a crime

Parole
The release of a prisoner from jail before the full term is served

---

Fig. 24.4 How Government Works

GOVERNMENT ONLINE
Audio Tour
Listen to a guided audio tour of this diagram at
PearsonSuccessNet.com

Choosing Executive Officers

Many jobs that are filled by the President in the federal government are filled by voters at the state level. *How do direct elections give citizens more power in state government?*

Federal Government

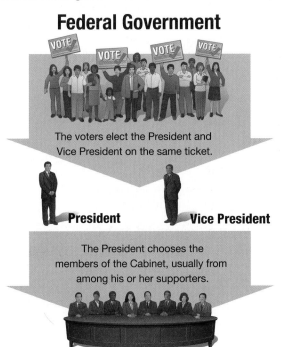

The voters elect the President and Vice President on the same ticket.

President   **Vice President**

The President chooses the members of the Cabinet, usually from among his or her supporters.

State Government

The voters elect the governor. In most states, the voters also elect the other executive officers independently.

Governor   **Lieutenant Governor**

Attorney General   **Secretary of State**   **State Treasurer**

What are some of the governor's other duties?

Other duties of the governor include welcoming important visitors, appearing at dedication ceremonies, and making speeches. Sometimes the governor is asked to travel, even to other countries. Governors also settle problems, such as trade or labor disputes.

Who are some other executive officers?

As shown in Figure 24.4 on page 617, the state officials are generally voted into office. The following are five key state officials.

- The lieutenant governor succeeds the governor if necessary.
- The attorney general is the chief legal officer in the state.
- The secretary of state keeps all records and publishes laws.
- The state treasurer collects taxes and pays bills.
- The superintendent of public instruction works with the board of education to carry out the laws.

Essential Questions Journal Go to your **Essential Questions Journal** to work on this chapter's Essential Question.

SECTION **3** ASSESSMENT

Quick Write

You have been asked to write a help-wanted ad for the job of governor for your state. You would place the ad in your state's newspapers. In the ad, list the qualifications, duties, and term of office.

1. **Guiding Question** Use your completed chart to answer this question: What are the roles and powers of a governor?

Key Terms and Comprehension

On a sheet of paper, match the sentence beginnings in Part 1 with the correct endings in Part 2.

Part 1 Beginning of Sentence

2. The executive branch of a state government . . .
3. As the state's chief legislator, the governor . . .
4. The lieutenant governor . . .
5. The attorney general . . .

Part 2 Ending of Sentence

A . . . succeeds the governor if necessary.
B . . . is headed by a governor.
C . . . is the chief legal officer in the state.
D . . . has the power to veto laws passed by the legislature.

Critical Thinking

6. **Draw Conclusions** Why do you think governors have the power to pardon people for crimes in certain cases?

7. **Analyze Information** Why do you think governors have the power to appoint department heads?

▲ Jury trial

SECTION 4

In the Courtroom

State constitutions give state governments the power to keep law and order within their borders. The legislative branch passes the laws. The executive branch sees that the laws are carried out. The judicial branch explains the laws and has the power to punish those who break the laws.

What kinds of laws are applied in state courts?

The following is a list of the types of laws applied in state courts.

- **Constitutional law** is based on the United States Constitution, the state constitutions, and court rulings on these documents. It is the highest form of law in the country.

- Statutory law is passed by legislative bodies and the people through the initiative or referendum. It includes laws passed by city councils and other local legislative bodies.

- **Administrative law** regulates federal and state government agencies not covered by constitutional law.

- **Common law** is unwritten law developed by judges over the years through many court cases. State courts can apply common law when it is not in conflict with written law. Once a decision is made, it becomes a precedent, or an example for similar cases to follow. Common law is not a list of fixed rules. In common law, the law is created or determined by judges. When there is a legal dispute to which no written law applies, judges use precedent to determine the law. If there is not a precedent for a case, the judge may create the law. Lawyers from both sides try to prove their cases using precedents from other similar cases.

- **Equity** is related to common law. Common law tries to make amends for a situation after it happens. Equity, on the other

Guiding Question

How do state and local courts apply different types of laws?
Use a flowchart similar to the one below to explain the significance of elements of the legal system.

State and Local Courts		
Kinds of Law	Criminal and Civil Law	Jury System
■ Common law	■ Felony	■ Grand jury
■	■	■
■	■	■

Objectives:

- Understand the kinds of law applied in state courts.
- Compare and contrast criminal law and civil law.
- Describe the purposes of juries and juror selection.

Constitutional law
Law based on the United States Constitution, the state constitutions, and court rulings on any part of these documents

Administrative law
Law that regulates federal and state government agencies not covered by constitutional law

Common law
Law based on customs or tradition

Equity
Law intended to stop wrongs before they happen

Criminal law
Law that regulates citizens' behavior and protects the public order

Felony
A serious crime

Misdemeanor
A minor crime

Civil law
Law that deals with citizens' behavior that does not involve a crime

Jury
A group of citizens chosen in a court to listen to both sides in a case and to make a decision

Prosecute
To bring legal action against a person or group

hand, attempts to prevent unjust actions *before* they happen. Suppose a new road or building is being constructed that takes away a person's property. The court is called on to decide if the construction can be done before any property is damaged or taken.

✓**Checkpoint**   What is the highest form of law in the country based on?

What are criminal and civil law?

There are other ways to describe laws as they are applied in courtrooms: criminal or civil.

Criminal law regulates citizens' behavior and protects the public order. The federal or state government brings a criminal case against a person who has broken a law. A crime is something that has been declared illegal because it threatens society. There are two types of crime a person can commit: **felony** or **misdemeanor.** A felony is a major crime, such as murder or burglary. Misdemeanors are minor crimes, such as littering or vandalism.

Civil law deals with citizens' behavior that does not involve a crime. Civil cases are usually disagreements between two or more individuals or groups. One person or group sues another person or group for damages. The state is not involved in civil cases because no law has been broken. For more on criminal and civil law, see **Figure 24.5.**

What is the jury system?

A **jury** is a group of people selected to hear evidence and make decisions in a court case. There are two types of juries in the legal system of the United States: the grand jury and the petit jury. For a list of some of the legal terms in this chapter, see **Figure 24.6** on page 622.

The grand jury is used in criminal trials and has from 6 to 23 persons. The grand jury has a foreman or forelady, the person in charge. The foreman or forelady is usually selected by the jurors but may be chosen by the judge. In large juries, at least 12 jurors must agree on the guilt of the accused. Even in small juries, a majority is needed to make a final decision.

In some states, the jurors may question the witnesses of the prosecuting attorney. The prosecuting attorney **prosecutes,** or brings legal action against, people who have broken county or state laws. The prosecuting attorney may also summon, or call, others to testify against the accused person. The grand jury then considers the evidence in private. Once they make a decision, they move to the courtroom and report their opinion to the court. A grand jury may also decide to send a case to a petit jury.

It is expensive to use a grand jury. Because of this, many states now use a process called **information.** An information is a charge filed by a prosecutor. It is used for minor and some major offenses, or crimes. Some states have decided that grand juries are not needed. This is because grand juries tend to follow the prosecutor's suggestions.

What is a petit jury?

A petit jury is a trial jury used in criminal and civil cases. There are usually 12 jurors in a petit jury. Sometimes states use only 6 jurors. Over one third of the states do not require a unanimous verdict in civil and minor criminal cases. In a unanimous verdict, all jurors agree on the decision. If a jury cannot decide on a verdict by whatever means the state decides, then another trial is held. Sometimes the matter is dropped by the parties involved.

What is a bench trial?

A judge, without a jury, can hold a **bench trial.** This type of trial is used for misdemeanors or civil cases involving small amounts of money. An accused person can waive, or give up, his or her right to a trial by jury. In that case, a bench trial will be held.

Information
A charge filed by the prosecutor

Bench trial
A case that is heard by a judge and not a jury

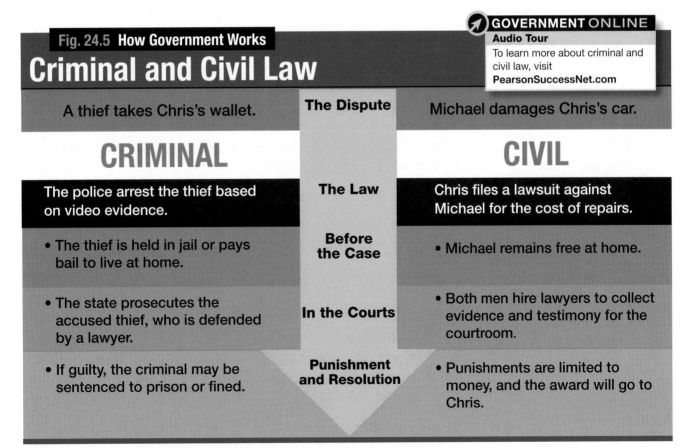

Fig. 24.5 How Government Works
Criminal and Civil Law

GOVERNMENT ONLINE
Audio Tour
To learn more about criminal and civil law, visit
PearsonSuccessNet.com

The Dispute	
A thief takes Chris's wallet.	Michael damages Chris's car.

CRIMINAL		CIVIL
The police arrest the thief based on video evidence.	**The Law**	Chris files a lawsuit against Michael for the cost of repairs.
• The thief is held in jail or pays bail to live at home.	**Before the Case**	• Michael remains free at home.
• The state prosecutes the accused thief, who is defended by a lawyer.	**In the Courts**	• Both men hire lawyers to collect evidence and testimony for the courtroom.
• If guilty, the criminal may be sentenced to prison or fined.	**Punishment and Resolution**	• Punishments are limited to money, and the award will go to Chris.

▲ This chart shows the different paths a criminal and a civil case could take. *Why don't civil cases lead to prison?*

Fig. 24.6 Legal Terms

Term	Purpose
Jury	To provide a fair trial before the accused's peers
Common law	To guide a judge's decisions with past examples
Equity	To stop wrongs before they occur
Criminal law	To protect the public order
Civil law	To resolve disputes between people and government

How are jurors selected?

Jurors are selected the same way in most states. A county official or group of officials makes a list of people who qualify as jurors. To qualify, a person must

- be between the ages of 18 and 70;

- be literate, or able to read;

- be healthy enough to serve; and

- have no criminal record.

The sheriff serves each person selected to be a juror with a court order. A judge then decides who will serve on the jury and who will be excused.

Some states are using trial jury less because of the cost and the number of errors made when making verdicts. The jury system has always been a part of the judicial system. Many people are in favor of keeping the jury system because it allows citizens to take part in the justice system.

Essential Questions Journal	Go to your **Essential Questions** Journal to work on this chapter's Essential Question.

SECTION 4 ASSESSMENT

Word Bank

civil law

common law

criminal law

statutory law

1. **Guiding Question** Use your completed table to answer this question: How do state and local courts apply different types of laws?

Key Terms and Comprehension

On a sheet of paper, write the type of law from the Word Bank that matches the description.

2. Law that makes certain behaviors, like murder, illegal

3. Law that deals with people's behavior that does not involve a crime, such as divorce

4. Unwritten law that is used as an example in similar cases

5. Law that can be passed by referendum

Critical Thinking

6. **Draw Conclusions** Most government processes in this country must take place in public. A grand jury, however, works in private. Why do you think this is so?

7. **Analyze Information** Being on a jury allows citizens to take part in the justice system. What do you think are some other reasons to keep the jury system?

What is it like to serve on a jury?

Serving on a jury is a chance to participate directly in the American justice system. The right to a trial by jury is a fundamental right in our democracy. It is given to citizens by the United States Constitution. As a juror, you become a major participant in the American judicial system. It is your duty to ensure that a fellow citizen receives justice.

Most jurors are chosen from voting lists, state department of motor vehicles records, or tax rolls. How long your jury duty lasts depends on the nature and difficulty of the case. It also depends on whether or not you are actually chosen to serve. Some people are excused from duty because of health issues or other hardships. And others are dismissed without having to serve at all.

If you were not excused, you become a potential juror. Lawyers from both sides question potential jurors. They hope to find a jury that will be helpful to their case. If they do not think you will be helpful, you may be dismissed.

Once chosen, you and other jurors will receive instructions before beginning a trial. These may include the following:

1. Do not be influenced by bias. Bias is when a person tends to favor or oppose something without reason. As a juror, you may have good or bad opinions about the people involved in the case. You must not let these opinions affect your decision about the case.

2. Follow the law exactly as it is explained to you. Your job as a juror is to determine if someone broke the law.

3. Remember that the defendant is presumed innocent. The government must prove that the defendant is guilty "beyond a reasonable doubt." If it fails to do so, the jury verdict must be "not guilty." If you feel that the government made its case, then you must find the defendant "guilty."

4. Keep an open mind. Do not form or state any opinions about the case until the trial is finished. Wait until you have heard all of the evidence and the lawyers' closing arguments.

5. During the trial, do not discuss the case. Do not talk about the case with anyone, including your fellow jurors. Only discuss the case in the jury room after the closing arguments, where others cannot hear your discussions. Avoid media coverage of the case once the trial has begun.

▶▶ What do you think?

1. What does "reasonable doubt" mean to you?
2. Jurors are instructed not to discuss the case and to avoid media coverage of it during the trial. Why do you think this is?

GOVERNMENT ONLINE
Citizenship Activity Pack
For activities on serving on a jury, go to **PearsonSuccessNet.com**

▲ Chief Justice Leah Sears, Supreme Court of Georgia

SECTION 5

State Courts and Their Judges

Guiding Question
How are state and local courts organized and staffed? Use a table similar to the one below to record information about the types of state and local courts.

Municipal Courts	Juvenile Courts	Justice and Magistrates' Courts
■ Civil cases ■ ■	■ Young people ■ ■	■ Urban areas ■ ■

Objectives:
- Understand how state courts are organized and describe the work that each type does.
- Examine the different ways judges are selected.

State and local courts deal with a variety of issues. Here, you will look at the way these courts are organized and how they work.

How is the court system organized?

The judicial branch, with its system of courts, applies the laws and punishes criminals. The three types of state courts are

- lower courts to handle lesser civil and criminal cases;
- general trial courts with a judge and jury for serious cases; and
- state supreme courts to handle appeals from the other courts.

What are Justices of the Peace?

The **Justices of the Peace**—JPs—are in charge of the low state courts called justice courts. Up until the mid-1900s, JPs were found in every part of the country. Today most states have done away with JPs, along with the justice courts. Some still can be found in small towns and rural areas.

A Justice of the Peace tries civil cases involving small sums of money, and also performs marriages. He or she also settles minor offenses such as **disorderly conduct,** which is a disturbance to public peace. In addition, JPs issue certain types of warrants. A **warrant** is a court order making an official action legal. It is usually issued for searches and arrests. Finally, JPs can hold preliminary hearings. A **preliminary hearing** is usually the first step in a criminal case. A judge hears the evidence and decides if the person can be held for the grand jury or a prosecutor.

What are magistrates' courts?

Magistrates' courts are located in urban areas. A magistrate presides over, or is in charge of, the court. A magistrate handles misdemeanors and small civil cases. Magistrates are elected for short terms in most areas. These courts perform some of the same functions as the justice courts in rural areas.

What are municipal courts?

A municipal court hears civil cases, minor criminal offenses, and probate cases. (Probate deals with the legal process of settling the affairs of a person who has died.) Municipal courts are separated according to the types of cases they hear. Some examples include criminal, civil, small claims, and traffic. A person can bring a claim to a small claims court for very little cost. The case may involve overdue bills, back rent, or other small debts. A judge will handle the case without attorneys.

What are juvenile courts?

A juvenile court is a court that hears cases of young people arrested for an offense. This court tries to help juveniles with problems. In very serious cases, the juvenile offenders are sent to adult criminal courts for trial. If a juvenile is tried as an adult, he or she will always be tried as an adult for any other offenses after that. This is true in over half of the states. For a look at the history of juvenile courts, see Figure 24.7.

✔ **Checkpoint** In what type of court might a thirteen-year-old be tried for a minor offense?

Justice of the Peace
A judge in charge of a justice court, the lowest part of the state judicial system

Disorderly conduct
Disturbing public peace

Warrant
A court order that makes an official action legal

Preliminary hearing
The first step in a criminal case; where the judge hears the evidence and decides if the person can be held for the grand jury or prosecutor

---

Fig. 24.7

Juvenile Justice

Juvenile courts arose at the state level to reform the criminal justice system. *Why did reformers seek separate prisons for young people?*

1800s Common law prefers to have parents discipline children for most crimes. Young people accused of serious crimes are jailed with adults. Those as young as seven can be tried and sentenced in criminal courts.

1899 Cook County, Illinois, founds the first juvenile court under the principle of "the state as parent." The court protects both the interest of public safety and the needs of the juveniles accused of crimes.

1974 Congress passes the Juvenile Justice and Delinquency Prevention Act requiring young people to be jailed separately from adults and encouraging states to develop alternatives to prisons.

Today While juvenile courts still flourish, most states allow juveniles accused of serious crimes to be tried and sentenced in adult courts.

Reading Strategy
Predicting
        Think about your
prediction in the previous section.
What details can you now add
to make your prediction more
specific?

What are general trial courts?

Trial courts handle important criminal and civil cases. A judge and jury hear most cases. A state is divided into districts and circuits that cover one or more counties. Most legal actions begin in a circuit court.

The cases are tried before a judge with a petit jury. A grand jury or prosecuting attorney sends criminal cases to these trial courts. Most of the time, the decision is final. If there is a dispute, the case may go to a higher state court.

What are the intermediate appellate courts?

States usually have intermediate appellate courts called courts of appeal. A disputed case will go to an appellate court before it is sent to the state supreme court. The courts of appeals do not hold trials. They study the case and listen to the lawyers' arguments. The court of appeals decides if the law was correctly applied in the lower court. Many times the decision of the appellate court is final. Sometimes cases are sent to the state supreme court.

What is the state supreme court?

The highest court in the state is usually called the state supreme court. In most cases, it is the court of last resort. Accused people who think their case was not tried fairly in a lower court may appeal to a higher court. When hearing or considering an appeal, the state supreme court does not hold a new trial. Instead the judges study the records and all the evidence. Then they vote on whether the accused person received a fair trial. Most of the time, the decision is final.

What is the unified court system?

In recent years, states have adopted a unified court system that is organized by types of cases. There is one court for the entire state, with different levels. There is a supreme court, intermediate appellate courts, and general trial courts. At each level there are divisions—criminal, juvenile, family relations, and others. Judges work in the divisions that interest them. A number of states have changed to this unified court system. The old system was organized geographically and heard every type of case in all areas of the law. Some cases took years to be heard. The unified court system is considered by some states to be faster.

✓ **Checkpoint** How is the unified court system organized?

How are judges selected?

Some state judges are elected by citizens. Elected judges can be voted out of office if voters do not agree with their decisions. Other judges are appointed by the governor. Some states combine both methods of judge selection in the following way. The governor appoints judges. Then, after a period of time, the judges must win election to keep their jobs. This way judges must win the approval of voters to stay in office.

What is the Missouri Plan?

The American Bar Association is in favor of a plan for the selection of judges. The plan was first used in Missouri and is known as the Missouri Plan.

The Missouri Plan, or part of it, is used in more than half of the states. The governor appoints all the judges in a state. Each appointment is made from a list of three given to the governor by a committee. Each new judge serves until election time and then must be approved by the voters. If the judge wins voter approval, he or she remains in the position for the number of years required. Trial court judges must stay in the position for 6 years and high court judges for 12 years.

Essential Questions Journal Go to your **Essential Questions Journal** to work on this chapter's Essential Question.

SECTION 5 ASSESSMENT

Word Bank

intermediate appellate courts

magistrates'

Missouri Plan

state supreme court

1. **Guiding Question** Use your completed table to answer this question: How are state and local courts organized and staffed?

Key Terms and Comprehension

On a sheet of paper, write the word from the Word Bank that best completes the sentence.

2. Accused people who do not think their trial was fair can appeal to the _____.

3. In the _____, the governor appoints a judge from a list of three.

4. _____ courts and justice courts perform similar functions.

5. Judges in _____ study records from a case and listen to lawyers' arguments. Then they decide if the law was correctly applied.

Critical Thinking

6. **Demonstrate Reasoned Judgment** How do you think judges should be selected? Why?

7. **Draw Conclusions** Should a judge who is appointed make important decisions that do not require a trial?

Chapter Summary

Section 1—State Constitutions

- State constitutions follow the same basic principles of the United States Constitution. These ideas are popular sovereignty, separation of powers, checks and balances, and limited government.

- Changes can be made to state constitutions by amendment or revision.

Section 2—State Legislatures

- The purpose of state legislatures is to make laws. Like Congress, most state legislatures are split into the senate and the house of representatives. Committees do most of the work of the legislature.

- State legislatures have powers that are not involved in the lawmaking process. Some examples are the power to maintain a police force, impeach a state official, or alter the state constitution.

Section 3—The Governor and State Administration

- A governor is the chief executive of the state. He or she can appoint heads of departments and write a state budget proposal.

- The governor acts as commander in chief of the National Guard. A governor can also pardon prisoners in certain cases and propose new laws to the legislature.

Section 4—In the Courtroom

- State courts apply the following types of law: constitutional law, statutory law, administrative law, common law, and equity. In the courtroom, laws can be described as either criminal or civil.

- The United States legal system has two types of juries: grand and petit. There are other alternatives to using the jury system. These include the process of information and a bench trial.

Section 5—State Courts and Their Judges

- Lower state courts handle lesser civil and criminal cases. These include justice courts, magistrates' courts, and municipal courts.

- General trial courts with a judge and a jury handle more serious cases.

- Intermediate appellate courts and state supreme courts handle appeals from other courts.

Guiding Question
Section 2 What are the defining traits and purpose of state legislatures?

Guiding Question
Section 3 What are the roles and powers of a governor?

Guiding Question
Section 4 How do state and local courts apply different types of laws?

Guiding Question
Section 1 What are the defining features of state constitutions?

CHAPTER 24

Essential Question
How much power should state government have?

Guiding Question
Section 5 How are state and local courts organized and staffed?

Document-Based Assessment

Governor of California's Inaugural Address

Arnold Schwarzenegger, a native of Austria, became an American citizen in 1983. He became California's 38th governor in 2003. Following are passages from his Inaugural Address.

Document at a Glance

- Speech outlining California's problems
- Request for citizens to help
- Inaugural address

My fellow citizens: Today is a new day in California. I did not seek this office to do things the way they've been done. What I care about is restoring your confidence in your government.

When I became a citizen . . . I had to learn about the history and principles of our republic. What I learned . . . is that sovereignty rests with the people—not with the government.

. . . I want the people to know that my administration is not about politics, it is about saving California. The state of California is in a crisis . . . we spent ourselves into the largest deficit in the nation. We have the worst credit rating . . . Next year we will have the highest unemployment insurance costs in the nation . . .

Our state has endured earthquakes, floods, and fires. The latest fires have destroyed lives, homes, businesses . . .

And just as California will come back from the fires, we will also come back from fiscal adversity . . .

There's a massive weight we must lift off our state. Alone, I cannot lift it. But together we can.

. . . I will not rest until our fiscal house is in order. I will not rest until California is a competitive job creating machine. I will not rest until the people of California come to see their government as a partner in their lives, not a roadblock to their dreams.

Today I ask all of you to join me in a new partnership for California.

Document-Based Questions

1. What does Governor Schwarzenegger want to restore?

2. According to Governor Schwarzenegger, California is in a crisis. What has contributed to the crisis?

3. What did Governor Schwarzenegger say he had to learn when he became a citizen?

4. What did Governor Schwarzenegger say about the California's credit rating?

5. **Make a prediction** How do you think residents of California reacted to this speech? Explain.

SOURCE: Governor Arnold Schwarzenegger's Inaugural Address, 2003

Chapter Assessment

Directions: On a sheet of paper, write the answer to each question. Use complete sentences.

Section 1—State Constitutions

1. What are fundamental laws?

2. What are two ways to change state constitutions?

3. **Critical Thinking** How might amendments and revisions contribute to the need for reform of state constitutions?

Section 2—State Legislatures

4. Who is the leader of the state house of representatives?

5. What is the difference between an initiative and a referendum?

6. **Critical Thinking** States have certain powers that the federal government does not have. Why do you think this is?

Section 3—The Governor and State Administration

7. What is the job of the attorney general?

8. What is the difference between the governor's power to parole and power of commutation?

9. Who is the chief executive of a state government? Name three duties of this chief executive.

10. **Critical Thinking** How do the governor's judicial powers demonstrate the principle of checks and balances?

Section 4—In the Courtroom

11. What is a civil case?

12. How does the legal charge of information save states money?

13. What are the origins of common law?

14. **Critical Thinking** The idea of a trial by jury has a long history in the United States. What does this say about American views of the role of citizens in the judicial process?

Section 5—State Courts and Their Judges

15. What are the similarities between JPs and magistrates?

16. Why have some states adopted unified court systems?

17. Critical Thinking Do you think the Missouri Plan is a fair and efficient way to select judges? Why or why not?

Apply What You've Learned

Exploring the Essential Question

18. Police power is a power that is typically saved for state legislatures to use. At times, Congress has used this power. Do you think this is appropriate or acceptable? Why or why not?

19. Should the federal government change its level of involvement in state governments?

Essential Questions Project

20. Work with a partner to write a proposed amendment to your state's constitution. Brainstorm ways that you could make your state government run more smoothly. Share this amendment with the class.

Essential Questions Journal

Go to your **Essential Questions Journal** to work on this chapter's Essential Question.

Test-Taking Tip

Restate the test directions in your own words. Tell yourself what you are expected to do.

▲ Mayor Michael Nutter in Philadelphia's City Hall, 2008

Local Government and Finance

Essential Question
How local should government be?

Reading Strategy: Text Structure
Readers can look at the organization of the text to help them identify the most important information.

- Before you begin reading about governing the states, look at the chapter title, the names of the sections, the boldfaced words, the photos, and the charts.

- You will notice that the section titles are in the form of questions. The answer to each question is provided in the paragraph(s) in that section. In this way, the text is structured in a question and answer format.

GOVERNMENT ONLINE
ON THE GO

To study anywhere, anytime, download these online resources at PearsonSuccessNet.com.
- **Political Dictionary**
- **Audio Review**
- **Downloadable Interactivities**

▲ Local governments provide fire protection and many other needed services.

SECTION 1

Counties, Towns, and Townships

Guiding Question

What are the similarities and differences of local governments, special districts, and tribal governments? Use a chart similar to the one below to record facts about counties, towns, and townships.

Types of Local Government		
Counties	Towns	Townships
■ Major unit of local government ■	■ Found in New England ■	■ Found in the Mid-Atlantic and Midwest ■

Objectives:

- Describe a typical county.
- Examine the structure of county government.
- Identify the functions of counties.
- Analyze the need for change in county government.
- Identify some services provided by tribal governments.
- Examine the governments of towns, townships, and special districts.

Local government comes in many shapes and sizes. Some local governments have only a few employees. Other local governments have tens of thousands of employees. Local governments provide many services and offer protection to citizens. People can easily participate in local government. They may attend public meetings to talk about their concerns or even run for public office.

What are counties?

During the early history of the United States, counties existed to take care of the rural areas. For people in areas far from a town, the **county** government was the only government they had. Today, the county government usually serves an area that has several towns or cities. In most states, it is the largest unit of local government. Sometimes, counties are divided into subdivisions. These subdivisions are called **townships.** Townships are most common in the Mid-Atlantic and Midwest states.

Counties are the main unit of government in most states. There are 3,033 county governments in the United States today. Although the number of counties varies in each state, the size of the state does not determine the number of counties. Connecticut and Rhode Island have no organized county government. Texas, on the other hand, has 254 counties.

✔ **Checkpoint** What is a township?

What is the government structure of counties?

In each county, a city or town serves as the county seat. A county seat is similar to a state capital. The county seat is where county officials have their offices. These offices are often in a county courthouse. The county may also own other buildings such as libraries and jails.

Each county is governed by a local body, often known as a county board. In addition to the county board, there are also many other elected officials. These people do the day-to-day work of the county. There are some three million people working in county government in the United States. The chart on this page (Figure 25.1) shows some of the county officials and the jobs that they do.

✔ **Checkpoint** What is the name of the governing body of a county?

County
A district into which a state is divided for purposes of local government

Township
A subdivision of a county

Reading Strategy
Text Structure
As you read, remember to use your chart to record facts about counties, towns, and townships.

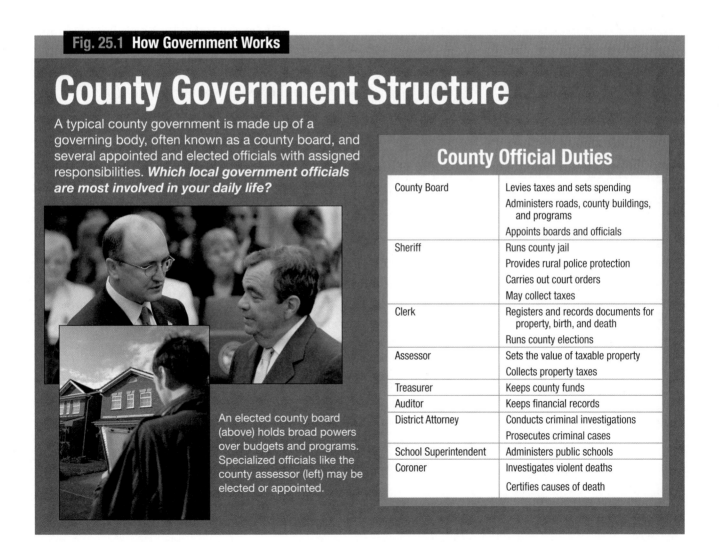

Fig. 25.1 How Government Works

County Government Structure

A typical county government is made up of a governing body, often known as a county board, and several appointed and elected officials with assigned responsibilities. *Which local government officials are most involved in your daily life?*

An elected county board (above) holds broad powers over budgets and programs. Specialized officials like the county assessor (left) may be elected or appointed.

County Official Duties

Official	Duties
County Board	Levies taxes and sets spending
	Administers roads, county buildings, and programs
	Appoints boards and officials
Sheriff	Runs county jail
	Provides rural police protection
	Carries out court orders
	May collect taxes
Clerk	Registers and records documents for property, birth, and death
	Runs county elections
Assessor	Sets the value of taxable property
	Collects property taxes
Treasurer	Keeps county funds
Auditor	Keeps financial records
District Attorney	Conducts criminal investigations
	Prosecutes criminal cases
School Superintendent	Administers public schools
Coroner	Investigates violent deaths
	Certifies causes of death

Fig. 25.2
Native American Reservations

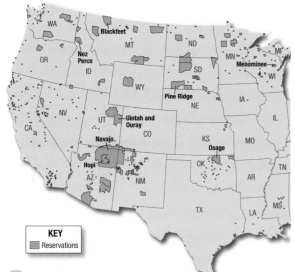

KEY
☐ Reservations

⏺ **GOVERNMENT** ONLINE
Interactive
To learn more about tribal governments, visit
PearsonSuccessNet.com

▲ Analyzing Maps Native American governments enjoy a sovereign status and a special relationship with the federal and state governments. **Why are reservations organized differently than other local governments?**

Reading Strategy
Text Structure
Study the map on this page. How does it help you better understand the location of tribal governments?

What are the functions of counties?

Counties enforce state and county laws. Most counties are interested in the concerns of rural areas. Common jobs of counties are peacekeeping, operating jails, collecting taxes, assessing property, and spending county money. Counties are also in charge of some roads, bridges, schools, and other public works. The county keeps legal documents for housing. Counties also supply licenses for marriage, hunting, and fishing. They also run all elections.

Counties with large populations offer services like those found in cities. These services include police and fire protection and medical services. Large counties often maintain airports and other mass transportation services. They may also provide money for sports stadiums and other recreational facilities.

Why is there a need to reform?

County governments have grown very large through the years. This often leads to confusion because authority is given to so many different people. Many officials are elected, not appointed. Voters may not be able to choose qualified people for each position. Some states have tried to reform these large county governments. The state may allow home rule for a large county. *Home rule* means that the county can set up its own government. Another way to reform is to use a county manager. A county manager is similar to a city manager. Yet another way is to combine county and city governments in one place.

What are tribal governments?

Native American tribes are sovereign nations. They govern their own people and are free from state or local control. They have a special relationship with the national government. All recognized tribes receive federal funds, and they use this money to provide services for their people. These services may include healthcare, education, and welfare. In the United States today there are 568 tribal governments, which include more than 1.7 million people. See Figure 25.2. Most tribes have an elected chairman and a council. Some, such as the Cherokee and Navajo, have a written constitution with three branches: executive, legislative, and judicial. Other tribes are small and not as well organized.

✔**Checkpoint** What services might tribal governments provide?

What are towns and townships?

Towns and townships are very common in the United States. They exist in about half of the states. Towns and townships are very common in the East and Midwest. For a view from above of a Midwestern township, see Figure 25.3.

The New England states are located in the northeastern part of the United States. Although the New England states are divided into counties, the towns are the basic unit of government. The town may have a form of government called direct democracy. A *direct democracy* means that all town voters meet to conduct the town's business. Town meetings are held once a year, or more often if necessary. The town's officers are elected at the yearly meeting.

This New England type of government began in colonial times. The Pilgrims landed at Plymouth Rock in 1620 as an organized congregation. They quickly set up a community in which their church and their government were almost one. Other Puritan groups followed this pattern as they settled in New England. In those days the meetings were popular events, and almost everyone attended. Today these gatherings are poorly attended, even though the towns have grown. Some towns now elect representatives to attend rather than counting on large numbers of citizens to participate.

Reading Strategy
Text Structure
Create a map that shows where in the United States you would find each type of local government talked about in this section.

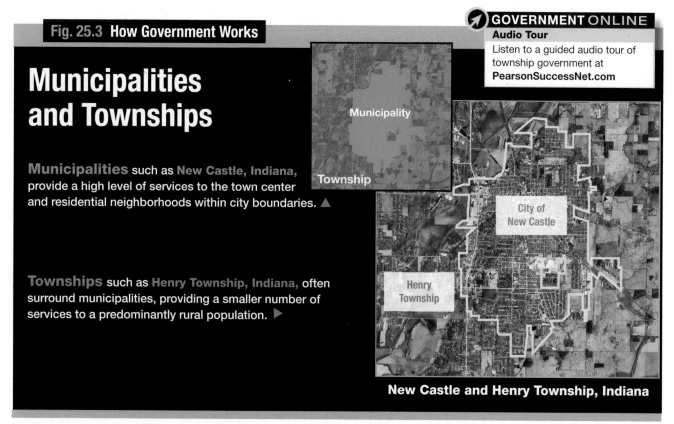

Fig. 25.3 How Government Works

Municipalities and Townships

Municipalities such as New Castle, Indiana, provide a high level of services to the town center and residential neighborhoods within city boundaries. ▲

Townships such as Henry Township, Indiana, often surround municipalities, providing a smaller number of services to a predominantly rural population. ▶

Municipality

Township

GOVERNMENT ONLINE
Audio Tour
Listen to a guided audio tour of township government at **PearsonSuccessNet.com**

City of New Castle

Henry Township

New Castle and Henry Township, Indiana

▲ Analyzing Maps *What services might a municipal government provide that a township would not?*

Municipality
A political unit within a township in an urban setting

Trustee
A person who is given power to act for others

Special district
An independent unit created to perform one or more related governmental functions at the local level

Some states in the Mid-Atlantic and Midwestern regions of the United States have township governments. In general, townships are found in rural parts of counties. A **municipality** is a political unit within a township in an urban setting. A municipality usually has its own separate government with more powers than a township. People of the township usually elect officials to serve on a board of commissioners or trustees. A **trustee** is a person who is given power to act for others. This board makes rules and regulations for the township. The board may include a tax collector, a clerk, and a justice of the peace.

What are special districts?

Special districts are units of government most often found in rural or suburban areas. These districts—the most common being school districts—perform a function of government. They may provide water, sewage removal, or electric power. Special districts may care for airports, bridges, libraries, and recreational facilities. They may take on issues such as housing, transportation, or soil conservation. Special districts are created to provide a service not handled by other local governments. User fees or federal grants may finance these special districts.

✔ **Checkpoint**   What is the most common type of special district?

Essential Questions Journal   Go to your **Essential Questions Journal** to work on this chapter's Essential Question.

SECTION 1 ASSESSMENT

1. **Guiding Question**   Use your completed chart to answer this question: What are the similarities and differences of local governments, special districts, and tribal governments?

Key Terms and Comprehension
On a sheet of paper, write the answer to each question. Use complete sentences.

2. What is the main purpose of a township?

3. Why do special districts exist?

4. Why are county governments in need of reform?

5. What is a trustee?

Critical Thinking

6. **Identifying Assumptions**   What does having a direct democracy type of government mean about the citizens of the town?

7. **Drawing Inferences**   What are two ways that these local governments might affect your day-to-day life? List and describe at least two examples.

▲ City of Rochester, New York

SECTION 2
Cities and Metropolitan Areas

Guiding Question

How do city governments serve the needs of residents and other Americans? Use an outline to take notes about the ways in which city governments serve citizens.

```
I.  America's Rural-Urban Shift
II. Incorporation and Charters
III. Forms of City Government
    A. Mayor-Council Form
        1. _____
        2. _____
    B. Commission Government
```

Objectives:

- Examine reasons for Americans moving from a rural to urban society.
- Explain the process of incorporation and the function of city charters.
- Understand the major forms of city government.
- Understand the need for city planning and list other municipal functions.
- Outline the challenges that face suburbs and metropolitan areas.

In 1790, most American citizens lived in rural areas on farms or in small towns. Over time, the population began shifting to the urban areas. One reason for this was the invention of the steam engine, steamboat, and locomotive. These inventions allowed raw materials to be sent anywhere. Factories became the new industrial centers, and cities grew around these centers. New farm tools were also invented. Fewer people were needed to work the farms. People moved to the cities to work in the factories. By 1920, more than 50 percent of the people of the United States lived in urban areas. Today, 80 percent of the population lives in cities and surrounding suburbs. City governments must now serve the needs of many people.

What are incorporations and charters?

State governments have authority over cities and other forms of local government. The state establishes a city legally by the process of **incorporation.** The rules for incorporation are in a state's constitution. Usually a state requires that a minimum number of people live in an area wanting to become a city. Cities are created at the request of the citizens, who want the services a city offers.

A city is run by a **charter.** A charter is the city's basic law. It allows the city to manage its own property. The charter also explains the city's form of government and how the city's finances are handled.

✔ **Checkpoint** What is the process of incorporation?

What are the forms of city government?

There are three basic forms of city government. Cities either have a **mayor-council government,** a **commission government,** or a **council-manager government.** The mayor-council is the most common type of city government. The commission and council-manager are further explained in Figure 25.4.

In a mayor-council city government, the chief executive or leader is called a mayor. The voters elect both the mayor and the council. Each member of the council may represent a ward. A ward is a small area or section of the city. In a strong-mayor government, the mayor writes the budget, hires city workers, and can veto laws. In a weak-mayor government, the mayor shares these powers with other officials and the council.

Usually the commission form of city government has no elected mayor. The city is run by a group of commissioners that people elect. Sometimes one commissioner will be chosen by the others to act as mayor. That person runs meetings and represents the commission at important ceremonies. With the commission type of government, each commissioner heads one of the city's departments.

A council-manager city government is also called the city manager plan. It has an elected council that acts as the city's lawmaking body. Under this system, the city is run very much like a business. The council hires a city manager who handles the city's business under the direction of the council. The city manager appoints department heads, who report to him or her. The city manager does not have to run for office. Many people think that this allows the city manager to do the best job possible.

✔**Checkpoint** What are the three basic forms of city government?

What is city planning?

Most cities were originally developed without a definite plan. Buildings, industrial plants, and other public facilities were put anywhere, usually on land that was cheap. Railroad lines and roads were run through crowded residential areas. Today, many cities are trying to correct these early mistakes. They have created planning agencies staffed with experts. The federal government will give grants and loans to cities for improvement projects.

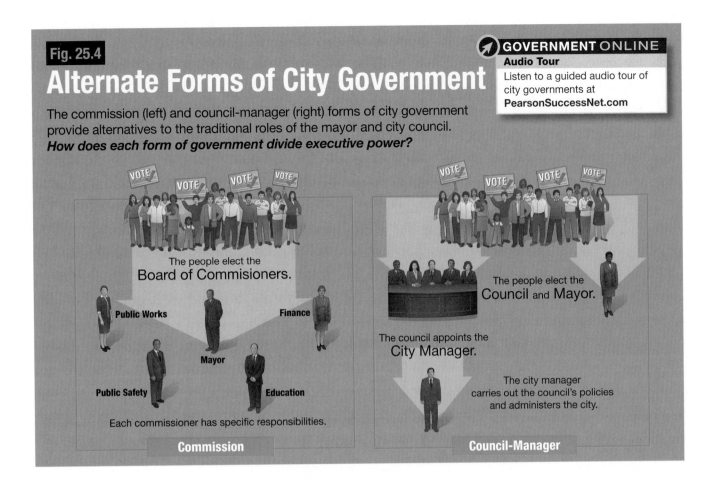

Fig. 25.4

Alternate Forms of City Government

The commission (left) and council-manager (right) forms of city government provide alternatives to the traditional roles of the mayor and city council. *How does each form of government divide executive power?*

The people elect the **Board of Commisioners.**

Public Works

Finance

Mayor

Public Safety

Education

Each commissioner has specific responsibilities.

Commission

The people elect the **Council and Mayor.**

The council appoints the **City Manager.**

The city manager carries out the council's policies and administers the city.

Council-Manager

Zoning
The process of determining where homes and businesses may be built

Zoning is the method a city uses to decide how property is used. Property may be zoned as residential, commercial, or industrial. Residential zones may be set up for single-family homes or multi-family homes. Zoning laws may also contain details about the sizes and heights of buildings, how close they can be to the street, and how far they must be from other buildings.

Some people oppose zoning, citing the 14th Amendment and state constitutions. These documents declare that a person may not be deprived of life, liberty, and property without due process of law.

✓ **Checkpoint** What is zoning?

What are municipal functions?

Cities must provide protection and other services for their residents. Cities maintain police and fire departments, streets, bridges, and all types of recreational facilities. Schools, correctional institutions, sewer facilities, and water treatment plants are concerns of cities. Some large cities operate hospitals, airports, and transportation systems. Cities also must provide sanitation services, water, gas, and electricity. Many other cities maintain public housing, docks, and tourist attractions.

■ ■ ■ ■ ■ ■ ■ ■ ■ ■ ■ ■ ■ ■ ■

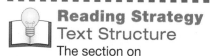

Reading Strategy
Text Structure
The section on
metropolitan areas talks about
a problem and the solution. Ask
yourself: What is the problem?
What is the solution?

What are metropolitan areas?

Cities—and the suburbs around them—are called **metropolitan areas.** After World War II, the movement in metropolitan areas from cities to suburbs began to rise. American families moved to the suburbs to escape crowded, noisy cities. They wanted better living conditions, better schools, lower taxes, and safer neighborhoods. Businesses, shopping centers, and industries also moved away from the cities. Cities were left with a population of elderly and low-income residents who needed many services.

Residents of the suburbs also had many needs. They needed water, sewage removal, electricity, police and fire protection, and other services. One way to meet these growing needs is through annexation by the cities. Annexation happens when suburbs near a city are included in the city's boundaries in order to share services.

Another way to help metropolitan areas meet their needs is to set up special districts called metropolitan districts. They handle several functions, such as waste disposal, for a large area. Another method to help suburbs is to increase the authority of counties. Miami-Dade County, Florida, is doing this successfully. It has a metropolitan government that operates countywide, providing many services. Miami and other cities within this area continue to carry out local functions.

✓ **Checkpoint**   Why did families move from the cities to suburbs? List three reasons.

Government in Your Life

┌ **City Governments Provide Police Protection** ┐

Of all the services provided by city governments, police protection is probably the most important and most expensive. As cities grow in size and population, police departments must expand and improve to meet these new demands.

City police departments, with money from the federal government, are teaching police officers the latest crime fighting and crime prevention methods. Police officers are now being taught how to investigate crimes. This makes cities safer and also reduces the cost of police protection.

Biography

Rudolph "Rudy" Guiliani (1944–)

Rudolph Guiliani was mayor of New York City when the World Trade Center was attacked on September 11, 2001. He became world-famous as "America's Mayor" for his skill in handling the results of this catastrophe. The Queen of England was one of his fans. She awarded him an honorary knighthood.

Guiliani was born in Brooklyn, New York, the son of Italian immigrants. He attended Catholic schools and graduated from Manhattan College in New York. He considered becoming a priest; instead he became a lawyer.

He held state and federal political offices as a Democrat, Independent, and Republican. He served two terms as mayor of New York. He received credit for reducing crime.

In 2008 Guiliani entered the race for President of the United States. He had many supporters. However, when other candidates did better in early primaries, he decided to drop out. He continues his career in law and lecturing.

Essential Questions Journal Go to your **Essential Questions Journal** to work on this chapter's Essential Question.

SECTION 2 ASSESSMENT

Word Bank

charter

commission

council-manager

mayor-council government

1. **Guiding Question** Use your completed outline to answer this question: How do city governments serve the needs of city residents and other Americans?

Key Terms and Comprehension

On a sheet of paper, use the words from the Word Bank to complete each sentence correctly.

2. A _____ government elects both a mayor and a council to represent a ward.

3. In a _____ government, a group of people work together to run the city's government.

4. A _____ government is run very much like a business.

5. A _____ is a city's basic law.

Critical Thinking

6. **Make Comparisons** Why do you think the mayor-council form of city government is a popular form of government?

7. **Compare Points of View** Zoning may be used to keep businesses that are popular with young people away from residential areas. Why do you think this is?

▲ Educational spending includes computers and books.

SECTION 3
Providing Vital Services

Guiding Question

What services do state and local governments provide?
Use a concept web similar to the one below to record information about state and local government services.

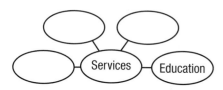

Objectives:

- Explain why state governments have a major role in providing important services.
- Identify the services that state and local governments provide.
- Analyze why the amount and types of services offered to citizens is different from state to state.

State and local governments provide many services citizens need. Each state is different in the amount and quality of services it provides. Most states provide services in the areas of education, public safety, welfare, roads, and public health.

What is the state government's role?

The Constitution gives the states all powers not given to the federal government. The states, like the federal government, try to follow the ideals of the Preamble: follow the law, keep peace, defend the country, and promote the general welfare of the citizens. To do all these things, the states need to spend money. See Figure 25.5.

✔ **Checkpoint** What services do most states provide?

What are state and local services?

States provide services either through state agencies and programs or through local governments in the state. These services fall into the following four categories.

Education

This is one of the most important state services. It is also the most expensive. Primary and secondary schools are taken care of by local governments and financed by taxes. The states help with funding. They also set guidelines for teacher qualifications, determine the length of the school year, and decide what is taught. Many states also have a statewide testing program.

Fig. 25.5 How Government Works

State and Local Spending

Public schools account for nearly three in ten dollars spent by state and local governments. *Why do you think state and local governments spend so much on education?*

29% Other

29% Education

6% Transportation

7% Health care

7% Utilities

7% Public safety

15% Public welfare

6% TRANSPORTATION needs drive governments to build and maintain roads, bridges, and trains.

7% HEALTH CARE spending includes Medicaid for low-income Americans.

7% PUBLIC SAFETY expenditures protect people from fires and crime.

GOVERNMENT ONLINE
Online Update
For current information on state and local spending, visit **PearsonSuccessNet.com**

Reading Strategy
Text Structure
Study Figure 25.5. How does it help you determine how state and local governments spend money?

Medicaid
A program managed by the state to provide to provide medical insurance to low-income families

Welfare
Cash assistance to the poor

Entitlement
A benefit that federal law says must be paid to all those who meet the eligibility requirements

At the college and university levels, states play an important role. Every state has a public higher education system. State colleges are less expensive than private colleges because states pay part of the cost. States also have a system of two-year community colleges.

Public Welfare
Public welfare includes such services as hospitals and direct care to citizens. Next to education, public welfare is the most expensive service for state and local governments. States manage **Medicaid** programs for low-income families. **Welfare,** which is cash assistance, is given to the poor. The government has used several programs for the benefit of some of its citizens. The first was Aid to Families with Dependent Children (AFDC). AFDC was an **entitlement** program. An entitlement program means that anyone that meets the requirements is entitled to the benefits. The AFDC program was replaced in 1996 by Temporary Assistance to Needy Families (TANF). This program limits people getting assistance to a total of five years of help in their lifetime. People getting this assistance also must work or participate in work training.

The number of people on welfare has been declining since the TANF program was started. There are also other welfare services managed by the states. These services include inspections of workplaces to keep workers safe and licensing of healthcare workers.

Public Safety

Every state has a number of police forces, which include well-trained state police. The state police monitor the roadways, investigate crimes, and train local law enforcement agents. Each state has its own corrections system for criminals. These prisons and other facilities are currently overcrowded with little room for more prisoners. Prisons are very expensive for the states. Some prisoners are now held in facilities that are privately owned and run.

Highways

Building roads and highways is very expensive for the states. The federal government helps the states build and maintain an interstate highway system, which began construction in 1956 and is almost finished. The federal government has paid about 90 percent of the cost. Many more roads are built with state funds. The state must keep these roadways in good condition. The state also sets speed limits, issues drivers' licenses, and conducts vehicle safety inspections.

Other services that are carried out by the states include managing parks and recreation, regulating businesses, and protecting consumers.

✔ **Checkpoint** What are two programs that help low-income families?

Essential Questions Journal Go to your **Essential Questions Journal** to work on this chapter's Essential Question.

SECTION 3 ASSESSMENT

1. **Guiding Question** Use your completed concept web to answer this question: What services do state and local governments provide?

Key Terms and Comprehension

On a sheet of paper, write the answer to each question. Use complete sentences.

2. What are the two largest spending categories in state and local budgets?

3. How was the AFDC program different from the TANF program?

4. What is welfare?

5. What are two services that state and local governments provide to keep the roads safer?

Critical Thinking

6. **Draw Conclusions** Why do you think the amount of services each state provides is different?

7. **Analyze Information** Which service provided by state and local governments is the most important? Why do you think so?

ISSUES OF OUR TIME

State Government Revenue and Spending

▶▶ Track the Issue

The United States was founded, in part, on opposition to taxation without representation. As unpopular as taxes are, governments have found many ways to raise money.

1646 The Massachusetts Bay Colony establishes the first property tax in the colonies.

1765 Prompted by the Stamp Act, the colonists declare "taxation without representation" to be illegal.

1862 The federal government provides for a temporary income tax to fund the Civil War.

1911 Wisconsin establishes the first state income tax.

1964 New Hampshire institutes the first modern-day state lottery to pay for programs.

1970s Voters in several states rebel against rising property taxes with laws limiting tax increases.

Governor Arnold Schwarzenegger (R., California).

▶▶ Perspectives

Many Americans complain that the government takes too much money out of their pockets in taxes. However, limits on taxes have contributed to deficit spending or cuts in services. What issues need to be considered when trying to balance budgets?

Raise Taxes	Cut Taxes
With California facing a possible $14 billion budget deficit, it is not surprising that legislators and the governor are considering tax increases. . . . The potential economic harm and unpopularity of tax increases should put spending increases on the back burner. . . . After all, it is spending increases, not tax breaks, that got the state in a financial mess. State taxes take a larger share of personal income than ever before.	[The governor's] budget all but ignores options for increasing revenues. . . . legislative leaders should adjourn and lock the doors for two weeks. That way, GOP lawmakers could go back to their districts and explain to voters why closing parks and plundering schools is preferable to closing tax loopholes. . . . Farsighted Republicans could agree to a one-year hike in taxes as part of a universal deal for long-term reform.
— Editorial, *Oakland Tribune*, January 2008	— Editorial, *Sacramento Bee*, January 2008

Connect to Your World

1. **Understand (a)** Why do you think taxes have increased in number and percentage since independence? **(b)** What is the central conflict between taxation and government services?

2. **Compare and Contrast (a)** How does the editor of the *Oakland Tribune* suggest that California balance its budget? **(b)** How does the editor of the *Sacramento Bee* think that goal should be accomplished? **(c)** With which viewpoint do you agree? Why?

⊙ GOVERNMENT ONLINE
In the News
To find out about how state budgets affects you, visit
PearsonSuccessNet.com

SECTION 4

Financing State and Local Government

▲ Sales taxes provide revenue (money) for state and local governments.

Guiding Question

How do state governments raise money to pay for services? Use a chart similar to the one below to record information about the sources of state revenue.

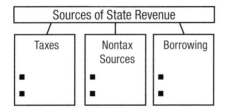

Sources of State Revenue

Taxes	Nontax Sources	Borrowing
▪	▪	▪
▪	▪	▪

Objectives:

- Describe the major federal and state limits on raising revenue.
- List the four principles of sound taxation.
- Identify major sources of state and local revenue.
- Explain the state budget process.

State and local governments need billions of dollars each year to operate. In total, state and local governments spend over $2 trillion per year. Most of this money comes from taxes. Some of the money comes from the federal government. In this section, you will learn more about how state and local governments pay for their services.

What are the limits on raising revenue?

The federal Constitution places some limits on the ability of state and local government to tax. According to the Constitution, there are three limits:

(1) States may not tax interstate or foreign commerce. Only Congress may do this.

(2) States may not tax the federal government or its agencies.

(3) States may only collect taxes that are fair, do not take property, and are only collected for public purposes.

Another federal limit comes from the Equal Protection Clause. It prevents unreasonable taxes based on race, religion, nationality, or political party membership.

State constitutions also limit the taxing power of state and local governments. State codes set maximum rates for sales and property taxes. Nonprofit groups are often exempt from taxes.

✔ **Checkpoint** What are the three limits placed on state and local governments?

What are the principles of sound taxation?

Adam Smith was a Scottish economist. In 1776, he wrote the book *The Wealth of Nations* in which he stated his four principles of **sound taxation.** His idea was that the tax burden should be spread fairly among the taxed. The principles are still respected by tax experts today. Here are Smith's four principles:

(1) All citizens should support the government according to their abilities and incomes.

(2) There should be a definite, fixed tax on revenue asked of each contributor.

(3) Taxes should be simple and easy to pay.

(4) No tax should be planned that would take more money from the taxpayer than is given to the public treasury.

✔ **Checkpoint** What are the four principles of sound taxation?

■ ■ ■ ■ ■ ■ ■ ■ ■ ■ ■ ■ ■ ■ ■ ■ ■

Reading Strategy
Text Structure
The section headings are written as questions. After you read each section, try to answer the question asked in the heading.

■ ■ ■ ■ ■ ■ ■ ■ ■ ■ ■ ■ ■ ■ ■ ■ ■

Sound taxation
Taxation that spreads the tax burden fairly among the taxed

Sales tax
A tax placed on the sale of various goods, paid by the purchaser

Regressive tax
A flat tax that is not based on the person's income or ability to pay

What are the sources of revenue?

The state legislature decides what taxes the state and its local governments will collect. The following are all the ways that states and local governments can raise revenue.

What is a sales tax?

About one third of the income to the states is sales tax. A **sales tax** is a tax paid when various goods or services are bought. It is paid by the purchaser. Sales taxes are either general or selective. A general sales tax is a tax on most items that are sold. A selective tax is a tax on only certain items. The general sales tax is used in 45 states. Items such as food, medicines, and newspapers are often not taxed. Some cities and counties also collect sales taxes, which are gathered along with the state tax. All states collect a selective sales tax on gasoline, alcoholic beverages, cigarettes, and insurance policies. Sales tax is easy to collect and a sure way for the state to get income. It is also a **regressive tax.** A regressive tax is not collected according to a person's income or ability to pay.

In recent years, Internet sales have increased. States are not allowed to tax most Internet purchases, because companies cannot tax items shipped to another state unless the company is also located in that state. See Figure 25.6 on page 650. The Supreme Court has upheld this many times. Congress may change the rule about Internet sales in the future, based on the commerce power given by the United States Constitution.

■ ■ ■ ■ ■ ■ ■ ■ ■ ■ ■ ■ ■ ■ ■ ■ ■

Reading Strategy
Text Structure
Use a graphic organizer to keep track of the different types of taxes in this section. The red headings in the text can help you to organize the information on taxes.

■ ■ ■ ■ ■ ■ ■ ■ ■ ■ ■ ■ ■ ■ ■ ■ ■

Income tax
A tax collected on the income of corporations and individuals

Progressive tax
A type of tax that is determined by the person's income

Property tax
A tax collected on real and personal property

What is an income tax?

About one third of the income to the states is income taxes. An **income tax** is a tax collected on the income of corporations and individuals. The individual income tax is a **progressive tax.** The higher a person's income, the more tax he or she pays. The rate of this tax is different in each state. Some states have no income tax. The rate can be 1 or 2 percent or be as high as 9 percent on the highest incomes. Taxpayers can usually get exemptions and deductions that may reduce the amount of tax they must pay. Corporate income taxes are usually set at a fixed rate, except in a few states that have a progressive corporate tax.

✓**Checkpoint**   What is the difference between a regressive tax and a progressive tax?

What is property tax?

About three fourths of the income to local governments is property tax. **Property tax** is a tax collected on real property or personal property. Real property includes land and buildings. Personal property includes such things as computers, cars, stocks and bonds, mortgages, or bank accounts. The property to be taxed is assessed before being taxed. This assessment sets the value of the property. Personal property is usually assessed yearly. Real property, for example homes, is usually assessed at least every four years. It is very difficult for local governments to be fair and equal when assessing property.

Fig. 25.6

▲ **Analyzing Political Cartoons** Study this cartoon about a man making a purchase over the Internet with his PDA. **What does this cartoon suggest about the sales tax as a state, not federal, source of revenue?**

What is inheritance or estate tax?

Every state has an **inheritance tax** or an **estate tax.** These taxes are sometimes called a "death tax." These taxes are paid by the person that is benefiting from the inheritance or estate. The inheritance tax is collected on a person's share of an estate. The estate tax is collected on the full estate.

What is business tax?

Business tax is an important source of income for most states. A number of states charge taxes on the removal of natural resources such as timber, oil, or fish. All states have license taxes. Certain businesses, for example, chain stores, taverns, and transportation companies, must have an operating license. In most states certain professionals need a license. These include doctors, lawyers, and barbers.

Many states collect document and stock transfer taxes on the recording and transferring of such things as mortgages and deeds. Some states collect capital stock taxes. These are paid by businesses on the stocks they issue.

State and local governments also collect payroll taxes. This money is held in trust funds for welfare programs. More than half of the states collect amusement taxes. All states collect license taxes for motor vehicles, hunting, fishing, and marriages.

What are other sources of income?

State and local governments receive over $1 trillion each year from the federal government. States, and the local governments within the states, also operate businesses. For example, many eastern states have toll roads. North Dakota sells flour. California operates a railroad line in San Francisco. Many cities operate their own water, electric, and bus systems. Some cities have farmers' markets and operate dams and docks. Sale of public land and fines collected in court are other nontax sources of income for local governments. See Figure 25.7 on page 652.

Many states, the District of Columbia, the U.S. Virgin Islands, and Puerto Rico run lotteries. These lotteries bring in over $17 billion a year. State and local government sometimes issue tax-free bonds to raise money. This money is often needed to complete large projects, such as bridges, highways, or public buildings. The amount of money that can be borrowed by the state is usually set by the state's constitution.

✔**Checkpoint**   What are two additional sources of income for states?

Inheritance tax
A tax collected on the beneficiary's share of an estate

Estate tax
A tax imposed on the assets of one who dies

Business tax
An additional tax collected on businesses for various services

What are state budgets?

A state **budget** is a financial plan for the spending of public money. It is also a statement of public policy. In the budget, the state lists how much money each agency will receive. In the early days, state agencies would appear before the legislature and request funds. Often the agencies had to compete for the money they needed. Politics played a part. Today, most states use an executive budget. This allows the governor to prepare the budget. The governor makes sure the agencies receive what they need. This budget process is similar to the one used by the federal government.

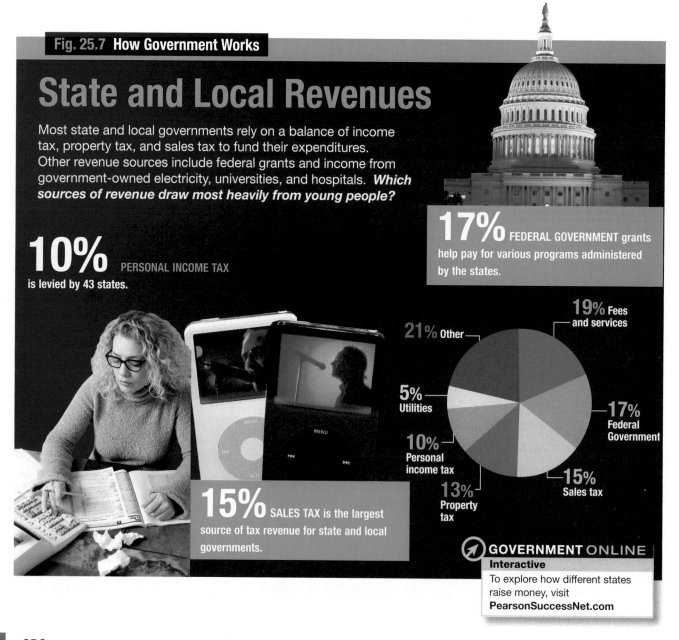

Fig. 25.7 How Government Works

State and Local Revenues

Most state and local governments rely on a balance of income tax, property tax, and sales tax to fund their expenditures. Other revenue sources include federal grants and income from government-owned electricity, universities, and hospitals. *Which sources of revenue draw most heavily from young people?*

10% PERSONAL INCOME TAX is levied by 43 states.

17% FEDERAL GOVERNMENT grants help pay for various programs administered by the states.

15% SALES TAX is the largest source of tax revenue for state and local governments.

21% Other
19% Fees and services
5% Utilities
17% Federal Government
10% Personal income tax
15% Sales tax
13% Property tax

GOVERNMENT ONLINE
Interactive
To explore how different states raise money, visit
PearsonSuccessNet.com

The following are the six main steps in the budget process.

(1) Each agency requests the money it needs for the upcoming year.

(2) Requests are studied by the budget agency.

(3) Revisions are made and put in a budget. This is given to the governor, who presents it to the legislature.

(4) The budget is worked on by the legislature, revised, and then passed.

(5) The governor supervises the spending of the money approved by the legislature.

(6) The budget is checked at the end of the fiscal year.

✔ **Checkpoint** How is a state's budget process similar to that of the federal government?

Essential Questions Journal Go to your **Essential Questions Journal** to work on this chapter's Essential Question.

SECTION 4 ASSESSMENT

Word Bank

budget

federal Constitution

sound taxation

state legislature

Quick Write

In your own words, describe each type of tax that is discussed in this section. Write an example of when each tax is used. For example, a sales tax is used when you buy a candy bar or a video game.

1. **Guiding Question** Use your completed chart to answer this question: How do state governments raise money to pay for services?

Key Terms and Comprehension

On a sheet of paper, use the words from the Word Bank to complete each sentence correctly.

2. A definite, fixed tax on revenue asked of each contributor is an example of _____.

3. The _____ places some limits on the ability of state and local government to tax.

4. A _____ is a financial plan for spending money.

5. The _____ decides what taxes the state and its local governments will collect.

Critical Thinking

6. **Determining Relevance** What are Adam Smith's four principles of sound taxation? What do you think makes each principle important?

7. **Identifying Alternatives** What might be the advantages and disadvantages of raising money by using a lottery? Explain your answer.

Chapter Summary

Section 1—Counties, Towns, and Townships

- County government usually serves several towns or cities. In each county, a city or town serves as the county seat.

- A group of elected officials usually runs the county government.

- Counties control state and county laws, take care of roads, schools, and public works, and supply licenses.

- Special districts perform one or more related governmental functions usually in rural or suburban areas.

Section 2—Cities and Metropolitan Areas

- Over time, the American population has shifted from rural areas to urban areas.

- Incorporation is the process by which a state establishes a city as a legal body; a charter is a city's basic law.

- The three basic forms of city government are mayor-council, commission, and council-manager.

- Many cities create planning agencies staffed with experts to decide how property is used.

Section 3—Providing Vital Services

- The state government has an interest in following the law, keeping peace, defending the country, and promoting the general welfare of its citizens.

- States provide many services. These services fall into four categories: education, public welfare, public safety, and highways.

Section 4—Financing State and Local Government

- The Federal Constitution places three limits on the state's ability to tax.

- Adam Smith's book, *The Wealth of Nations,* stated four principles for sound taxation that are still used today.

- The most common ways that states and local governments can raise revenue are sales tax, income tax, and property tax, inheritance tax, estate tax, and business tax.

- A state budget is a financial plan for spending of public money.

Guiding Question
Section 2 How do city governments serve the needs of residents and other Americans?

Guiding Question
Section 3 What services do state and local governments provide?

Guiding Question
Section 1 What are the similarities and differences of local governments, special districts, and tribal governments?

Guiding Question
Section 4 How do state governments raise money to pay for services?

CHAPTER 25

Essential Question
How local should government be?

Document-Based Assessment

What Is City Government?

"Phoenix Is Your City" is a Web site that was developed as a resource for teaching about Phoenix city government. This material can be used to show how any city government affects our lives. The following are excerpts from the part of this program entitled "What Is City Government and What Can It Do?":

Document at a Glance
- Web site about Phoenix city government
- Tells how government affects our lives

. . . Before you know what city government is, you need to know what it is not . . . The government for the whole country is called the federal government . . . [which] provides some services directly to the people, but more often it makes decisions.

Each state has powers to create its own programs to serve its citizens . . . the programs and services may vary from one state to the other. Each state has its own government, too.

. . . One of the jobs of county government is to work with cities located near one another and provide services that affect more than one city. County government also provides services to people who live in areas that are not within any particular city.

. . . City government is the smallest, most local form of government. Cities have boundaries or city limits. States give cities the right to form governments to meet the needs of their citizens and to make laws for the people who live there. A city can form a government according to directions provided by the state—that's called "general law." Or a city can form a government of its own design—that's called "home rule." City government has the power to make laws on any issues not already decided by the state or federal government and has the power to fund and provide any services to the citizens living within its boundaries. However, local laws can't break state or federal laws.

Document-Based Questions

1. For what purpose was the "Phoenix Is Your City" program developed?

2. What are some services provided by city government?

3. What does the federal government most often do besides providing some services directly to the people?

4. Where does a city's right to form a government come from?

5. What term is used when a city forms a government according to directions provided by the state? According to own design?

Source: Phoenix Youth and Education Programs Office; phoenix.gov/EDUCATN/whatcity.html

Chapter Assessment

GOVERNMENT ONLINE
Self-Test
To test your understanding of
key terms and main ideas, visit
PearsonSuccessNet.com

Directions: Choose the letter of the best answer
or write the answer using complete sentences.

Section 1—Counties, Towns, and Townships

1. How are counties different from townships?

2. How are tribal governments similar to the federal
government?

3. What is the purpose of a New England town meeting?

4. Critical Thinking How could you make sure that a trustee for
your county is acting on behalf of the citizens?

Section 2—Cities and Metropolitan Areas

5. Why did Americans start moving from rural areas to urban
areas after 1790?

6. A new development of homes being built would be an
example of what type of zoning?

7. What might large city governments provide that smaller city
governments do not?

8. What do mayors do?

9. Critical Thinking Why might citizens want their city
incorporated?

Section 3—Providing Vital Services

10. How do states try to ensure the public safety of their citizens?

11. Providing medical service to low-income families is an
example of which program?

12. Why is a state college less expensive than a private college?

13. Critical Thinking Why might states limit assistance to needy
families to only a certain number of years?

Section 4—Financing State and Local Government

14. What is the Equal Protection Clause and how does it affect taxes?

15. What is a progressive tax?

16. Why do most states now use an executive budget?

17. Critical Thinking Why might states prefer other sources of income instead of money raised by taxes?

Apply What You've Learned

Exploring the Essential Question

18. What do you think life would be like if there were no state governments, but only government at a federal level?

19. Do you think that national government could provide services as well as your local government? Why or why not?

Essential Question Project

20. Prepare an election brochure that answers the Essential Question: **How local should government be?** Use the content of the chapter and your answers to the questions above to help you. Create a brochure for a fictional candidate for local office. Include the responsibilities of the job and explain how the candidate will solve key issues.

> **Essential Questions**
> **Journal**
>
> Go to your **Essential Questions Journal** to work on this chapter's Essential Question.

Test-Taking Tip

When you review your notes to prepare for an exam, use a marker to highlight key words and examples.

Essential Question

What is the right balance of local, state, and federal government?

The U.S. federal system divides power among multiple levels of government. Elected officials at each level have sought more power and authority for their governments—or to spread responsibilities to others.

ON THE ROLE OF THE FEDERAL GOVERNMENT:

"It is my intention to curb the size and influence of the federal establishment and to demand recognition of the distinction between the powers granted to the federal government and those reserved to the states or to the people. All of us need to be reminded that the federal government did not create the states; the states created the federal government.

—Ronald Reagan, First Inaugural Speech, 1981

ON THE KEY ISSUES FACING THE STATES:

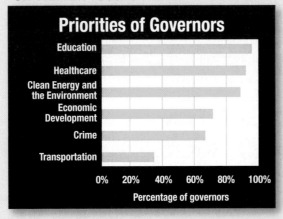

Priorities of Governors

- Education
- Healthcare
- Clean Energy and the Environment
- Economic Development
- Crime
- Transportation

0% 20% 40% 60% 80% 100%

Percentage of governors

Each year, the National Association of Governors tracks the governors' State of the State addresses and identifies the subjects mentioned by the most governors.

ON THE VALUE OF MAYORS:

"As CEOs of the nation's cities, mayors know all too well the challenges American families face daily, so we are in the best position to offer solutions to local problems.

—Mayor Douglas Palmer, Trenton, New Jersey

Essential Question Warmup

Throughout this unit, you studied the roles, responsibilities, and powers of state and local government. Use what you have learned and the quotations, data, and opinions above to answer the following questions. Then go to your **Essential Questions Journal.**

1. Which issues are best handled at the local, state, and federal levels, respectively?

2. How do taxes, spending, and various programs link different levels of government?

3. Is any level of government more responsive and democratic than others?

4. What are the advantages and disadvantages of centralizing power?

Essential Questions Journal

To continue to build a response to the unit Essential Question, go to your **Essential Questions Journal.**

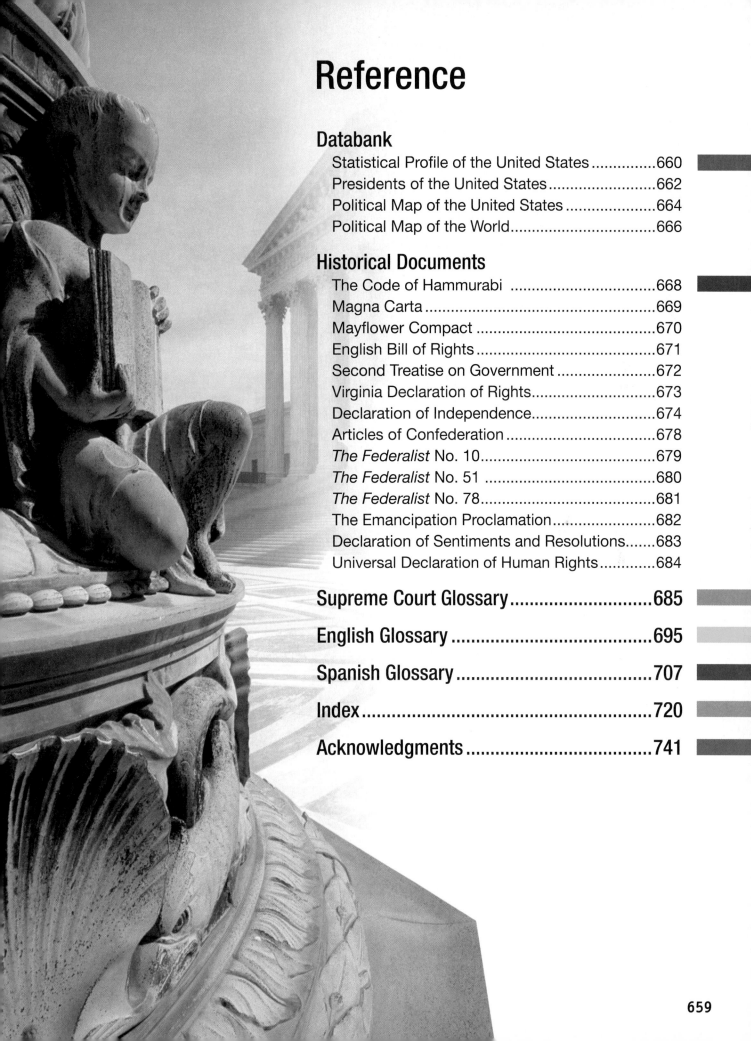

Reference

A Statistical Profile of the United States

| State | Capital | Population (in thousands) | | | | | Land Area in Sq. Mi. | Population per Sq. Mi |
		Year 2000	% Urban	African American	Hispanic Origin	% Foriegn Born		
United States	Washington, D.C.	281,422	80.1	34,862	31,337	7.9	3,536,278	79.6
Alabama	Montgomery	4,447	70.1	1,139	45	1.1	50,750	87.6
Alaska	Juneau	627	41.5	24	25	4.5	570,374	1.1
Arizona	Phoenix	5,131	87.8	176	1,084	7.6	113,642	45.2
Arkansas	Little Rock	2,673	48.6	411	54	1.1	52,075	51.3
California	Sacramento	33,872	96.7	2,487	10,460	21.7	155,973	217.2
Colorado	Denver	4,301	84.0	176	604	4.3	103,729	41.5
Connecticut	Hartford	3,406	95.6	309	279	8.5	4,845	703.0
Delaware	Dover	784	81.6	149	28	3.3	1,955	401.0
Florida	Tallahassee	15,982	93.0	2,333	2,334	12.9	53,937	296.3
Georgia	Atlanta	8,186	68.9	2,236	240	2.7	57,919	141.3
Hawaii	Honolulu	1,212	73.1	34	95	14.7	6,423	188.7
Idaho	Boise	1,294	38.3	8	93	2.9	82,751	15.6
Illinois	Springfield	12,419	84.5	1,854	1,276	8.3	55,593	223.4
Indiana	Indianapolis	6,080	71.7	498	154	1.7	35,870	169.5
Iowa	Des Moines	2,926	44.6	58	62	1.6	55,875	52.4
Kansas	Topeka	2,688	56.4	157	148	2.5	81,823	32.9
Kentucky	Frankfort	4,042	48.3	288	35	0.9	39,732	101.7
Louisiana	Baton Rouge	4,469	75.2	1,415	119	2.1	43,566	102.6
Maine	Augusta	1,275	35.8	6	9	3.0	30,865	41.3
Maryland	Annapolis	5,296	92.7	1,454	199	6.6	9,775	541.8
Massachusetts	Boston	6,349	96.1	405	391	9.5	7,838	810.0
Michigan	Lansing	9,938	82.6	1,415	276	3.8	56,809	174.9
Minnesota	St. Paul	4,919	70.1	149	93	2.6	79,617	61.8
Mississippi	Jackson	2,845	35.9	1,010	24	0.8	46,914	60.6
Missouri	Jefferson City	5,595	68.0	617	91	1.6	68,898	81.2

State	Capital	Population (in thousands)					Land Area in Sq. Mi.	Population per Sq. Mi
		Year 2000	% Urban	African American	Hispanic Origin	% Foriegn Born		
Montana	Helena	902	33.4	3	16	1.7	145,556	6.2
Nebraska	Lincoln	1,711	51.8	68	77	1.8	76,878	22.3
Nevada	Carson City	1,998	86.1	140	304	8.7	109,806	18.2
New Hampshire	Concord	1,236	60.2	9	20	3.7	8,969	137.8
New Jersey	Trenton	8,414	100.0	1,197	1,027	12.5	7,419	1,134.1
New Mexico	Santa Fe	1,819	57.0	46	708	5.3	121,364	15.0
New York	Albany	18,976	91.9	3,222	2,661	15.9	47,224	401.8
North Carolina	Raleigh	8,049	67.1	1,686	176	1.7	48,718	165.2
North Dakota	Bismarck	642	43.1	4	7	1.5	68,994	9.3
Ohio	Columbus	11,353	81.0	1,304	185	2.4	40,953	277.2
Oklahoma	Oklahoma City	3,451	60.5	262	137	2.1	68,679	50.2
Oregon	Salem	3,421	72.7	62	213	4.9	96,002	35.6
Pennsylvania	Harrisburg	12,281	84.5	1,170	326	3.1	44,820	274.0
Rhode Island	Providence	1,048	93.8	50	69	9.5	1,045	1,002.9
South Carolina	Columbia	4,012	70.0	1,157	54	1.4	30,111	133.2
South Dakota	Pierre	755	34.0	5	9	1.1	75,896	9.9
Tennessee	Nashville	5,689	67.8	913	67	1.2	41,219	138.0
Texas	Austin	20,852	84.5	2,470	6,045	9.0	261,914	79.6
Utah	Salt Lake City	2,233	76.7	19	151	3.4	82,168	27.2
Vermont	Montpelier	609	27.9	3	5	3.1	9,249	65.8
Virginia	Richmond	7,079	78.1	1,385	266	5.0	39,598	178.8
Washington	Olympia	5,894	82.9	204	377	6.6	66,581	88.5
West Virgina	Charleston	1,808	41.9	56	10	0.9	4,087	75.1
Wisconsin	Madison	5,364	67.8	293	140	2.5	54,314	98.8
Wyoming	Cheyenne	494	29.6	4	29	1.7	97,105	5.1
Washington, D.C.		572	100.0	319	38	9.7	61	9,377.0

George Washington Zachary Taylor Abraham Lincoln Ulysses S. Grant Chester A. Arthur

Presidents of the United States

Name	Party	State [a]	Entered Office	Age On Taking Office	Vice President(s)
George Washington (1732–1799)	Federalist	Virginia	1789	57	John Adams
John Adams (1735–1826)	Federalist	Massachusetts	1797	61	Thomas Jefferson
Thomas Jefferson (1743–1826)	Dem-Rep	Virginia	1801	57	Aaron Burr/George Clinton
James Madison (1751–1836)	Dem-Rep	Virginia	1809	57	George Clinton/Elbridge Gerry
James Monroe (1758–1831)	Dem-Rep	Virginia	1817	58	Daniel D. Tompkins
John Q. Adams (1767–1848)	Dem-Rep	Massachusetts	1825	57	John C. Calhoun
Andrew Jackson (1767–1845)	Democrat	Tennessee (SC)	1829	61	John C. Calhoun/Martin Van Buren
Martin Van Buren (1782–1862)	Democrat	New York	1837	54	Richard M. Johnson
William H. Harrison (1773–1841)	Whig	Ohio (VA)	1841	68	John Tyler
John Tyler (1790–1862)	Democrat	Virginia	1841	51	none
James K. Polk (1795–1849)	Democrat	Tennessee (NC)	1845	49	George M. Dallas
Zachary Taylor (1784–1850)	Whig	Louisiana (VA)	1849	64	Millard Fillmore
Millard Fillmore (1800–1874)	Whig	New York	1850	50	none
Franklin Pierce (1804–1869)	Democrat	New Hampshire	1853	48	William R. King
James Buchanan (1791–1868)	Democrat	Pennsylvania	1857	65	John C. Breckinridge
Abraham Lincoln (1809–1865)	Republican	Illinois (KY)	1861	52	Hannibal Hamlin/Andrew Johnson
Andrew Johnson (1808–1875)	Democrat	Tennessee (NC)	1865	56	none
Ulysses S. Grant (1822–1885)	Republican	Illinois (OH)	1869	46	Schuyler Colfax/Henry Wilson
Rutherford B. Hayes (1822–1893)	Republican	Ohio	1877	54	William A. Wheeler
James A. Garfield (1831–1881)	Republican	Ohio	1881	49	Chester A. Arthur
Chester A. Arthur (1829–1896)	Republican	New York (VT)	1881	51	none
Grover Cleveland (1837–1908)	Democrat	New York (NJ)	1885	47	Thomas A. Hendricks
Benjamin Harrison (1833–1901)	Republican	Indiana (OH)	1889	55	Levi P. Morton
Grover Cleveland (1837–1908)	Democrat	New York (NJ)	1893	55	Adlai E. Stevenson

William Howard Taft Harry S Truman Lyndon B. Johnson Ronald Reagan Barack Obama

Name	Party	State [a]	Entered Office	Age On Taking Office	Vice President(s)
William McKinley (1843–1901)	Republican	Ohio	1897	54	Garret A. Hobart/ Theodore Roosevelt
Theodore Roosevelt (1858–1919)	Republican	New York	1901	42	Charles W. Fairbanks
William H. Taft (1857–1930)	Republican	Ohio	1909	51	James S. Sherman
Woodrow Wilson (1856–1924)	Democrat	New Jersey (VA)	1913	56	Thomas R. Marshall
Warren G. Harding (1865–1923)	Republican	Ohio	1921	55	Calvin Coolidge
Calvin Coolidge (1872–1933)	Republican	Massachusetts (VT)	1923	51	Charles G. Dawes
Herbert Hoover (1874–1964)	Republican	California (IA)	1929	54	Charles Curtis
Franklin Roosevelt (1882–1945)	Democrat	New York	1933	51	John N. Garner/ Henry A. Wallace/Harry S Truman
Harry S Truman (1884–1972)	Democrat	Missouri	1945	60	Alben W. Barkley
Dwight D. Eisenhower (1890–1969)	Republican	New York (TX)	1953	62	Richard M. Nixon
John F. Kennedy (1917–1963)	Democrat	Massachusetts	1961	43	Lyndon B. Johnson
Lyndon B. Johnson (1908–1973)	Democrat	Texas	1963	55	Hubert H. Humphrey
Richard M. Nixon (1913–1994)	Republican	New York (CA)	1969	56	Spiro T. Agnew [d]/Gerald R. Ford [e]
Gerald R. Ford (1913– 2006)	Republican	Michigan (NE)	1974	61	Nelson A. Rockefeller [f]
James E. Carter (1924–)	Democrat	Georgia	1977	52	Walter F. Mondale
Ronald W. Reagan (1911–2004)	Republican	California (IL)	1981	69	George H. W. Bush
George H.W. Bush (1924–)	Republican	Texas (MA)	1989	64	J. Danforth Quayle
William J. Clinton (1946–)	Democrat	Arkansas	1993	46	Albert Gore, Jr.
George W. Bush (1946–)	Republican	Texas	2001	54	Richard B. Cheney
Barack Obama (1961–)	Democrat	Illinois (Hawaii)	2009	47	Joseph R. Biden

[a] State of residence when elected; if born in another State, that State in parentheses.
[b] Democratic-Republican
[c] Johnson, a War Democrat, was elected Vice-President on the coalition Union Party ticket.
[d] Resigned October 10, 1973.

[e] Nominated by Nixon, confirmed by Congress on December 6, 1973.
[f] Nominated by Ford, confirmed by Congress on December 19, 1974.

Political Map of the United States

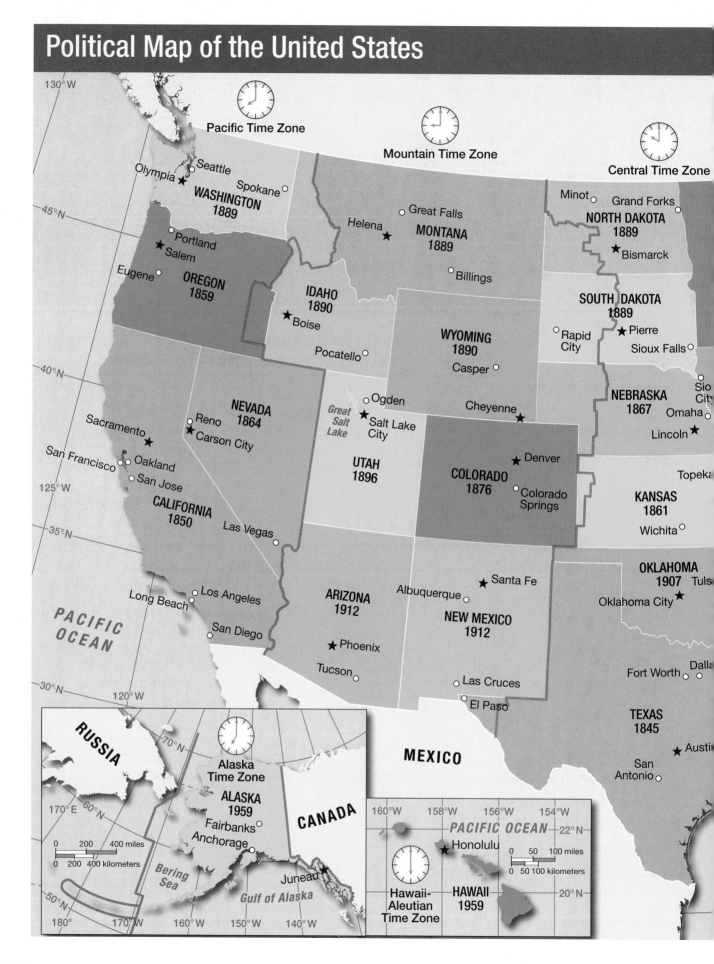

Pacific Time Zone

Mountain Time Zone

Central Time Zone

130° W

Olympia ★ · Seattle
· Spokane ○
WASHINGTON
1889

45° N

· Portland
★ Salem
OREGON
1859
Eugene ○

Great Falls ○
Helena
★ MONTANA
1889

· Billings ○

Minot ○ · Grand Forks ○
NORTH DAKOTA
1889
★ Bismarck

IDAHO
1890
★ Boise
Pocatello ○

WYOMING
1890
Casper ○

SOUTH DAKOTA
1889
Rapid ○ ★ Pierre
City
Sioux Falls ○

40° N

Sacramento ★
San Francisco ○ · Oakland ○
· San Jose ○
125° W

NEVADA
1864
Reno ○
★ Carson City

Great
Salt
Lake
★ Ogden ○
★ Salt Lake
City
UTAH
1896

Cheyenne ★

NEBRASKA
1867
Sio
Cit
Omaha ○

Lincoln ★

35° N

CALIFORNIA
1850
Las Vegas ○

★ Denver
COLORADO
1876
○ Colorado
Springs

Topeka

KANSAS
1861
Wichita ○

PACIFIC
OCEAN

Long Beach ○ · Los Angeles ○
· San Diego ○

ARIZONA
1912

Albuquerque ○
★ Santa Fe

NEW MEXICO
1912

OKLAHOMA
1907 Tuls

Oklahoma City ★

30° N

120° W

★ Phoenix
Tucson ○

Las Cruces ○
El Paso ○

Fort Worth ○ Dalla ○

TEXAS
1845

MEXICO

RUSSIA

70° N

Alaska
Time Zone
ALASKA
1959
Fairbanks ○
Anchorage ·

CANADA

160° W   158° W   156° W   154° W

PACIFIC OCEAN 22° N
Honolulu ★

Austi ★

San
Antonio ○

170° E
60° N
60° N

0   200   400 miles
0   200   400 kilometers

Bering
Sea

0   50   100 miles
0   50 100 kilometers

HAWAII
1959

20° N

50° N

180°   170° W   160° W   150° W   140° W

Juneau ★
Gulf of Alaska

Hawaii-
Aleutian
Time Zone

DATABANK: Political Map of the United States

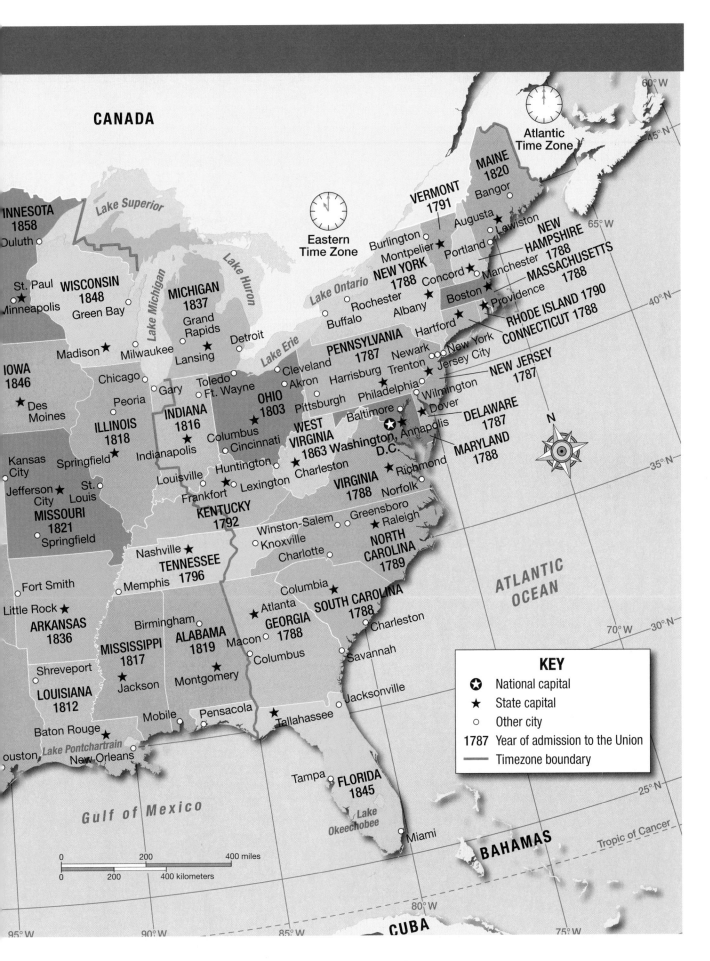

CANADA

Lake Superior

Atlantic
Time Zone

Eastern
Time Zone

MINNESOTA 1858
Duluth

WISCONSIN 1848
St. Paul ★
Minneapolis ★
Green Bay

Lake Michigan

Lake Huron

MICHIGAN 1837
Grand Rapids
Detroit
Lansing ★

Madison ★ Milwaukee

IOWA 1846
Des Moines ★

Chicago
Peoria
Gary

ILLINOIS 1818
Springfield ★

INDIANA 1816
Toledo
Ft. Wayne
Indianapolis ★

Lake Erie

OHIO 1803
Cleveland
Akron
Columbus ★
Cincinnati

Pittsburgh

Lake Ontario

VERMONT 1791
Burlington
Montpelier ★

NEW YORK 1788
Rochester
Buffalo
Albany ★

MAINE 1820
Bangor
Augusta ★
Portland
Lewiston

NEW HAMPSHIRE 1788
Concord ★
Manchester

MASSACHUSETTS 1788
Boston ★
Providence

RHODE ISLAND 1790
CONNECTICUT 1788

Hartford

PENNSYLVANIA 1787
Newark
Harrisburg ★
Philadelphia

Trenton ★
New York
Jersey City

NEW JERSEY 1787

Wilmington
Dover ★

DELAWARE 1787

Baltimore
Washington, D.C. ⊛
Annapolis ★

MARYLAND 1788

N

KANSAS
Kansas City

MISSOURI 1821
Jefferson City ★
St. Louis
Springfield

Springfield ★

KENTUCKY 1792
Louisville
Frankfort ★
Lexington
Huntington

WEST VIRGINIA 1863
Charleston ★

VIRGINIA 1788
Richmond ★
Norfolk

ARKANSAS 1836
Fort Smith
Little Rock ★

TENNESSEE 1796
Nashville ★
Memphis
Knoxville
Charlotte

Winston-Salem

NORTH CAROLINA 1789
Greensboro
Raleigh ★

MISSISSIPPI 1817
Shreveport
Jackson ★

Birmingham

ALABAMA 1819
Macon
Montgomery ★

GEORGIA 1788
Atlanta ★
Columbus

SOUTH CAROLINA 1788
Columbia ★
Charleston

LOUISIANA 1812
Baton Rouge ★
Houston
New Orleans

Mobile
Pensacola
Tallahassee ★

Lake Pontchartrain

ATLANTIC OCEAN

Gulf of Mexico

Tampa

FLORIDA 1845
Lake Okeechobee

Jacksonville

Savannah

Miami

BAHAMAS

Tropic of Cancer

CUBA

KEY

⊛ National capital
★ State capital
○ Other city
1787 Year of admission to the Union
— Timezone boundary

0   200   400 miles
0   200   400 kilometers

60° W
45° N
65° W
40° N
35° N
70° W   30° N
25° N
80° W
75° W
85° W
90° W
95° W

Political Map of the World

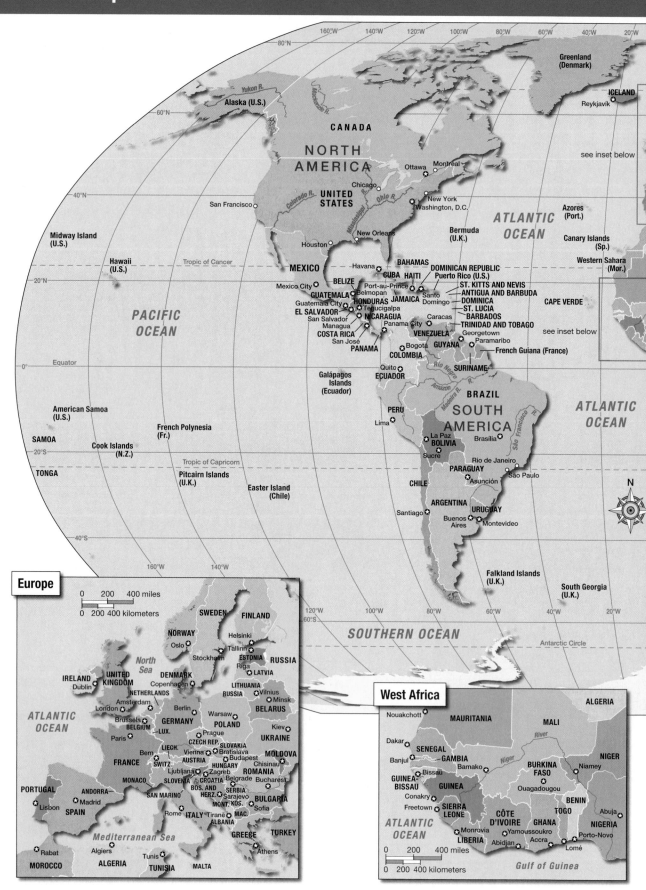

Europe

0   200   400 miles
0   200 400 kilometers

West Africa

0   200   400 miles
0   200 400 kilometers

KEY
- ✪ National capital
- ○ Other city

0   1,000   2,000 miles
0   1,000   2,000 kilometers

Middle East

0   400 miles
0   400 kilometers

▶ The Code of Hammurabi

The Code of Hammurabi, believed to date before 1750 B.C., is a series of laws decreed by Hammurabi. He was the ruler of Babylon when that ancient city was at the peak of its power. Inscribed on stone columns over seven feet high, the Code consisted of 280 sections. Selected sections are excerpted below:

- If a man practice (robbery) and be captured, that man shall be put to death. . . .
- If a man has come forward in a lawsuit for the witnessing of false things, and has not proved the thing that he said, if that lawsuit is a capital case, that man shall be put to death. If he came forward for witnessing about corn or silver, he shall bear the penalty (which applies to) that case.
- If a man has concealed in his house a lost slave or slave-girl belonging to the Palace or to a subject, and has not brought him (or her) out at the proclamation of the Crier, the owner of the house shall be put to death.
- If a fire has broken out in a man's house, and a man who has gone to extinguish it has cast his eye on the property of the owner of the house and has taken the property of the owner of the house, that man shall be thrown into the fire.
- If a man is subject to a debt bearing interest, and Adad (the Weather-god) has saturated his field or a high flood has carried (its crop) away, or because of lack of water he has not produced corn in that field, in that year he shall not return any corn to (his) creditor. He shall . . . not pay interest for that year.
- If a man has donated field, orchard or house to his favourite heir and has written a sealed document for him (confirming this), after the father has gone to his doom, when the brothers share he (the favorite heir) shall

▲ Stone pillar with Hammurabi's Code

take the gift that his father gave him, and apart from that they shall share equally in the property of the paternal estate.
- If an artisan has taken a child for bringing up, and has taught him his manual skill, (the child) shall not be (re)claimed. If he has not taught him his manual skill, that pupil may return to his father's house.
- If a man aid a male or female slave . . . to escape from the city gates, he shall be put to death. . . .
- If a man be in debt and sell his wife, son, or daughter, or bind them over to service, for three years they shall work in the house of the purchaser or master; in the fourth year they shall be given their freedom. . . .
- If a builder has made a house for a man but has not made his work strong, so that the house he made falls down and causes the death of the owner of the house, that builder shall be put to death. If it causes the death of the son of the owner of the house, they shall kill the son of the builder.

Analyzing Documents

Use the passage on this page to answer the following questions.
1. With what general topics is the Code concerned?
2. Why do you suppose the laws were written down and codified?

▶ Magna Carta

Signed by England's King John in 1215, the Magna Carta (Great Charter) was the first document to limit the power of England's monarchs. The Magna Carta established the principle that rulers are subject to law—a major step toward constitutional government.

We . . . by this our present Charter have confirmed, for us and our heirs forever—

1. That the English Church shall be free and shall have her whole rights and her liberties inviolable. . . .

9. Neither we nor our bailiffs shall seize any land or rent for any debt while the chattels [possessions] of the debtor are sufficient for the payment of the debt. . . .

12. No scutage [tax] or aid [subsidy] shall be imposed in our kingdom, unless by the common counsel of our kingdom. . . .

▲ King John signs the Magna Carta.

14. And also to have the common council of the kingdom to assess and aid, . . . and for the assessing of scutages, we will cause to be summoned the archbishops, bishops, abbots, earls, and great barons, . . . And besides, we will cause to be summoned . . . all those who hold of us in chief, at a certain day . . . and to a certain place; and in all the letters of summons, we will express the cause of the summons; and the summons being thus made, the business shall proceed on the day appointed, according to the counsel of those who shall be present, although all who have been summoned have not come.

39. No free-man shall be seized, or imprisoned, or dispossessed, or outlawed, or in any way destroyed; nor will we condemn him, nor will we commit him to prison, excepting by the legal judgment of his peers, or by the laws of the land.

40. To none will we sell, to none will we deny, to none will we delay right or justice.

41. All merchants shall have safety and security in coming into England, and going out of England, and in staying and in traveling through England . . . to buy and sell, . . . excepting in the time of war, and if they be of a country at war against us. . . .

42. It shall be lawful to any person to go out of our kingdom . . . and to return safely and securely, by land or by water, saving his allegiance to us, unless it be in time of war, for some short space, for the common good of the kingdom. . . .

52. If any have been disseised [deprived] or dispossessed by us, without a legal verdict of their peers, of their lands, castles, liberties, or rights, we will immediately restore these things to them. . . .

63. Wherefore our will is . . . that the men in our kingdom have and hold the aforesaid liberties, rights, and concessions . . . fully and entirely, to them and their heirs, . . . in all things and places forever.

Analyzing Documents

Use the passage on this page to answer the following questions.

1. What basic American right has its origins in Article 39 of the Magna Carta?
2. Which article provides the basis for the Fifth Amendment to the Constitution, which states that no person can "be deprived of life, liberty, or property, without due process of law"?
3. What limits does Article 12 place on the king's power to tax?

▶Mayflower Compact

The *Mayflower* landed in present-day Cape Cod in November 1620. The document that became know as the Mayflower Compact contained the first written laws for the new land. It also established a government created by those who were to be governed. It was signed by 41 adult men.

In the name of God, Amen. We, whose names are underwritten, the Loyal Subjects of our dread Sovereign Lord, King James, by the Grace of God, of England, France and Ireland, King, Defender of the Faith, e&.

Having undertaken for the Glory of God, and Advancement of the Christian Faith, and the Honour of our King and Country, a voyage to plant the first colony in the northern parts of Virginia; do by these presents, solemnly and mutually in the Presence of God and one of another, covenant and combine ourselves together into a civil Body Politick, for our better Ordering and Preservation, and Furtherance of the Ends aforesaid; And by Virtue hereof to enact, constitute, and frame, such just and equal Laws, Ordinances, Acts, Constitutions and Offices, from time to time, as shall be thought most meet and convenient for the General good of the Colony; unto which we promise all due submission and obedience.

In Witness whereof we have hereunto subscribed our names at Cape Cod the eleventh of November, in the Reign of our Sovereign Lord, King James of England, France and Ireland, the eighteenth, and of Scotland the fifty-fourth. Anno Domini, 1620.

Analyzing Documents

Use the passage on this page to answer the following questions.
1. What goals are laid out in this document?
2. Why was this document necessary?
3. What might have happened if the Mayflower Compact had not be written?

▲ Selected signatures on the Mayflower Compact

Signing the Mayflower Compact aboard ship ▶

▶ English Bill of Rights

When the Catholic king, James II, was forced from the English throne in 1688, Parliament offered the crown to his Protestant daughter Mary and her husband, William of Orange. Parliament, however, insisted that William and Mary submit to a bill of rights. This document sums up the powers that Parliament had been seeking since the Petition of Right in 1628.

Whereas, the late King James II . . . did endeavor to subvert and exirpate [eliminate] the Protestant religion and the laws and libertyies of this kingdom . . . and whereas the said late king James II having abdicated the government, and the throne being vacant. . . .

The said Lords [Parliament] . . . being now assembled in a full and free representative [body] of this nation . . . do in the first place . . . declare

- That the pretended [untruthfully claimed] power of suspending the laws or the execution of laws by regal authority without consent of Parliament is illegal;

- That the pretended power of dispensing with laws or the execution of laws by regal authority, as it hath been assumed and exercised of late, is illegal; . . .

- That levying money for or to the use of the Crown by pretence of prerogative, without grant of Parliament, for longer time, or in other manner than the same is or shall be granted, is illegal;

- That it is the right of the subjects to petition the king, and all commitments and prosecutions for such petitioning are illegal;

- That the raising or keeping a standing army within the kingdom in time of peace, unless it be with consent of Parliament, is against law;

- That the subjects which are Protestants may have arms for their defence suitable to their conditions and as allowed by law;

- That election of members of Parliament ought to be free;

- That the freedom of speech and debates or proceedings in Parliament ought not to be impeached or questioned in any court or place out of Parliament;

- That excessive bail ought not to be required, nor excessive fines imposed, nor cruel and unusual punishments inflicted;

- That jurors ought to be duly impanelled and returned, and jurors which pass upon men in trials for high treason ought to be freeholders [property owners with unconditional rights];

- That all grants and promises of fines and forfeitures of particular persons before conviction are illegal and void;

- And that for redress of all grievances, and for the amending, strengthening and preserving of the laws, Parliaments ought to be held frequently.

Analyzing Documents

Use the passage on this page to answer the following questions.

1. Which rights and freedoms listed above do you think are most important? Explain your choices.
2. Review the American Declaration of Independence. What similarities do you see between the two documents?
3. What is the importance of this document for American government?

▶ Second Treatise on Government

As you learned in Chapter 1, English philosopher John Locke (1632–1704) produced two treatises (essays) on government in 1690. In his second treatise, he discussed the responsibilities of a government and claimed that the people have the right to overthrow an unjust government. Locke's ideas greatly influenced Thomas Jefferson and other supporters of the American Revolution. In this selection, Locke explains why people form governments.

To understand political power aright . . . we must consider what estate all men are naturally in, and that is, a state of perfect freedom to order their actions, and dispose of their possessions. . . . Men being . . . by nature, all free, equal and independent, no one can be put out of this estate and subjected to the political power of another without his own consent, which is done by agreeing with other men, to join and unite into a community for their comfortable, safe and peaceable living, one amongst another, in a secure enjoyment of their properties, and a greater security against any that are not of it. . . .

When any number of men have, by the consent of every individual, made a community, they have thereby made that community one body, with a power to act as one body, which is only by the will and determination of the majority. . . . . And thus every man, by consenting with others to make one body politic under one government, puts himself under an obligation to every one in that society to submit to the determination of the majority, and to be concluded by it. . . .

If man in the state of nature . . . be absolute lord of his own person and possessions, equal to the greatest and subject to nobody, why will he part with his freedom, this empire, and subject himself to the dominion and control

▲ John Locke

of any other power? . . . It is obvious to answer that though in the state of nature he hath such a right, yet the enjoyment of it is very uncertain and constantly exposed to the invasion of others; for all being kings as much as he, every man his equal, . . . the enjoyment of the property he has in this state is very unsafe, very insecure. This makes him willing to quit this condition which, however free, is full of fears and continual dangers; and it is not without reason that he seeks out and is willing to join in society with others . . . for the mutual preservation of their lives, liberties and estates, which I call by the general name—property.

The great and chief end, therefore, of men uniting into commonwealths, and putting themselves under government, is the preservation of their property. . . .

Analyzing Documents

Use the passage on this page to answer the following questions.
1. What freedoms did people have before the founding of governments?
2. How are governments formed?
3. What trade-off does Locke say occurs when people live under government?

▶Virginia Declaration of Rights

The Virginia Declaration of Rights was largely the work of George Mason (1725–1792). He was one of Virginia's wealthiest planters and a neighbor and friend of George Washington. The Declaration was adopted unanimously by the Virginia Convention of Delegates on June 12, 1776. It influenced a number of later documents, including the Declaration of Independence and the Bill of Rights. Selected articles are excerpted below:

A declaration of rights made by the representatives of the good people of Virginia, assembled in full and free convention; which rights do pertain to them and their posterity, as the basis and foundation of government.

I That all men are by nature equally free and independent, and have certain inherent rights, of which, . . . they cannot, by any compact, deprive or divest their posterity; namely, the enjoyment of life and liberty, with the means of acquiring and possessing property, and pursuing and obtaining happiness and safety.

II That all power is vested in, and consequently derived from, the people; that magistrates are their trustees and servants, and at all times amenable to them.

▲ George Mason

V That the legislative and executive powers of the state should be separate and distinct from the judicative; and, that the members of the two first may be restrained from oppression by feeling and participating the burthens of the people, they should, at fixed periods, be reduced to a private station . . . .

VII That all power of suspending laws, or the execution of laws, by any authority without consent of the representatives of the people is injurious to their rights and ought not to be exercised.

VIII That in all capital or criminal prosecutions a man hath a right to demand the cause and nature of his accusation to be confronted with the accusers and witnesses, to call for evidence in his favor, and to a speedy trial by an impartial jury of his vicinage . . . .

IX That excessive bail ought not to be required, nor excessive fines imposed; nor cruel and unusual punishments inflicted.

XII That the freedom of the press is one of the greatest bulwarks of liberty and can never be restrained but by despotic governments.

XIV That the people have a right to uniform government; and therefore, that no government separate from, or independent of, the government of Virginia, ought to be erected or established within the limits thereof.

XVI That religion, or the duty which we owe to our Creator and the manner of discharging it, can be directed by reason and conviction, not by force or violence; and therefore, all men are equally entitled to the free exercise of religion . . . .

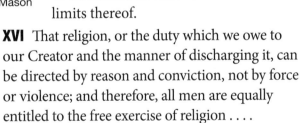

Analyzing Documents

Use the passage on these pages to answer the following questions.

1. What similarities do you see in language and ideas between the Virginia Declaration of Rights and the Declaration of Independence?

2. Choose one of the articles from the Virginia Declaration and explain the importance of the right that it describes.

▶Declaration of Independence

By signing the Declaration of Independence, the Continental Congress sent a clear message to Britain that the American colonies were free and independent states. The document spells out all the reasons the people in the United States had a right to break away from Britain.

▶ **When in the Course of human events** it becomes necessary for one people to dissolve the political bands which have connected them with another, and to assume among the powers of the earth, the separate and equal station to which the Laws of nature and of nature's God entitle them, a decent respect to the opinions of mankind requires that they should declare the causes which impel them to the separation.

▶ We hold these truths to be self-evident, that all men are created equal, that they are endowed by their Creator with certain unalienable Rights, that among these are Life, Liberty and the Pursuit of Happiness. That to secure these rights, Governments are instituted among Men, deriving their just powers from the consent of the governed; That whenever any Form of Government becomes destructive of these ends it is the Right of the People to alter or to abolish it, and to institute new Government, laying its foundation on such principles and organizing its powers in such form, as to them shall seem most likely to effect their Safety and Happiness. Prudence, indeed, will dictate that Governments long established should not be changed for light and transient causes; and accordingly all experience hath shown, that mankind are more disposed to suffer, while evils are sufferable, than to right themselves by abolishing the forms to which they are accustomed. But when a long train of abuses and usurpations, pursuing invariably the same Object evinces a design to reduce them under absolute Despotism, it is their right, it is their duty, to throw off such Government, and to provide new Guards for their future security.

▶ Such has been the patient sufferance of these Colonies; and such is now the necessity which constrains them to alter their former Systems of Government. The history of the present King of Great Britain is a history of repeated injuries and usurpations, all having in direct object the establishment of an absolute Tyranny over these States. To prove this, let Facts be submitted to a candid world.

He has refused his Assent to Laws, the most wholesome and necessary for the public good.

He has forbidden his Governors to pass Laws of immediate and pressing importance, unless suspended in their operation till his Assent should be obtained; and when so suspended, he has utterly neglected to attend to them.

▶ He has refused to pass other Laws for the accommodation of large districts of people, unless those people would relinquish the right of Representation in the Legislature, a right inestimable to them and formidable to tyrants only.

He has called together legislative bodies at places unusual, uncomfortable, and distant from the depository of their Public Records, for the sole purpose of fatiguing them into compliance with his measures.

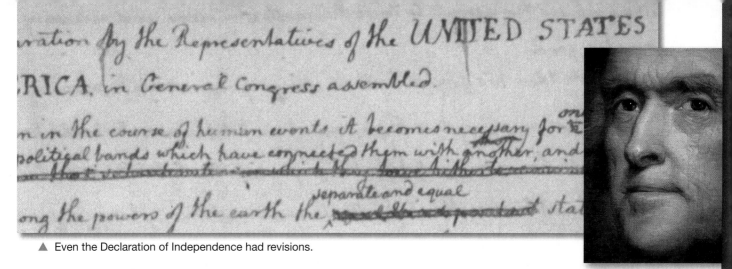

▲ Even the Declaration of Independence had revisions.

▲ Thomas Jefferson

▶ He has dissolved Representative Houses repeatedly, for opposing with manly firmness his invasions on the rights of the people.

He has refused for a long time, after such dissolutions, to cause others to be elected; whereby the Legislative powers, incapable of Annihilation, have returned to the People at large for their exercise; the State remaining in the mean time exposed to all the dangers of invasions from without, and convulsions within.

▶ He has endeavored to prevent the population of these States; for that purpose obstructing the Laws for Naturalization of Foreigners; refusing to pass others to encourage their migration hither, and raising the conditions of new Appropriations of Lands.

He has obstructed the Administration of Justice, by refusing his Assent to Laws for establishing Judiciary powers.

▶ He has made Judges dependent on his Will alone for the tenure of their offices, and the amount and payment of their salaries.

He has erected a multitude of New Offices, and sent hither swarms of Officers to harass our people and eat out their substance.

He has kept among us in time of peace, Standing Armies, without the Consent of our legislatures.

He has affected to render the Military independent of, and superior to, the Civil Power.

He has combined with others to subject us to a jurisdiction foreign to our constitutions, and unacknowledged by our laws; giving his Assent to their Acts of pretended Legislation:

▶ For quartering large bodies of armed troops among us;

For protecting them, by a mock Trial, from punishment for any Murders which they should commit on the Inhabitants of these States;

For cutting off our Trade with all parts of the world;

For imposing Taxes on us without our Consent;

For depriving us, in many cases, of the benefits of Trial by Jury;

For transporting us beyond Seas to be tried for pretended offenses;

▶ For abolishing the free System of English Laws in a neighboring Province, establishing therein an Arbitrary government, and enlarging its Boundaries so as to render it at once an example and fit instrument for introducing the same absolute rule into these Colonies;

For taking away our Charters, abolishing our most valuable Laws, and altering fundamentally the Forms of our Governments;

For suspending our own Legislatures, and declaring themselves invested with Power to legislate for us in all cases whatsoever.

He has abdicated Government here, by declaring us out of his Protection, and waging War against us.

He has plundered our seas, ravaged our Coasts, burned our towns, and destroyed the lives of our people.

He is at this time transporting large Armies of foreign mercenaries to complete the works of death, desolation and tyranny, already begun with circumstances of Cruelty and perfidy scarcely paralleled in the most barbarous ages, and totally unworthy of the Head of a civilized nation.

▶ He has constrained our fellow Citizens taken Captive on the high Seas to bear Arms against their Country, to become the executioners of their friends and Brethren, or to fall themselves by their Hands.

He has excited domestic insurrections amongst us, and has endeavored to bring on the inhabitants of our frontiers the merciless Indian Savages whose known rule of warfare, is an undistinguished destruction of all ages, sexes, and conditions.

▶ In every stage of these Oppressions We have Petitioned for Redress in the most humble terms. Our repeated Petitions have been answered only by repeated injury. A Prince, whose character is thus marked by every act which may define a Tyrant, is unfit to be the ruler of a free People.

▶ Nor have We been wanting in attentions to our British brethren. We have warned them from time to time of attempts by their legislature to extend an unwarrantable jurisdiction over us. We have reminded them of the circumstances of our emigration and settlement here. We have appealed to their native justice and magnanimity, and we have conjured them by the ties of our common kindred to disavow these usurpations, which, would inevitably interrupt our connections and correspondence. They too have been deaf to the voice of justice and of consanguinity. We must, therefore, acquiesce in the necessity, which denounces our Separation, and hold them, as we hold the rest of mankind, Enemies in War, in Peace Friends.

▶ We, therefore, the Representatives of the United States of America, in General Congress, Assembled, appealing to the Supreme Judge of the world for the rectitude of our intentions, do, in the Name, and by the Authority of the good People of these Colonies, solemnly publish and declare, That these United Colonies are, and of right ought to be Free and Independent States; that they are Absolved from all Allegiance to the British Crown, and that all political connection between them and the State of Great Britain, is and ought to be totally dissolved, and that as Free and Independent States, they have full Power to levy War, conclude Peace, contract Alliances, establish Commerce, and to do all other Acts and Things which Independent States may of right do. And for the support of this Declaration, with a firm reliance on the protection of Divine Providence, we mutually pledge to each other our Lives, our Fortunes, and our sacred Honor.

John Hancock

New Hampshire:
Josiah Bartlett
William Whipple
Mathew Thornton

Massachusetts Bay:
John Hancock
Samuel Adams
John Adams
Robert Treat Paine
Elbridge Gerry

Rhode Island:
Stephan Hopkins
William Ellery

Connecticut:
Roger Sherman
Samuel Huntington
William Williams
Oliver Wolcott

New York:
William Floyd
Philip Livingston
Francis Lewis
Lewis Morris

New Jersey:
Richard Stockton
John Witherspoon
Francis Hopkinson
John Hart
Abraham Clark

Delaware:
Caesar Rodney
George Read
Thomas M'Kean

Maryland:
Samuel Chase
William Paca
Thomas Stone
Charles Carroll
of Carrollton

Virginia:
George Wythe
Richard Henry Lee
Thomas Jefferson
Benjamin Harrison
Thomas Nelson, Jr.
Francis Lightfoot Lee
Carter Braxton

Pennsylvania:
Robert Morris
Benjamin Rush
Benjamin Franklin
John Morton
George Clymer
James Smith
George Taylor
James Wilson
George Ross

North Carolina:
William Hooper
Joseph Hewes
John Penn

South Carolina:
Edward Rutledge
Thomas Heyward, Jr.
Thomas Lynch, Jr.
Arthur Middleton

Georgia:
Button Gwinnett
Lyman Hall
George Walton

▲ As president of the Second Continental Congress, John Hancock was the first to sign the Declaration of Independence, approving it with his now-famous signature.

Analyzing Documents

Use the passage on these pages to answer the following questions.
1. What are the three "unalienable rights" listed in the Declaration of Independence?
2. According to the Declaration, what powers belong to the United States as "Free and Independent States"?

▶Articles of Confederation

The Articles of Confederation were approved on November 15, 1777. The 13 Articles were in effect from March 1, 1781, when they were finally ratified by all 13 States, until March 4, 1789. They established a weak central government, which led to conflicts among the States. Demand soon grew for a stronger central government, leading to the creation of the United States Constitution. Selected articles are excerpted below:

[ART. I.] The Stile of this confederacy shall be "The United States of America."

[ART. II.] Each state retains its sovereignty, freedom and independence . . .

[ART. III.] The said states hereby severally enter into a firm league of friendship with each other, for their common defence . . .

[ART. IV.] The better to secure and perpetuate mutual friendship and intercourse among the people of the different states in this union, the free inhabitants of each of these states, paupers, vagabonds and fugitives from Justice excepted, shall be entitled to all privileges and immunities of free citizens in the several states . . .

If any Person guilty of, or charged with treason, felony, or other high misdemeanor in any state, shall flee from Justice, and be found in any of the united states, he shall upon demand of the Governor or executive power, of the state from which he fled, be delivered up and removed to the state having jurisdiction of his offence.

[ART. V.] For the more convenient management of the general interests of the united states, delegates shall be annually appointed in such manner as the legislature of each state shall direct, to meet in Congress . . .

[ART. VI.] No state without the Consent of the united states in congress assembled, shall send any embassy to, or receive any embassy from, or enter into any conference, agreement, or alliance or treaty with any King . . .

[ART. VII.] . . . officers of or under the rank of colonel, shall be appointed by the legislature of each state . . .

[ART. VIII.] All charges of war, and all other expences that shall be incurred for the common defence or general welfare, and allowed by the united states in congress assembled, shall be defrayed out of a common treasury, which shall be supplied by the several states, in proportion to the value of all land within each state . . .

[ART. IX.] The united states in congress assembled, shall have the sole and exclusive right and power of determining on peace and war . . .

[ART. X.] The committee of the states, or any nine of them, shall be authorised to execute, in the recess of congress, such of the powers of congress as the united states in congress assembled, by the consent of nine states . . .

[ART. XI.] Canada acceding to this confederation, and joining in the measures of the united states, shall be admitted into, and entitled to all the advantages of this union . . .

[ART. XII.] All . . . debts contracted by, or under the authority of congress, before the assembling of the united states, in pursuance of the present confederation, shall be deemed and considered as a charge against the united states . . .

[ART. XIII.] Every state shall abide by the determinations of the united states in congress assembled . . .

Analyzing Documents

Use the passage on this page to answer the following questions.
1. What is the provision of Article I?
2. What are two of the provisions of Article IV?

HISTORICAL DOCUMENTS

▶ *The Federalist* No. 10

This is one of the 29 essays believed to have been written by James Madison. It is the tenth of *The Federalist* papers that presents Madison's observations on dealing with the "mischiefs of faction" and the advantages of a republican (representative) form of government over that of a pure democracy. This essay was first published on November 23, 1787. Below is an excerpt of the essay.

Among the numerous advantages promised by a well-constructed Union, none deserves to be more accurately developed than its tendency to break and control the violence of faction

. . . There are two methods of curing the mischiefs of faction: the one, by removing its causes; the other, by controlling its effects.

There are again two methods of removing the causes of faction: the one, by destroying the liberty which is essential to its existence; the other, by giving to every citizen the same opinions, the same passions, and the same interests.

. . . From this view of the subject it may be concluded that a pure democracy, by which I mean a society consisting of a small number of citizens who assemble and administer the government in person, can admit of no cure for the mischiefs of faction. A common passion or interest will, in almost every case, be felt by a majority of the whole; a communication and concert result from the form of government itself; and there is nothing to check the inducements to sacrifice the weaker party or an obnoxious individual. Hence it is that such democracies have ever been spectacles of turbulence and contention; have ever been found incompatible with personal security or the rights of property; and have in general been as short in their lives as they have been violent in their deaths.

A republic, by which I mean a government in which the scheme of representation takes place, opens a different prospect and promises the cure for which we are seeking. Let us examine the points in which it varies from pure democracy, and we shall comprehend . . . the nature of the cure . . . .

The two great points of difference between a democracy and a republic are: first, the delegation of the government, in the latter, to a small number of citizens elected by the rest; secondly, the greater number of citizens, and greater sphere of country, over which the latter may be extended. . . .

. . . The influence of factious leaders may kindle a flame within their particular States but will be unable to spread a general conflagration through the other States. . . . A rage for paper money, for an abolition of debts, for an equal division of property, or for any other improper or wicked project will be less apt to pervade the whole body of the Union than a particular member of it; in the same proportion as such a malady is more likely to taint a particular county or district than an entire State.

In the extent, and proper structure of the Union, therefore, we behold a republican remedy for the diseases most incident to republican government. And according to the degree of pleasure and pride we feel in being republicans, ought to be our zeal in cherishing the spirit and supporting the character of Federalists.

Analyzing Documents

Use the passage on these pages to answer the following questions.
1. What does Madison mean by "the mischief of faction"?
2. Why does Madison support a republican form of government?

▶ *The Federalist* No. 51

As you learned in Chapter 2, *The Federalist* No. 51 was first published on February 8, 1788. Here, Madison discusses the need for a system of checks and balances to guard against an oppressive government.

. . . It is of great importance in a republic not only to guard the society against the oppression of its rulers, but to guard one part of the society against the injustice of the other part. Different interests necessarily exist in different classes of citizens. If a majority be united by a common interest, the rights of the minority will be insecure. There are but two methods of providing against this evil: The one by creating a will in the community independent of the majority—that is, of the society itself; the other, by comprehending in the society so many separate descriptions of citizens as will render an unjust combination of a majority of the whole very improbable, if not impracticable. The first method prevails in all governments possessing an hereditary or self appointed authority. This, at best, is but a precarious security; because a power independent of the society may as well espouse the unjust views of the major as the rightful interests of the minor party, and may possibly be turned against both parties. The second method will be exemplified in the federal republic of the United States. Whilst all authority in it will be derived from and dependent on the society, the society itself will be broken into so many parts, interests, and classes of citizens, that the rights of individuals, or of the minority, will be in little danger from interested combinations of the majority. In a free government the security for civil rights must be the same as that for religious rights. It consists in the one case in the multiplicity of interests, and in the other in the multiplicity of sects. The degree of security in both cases will depend on the number of interests and sects; and this may be presumed to depend on the extent of country and number of people comprehended under the same government.

This view of the subject must particularly recommend a proper federal system to all the sincere and considerate friends of republican government, since it shows that in exact proportion as the territory of the Union may be formed into more circumscribed Confederacies, or States, oppressive combinations of a majority will be facilitated: the best security, under the republican forms, for the rights of every class of citizens, will be diminished; and consequently, the stability and independence of some member of the government, the only other security, must be proportionally increased. Justice is the end of government. It is the end of civil society. It ever has been and ever will be pursued until it be obtained, or until liberty be lost in the pursuit. In a society under the forms of which the stronger faction can readily unite and oppress the weaker, anarchy may as truly be said to reign as in a state of nature, where the weaker individual is not secured against the violence of the stronger: And as, in the latter state, even the stronger individuals are prompted by the uncertainty of their condition to submit to a government which may protect the weak as well as themselves. So, in the former state, will the more powerful factions or parties be gradually induced, by a like motive, to wish for a government which will protect all parties, the weaker as well as the more powerful.

Analyzing Documents

Use the passage on these pages to answer the following question.

How will the new government guard against placing too much power in the hands of one individual or government body?

▶ *The Federalist* No. 78

The Federalist papers were the brainchild of Alexander Hamilton, who conceived them and recruited James Madison and John Jay to the project. Hamilton is usually credited as the author of 51 of the 85 essays in the collection. First published in April 11, 1788, this paper discusses the national judiciary to be established by Article III in the proposed Constitution. Hamilton emphasizes the need for an independent judiciary. He also discusses its role in the interpretation of laws and the determination of their constitutionality.

We proceed now to an examination of the judiciary department of the proposed government. . . .

The manner of constituting it seems to embrace these several objects: 1st. The mode of appointing the judges. 2nd. The tenure by which they are to hold their places. 3rd. The partition of the judiciary authority between different courts and their relations to each other.

First. As to the mode of appointing the judges: this is the same with that of appointing the officers of the Union in general and has been so fully discussed in the two last numbers that nothing can be said here which would not be useless repetition.

Second. As to the tenure by which the judges are to hold their places: this chiefly concerns their duration in office, the provisions for their support, the precautions for their responsibility. . . .

. . . It has been frequently remarked with great propriety that a voluminous code of laws is one of the inconveniences necessarily connected with the advantages of a free government. To avoid an arbitrary discretion in the courts, it is indispensable that they should be bound down by strict rules and precedents which serve to define and point out their duty in every particular case that comes before them; and it will readily be conceived from the variety of controversies which grow out of the folly and wickedness of mankind that the records of those precedents must unavoidably swell to a very considerable bulk and must demand long and laborious study to acquire a competent knowledge of them. Hence it is that there can be but few men in the society who will have sufficient skill in the laws to qualify them for the stations of judges. And making the proper deductions for the ordinary depravity of human nature, the number must be still smaller of those who unite the requisite integrity with the requisite knowledge. These considerations apprise us that the government can have no great option between fit characters; and that a temporary duration in office which would naturally discourage such characters from quitting a lucrative line of practice to accept a seat on the bench would have a tendency to throw the administration of justice into hands less able and less well qualified to conduct it with utility and dignity.

Upon the whole, there can be no room to doubt that the convention acted wisely in copying from the models of those constitutions which have established *good behavior* as the tenure of their judicial offices, in point of duration; and that so far from being blamable on this account, their plan would have been inexcusably defective if it had wanted this important feature of good government. The experience of Great Britain affords an illustrious comment on the excellence of the institution.

Analyzing Documents

Use the passage on these pages to answer the following questions.
1. Who wrote *Federalist No. 78*?
2. What department does the writer discuss?

▶ The Emancipation Proclamation

President Abraham Lincoln issued the Emancipation Proclamation on January 1, 1863, at the beginning of the third year of the bloody Civil War. The proclamation declared "that all persons held as slaves" within the rebellious states "are, and henceforward shall be free." Below is an excerpt from the Emancipation Proclamation.

HISTORICAL DOCUMENTS

"That on the 1st day of January, A.D. 1863, all persons held as slaves within any State or designated part of a State the people whereof shall then be in rebellion against the United States shall be then, thenceforward, and forever free; and the Executive Government of the United States, including the military and naval authority thereof, will recognize and maintain the freedom of such persons and will do no act or acts to repress such persons, or any of them, in any efforts they may make for their actual freedom. . . .
Now, therefore, I, Abraham Lincoln, President of the United States, by virtue of the power in me vested as Commander-in-Chief of the Army and Navy of the United States in time of actual armed rebellion against the authority and government of the United States, and as a fit and necessary war measure for suppressing said rebellion, do, on this 1st day of January, A.D. 1863, and in accordance with my purpose so to do, publicly proclaimed for the full period of one hundred days from the first day above mentioned, order and designate as the States and parts of States wherein the people thereof, respectively, are this day in rebellion against the United States the following, to wit:

Arkansas, Texas, Louisiana (except the parishes of St. Bernard, Plaquemines, Jefferson, St. John, St. Charles, St. James, Ascension, Assumption, Terrebonne, Lafourche, St. Mary, St. Martin, and Orleans, including the city of New Orleans), Mississippi, Alabama, Florida, Georgia, South Carolina, North Carolina, and Virginia (except the forty-eight counties designated as West Virginia, and also the counties of Berkeley, Accomac, Northhampton, Elizabeth City, York,

Princess Anne, and Norfolk, including the cities of Norfolk and Portsmouth), and which excepted parts are for the present left precisely as if this proclamation were not issued.

. . . I do order and declare that all persons held as slaves within said designated States and parts of States are, and henceforward shall be, free; and that the Executive Government of the United States, including the military and naval authorities thereof, will recognize and maintain the freedom of said persons.

And I hereby enjoin upon the people so declared to be free to abstain from all violence, unless in necessary self-defense; and I recommend to them that, in all cases when allowed, they labor faithfully for reasonable wages.

And I further declare and make known that such persons of suitable condition will be received into the armed service of the United States to garrison forts, positions, stations, and other places, and to man vessels of all sorts in said service.

And upon this act, sincerely believed to be an act of justice, warranted by the Constitution upon military necessity, I invoke the considerate judgment of mankind and the gracious favor of Almighty God.

Analyzing Documents

Use the passage on this page to answer the following questions.
1. In addition to proclaiming an end to slavery, what other action does the Proclamation declare? Why is this action significant?
2. Why was the Proclamation important even though no slaves were freed immediately?

▶ Declaration of Sentiments and Resolutions

As you have read in Chapter 19, Elizabeth Cady Stanton and Lucretia Mott were two activists in the movement to abolish slavery. They called together the first conference to address women's rights and issues in Seneca Falls, New York, in 1848. Using the Declaration of Independence as a model, the Declaration of Sentiments and Resolutions demanded that the rights of women be acknowledged and respected. Below is an excerpt from the declaration:

We hold these truths to be self-evident: that all men and women are created equal; that they are endowed by their Creator with certain inalienable rights; that among these are life, liberty, and the pursuit of happiness . . . The history of mankind is a history of repeated injuries and usurpations on the part of man toward woman, having in direct object the establishment of an absolute tyranny over her. To prove this, let facts be submitted to a candid world.

- He has never permitted her to exercise her inalienable right to the elective franchise.

- He has compelled her to submit to laws, in the formation of which she had no voice.

- He has withheld from her rights which are given to the most ignorant and degraded men—both natives and foreigners.

- Having deprived her of this first right of a citizen, the elective franchise, thereby leaving her without representation in the halls of legislation, he has oppressed her on all sides.

- He has made her, if married, in the eye of the law, civilly dead.

- He has taken from her all right in property, even to the wages she earns.

- He has made her, morally, an irresponsible being, as she can commit many crimes with impunity, provided they be done in the presence of her husband. In the covenant of marriage, she is compelled to promise obedience to her husband, he becoming, to all intents and purposes, her master—the law giving him power to deprive her of her liberty, and to administer chastisement.

- He has so framed the laws of divorce, as to what shall be the proper causes, and in case of separation, to whom the guardianship of the children shall be given, as to be wholly regardless of the happiness of women— the law, in all cases, going upon a false supposition of the supremacy of man, and giving all power into his hands.

- After depriving her of all rights as a married woman, if single, and the owner of property, he has taxed her to support a government which recognizes her only when her property can be made profitable to it.

- He has monopolized nearly all the profitable employments, and from those she is permitted to follow, she receives but a scanty remuneration.

- He closes against her all the avenues to wealth and distinction which he considers most honorable to himself. As a teacher of theology, medicine, or law, she is not known.

- He has denied her the facilities for obtaining a thorough education, all colleges being closed against her.

Analyzing Documents

Use the passage on this page to answer the following questions.
1. Why did Mott and Stanton base their declaration on the Declaration of Independence?
2. The Declaration of Sentiments and Resolutions attracted much controversy when it was first published? Why might this have been so?

▶Universal Declaration of Human Rights

The General Assembly of the United Nations adopted this declaration on December 10, 1948. The document sets forth the basic liberties and freedoms to which all people are entitled.

Article 1 All human beings are born free and equal in dignity and rights. They are endowed with reason and conscience and should act toward one another in a spirit of brotherhood.

Article 2 Everyone is entitled to all the rights and freedoms set forth in this Declaration, without distinction of any kind, such as race, colour, sex, language, religion, political or other opinion, national or social origin, property, birth or other status. . . .

Article 3 Everyone has the right to life, liberty and security of person.

Article 4 No one shall be held in slavery or servitude. . . .

Article 5 No one shall be subjected to torture or to cruel, inhuman or degrading treatment or punishment.

Article 9 No one shall be subjected to arbitrary arrest, detention or exile.

Article 13 Everyone has the right to freedom of movement. . . .

Article 18 Everyone has the right to freedom of thought, conscience and religion. . . .

Article 19 Everyone has the right to freedom of opinion and expression. . . .

Article 20 Everyone has the right to freedom of peaceful assembly and association. . . .

Article 23 Everyone has the right to work, to free choice of employment, to just and favourable conditions of work and to protection against unemployment. . . .

Article 25 Everyone has the right to a standard of living adequate for the health and well-being of himself and of his family, including food, clothing, housing and medical care and necessary social services, and the right to security in the event of unemployment, sickness, disability, widowhood, old age or other lack of livelihood in circumstances beyond his control.

Article 26 Everyone has the right to education. Education shall be free, at least in the elementary and fundamental stages. . . .

Analyzing Documents

Use the passage on this page to answer the following questions.
1. Which of the above rights are reflected in the Bill of Rights in the U.S. Constitution?
2. What additional rights are included in these excerpts? Why do you think these rights are not spelled out in the U.S. Constitution?
3. In what ways might the existence of this declaration benefit people living under an oppressive regime?

▲ A young girl carries water in Chennai, India

Supreme Court Glossary

Abrams v. United States (1919)

Decision: The Court ruled 7-2 that Congress could make it illegal to criticize the United States government and to encourage others not to obey the laws. When the defendants were convicted of distributing pamphlets that opposed certain U.S. military policies during World War I and urging people not to participate in the war effort, they were sentenced to 20 years imprisonment. The Court upheld their convictions. In his dissent, Justice Oliver Wendell Holmes argued that "the surreptitious publishing of a silly leaflet by an unknown man" did not create a clear and imminent danger to the United States and therefore should be protected by the First Amendment. The case was essentially overruled 50 years later in *Brandenburg v. Ohio*, which held that "mere advocacy" is constitutionally protected unless it is actually likely to produce imminent lawless action.

Agostini v. Felton (1997)

Decision: The Court decided that it was appropriate to reconsider *Aguilar v. Felton* as subsequent cases had undermined several of the assumptions, for example that public employees placed at parochial schools would "inevitably inculcate religion," upon which the decision was based. The Court then found that New York City's Title I Program did not violate any of the criteria used "to evaluate whether government aid has the effect of advancing religion: it does not result in governmental indoctrination; define its recipients by reference to religion; or create an excessive entanglement." As a result, the Court concluded that "a federally funded program providing supplemental, remedial instruction to disadvantaged children on a neutral basis is not invalid under the Establishment Clause when such instruction is given on the premises of sectarian schools by government employees pursuant to a program containing safeguards" against excessive entanglement between government and religion.

Alden v. Maine (1999)

Decision: In a 5-4 decision, the Court held that Congress does not have the power to force States to submit to being sued in their own courts without their consent. The structure of the Constitution and the Eleventh Amendment give the States "sovereign immunity" that allows the States to prevent people from suing them in their own courts, and Congress does not have the power to override this immunity.

American Insurance Association v. Garamendi (2003)

Decision: California's Holocaust Victim Insurance Relief Act interferes with the President's conduct of the nation's foreign policy and is therefore unconstitutional. Although the executive agreements do not specifically prohibit State action, they do pre-empt (override) the State's authority to act on the same subject matter, even in the absence of any direct conflict.

Baker v. Carr (1962)

Decision: Although in past decisions, the Court had called apportionment cases a "political thicket" and declined to intervene, in *Baker*, the Court held that it was within the scope of the judicial branch of government to rule on matters of legislative apportionment. The Court further ruled that Baker and other Tennessee citizens were entitled to a trial deciding whether their constitutionally guaranteed right to equal protection of the law (14th Amendment) had been denied. *Baker* opened the door to later cases on apportionment which led to the eventual reapportioning of nearly every State legislature according to population.

Board of Estimate of City of New York v. Morris (1989)

Decision: The reapportionment requirement of "one-person, one-vote" applies to the Board of Estimate. The Board has sufficient legislative functions that its composition must fairly represent city voters on an approximately equal basis. The fact that some members are elected citywide is one factor to be considered in evaluating the fairness of the electoral structure, but it is not determinative. The City's expressed interests—that the Board be effective and that it accommodate natural and political boundaries as well as local interests—does not justify the size of the deviation from the "one-person, one-vote" ideal. The City could structure the Board in other ways that would further these interests while minimizing the discrimination in voting power.

Bob Jones University v. United States (1983)

(14th Amendment in conflict with 1st Amendment) Bob Jones University, a private school, denied admission to applicants in an interracial marriage or who "espouse" interracial marriage or dating. The Internal Revenue Service then denied tax exempt status to the school because of racial discrimination. The university appealed, claiming their policy was based on the Bible. The Court upheld the IRS ruling, stating that ". . . Government has a fundamental overriding interest in eradicating racial discrimination in education."

Brandenburg v. Ohio (1969)

Decision: The Court ruled unanimously that advocacy is protected under the First Amendment "except where such advocacy is directed to inciting or producing imminent lawless action and is likely to incite or produce such action." Therefore a Ku Klux Klan leader could not be convicted under an Ohio statute that prohibited advocating violence. The opinion effectively overruled prior Supreme Court cases such as *Whitney v. California* and *Abrams v. United States* that had allowed criminal convictions merely for urging violence or other unlawful acts.

Brown v. Board of Education of Topeka (1954)

(14th Amendment, Equal Protection Clause) Probably no twentieth century Supreme Court decision so deeply stirred and changed life in the United States as *Brown*. A 10-year-old Topeka girl, Linda Brown, was not permitted to attend her neighborhood school because she was an African American. The Court heard arguments about whether segregation itself was a violation of the Equal Protection Clause and found that it was, commenting that "in the field of public education the doctrine of 'separate but equal' has no place. . . . Segregation is a denial of the equal protection of the laws." The decision overturned *Plessy v. Ferguson*, 1896.

City of Boerne, Texas v. Flores (1997)

Decision: A 6-3 majority ruled that the Religious Freedom Restoration Act was unconstitutional. The majority concluded that the Act was not a legitimate attempt by Congress to implement the Free Exercise Clause of the First Amendment but was really an attempt to change constitutional law as previously determined by the Court. The Act therefore violated separation of powers.

The Civil Rights Cases (1883)

(14th Amendment, Equal Protection Clause) The Civil Rights Act of 1875 included punishments of businesses that practiced discrimination. The Court ruled on a number of cases involving the Acts in 1883, finding that the Constitution, "while prohibiting discrimination by governments, made no provisions . . . for acts of racial discrimination by private individuals." The decision limited the impact of the Equal Protection Clause, giving tacit approval for segregation in the private sector.

Cruzan v. Missouri (1990)

(14th Amendment, Due Process Clause) After Nancy Beth Cruzan was left in a "persistent vegetative state" by a car accident, Missouri officials refused to comply with her parents' request that the hospital terminate life-support. The Court upheld the State policy under which officials refused to withdraw treatment, rejecting the argument that the Due Process Clause of the 14th Amendment gave the parents the right to refuse treatment on their daughter's behalf. Although individuals have the right to refuse medical treatment, "incompetent" persons are not able to exercise this right; without "clear and convincing" evidence that Cruzan desired the withdrawal of treatment, the State could legally act to preserve her life.

Dennis v. United States (1951)

(1st Amendment, freedom of speech) The Smith Act of 1940 made it a crime for any person to work for the violent overthrow of the United States in peacetime or war. Eleven Communist party leaders, including Dennis, had been convicted of violating the Smith Act, and they appealed. The Court upheld the Act.

District of Columbia v. Heller (2008)

Decision: The Court ruled 5 to 4 that Washington, D.C.'s gun law was unconstitutional. The majority concluded that the Second Amendment "right of the people to keep and bear Arms" meant that individuals could have weapons for self-defense. An outright ban on gun ownership was therefore unconstitutional. In addition, since dismantled or disabled weapons would not be useful for self-defense, the part of the law requiring that all guns, including shotguns and rifles, be kept unloaded and either taken apart or disabled by a trigger lock was also unconstitutional. In dissent, Justice Breyer suggested a balancing test, under which gun control laws could be constitutional when they supported a compelling governmental interest in preventing crime.

Dred Scott v. Sandford (1857)

(5th Amendment, individual rights) This decision upheld property rights over human rights by saying that Dred Scott, a slave, could not become a free man just because he had traveled in "free soil" States with his master. A badly divided nation was further fragmented by the decision. "Free soil" federal laws and the Missouri Compromise line of 1820 were held unconstitutional because they deprived a slave owner of the right to his "property" without just compensation. This narrow reading of the Constitution, a landmark case of the Court, was most clearly stated by Chief Justice Roger B. Taney, a States' rights advocate.

Engel v. Vitale (1962)

(1st Amendment, Establishment Clause) The State Board of Regents of New York required the recitation of a 22-word nonsectarian prayer at the beginning of each school day. A group of parents filed suit against the required prayer, claiming it violated their 1st Amendment rights. The Court found New York's action to be unconstitutional, observing, "There can be no doubt that. . . religious beliefs [are] embodied in the Regent's prayer."

Edwards v. South Carolina (1963)

(1st Amendment, freedom of speech and assembly) A group of mostly African American civil rights activists held a rally at the South Carolina State Capitol, protesting segregation. A hostile crowd gathered and the rally leaders were arrested and convicted for "breach of the peace." The Court overturned the convictions, saying, "The Fourteenth Amendment does not permit a State to make criminal the peaceful expression of unpopular views."

Escobedo v. Illinois (1964)

(6th Amendment, right to counsel) In a case involving a murder confession by a person known to Chicago-area police who was not afforded counsel while under interrogation, the Court extended the "exclusionary rule" to illegal confessions in State court proceedings. Carefully defining an "Escobedo Rule," the Court said, "where. . . the investigation is no longer a general inquiry . . . but has begun to focus on a particular suspect . . . (and where) the suspect has been taken into custody . . . the suspect has requested . . . his lawyer, and the police have not . . . warned him of his right to remain silent, the accused has been denied . . . counsel in violation of the Sixth Amendment."

Ex parte Milligan (1866)

(Article II, executive powers) An Indiana man was arrested, treated as a prisoner of war, and imprisoned by a military court during the Civil War under presidential order. He claimed that his rights to a fair trial were interfered with and that military courts had no authority outside of "conquered territory." He was released because, "the Constitution . . . is a law for rulers and people, equally in war and peace, and covers . . . all . . . men, at all times, and under all circumstances." The Court held that presidential powers to suspend the writ of habeas corpus in time of war did not extend to creating another court system run by the military.

Flast v. Cohen (1968)

Decision: The Supreme Court concluded that the rule announced in *Frothingham* v. *Mellon* expressed a practical policy of judicial self-restraint rather than an absolute constitutional limitation on the power of federal courts to hear taxpayer suits. While mere status as a federal taxpayer ordinarily will not give sufficient "standing" to allow a person to challenge the constitutionality of a federal law, there may be times when taxpayers are appropriate plaintiffs. *Flast* v. *Cohen*, in which plaintiffs argued that the First Amendment specifically prohibited taxing them in order to support religious activities, was one in which their role as taxpayers was well suited to the challenge they sought to assert. The Court ruled that they had standing to sue, and allowed them to proceed with their case.

Furman v. Georgia (1972)

(8th Amendment, capital punishment) Three different death penalty cases, including *Furman,* raised the question of racial imbalances in the use of death sentences by State courts. Furman had been convicted and sentenced to death in Georgia. In deciding to overturn existing State death-penalty laws, the Court noted that there was an "apparent arbitrariness of the use of the sentence. . . ." Many States rewrote their death-penalty statutes and these were generally upheld in *Gregg* v. *Georgia,* 1976.

Gibbons v. Ogden (1824)

(Supremacy Clause) This decision involved a careful examination of the power of Congress to "regulate interstate commerce." Aaron Ogden's exclusive New York ferry license gave him the right to operate steamboats to and from New York. He said that Thomas Gibbons's federal "coasting license" did not include "landing rights" in New York City. The Court invalidated the New York licensing regulations, holding that federal regulations should take precedence under the Supremacy Clause. The decision strengthened the power of the United States to regulate any interstate business relationship. Federal regulation of the broadcasting industry, oil pipelines, and banking are all based on *Gibbons.*

Gideon v. Wainwright (1963)

(6th Amendment, right to counsel) In 1961 a Florida court found Clarence Earl Gideon guilty of breaking and entering and sentenced him to five years in prison. Gideon appealed his case to the Supreme Court on the basis that he had been unconstitutionally denied counsel during his trial due to Florida's policy of only providing appointed counsel in capital cases. The Court granted Gideon a new trial, and he was found not guilty with the help of a court-appointed attorney. The "Gideon Rule" upheld the 6th Amendment's guarantee of counsel of all poor persons facing a felony charge, a further incorporation of Bill of Rights guarantees into State constitutions.

Gitlow v. New York (1925)

(1st Amendment, freedom of speech) A New York socialist, Gitlow, was convicted under a State law on "criminal anarchy" for distributing copies of a "left-wing manifesto." For the first time, the Court considered whether the 1st Amendment applied to State laws. The case helped to establish what came to be known as the "incorporation" doctrine, under which, it was argued, the provisions of the 1st Amendment were "incorporated" by the 14th Amendment, thus applying to State as well as federal laws. Although New York law was not overruled in this case, the decision clearly indicated that the Supreme Court could make such a ruling. See also *Powell* v. *Alabama,* 1932.

Goss v. Lopez (1975)

(14th Amendment, Due Process Clause) Ten Ohio students were suspended from their schools without hearings. The students challenged the suspensions, claiming that the absence of a preliminary hearing violated their 14th Amendment right to due process. The Court agreed, holding that "having chosen to extend the right to an education. . . Ohio may not withdraw that right on grounds of misconduct, absent fundamentally fair procedures to determine whether the misconduct has occurred, and must recognize a student's legitimate entitlement to a public education as a property interest that is protected by the Due Process Clause."

Gregg v. Georgia (1976)

(8th Amendment, cruel and unusual punishment) A Georgia jury sentenced Troy Gregg to death after finding him guilty on two counts each of murder and armed robbery. Gregg appealed the sentence, claiming that it violated the "cruel and unusual punishment" clause of the 8th Amendment and citing *Furman v. Georgia*, 1972, in which the court held that Georgia's application of the death penalty was unfair and arbitrary. However, the Court upheld Gregg's sentence, stating for the first time that "punishment of death does not invariably violate the Constitution."

Griswold v. Connecticut (1965)

(14th Amendment, Due Process Clause) A Connecticut law forbade the use of "any drug, medicinal article, or instrument for the purpose of preventing conception." Griswold, director of Planned Parenthood in New Haven, was arrested for counseling married persons and, after conviction, appealed. The Court overturned the Connecticut law, saying that "various guarantees (of the Constitution) create zones of privacy. . ." and questioning, ". . .would we allow the police to search the sacred precincts of marital bedrooms. . . ?" The decision is significant for raising for more careful inspection the concept of "unenumerated rights" in the 9th Amendment, later central to *Roe* v. *Wade*, 1973.

Grutter v. Bollinger; Gratz v. Bollinger (2003)

Decision: (*Gratz*) The policy of the University of Michigan, giving undergraduate applicants twenty points just for being a member of a racial or ethnic group, violates the Equal Protection Clause of the 14th Amendment. The policy discriminates on the basis of race, but is not narrowly tailored to create a diverse student body. (*Grutter*) The policy of the University of Michigan's law school, considering an applicant's racial or ethnic background as just one factor in attempting to admit a diverse student body, is constitutional. Because the law school considers each applicant individually, and does not assign an inflexible value for race, the policy creates a diverse student body without discriminating on the basis of race.

Hazelwood School District v. Kuhlmeier (1988)

(1st Amendment, freedom of speech) In 1983, the principal of Hazelwood East High School in Missouri removed two articles from the upcoming issue of the student newspaper, deeming their content "inappropriate, personal, sensitive, and unsuitable for student readers." Several students sued, claiming that their right to freedom of expression had been violated. The Court upheld the principal's action: "a school need not tolerate student speech that is inconsistent with its basic educational mission, even though the government could not censor similar speech outside the school." School officials had full control over school-sponsored activities "so long as their actions are reasonably related to legitimate pedagogical concerns. . . ."

Heart of Atlanta Motel, Inc. v. United States (1964)

Decision: The Court ruled that Congress could outlaw racial segregation of private facilities that are engaged in interstate commerce. The Court's decision stated, "If it is interstate commerce that feels the pinch, it does not matter how 'local' the operation which applies the squeeze. . . . The power of Congress to promote interstate commerce also includes the power to regulate the local incidents thereof, including local activities. . . which have a substantial and harmful effect upon that commerce."

Hutchinson v. Proxmire (1979)

Decision: The Court held that the Speech or Debate Clause gives members of Congress immunity from suit for defamatory statements made within the legislative chambers, but the privilege does not extend to comments made in other locations, even if they merely repeat what was said in Congress. The newsletters and press release were not within the deliberative process nor were they essential to the deliberation of the Senate. They also were not part of the "informing function" of members of Congress, since they were not a part of legislative function or process. The comments were merely designed to convey information on the Senator's individual positions and beliefs. Finally, although Hutchinson had received extensive attention in the media as a result of his receipt of the Golden Fleece Award, he was not a public figure prior to that controversy and thus is entitled to the greater protection against defamation that is extended to non-public figures. The fact that the public may have an interest in governmental expenditures does not make Hutchinson himself a public figure.

Illinois v. Wardlow (2000)

Decision: The Supreme Court refused to say that flight from the police will always justify a stop or that it will never do so. Instead, the Court ruled that flight can be an important factor in determining whether police have "reasonable suspicion" to stop a suspect. The trial court will have to determine in each case whether the information available to the police officers, including the fact of a suspect's flight, was sufficient to support the stop.

In Re Gault (1966)

(14th Amendment, Due Process Clause) Prior to the *Gault* case, proceedings against juvenile offenders were generally handled as "family law," not "criminal law" and provided few due process guarantees. Gerald Gault was assigned to six years in a State juvenile detention facility for an alleged obscene phone call. He was not provided counsel and not permitted to confront or cross-examine the principal witness. The Court overturned the juvenile proceedings and required that States provide juveniles "some of the due process guarantees of adults," including a right to a phone call, to counsel, to cross-examine, to confront their accuser, and to be advised of their right to silence.

Johnson v. Santa Clara Transportation Agency (1987)

(Discrimination) Under their affirmative action plan, the Transportation Agency in Santa Clara, California, was authorized to "consider as one factor the sex of a qualified applicant" in an effort to combat the significant underrepresentation of women in certain job classifications. When the Agency promoted Diane Joyce, a qualified woman, over Paul Johnson, a qualified man, for the job of road dispatcher, Johnson sued, claiming that the Agency's consideration of the sex of the applicants violated Title VII of the Civil Rights Act of 1964. The Court upheld the Agency's promotion policy, arguing that the affirmative action plan created no "absolute bar" to the advancement of men but rather represented "a moderate, flexible, case-by-case approach to effecting a gradual improvement in the representation of minorities and women ... in the Agency's work force, and [was] fully consistent with Title VII."

Korematsu v. United States (1944)

Decision: The Court upheld the military order in light of the circumstances presented by World War II. "Pressing public necessity may sometimes justify the existence of restrictions which curtail the civil rights of a single racial group." The Court noted, however, that racial antagonism itself could never form a legitimate basis for the restrictions.

Lemon v. Kurtzman (1971)

(1st Amendment, Establishment Clause) In overturning State laws regarding aid to church-supported schools in this and a similar Rhode Island case, the Court created the Lemon test limiting "... excessive government entanglement with religion." The Court noted that any State law about aid to religion must meet three criteria: (1) purpose of the aid must be clearly secular, (2) its primary effect must neither advance nor inhibit religion, and (3) it must avoid "excessive entanglement of government with religion."

Mapp v. Ohio (1962)

(4th and 14th Amendments, illegal evidence and Due Process Clause) Admitting evidence gained by illegal searches was permitted by some States before *Mapp*. Cleveland police raided Dollree Mapp's home without a warrant and found obscene materials. She appealed her conviction, saying that the 4th and 14th Amendments protected her against improper police behavior. The Court agreed, extending "exclusionary rule" protections to citizens in State courts, saying that the prohibition against unreasonable searches would be "meaningless" unless evidence gained in such searches was "excluded." *Mapp* developed the concept of "incorporation" begun in *Gitlow* v. *New York*, 1925.

Marbury v. Madison (1803)

(Article III, judicial powers) After defeat in the 1800 election, President Adams appointed many Federalists to the federal courts, but James Madison, the new secretary of state, refused to deliver the commissions. William Marbury, one of the appointees, asked the Supreme Court to enforce the delivery of his commission based on a provision of the Judiciary Act of 1789 that allowed the Court to hear such cases on original jurisdiction. The Court refused Marbury's request, finding that the relevant portion of the Judiciary Act was in conflict with the Constitution. This decision, written by Chief Justice Marshall, established the evaluation of federal laws' constitutionality, or "judicial review," as a power of the Supreme Court.

McCulloch v. Maryland (1819)

(Article I, Section 8, Necessary and Proper Clause) Called the "Bank of the United States" case. A Maryland law required federally chartered banks to use only a special paper to print paper money, which amounted to a tax. James McCulloch, the cashier of the Baltimore branch of the bank, refused to use the paper, claiming that States could not tax the Federal Government. The Court declared the Maryland law unconstitutional, commenting ". . . the power to tax implies the power to destroy."

Miranda v. Arizona (1966)

(5th, 6th, and 14th Amendments, rights of the accused) Arrested for kidnapping and sexual assault, Ernesto Miranda signed a confession including a statement that he had "full knowledge of [his] legal rights. . . ." After conviction, he appealed, claiming that without counsel and without warnings, the confession was illegally gained. The Court agreed with Miranda that "he must be warned prior to any questioning that he has the right to remain silent, that anything he says can be used against him in a court of law, that he has the right to. . . an attorney and that if he cannot afford an attorney one will be appointed for him. . . ." Although later modified by *Nix* v. *Williams,* 1984, and other cases, *Miranda* firmly upheld citizen rights to fair trials in State courts.

New Jersey v. T.L.O. (1985)

(4th and 14th Amendments) After T.L.O., a New Jersey high school student, denied an accusation that she had been smoking in the school lavatory, a vice-principal searched her purse and found cigarettes, marijuana, and evidence that T.L.O. had been involved in marijuana dealing at the school. T.L.O. was then sentenced to probation by a juvenile court, but appealed on the grounds that the evidence against her had been obtained by an "unreasonable" search. The Court rejected T.L.O.'s arguments, stating that the school had a "legitimate need to maintain an environment in which learning can take place," and that to do this "requires some easing of the restrictions to which searches by public authorities are ordinarily subject..." The Court thus created a "reasonable suspicion" rule for school searches, a change from the "probable cause" requirement in the wider society.

New York Times v. United States (1971)

(1st Amendment, freedom of the press) In 1971 The New York Times obtained copies of classified Defense Department documents, later known as the "Pentagon Papers," which revealed instances in which the Johnson Administration had deceived Congress and the American people regarding U.S. policies during the Vietnam War. A U.S. district court issued an injunction against the publication of the documents, claiming that it might endanger national security. On appeal, the Supreme Court cited the 1st Amendment guarantee of a free press and refused to uphold the injunction against publication, observing that it is the obligation of the government to prove that actual harm to the nation's security would be caused by the publication. The decision limited "prior restraint" of the press.

New York Times v. Sullivan (1964)

Decision: A unanimous Court announced that a public official could not win a suit for defamation (false statement) unless the statement was made with "actual malice," meaning either with the knowledge that it was false or with "reckless disregard" of the truth. The Court found a national commitment to "uninhibited, robust, and wide-open" debate on issues of public concern—even when this included "vehement, caustic, and sometimes unpleasantly sharp attacks on government and public officials." Without an "actual malice" standard, citizens might be unwilling to criticize elected officials for fear of being sued if something they said turned out to be inaccurate.

Nixon v. Fitzgerald (1982)

Decision: The Court ruled that a President or former President is entitled to absolute immunity from liability based on his official acts. The President must be able to act forcefully and independently, without fear of liability. Diverting the President's energies with concerns about private lawsuits could impair the effective functioning of government. The President's absolute immunity extends to all acts within the "outer perimeter" of his duties of office, since otherwise he would be required to litigate over the nature of the acts and the scope of his duties in each case. The remedy of impeachment, the vigilant scrutiny of the press, the Congress, and the public, and presidential desire to earn reelection and concern with historical legacy all protect against presidential wrongdoing.

Nixon v. Shrink Missouri Government PAC (2000)

Decision: In *Buckley* v. *Valeo*, 1976, the Supreme Court had upheld a $1000 limit on contributions by individuals to candidates for federal office. In *Nixon* v. *Shrink Missouri Government PAC*, the Court concluded that large contributions will sometimes create actual corruption, and that voters will be suspicious of the fairness of a political process that allows wealthy donors to contribute large amounts. The Court concluded that the Missouri contribution limits were appropriate to correct this problem and did not impair the ability of candidates to communicate their messages to the voters and to mount an effective campaign.

Olmstead v. United States (1928)

(4th Amendment, electronic surveillance) Olmstead was engaged in the illegal sale of alcohol. Much of the evidence against him was gained through a wiretap made without a warrant. Olmstead argued that he had "a reasonable expectation of privacy," and that the *Weeks* v. *United States* decision of 1914 should be applied to exclude the evidence gained by the wiretap. The Court disagreed, saying that Olmstead intended "to project his voice to those quite outside . . . and that . . . nothing tangible was taken." Reversed by subsequent decisions, this case contains the first usage of the concept of "reasonable expectation of privacy" that would mark later 4th Amendment decisions.

Oregon v. Mitchell (1970)

Decision: The Supreme Court was unable to issue a single opinion of the Court supported by a majority of the justices. However, in a series of separate opinions, differing majority groups agreed that (1) the 18-year-old minimum-age requirement of the Voting Rights Act Amendments is valid for national elections but not for State and local elections; (2) the literacy test provision is valid in order to remedy discrimination against minorities; and (3) the residency and absentee balloting provisions are a valid congressional regulation of presidential elections.

Plessy v. Ferguson (1896)

(14th Amendment, Equal Protection Clause) A Louisiana law required separate seating for white and African American citizens on public railroads, a form of segregation. Homer Plessy argued that his right to "equal protection of the laws" was violated. The Court held that segregation was permitted if facilities were equal. The Court interpreted the 14th Amendment as "not intended to give Negroes social equality but only political and civil equality. . . ." The Louisiana law was seen as a "reasonable exercise of (State) police power. . ." Segregated public facilities were permitted until *Plessy* was overturned by the *Brown* v. *Board of Education* case of 1954.

Powell v. Alabama (1932)

(6th Amendment, right to counsel) The case involved the "Scottsboro boys," seven African American men accused of sexual assault. This case was a landmark in the development of a "fundamentals of fairness" doctrine of the Court over the next 40 years. The Scottsboro boys were quickly prosecuted without the benefit of counsel and sentenced to death. The Court overturned the decision, stating that poor people facing the death penalty in State courts must be provided counsel, and commenting, ". . . there are certain principles of Justice which adhere to the very idea of free government, which no [State] may disregard." The case was another step toward incorporation of the Bill of Rights into State constitutions.

Printz v. United States (1997)

Decision: The Court ruled that the Brady Act's interim provision requiring certain State or local law enforcement agents to perform background checks on prospective handgun purchasers was unconstitutional. Although no provision of the Constitution deals explicitly with federal authority to compel State officials to execute federal law, a review of the Constitution's structure and of prior Supreme Court decisions leads to the conclusion that Congress does not have this power.

Reno v. American Civil Liberties Union (1997)

Decision: The Supreme Court unanimously ruled that the anti-obscenity provisions of the Communications Decency Act (CDA) abridged the freedom of speech protected under the First Amendment. Those parts of the CDA were intended to keep minors from "patently offensive" or "indecent" communications on the Internet. While the Court recognized the importance of Congress's goal of protecting children, it concluded that the terms "patently offensive" and "indecent" were too vague to be enforceable, especially since information on the Internet is easily transmitted to many different parts of the country where community standards of decency may vary. The decision suggested that the Court saw the Internet as more like books or newspapers, which have high First Amendment protection, rather than like radio and television, where content can be more closely regulated by the government.

Reno v. Condon (2000)

Decision: The Court upheld the federal law that forbids States from selling addresses, telephone numbers, and other information that drivers put on license applications. They agreed with the Federal Government that information, including motor vehicle license information, is an "article of commerce" in the interstate stream of business and therefore is subject to regulation by Congress. The Court emphasized that the statute did not impose on the States any obligation to pass particular laws or policies and thus did not interfere with the States' sovereign functions.

Republican Party of Minnesota v. White (2002)

Decision: The Supreme Court decided that the State prohibition on "announcing" a judicial candidate's views violates the 1st Amendment. It unduly restricts the candidates' rights of free speech without adequately furthering the expressed goal of improving judicial impartiality and the appearance of impartiality. The government may not restrict speech based on its content, as this rule does. In addition, the government may not restrict speech about candidates' qualifications for office, which the rule also does. In addition, the rule is not well designed to preserve impartiality, since

it has no effect on the candidate's beliefs. Finally, the lack of any longstanding tradition of such a rule shows there is no historical presumption of constitutionality.

Roe v. Wade (1973)

(9th Amendment, right to privacy) A Texas woman challenged a State law forbidding the artificial termination of a pregnancy, saying that she "had a fundamental right to privacy." The Court upheld a woman's right to choose in this case, noting that the State's "important and legitimate interest in protecting the potentiality of human life" became "compelling" at the end of the first trimester, and that before then, ". . . the attending physician, in consultation with his patient, is free to determine, without regulation by the State, that . . . the patient's pregnancy should be terminated." The decision struck down the State regulation of abortion in the first three months of pregnancy and was modified by *Planned Parenthood of Southeastern PA v. Casey,* 1992.

Rostker v. Goldberg (1981)

Decision: The Court ruled that women did not have to be included in the draft registration. The purpose of having draft registration was to prepare for the actual draft of combat troops if they should be needed. Since Congress and the President had both consistently decided not to use women in combat positions, it was not necessary for women to register either. The Court also noted that the role of women in the armed services had been debated extensively in the Congress, and concluded that the legislature had reached a thoughtful, reasoned conclusion on this issue.

Roth v. United States (1951)

(1st Amendment, freedom of the press) A New York man named Roth operated a business that used the mail to invite people to buy materials considered obscene by postal inspectors. The Court, in its first consideration of censorship of obscenity, created the "prevailing community standards" rule, which required a consideration of the work as a whole. In its decision, the Court defined as obscene that which offended "the average person, applying contemporary community standards." In a case decided the same day, the Court applied the same "test" to State obscenity laws.

Rush Prudential HMO, Inc. v. Moran (2002)

Decision: The Supreme Court decided that ERISA does not preempt the Illinois medical-review statute. The statute regulates insurance, which is one of the functions HMOs perform. Although HMOs provide healthcare as well as insurance, the statute does not require choosing a single or primary function of an HMO. Congress has long recognized that HMOs are risk-bearing organizations subject to state regulation. Finally, allowing States to regulate the insurance aspects of HMOs will not interfere with the desire of Congress for uniform national standards under ERISA.

Schenck v. United States (1919)

(1st Amendment, freedom of speech) Charles Schenck was an officer of an antiwar political group who was arrested for alleged violations of the Espionage Act of 1917, which made active opposition to the war a crime. He had urged thousands of young men called to service by the draft act to resist and to avoid induction. The Court limited free speech in time of war, stating that Schenck's words, under the circumstances, presented a "clear and present danger. . . ." Although later decisions modified the decision, the *Schenck* case created a precedent that 1st Amendment guarantees were not absolute.

School District of Abington Township, Pennsylvania v. Schempp (1963)

(1st Amendment, Establishment Clause) A Pennsylvania State law required reading from the Bible each day at school as an all-school activity. Some parents objected and sought legal remedy. When the case reached the Court, the Court agreed with the parents, saying that the Establishment Clause and Free Exercise Clause both forbade States from engaging in religious activity. The Court created a rule holding that if the purpose and effect of a law "is the advancement or inhibition of religion," it "exceeds the scope of legal power."

Shelley v. Kraemer (1948)

Decision: The Court ruled that "in granting judicial enforcement of the restrictive agreements . . . the States have denied petitioners the equal protection of the laws. . . ." No individual has the right under the Constitution to demand that a State take action that would result in the denial of equal protection to other individuals. The Court rejected the respondents' argument that, since State courts would also enforce restrictive covenants against white owners, enforcement of covenants against black owners did not constitute a denial of equal protection. "Equal protection of the laws is not achieved through indiscriminate imposition of inequalities."

Sheppard v. Maxwell (1966)

(14th Amendment, Due Process Clause) Dr. Samuel Sheppard was convicted of murdering his wife in a trial widely covered by national news media. Sheppard appealed his conviction, claiming that the pretrial publicity had made it impossible to get a fair trial. The Court rejected the arguments about "press freedom," overturned his conviction, and ordered a new trial. As a result of the *Sheppard* decision, some judges have issued "gag" orders limiting pretrial publicity.

Tahoe-Sierra Preservation Council v. Tahoe Regional Planning Agency (2002)

Decision: The 32-month moratorium imposed by the Tahoe Regional Planning Agency on development in the Lake Tahoe Basin between Nevada and California is not a taking of property for which compensation is required. It is impossible in the abstract to say how long a restriction would be permissible. Although 32 months is a long moratorium, it is not unreasonable in this case and does not restrict the property owners' economic use of their property sufficiently to amount to a taking for which compensation must be paid.

Tennessee Valley Authority v. Hill (1978)

(Article I, Section 8, Necessary and Proper Clause) In 1975 the secretary of the interior found that the Tennessee Valley Authority's work on the Tellico Dam would destroy the endangered snail darter's habitat in violation of the Endangered Species Act of 1975. When the TVA refused to stop work on the project, local residents sued and won an injunction against completion of the dam from the federal court of appeals. The TVA appealed, arguing that the project should be completed since it had already been underway when the Endangered Species Act had passed and, with full knowledge of the circumstances of the endangered fish, Congress had continued to appropriate money for the dam in every year since the Act's passage. However, the Supreme Court found the injunction against the TVA's completion of the dam to be proper, stating "examination of the language, history, and structure of the legislation . . . indicates beyond doubt that Congress intended endangered species to be afforded the highest of priorities."

Texas v. White (1869)

Decision: The Court held, in a 5–3 decision, that Texas had the right to bring suit as a "State" in the Supreme Court, even though it had claimed to secede from the United States in 1862. Writing after the end of the Civil War, with military rule imposed in Texas under the Reconstruction Acts of 1867, the majority concluded that the United States was "an indestructible Union, composed of indestructible States," so that Texas had never actually left the Union.

Tinker v. Des Moines School District (1969)

Decision: The Court upheld the students' First Amendment rights. Because students do not "shed their constitutional rights to freedom of speech or expression at the schoolhouse gate," schools must show a possibility of "substantial disruption" before free speech can be limited at school. Students may express personal opinions as long as they do not materially disrupt classwork, create substantial disorder, or interfere with the rights of others. In this case, the wearing of black armbands was a "silent, passive expression of opinion" without these side effects and thus constitutionally could not be prohibited by the school.

U.S. Term Limits, Inc. v. Thornton (1995)

Decision: The Arkansas amendment preventing any person who had already served three terms as U.S. representative or two terms as U.S. senator from being listed on the ballot violates Article I, Section 2, Clause 2 and Section 3, Clause 3 of the Federal Constitution. The Arkansas law in effect established term limits for members of Congress, but the Constitution is the sole source of qualifications for membership. Such limits can only be set by an amendment to the Federal Constitution.

United States v. American Library Association (2003)

Decision: Requiring public libraries to install filters to block obscene or pornographic Internet sites as a condition for obtaining federal funds for Internet access does not violate the 1st Amendment. Congress's substantial interest in protecting children from harmful materials justifies the minimal interference with free speech caused when library users are forced to request access to a specific site.

United States v. Amistad (1841)

In 1839 two Spaniards purchased a group of kidnapped Africans and put them aboard the schooner *Amistad* for a journey from Cuba to Principe. The Africans overpowered the ship's crew, killing two men, and ordered the Spaniards to steer towards Africa. The crew steered instead toward the United States coast, where the U.S. brig *Washington* seized the ship, freeing the Spaniards and imprisoning the Africans. A series of petitions to the courts ensued, in which the Spaniards claimed the Africans as their property, and the Americans who had seized the ship claimed a share of the cargo, including the Africans, as their lawful salvage. The Court, however, declared that the Africans were not property and issued a decree that the unlawfully kidnapped Africans "be and are hereby declared to be free."

United States v. Eichman (1990)

Decision: The Court agreed with the trial courts' rulings that the Flag Protection Act violated the 1st Amendment. Flag-burning constitutes expressive conduct, and thus is entitled to constitutional protection. The Act prevents protesters from using the flag to express their opposition to governmental policies and activities. Although the protesters' ideas may be offensive or disagreeable to many people, the government may not prohibit them from expressing those ideas.

United States v. General Dynamics Corp. (1974)

A deep-mining coal producer, General Dynamics Corp., acquired control of a strip-mining coal producer, United Electric Coal Companies. The Government filed suit against the company, claiming that the acquisition violated the Clayton Act by limiting competition in coal sales and production. The Court rejected the Government's argument, finding that, although the acquisition may have increased concentration of ownership, it did not threaten to substantially lessen competition and was therefore not in violation of the Clayton Act.

United States v. Leon (1984)

(4th Amendment, exclusionary rule) Police in Burbank, California, gathered evidence in a drug-trafficking investigation using a search warrant issued by a State court judge. Later a District Court found that the warrant had been improperly issued and granted a motion to suppress the evidence gathered under the warrant. The Government appealed the decision, claiming that the exclusionary rule should not apply in cases where law enforcement officers acted in good faith, believing the warrant to be valid. The Court agreed and established the "good-faith exception" to the exclusionary rule, finding that the rule should not be applied to bar evidence "obtained by officers acting in reasonable reliance on a search warrant issued by a detached and neutral magistrate but ultimately found to be invalid."

United States v. Lopez (1990)

(Article I, Section 8, Commerce Clause) Alfonzo Lopez, a Texas high school student, was convicted of carrying a weapon in a school zone under the Gun-Free School Zones Act of 1990. He appealed his conviction on the basis that the Act, which forbids "any individual knowingly to possess a firearm at a place that [he] knows . . . is a school zone," exceeded Congress's legislative power under the Commerce Clause. The Court agreed that the Act was unconstitutional, stating that to uphold the legislation would "bid fair to convert congressional Commerce Clause authority to a general police power of the sort held only by the States."

United States v. Nixon (1974)

(Separation of powers) During the investigation of the Watergate scandal, in which members of President Nixon's administration were accused of participating in various illegal activities, a special prosecutor subpoenaed tapes of conversations between Nixon and his advisors. Nixon refused to release the tapes but was overruled by the Court, which ordered him to surrender the tapes, rejecting his arguments that they were protected by "executive privilege." The President's "generalized interest in confidentiality" was subordinate to "the fundamental demands of due process of law in the fair administration of criminal justice."

Wallace v. Jaffree (1985)

(1st Amendment, Establishment Clause) An Alabama law authorized a one-minute period of silence in all public schools "for meditation or voluntary prayer." A group of parents, including Jaffree, challenged the constitutionality of the statute, claiming it violated the Establishment Clause of the 1st Amendment. The Court agreed with Jaffree and struck down the Alabama law, determining that "the State's endorsement . . . of prayer activities at the beginning of each schoolday is not consistent with the established principle that the government must pursue a course of complete neutrality toward religion."

Walz v. *Tax Commission of the City of New York* (1970)

(1st Amendment, Establishment Clause) State and local governments routinely exempt church property from taxes. Walz claimed that such exemptions were a "support of religion," a subsidy by government. The Court disagreed, noting that such exemptions were just an example of a "benevolent neutrality" between government and churches, not a support of religion. Governments must avoid taxing churches because taxation would give government a "control" over religion, prohibited by the "wall of separation of church and state" noted in *Everson* v. *Board of Education,* 1947.

Watchtower Bible & Tract Society v. *Village of Stratton* (2001)

Decision: The Court ruled the Village's ordinance requiring canvassers to get a permit to be unconstitutional. Although a municipality may have a legitimate interest in regulating door-to-door solicitation, there must be a balance between furthering that interest and restricting 1st Amendment rights. The ordinance restricts religious or political speech, and thus needs strong justification to be valid. Because the ordinance is not restricted to commercial activities, it is broader than necessary to protect fraud. Residents have other ways to protect their privacy—they can post "no solicitation" signs or refuse to talk with unwelcome visitors. Finally, the 1st Amendment protects the right to anonymous expressions of religious or political belief.

Watkins v. *United States* (1957)

Decision: The Court held that Watkins was not given a fair opportunity to determine whether he was within his rights in refusing to answer the Committee's questions. Congress has no authority to expose the private affairs of individuals unless justified by a specific function of Congress. Congress's investigative powers are broad but not unlimited, and must not infringe on 1st Amendment rights of speech, political belief, or association. When witnesses are forced by subpoena to testify, the subject of Congressional inquiry must be articulated in the Committee's charter or explained at the time of testimony if 1st Amendment rights are in jeopardy.

West Virginia Board of Education v. *Barnette* (1943)

(1st Amendment, freedom of religion) During World War II the West Virginia Board of Education required all students to take part in a daily flag-saluting ceremony or else face expulsion. Jehovah's Witnesses objected to the compulsory salute, which they felt would force them to break their religion's doctrine against the worship of any "graven image." The Court struck down the rule, agreeing that a compulsory flag salute violated the 1st Amendment's exercise of religion clause and stating that "No official, high or petty, can prescribe what shall be orthodox in politics, nationalism, religion, or other matters of opinion. . . ."

Board of Education of Westside Community Schools v. *Mergens* (1990)

(1st Amendment, Establishment Clause) A request by Bridget Mergens to form a student Christian religious group at school was denied by an Omaha high school principal. Mergens took legal action, claiming that a 1984 federal law required "equal access" for student religious groups. The Court ordered the school to permit the club, stating, "a high school does not have to permit any extracurricular activities, but when it does, the school is bound by the . . . [Equal Access] Act of 1984. Allowing students to meet on campus and discuss religion is constitutional because it does not amount to 'State sponsorship of a religion.' "

Wisconsin v. *Yoder* (1972)

(1st Amendment, Free Exercise Clause) Members of the Amish religious sect in Wisconsin objected to sending their children to public schools after the eighth grade, claiming that such exposure of the children to another culture would endanger the group's self-sufficient agrarian lifestyle essential to their religious faith. The Court agreed with the Amish, while noting that the Court must move carefully to weigh the State's "legitimate social concern when faced with religious claim for exemption from generally applicable educational requirements."

Glossary

A

Absentee voting (ab sən tē´vōting) The process by which people can vote without going to polling places on election day

Acquit (ə kwit´) Find not guilty of a charge

Act of admission (akt ov ad mis´shən) A congressional act admitting a new state to the Union

Adjourn (a jėrn´) To bring a meeting to an end

Administrative law (ad min´ə strā´tiv lò) Law that regulates federal and state government agencies not covered by constitutional law

Affirmative action (ə fèr´mə tiv ak´shən) A policy that requires most employers to take positive steps to make better the effects of past discrimination

Albany Plan of Union (òl´bə nē plan ov yü´nyən) Plan made by Benjamin Franklin that would unite colonies for trade and war decisions

Alien (ā´lyən) A person who lives in a country but is a citizen of another country

Ambassador (am bas´ə dər) A person appointed by the President to represent the United States in a foreign country

Amendment (ə mend´mənt) A change in, or addition to, a constitution

Amicus curiae brief (uh mē kuhs kyür ē brēf) Latin for "friend of the court;" a brief that supports one of the sides in a case being

Amnesty (am´nə stē) A pardon that affects many people

Ancient (ān´shənt) Many years ago; belonging to early history

Anti-Federalist (an´tē fed´ər ə list) A person who favored state and individual rights

Appellate jurisdiction (ə pel´it jùr´is dik´shən) The authority of a court to review decisions of inferior (lower) courts

Appoint (ə point´) To name or choose a person for an office, but not by election

Appropriate (u prō´prē ātz) To assign to a particular use

Article (är´tə kəl) A numbered section of a document such as the Constitution

Assembly (ə sem´blē) A coming together for a common purpose

Assimilation (ə sim´ə lā´shən) The process by which people of one culture become a part of another culture

At-large (at lärj) Describes an election of a candidate by the whole state rather than a single district

Attorney General (ə tėr´nē jen´ər əl) The head of the Department of Justice

Authority (ə thôr´ə tē) The power or right to command or make final decisions

Autocracy (ò tok´rə sē) A government in which one person holds unlimited political power

B

Bail (bāl) Money paid to the court by an accused person to guarantee that the person will show up for trial

Balance the ticket (bal´əns Ŧнə tik´it) The practice of choosing a presidential running mate who can strengthen a presidential candidate's chance of being elected

Ballot (bal´ət) The tool voters use to select a candidate in an election

Ballot fatigue (bal´ət fə tēg´) A general rule that the farther down the ballot an office is, the fewer number of votes that will be cast for it

Bankruptcy (bang´krupt sē) The legal procedure in which the bankrupt's assets are paid to those to whom a debt is owed

Battleground State (bat´l ground stāt´) States in which the outcome is too close to call and either candidate could win

Bench trial (bench tri´əl) A trial that is heard by a judge without a jury

Bicameral (bī kam´ər əl) A legislative body made up of two parts, or chambers

Bill (bil) A proposed law

Bill of attainder (bil ov ə tān´dər) A legislative act that inflicts punishment on a person without a court trial

Bipartisan (bī pär´tə zən) Supported by two parties

Blanket primary (blang´kit prī´mer i) An election in which voters receive a long ballot containing the names of all contenders, regardless of party, and can vote however they choose

Block grants (blok grantz) Grants made by the federal government for some particular but broadly defined area of public policy

Budget (buj´it) A financial plan for spending money

Bureaucracy (byrok´rə sē) A large, complex structure that handles the everyday business of an organization

Bureaucrat (byòr´ə krat) A person who works for a bureaucratic organization

Business tax (biz´nis taks) An additional tax collected on businesses for various services

C

Cabinet (kab´ə nit) A group of advisors to the President made up of heads of the executive departments

a	hat	e	let	ī	ice	ô	order	ù	put	sh	she		a	in about
ā	age	ē	equal	o	hot	oi	oil	ü	rule	th	thin		e	in taken
ä	far	ėr	term	ō	open	ou	out	ch	child	ŦH	then	ə	i	in pencil
â	care	i	it	ò	saw	u	cup	ng	long	zh	measure		o	in lemon
													u	in circus

GLOSSARY

Campaign (kam pān´) The activities connected to trying to get a person elected to a political office

Candidate (kan´də dāt) A person who hopes to be elected to a public office

Capital (kap´ə təl) Human-made resources: buildings, machines, and money

Capitalism (kap´ə tə liz əm) An economic system in which people and businesses own and control production

Capital punishment (kap´ə təl pun´ ish mənt) The death penalty

Categorial grants (kat´ə gôr´ə kəl grantz) Grants made by the federal government for a specific purpose

Caucus (kȯ kəs) A group of like-minded people who meet to select candidates they will support in an upcoming election

Censure (sen´shər) Issue a formal disproval

Census (sen´səs) A count of population

Charter (chär´tər) A document that states a group's purpose and plan; a city's basic law; its constitution

Checks and balances (cheks and bal´əns əs) A system in which each branch of government checks the others to prevent one branch from becoming too powerful

Chief administrator (chēf ad min´ə strā´tər) The President as the leader of the executive branch of the federal government

Chief citizen (chēf sit´ə zən) The President as the representative of all the people

Chief diplomat (chēf dip´lə mat) The President as the main architect of American foreign policy and the nation's chief spokesperson to other countries

Chief executive (chēf eg zek´yə tiv) The President as the holder of the executive power of the United States

Chief legislator (chēf lej´ə slā´ tər) The President as the main author of public policy

Chief of party (chēf ov pär´tē) The President as the leader of his or her political party

Chief of state (chēf ov stāt´) The President as ceremonial head of the United States

Citizen (sit´ə zən) A person given certain rights, duties, and privileges because he or she was born in or chooses to live in a certain place

Civil case A case involving a noncriminal matter

Civilian (sə vil´yən) A person not on active duty in a military, police, or fire-fighting force

Civilian tribunal (sə vil´yən trī´ byü´nl) A court operating as part of the judicial branch, separate from the military establishment

Civil law (siv´əl lȯ) Law that deals with citizens' behavior that does not involve a crime

Civil liberties (siv´əl lib´ər tē) Guarantees of personal freedoms against possible threats from government

Civil rights (siv´əl rīts) Acts of government that make the constitutional guarantees of freedom a reality

Civil service (siv´əl sėr´vis) Civilian employees whose hiring and pay are regulated by Congress

Clemency (klem´ən sē) Mercy granted to an offender

Closed primary (klōsd prī´mer i) A party nominating election in which only declared party members can vote

Cloture (klō´chər) Limiting debate

Coalition (kō ə lish´ən) A temporary coming together of several groups to form a majority in order to control a government

Coattail effect (kōt´tāl ə fekt´) The effect of a strong candidate running for an office at the top of a ballot helping to attract voters to other candidates on the party's ticket

Cold war (kōld wôr) A period of 40 years during which the United States and Soviet Union were unfriendly toward each other

Collective security (kü lek´tiv si kyûr´ə tē) Principle that calls for countries to act together to promote peace and security

Collectivization (kə lek´tiv i zā´shən) Collective or state ownership of the means of production; refers largely to agriculture

Colonialism (kə lō´nē ə liz´əm) Control of foreign lands by one nation

Colonist (kol´ə nist) Person who lives in a new land that keeps ties with the home country

Command economy (kə mand´ i kon´ə mē) An economy in which the government plans what to produce and how much money to invest

Commander (kə man´dər) A person who has full control of a group

Commander in chief (kə man´dər in chēf) A top person in charge of a nation's armed forces; in the United States, the President

Commerce power (kom´ərs pou´ ər) Exclusive power of Congress to regulate trade between states and foreign countries

Commercial speech (kə mėr´shəl spēch) Speech for business purposes, most often for advertising

Commission government (kə mish´ən guv´ərn mənt) A government formed by heads of different departments who are popularly elected to form the city council

Committee chairmen (kə mit´ē chär´mən) Congress member who leads a standing committee

Common law (kom´ən lȯ) Law based on customs or tradition

Communism (kom´yə niz əm) An economic and government system in which government owns all property and business

Communist Manifesto, The (the kom´yə nist man´ə fes´tō) A document ritten by Karl Marx and Friedrich Engels that criticized the Industrial Revolution

Commutation (kom´yə tā´ shən) Reducing the sentence given by the court for a crime

Compromise (kom´prə mīz) A settlement of differences in which each side gives up some of its demands

Concurrent jurisdiction (kən kėr´ənt jür´is dik´shən) The power shared by federal and state courts to hear certain cases

Concurrent powers (kən kėr´ənt pou´ərz) Powers that both the national government and the states share

Concurrent resolution (kən kėr´ənt rez´ə lü´shən) Explains the government's position; require the House and Senate to act together

Concurring opinion (kən kėr´ing ə pin´yən) Written explanation of the views of one or more judges who support the majority of the court

Confederation (kən fed´ə rā´shən) A form of government in which several states join together for a common purpose

Conference committee (kon´fər əns kə mit´ ē) A committee that settles Senate and House differences in a bill

Conservative (kon sər´və tiv) A person who believes in less government control and more individual responsibility

Constituent power (kən stich´ú ənt pou´ər) The nonlegislative power to revise or amend the constitution

Constitution (kon´stə tü´shən) A plan for government

Constitutional law (kon´stə tü´shə nəl lò) Law based on the United States Constitution, the state constitutions, and court rulings on any part of these documents

Containment (kən tān´mənt) A policy based on the belief that if communism could be kept within its existing boundaries, it would collapse

Content neutral (kon´tent nü´trəl) The government many not regulate assemblies on a basis of what might be said

Continuing resolution (kən tin´yü ing rez´ ə lü´shən) An emergency spending bill that allows agencies to continue working based on the previous year's appropriations

Continuous body (kən tin´yü əs bod´ē) A government body whose seats are never up for election all at the same time

Controllable spending (kən trōl´la bəl spend ing) An amount determined by Congress and the President to be spent on many individual government costs

Convention (kən ven´ shən) A formal meeting called for a special purpose

Copyright (kop´ē rīt) The exclusive right of a person or company to reproduce, publish, and sell a creative work

Council-manager government (koun´səl man´ə jər guv´ərn mənt) A government with a strong council that is popularly elected and a city manager that is chosen by the council

County (koun´tē) A district into which a state is divided for purposes of local government

Court-martial (kôrt´mär´shəl) A court composed of military personnel, for the trial of those accused of violating military law

Criminal case (krim´ə nəl kās) A case in which a defendant is tried for breaking the law

Criminal law (krim´ə nəl lò) Law that regulates citizens' behavior and protects the public order

Custom duties (kus´təm dü´tēz) Taxes levied on goods brought into the United States from other countries

D

De facto segregation (di fak´tō seg´rə gā´shủn) Segregation even if no law requires it

De jure segregation (di jûr´ē seg´rə gā´shən) Segregation by law

Defendant The person against whom a complaint is made

Deficit (def´ə sit) The shortfall between money taken in and money spent

Deficit spending (def´ə sit spend´ing) Spending more money than is taken in

Deflation (di flā´ shən) A general decrease in prices

Delegate (del´ə git) A person chosen to speak or act for another person in a group

Delegated powers (del´ə gāt d pou´ərz) Those powers—expressed, implied, or inherent—granted to the national Government by the Constitution

Demand-side economics (di mand sīd ek ə nom´iks) Part of Keynesian economics; belief that government should spend more in times of high unemployment to bring in more jobs, and thus, more in taxes

Democracy (di mok rə sē) A form of government in which people hold the power

Democratic consolidation (dem´ə krat´ik kən sol´ə dā´shən) The process where all the factors necessary for a democracy are put in place

Democratization (di mok´rə ti zā´shən) The change from a dictatorship to a democracy

Denaturalization (dē nach ər əl i zā´shən) Citizenship taken away by court order

Deportation (dē´pôr tā´shən) A legal process by which aliens are removed from the country

Détente (dā tänt´) A relaxation of tensions

Deterrence (di tėr´əns) Building a strong military to discourage any attacks against the country

Dictatorship (dik´tā tər ship) A person or small group of people ruling a country with total control

Diplomat (dip´lə mat) A person whose work is to manage relations between nations

GLOSSARY

a	hat	e	let	ī	ice	ô	order	ủ	put	sh	she		a	in about
ā	age	ē	equal	o	hot	oi	oil	ü	rule	th	thin		e	in taken
ä	far	ėr	term	ō	open	ou	out	ch	child	ҭн	then	ə	i	in pencil
â	care	i	it	ȯ	saw	u	cup	ng	long	zh	measure		o	in lemon
													u	in circus

GLOSSARY

Diplomatic immunity (dip´lə mat´ik i myü´nə tē) Rule that says an ambassador is not bound by the laws of the country where he or she is serving

Direct popular election (də rekt´pop´yə lər i lek´shən) Proposal to do away with the electoral college and allow the people to vote directly for President and Vice President

Direct primary (də rekt´ prī ´mer ē) An election held within a party to pick that party's candidates for the general election

Discharge petition (dis´chärj pə tish´ ən) A petition that releases a bill from being pigeonholed

Discount rate (dis´kount rāt) Rate of interest a bank must pay when it borrows money from the Federal Reserve Bank

Discrimination (dis krim´ə nā´shən) Treating people unfairly because of their race, sex, age, religion, or physical condition

Disenfranchised (dis´en fran´ chīzd) Not allowed to vote

Disorderly conduct (dis ôr´dər lē kon´duckt) Disturbing public peace

Dissenting opinion (di sent´ing ə pin´yən) Written explanation of the views of one or more judges who disagree with a decision reached by the majority of the court

District plan (dis´trikt plan) Proposal for choosing presidential electors by which two electors would be selected in each state according to the statewide popular vote and the other electors would be selected separately in each of the state's congressional districts

Divine right of kings (də vīn´rīt ov kingz) The belief that monarchs had the right to rule because God had granted them the authority

Division of Power (də vizh´ən ov pou´ər) The constitutional provisions by which government powers are divided between the national government and the states

Domestic affairs (də mes´tik ə fâr´z) All matters not directly connected to foreign affairs; events that happen at home

Double jeopardy (dub´əl jep´ ər dē) Being tried twice for the same crime

Draft (draft) Choosing individuals from a group; required military service

Due process (dü pros´es)The government must act fairly and follow established rules

Due Process Clause (dü pros´es klòz) Part of the 14th Amendment that guarantees that no state deny basic rights to its people

E

Economic protest party (ek ə nom´ik prō´test pär´tē) A political party that forms during difficult economic times; often upset with current problems and demand reforms

Electioneering (i lek´shə nir´ing) Working to get someone elected to office

Electoral college (i lek´tər əl kol´ij) Group of persons chosen in each state and the District of Columbia every four years who make a formal selection of the President and Vice President

Electoral vote (i lek´tər əl vōt) Vote cast by electors in the electoral college

Electorate (i lek´tər it) All of the people allowed to vote in an election

Eminent domain (em´ə nənt dō mān´) Power of a government to take private property for public use

Enabling act (en ā´bəling akt) A congressional act directing the people of a territory to write a state constitution as a step toward admission to the Union

Encomienda (en kō mē en′dä) A system used by the Spanish government to force the Indian population to work in the mines and on farms

Endowed (en dou´d) Given as a gift

English Bill of Rights (ing´glish bil ov rītz) Document written by Parliament to prevent abuse of power by English rulers

Entitlement (en tī´tl mənt) A benefit that federal law says must be paid to all those who meet the eligibility requirements

Entrepreneur (än´trə prə nėr) An individual who combines land, labor, and capital resources to produce goods or services

Enumerated powers (i nü´mə rāt´d pou´ ərz) The 18 powers of Congress numbered from 1 to 18 in the Constitution

Equity (ek´wə tē) Laws intended to stop wrongs before they happen

Espionage (es´pē ə näzh) Spying

Essay (es´ ā) A short writing on a subject

Establishment Clause (e stab´lish mənt klòz) Separates church and state

Estate tax (e stāt taks) A levy imposed on the assets (the estate) of a person who dies

Ex post facto law (eks pōst fakt ō lò) "After the fact" law; a criminal law that applies to a crime committed before the law was passed

Excise tax (ek´sīz taks) Tax on the manufacture, sale, or use of goods and services

Exclusionary rule (ik sklü´zhə ner´ē) A rule that states that if police find evidence as the result of an illegal act, this evidence cannot be used in court

Exclusive jurisdiction (ek sklü´siv jùr´is dik´shən) The power of the federal courts alone to hear certain cases

Exclusive powers (ek sklü´siv pou´ ərz) Powers that are only given to the federal government

Executive agreement (eg zek´yə tiv ə grē´mənt) A pact between the President and the head of a foreign country

Executive departments (eg zek´yə tiv di pärt´mənt) Often called the Cabinet departments, they are traditional units of federal administration

Executive Office of the President (eg zek´yə tiv ò´fis ov the prez´ə dənt) An organization of several agencies staffed by the President's closest advisors

Executive order (eg zek´yə tiv ôr´dər) An order the President gives based on the authority of the Constitution or that given by Congress

Executive power (eg zek´yə tiv pou´ər) The power to carry out laws

Expatriation (ek spā´trē ā´shən) The legal process of giving up citizenship

Expelled (ek spel´d) forced to leave

Exports (ek´spôrtz) Goods sold and shipped to foreign countries

Expressed powers (ek spres´d pou´ərz) The delegated powers of the national government that are written plainly in the Constitution

Extradition (ek´strə dish´ən) The legal process by which a fugitive from justice in one state is returned to that state

F

Factors of production (fak´tərz ov prə duk´shən) Basic resources that are used to make all goods and services

Failed state (fāld stāt) A country that does not have government control

Fascism (fash´iz əm) A political system based on a strong racist government

Federal government (fed´ər əl guv´ərn mənt) A form of government in which powers are divided between a central government and several local governments

Federalism (fed´ər ə liz´əm) A government system in which power is divided between the federal and the state governments

Federalist (fed´ər ə list) A person who favored the Constitution

Felony (fel´ə nē) A serious crime

Feudalism (fyü´dl iz əm) A system in which a feudal lord gave protection to the people who lived and worked on his land in return for their services

Filibuster (fil´ə bus´tər) An effort to keep talking long enough to prevent a vote on a bill

Fiscal policy (fis´kəl pol´ə sē) The Federal government's powers to tax and spend as a way to control the economy

Five-year plan (fīv yir plan) A plan that projects economic development over the next five years

Floor consideration (flôr kən sid´ə rā´shən) The consideration of and action on a bill by the full membership of the House or Senate

Floor leaders (flôr lē´darz) Political party leaders in Congress

Foreign affairs (fôr´ən ə fârz´) A nation's relationship with other countries

Foreign aid (fôr´ən ād) Economic and military aid given to other countries

Foreign policy (fôr´ən pol´ə sē) The plan a country follows in dealing with other countries

Franchise (fran´chīz) A synonym for suffrage; the right to vote

Franking privilege (frangk ing priv´ə lij) A benefit for members of Congress to mail letters and other materials for free

Free enterprise system (frē en´tər priz sis´təm) Freedom of private businesses to operate with few government rules

Free Exercise Clause (frē ek´sər sīz klôz) Guarantees the right to each person to believe whatever he or she chooses about religion

Free market (frē mär´kit) Buyers and sellers are free to buy and sell wóat they want

Full Faith and Credit Clause (fúl fāth and kred´it klôz) Constitution's requirement that each state accept the public acts, records, and judicial proceedingò of every other state

Fundamental law (fun´də men´tl lôz) Law of basic and lasting importance which may not easily be changed

G

Gender gap (jen´dər gap) The difference between how men and women vote for candidates

General election (jen´ər əl i lek´shən) The regularly scheduled election at which voters make a final selection of officeholders

Genocide (jen´ə sīd) An attempt to eliminate an entire race of people

Gerrymandering (jer´ē man dər ing) Unfair drawing of district lines

Gift tax (gift taks) A tax on a gift from one living person to another

Globalization (glō bəl lə zā´shən) The act of making something worldwide

Government (guv´ərn mənt) The group of people and agencies entrusted with making and carrying out laws and policòes agreed upon by the larger population

Grand jury (grand jùr´ē) A group of persons from a federal district court

Grant-in-aid program (grant in ād prō´gram) Grants of federal money or other resources to states, cities, counties, and other local units

Grass-roots pressure (gras rütz presh´ər) Process of putting demands on government from all the members of a group

Great Leap Forward (grāt lēp fôr´wərd) The five-year plan in 1958 that was an attempt to quickly modernize China

a	hat	e	let	ī	ice	ô	order	ù	put	sh	she	ə	a	in about
ā	age	ē	equal	o	hot	oi	oil	ü	rule	th	thin		e	in taken
ä	far	ėr	term	ō	open	ou	out	ch	child	ᴛʜ	then		i	in pencil
â	care	i	it	ȯ	saw	u	cup	ng	long	zh	measure		o	in lemon
													u	in circus

Grievance (grē´vəns) A complaint

Gross domestic product (grōs nash´ə nəl prod´əkt) The total value of goods and services in one year

Guarantee (gar ən tē´) An agreement to protect a possession or right

Guerilla warfare (gə ril´ə wôr´fâr´) Fighting that is carried out by small groups in hit-and-run raids

H

Hard-liners (härd līn ėr) Group that fights to keep government the same

Hard money (härd mun´e) Campaign money given directly to candidates and subject to FEC regulations

Heterogeneous (het´ər ə jē´nē əs) Made up of different races or genders; from the Greek meaning "different kinds"

I

Ideological party (ī´dē o ləj´kəl pär´tē) A political party based on a certain set of beliefs, such as political or economic issues

Immigrant (im´ə grant) An alien admitted to the United States as a legal resident

Impeach (im pēch) To bring formal charges against a public official

Impeachment A charge of wrongful conduct of a public official

Implied powers (im plī´d pou´ərz) Powers the national government is presumed to have because it is the government of a sovereign state in the world community

Import quota (im´port kwō´tə) A set limit on the number of goods a foreign country may sell in the United States

Imports (im´pôrtz) Goods brought from foreign countries

Income tax (in´kum taks) A tax collected on the income of corporations and individuals

Incorporation (in kôr´pə rā´shən) The process by which a state establishes a city as a legal body

Incumbent (in kum´bənt) A person who holds an office

Independent (in´di pen´dənt) Person who does not belong to a political party

Independent agencies (in´di pen´dənt ā´jən sē) Agencies created by Congress located outside of the Cabinet departments

Independent regulatory commissions (in´di pen´dənt reg´yə lə tôr´ē kə mish´ən) Independent agencies created by Congress to regulate important aspects of the nation's economy

Indictment (in dīt´mənt) A formal complaint before a grand jury which charges the accused of one or more crimes

Inferior courts The lower federal courts, beneath the Supreme Court

Inflation (in flā´shən) A general increase in prices

Information (in´fər mā´shən) A formal charge filed by the prosecutor without the action of a grand jury

Inherent powers (in hir´ənt pou´ərz) Powers the Constitution is presumed to have given to the national government because it is the government of a sovereign state within the world community

Inheritance tax (in her´ə təns taks) A tax collected on the beneficiary's share of an estate

Initiative The process of proposing a law through a petition and then voting on it

Injunction (in jungk´shən) A court order that forces or limits the performance of some act by a private individual or a public official

Integration (in´ tə grā´shən) The process of bringing a group of people into the mainstream of society

Interest (in´tər ist) A fee charged for borrowing money

Interest group (in´tər ist grüp) Group whose members share the same viewpoint and work to shape public policy on certain issues

Interstate (in´tər stāt´) Between or connecting two or more states

Interstate compact (in´tər stāt´ kom´pakt) Agreements made between two or more states

Intolerable Acts (in tol´ər ə bəl aktz) New laws passed by British Parliament to punish the colonists

Involuntary servitude (in vol´əú ter´ē sėr´və tüd) Forced labor

Isolationism (ī´sə lā´shə niz´ əm) A refusal to be involved with other countries

Item veto (ī´təm vē´tō) The power to elimióate or remove certain parts of a bill

J

Jim Crow law (jim´ krō lò) A law that separates people on the basis of race

Joint committee (joint kə mit´ē) A committee made up of members of both parts of Congress

Joint resolution (joint rez´ə lü´shən) A proposal for action that has the force of law when passed

Judicial activism (jü dish´əl ak´ti vi zəm) A belief that the courts should take an active role in deciding cases related to politics and social issues

Judicial power (jü dish´əl pou´ər) The power to settle arguments and decide the meaning of laws

Judicial restraint (jü dish´əl ri strānú´) A belief that the courts should decide cases based on the original intent of a law and on precedent

Judicial review (jü dish´əl ri vyü´) The power of the courts óo decide whether or not a government action is constitutional

Jury (jùr´ē) A group of citizens chosen in a court to listen to both sides in a case and to make a decision

Jus sanguinis (jü sän gwə nəs) The law of blood, which determines citizenship based on one's parents' citizenship

Jus soli (jü sō lē) The law of soil, which determines citizenship based on where a person is born

Justice (jus´tis) Fair and equal treatment under the law; the use of authority to uphold what is right and lawful

Justice of the Peace (jus´tis ov the pēs) A judge in charge of a justice court; the lowest part of the state judicial system

K

Keynote address (kē´nōt ə dres´) Speech given at a party convention to set the tone for the convention and the campaign to come

L

Labor (lā´bər) Human activity that provides goods or services

Labor union (lā´bər yü´nyen) A group of workers who join together to advance their wages, benefits, and safety

Laissez-faire theory (les ā fer´) A theory that government should take a very limited part in society

Law of supply and demand (lô ov sə plī´ and di mand´) When goods are plentiful, prices are lower. When goods become limited, prices are higher.

Legal tender (lē´gəl ten´dər) Any kind of money that a creditor must by law accept in payment for debts

Legislative power (lej´ə slā´tiv pou´ər) The power to make laws

Legitimacy (lə jit´ə mə sē) The belief of a people that a government has the right to make public policy

Libel (lī´bəl) False or unjust statements in writing

Liberal (lib´ər əl) A person who is less concerned about the amount of government control and more open to change

Liberal constructionist (lib´ər əl kən struk´shən ist) One who believes government should be able to create new power when needed

Limited government (lim´ə tid guv´ərn mənt) A government that has certain restrictions and gives certain rights to individuals

Line agency (līn ā´jən sē) An agency that performs tasks to meet its goals

Line-item veto (līn i´təm vē´tō) A President's cancellation of specific dollar amounts (line items) from a congressional spending bill

Literacy (lit´ər ə sē) The ability to read or write

Lobbying (lob´ē ing) Trying to influence members of a lawmaking group

Lobbyist (lob´ē ist) A person that tries to influence members of a lawmaking group

M

Magna Carta (mag´nə kär´ tə) Great Charter; a document that grants rights

Major party (mā´jər pär´tē) In American politics, the Republican and Democratic parties

Majority leader (mə jôr´ə tē lē´dar) The floor leader of the party that holds the majority of seats in each house of Congress

Majority opinion (mə jôr´ə tē ə pin´yən) Officially called the Opinion of the Court; announces the Court's decision and sets out the reasoning upon which it is based

Majority rule (mə jôr´ə tē rül) A belief that a majority will be just more often than they will be unjust

Mandate (man´dāt) The instructions or commands of the people given to their elected officials

Mass media (mas mē´dē ə) Types of communication that reach large audiences at the same time, especially television, radio, printed publications, and the Internet

Mayor-council government (mā´ər koun´səl guv´ərn mənt) A government with an elected mayor as the chief executive and an elected council as the legislative body

Medicaid (med´ə kād´) A program managed by the state to provide medical insurance to low-income families

Medium (mē´dē əm) A means of communication

Mercantilism (mėr´kən ti liz əm) The belief that money is the chief source of wealth

Metropolitan areas (met´rə pol´ə tən âr´ē əz) A city and the area around it

Ministers (min´ə st ərz) Cabinet members, usually of the House of Commons

Minority leader (mə nôr´ə tē lē´dar) The floor leader of the party that holds the minority of the seats in each house of Congress

Minor party (mī´nər pär´tē) A political party that is not supported by a large number of people

Minutemen (min´it men) A group of armed men who fought in the Revolutionary War

Miranda Rule (mə ran´də rül) Rule that states that a person must be told of his or her rights before being questioned

Misdemeanor (mis di mē´nər) A minor crime

Monetary policy (mon´ə ter ē pol´ə sē) Policy that involves the money supply and how much credit is available in the economy

Monopoly (mə nop´ə lē) One company controls the production of a specific good or service

GLOSSARY

a	hat	e	let	ī	ice	ô	order	u̇	put	sh	she		a	in about
ā	age	ē	equal	o	hot	oi	oil	ü	rule	th	thin		e	in taken
ä	far	ėr	term	ō	open	ou	out	ch	child	ᴛʜ	then	ə	i	in pencil
â	care	i	it	ȯ	saw	u	cup	ng	long	zh	measure		o	in lemon
													u	in circus

Multiparty system (mul´ti pär´tē sis´təm) A system in which several major and many minor parties compete for and win public offices

Municipality (myü nis´ə pal´ə tē) A political unit within a township in an urban setting

N

NAFTA (naf´tə) An agreement of free trade among the United States, Canada, and Mexico

National convention (nash´ə nəl kən ven´shən) Meeting at which a party's delegates pick the presidential and vice-presidential candidates

National popular vote plan (nash´ə nəl pop´yə lər vōt plan) Proposal for electing the President whereby each state's election laws would provide for all of the state's electoral vote and enter into an interstate compact agreeing to elect the President by national popular vote

NATO (nā´tō) North Atlantic Treaty Organization

Naturalization (nach ər əl i zā´shən) The process of giving full citizenship to a person born in another country

Necessary and Proper Clause (nes´ə ser´ē and prop´er klȯ z) Gives Congress the power to make all laws "necessary and proper" for executing its powers

Nominate (nom´ə nāt) To select a candidate to run for a political office

Nomination (nom´ə nā´shən) The process of candidate selection in an electoral system

Nonpartisan election (non pär´tə zən i lek´shən) Elections ȯn which candidates are not identified by party labels

O

Oath of office (ōth ov ȯ´fis) Oath taken by the President on the day he takes oȯfice

Obscenity (əb sen´ə tē) Disgusting to the senses; offensive

Off-year election (ȯf yir i lek´shən) An election for Congress that takes place between presidential election years

Oligarchy (oli gär´kē) A government in which a small group of people hold unlimited political power

One-party system (wun pär´tē sis´təm) A political system in which only one party exists

Open market operations (ō´pən mär´kit op´ə rā´shən) The buying back of government securities (such as bonds) by the Fed from banks

Open primary (ō´pən prī´mer i) A party nominating election in which any qualified voter can vote

Opinion leader (ə pin´yən lē´dar) A person who has strong influence on others

Ordered government (ȯr´dər d guv´ərn mənt) The regulated government that consists of specific offices and units

Ordinance power (ȯrd´n əns pou´ ər) Power of the President to issue executive orders

Original jurisdiction (ə rij´ə nəl jur´is dik´shən) The power of a court to hear a case first, before any other court

P

Pardon (pärd´n) Legal forgiveness of a crime

Parliamentary government (pär´lə men´tər ē guv´ərn mənt) A form of government in which the executive branch is made up of a prime minister and his or her cabinet and is part of the legislature

Parochial (pə rō´kē əl) Church-related, as in a parochial school

Parole (pə rōl´) The release of a prisoner from jail before the full term is served

Partisan (pär´tə zən) A person that votes by the ȯarty line

Partisanship (pär´tə zən ship) Strong support of a political party

Party caucus (pär´tē kȯ´kəs) A closed meeting of a party's House or Senate members

Party identification (pär´tē ī den´tə fə kā shən) Loyalty of people to a political party

Passport (pas´pȯrt) A legal document issued by a state that identifies a person as a citizen of that state

Patent (pat´nt) A license issued to an inventor granting the exclusive right to use or sell the invention for a limited period of time

Patricians (pə trish´ənz) The rich, upper-class, landowning people of the Roman Republic

Patronage system (pā´trə nij sis´təm) The practice of giving jobs to supporters and friends

Payroll tax (pā´rōl´taks) A tax withheld from an employee's paycheck

Peer group (pir grüp) People with whom one regularly associated, including friends, classmates, neighbors, and co-workers

Perjury (pėr´jər ē) The act of lying under oath

Persona non grata (per sō´nə non grätə) An unwelcome person

Petition (pə tish´ən) Written request to the government for a right or benefit

Petition of Right (pə tish´ən ov rīt) A written document asking for a limit to the king's power

Picketing (pik´it ing) The gathering of striking workers at a business site as a sign of protest

Pigeonholed (pij´ən hōl´d) To set aside a bill that is no longer being considered

Plaintiff (plān´tif) In civil law, the party who brings a suit or some other legal action against another (the defendant) in court

Platform (plat´fȯrm) A political party's statement of ideas, policies, and beliefs

Plebians (pli bē´ənz) The common people of the Roman Republic

Pocket veto (pok´it vē´tō) The President's indirect veto of a bill by not acting on it

Police power (pə lēs´ pou´ər) The authority of each state to guard the safety, health, and welfare of its citizens

Political (pə lit´ə kəl) Having to do with government or the actions of the government

Political Action Committee (pə lit´ə kəl ak´shən kə mit´ē)The political extension of special interest groups

Political efficacy (pə lit´ə kəl ef´ə kú sē) One's ability to make a political difference

Political party (pə lit´ə kəl pär´tē) A group of people that tries to control the government by getting its candidates elected

Political socialization (pə lit´ə kəl sō´shəl ī zā´shən) The way people get their political attitudes and opinions

Politico (pə lit´ə kō) A person that tries to balance being a delegate, trustee, and partisan

Poll book (pōl búk) A list of all registered voters in each precinct

Poll tax (pōl taks) A tax paid to vote

Polling place (pō ling plās) The place where the voters who live in a precinct go to vote

Popular sovereignty (pop´ yə lər sov´rən tē) A basic principle of American government in which the people hold all of the political power

Preamble (prē´am bəl) The beginning of the Constitution that outlines the goals of the government

Precedent A court decision that stands as an example to be followed in the future

Precinct (prē´singkt) A very small unit where all voters report to one place

Preclearance (prē klir´əns) The prior approval by the Justice Department of changes to or new election laws by certain states

Preliminary hearing (pri lim´ə ner ē hi ring) The first step in a criminal case; where the judge hears the evidence and decides if the person can be held for the grand jury or prosecutor

President of the Senate (prez´ə dənt ov the sen´it) The leading officer of the Senate, the Vice President of the United States

President pro tempore (prez´ə dənt prō tem´pə rē) The member of the Senate chosen to take the place of the Vice President when he or she is absent

Presidential elector (prez´ə dən´shəl i lek´tər) A person elected by the voters to represent them in making a formal selection of the Vice President and President

Presidential government (prez´ə dən´shəl guv´ərn mənt) A form of government in which the executive and legislative branches are separate and equal

Presidential primary (prez´ə dən´shəl prī´mer i) An election in which a party's voters (1) choose a state party organization's delegates to their national convention, and/or (2) express a preference for their party's presidential nomination

Presidential succession (prez´ə dən´shəl sək sesh´ən) Scheme by which a presidential vacancy is filled

Presidential Succession Act of 1947 (prez´ə dən´shəl sək sesh´ən akt ov 1947) Law specifying the order of presidential succession following the Vice President

Presiding (pri zīd ing) Acting as a leader or official

Preventative detention (pri ven´tə tiv di ten´shən) A law that allows judges to order an accused person to stay in jail without bail when there is good reason to believe that the person will commit another serious crime before trial

Primary election (prī´mer i ə lek´shən)An election to choose candidates or select delegates to a party convention

Principle (prin´ sə pəl) A basic truth, law, or ideal of behavior

Prior restraint (prī´ər ri strānt´) Placing a ban on written or spoken words before they are expressed

Privatization (prī´vu tīz ā shən) The process of returning ȯ ationalized enterprises to private ownership

Privileges and Immunities Clause (priv´ə lijz and imyü´nə tēz klȯz) Constitution's stipulation that all citizens are ȯntitled to certain "privileges and immunities" regardless of their state of residence

Probable cause (prob´ə bəl kȯz) Real suspicion of a crime

Procedural due process (prə sē´jər il dü pros´ es) The government must use fair procedures and methods

Process of incorporation (pros´es ov in kȯr´pə rā´ shən) The process of incorporating, or including, most of the guarantees in the Bill of Rights into the 14th Amendment's Due Process Clause

Progressive tax (prə gres´iv taks) A type of tax that is determined by the person's income

Project grants (proj´ekt grantz) Grants made by the federal government for specific projects to States, localities, and private agencies that apply for them

Propaganda (prop´ə gan´də) A method of persuasion used to influence individuals or groups

Property tax (prop´ər tē taks) A tax collected on real and personal property

Proportional plan (prə pȯr´shə nəl plan) Proposal by which each presidential candidate would receive the same share of a state's electoral vote as he or she received in the state's popular vote

Proportional representation (prə pȯr´shə nəl rep´ ri zen tā´shən) Rule applied in Democratic primaries whereby any candidate who wins at least 15 percent of the votes gets the number of that state's Democratic convention delegates based on his or her share of that primary vote

GLOSSARY

a	hat	e	let	ī	ice	ô	order	ú	put	sh	she	ə	a	in about
ā	age	ē	equal	o	hot	oi	oil	ü	rule	th	thin		e	in taken
ä	far	ėr	term	ō	open	ou	out	ch	child	ᴛʜ	then		i	in pencil
â	care	i	it	ȯ	saw	u	cup	ng	long	zh	measure		o	in lemon
													u	in circus

Proprietary (prə prī′ə ter′ē) Organized by a person who was given land by the king

Prosecute (pros′ə kyüt) To bring legal action against a person or group

Protectionism (prə tek′shə nism) The effort of countries to protect their industries from foreign competition

Public affairs (pub′lik ə fâr′z) Issues and events that concern the people at large

Public agenda (pub′lik ə jen′də) The public issues on which the people's attention is focused

Public debt (pub′lik det) All the money borrowed by the government and not yet repaid plus the interest owed on that money; also called the national debt or the federal debt

Public-interest group (pub′lik in′tər ist grüp) An interest group that works for the benefit of all citizens

Public opinion (pub′lik ə pin′yən) The attitudes shared by many people about government and politics

Public opinion poll (pub′lik ə pin′yən pōl) Devices that attempt to collect information by asking people questions

Public Policy (pub′lik pol′ə sē) The laws and goals that government follows or pursues

Purge (pèrj) The process of reviewing lists of registered voters and removing the names of those no longer eligible to vote

Q

Quorum (kwôr′əm) A majority

Quota (kwō′tə) A rule requiring set numbers of jobs or promotions for members of a certain group

Quota sample (kwō′tə sam′pəl) A sample constructed to reflect the major characteristics of a given population

R

Random sample (ran′dəm sam′pəl) A sample in which each member of the universe has an equal chance of being included

Ratify (rat′ə fī) To approve

Rational basis test (rash′ə nəl bā′sis test) A test that measures if the action of the government achieves a fair purpose

Reapportionment (rē′ə pôr′shən mənt) To distribute differently

Recall (ri kȯl′) The process of removing a public official from office by a vote

Recession (ri sech′ən) A time of no economic growth and a shrinking economy

Recognition (rek′ əg nish′ən) To accept the legal existence of another country

Referendum (ref ə ren′dəm) The act of submitting a matter to direct vote

Refugee (ref yə jē′) A person that flees from a different country to a safer place

Regional security alliances (rē′ jə nəl si kyủr′ə tē ə lī′ənsz) Agreement among nations to act together to meet any attack against any member

Registration (rej′ə strā′sh ən) Procedure of voter identification intended to stop voter fraud

Regressive tax (ri gres′iv taks) A flat tax that is not based on the person's income or ability to pay

Repeal (ri pēl′) To recall or take back

Representative government (rep′ri zen tā′tə tiv guv′ərn mənt) A government in which the people have a say

Reprieve (ri′prēv′) Delay in carrying out

Reservation (rez′ər vā′shən) Public land set aside by the government for use by Native American tribes

Reserve requirement (ri zèrv′ri kwīr′mənt) Amount of money that a bank must keep on hand

Reserved powers (ri zèrv′d pou′ərz) The powers that the Constitution does not grant to the national government and does not deny to the states

Resign (ri zīn′) To give up an office or position

Resolution (rez′ə lü′ shən) A measure dealing with some matter in one house; does not have the force of law and does not require the President's signature

Reverse discrimination (ri vèrs′ dis krim′ə nā shən) Discrimination against the majority group

Revision A change that affects a written plan

Rider (rī′dər) Unrelated provision added to an important bill so that it will "ride" through the legislative process

Right of association Citizens may freely associate with others to promote a cause

Right of legation (rīt ov li gā′shən) The right to senȯ and receive diplomatic representatives

Rule of law (rül ov lȯ) The principle that government must obey the law

Runoff primary (run′ȯf′ prī′mer i) A primary in which the top two vote getters in the first primary face one another

S

Sales tax (sālz taks) A tax placed on the sale of various goods, paid by the purchaser

Sample (sam′pəl) A representative portion of the total universe

Search warrant (sèrch wôr′ənt) A court order authorizing a search

Secretary (sek′rə ter′ē) An official in charge of a department of government

Security Council (si kyủr′ə tē koun′səl) A 15-member panel that has the major responsibility for keeping international peace

Sedition (si dish′ shən) An effort of people or groups to overthrow or harm the government using violence

Seditious speech (si dish´əs spēch) Speech that encourages an effort of people or groups to overthrow or harm the government using violence

Segregation (seg´rə gā´shən) To separate or set apart from others

Select committee (si lekt´ kə mit´ē) A House or Senate committee that is set up for a limited time

Self-announcement (self ə nouns´mənt) Nominating method in which a person announces an intention to run for public office

Self-incrimination (self in krim´ə nā shən) A person forced to be a witness against him- or herself

Senate (sen´ it) A governing body that makes rules and laws

Seniority rule (sē nyôr´ə tē rül) A custom that gives the most important jobs in Congress to the members who have served the longest

"Separate-but-equal" doctrine (sep´ ər it but ē´kwəl) A constitutional basis for laws that separate one group from another on the basis of race

Separation of powers (sep ə rā´ shən ov pou´ərz) The division of government into three branches--the legislative, executive, and judicial branches

Session (sesh´ən) The period of time each year when Congress meets

Shadow cabinet (shad´ō kab´ə nit) Members of opposition parties who watch, or shadow, particular Cabinet members, and would be ready to run for government

Shield laws (shēld lòz) Laws that give reporters some protection against having to reveal their sources

Signing statements (sīn ing stat´məntz) Statements used to point out problems in a new law

Single-issue party (sing´gəl ish´ü pär´tē) A political party that focuses on one main concern

Slander (slan´dər) False or uójust statements in speech

Socialism (sō´shə liz əm) An economic system in which government òwns large industries and provides many benefits

Soft-liners (sòft līn ėr) Group that fights to have government change or be open to policy reform

Soft money (sòft mun´ ē) Money given to parties or other political organizations in unlimited amounts

Sound bite (sound bīt) Short, sharply focused reports that can be aired in 30 or 40 seconds

Sound taxation (sound tak sā´shən) Taxation that spreads the tax burden fairly among the taxed

Sovereignty (sov´rən tē) The authority to make decisions and keep peace

Speaker of the House (spē´kər ov the hous) The leading officer of the House of Representatives, chosen by and from the majority party in the House

Special district (spesh´əl dis´trikt) An independent unit created to perform one or more related governmental functions at the local level

Special session (spesh´əl sesh´ ən) A session called to deal with an emergency

Splinter party (splin´tər pär´tē) A political party that has broken away from one of the major parties

Split-ticket voting (split tik´it vō´tər) Voting for candidates of different parties in an election

Spoils system (spoilz sis´təm) The practice of giving government jobs to loyal supporters

Staff agency (staf ā´jən sē) An agency that supports the chief executive and other administrators

Standing Committee (stan´ding kə mit´ ē) Permanent committees that consider certain topics

State (stāt´) A group of people living in a defined, having a government with absolute power within its territory to decide its own policies

Statutory law (stach´ü er´ē lòz) Ordinary regulations passed by the legislature

Straight-ticket voting (strāt tik´it vō´tər) Voting for candidates of only one party in an election

Straw vote (strò vōt) Polls that seek to read the public's mind by asking the same question of a large number of people

Strict constructionist (strict kən struk´shən ist) One who wants Congress to only use powers written in the Constitution

Strict scrutiny test (strict skrüt´n ē test) The requirement that a law must show a "compelling government interest" for treating groups of people differently

Subcommittee (sub´kə mit´ē) A smaller part of a standing committee

Subpoena (sə pē´nə) A legal order to appear or give evidence to the court

Subpoenaed (sə pē´nə d) Forced to appear in court

Subsidy (sub´sə dē) A grant of money

Substantive due process (sub´stən tiv dü pros´es) The government must create fair policies and laws

Suffrage (suf´rij) The right to vote

Supply-side economics (sə plī´sīd ek ə nom´iks) A belief that lowering taxes will result in a stronger economy

a	hat	e	let	ī	ice	ô	order	ù	put	sh	she		a	in about
ā	age	ē	equal	o	hot	oi	oil	ü	rule	th	thin	ə	e	in taken
ä	far	ėr	term	ō	open	ou	out	ch	child	ᴛʜ	then		i	in pencil
â	care	i	it	ò	saw	u	cup	ng	long	zh	measure		o	in lemon
													u	in circus

Supremacy Clause (sə prem´ə sē klòz) A clause in the Constitution that states that the Constitution is above all other laws

Surplus (sėr pləs) An amount over what is needed; extra

Swing voter (swing võ´tər) Those voters who have not yet decided which candidate they will support at the start of the campaign and who are open to persuasion by either side

Symbolic speech (sim bol´ik spēch) Communicating ideas through facial expressions, body language, or by carrying a sign or wearing an arm band

T

Tariff (tar´ if) Taxes charged by a country on goods coming into a country, sometimes called a duty

Tax (taks) A charge collected by government on persons or property to meet public needs

Term (tėrm) An assigned period of time for an elected official to serve

Territory (ter´ə tôr´ē) A part of the United States not included in any state but organized with a separate system of government

Terrorism (ter´ə riz´ əm) The use of violence or force to achieve political goals

Township (toun´ship) A subdivision of a county

Trade association (trād ə sō´sē ā´shən) Interest group within the business community

Trade embargo (trād em bär´gō) Stopping trade with a county

Transient (tran´shənt) Person living in a state for only a short time, without legal residence

Treason (trē´zn) Betrayal of one's country; making war against the United States or giving aid to enemies of the United States

Treaty (trē´tē) An agreement between two or more countries or states about trade, peace, or other matters

Tribunal (trī byü´nl) A court of forum of justice

Trust (trust) Several corporations in the same business working to eliminate competition and regulate prices

Trustee (tru stē´) A person who is given power to act for others

U

Unalienable (un ā´lyə nə bəl) Unable to be surrendered

Unconstitutional (un kon stə tü´shə nəl) Against the Constitution

Uncontrollable spending (un kən trō´lə bəl spend ing) Spending that Congress and the President have no power to change directly

Unitary government (yü´nə ter´ē guv´ərn mənt) A system of government that gives all key powers to the national or central government

United Nations (yü nī ´tid nā´shənz)An international organization of 180 member nations created to develop peace and friendly relations, and to protect human rights worldwide

Universe (yü´nə vèrs´) The entire population that a poll wants to measure

V

Veto (vē´tō)To reject a proposed law

Visa (vē´zə) A permit to enter another state; must be obtained from the country the person wants to enter

W

Ward (wôrd) A unit into which cities are divided for the election of city council members

Warrant (wôr´ənt) A court order that makes an official action legal

Weblog (web´lôg) A Website posting, usually devoted to a specific subject

Welfare (wel´fâr) Cash assistance to the poor

Welfare State (wel´fâr stāt´) A country whose governmònt provides many services, including pensions, healthcare, education, and housing

Whips (wipz) Assistants to the floor leaders in the House and Senate

Winner-take-all (win´ər tāk òl) An almost obsolete system whereby a presidential candidate who won the preference vote in a primary automatically won all the delegates chosen in the primary

World Trade Organization (wėrld trād ə ôr´gə nə zā´shən) An organization that oversees international trade and helps settle trade disagreements between countries; created in 1995

Writ of habeas corpus (writ ov ha´be əs kôr´pəs) A court order telling an officer to bring his or her prisoner to the court

Z

Zoning (zōn´ing) The act of determining where homes and businesses may be built

Spanish Glossary

A

Absentee voting/Votación en ausencia El proceso mediante el cual las personas pueden votar sin trasladarse a la caseta de votación el día de la elección

Acqui/Absolver Hallar a un acusado inocente del cargo que se le imputa

Act of admissio/Ley de admisión Una ley del congreso que admite a un nuevo estado en la Unión

Adjour/Levantar la sesión Concluir una reunión

Administrative la/Ley administrativa Ley que regula las agencias de los gobiernos federal y estatal que no están cubiertas por el derecho constitucional

Affirmative action/Acción afirmativa Una política que establece que la mayoría de los empleadores deben llevar a cabo acciones para mitigar los efectos de discriminación previa

Albany Plan of Union/Plan de Unión de Albany Plan formulado por Benjamin Franklin que uniría a las colonias en la toma de decisiones sobre comercio y guerra

Alien/Extranjero Una persona que vive en un país pero es ciudadano de otro país

Ambassador/Embajador Una persona designada por el presidente para representar a los Estados Unidos en otro país

Amendment A change in, or addition to, a constitution

Enmienda Una modificación, o adición, a una constitución

Amicus curiae brief/Informe Amicus curiae Latín que significa "amigo de la corte"; un informe que apoya uno de los lados en un juicio

Amnesty/Amnistía Un perdón que se aplica a muchas personas

Ancient/Antiguo Hace mucho años; que pertenece a la historia temprana

Anti-Federalist/Antifederalista Una persona que estaba a favor de los derechos estatales individuales

Appellate jurisdiction/Jurisdicción de Apelación La autoridad de un tribunal de revisar las decisiones de tribunales inferiores

Appoint/Designar Nombrar o elegir a una persona para un cargo público, pero no mediante una elección

Appropriate/Asignar Destinar a un uso particular

Article/Artículo Una sección numerada de un documento, como la Constitución

Assembly/Asamblea Una reunión con un propósito común

Assimilation/Asimilación El proceso mediante el que personas de una cultura se vuelven parte de otra cultura

At-large/En conjunto Describe una elección en la que un candidato es elegido por todo el estado, y no sólo por un distrito

Attorney General/Fiscal General El jefe del Departamento de Justicia

Authority/Autoridad El poder o derecho de comandar o de tomar las decisiones finales

Autocracy/Autocracia Un gobierno en el que una persona detenta un poder político ilimitado

B

Bail/Fianza Dinero que un acusado paga a un tribunal como garantía de que se presentará al juicio

Balance the ticket/Equilibrar la candidatura La práctica de elegir un compañero de candidatura en una elección presidencial que puede fortalecer la probabilidad que tiene un candidato de resultar electo

Ballot/Papeleta electoral El medio que los votantes usan para elegir a un candidato en una elección

Ballot fatigue/Fatiga del votante Una regla general que indica que entre más abajo aparezcan los cargos de elección popular en la papeleta electoral, menos serán los votos que esos cargos reciban

Bankruptcy/Bancarrota El procedimiento legal mediante el cual se usan los activos de quien se declara en bancarrota para pagar a aquellos con quienes tiene deudas

Battleground State/Estado clave Estados en los que es muy difícil predecir el resultado de la elección y en los que cualquier candidato podría ganar

Bench trial/Juicio sin jurado Un juicio que es atendido por un juez sin un jurado

Bicameral/Bicameral Un cuerpo legislativo compuesto por dos partes, o cámaras

Bill/Proyecto de ley Una ley propuesta

Bill of attainder/Escrito de proscripción y confiscación Un acto legislativo que inflinge castigo a una persona sin que medie un juicio en tribunales

Bipartisan/Bipartidista Respaldado por dos partidos

Blanket primary/Primaria comprensiva Una elección en la que los votantes reciben una larga papeleta electoral que contiene los nombres de todos los contendientes, sin importar el partido, y en la que pueden votar de la manera que ellos prefieran

Block grants/Subvención en bloque Subvenciones hechas por el gobierno federal para una área particular de políticas públicas, pero definida con amplitud

Budget/Presupuesto Un plan financiero para gastar dinero

Bureaucracy/Burocracia Una estructura grande y compleja que se ocupa del funcionamiento diario de una organización

Bureaucrat/Burócrata Una persona que trabaja para una organización burocrática

Business tax/Impuesto sobre los negocios Un impuesto adicional que se recauda sobre varios servicios de los negocios

C

Cabinet/Gabinete Un grupo de asesores del presidente, compuesto por los encargados de los departamentos del ejecutivo

Campaign/Campaña Las actividades relacionadas con el intento de lograr que una persona sea elegida a un cargo político

Candidate/Candidato Una persona que quiere ser elegida a un cargo público

Capital/Capital Recursos hechos por los seres humanos: edificios, máquinas o dinero

Capital punishment/Pena capital La pena de muerte

Capitalism/Capitalismo Un sistema económico en el que las personas y los negocios son propietarios de, y controlan, los medios de producción

Categorial grants/Subvenciones categóricas Subvenciones hechas por el gobierno federal con un propósito específico

Caucus/Asamblea electoral Un grupo de personas que tiene ideas en común y que se reúne para seleccionar candidatos a los que apoyarán en una próxima elección

Census/Censo Un recuento de la población

Censure/Censurar Emitir una desaprobación formal

Charter/Carta Un documento que establece el propósito y plan de un grupo

Checks and balances/Control y equilibrio de poderes Un sistema en el que cada rama del gobierno controla a las otras, para impedir que una se vuelva demasiado poderosa

Chief administrator/Administrador en Jefe El Presidente como el líder del poder ejecutivo del gobierno federal

Chief citizen/Ciudadano en Jefe El presidente como el representante de todo el pueblo

Chief diplomat/Diplomático en Jefe El presidente como el arquitecto principal de la política pública estadounidense y como el vocero principal de la nación respecto de otros países

Chief executive/Jefe del Ejecutivo El presidente como quien detenta el poder ejecutivo en los Estados Unidos

Chief legislator/Legislador en Jefe El presidente como el autor principal de las políticas públicas

Chief of party/Jefe del partido El presidente como el líder de su partido

Chief of state/Jefe de Estado El presidente como cabeza ceremonial de los Estados Unidos

Citizen/Ciudadano Una persona que tiene ciertos derechos, deberes y privilegios porque él o ella nació en, o elige vivir en, cierto lugar

Civil case/Caso civil Un caso que se ocupa de un asunto que no es criminal o penal

Civil law/Ley civil La ley que se ocupa del comportamiento de los ciudadanos que no esté relacionado con un crimen

Civil liberties/Libertades civiles Garantías de libertades personales en prevención de posibles amenazas por parte del gobierno

Civil rights/Derechos civiles Actos del gobierno que hacen una realidad las garantías constitucionales de libertad

Civilian/Civil Una persona que no tiene deberes activos en una fuerza militar, de policía o de bomberos

Civilian tribunal/Tribunal civil Un tribunal que opera como parte del poder judicial, separado del ámbito militar

Clemency/Clemencia Indulgencia que se otorga a un criminal

Civil service/Servicio civil Empleados civiles cuya contratación y salario están regulados por el Congreso

Closed primary/Primaria cerrada Una elección para nominar a candidatos de un partido en la que sólo pueden votar los miembros declarados de ese partido

Cloture/Clausura Limitar la duración del debate

Coalition/Coalición Una asociación temporal de varios grupos para formar una mayoría cuyo objetivo es controlar un gobierno

Coattail effect/Efecto de arrastre El efecto que tiene un candidato fuerte, cuya candidatura ha sido colocada en la parte superior de la papeleta electoral, de atraer votos a otros candidatos de la plantilla de su partido

Cold war/Guerra fría Un periodo de 40 años durante el que los Estados Unidos y la Unión Soviética mantuvieron un estado de conflicto latente

Collective security/Seguridad colectiva El principio que hace un llamado a los países a que actúen unidos para promover la paz y la seguridad

Collectivization/Colectivización Propiedad colectiva o estatal de los medios de producción; se refiere principalmente a la agricultura

Colonialism/Colonialismo Control que una nación ejerce sobre territorios extranjeros

Colonist/Colono Una persona que vive en un nuevo territorio y que mantiene lazos con su patria

Command economy/Economía controlada Una economía en la que el gobierno planea lo que se produce y cuándo dinero se invierte

Commander/Comandante Una persona que tiene el control total de un grupo

Commander in chief/Comandante en jefe La persona de mayor rango encargada de las fuerzas armadas de una nación

Commerce power/Poder de regular el comercio Poder exclusivo del Congreso, que le otorga el derecho de regular el comercio entre estados y con otros países

Commercial speech/Discurso comercial Discurso con propósito de negocios, usualmente propaganda

Commission government/Gobierno por comisión Un gobierno formado por los jefes de diferentes departamentos que son elegidos por voto popular para formar el consejo de la ciudad

Committee chairmen/Presidentes de Comité Miembros del Congreso que dirigen un comité permanente

Common law/Ley consuetudinaria Ley basada en costumbres o tradición

Communism/Comunismo Un sistema económico y de gobierno en el que el gobierno posee toda la propiedad y todos los negocios

The Communist Manifesto/El Manifiesto del Partido Comunista Un documento escrito por Karl Marx y Friedrich Engels que critica la Revolución Industrial

Commutation/Conmutación Reducir la sentencia que impone el tribunal por un crimen

Compromise/Compromiso Una solución de disputas en la que cada lado renuncia a algunas de sus demandas

Concurrent jurisdiction/Jurisdicción concurrente El poder compartido por los tribunales federales y estatales de atender ciertos casos

Concurrent powers/Poderes concurrentes Poderes que comparten el gobierno nacional y los estados

Concurrent resolution/Resolución concurrente Explica la posición del gobierno; requiere que la Cámara de Representantes y el Senado actúen en conjunto

Concurring opinion/Opinión concurrente Explicación escrita de los puntos de vista de uno o más jueces que apoyan la decisión de la mayoría de la corte

Confederation/Confederación Una forma de gobierno en la que varios estados se unen con un propósito en común

Conference committee/Comité de conferencia Un comité que dirime las diferencias entre los proyectos de ley del Senado y de la Cámara de representantes

Conservative/Conservador Una persona que cree en menor control del gobierno y mayor responsabilidad individual

Constituent power/Poder constituyente El poder no legislativo de revisar o enmendar la Constitución

Constitution/Constitución Un plan de gobierno

Constitutional law/Ley constitucional Ley basada en la Constitución de los Estados Unidos, las constituciones estatales y las decisiones de los tribunales sobre cualquier parte de estos documentos

Containment/Contención Una política basada en la creencia de que si se lograba mantener al comunismo al interior de las fronteras que ya controlaba, colapsaría

Content neutral/Neutral respecto del contenido El gobierno no puede regular asambleas con base en lo que podría discutirse en ellas

Continuing resolution/Resolución continua Un proyecto de ley de gasto de emergencia que permite que las agencias funcionen con base en las asignaciones del año anterior

Continuous body/Cuerpo continuo Un cuerpo gubernamental cuyos escaños nunca están sujetos a una elección en su totalidad al mismo tiempo

Controllable spending/Gasto controlable Una cantidad que el Congreso y el presidente determinan y que se debe gastar en muchos costos individuales del gobierno

Convention/Convención Una reunión formal convocada con un propósito especial

Copyright/Derechos de autor El derecho exclusivo de una persona o compañía de reproducir, publicar y vender trabajo creativo

Council-manager government/Gobierno de consejo y gerente Un gobierno con un consejo fuerte que es elegido por voto popular y un gerente de la ciudad que es seleccionado por el consejo

County/Condado Un distrito en el que se divide un estado para propósitos del gobierno local

Court-martial/Corte marcial Una corte compuesta por personal militar, establecida para juzgar a quienes se acusa de violar la ley militar

Criminal case/Caso criminal Un caso en el que el acusado es juzgado por violar la ley

Criminal law/Ley penal Ley que regula el comportamiento de los ciudadanos y que protege el orden público

Custom duties/Aranceles aduaneros Impuestos que se aplican a bienes que ingresan a los Estados Unidos desde otro países

De facto segregation/Segregación De facto Segregación aún si no hay ley que la requiera

De jure segregation/Segregación De jure Segregación dispuesta por la ley

Defendant/Acusado La persona en contra de la que se hace una denuncia

Deficit/Déficit La diferencia entre la cantidad de dinero que se ingresa y la que se gasta

Deficit spending/Gasto deficitario Gastar más de lo que se ingresa

Deflation/Deflación Un descenso general en los precios

Delegate/Delegado Una persona elegida para hablar o actuar en nombre de otra persona en un grupo

Delegated powers/Poderes delegados Aquellos poderes (expresos, implícitos o inherentes) que la Constitución otorga al gobierno nacional

Demand-side economics/Economía de la demanda Parte de la economía keynesiana; la creencia de que el gobierno debe gastar más en épocas de alto desempleo para producir más puestos de trabajo y, con ello, más impuestos

Democracy/Democracia Una forma de gobierno en la que el pueblo tiene el poder

Democratic consolidation/Consolidación democrática El proceso mediante el cual se establecen todos los factores necesarios para producir una democracia

Democratization/Democratización El cambio de una dictadura a una democracia

Denaturalization/Desnaturalización Sucede cuando se quita la ciudadanía por orden de un tribunal

Deportation/Deportación El proceso legal mediante el que los extranjeros son expulsados de un país

Détente/Distensión Una relajación de las tensiones

Deterrence/Disuasión El desarrollo de fuerzas armadas poderosas para disuadir a otros de atacar el país

Dictatorship/Dictadura Una persona o un grupo pequeño de personas que gobiernan a un país ejerciendo un control total

Diplomat/Diplomático Una persona cuyo trabajo consiste en establecer y administrar relaciones entre naciones

Diplomatic immunity/Inmunidad diplomática La regla que dice que un embajador no está sujeto a las leyes del país en el que él o ella sirve

Direct popular election/Elección popular directa Propuesta que propone la desaparición del colegio electoral y que permitiría al pueblo votar directamente por el presidente y por el vicepresidente

Direct primary/Primaria directa Una elección que se lleva a cabo al interior de un partido para elegir a los candidatos de ese partido a la elección general

Discharge petition/Petición de descarga Una petición que libera a un proyecto de ley del carpetazo que había recibido

Discount rate/Tasa de descuento La tasa de interés que un banco debe pagar cuando pide dinero prestado al Banco de la Reserva Federal

Discrimination/Discriminación Tratar a las personas injustamente debido a su raza, sexo, edad, religión o condición física

Disenfranchised/Sin derecho al voto No se le permite votar

Disorderly conduct/Alteración del orden público Perturbar la paz social

Dissenting opinion/Opinión disidente Una explicación escrita de los puntos de vista de uno o más jueces que no están de acuerdo con la decisión de la mayoría de la corte

District plan/Plan por distritos Una propuesta para elegir a electores presidenciales que propone que dos electores serían seleccionados en cada estado con base en el voto popular de todo el estado, y los demás electores serían seleccionados en cada uno de los distritos del Congreso del estado

Divine right of kings/Derecho divino de los reyes La creencia de que los monarcas tenían el derecho de gobernar porque Dios les había dado la autoridad

Division of Power/División de poderes Las disposiciones constitucionales que establecen qué poderes del gobierno están divididos entre el gobierno nacional y lo estados

Domestic affairs/Asuntos internos Todas las cuestiones que no están directamente conectadas con las relaciones internacionales; los eventos que tienen lugar en el propio país

Double jeopardy/Excepción de cosa juzgada Ser juzgado dos veces por el mismo crimen

Draft/Reclutamiento Seleccionar a ciertos individuos de un grupo; servicio militar obligatorio

Due process/Debido proceso El gobierno debe actuar con justicia y seguir reglas establecidas

Due Process Clause/Cláusula de Debido Proceso Parte de la Enmienda 14 que garantiza que ningún estado puede negar los derechos básicos a sus ciudadanos

Economic protest party/Partido de protesta económica Un partido político que se forma durante periodos de crisis económica; suele estar a disgusto con la situación actual y exige reformas

Electioneering/Electoralismo Trabajar para que alguien gane una elección

Electoral college/Colegio electoral Grupo de personas seleccionadas en cada estado y el Distrito de Columbia cada cuatro años, para llevar a cabo la elección formal del presidente y del vicepresidente

Electoral vote/Voto electoral Voto emitido por los electores en el colegio electoral

Electorate/Electorado Todas las personas que tienen derecho al voto en una elección

Eminent domain/Dominio eminente El poder de un gobierno de requisar la propiedad privada para destinarla a uso público

Enabling act/Ley de autorización Una ley del Congreso que establece que las personas que viven en un territorio deben redactar una constitución estatal como un paso hacia su admisión en la Unión

Encomienda/Encomienda Un sistema usado por el gobierno español que obligaba a la población indígena a trabajar en las minas y en las granjas

Endowed/Donado Entregado como un regalo

English Bill of Rights/Declaración de Derechos de Inglaterra Documento escrito por el Parlamento para impedir el abuso de poder de parte de los gobernantes ingleses

Entitlement/Derecho consuetudinario Un beneficio que establece la ley federal y que establece que se debe otorgar a todos aquellos que cumplen con los requisitos

Entrepreneur/Empresario Un individuo que combina tierra, trabajo y recursos de capital para producir bienes o servicios

Enumerated powers/Poderes enumerados Los 18 poderes que el Congreso enumeró del 1 al 18 en la Constitución

Equity/Equidad Leyes cuyo objetivo es impedir conductas incorrectas antes de que sucedan

Espionage/Espionaje Espiar

Essay/Ensayo Un escrito corto sobre un tema

Establishment Clause/Cláusula de establecimiento Separa a la iglesia del Estado

Estate tax/Impuesto de sucesión Un impuesto a los activos (la sucesión o herencia) de una persona que muere

Ex post facto law/Ley ex post facto "Después de los hechos"; una ley penal que se aplica a crímenes cometidos antes de que esa ley fuera aprobada

SPANISH GLOSSARY

Excise tax/Impuesto sobre artículos de uso y consumo Un impuesto a la manufactura, venta o uso de bienes y servicios

Exclusionary rule/Regla de exclusión Una regla que establece que si la policía halla evidencia como resultado de un acto ilegal, esta evidencia no puede ser usada en tribunales

Exclusive jurisdiction/Jurisdicción exclusiva El derecho que pertenece sólo a los tribunales federales de atender ciertos casos

Exclusive powers/Poderes exclusivos Poderes que se otorgan sólo al gobierno federal

Executive agreement/Acuerdo presidencial Un pacto entre el presidente y el líder de otro país

Executive departments/Departamentos ejecutivos Unidades tradicionales de la administración federal, a las que se suele llamar departamentos de gabinete

Executive Office of the President/Oficina Ejecutiva del Presidente La organización que reúne a varias agencias cuyo personal está formado por los asesores más cercanos al presidente

Executive order/Orden presidencial Una orden que emite el presidente con base en la autoridad que le otorga la Constitución, o en la que le da el Congreso

Executive power/Poder ejecutivo El poder de aplicar las leyes

Expatriation/Expatriación El proceso legal de renunciar a la ciudadanía

Expelled/Expulsado Obligado a salir

Exports/Exportaciones Bienes que se venden y se envían a otros países

Expressed powers/Poderes expresos Los poderes delegados del gobierno nacional que están escritos expresamente en la Constitución

Extradition/Extradición El proceso legal mediante el cual un fugitivo de la justicia en un estado es devuelto a ese estado

F

Factors of production/Factores de la producción Recursos básicos que se usan para producir todos los bienes y servicios

Failed state/Estado fallido Un país en el que el gobierno no ejerce el control

Fascism/Fascismo Un sistema político basado en un fuerte gobierno racista

Federal government/Gobierno federal Una forma de gobierno en la que los poderes están divididos entre un gobierno central y varios gobiernos locales

Federalism/Federalismo Un sistema de gobierno en el que el poder está dividido entre el gobierno federal y el estatal

Federalist/Federalista Una persona que estaba a favor de la Constitución

Felony/Felonía Un delito mayor

Feudalism/Feudalismo Un sistema en el que un señor feudal daba protección a las personas que vivían y trabajaban en sus tierras, a cambio de sus servicios

Filibuster/Táctica obstruccionista El intento de prolongar la discusión de un proyecto de ley por suficiente tiempo para impedir que se pueda poner a votación

Fiscal policy/Política fiscal Los poderes del gobierno federal para cobrar impuestos y gastar para controlar la economía

Five-year plan/Plan quinquenal Un plan que hace una proyección del desarrollo económico para los siguientes cinco años

Floor consideration/Consideración en el pleno La revisión y la decisión sobre un proyecto de ley por todos los miembros de la Cámara de Representantes o del Senado

Floor leaders/Líderes de partido Líderes de los partidos políticos en el Congreso

Foreign affairs/Asuntos exteriores La relación de una nación con otros países

Foreign aid/Ayuda internacional Ayuda económica y militar que se otorga a otros países

Foreign policy/Política exterior El plan que sigue un país en sus relaciones con otros países

Franchise/Derecho al voto Sinónimo de voto; el derecho al voto

Franking privilege/Privilegio de franqueo Una prerrogativa que reciben los miembros del Congreso que les permite enviar gratis cartas y otros materiales por correo

Free enterprise system/Sistema de libre empresa La libertad que tienen los negocios privados de operar con pocas reglas del gobierno

Free Exercise Clause/Cláusula de libre ejercicio Garantiza el derecho de cada persona de creer en cualquier religión que elija

Free market/Mercado libre Los compradores y los vendedores tienen la libertad de vender y comprar lo que quieran

Full Faith and Credit Clause/Cláusula de entera fe y crédito Un requerimiento de la Constitución que establece que cada estado debe aceptar las actas públicas, registros y procedimientos judiciales de todos los demás estados

Fundamental law/Ley fundamental Ley de importancia fundamental y duradera que no puede ser cambiada con facilidad

G

Gender gap/Brecha de género La diferencia en la manera en que hombres y mujeres votan por los candidatos

General election/Elección general Una elección programada regularmente en la que los votantes hacen una selección final de candidatos a cargos públicos

Genocide/Genocidio El intento de eliminar una raza entera

Gerrymandering/Gerrymandering Trazar de manera injusta los límites de los distritos

SPANISH GLOSSARY

Gift tax/Impuesto sobre donaciones Un impuesto que se aplica a un obsequio que una persona viva hace a otra

Globalization/Globalización El proceso de producir algo a nivel mundial

Government/Gobierno El grupo de personas y agencias encargadas de hacer y aplicar leyes y políticas públicas que han sido aceptadas por la población en general

Grand jury/Gran Jurado Un grupo de personas de un tribunal federal de distrito

Grant-in-aid program/Programa de subvenciones Subvenciones con recursos federales, u otro tipo de recursos, otorgadas a los estados, ciudades, condados y otras unidades locales

Grass-roots pressure/Presiones de organizaciones populares El proceso de presentar demandas a un gobierno de parte de todos los miembros de un grupo

Great Leap Forward/El Gran Salto Adelante El plan de cinco años presentado en 1958 y que fue un intento de modernizar rápidamente a China

Grievance/Queja Una disconformidad

Gross domestic product/Producto interno bruto El valor total de los bienes y servicios en un año

Guarantee/Garantía Un acuerdo para proteger una posesión o un derecho

Guerilla warfare/Guerra de guerrillas Lucha que pequeños grupos llevan a cabo usando la estrategia de golpear y correr

H

Hard-liners/Intransigentes Grupo que lucha para mantener el gobierno tal y como está

Hard money/Dinero duro Dinero para campañas entregado directamente a los candidatos y sujeto a las regulaciones de la FEC (Comisión Federal de Elecciones, por sus siglas en inglés)

Heterogeneous/Heterogéneo Compuesto por diferentes razas o géneros; del griego que significa "diferentes tipos"

I

Ideological party/Partido ideológico Un partido político basado en un conjunto particular de creencias, como asuntos políticos o económicos

Immigrant/Inmigrante Un extranjero que es admitido en los Estados Unidos como un residente legal

Impeach/Acusación por responsabilidades oficiales Presentar cargos formales en contra de un funcionario público

Impeachment/Acusación por responsabilidades oficiales Un cargo de conducta incorrecta levantado a un funcionario público

Implied powers/Poderes implícitos Poderes que el gobierno nacional presume tener porque es el gobierno de un estado soberano en la comunidad mundial

Import quota/Cuota de importaciones Un límite fijo en el número de bienes que otro país puede vender a los Estados Unidos

Imports/Importaciones Bienes que se traen de otros países

Income tax/Impuesto sobre la renta Un impuesto que se recauda a partir del ingreso de las corporaciones y los individuos

Incorporation/Incorporación El proceso mediante el cual un estado establece una ciudad como un cuerpo legal

Incumbent/Titular Una persona que ocupa un cargo público

Independent/Independiente Persona que no pertenece a un partido político

Independent agencies/Agencias independientes Agencias creadas por el Congreso y que están situadas fuera de los departamentos del gabinete

Independent regulatory commissions/Comisiones regulatorias independientes Agencias independientes creadas por el Congreso para regular aspectos importantes de la economía nacional

Indictment/Imputación Una querella formal presentada ante un gran jurado que inculpa al acusado de uno o más crímenes

Inferior courts/Cortes inferiores Los tribunales federales inferiores, por debajo de la Corte Suprema

Inflation/Inflación Un aumento general en los precios

Information/Información Una querella formal presentada por el fiscal sin la acción de un gran jurado

Information/Información Un cargo presentado por el fiscal

Inherent powers/Poderes inherentes Poderes que se presume que la Constitución otorga al gobierno nacional porque es el gobierno de un estado soberano en la comunidad internacional

Inheritance tax/Impuesto sobre la herencia Un impuesto que se recauda sobre la parte de una herencia que es asignada al beneficiario

Initiative/Iniciativa El proceso de proponer una ley a través de la petición, y de luego votar por ella

Injunction/ Interdicto Una orden de los tribunales que obliga a un individuo, o a un funcionario público, a llevar a cabo un acto; también puede limitar la capacidad de actuar de individuos o funcionarios

Integration/Integración El proceso de atraer a un grupo de personas al seno de la sociedad en general

Interest/Interés Una cuota que se cobra por recibir dinero prestado

Interest group/Grupo de interés Grupo de personas que comparte los mismos puntos de vista sobre asuntos públicos y que trabaja para influir en las políticas públicas

Interstate/Interestatal Que está situado entre, o conecta a, dos o más estados

Interstate compact/Convenio interestatal Acuerdos hechos entre dos o más estados

Intolerable Acts/Leyes Intolerables Leyes nuevas aprobadas por el Parlamento británico para castigar a los colonos

Involuntary servitude/Servidumbre involuntaria Trabajo forzado

Isolationism/Aislacionismo La negativa a involucrarse con otros países

Item veto/Veto de partidas El derecho de eliminar ciertas partes de un proyecto de ley

J

Jim Crow law/Ley Jim Crow Una ley que separa a las personas con base en la raza

Joint committee/Comité conjunto Un comité compuesto por miembros de ambas cámaras del Congreso

Joint resolution/Resolución conjunta Una propuesta de acción que tiene la fuerza de la ley cuando es aprobada

Judicial activism/Activismo judicial La creencia de que los tribunales deben tomar un rol activo al decidir casos relacionados con asuntos políticos y sociales

Judicial power/Poder judicial El poder de resolver disputas y establecer el significado de las leyes

Judicial restraint/Restricción judicial La creencia de que los tribunales deben decidir casos con base en la intención original de la ley y en los precedentes

Judicial review/Revisión judicial El poder de los tribunales de decidir si una acción de un gobierno es constitucional

Jury/Jurado Un grupo de ciudadanos elegido por un tribunal para atender los dos lados de un caso y tomar una decisión

Jus sanguinis/Jus sanguinis La ley de sangre, que determina la ciudadanía con base en la ciudadanía de los padres

Jus soli/Jus soli La ley del terreno, que determina la ciudadanía con base en el lugar en que nace una persona

Justice/Justicia Tratamiento justo y equitativo bajo la ley; el uso de la autoridad para defender lo que es justo y legal

Justice of the Peace/Juez de Paz Un juez a cargo de un tribunal de justicia; el nivel más bajo del sistema judicial estatal

K

Keynote address/Discurso inaugural Discurso que se hace en una convención y que establece el tono tanto de la convención como de la futura campaña

L

Labor/Trabajo Actividad humana que proporciona bienes o servicios

Labor union/Sindicato de trabajadores Un grupo de trabajadores que se unen para defender sus salarios, beneficios y seguridad

Laissez-faire theory/Teoría Laissez-faire Una teoría que sostiene que el gobierno debe tener una participación muy limitada en la sociedad

Law of supply and demand/Ley de la oferta y la demanda Cuando hay muchos bienes, los precios son menores Cuando hay una cantidad limitada de bienes, los precios son mayores

Legal tender/Moneda de curso legal Cualquier tipo de moneda que un acreedor debe aceptar por ley en pago de deudas

Legislative power/Poder legislativo El poder de hacer leyes

Legitimacy/Legitimidad La creencia de parte del pueblo de que el gobierno tiene el derecho de hacer políticas públicas

Libel/Libelo Afirmaciones falsas o injustas presentadas por escrito

Liberal/Liberal Una persona a la que no le preocupa mucho el grado de control que ejerce el gobierno, y que está más abierta al cambio

Liberal constructionist/Construccionista liberal Persona que cree que el gobierno debe tener la capacidad de crear nuevos poderes cuando sea necesario

Limited government/Gobierno limitado Un gobierno que tiene ciertas restricciones y otorga ciertos derechos a los individuos

Line agency/Departamento de operaciones Una agencia que lleva a cabo tareas para alcanzar sus objetivos

Line-item veto/Veto de partidas Poder del presidente para cancelar cantidades específicas de dólares (partidas) sobre un proyecto de ley de presupuesto presentado por el Congreso

Literacy/Alfabetismo La capacidad de leer o escribir

Lobbying/Cabildear Intento de influenciar a los miembros de un grupo legislativo

Lobbyist/Cabildero Una persona que trata de influenciar a miembros de un grupo legislativo

M

Magna Carta/Magna Carta Gran Carta; un documento que otorga derechos

Major party/Partido principal En la política de los Estados Unidos, los partidos Republicano y Demócrata

Majority leader/Líder de la mayoría El líder del pleno del partido que tiene la mayoría de escaños en cada cámara del Congreso

Majority opinion/Opinión de la mayoría Se le llama oficialmente Opinión de la Corte; anuncia la decisión de la Corte y presenta el razonamiento en que se basa

Majority rule/Gobierno de mayoría La creencia de que la mayoría será justa con mayor frecuencia de lo que será injusta

Mandate/Mandato Las instrucciones u órdenes que el pueblo da a las personas que obtuvieron cargos de elección popular

Mass media/Medios de comunicación masiva Tipos de comunicación que llegan a grandes audiencias al mismo tiempo; en especial televisión, radio, publicaciones impresas e Internet

Mayor-council government/Gobierno de alcalde y consejo Un gobierno con un alcalde elegido como jefe del ejecutivo y un consejo elegido como cuerpo legislativo

SPANISH GLOSSARY

SPANISH GLOSSARY

Medicaid/Medicaid Un programa administrado por el estado para proporcionar seguro médico a familias de bajos recursos

Medium/Medio Una forma de comunicación

Mercantilism/Mercantilismo La creencia de que el dinero es la fuente primaria de la riqueza

Metropolitan areas/Áreas metropolitanas Una ciudad y el área que la circunda

Ministers/Ministros Miembros del gabinete, usualmente de la Cámara de los Comunes

Minor party/Partido menor Un partido político que no tiene el apoyo de un gran número de personas

Minority leader/Líder de la minoría El líder del pleno del partido que tiene la minoría de escaños en cada cámara del Congreso

Minutemen/Minutemen (milicianos) Un grupo de hombres armados que peleó en la Guerra de Independencia

Miranda Rule/Regla Miranda Regla que establece que se debe leer los derechos a una persona antes de que sea interrogada

Misdemeanor/Delito menor Un delito menor

Monetary policy/Política monetaria Una política que incluye la oferta de dinero y cuánto crédito hay disponible en la economía

Monopoly/Monopolio Una compañía controla la producción de un bien o servicio específico

Multiparty system/Sistema pluripartidista Un sistema en el que varios partidos principales y menores compiten y obtienen cargos públicos

Municipality/Municipalidad Una unidad política al interior de un territorio comunal, pero en un medio urbano

N

NAFTA/TLCAN Un acuerdo de libre comercio entre los Estados Unidos, Canadá y México (por sus siglas en español; Tratado de Libre Comercio de América del Norte)

National convention/Convención nacional Reunión en la que los delegados de un partido eligen a los candidatos a la presidencia y a la vicepresidencia

National popular vote plan/Plan del voto nacional popular Propuesta para elegir al presidente en la que las leyes electorales de cada estado aceptarían el voto electoral completo de cada estado; los estados, además, establecerían un contrato con otros estados, en el que aceptarían elegir al presidente con base en el voto nacional popular

NATO/OTAN Organización del Tratado del Atlántico Norte

Naturalization/Naturalización El proceso mediante el cual se otorga ciudadanía completa a una persona nacida en otro país

Necessary and Proper Clause/Cláusula necesaria y justa Concede al Congreso el poder de hacer todas las leyes "necesarias y justas" para aplicar sus poderes

Nominate/Nominar Seleccionar a un candidato que se presentará a una elección por un cargo público

Nomination/Nominación El proceso de selección de un candidato en un sistema electoral

Nonpartisan election/Elección no partidista Elecciones en las que los candidatos no se identifican por etiquetas partidistas

O

Oath of office/Juramento de toma de posesión presidencial El juramento que toma el presidente el día que toma posesión

Obscenity/Obscenidad Repugnante a los sentidos; ofensivo

Off-year election/Elección intermedia Una elección para el Congreso que tiene lugar entre dos elecciones presidenciales

Oligarchy/Oligarquía Un gobierno en el que un pequeño grupo de personas detentan un poder político ilimitado

One-party system/Sistema unipardista Un sistema político en el que sólo existe un partido

Open market operations/Operaciones de mercado abierto La compra de instrumentos de crédito del gobierno (como bonos) que hace la Reserva Federal a los bancos

Open primary/Primaria abierta Una elección para nominar a candidatos de un partido en la que cualquier votante calificado puede votar

Opinion leader/Líder de opinión Una persona que tiene mucha influencia sobre otros

Ordered government/Gobierno ordenado El gobierno regulado conformado por oficinas y unidades específicas

Ordinance power/Poder de ordenanza Poder del presidente de emitir órdenes ejecutivas

Original jurisdiction/Jurisdicción original El derecho de un tribunal de atender primero un caso, antes que cualquier otro tribunal

P

Pardon/Perdón Absolución legal de un crimen

Parliamentary government/Gobierno parlamentario Una forma de gobierno en la que el poder ejecutivo se compone de un primer ministro y su gabinete, y es parte del poder legislativo

Parochial/Parroquial Relacionado con la iglesia, como en una escuela parroquial

Parole/Libertad condicional La liberación de un prisionero antes de que cumpla con la totalidad de su condena en la cárcel

Partisan/Partidista Una persona que vota siguiendo la línea del partido

Partisanship/Partidismo Fuerte apoyo a un partido político

Party caucus/Grupo legislativo Una reunión cerrada de miembros de un partido de la Cámara de Representantes o del Senado

Party identification/Identificación partidista La lealtad de las personas hacia un partido político

Passport/Pasaporte Un documento legal expedido por un Estado y que identifica a una persona como ciudadano de ese Estado

Patent/Patente Una licencia que se otorga a un inventor y que concede el derecho exclusivo de usar o vender un invento por un periodo limitado de tiempo

Patricians/Patricios Los ricos terratenientes, miembros de la clase alta, de la república romana

Patronage system/Clientelismo La práctica de dar trabajos a partidarios y amigos

Payroll tax/Impuesto sobre la nómina Un impuesto que se retiene del salario de un empleado

Peer group/Grupo de pares Personas con las que uno se asocia regularmente, incluyendo amigos, compañeros de clase, vecinos y colegas

Petition /Petición Una solicitud que se hace al gobierno por escrito

Perjury/Perjurio El acto de mentir bajo juramento

Persona non grata/Persona non grata Una persona que no es bienvenida

Petition/Petición Un documento escrito o informe jurídico que pide a quienes detentan el poder un derecho o beneficio

Petition of Right/Petición de Derechos Un documento escrito que pide la limitación del poder del rey

Picketing/Protesta Congregar a trabajadores en huelga frente a su lugar de trabajo como señal de descontento

Pigeonholed/Dar carpetazo Archivar un proyecto de ley que ya no está siendo considerado

Plaintiff/Demandante En la ley civil, la parte que presenta una acusación u cualquier otra acción legal en contra de alguien (el acusado) en corte

Platform/Plataforma La declaración de las ideas, políticas y creencias de un partido político

Plebeians/Plebeyos El pueblo llano de la república romana

Pocket veto/Veto indirecto Una forma indirecta que tiene el presidente de ejercer un veto; simplemente no actúa sobre el proyecto de ley que se le presenta

Police power/Poder regulador La autoridad de cada estado de salvaguardar la seguridad, la salud y el bienestar de sus ciudadanos

Political/Política Tiene que ver con el gobierno o las acciones del gobierno

Political Action Committee/Comité de acción política La extensión política de grupos de interés

Political efficacy/Eficacia política La habilidad de una persona de tener influencia en política

Political party/Partido político Un grupo de personas que trata de controlar el gobierno presentando candidatos a puestos de elección popular

Political socialization/Socialización política La manera en que las personas obtienen sus actitudes y opiniones políticas

Politico/Político Una persona que intenta combinar las funciones de delegado, síndico y partidista

Poll book/Lista electoral Una lista de todos los votantes registrados en cada circunscripción

Poll tax/Impuesto al voto Un impuesto que se paga para poder votar

Polling place/Caseta de votación El lugar en el que los votantes que viven en una circunscripción van a votar

Popular sovereignty/Soberanía popular Un principio básico del gobierno estadounidense que sostiene que todo el poder político reside en el pueblo

Preamble/Preámbulo El preludio de la Constitución, que presenta los objetivos del gobierno

Precedent/Precedente Una decisión de la Corte que se mantiene como un ejemplo a seguir en el futuro

Precinct/Circunscripción Una unidad de votación muy pequeña en la que todos los votantes votan en un mismo lugar

Preclearance/Preaprobación La aprobación previa que otorga el Departamento de Justicia tanto a cambios en las leyes electorales de los estados, como a una nueva ley

Preliminary hearing/Audiencia preliminar El primer paso en un caso penal; el juez recibe la evidencia y decide si la persona puede ser detenida y enviada ante el gran jurado o el fiscal

President pro tempore/Presidente pro tempore El miembro del Senado elegido para tomar el lugar del vicepresidente cuando él o ella estén ausentes

President of the Senate/Presidente del Senado El líder del Senado, es decir, el vicepresidente de los Estados Unidos

Presidential elector/Elector presidencial Una persona seleccionada por los votantes como su representante para hacer la elección formal del presidente y del vicepresidente

Presidential government/Gobierno presidencial Una forma de gobierno en la que los poderes ejecutivo y legislativo están separados pero son iguales

Presidential primary/Primaria presidencial expresan su preferencia por la nominación presidencial de su partido

Presidential succession/Sucesión presidencial Un proceso mediante el cual se ocupa el puesto vacante de la presidencia

Presidential Succession Act of 1947/Ley de la Sucesión Presidencial de 1947 Una ley que especifica el orden de la sucesión presidencial, del vicepresidente en adelante

Presiding/Presidir Actuar como un líder o funcionario oficial

Preventative detention/Detención preventiva Una ley que permite a los jueces ordenar que un acusado permanezca en la cárcel sin fianza, cuando hay buenas razones para creer que la persona cometerá un crimen serio antes de su juicio

Primary election/Elección primaria Una elección para elegir candidatos o seleccionar delegados para una convención de partido

Principle/Principio Una verdad, ley o comportamiento ideal básicos

Prior restraint/Restricción previa Aplicar una prohibición sobre un discurso escrito o hablado antes de que sea hecho público

SPANISH GLOSSARY

Privatization/Privatización El proceso de devolver las empresas nacionalizadas a manos privadas

Privileges and Immunities Clause/Cláusula de privilegios e inmunidades Una estipulación de la Constitución que establece que todos los ciudadanos tienen derecho a ciertos "privilegios e inmunidades", sin que importe en qué estado residan

Probable cause/Causa probable Sospecha real de un crimen

Prosecute/Procesar Presentar una acción legal en contra de una persona o grupo

Procedural due process/Debido proceso procesal El gobierno debe usar procedimientos y métodos justos

Process of incorporation/Proceso de incorporación El proceso de incorporar, o incluir, la mayoría de las garantías que establece la Declaración de Derechos en la Cláusula de Debido Proceso de la Enmienda 15

Progressive tax/Impuesto progresivo Un tipo de impuesto que es determinado por el ingreso de la persona

Propaganda/Propaganda Un método de persuasión que se usa para influenciar a individuos o grupos

Property tax/Impuesto sobre la propiedad Un impuesto que se recauda sobre la propiedad personal y bienes raíces

Proportional plan/Plan proporcional Propuesta que propone que cada candidato presidencial recibiría la misma parte del voto electoral de un estado que haya recibido en el voto popular de ese estado

Proportional representation/Representación proporcional Una regla que se aplica en primarias del partido Demócrata y que señala que cualquier candidato que obtenga al menos 15 por ciento de los votos, obtiene un número de los delegados de ese estado a la convención Demócrata correspondiente al porcentaje del voto que obtuvo en la elección primaria

Proprietary/Colonia de Propietarios Organizada por una persona a la que el rey otorgó terrenos

Protectionism/Proteccionismo El esfuerzo que hacen los países por proteger sus industrias de la competencia extranjera

Public affairs/Asuntos públicos Cuestiones y eventos que conciernen a las personas en general

Public agenda/Agenda pública Los asuntos públicos en los que se concentra la atención de la gente

Public debt/Deuda pública Todo el dinero que el gobierno pide prestado y que no ha pagado, más el interés sobre ese dinero

Public-interest group/Grupo de interés público Un grupo de interés que trabaja en beneficio de todos los ciudadanos

Public opinion/Opinión pública Las actitudes que comparten muchas personas sobre el gobierno y la política

Public opinion poll/Encuesta de opinión pública Procedimientos que pretenden recolectar información haciendo preguntas a las personas

Public Policy/Política pública Las leyes y objetivos que el gobierno se plantea o persigue

Purge/Purga El proceso de revisar las listas de votantes registrados y de eliminar los nombres de aquellos que ya no tienen derecho al voto

Q

Quorum/Quórum Una mayoría

Quota/Cuota Una regla que exige la otorgación de una cantidad fija de trabajos o promociones a los miembros de cierto grupo

Quota sample/Muestra del cupo Una muestra construida para reflejar las características principales de una población dada

R

Random sample/Muestra aleatoria Una muestra en la que cada miembro del universo tiene la misma oportunidad de ser incluido

Ratify/Ratificar Aprobar

Rational basis test/Prueba de fundamento razonable Una prueba que mide si la acción del gobierno alcanza un propósito justo

Reapportionment/Redistribuir Distribuir de manera diferente

Recall/Destituir El proceso de separar a un funcionario público de su cargo mediante un voto

Recession/Recesión Un periodo en el que no hay crecimiento económico y se reduce el tamaño de la economía

Recognition/Reconocimiento Aceptar la existencia legal de otro país

Referendum/Referéndum El acto de someter una cuestión al voto directo

Refugee/Refugiado Una persona que huye de un país hacia un lugar más seguro

Regional security alliances/Alianzas de defensa colectiva Un acuerdo entre naciones de actuar unidas para enfrentar cualquier ataque contra cualquier miembro

Registration/Registro Procedimiento de identificación del votante cuyo objetivo es impedir el fraude electoral

Regressive tax/Impuesto regresivo Un impuesto fijo que no está basado en el ingreso de las personas o en su capacidad de pago

Repeal/Revocar Retirar o recuperar

Representative government/Gobierno representativo Un gobierno en el que el pueblo tiene voz

Reprieve/Prórroga Aplazamiento en la ejecución de algo

Reservation/Reservación Terrenos públicos destinados por el gobierno para el uso de tribus de indígenas norteamericanos

Reserve requirement/Encaje La cantidad de dinero que un banco debe tener a mano

Reserved powers/Poderes reservados Los poderes que la Constitución no otorga al gobierno nacional y no niega a los estados

Resign/Renunciar Dimitir a un cargo o puesto público

Resolution/Resolución Una medida que se ocupa de un asunto en una de las cámaras; no tiene la fuerza de la ley y no requiere la firma del presidente

Reverse discrimination/Discriminación positiva Discriminación en contra del grupo mayoritario

Revision/Revisión Un cambio que afecta a un plan escrito

Rider/Cláusula añadida Una disposición no relacionada con un proyecto de ley importante, pero que se añade para que "siga el mismo curso" a través del proceso legislativo; su nombre en inglés es Rider, que proviene de Ride, viajar

Right of association/Derecho de asociación Los ciudadanos pueden asociarse libremente con otros para promover una causa

Right of legation/Derecho de legación El derecho de enviar y recibir representantes diplomáticos

Rule of law/Imperio de la ley El principio que sostiene que el gobierno debe obedecer la ley

Runoff primary/Primaria de segunda vuelta Una elección primaria en la que los dos candidatos que obtuvieron el mayor número de votos en la primaria original se enfrentan nuevamente

Sales tax/Impuesto a las ventas Un impuesto que se carga a la venta de varios bienes, y que es pagado por el comprador

Sample/Muestra Una porción representativa del universo total

Search warrant/Orden de registro Un registro autorizado por un tribunal

Secretary/Secretario(a) Un funcionario encargado de un departamento del gobierno

Security Council/Consejo de seguridad Un panel de 15 miembros que tiene la responsabilidad de mantener la paz internacional

Sedition/Sedición El esfuerzo que hace una persona o grupos por derrocar o dañar al gobierno por medio de la violencia

Seditious speech/Discurso sedicioso Discurso que alienta el esfuerzo de personas o grupos por derrocar o dañar al gobierno mediante la violencia

Segregation/Segregación Separar o apartar de otros

Select committee/Comité especial Un comité de la Cámara de Representantes o del Senado que se establece por un periodo limitado de tiempo

Self-announcement/Autoproclamación Método de nominación en el que una persona anuncia su intención de presentarse como candidato a un cargo público

Self-incrimination/Autoincriminación Una persona obligada a dar testimonio en contra de sí misma

Senate/Senado Un cuerpo gubernamental que hace reglas y leyes

Seniority rule/Derecho de antigüedad Una costumbre que preserva los puestos más importantes del Congreso a los congresistas que tienen más años de servicio

"Separate-but-equal" doctrine/Doctrina "separados pero iguales" Una base constitucional para leyes que separan a un grupo de otro con base en la raza

Separation of powers/Separación de poderes La división del gobierno en tres poderes: legislativo, ejecutivo y judicial

Session/Sesión El periodo de tiempo en el que el Congreso se reúne cada año

Shadow cabinet/Gabinete fantasma Miembros de partidos de la oposición que vigilan, o persiguen como sombras o fantasmas, a miembros particulares del gabinete y que están listos para presentarse a elecciones

Shield laws/Leyes escudo Leyes que protegen a los reporteros de tener que revelar sus fuentes

Signing statements/Aclaración al firmar Corrección que se hace para señalar problemas en una nueva ley

Single-issue party/Partido de un solo tema Un partido político que se enfoca en un asunto principal

Slander/Difamar Afirmaciones falsas o injustas hechas de viva voz

Socialism/Socialismo Un sistema económico en el que el gobierno posee industrias importantes y proporciona muchos beneficios

Soft-liners/Reformistas Grupo que lucha para lograr que el gobierno cambie o que esté abierto a reformas en sus políticas

Soft money/Dinero blando Dinero entregado a partidos u otras organizaciones políticas en cantidades ilimitadas

Sound bite/Eslogan Frases cortas y concisas, o fórmulas, que se pueden pasar al aire en 30 ó 40 segundos

Sound taxation/Política fiscal equitativa La política fiscal que distribuye la carga de impuestos de manera equitativa entre quienes pagan impuestos

Sovereignty/Soberanía La autoridad de tomar decisiones y mantener la paz

Speaker of the House/Presidente de la Cámara de Representantes El líder de la Cámara de Representantes, elegido por, y miembro del partido que tiene la mayoría en la Cámara

Special district/Distrito especial Una unidad independiente creada para llevar a cabo una o más funciones gubernamentales a nivel local

Special session/Sesión extraordinaria Una sesión del Congreso que se convoca para enfrentar una emergencia

Splinter party/Partido disidente Un partido político que se ha separado de uno de los partidos principales

Split-ticket voting/Voto dividido Votar por candidatos de diferentes partidos en una elección

Spoils system/Sistema de despojos La práctica de dar trabajos en el gobierno a partidarios leales

Staff agency/Agencia administrativa Una agencia que apoya al jefe del ejecutivo y a otros administradores

Standing Committee/Comité permanente Comités fijos que consideran ciertos tópicos

State/Estado Un grupo de personas que viven en un territorio definido, con un gobierno que tiene poder absoluto al interior del territorio para decidir sus propias políticas

Statutory law/Ley estatutaria Regulaciones ordinarias que aprueba la legislatura

Straight-ticket voting/Voto de partido completo Votar por candidatos de un sólo partido en una elección

Straw vote/Votación extraoficial Encuestas que pretenden leer la mente del público haciendo la misma pregunta a un gran número de personas

Strict constructionist/Construccionista estricto Persona que quiere que el Congreso sólo use los poderes que aparecen escritos en la Constitución

Strict scrutiny test/Prueba de escrutinio estricto El requisito que exige que una ley demuestre un "interés gubernamental de peso" para tratar a grupos de personas de manera distinta

Subcommittee/Subcomité Una parte más pequeña de un comité permanente

Subpoena/Citatorio Una orden legal de presentación o de entrega de evidencia a un tribunal

Subpoenaed/Citado Obligado a aparecer en tribunales

Subsidy/Subsidio Una subvención monetaria

Substantive due process/Debido proceso sustantivo El gobierno debe crear políticas y leyes justas

Suffrage/Sufragio El derecho al voto

Supply-side economics/Economía por el lado de la oferta La creencia de que reducir impuestos tendrá como resultado una economía más fuerte

Supremacy Clause/Cláusula de supremacía Una cláusula de la Constitución que establece que la Constitución está por encima de todas las demás leyes

Surplus/Superávit Una cantidad superior a la que se necesita; extra

Swing voter/Votante indeciso Aquellos votantes que aún no deciden a qué candidato van a apoyar al inicio de la campaña, y que están dispuestos a escuchar los argumentos de ambos lados

Symbolic speech/Discurso simbólico Comunicar ideas a través de expresiones faciales, de lenguaje corporal, de llevar un letrero o de usar una banda en el brazo

T

Tariff/Arancel Impuestos que un país cobra a los bienes que importa de otro país; un tipo de impuesto

Tax/Impuesto Un cargo que el gobierno hace a las personas o sobre la propiedad para satisfacer necesidades públicas

Term/Periodo Tiempo durante el cual debe servir un funcionario público en el cargo para el que fue elegido

Territory/Territorio Una parte de los Estados Unidos que no forma parte de un estado, sino que está organizada con un sistema de gobierno propio

Terrorism/Terrorismo El uso de la violencia o fuerza para alcanzar objetivos políticos

Township/Territorio comunal Una subdivisión de un condado

Trade association/Asociación comercial Grupo de interés al interior de la comunidad empresarial

Trade embargo/Embargo comercial Detener el comercio con un país

Transient/Transeúnte Una persona que vive en un estado por un periodo corto de tiempo, sin tener residencia legal

Treason/Traición Ser desleal a su propio país; hacer la guerra a los Estados Unidos o dar ayuda a los enemigos de los Estados Unidos

Treaty/Tratado Un acuerdo entre dos o más países o estados sobre comercio, paz u otros asuntos

Tribunal/Tribunal Una corte o foro de justicia

Trust/Trust Cuando varias corporaciones que están en el mismo negocio se unen para eliminar la competencia y regular los precios

Trustee/Síndico Una persona a quien se entrega el poder de actuar en nombre de otros

U

Unalienable/Inalienable Algo a lo que uno no puede renunciar

Unconstitutional/Inconstitucional En contra de la Constitución

Uncontrollable spending/Gasto no controlable El gasto sobre el que ni el Congreso ni el presidente tienen la capacidad de cambiar directamente

Unitary government/Gobierno unitario Un sistema de gobierno que otorga todos los poderes clave a un gobierno central o nacional

United Nations/Naciones Unidas Una organización internacional de 180 naciones creada para desarrollar la paz y las relaciones amistosas, y para proteger los derechos humanos en todo el mundo

Universe/Universo La población entera que una encuesta desea medir

V

Veto/Veto Rechazar una propuesta de ley

Visa/Visa El permiso de entrar a otro Estado; debe ser expedido por el país al que la persona desea ingresar

W

Ward/Distrito electoral municipal Una unidad en la que se dividen las ciudades para la elección de miembros del consejo de la ciudad

Warrant/Orden judicial Una orden de los tribunales que hace que una acción oficial sea legal

Weblog/Ciberbitácora Un escrito presentado en un sitio de la Internet que usualmente se ocupa de un tema específico

Welfare/Asistencia social Asistencia en efectivo a los pobres

Welfare State/Estado de bienestar Un país cuyo gobierno proporciona muchos servicios, incluyendo pensiones, salud, educación y vivienda

Whips/Whips Asistentes a los líderes de los partidos en la Cámara de Representantes y el Senado

Winner-take-all/El ganador lo toma todo Un sistema casi obsoleto en el cual un candidato presidencial que ganó el voto preferencial en una primaria obtiene automáticamente todos los delegados que se seleccionan en esa primaria

World Trade Organization/Organización Mundial de Comercio Una organización que supervisa el comercio internacional y que ayuda a resolver disputas entre países; fue creada en 1995

Writ of habeas corpus/Auto de habeas corpus Una orden de los tribunales que indica a un funcionario que presente a su prisionero(a) en el tribunal

Z

Zoning/Zonificar El acto de determinar el lugar en el que se pueden construir viviendas y negocios

Index

INDEX

INDEX

Acknowledgments

The people who made up the **Foundations American Government** team—representing design services, editorial, editorial services, education technology, fact-checking, manufacturing and inventory planning, marketing services, product management, and production management—are listed below.

Courtney Alexander, Alyssa Boehm, Peter Brooks, Lynn Burke, Lori-Anne Cohen, Laura Edgerton-Riser, Thomas Ferreira, Patricia Fromkin, Andrea Golden, Thomas Guarino, Susan Hersch, Paul Hughes, Katharine Ingram, Stephanie Krol, Courtney Markham, Dotti Marshall, Grace Massey, Laurie McKenna, Jennifer Paley, Judi Pinkham, Jennifer Ribnicky, Alexandra Sherman, Mark Staloff, Kara Stokes, Kristen VanEtten, Paula Wehde

Art Credits

Maps: XNR Productions, Inc.

Cover Image

Getty Images

Illustration

Kenneth Batelman, Kerry Cashman, Daniel Guidera, Gillian Kahn, Rich McMahon, Jen Paley, Cyndy Patrick, Ted Smykal, Robin Storesund

Picture Research

Kara Stokes

Photography

FRONT MATTER Page xiii Danny Kerr; **xiv B** istockphoto.com; **xiv M** istockphoto.com; **xiv T** Getty Images; **1** Catherine Karnow/CORBIS; **1** Charles Barsotti/The Cartoon Bank.

UNIT 1 Page 1 Free Agents Limited/CORBIS; **2-3** Larry Chiger/ SuperStock; **4 L** ©Jupiter Images/Comstock RF; **4 R** ©Jupiter Images/ Comstock RF; **4 TR** Romilly Lockyer/The Image Bank/Getty Images, Inc.; **5 B** SANDY SCHAEFFER/MAI /Landov; **5 M** Brooks Kraft/Corbis; **5 T** REUTERS/Larry Downing /Landov; **8** Ed Fischer/CartoonStock; **9 M** Tim Graham/Getty Images; **9 L** ©Jupiter Images/Comstock RF; **9 R** ©Jupiter Images/Comstock RF; **10 R** AP Photo/Harry Cabluck; **10 L** AP Photo/Toby Talbot; **12** The Granger Collection, New York; **13** AP Photo/Mike Stone; **14 M** Richard B. Levine; **14 R** ©Jupiter Images/Comstock RF; **15 L** ©Jupiter Images/Comstock RF; **17** Comstock, Inc.; **20-021** The Battle of Lexington, 19th April 1775, 1910 (oil on canvas), Wollen, William Barnes (1857-1936) / National Army Museum, London, / The Bridgeman Art Library International; **22 R** ©Jupiter Images/Comstock RF; **22 R** The Granger Collection, New York; **24** William Sumits//Time Life Pictures/Getty Images; **27 B** Peter Andrews/Reuters/Corbis; **27 L** Getty Images, Inc.; **27 R** Getty Images, Inc.; **28 R** HIP / Art Resource, NY; **28 L** ©Jupiter Images/Comstock RF; **28 R** ©Jupiter Images/Comstock RF; **33 L** ©Jupiter Images/Comstock RF; **33 R** ©Jupiter Images/Comstock RF; **33 R** The Granger Collection, New York; **34** The Granger Collection, New York; **35 R** Kord/Getty Images/Retrofile; **36 L** ©Jupiter Images/Comstock RF; **36 R** ©Jupiter Images/Comstock RF; **36 R** The Granger Collection, New York; **37 BM** VisionsofAmerica/Joe Sohm; **37 BR** Photo by George Skadding/Time & Life Pictures/Getty Images; **37 L** Purestock/Getty Images, Inc.; **37 BL** Bettmann/CORBIS; **37 TM** The Granger Collection, New York; **37 TR** Burazin/Getty Images; **39** Reunion des Musees Nationaux/Art Resource, NY; **41 L** ©Jupiter Images/Comstock RF; **41 R** ©Jupiter Images/Comstock RF; **41 R** Picture History; **45** Comstock, Inc.; **48-49** age fotostock / SuperStock ; **52-53** all ©Steve Artley/www.artleytoons. com; **58 BL** James Madison (oil on canvas), American School, (19th century) / Musee Franco-Americaine, Blerancourt, Chauny, France, Giraudon / The Bridgeman Art Library; **58 BM** The Granger Collection, New York; **58 TL** Purestock/Getty Images, Inc.; **59 BR** The Granger Collection, New York; **60 L** ©Jupiter Images/Comstock RF; **60 R** ©Jupiter Images/Comstock RF; **60 M** Bettmann/CORBIS; **063** © Mark Parisi, reprint by permission; **064 R** Bettmann/CORBIS; **65 R** Bettmann/CORBIS; **67** image100/Corbis; **68 L** ©Jupiter Images/Comstock RF; **68 M** Tom Fox/Dallas Morning News/ Corbis; **68 R** ©Jupiter Images/Comstock RF; **69** AP Photo; **70** JASON REED/Reuters/Corbis; **73** Comstock, Inc.; **76-77** EMMANUEL DUNAND/ AFP/Getty Images; **78 L** ©Jupiter Images/Comstock RF; **78 M** choice of two: **369_8476.jpg; vets_0574.jpg; 78 R** ©Jupiter Images/Comstock RF; **79 L** Richard Ellis / The Image Works; **79 R** Bettmann/CORBIS; **80** Image

by © Michael Urban/POOL/epa/Corbis; **82 L** David R. Frazier / Photo Researchers, Inc.; **82 R** LUKE FRAZZA/AFP/Getty Images; **84** The Granger Collection, New York; **85 L** ©Jupiter Images/Comstock RF; **85 M** AP Photo/ Nancy Bannick Collection, Hawaii State Archives; **85 R** ©Jupiter Images/ Comstock RF; **90 B** AP Photo/Energy Star, John Harrington; **90 L** Getty Images, Inc.; **90 R** Getty Images, Inc.; **91 L** ©Jupiter Images/Comstock RF; **91 M** Corbis / SuperStock; **91 R** ©Jupiter Images/Comstock RF; **93** Courtesy of West Virginia Senate Office.; **95** Comstock, Inc; **98** Free Agents Limited/CORBIS.

UNIT 2: Page 100-101 AP Photo/Stephan Savoia; **102 L** ©Jupiter Images/ Comstock RF; **102 R** AP Photo/Victoria Arocho; **102 R** ©Jupiter Images/ Comstock RF; **104 TR** Carolyn Chappo; **106** J.B. Handelsman/The Cartoon Bank; **108 L** ©Jupiter Images/Comstock RF; **108 R** Bridgeman Art Library; **108 R** ©Jupiter Images/Comstock RF; **108 FR** Archivo Iconografico, S.A./ CORBIS; **113 L** ©Jupiter Images/Comstock RF; **113 R** Bettmann/CORBIS; **113 R** ©Jupiter Images/Comstock RF; **116** AP/Wide World Photos; **117** (AP Photo/Kevork Djansezian); **118 L** ©Jupiter Images/Comstock RF; **118 R** Chris Kleponis/Zuma/Corbis; **118 R** ©Jupiter Images/Comstock RF; **119** Copley News Service; **119** REUTERS/Jason Reed; **120** AP Photo/ Kiichiro Sato; **123** Comstock, Inc.; **126-127** AP Photo/Springfield News-Leader, Christina Dicken; **128 L** ©Jupiter Images/Comstock RF; **128 M** LOU DEMATTEIS/Reuters/Corbis; **128 R** ©Jupiter Images/Comstock RF; **129 L** George Caleb Bingham/Bridgeman Art Library/Getty Images, Inc.; **129 M** The Granger Collection, New York; **129 R** AP Photo; **132 L** ©Jupiter Images/ Comstock RF; **132 M** Barbara Davidson/Dallas Morning News/Corbis; **132 R** ©Jupiter Images/Comstock RF; **133 L** AP Photo/Chuck Burton; **133 R** AP Photo/Khampha Bouaphanh; **134 B** Jonathan Nourok / Photo Edit; **134 M** AP Photo/Bill Waugh; **134 T** AP Photo/ Robert E. Klein; **136** Tamio Wakayama/Take Stock Images; **138 L** ©Jupiter Images/Comstock RF; **138 M** Bettmann/CORBIS; **138 R** ©Jupiter Images/Comstock RF; **140 L** The Granger Collection, New York; **140 M** CORBIS; **140 R** AP Photo; **141 L** AP Photo; **141 R** Jacques M. Chenet/CORBIS; **143** Jim West / Alamy; **144 L** ©Jupiter Images/Comstock RF; **144 M** Peter Turnley/Corbis; **144 R** ©Jupiter Images/Comstock RF; **146** Kara Stokes; **147** © Copyright (2008) Jeff Parker/Cagle Cartoons. All rights reserved.; **148** EMMANUEL DUNAND/ AFP/Getty Images; **149** © CORBIS; **151** Comstock, Inc.; **154-155** Elaine Thompson/AP Images; **156 L** ©Jupiter Images/Comstock RF; **156 M** AP Photo/Janet Hostetter; **156 R** ©Jupiter Images/Comstock RF; **157** Jack Ohman/Tribune Media Services; **158** Official congressional portrait; **160 B** AP Photo/Amy E. Powers; **160 M** REUTERS/Eric Miller /Landov; **163 L** ©Jupiter Images/Comstock RF; **163 M** Justin Sullivan/Getty Images; **163 R** ©Jupiter Images/Comstock RF; **164** AP Photo/Elaine Thompson; **168 B** AP Photo/Lawrence Jackson; **168 L** Getty Images, Inc.; **168 R** Getty Images, Inc.; **169 L** ©Jupiter Images/Comstock RF; **169 M** AP Photo/Ben Margot; **169 R** ©Jupiter Images/Comstock RF; **170 M** Jason Reed/Reuters/Corbis; **170 R** Jason Reed/Reuters/Corbis; **172 L** Joe Raedle/Getty Images; **172 R** Joe Raedle/Getty Images; **173 L** Getty Images/Richard Ellis; **174** credit as art or photo? ask Jen (Steve Artley); **177** Comstock, Inc.; **180 M** Mario Tama/Getty Images; **182 L** ©Jupiter Images/Comstock RF; **182 R** ©Jupiter Images/Comstock RF; **182 M** Alex Wong/Getty Images for Meet the Press; **184 B** Dave Carpenter/Cartoon Stock; **186 L** ©Jupiter Images/Comstock RF; **186 R** ©Jupiter Images/Comstock RF; **186 M** Billy E. Barnes / Photo Edit -- All rights reserved.; **187 R** AP Photo/Shawn Patrick Ouellette; **192 B** Tom Carter / Photo Edit -- All rights reserved.; **193 L** ©Jupiter Images/ Comstock RF; **193 M** Masterfile; **193 R** ©Jupiter Images/Comstock RF; **196 L** Bettmann/CORBIS; **196 R** Yale Joel//Time Life Pictures/Getty Images; **197** Campbell/epa/Corbis; **199** Getty Images; **200** Comstock, Inc.; **204-205** Frances Roberts/Levine Roberts; **206 L** ©Jupiter Images/Comstock RF; **206 M** Frances Roberts/Levine Roberts; **206 R** ©Jupiter Images/Comstock RF; **207 BL** Minnesota Historical Society; **207 BML** New York Public Library; **207 BM** The Granger Collection, New York; **207 TL** J. R. Eyerman// Time Life Pictures/Getty Images; **207 TML** Library of Congress; **208** Dave Coverly/The Cartoonist Group; **210 L** ©Jupiter Images/Comstock RF; **210 R** ©Jupiter Images/Comstock RF; **210 TM** AP Photo/Mark Humphrey; **212 B** PRNewsFoto/Panasonic Corporation of North America; **212 T** Bettmann/ CORBIS; **214 B** Scott Nelson/Getty Images; **214 T** Photo by Gary Dineen/ NBAE via Getty Images; **215** © James Leynse/Corbis; **216 BL** Ian Wagreich Photography / www.iwphoto.com; **216 L** Getty Images, Inc.; **216 R** Getty Images, Inc.; **217 L** ©Jupiter Images/Comstock RF; **217 R** ©Jupiter Images/Comstock RF; **217 TM** Scott J. Ferrell/Newscom; **22 L** ©Jupiter Images/Comstock RF; **220 B** Polka Dot Images / SuperStock ; **220** Bkgrnd Momatiuk - Eastcott/Corbis; **220 BM** Alan Schein Photography/Corbis; **220 M** www.avaaz.com; **220 T** Jupiter Images; **220 TM** Getty Images, Inc.; **225** Comstock, Inc.

UNIT 3: Page 229 DAVID NOBLE PHOTOGRAPHY / Alamy; **230-231** Shawn Thew/epa/Corbis; **232 L** ©Jupiter Images/Comstock RF; **232 R** ©Jupiter Images/Comstock RF; **232 M** AP Photo/Susan Walsh; **235** Bonnie Kamin / Photo Edit; **236 L** ©Jupiter Images/Comstock RF; **236 R** ©Jupiter Images/

ACKNOWLEDGMENTS

Comstock RF; **236 TL** Stefan Zaklin/epa/Corbis; **240 L** ©Jupiter Images/ Comstock RF; **240 M** UPI Photo/Kevin Dietsch; **240 R** ©Jupiter Images/ Comstock RF; **242 L** ©Jupiter Images/Comstock RF; **242 M** REUTERS/ Jason Reed; **242 R** ©Jupiter Images/Comstock RF; **244 L** © Marvin Koner/ CORBIS; **247** Comstock, Inc.; **250-251** Mark Wilson/Getty Images; **252 L** ©Jupiter Images/Comstock RF; **252 M** AP Photo/Roberto Borea; **252 R** ©Jupiter Images/Comstock RF; **259 L** ©Jupiter Images/Comstock RF; **259 R** Harris and Ewing/Corbis; **259 R** ©Jupiter Images/Comstock RF; **260** James Madison (**1751-1836**) published by Nathaniel Currier (**1813-88**) (colour litho), Stuart, Gilbert (1755-1828) (after) / Private Collection, Peter Newark American Pictures / The Bridgeman Art Library; **262 BM** Alexander Hamilton, c.**1804** (oil on canvas), Trumbull, John (**1756-1843**) / © Collection of the New-York Historical Society, USA, / The Bridgeman Art Library; **262 BL** Corbis Premium RF / Alamy; **262 TL** UpperCut Images/Getty Images, Inc.; **262 BM** Getty Images, Inc.; **262 BR** Getty Images, Inc.; **262 TR** DK Stock/Getty Images, Inc.; **264 BL** Corbis Super RF / Alamy; **265 R** Sandy Felsenthal/CORBIS; **266 L** ©Jupiter Images/Comstock RF; **266 R** AP Photo/ Khampha Bouaphanh; **266 R** ©Jupiter Images/Comstock RF; **268 B** AP Photo/Jason Hunt; **268 R** Jeff Greenberg/Jupiter images; **268 T** A.Y. Owen/ Time Life Pictures/Getty Images; **269** J.B. Handelsman/Cartoonbank; **271 B** Chris Hondros/Getty Images; **271 TL** Getty Images, Inc.; **271 TR** Getty Images, Inc.**;** **272 L** AP Photo; **272 L** ©Jupiter Images/Comstock RF; **272 R** ©Jupiter Images/Comstock RF; **275 BL** Mark Wilson/Getty Images, Inc.; **275 M** AP Photo/Khue Bui; **275 TR** Wally McNamee/CORBIS; **275 MR** George Waldman/Getty Images, Inc.; **275 TM** Najlah Feanny/Corbis; **275 T** LUKE FRAZZA/AFP/Getty Images; **279** Comstock, Inc.; **283** Scott J. Ferrell/ Congressional Quarterly/Getty Images; **284 L** ©Jupiter Images/Comstock RF; **284 M** Shawn Thew/epa/Corbis; **284 R** ©Jupiter Images/Comstock RF; **285** © Ron Sachs/CNP/Corbis; **285 BL** Courtesy James Clyburn; **285 BML** Courtesy Roy Blunt; **285** BMR Courtesy Dick Durbin; **285 BR** Courtesy Jon Kyl; **285 BR** Public domain This United States Congress image is in the public domain. http://cantor.house.gov/images/cantorheadshot.JPG; **285 ML** Courtesy Steny Hoyer; **285** MML Courtesy John Boehner; **285** MMR Courtesy Harry Reid; **285 MR** Courtesy Mitch McConnell; **285 TL** Courtesy Nancy Pelosi; **285 TM** Courtesy Joe Biden (BIDEN CHOICE); **285 TR** Courtesy Robert Byrd; **289 L** ©Jupiter Images/Comstock RF; **289 M** Ken Cedeno/Corbis; **289 R** ©Jupiter Images/Comstock RF; **294 L** ©Jupiter Images/Comstock RF; **294 R** ©Jupiter Images/Comstock RF; **294 M** Scott J. Ferrell/Congressional Quarterly; **295** Mark Wilson/Getty Images; **297 L** Getty Images, inc.; **297 R** Chip Somodevilla/Getty Images; **298** Jack Ziegler/ The Cartoon Bank, Inc.; **299** Bettmann/CORBIS; **300 L** Getty Images, Inc.; **300 TR** Getty Images, Inc.**;** **301 L** ©Jupiter Images/Comstock RF; **301 M** Scott J. Ferrell/Congressional Quarterly/Newscom; **301 R** ©Jupiter Images/ Comstock RF; **302** Newscom; **303** Brooks Kraft/Corbis; **307** Comstock, Inc.; **310 L** Free Agents Limited/CORBIS; **310 R** Nick Anderson.

UNIT 4: Page 312-313 REUTERS/Jim Young (OBAMA OPTION); **314 L** ©Jupiter Images/Comstock RF; **314 M** David Hume Kennerly/Getty Images; **314 R** ©Jupiter Images/Comstock RF; **315** Reuters/CORBIS; **317** Courtesy Ronald Reagan Library.; **318** Michael Newman / Photo Edit -- All rights reserved.; **319 M** Bettmann/CORBIS; **319 L** ©Jupiter Images/Comstock RF; **319 R** ©Jupiter Images/Comstock RF; **320** National Archives/Handout/ Getty Images, Inc.; **322 L** ©Jupiter Images/Comstock RF; **322 ML** ©Private Collection/ Peter Newark American Pictures/ The Bridgeman Art**; 322 MR** ©Bristol City Museum and Art Gallery, UK/ The Bridgeman Art Library; **322 R** ©Jupiter Images/Comstock RF; **325 L** ©Jupiter Images/Comstock RF; **325 M** Spencer Platt/Getty Images; **325 R** ©Jupiter Images/Comstock RF; **331 L** ©Jupiter Images/Comstock RF; **331 M** Courtesy Rock the Vote; **331 R** ©Jupiter Images/Comstock RF; **337** Comstock, Inc.; **340-341** Bettmann/ CORBIS; **342 L** ©Jupiter Images/Comstock RF; **342 M** Christie's Images/ Corbis; **342 R** ©Jupiter Images/Comstock RF; **345 B** Brooks Kraft/Corbis; **345 L** Getty Images, Inc.; **345 R** Getty Images, Inc.**;** **346 L** ©Jupiter Images/ Comstock RF; **346 M** AP Photo/Ron Edmonds; **346 R** ©Jupiter Images/ Comstock RF; **347** Dwayne Booth; **350 BL** Joseph Sohm/Visions of America/Corbis; **350 BR** AP Photo/stf; **350 TL** Purestock/Getty Images, Inc.; **351 BL** AP Photo/The Herald-Sun, Christine T. Nguyen; **351 R** Owen Franken/CORBIS; **352 L** ©Jupiter Images/Comstock RF; **352 R** ©Jupiter Images/Comstock RF; **352 M** Bettmann/CORBIS; **354; 355 L** ©Jupiter Images/Comstock RF; **355 R** © Brooks Kraft/CORBIS; **355 R** ©Jupiter Images/Comstock RF; **356** TR/B Bettmann/CORBIS; **361** AP Photo/Doug Mills; **362-363** Melanie Steton Freeman/The Christian Science Monitor via Getty Images; **364 L** ©Jupiter Images/Comstock RF; **364 R** ©Jupiter Images/Comstock RF; **365** both UPI Photo/Roger L. Wollenberg; **366** Jon Arnold Images Ltd / Alamy; **368 L** ©Jupiter Images/Comstock RF; **368 R** Eric Draper/White House/Handout/Reuters/Corbis; **368 R** ©Jupiter Images/ Comstock RF; **369** Brooks Kraft/Corbis; **370** SAUL LOEB/AFP/Getty Images; **371 L** AP/Wide World Photos; **371 R** AP/Wide World Photos; **373 L** ©Jupiter Images/Comstock RF; **373 R** AP Photo/Tim Larsen; **373 R** ©Jupiter Images/ Comstock RF; **376 B** Bettmann/CORBIS; **376 T** AP Photo/White House, Paul Morse; **379 L** REUTERS/Jessie Cohen/Smithsonian's National Zoo /Landov; **379 M** AP Photo/Rich Pedroncelli; **379 R** REUTERS/Bob Care/Florida Keys News Bureau/HO /Landov; **380 B** AP Photo/Keith Srakocic; **380 L** Brooks Kraft/Sygma/Corbis; **380 R** David Frazier / Photo Edit -- All rights reserved.; **380 T** Comstock/Corbis; **382** Gary McCoy/Cagle Cartoons; **383 B** Cynthia Johnson/Time Life Pictures/Getty Images; **383 L** Getty Images, Inc.; **383 R** Getty Images, Inc.**;** **385** Comstock, Inc.; **388-389** GREG DERR photos/ The Patriot Ledger; **390 L** ©Jupiter Images/Comstock RF; **390 M** Monika Graff/Getty Images; **390 R** ©Jupiter Images/Comstock RF; **391** Harley Schwadron/Cartoon Stock; **393 L** ©Jupiter Images/Comstock RF; **393 M** Minnesota Historical Society/CORBIS; **393 R** ©Jupiter Images/Comstock RF; **394** © Bettmann/CORBIS; **396 L** ©Jupiter Images/Comstock RF; **396 M** Najlah Feanny/Corbis; **396 R** ©Jupiter Images/Comstock RF; **399** Getty Images, Inc.; **400 L** ©Jupiter Images/Comstock RF; **400 M** Scott J. Ferrell/ Congressional Quarterly/Getty Images; **400 R** ©Jupiter Images/Comstock RF; **403** Comstock, Inc.; **406-407** Bettmann/CORBIS; **408 L** ©Jupiter Images/Comstock RF; **408 M** Howard Sochurek/Time Life Pictures/Getty Images; **408 R** ©Jupiter Images/Comstock RF; **409** Jim Borgman/Courtesy Cincinatti Enquirer; **410 BL** Voice of America; **410 BR** Dimas Ardian/Getty Images; **410 TL** Marwan Assaf/REUTERS/Corbis; **410 TR** Courtesy United States Government, State Department; **411** Courtesy Skidmore, Owings & Merrill LLP; **412 T** MPI/Getty Images); **414 L** ©Jupiter Images/Comstock RF; **414 M** Shawn Thew/AFP/Getty Images; **414 R** ©Jupiter Images/Comstock RF; **417** Brad Loper/Dallas Morning News/Corbis; **419 BL** Tom Pennington/ Fort Worth Star-Telegram/MCT/Newscom**;** **419 BM** Brooks Kraft/Corbis **; 419 BR** NyxoLyno Cangemi/U.S. Coast Guard via Getty Images**;** **419 T** Gerald French/CORBIS; **421 L** ©Jupiter Images/Comstock RF; **421 M** Library of Congress **;** **421 R** ©Jupiter Images/Comstock RF; **422 L** Bettmann/ CORBIS; **427 T** Bettmann/CORBIS; **430 B** Sgt Andres Alcaraz/epa/Corbis; **430 L** Getty Images, Inc.; **430 R** Getty Images, Inc.**;** **431 L** ©Jupiter Images/ Comstock RF; **431 M** Bettman/Corbis; **431 R** ©Jupiter Images/Comstock RF; **435** © ADREES LATIF/Reuters/Corbis; **437** Comstock, Inc.; **440 L** Free Agents Limited/CORBIS; **440 R** ©John Deering.

UNIT 5: Page 441 Catherine Karnow/CORBIS; **442-443** AP Photo/Evan Vucci; **444 L** ©Jupiter Images/Comstock RF; **444 R** ©Jupiter Images/ Comstock RF; **444 R** SCOTT J. FERREL/Congressional Quarterly Inc./ Newscom; **447** Corbis; **449 B** Image by ©Ron Sachs/CNP/Corbis; **449 L** Getty Images, Inc.; **449 R** Getty Images, Inc.**;** **450 L** ©Jupiter Images/ Comstock RF; **450 R** Jerry Talfer/San Francisco Chronicle/Corbis; **450 R** ©Jupiter Images/Comstock RF; **454 L** ©Jupiter Images/Comstock RF; **454 R** ©Jupiter Images/Comstock RF; **454 R** Stock Montage/Getty Images; **457** Brooks Kraft/Corbis; **458 L** ©Jupiter Images/Comstock RF; **458 R** AP Photo/U.S. Army, Pvc Ben Brody; **458 R** ©Jupiter Images/Comstock RF; **459** ©Copyright 2007 Paresh Nath /Cagle Cartooons. All rights reserved.; **461** ©Jeff Topping/Reuters/Corbis; **463** Comstock, Inc.; **466-467** Levine Roberts Photography; **468 L** ©Jupiter Images/Comstock RF; **468 R** AP Photo; **468 R** ©Jupiter Images/Comstock RF; **469** Michael Newman / Photo Edit -- All rights reserved.; **472 L** ©Jupiter Images/Comstock RF; **472 M** JUPITERIMAGES/ Brand X / Alamy; **472 R** ©Jupiter Images/Comstock RF; **473** AP Photo/Douglas C. Pizac; **475** AP Photo/The News-Tribune, Bob King; **477 L** ©Jupiter Images/Comstock RF; **477 M** ©Jupiter Images/ Comstock RF; **477 R** New York Times Pictures; **479; 483** Tony Freeman / Photo Edit, Inc.; **484 L** ©Jupiter Images/Comstock RF; **484 R** AP Photo/Nick Ut; **484 R** ©Jupiter Images/Comstock RF; **486 L** Najlah Feanny/CORBIS SABA; **486 R** AP Photo/Ric Francis; **493** Steve Hamblin / Alamy; **494 L** ©Jupiter Images/Comstock RF; **494 R** ©Jupiter Images/Comstock RF; **494 M** Mark Harmel/Getty Images, Inc.; **495 B** Stockbyte/Getty Images, Inc.; **495 T** Jon Shireman/Getty Images, Inc.; **498 L** ©Jupiter Images/Comstock RF; **498 M** Masterfile; **498 R** ©Jupiter Images/Comstock RF; **499** New York Public Library; **50 L** ©Jupiter Images/Comstock RF; **50 M** ROBERTO SCHMIDT/AFP/Getty Images; **50 R** ©Jupiter Images/Comstock RF; **502** Dwight Carter; **504 L** Getty Images, Inc.; **504 R** Getty Images, Inc.**;** **505 L** ©Jupiter Images/Comstock RF; **505 R** Douglas C. Pizac-Pool/Getty Images; **505 R** ©Jupiter Images/Comstock RF; **51** Visions of America, LLC / Alamy; **510 BL** Bettmann/CORBIS; **510 BR** John Loengard//Time Life Pictures/Getty Image; **510 L** Getty Images; **511 BL** Michael Newman / Photo Edit -- All rights reserved.; **511 BM** Getty Images; **511 BR** AP Photo/Robert Houston; **512 L** ©Jupiter Images/Comstock RF; **512 M** AP Photo/Nathan Martin; **512 R** ©Jupiter Images/Comstock RF; **513 BR** Dave Parker/Cartoon Stock; **517** Comstock, Inc.; **520-521** Bruce Davidson/Magnum Photos; **522 L** ©Jupiter Images/Comstock RF; **522 M** Chuck Savage/CORBIS; **522 R** ©Jupiter Images/Comstock RF; **524** Getty Images; **525** Getty Images; **526** Clay Bennett, The Christian Science Monitor; **527 L** ©Jupiter Images/Comstock RF; **527 M** AP Photo/Marcy Nighswander; **527 R** ©Jupiter Images/Comstock RF; **529 L** ©Najlah Feanny/Corbis; **529 R** AP/Wide World Photos**; 530 BR** Hulton Archive/Getty Images; **530 L** New York Times Co./Getty Images; **530 TR** Center for American History, UT-Austin; **532 L** Bettmann/CORBIS; **532 R** Carl Iwasaki//Time Life Pictures/Getty Images; **532 TL** Purestock/ Getty Images, Inc.; **533 L** AP Photo; **533 M** Bettmann/CORBIS; **533 R** Bettman/Corbis; **534 L** ©Jupiter Images/Comstock RF; **534 M** AP Photo/ File; **534 R** ©Jupiter Images/Comstock RF; **536** Jack Moebes/CORBIS; **537** Doug Pensinger/Getty Images; **539** Newmann/zefa/Corbis; **540 L** ©Jupiter Images/Comstock RF; **540 M** Carlos Barria/Reuters/Corbis; **540 R** ©Jupiter Images/Comstock RF; **548 L** Free Agents Limited/Corbis; **548 R** Bob/Tom Thaves/ Cartoonist Group.

UNIT 6: Page 549 Zhukov Sergei/ITAR-TASS/Corbis; **550-551** Lan Hongguang/Xinhua Press/Corbis; **552 M** Jon Arnold Images Ltd / Alamy; **552 L** ©Jupiter Images/Comstock **RF**; **552 R** ©Jupiter Images/Comstock

742 Acknowledgments

Text Acknowledgments

Grateful acknowledgment is made to the following for copyrighted material:

The Associated Press "Major Provisions of the Lobbying Bill" by The Associated Press from http://www.washingtonpost.com/wp-dyn/content/article/2006/03/29/AR2006032901950.html.

"School's Integration Legacy Looms Large" by Andrew DeMillo, The Associated Press from http://www.usatoday.com/news/nation/2007-09-22-littlerock_N.htm. Copyright © 2008 The Associated Press. Used by permission.

League of Women Voters "Ethics and Lobbying Reform" from http://www.lwv.org/AM/Template.cfm?Section=Lobby_Reform_and_Ethics. Copyright © 2008 The League of Women Voters of the United States. Used by permission.

The Honorable Lee H. Hamilton "Whose Team Should a Member of Congress Be On?" by Lee H. Hamilton from http://www.centeroncongress.org/radio_commentaries/whose_team.php. Copyright © Lee Hamilton. Used by permission.

The New York Times "Fewer Youths Jump Behind the Wheel at 16" by Mary M. Chapman and Micheline Maynard from The New York Times, February 25th, 2008. Copyright © 2008 by The New York Times. All rights reserved. Used by permission and protected by the Copyright Laws of the United States. The printing, copying, redistributing, or retransmission of the Material without express written permission is prohibited.

The Oakland Tribune "Don't Balance California's State Budget by Raising Taxes" from The Oakland Tribune, January 2nd, 2008. Copyright © The Oakland Tribune/Zuma Press. Used by permission.

The Sacramento Bee "A new GI bill for a new generation of veterans" from The Sacramento Bee, May 26th, 2008. Copyright © The Sacramento Bee. Used by permission conveyed through Copyright Clearance Center.

"If you're into pain, you'll love this state budget" from The Sacramento Bee, January 11, 2008. Copyright © The Sacramento Bee.

The San Francisco Chronicle "Homeless project's army of citizens calls year success" by Kevin Fagan from The San Francisco Chronicle, October 19th, 2005. Copyright © The San Francisco Chronicle. Used by permission.

Writers House "I have a dream" by Dr. Martin Luther King Jr. Copyright © 1963 Dr. Martin Luther King Jr.; copyright © renewed 1991 Coretta Scott King. Used by arrangement with The Heirs to the Estate of Martin Luther King Jr., c/o Writers House as agent for the proprietor New York, NY.

Note: Every effort has been made to locate the copyright owner of material reproduced on this component. Omissions brought to our attention will be corrected in subsequent editions.